Peasants Making History

Peasants Making History

Living in an English Region 1200–1540

CHRISTOPHER DYER

OXFORD
UNIVERSITY PRESS

Great Clarendon Street, Oxford, OX2 6DP,
United Kingdom

Oxford University Press is a department of the University of Oxford.
It furthers the University's objective of excellence in research, scholarship,
and education by publishing worldwide. Oxford is a registered trade mark of
Oxford University Press in the UK and in certain other countries

© Christopher Dyer 2022

The moral rights of the author have been asserted

First Edition published in 2022

Impression: 2

All rights reserved. No part of this publication may be reproduced, stored in
a retrieval system, or transmitted, in any form or by any means, without the
prior permission in writing of Oxford University Press, or as expressly permitted
by law, by licence or under terms agreed with the appropriate reprographics
rights organization. Enquiries concerning reproduction outside the scope of the
above should be sent to the Rights Department, Oxford University Press, at the
address above

You must not circulate this work in any other form
and you must impose this same condition on any acquirer

Published in the United States of America by Oxford University Press
198 Madison Avenue, New York, NY 10016, United States of America

British Library Cataloguing in Publication Data

Data available

Library of Congress Control Number: 2021952504

ISBN 978-0-19-884721-2

DOI: 10.1093/oso/9780198847212.001.0001

Printed and bound by
CPI Group (UK) Ltd, Croydon, CR0 4YY

Links to third party websites are provided by Oxford in good faith and
for information only. Oxford disclaims any responsibility for the materials
contained in any third party website referenced in this work.

Contents

List of figures	vii
List of tables	ix
Preface	xi
Notes on boundaries and measures	xiii
Abbreviations	xv
1. Introduction	1
2. Peasants and landscapes	10
The west-midland region	10
Human impacts on the land	19
Lords and landscapes	20
Peasants and the making of the landscape	27
Peasants, lords, and the changing landscape after 1350	41
Conclusion	45
3. Peasant society: Landholding and status	47
Holding land before 1349	49
Changing circumstances: Entry fines	60
Landholding 1349–1540	64
Serfdom, 1200–1540	73
Conclusion	82
4. Peasants changing society	85
Migration	85
Social mobility	92
Poverty	97
Village community	102
Conclusion	111
5. Family and household	113
The size and composition of the household	113
Space for households	121
The character of family life	133
Conclusion	144
6. Peasants and their crops	145
Fields and their regulation	145
Changing agriculture: Managing the fields	150
Crops and their use	159
Arable husbandry	165
Farming methods and techniques	168

Conclusion on husbandry and techniques	178
Arable and pasture: Managing change	180
Conclusion	187

7. Peasant farming: Livestock and pasture — 188
Horses	188
Cattle	193
Sheep	197
Goats	203
Pigs	204
Poultry	207
Bees	209
Animal husbandry on the peasant holding	211
Animal welfare	215
Marketing animals and animal products	222
Conclusion	226

8. Peasants and towns — 228
Origins of towns	228
Peasant migration into towns	236
Occupations and commerce: Peasant influence on towns	243
Peasant consumption and towns	250
Peasants and changing fortunes of towns	255
Peasants and money	260
Town and country: Cultural connections	262
Conclusion	269

9. Peasants and industry — 271
The role of lords in creating industry	273
Urban entrepreneurs and rural industry	278
Poverty and industry	283
Industry within peasant society	289
Conclusion	303

10. Peasant outlook, values, perceptions, and attitudes — 305
Piers Plowman	305
Peasants and the state	307
Peasants and lords	314
Peasants and religion	320
Peasants and the environment	328
Individuals and communities	334
Conclusion	341

Conclusion	342
Glossary	347
Bibliography	353
Index	367

List of figures

2.1	Topography of the west midland region	11
2.2	Landscape divisions of the west midland region	13
2.3	Pendock, Worcestershire	15
2.4	Aston Blank, Gloucestershire	16
2.5	Westcote in Tysoe, Warwickshire	23
2.6	Northfield, Worcestershire	26
2.7	Malvern Hills and adjoining parishes	28
2.8	Ufton, Warwickshire	32
2.9	Wolverley, Worcestershire	36
2.10	Forest of Dean, Gloucestershire	37
3.1	Gloucestershire. Places named	49
3.2	Warwickshire. Places named	51
3.3	Worcestershire. Places named	53
4.1	Continuity of names at Romsley, Worcestershire	86
4.2	Migration patterns in Warwickshire, 1279–1332	89
5.1	Plans of house plots	122
5.2	Plans of excavated houses (Burton Dassett Southend, Upton, Pinbury, Coton)	124
5.3	Standing buildings (Stoneleigh, Defford)	126
6.1	Compton Verney, Warwickshire	146
6.2	Crops from tithe receipts, mainly Worcestershire	160
6.3	Peasant barns, Burton Dassett Southend	176
6.4	Cleeve Prior, Worcestershire	186
7.1	Remote pastures, transhumance, and droving	218
8.1	Towns in the west midlands	230
8.2	Plan of Coleshill, Warwickshire	232
8.3	Plan of Alcester, Warwickshire	234
8.4	Migration into Chipping Campden, Gloucestershire	237
8.5	Origins of apprentices at Bristol, 1532–9	241
8.6	Hinterland of Alcester	247
9.1	Industries in the region	272

9.2	Smith's tenement at Burton Dassett Southend	277
9.3	Distribution of fulling mills	279
9.4	Hanley Castle. Potters in a landscape	285
9.5	Masons and carpenters in Worcestershire in 1275	294
10.1	Halesowen parish	323
10.2	Woods in Balsall and Berkswell, Warwickshire	332

List of tables

3.1	Transfers of free land	55
3.2	Subletting arrangements on Worcester Priory manors	58
3.3	Entry fines on two Worcester Priory manors	62
3.4	Transfers of land between tenants on the Worcester Cathedral Priory estate	68
3.5	Transfers of land by surrender and grant	72
4.1	Distances between taxpayers' locations, and the places from which their surnames derive	87
4.2	Distances from home manor to destinations of *nativi*	88
4.3	Holdings of land linked with those identified as paupers in manorial records, 1200–1540	98
5.1	Servants taxed in 1525	118
5.2	Moral offences reported to west midland church courts	136
6.1	Land use in Gloucestershire from final concords	182
6.2	Reduction in the quantity of crops	183
7.1	Estimates of the size of the flocks of those selling wool to John Heritage	199
8.1	Occupations in Alcester	244
8.2	Peasant possessions, classified by materials	251
8.3	Households and expenditure in the hinterland of Alcester	255
8.4	Single coin finds from Warwickshire	262
8.5	Single coin finds from Alcester parish	263
10.1	Tax assessments at Brandon, Warwickshire	311

Preface

This book is the result of research over many years, and in acknowledging help that has been received I will focus on those who have participated or have given advice in the period of active preparation since 2011. Initial progress was made possible by a Leverhulme Trust Emeritus Fellowship for which I was grateful because it enabled me to visit archives intensively, and to gain from the reliable and skilful services of Matthew Tompkins. The Aurelius Charitable Trust funded the preparation of the figures, which were drawn expertly by Andy Isham. During the period of preparation, I became involved in a number of short-term projects which were relevant to the themes of the book. They encouraged me to embark on specialized aspects of my theme, and stimulated me with contacts with other scholars. These included work on the Inquisitions Post Mortem on a project led by Michael Hicks, and investigations of social mobility with Sandro Carocci. Conference papers at the University of Western Australia and the Leeds Medieval Congress made me pull together my thinking about poverty. I learnt more about open fields from a symposium hosted by Erik Thoen, and I found the discussions on serfdom at the Anglo-American conference organized by Phillipp Schofield in 2019 very helpful. The theme of migration figures prominently in this book mainly because of my involvement in a project devised by Jo Story and the late Mark Ormrod. Umberto Albarella, by inviting me to a conference on the archaeology of birds, encouraged me to study poultry more closely. Invitations to contribute to conferences and books by Phillipp Schofield and Martin Allen encouraged me to work on tithes and earnings. Early versions of Chapter 2 were delivered in a lecture to the Institute of Historical Research, a lecture at Taunton in memory of Mick Aston, and to the Friends of the Centre for English Local History at Leicester. Parts of other chapters were given to the economic history seminars at Cambridge and the London School of Economics, and in presentations to the Institute of Archaeology in London, the Flaran conference, and the Berne conference of the European Agricultural History Organisation.

This is a book about a region, and I have always welcomed the opportunity to talk to local societies and groups, who have sometimes allowed me to try out the general themes of this book; for example, at occasions organized by the Bristol and Gloucestershire Archaeological Society and the Worcestershire Archaeological Society, and also by the Nuneaton branch of the Historical Association and the Gotherington Local History Society. Invitations from the local history societies and heritage groups at Alcester, Bidford-on-Avon, Chipping Campden, the Forest of Dean, Thornbury, Welford-on-Avon, Winterbourne, Yate (near Chipping

Sodbury), and the Victoria County History Trust of Herefordshire, have all encouraged me to focus enquiries on particular places and themes, which are reflected in this book. Invariably at both the academic events and the talks to local groups, questions were posed which made me think harder.

This book uses archaeological evidence, much of which has been published quite recently, and I have also done fieldwork, but rarely on my own. My collaborators, who have contributed to interpretations as well as in practical matters, were David Aldred, Jenny Dyer, Bryn Gethin, Paul Hargreaves, Pat Lacy, and Sarah Wager.

The research includes work in specialist areas and I have had the benefit of advice from experts, notably Umberto Albarella, Laura Ashe, Jonathan Hart, Rose Hewlett, Matilda Holmes, Derek Hurst, Michael Lewis, David Pannett, Stephanie Ratkai, and Terry Slater. The contacts and conversations with fellow historians are too numerous for all to be mentioned, but I have gained specific benefits from Jean Birrell, Spencer Dimmock, Susan Kilby, Steve Rigby, and Andrew Watkins.

I do not have the space to thank individually all of the archivists (in 25 depositories), librarians, and custodians of Historic Environment Records of the three counties who have given me access to sources and information. Worcester Cathedral Library in the care of David Morrison has been especially welcoming. During the Covid-19 pandemic, special help has been provided by the David Wilson Library at the University of Leicester and the Wohl Library in the Institute of Historical Research, University of London. Worcestershire Archives and the Society of Antiquaries took trouble to answer queries.

Documents have been used by kind permission of the President and Fellows, Magdalen College, Oxford. I was also able to use the archives of Corpus Christi College Oxford and King's College Cambridge. Figure 2.8 is reproduced by kind permission of the Master and Fellows of Balliol College Oxford. I am grateful for the hospitality and facilities of the library of Raynham Hall, Norfolk, provided by the Marquess Townshend. Documents from the Badminton archive can be cited by kind permission of the Duke of Beaufort.

Theses and unpublished typescripts by various authors have provide useful information and are acknowledged at the appropriate places: they are M. Andrews, S. Dickson, R. Field, D. Greenblatt, C. Hart, T. Lloyd, G. Scardellato, G. Smyth, A. Sutherland, J. Toomey, and E. Vose.

I appreciate greatly the patience and expertise of the staff of the Oxford University Press, and in particular my main contact, Cathryn Steele.

As always, my wife supports and encourages my work in many ways, including reading drafts, compiling the index, and contributing to my understanding of history.

Christopher Dyer
Oadby, November 2021

Notes on boundaries and measures

The region covers three counties, but their boundaries have changed over time. I have tried to use as much as possible the boundaries that existed between 1935 and 1974. Accordingly, the short-lived county of Avon is not mentioned, enabling villages to the north of Bristol to be described as in Gloucestershire. In the once complicated area at the meeting point of Gloucestershire, Warwickshire, and Worcestershire the boundaries after the reforms of the 1930s are used, so that Alderminster, Quinton, Shipston-on-Stour, and Welford-on-Avon are all here located in Warwickshire, and Blockley in Gloucestershire. The Birmingham area is more entangled in changes in local government, but the post-1974 West Midlands can be ignored, and Solihull for example is here regarded as in Warwickshire. Birmingham's modern absorption of parts of Worcestershire and Staffordshire are set aside, and King's Norton, Northfield, and Yardley are restored to Worcestershire. Halesowen, once in Shropshire, is treated as part of Worcestershire, as is Mathon, now in Herefordshire. Chaceley is now in Gloucestershire, having previously been in Worcestershire.

Measures

Distances are given in miles as these are most readily understood in the UK, but metric equivalents are indicated on maps. The metric system (metres and centimetres) is in universal use by archaeologists, so all references to dimensions of settlements, buildings, artefacts, etc. are metric. Measures used in the past (yards for cloth, acres for land), are retained, as also are sums of money in £ s d and marks. Some measures appear in the glossary.

Abbreviations

AgHR	*Agricultural History Review*
BAH	Birmingham Archives and Heritage
BGAS	Bristol and Gloucestershire Archaeological Society
CBA	Council for British Archaeology
Cov Reg	P. Coss and J.C. Lancaster Lewis, eds., *Coventry Priory Register* (DS, 46, 2013)
CR Elmley	R.K. Field, ed., *Court Rolls of Elmley Castle, Worcestershire 1347–1564* (WHS, new series, 20, 2004)
CR Romsley	M. Tompkins, ed., *Court Rolls of Romsley 1279–1643* (WHS, new series, 27, 2017)
DS	Dugdale Society
EcHR	*Economic History Review*
GA	Gloucestershire Archives
GRS	Gloucestershire Record Series
Hist Glouc	W. Hart, ed., *Historia et Cartularium Monasterii Sancti Petri Gloucestriae*, 3 vols (London, Rolls Series, 1867)
HTC	M. Chibnall, ed., *Charters and Custumals of the Abbey of Holy Trinity Caen* (British Academy Records of Social and Economic History, new series, 5, 1982)
IPM	*Inquisitions Post Mortem*
Med Arch	*Medieval Archaeology*
P&P	*Past and Present*
PT	C. Fenwick, ed., *The Poll Taxes of 1377, 1379 and 1381*, 3 parts (British Academy Records of Social and Economic History, new series, 27, 29, 37, 1998, 2001, 2005)
Rec Feck For	J.R. Birrell, ed., *Records of Feckenham Forest, Worcestershire, c.1236–1377* (WHS, new series, 21, 2006)
Rec Hanley	J. Toomey, ed., *Records of Hanley Castle, Worcestershire, c.1147–1547* (WHS, new series, 18, 2001)
RBW	M. Hollings, ed., *Red Book of Worcester* (WHS, 1934–50).
Reg Guild	M. Macdonald, ed., *The Register of the Guild of the Holy Cross, Stratford-upon-Avon* (DS, 42, 2007)
Reg Wig	W. Hale, ed., *Registrum Prioratus Beatae Mariae Wigorniensis* (Camden Society, 1865)
SCLA	Shakespeare Centre Library and Archives, Stratford-upon-Avon
SRO	Staffordshire Record Office
TNA	The National Archives
TBGAS	*Transactions of the Bristol and Gloucestershire Archaeological Society*
TBAS	*Transactions of the Birmingham Archaeological Society*

TBWAS	*Transactions of the Birmingham and Warwickshire Archaeological Society*
UNMSC	University of Nottingham Manuscripts and Special Collections
VCH Glouc, Warw, Worc	*Victoria County History (Gloucestershire, Warwickshire, Worcestershire)*
VE	J. Caley and J. Hunter, eds., *Valor Ecclesiasticus temp Henry VIII* (Record Commission, 6 vols. 1810–34)
WAM	Westminster Abbey Muniments
WCRO	Warwickshire County Record Office
WHR	T. John, ed., *The Warwickshire Hundred Rolls of 1279–80* (Records of Social and Economic History, new series, 19, 1992)
WCL	Worcester Cathedral Library
WA	Worcestershire Archives
WHS	Worcestershire Historical Society

1
Introduction

This book is not a response to the neglect of peasants by historians. Their historical significance has often been demonstrated, but this book is a new venture in the sense that no one has attempted an overview of the importance of peasants over a wide range of themes, from agriculture to religion.[1] The approach is peasant-centred, so it seeks to identify their contributions, and the changes in which they participated, from their perspective. It is concerned with peasants' ideas and outlook, the controversies in which they became embroiled, the decisions that they made, and the actions that they took. Peasants were not gifted with free choices but were under pressure from external forces, such as the demands of their lords and the state, demographic movements, the hidden hand of the market, economic growth and recession, environmental factors including disasters, and political and religious movements. However, plenty has been written about these long-term tendencies, and my purpose is to give attention to peasants and their communities as they experienced these changes, resisted or accommodated them, and took advantage of opportunities they presented. Peasants varied greatly, and among them many different life chances and experiences can be found. Viewed as a mass, if we ignore their names or individual identities, they can be depicted as weak, miserable, poverty-stricken, ignorant, and unchanging. The narrative is often a negative account of crisis and decline. However, if disaggregated into individuals or small groups, a very different picture emerges of people with varied ambitions, concerns, knowledge, and the ability to make something of their lives.

Doubts about the use of the word 'peasant' were voiced briefly in the late twentieth century. It was alleged that the term could not be applied in medieval or modern England because the defining characteristics of peasants were their subordination to the family group, and their lack of participation in the market.[2] For

---

[1] G.C. Homans, *English Villagers of the Thirteenth Century* (Cambridge, MA, 1941); R.H. Hilton, *The English Peasantry in the Later Middle Ages* (Oxford, 1975); P.D.A. Harvey, ed., *The Peasant Land Market in Medieval England* (Oxford, 1984); R.M. Smith, ed., *Land, Kinship and Life-Cycle* (Cambridge, 1984); B.A. Hanawalt, *The Ties that Bound: Peasant Families in Medieval England* (Oxford, 1986); J. Whittle, *The Development of Agrarian Capitalism: Land and Labour in Norfolk, 1440–1580* (Oxford, 2000); P.R. Schofield, *Peasant and Community in Medieval England, 1200–1500* (Basingstoke, 2003); P.R. Schofield, *Peasants and Historians: Debating the Medieval English Peasantry* (Manchester, 2016). For continental Europe, see M.M. Postan, ed., *The Agrarian Life of the Middle Ages* (Cambridge Economic History of Europe, vol. 1, 2nd edn, 1966); W. Rösener, *Peasants in the Middle Ages* (Cambridge, 1985); T. Scott, ed., *The Peasantries of Europe* (Harlow, 1998).
[2] A. Macfarlane, *The Origins of English Individualism* (Oxford, 1978).

a time the rejection of the term peasants had some influence, and historians experimented with an alternative vocabulary, such as 'villagers' or even 'agriculturalists', but wiser views eventually prevailed and it was realized that the rural population across the world and over long periods could have different ways of life, but bore enough resemblance to one another to be usefully described as peasants.[3]

'Peasant' can be applied to a wide range of country people who possessed land in relatively small quantities (as small as the plot attached to a cottage, as large as 50 acres). They often produced their own food using family labour, so to some extent they were not dependent on the market. They were relatively poor and were socially subordinate, though they gained some benefit from belonging to communities. They were not farmers, who were a special category of leaseholders, often holding large amounts of land, employing labour and producing for the market. Some peasants can also be called labourers because they earned wages part-time, but most of them lived partly on the produce of their holdings. Many peasants were also serfs, but their servile status did not define them, as there were numerous free peasants. 'Villagers' is an alternative term of limited value, because although all rural people lived in units of government called villages or vills, the word village is often reserved for large compact settlements, and most people lived in hamlets or scattered farms. Peasants were not all male, because wives, daughters, and female servants formed part of the household and did much of the labour on the holding, and in some circumstances, especially widowhood, women were in charge. Peasants were involved in agriculture, but they did not disqualify themselves from the category of peasant by working also in crafts or retail trade.[4] All of this is written in the past tense, because the example of late medieval England is in the forefront of the author's attention. However, the definition can be applied widely. In the fourteenth century the majority of the English, European, and Eurasian population can be described as peasants, and although they have become extinct in modern England, and have greatly diminished in continental Europe (though still surviving in some countries and can be known as 'family farmers'), in Asia, Africa, and much of South America they have modernized and are active in great numbers, accounting according to one estimate for a third of the world's population.[5]

By including the term *peasant* in our historical vocabulary, it is much easier to communicate with other disciplines because the word is used and understood by social scientists, archaeologists, and geographers. International comparisons are

---

[3] P.R. Schofield, *Peasants and Historians*, pp. 22–3; T. Shanin, ed. *Peasants and Peasant Societies* (Harmondsworth, 1971), pp. 14–17.
[4] For a useful definition in a European context, see P. Freedman, *Images of the Medieval Peasant* (Stanford, CA, 1999), pp. 9–12.
[5] Hilton, *English Peasantry*, pp. 12–13; F. Ellis, *Peasant Economics* (Cambridge, 1993); E. Vanhaute, *Peasants in World History* (London, 2021).

also helped by sharing terminology; if we can agree on the types of people under discussion, similarities and differences can be more easily identified. An argument for 'English exceptionalism', that is, the belief that England was uniquely different in having no peasantry (and in many other ways), prevents any attempt at comparison.

This book has been made possible by a recent tendency in historical writing to give medieval peasants more prominence. For a long time, historians were using such phrases as 'lords and peasants' and tended to focus on peasants in their role as tenants, so they were seen as payers of rent, performers of labour services, and attenders at the lords' courts. Lords were imagined to have been the main producers and innovators. It was widely assumed that the planning of villages, the organization of field systems, farming methods, and much else followed mainly from initiatives by lords. Now we have learnt not to regard peasants as appendages of the seigneurial regime, nor as its victims, but as players in their own right, with resources, traditions, and ideas of their own.

The 'peasant-centred' approach has come from a number of different directions. An important influence has been historians on the left, who are associated with the 'history from below' approach. Peasant revolts, and especially the English Rising of 1381 has attracted interest from the progressive historians since the 1890s.[6] Although historians from a Marxist perspective have written about rebellious peasants, they have not been as 'peasant-centred' as might be expected. One obstacle has been Marx's assumption that the industrial working class was uniquely capable of revolution, so that other discontented plebeians were overshadowed. Also, the analysis of the 'feudal mode of production' focusses attention on the 'struggle for rent' between lords and peasants, which is portrayed as giving feudal society its dynamic capacity to change.[7] This is difficult to reconcile with an agenda to give pride of place to social differences within the village, peasant culture, and interactions among peasants. It is, however, important to be reminded that lordship was a presence and a strong influence throughout, which some enthusiasts for peasant autonomy are prone to forget.

Since the 1970s an important development in studies of peasants in the Middle Ages has been the interest of historians and historical geographers with a strong social science background, based mainly at Cambridge. Their initial agenda was to investigate the extent to which the demographic regime of early modern northwestern Europe, based on the European Marriage Pattern, went back before the sixteenth century. This research broadened to include not just marriage, but such

---

[6] E. Powell, *The Rising in East Anglia in 1381* (Cambridge, 1896); R.H. Hilton, *Bond Men Made Free: Medieval Peasant Movements and the English Rising of 1381* (London, 1973).
[7] C.J. Wickham, 'How Did the Feudal Economy Work? The Economic Logic of Medieval Societies', *P&P* 251 (2021), pp. 3–40.

subjects as the land market, inheritance, social welfare, servants, and credit.[8] The main sources were manorial court rolls, and the lords' presence is fully acknowledged in these investigations. Beginning rather earlier than the Cambridge research, the Toronto school of historians were also approaching peasants from a social science perspective, and they carried out comprehensive analyses of village life, with a special concern for office holding and stratification.[9]

The history of women and gender in general has drawn on the abundant sources relating to the aristocracy, nunneries, and urban society, but peasant women have received a good deal of attention. In particular their leading role in brewing and selling ale has been highlighted, and also their contribution to rural labour, raising issues relating to pay differences between male and female workers.[10] A controversial view, applied more to urban than peasant women, suggests that in the shortage of labour after 1349 women became more independent, their marriages were delayed, prolonging the demographic recession, and in the long term they made an important contribution to the supply of workers.[11]

Economic historians tend to be drawn to the abundant manorial accounts and surveys which have primarily provided information about lords' demesnes and rent income. They include receipts from tithes, which as they represent a tenth of the crops of each parish, are a guide to peasant crops. Notable work on tithes came from a study of peasant grain production in Durham over two centuries. Among other findings, it was shown that peasants changed the acreage of types of grain in relation to price movements.[12] Mills were an important source of revenue for lords, who usually leased out the mill for a substantial sum of money. The miller drew an income and paid the rent from the tolls paid by the peasants who were compelled to take their grain to their lords' mill. However, some mills escaped from close supervision, mainly before 1200, and the peasant tenants who paid a modest rent for a mill outside manorial control had the chance of profiting from the toll revenue.[13] A sophisticated study of demesne policy in the fourteenth

---

[8] R.M. Smith, *Land, Kinship and Lifecycle*; L.R. Poos, *A Rural Society after the Black Death: Essex 1350–1525* (Cambridge, 1991); Z. Razi and R.M. Smith, eds., *Medieval Society and the Manor Court* (Oxford, 1996); R.M. Smith, 'The English Peasantry, 1250–1650', in T. Scott, ed., *Peasantries*; C. Briggs, *Credit and Village Society in Fourteenth-Century England* (Oxford, 2009).

[9] J.A. Raftis, *Tenure and Mobility. Studies in the Social History of the Medieval English Village* (Toronto, 1964); E. Britton, *The Community of the Vill* (Toronto, 1977).

[10] J.M. Bennett, *Women in the Medieval English Countryside: Gender and Household in Brigstock before the Plague* (Oxford, 1987); J.M. Bennett, *Ale, Beer and Brewsters in England* (Oxford, 1996); M.E. Mate, *Daughters, Wives and Widows after the Black Death: Women in Sussex, 1350–1535* (Woodbridge, 1998).

[11] PJ.P. Goldberg, *Women, Work, and Life Cycle in a Medieval Economy. Women in York and Yorkshire c.1300–1520* (Oxford, 1992); T. de Moor and J.L van Zanden, 'Girl Power: The European Marriage Pattern and Labour Market in the North Sea Region in the Late Medieval and Early Modern Period', *EcHR* 63 (2010), pp. 1–33.

[12] B. Dodds, *Peasants and Production in the Medieval North-East. The Evidence of Tithes, 1270–1536* (Woodbridge, 2007).

[13] R. Holt, 'Whose were the Profits of Corn Milling? The Abbots of Glastonbury and their Tenants, 1086–1350', *P&P* 116 (1987), pp. 3–23.

century, which explained the various decisions about agricultural management made by lords' officials (many of them peasant reeves), made comparisons between demesnes and peasant holdings. An important finding was that peasants who seemed to have small numbers of animals actually kept a higher density of livestock than many lords. Similar conclusions have emerged from peasant animals recorded in tax records.[14] The historian who had done the most thorough study of lords' agriculture based mainly on manorial accounts turned to assess our understanding of the peasant economy in the early fourteenth century, and concluded that tenants could derive advantages from fixed rents, and could profitably sublet their land.[15]

These are just some examples of the growing appreciation of the need to include peasants in any analysis of medieval society and economy, and they are selected from dozens of publications which give peasants careful attention. There are useful contributions to peasant history in the *Agrarian Histories*, general surveys of medieval economy and society, and the various handbooks aimed at both students and general readers.[16] Taking peasants seriously as historical players in their own right is a feature of work on the early medieval period, for which sources are not so thin as is sometimes supposed.[17]

Specialized fields of historical enquiry have also extended their scope to include the ordinary people of the medieval countryside. Legal historians whose concern was understandably focussed on parliament, the Westminster courts, and the workings of the common law have devoted more attention to manorial courts. This has led to them analysing customary law, exploring procedures such as the role of juries, and examining issues of tenure. All of these were directly the concern of peasants, and have led to legal historians appreciating the knowledge and understanding shown by peasant litigants and officials.[18] Peasants were by no means confined to their local courts, and had a role as jurors in royal courts.[19] Canon law courts, so important in their influence on marriage, were dependent like the secular courts on ordinary people prepared to report on their neighbours'

---

[14] D. Stone, *Decision-Making in Medieval Agriculture* (Oxford, 2005), pp. 262-72. P. Slavin, 'Peasant Livestock Husbandry in Late Thirteenth-Century Suffolk: Economy, Environment and Society', in *Peasants and Lords in the Medieval English Economy*, edited by M. Kowaleski, J. Langdon, and P.R. Schofield (Turnhout, 2015), pp. 3-26.

[15] B.M.S. Campbell, 'The Agrarian Problem in the Early Fourteenth Century', *P&P* 188 (2005), pp. 3-70.

[16] H.E. Hallam, ed., *Agrarian History of England and Wales*, 2, 1042-1350 (Cambridge, 1988); E. Miller, ed., *Agrarian History of England and Wales*, 3, 1350-1500 (Cambridge, 1991); R.H. Britnell, *Britain and Ireland, 1050-1530* (Oxford, 2004); S.H. Rigby, ed., *A Companion to Britain in the Later Middle Ages* (Oxford, 2003).

[17] C. Wickham, *Framing the Early Middle Ages. Europe and the Mediterranean 400-800* (Oxford, 2005), pp. 383-588.

[18] J.S. Beckerman, 'Procedural Innovation and Institutional Change in Medieval English Manorial Courts', *Law and History Review* 10 (1992), pp. 197-252; L.R. Poos and L. Bonfield, eds., *Select Cases in Manorial Courts* (Selden Society, 114 (1998).

[19] J. Masschaele, *Jury, State and Society in Medieval England* (Basingstoke, 2008).

behaviour, and on those bringing forward litigation.[20] A similar development among historians of religion has led them to give more attention to 'popular' religion, and to take more seriously expressions of piety from all ranks of the laity. Participation by peasants in the life of the church has resulted from greater interest in parish churches and the parish in general.[21] The study of late medieval English literature has traditionally been focussed on works intended for an elite audience, and historians rather than literary scholars showed more interest in such popular work as the Robin Hood ballads and the shorter pieces sometimes called 'political songs'. Historical interest has been maintained, but literary scholars have shown more concern for works appreciated by a large general audience.[22] Linguistic studies were always anchored in everyday speech, but without explicit links being made to peasant society. The interaction between social historians and place-name scholars has enabled local names to be explored more directly as evidence for peasant perceptions of their surroundings.[23]

Medieval archaeology and its close allies, landscape history and vernacular architecture, began together in the mid twentieth century in a surge of interest in villages, fields, and rural non-elite houses. The practitioners proclaimed their objectives of discovering authentic peasant houses and exploring the daily lives of peasants.[24] To some extent that initial focus has shifted, as the study of castles, churches, monasteries, and above all towns occupied important places on the agenda. The archaeology of the peasantry has survived with the 'peasant house' still a central concern but now with more interest in material culture and the environmental context. Landscape history (or landscape archaeology as it is often called) has not lost its early enthusiasm for rural settlements, fields, and associated sites.[25]

This book can draw on the insights and achievements of many scholars, and they indicate the possibility of a broad enquiry into the full peasant experience, giving a more complete picture of the peasant contribution to late medieval life. Such a survey is more difficult to achieve if it is spread over a very large geographical area, and so is focussed here on one region, the west midlands. This

---

[20] R.H. Helmholz, *Marriage Litigation in Medieval England* (Cambridge, 1974); L.R. Poos, ed., *Lower Ecclesiastical Jurisdiction in Late-Medieval England* (British Academy Records of Social and Economic History, New Series, 32, 2001).

[21] A.D. Brown, *Popular Piety in Late Medieval England: The Diocese of Salisbury, 1200–1550* (Oxford, 1995); K.L. French, *The People of the Parish: Community Life in a Late Medieval Diocese* (Philadelphia, PA, 2001); B. Kumin, *The Shaping of a Community: The Rise and Reformation of the English Parish c.1400–1560* (Aldershot, 1996).

[22] S. Knight, *Robin Hood: A Complete Study of the English Outlaw* (Oxford, 1994).

[23] S. Kilby, *Peasant Perspectives on the Medieval Landscape* (Hatfield, 2020).

[24] C. Gerrard, *Medieval Archaeology. Understanding Traditions and Contemporary Approaches* (London, 2003), pp. 95–132).

[25] N. Christie and P. Stamper, eds., *Medieval Rural Settlement. Britain and Ireland, AD 800–1600* (Oxford, 2012); M. Gardiner and S. Rippon, eds., *Medieval Landscapes* (Macclesfield, 2007); S. Mileson, 'Openness and Closure in Later Medieval Villages', *P&P* 234 (2017), pp. 3–37.

region, consisting of the counties of Gloucestershire, Warwickshire, and Worcestershire, was an obvious choice because the author is familiar with its documents and landscape. Treating the three counties together was not an original idea, because it was chosen by Rodney Hilton for his study, modelled on French regional surveys, which covers the whole social spectrum concentrating on the period around 1300.[26] Writing this book has been aided not only by many works of Hilton's, but also by a dozen other scholars who have researched and written about the region and edited major texts, many of them influenced by him.

The region offers many other advantages. Its landscape is very varied, which allows comparisons to be made between open-field country with large villages, and woodlands where people lived in hamlets and in isolation, with some high ground (though no mountains) and areas of wetland. No region is typical, but the west midland region is free of idiosyncratic or very specialized characteristics. It was not dominated by a powerful lord, like county Durham, nor was it as urbanized as Suffolk, or as densely populated or intensively farmed as Norfolk, nor as unusually free as in Kent, nor as industrialized as parts of the south-west.

The period covered is divided into equal parts by the plague epidemic of 1349, and the content of the book reflects the differences between the growth of the thirteenth century which slowed or ended between 1300 and 1350, and the subsequent period of retreat but also new developments. We might be drawn into the belief that the Black Death was an overwhelming disaster and a decisive turning point, and certainly the west midlands suffered a very high mortality in what one source calls 'the first pestilence' (in the context of the subsequent lesser outbreak in 1361–2). However, many developments began well before the fateful year and continued, such as the advance of peasant freedom, the rise of peasants with larger holding, the desertion of villages and abandonment of cultivated land, and the growth of some towns and industries. It is often said that women advanced their status and independence after 1349, but the records used for this book show women behaving decisively in the management of their inheritance in the early fourteenth century.

How can we write peasant-centred history, emphasizing their contribution to change without any sources written by them? There are no letters, diaries, or autobiographies. Instead, the main sources were written by clerks working in the administration of lords, church, and state and serving their purposes. We must use skill and imagination to counter the perspectives of the institutions which filtered and coloured the information that they provide. This is not so difficult because behind many of the sources lie the spoken words of peasants. They reported to the courts, and as litigants argued their cases, and some of their words formed the basis of the written record. When a peasant's will was recorded, he or

---

[26] R.H. Hilton, *A Medieval Society: The West Midlands at the End of the Thirteenth Century* (revised edition, Cambridge, 1983).

she was often suffering a last illness, but could still make bequests to be written by the clerk, though the details may have been prompted by the clerk's suggestions. A manorial account was based on the spoken words of the reeve, an unfree peasant, with the help of aids to memory such as tally sticks. The document was prepared by the clerk using a template. For us to hear the voice of the peasant is not always an effort of imagination, as English phrases were included in the documents when the clerk's Latin failed him. Cattle grazing illicitly on a common because a peasant had sold his rights to a butcher were called 'chapman's wares'. Landmarks in deeds might include 'a nether hadelond' or a 'wateryngplace'. A marriage agreed by mutual consent was called a 'handfasting'. These glimpses of everyday speech are very satisfying, but almost all written records were Latin texts recording legal processes in conventional formulae. They were written for the lords or the government for particular ends, rarely for the benefit of the peasants, and never to help future historians.

Archaeological evidence appears to give us direct access to the illiterate and underprivileged. If a village, or part of one, is excavated and its surroundings surveyed the houses, fields, material goods (pottery and metalwork) and animal bones and plant remains are laid out before us as they were abandoned by the peasant occupants. Of course the meaning of the surviving data is by no means straightforward. The record is incomplete because organic building materials and artefacts of wood, leather, and cloth have not survived. We cannot be sure how the house was occupied, and we have no information about the status of the tenant or builder. The dates of building and abandonment are based usually on pottery which is often imprecise, and the material from the final phases is mingled with debris from earlier periods. The surrounding landscape has much evidence of boundaries and some for the use of land, but ownership, tenancy, and management are matters for conjecture.

This book is based on a sample of evidence. Every major collection of manuscripts has been visited, and transcripts and notes made, but much has had to be left unread. The largest collection is in Worcester Cathedral Library, which includes a series of court rolls for eighteen of its larger manors for most of the years between 1314 and 1520. All of the rolls for six sample years have been read, and all of the rolls for two manors, Blackwell and Shipston and Cleeve Prior. Many of the other rolls have been used in parts.

A higher proportion of the contents of other archives of manorial records have been transcribed or summarized, but rarely all those surviving for one place or estate. Some public records in print such as the Hundred Rolls, the lay subsidies, the poll taxes, the inquisitions post mortem, and the Valor Ecclesiasticus have been used often, but the voluminous unpublished records of the courts of King's Bench and Common Pleas have been barely scratched.

All of the archaeological reports with relevant material—that is, relating to villages and other peasant sites—have been consulted, and also surveys and reports resulting from landscape history projects. The author has done field work, mostly in south Warwickshire, the north Cotswolds, and in parts of woodland Worcestershire.

The purpose of this book is to use as much evidence as possible, hopefully overcoming the many problems of interpretation, in order to answer the central questions about the parts that peasants played in creating, promoting, and resisting change in a representative region between 1200 and 1540.

2
Peasants and landscapes

Landscapes provide the physical setting for people's lives, and geology and topography had a strong influence on farming, housing, communications, and economy. On the other hand, people could make choices about settlements and the organization and use of land which had an impact on the landscape. Two questions arise from this interaction between society and the land: How important was the human factor in forming landscapes, and which sections of society exerted most influence; in particular what was the peasants' role? Before addressing these questions the region and its various landscapes, must be introduced.

The west-midland region

The west-midland region is defined here as the counties of Gloucestershire, Warwickshire, and Worcestershire, three modern shires with origins before 1066 (Figure 2.1). The boundaries of these shires began to be established by the seventh century, when the kingdom of the Hwicce had been assigned a bishop based at Worcester. The kingdom died in the ninth century, but its frontiers were fossilized in those of the Worcester diocese. Four shires were formed from this territory in the tenth and eleventh centuries; originally Winchcomb in the north Cotswolds was the head of a separate shire, which was subsequently absorbed into Gloucestershire.[1] Worcestershire was extended to the north-west along the Teme valley beyond the boundary of the diocese. The western parts of Warwickshire had been in the kingdom of the Hwicce, but when the shire boundary was drawn it took in a large area to the east up to Watling Street. Gloucestershire largely coincided with the southern end of the kingdom and its diocese, except that it took in land to the west of the Severn, including the Forest of Dean which came under the ecclesiastical jurisdiction of the bishops of Hereford. These units of local government were political institutions designed to perform specific tasks, but they

---

[1] A.H. Smith, 'The Hwicce', in *Franciplegius: Medieval and Linguistic Studies in Honour of F.P. Magoun*, edited by J.B. Bessinger and R.P. Creed (New York, 1965), pp. 56–65. D. Hooke, *The Anglo-Saxon Landscape: The Kingdom of the Hwicce* (Manchester, 1985); J. Whybra, *A Lost English County: Winchcombshire in the Tenth and Eleventh Centuries* (Woodbridge, 1990). The idea of using these three counties as a regional entity was advanced in R.H. Hilton, *A Medieval Society. The West Midlands at the End of the Thirteenth Century* (reissue Cambridge, 1983), pp. 7–14.

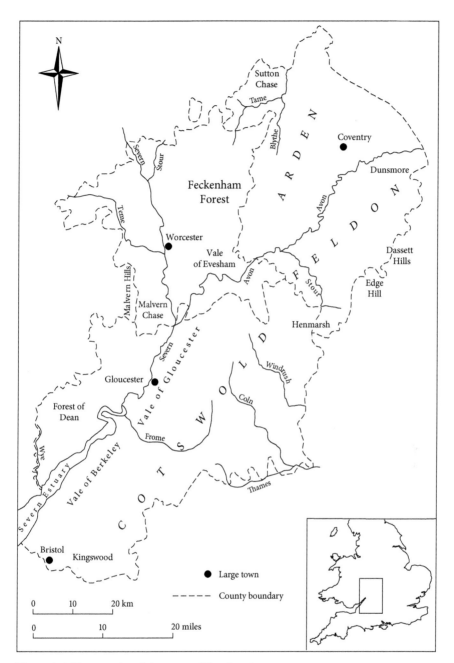

Figure 2.1 Topography of the west midland region.

derived some unity from the inclusion within their borders of the River Severn and its tributaries, in the east the Warwickshire Avon, and its tributaries such as the Arrow, Stour, and Dene, and in the west the Leadon, Teme, and Worcestershire Stour. South of Gloucester the Severn was fed by small rivers that flowed from east to west from the Cotswolds, notably the Frome, the Cam, and the Little Avon. Observers could stand on high ground, such as the Malvern Hills, the Birmingham plateau and its outliers to the north, Edge Hill to the east and the Cotswold escarpment to the south, and overlook a shallow bowl of valley land 36 miles across. Not all of the rivers flowed into the Severn, as in the north of Warwickshire the waters of the Blythe and Tame ended in the Trent, and most of the Gloucestershire Cotswolds were drained by the Evenlode, Windrush, Coln, and Churn which flowed southward into the Thames. The bulk of the land could be cultivated. The predominant soils are heavy, either the reddish marls associated with Mercian mudstone to the west and north of the region, or the grey lias clays of the eastern lowlands. The Cotswolds have 'calcareous earths' containing chips of oolitic limestone. Light alluvial soils occur mostly in the river valleys, though there are occasional patches of sand. The western edge of the region, notably Dean and Malvern, are characterized by ancient rocks and a variety of soils.[2]

The people of the three shires in the later Middle Ages must have been well aware of the unifying river valleys and the religious centre at Worcester. Together with their dialect of English these may have given them a sense of attachment to the region. They would also have recognized very clearly the varieties of countryside, with which we are familiar from the writings of the early modern topographers and county historians such as Leland, Camden, Habington, and Dugdale: they used such terms as forest, woodland, wold, champion, and Feldon (Figure 2.2).

Areas of land devoted to large trees and underwood were especially prominent in 'the Forest', that is the Forest of Dean. Royal forests occupied much of Worcestershire, notably in Feckenham in the east and Malvern to the west, and the short-lived Ombersley and Horwell. In south-western Gloucestershire lay Kingswood. These were legally defined hunting reserves, which gave the king the opportunity to hunt but also to raise revenue by fining the inhabitants for offences against the beasts of the chase and the vegetation that gave them shelter. Ombersley and Horwell ceased to be forests in 1218, and Malvern became a chase, a private forest of the earls of Gloucester. In north Warwickshire Sutton Chase

---

[2] H.C. Darby and I.B. Terrett, *The Domesday Geography of Midland England* (Cambridge, 1954); B. Hains and A. Horton, *British Regional Geology. Central England* (London, 1969); J.M. Ragg et al., *Soils and their Use in Midland and Western England*, Soil Survey of England and Wales, Bulletin no. 12 (1984); D.C. Findlay et al., *Soils and their Use in South-West England*, Soil Survey of England and Wales, Bulletin no. 14 (1984).

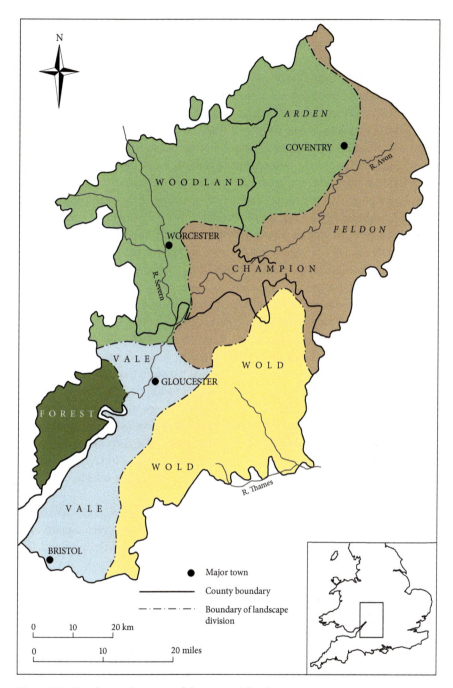

Figure 2.2 Landscape divisions of the west midland region.

belonged to the earls of Warwick.[3] The boundaries of the forests and chases included some important woods, but also many settlements and fields with few trees or deer.

'Woodland' described a large area of the west and north of the region, where important features as well as trees, were the areas of pasture, often in extensive greens, heaths, commons, and moors. In the woodlands the arable lay in small open fields, often with five or more in a single township, and in enclosed crofts; the land was farmed from hamlets (often called greens and ends) and single farmsteads. Figure 2.3 shows the oddly shaped parish of Pendock, with houses strung along winding lanes, with an occasional cluster. The land included six fields, many crofts, parcels of assarts bearing distinctive clearance names like rudding and Newland, with access to large meadows and a moor for summer grazing. The country along the Severn in Gloucestershire below the hills, the Vale, resembled woodland landscapes in many ways, with dispersed settlements and many enclosed parcels. Similarly the wold shared many characteristics with champion country, as both types of landscape cultivated large areas of open field land, often divided into two fields, and their settlements were usually nucleated villages with between twelve and forty households. Figure 2.4 shows the village of Aston Blank and its original two fields, later divided into four, typically with a small grove.[4] 'Wold' originally meant 'woodland', and extensive woods occupied parts of the Cotswolds and still do, but 'wold' for medieval people referred to high ground with extensive cultivation, though having access to hill pasture. Champion ran eastwards from the confluence of the Avon and Severn along the Avon valley and below the Cotswold edge, including the Vale of Evesham ('the granary of Worcestershire') and parts of central Worcestershire, and then extended across south and east Warwickshire. Here it was called the Feldon—in fact, the English equivalent of champion as both English *feld* and French *champ* refer to the abundance of arable land in open fields.[5]

The four types of landscape—woodland, vale, wold, and champion—contained some distinctive subdivisions, such as the wetlands along the Severn estuary, and the less extensive marshes of Longdon marsh (in west Worcestershire) and the

---

[3] C.R. Young, *The Royal Forests of Medieval England* (Leicester, 1979), pp. 62–3 reproduces an incomplete map compiled in 1921. John Langton is preparing an atlas of forests and chases in England and Wales: info. sjc.ox.ac.uk/Forest/maps.html.

[4] C. Dyer, 'Dispersed Settlements in Medieval England: A Case Study of Pendock, Worcestershire', *Med. Arch.* 34(1990), pp. 97–121; C. Dyer, 'The Rise and Fall of a Medieval Village: Little Aston (in Aston Blank)', *TBGAS* 105(1987), pp. 165–81.

[5] This is based on a variety of sources, such as Hooke, *Anglo-Saxon Landscape*; H.C. Darby and I B. Terrett, *The Domesday Geography of Midland England* (Cambridge, 1954); various essays in *Field and Forest. An Historical Geography of Warwickshire and Worcestershire*, edited by T.R. Slater and P.J. Jarvis (Norwich, 1982); H.P.R. Finberg, *Gloucestershire: An Illustrated Essay on the History of the Landscape* (London, 1955); O. Rackham, *The History of the Countryside* (London, 1986); B.K. Roberts and S. Wrathmell, *Region and Place: A Study of English Rural Settlement* (London, 2002); J. Thirsk, ed., *Rural England: An Illustrated History of the Landscape* (Oxford, 2000).

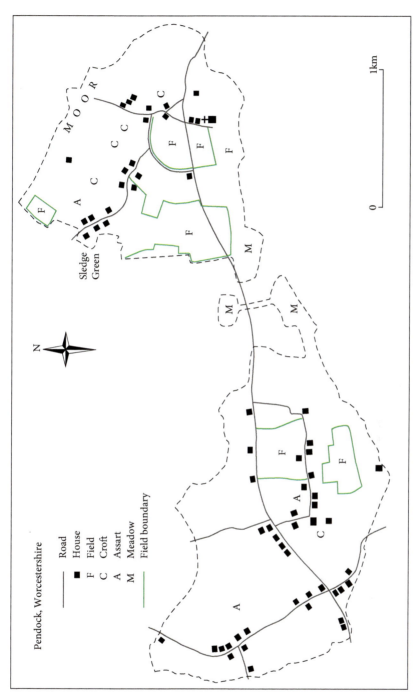

Figure 2.3 Pendock, Worcestershire. This parish was taken out of a larger land unit before the Conquest in a process that left it in two pieces. It lay within Malvern Chase. This reconstruction of its landscape in c.1300 shows scattered houses, winding roads, fields, crofts, assarts, meadows, and a moor. Its detached wood was in another parish (source: note 4).

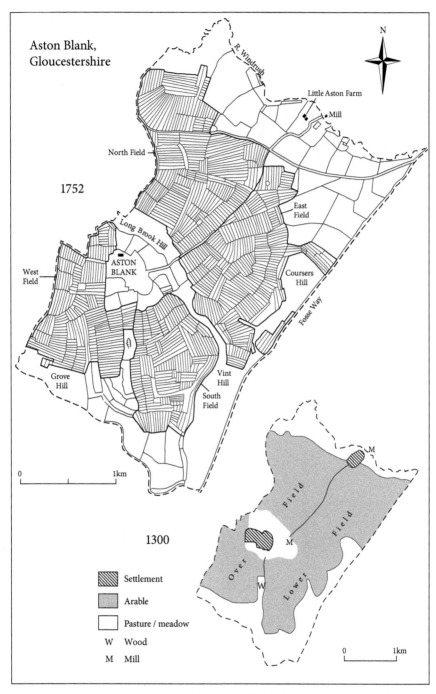

Figure 2.4 Aston Blank, Gloucestershire (also called Cold Aston—it was sited on high ground in the Cotswolds). In c.1300, two settlements shared arable in two fields, with pasture and a small grove. By 1752, when the map shows the strips (selions) and furlongs, a single settlement was cultivating arable in four fields, and the northern area was enclosed (see Figures 6.1 and 6.4 for open-field villages in champion areas) (source: note 4).

Henmarsh near Moreton in north-east Gloucestershire. Distinctive wooded valleys were an important feature of the mid Cotswolds, around Stroud, Woodchester, and Painswick. Relatively flat country is seen as the Cotswolds dip gently into the Thames valley around Lechlade. Some of the landscape boundaries were and are sharp and distinct, like the 'edge' to the north and west of the Cotswolds, but sometimes we find hybrid frontier zones, leaving us uncertain as to how to classify, for example, the villages on the northern and western sides of the valley of the Warwickshire Avon.

Historic landscapes can partly be characterized from their topography of hills and valleys, and from the management of their land, but they were inhabited and a full assessment of the character of landscapes needs to take into account the human and social dimension. Peasants held land as tenants, and were subordinated to lords, and these social conditions had implications for their settlements and lands. Large church landlords, who were especially prominent in the southern parts of the region, had developed combinations of manors located in champion, woodland, and wold, as the varied resources of these landscapes benefited the estates' production and consumption. However, champion and wold lands predominated, and as bishops and Benedictine monasteries exercised considerable social power, strengthened by continuous control over centuries, their lordship involved a high proportion of servile or customary tenants, who owed regular labour services in addition to cash payments for annual rent and extra dues. In the woodlands lay lords, especially knights and gentry, and smaller church institutions held much of the land and were more likely to gather rent in cash from freeholders or lightly burdened customary tenants. The obligations of tenants were not determined by their lords, as much depended on the productive capacity of their land, and the pull of the market. So it was a complex combination of factors that led customary tenants in the Vale of Berkeley and along the Severn estuary to be paying 12*d* per acre, while 4*d*–8*d* per acre is encountered more often in the Cotswolds and south Worcestershire, but 5*d*–6*d* in south-east Warwickshire. In the woodlands they might dip as low as 2*d*–4*d*.[6] By a paradox that surprises those who expect the unfree to be poor, servile tenants often occupied larger and middling holdings, while many free tenants were smallholders. Although nucleated villages were often inhabited by unfree or customary tenants, there is no exact coincidence between settlements and the powers of their lords. So the unfree tenants with heavy obligations near the Severn estuary lived in straggling hamlets and farms.

---

[6] Many observations are involved in this generalization, but published works dealing with the issue include J. Kanzaka, 'Villein Rents in Thirteenth-Century England: an Analysis of the Hundred Rolls of 1279–80', *EcHR* 55 (2002), pp. 593–618; B.M.S. Campbell and K. Bartley, *England on the Eve of the Black Death. An Atlas of Lay Lordship, Land and Wealth 1300–49* (Manchester, 2006), pp. 251–68.

A distinctive landscape was created from a combination of influences. On the Birmingham plateau in such Worcestershire parishes as Northfield, King's Norton, and Yardley the poor soils and damp climate encouraged pastoral farming. People lived in dispersed hamlets and farms, cultivated in many small enclosed fields as well as areas of open field, and their livestock could feed in the closes and on large areas of common pasture, often called heaths. The peasants, many of whom were smallholders, tended to hold land by free tenure under lay lords, including the king, a baronial family, and a rich knight; the estates of lesser lords are represented in the physical landscape by moats which had surrounded once prominent houses. Pastoral agriculture in the later Middle Ages was often aimed at the market, and both the country and the towns had a strong industrial dimension.[7]

A similar group of villages including Cropthorne, Fladbury, Netherton, and Elmley Castle were placed between the river Avon and Bredon Hill, the inhabitants of which produced grain and legumes on both clay and alluvial soils of high quality in open fields. Two of the villages could feed animals on the hay from large riverside meadows, and Bredon Hill provided pasture for the others. The peasants lived in nucleated villages, many with standard holdings of about 15 or 30 acres, made up of strips scattered over the open fields. The majority were customary tenants owing labour services and cash rents to large church estates and, in the case of Elmley powerful lay lords, the earls of Warwick. With little scope for industry the inhabitants lived from agriculture and especially arable farming, sending a surplus of crops and animal products, especially wool, to nearby market towns, Evesham and Pershore.[8]

The countryside could only function with communications, which in most of the medieval west midlands means roads, lanes, tracks, and paths. These mattered at the most local level: Admington (Warwickshire), a champion village with extensive open fields, was provided with more than 18 miles of access routes to connect its thirty houses with hundreds of small strips. Admington now contains within its boundaries 3 miles of public roads. A woodland settlement of comparable size required a close network of routes for access to scattered small settlements, enclosed parcels, and strips of land in open fields, resulting in more roads than exist today.

Long-distance journeys were most easily made by rivers, but in the region only the Severn was navigable for many miles, though in addition the Bristol Avon

---

[7] G. Demidowicz, *Medieval Birmingham: The Borough Rentals of 1296 and 1344-5* (DS Occasional Paper 48, 2008), pp. 31-4; G. Demidowicz and S. Price, *King's Norton. A History* (Chichester, 2009); T.R. Slater, *Edgbaston. A History* (Chichester, 2002); V. Skipp, *Medieval Yardley* (Chichester, 1970).

[8] *CR Elmley*, pp. xi—xvi; R.K. Field, 'The Beauchamp Earls of Warwick and the Castle of Elmley', *Transactions of the Worcestershire Archaeological Society*, 3rd ser, 15 (1996), pp. 135-46; E.K. Vose, 'The Estates of Worcester Cathedral Priory in the Later Middle Ages' (typescript, University of Birmingham, 1990), pp. 104-40; *RBW*, pp. 125-50.

connected Bristol to the sea. Some roads were survivals from the Roman network, and the Fosse Way and the route from Bristol to Worcester, and then northwards towards Birmingham and Lichfield attracted much traffic. Hubs for long-distance roads included Cirencester, with connections to London, Gloucester, and Bristol. Droitwich sent salt out over the whole region and beyond on a network of roads. Coventry, the only regional capital in England not situated on a navigable river, had connections with coastal ports as well as smaller places in the region.[9] Contrary to modern prejudice, medieval roads could cope with heavy traffic and for example there was regular cart traffic in the fifteenth century between Southampton and west midland towns.[10] Towns were connected to one another, and to their surrounding villages by roads of varying quality. Many peasants owned carts, and even more used packhorses, and these were the main users of the region's road system (see 'Horses' in Chapter 7). Costly bridges to take major roads over wide rivers, which increased in number in the thirteenth century, were funded by lords and towns. More numerous minor bridges were maintained, and presumably built, together with the metalling of roads, by peasants co-ordinated by villages (see 'Village community' in Chapter 4).

Human impacts on the land

The road network is only one case of human intervention in the making of the landscape. A distinctive section of landscape in the south-western corner of the region is the low-lying south bank of the Severn estuary between the mouth of the Bristol Avon and Slimbridge Warth (Figure 2.1). This strip of land, a mile or two wide and 22 miles long, resembles parts of the Netherlands in that the inhabitants exposed themselves to the danger of flooding, but learnt to endure the occasional inundation. They protected themselves from rising water level with sea walls and drainage ditches. They were rewarded for their skill, vigilance, and communal co-operation by being able to take advantage of the wetland resources. They could benefit from lush meadows and good arable land. Beyond the sea wall, the salt marshes were managed to provide plentiful summer grazing, and access to the sea enabled them to profit from salt pans and fisheries. Flooding was not the only hazard, as the inhabitants were probably prone to malaria. The adaptations to the land are still visible, to the east of modern industrial Avonmouth, in a largely man-made countryside, with the ridge and furrow of former cultivation, small irregular fields defined by curving drainage ditches (once creeks in the marsh), and drove roads to give livestock access to reclaimed

---

[9] B.P. Hindle, *Medieval Roads* (Princes Risborough, 1982); Hilton, *Medieval Society*, pp. 10–13.
[10] M. Hicks, ed., *English Inland Trade 1430–1540. Southampton and its Region* (Oxford, 2015), pp. 105–7, 108–9; a carrier connected London and Worcester by regular cart journeys: E.S. Fegan, ed., *Journal of Prior More* (WHS, 1914), pp. 208, 260.

land (formerly salt marsh). The sea walls, water courses (called ditches, pills, and rhines), and gouts (water courses fitted with doors), still guard against incursions by the sea and flows of water from higher ground.[11] The general message deriving from this example is that material conditions have profound consequences, but that people adapt and create appropriate landscapes. The same is true of the rest of the west midland region, even though dry land did not pose such great challenges and require such elaborate precautions.

Lords and landscapes

Many landscape features emerged in a period well before 1200, when evidence is very thin. It has been said that the lords must have been responsible for settling tenants and dependents in villages, and laying out fields which maximized orderly cultivation and economic efficiency. This could have happened as late as the eleventh century, but formation of nucleated villages could date back to the period before 1000, even before 800. No direct evidence from the early medieval period has been discovered for this process, though some excavated sites in other parts of England of *c*. 650–850 have quite regular arrangements of rectangular ditched enclosures.[12] For a later period the planned streets of some nucleated villages, such as the very regular single street with rows of house plots on each side at Elmley Castle, suggests the work of a single authority. The regular plan might have coincided with the development of a market in the thirteenth century when houses were located on both sides of a wide village street which served as a marketplace. Villages, whether with a regular or irregular plans, were often associated with open fields. Were those devised by the lords also? Elmley happens to be a case where in the middle of the fourteenth century the lord can be observed exercising some control over the management of the open fields attached to the village. If a neighbouring village which had access to common pasture on Elmley's fields wished to enclose part of the fallow, they had to obtain permission from the lord of Elmley.[13]

---

[11] S. Rippon, *The Severn Estuary. Landscape Evolution and Wetland Reclamation* (Leicester, 1997), pp. 186–267; J. Allen, 'A Short History of Salt-Marsh Reclamation at Slimbridge Warth and Neighbouring Areas, Gloucestershire', *TBGAS* 104 (1986), pp. 139–55; R. Hewlett, ed., *The Gloucestershire Court of Sewers 1583–1642* (GRS, 35, 2020), pp. xxx–xxxv, xli–xlv, xlix–lix; P. Franklin, 'Malaria in Medieval Gloucestershire: an Essay in Epidemiology', *TBGAS*, 101 (1983), pp. 111–22.

[12] R. Jones and C. Lewis, 'The Midlands: Medieval Settlements and Landscapes', in *Medieval Rural Settlement. Britain and Ireland AD 800–1600*, edited by N. Christie and P. Stamper (Oxford, 2012), pp. 197–201; T. Williamson, R. Liddiard, and T. Partida, *Champion. The Making and Unmaking of the English Midland Landscape* (Liverpool, 2013), pp. 74–100; C. Dyer, 'Rural Settlement in Medieval Warwickshire', *TBWAS* 100 (1996), pp. 117–32; C. Dyer, 'Villages and Non-Villages in the Medieval Cotswolds', *TBGAS* 120 (2002), pp. 11–35; H. Hamerow, *Rural Settlements and Society in Anglo-Saxon England* (Oxford, 2012), pp. 67–98.

[13] *CR Elmley*, pp. xi–xiii, xxi.

Lords have also been regarded as playing a decisive part in the expansion of settlement and cultivation of land in the woodlands, which was still a very active process in the thirteenth century. The evidence comes from grants made by lords to tenants who were expected to bring the land into cultivation.[14] For example the charters issued by Thomas, earl of Warwick between 1229 and 1242 include twenty-two grants of land in two very large, thinly populated manors in the Arden of north-west Warwickshire, Sutton Coldfield and Tanworth-in-Arden. Most of the land was in parcels of between 2 and 12 acres, often described as heath, and in four cases the new tenant was given permission to enclose or ditch the parcel, and to clear or assart it in preparation for cultivation. In most of the grants no reference is made to a previous tenant, which leads us to believe that the land lay in an undeveloped state, and formed part of the open common waste on which livestock had been grazed. The impression that these were new parcels that were being precisely defined for the first time comes from the boundary descriptions which used as landmarks rivers, streams, roads, and the hedges and ditches around other parcels of land described as assarts. The lord gained only a modest rent of between 5*d* and 2*s* each, or about 2*d* per acre, but he may also have been rewarding a servant, or anticipating future services. A few of the new tenants also paid a more substantial initial sum to gain possession, between a mark and 15 marks (13*s* 4*d* and £10).[15] In most cases the land was being granted rather than sold, and the impression is given that the lord was anxious to develop and populate his manor, offering low rents to encourage new settlers and cultivators. From the boundary descriptions we see a landscape filling up as new plots of land being added to clusters of closes and clearings. The main beneficiaries would have been the new tenants, once they had struggled through the hard work of removing vegetation and digging out tree stumps.

Only occasionally do the grants made by lords refer to the clearance of land by the lords themselves—only one of the group of documents analysed above mentions an assart of the earl of Warwick. In royal forests lords would be reported to the justices of the forest for appropriating land in purprestures, or removing the vegetation in assarts, sometimes in large quantities of 50 acres or more in a single episode. In the case of Westminster Abbey at Knowle in Warwickshire the costs of assarting by a lord appears in the reeve's account, with £1 'for assarting by a certain contract' in 1293–4, and a total of 16*s* 6*d* on labour and repairs to a plough in the following year. In this case one of the assarts lay within a park, demonstrating the versatility of these private landscapes.[16] The act of enclosing land that had previously been open pasture or wood pasture often caused controversy, and the

---

[14] B.K. Roberts, 'A Study of Medieval Colonization in the Forest of Arden, Warwickshire', *AgHR* 16 (1968), pp. 101–13.
[15] D. Crouch, ed., *The Newburgh Earldom of Warwick and its Charters 1088–1253* (DS, 48, 2015), pp. 223–50.
[16] WAM 27693, 27694.

lord had to deal with lawsuits brought against him under the assize of novel disseisin, which sought to prevent the loss of common pasture. Disputes could reach a pitch which led the defenders of common rights to assemble (commonly at night) and remove the hedges and fences and fill in the ditches around the newly appropriated land. At King's Norton Wood in 1332, a great crowd of people from King's Norton (Worcestershire) and adjoining Yardley and Solihull destroyed a bank and ditch which had been constructed by Roger Mortimer across a shared common pasture.[17] To avoid such confrontations, some lords would make agreements with those exercising common rights, and even buy off those who had been deprived of grazing.

The role of lords in the planning of villages and clearing land should not be exaggerated. If lords were ordering their tenants into planned villages one might expect to see some resemblances between villages across a large and powerful estate such as that of Evesham Abbey or Worcester Priory, but their settlements seem rather varied. The neat and regular plan of Westcote in Tysoe in Warwickshire, which consisted essentially of a single street with rows of houses on each side, can be seen with particular clarity because it was abandoned in the fifteenth century, with its plan frozen in time (Figure 2.5). Westcote was recorded in 1279 as having tenants under the lordship of four church institutions and two laymen.[18] At the time when the village was laid out in an orderly fashion at an unknown earlier date there may have been two or three lords, but planning here and elsewhere would have needed agreement from a number of interested parties, and the source of the initiative is not known. Nor is it clear what lords would have gained from the complex processes of settling the inhabitants in new houses in neat plots. In the open fields the lords had an obvious interest in maintaining a systematic sequence of crops and fallow if the lord's demesne and the tenants' holdings were intermingled across the furlongs of the field system, and both had to follow the same routine. Often, however, the lord's land was located in a block, and did not have to observe the same rotations as the village fields, and some lords had no demesne at all. The case for identifying lords as the usual organizers and planners of villages would be stronger if they were ever in the situation of starting a village from new, and bringing settlers into an empty countryside, such as an area of moorland. In the midlands the countryside was invariably inhabited, and nucleation and planning involved re-organization, with people being persuaded or ordered to move, coinciding with increased density of population and intensity in land use.

In the woodlands there is more evidence for identifying lords as changing the land by promoting the colonization of wastes. However the charters and legal disputes may be misleading us in presenting the lord as the activist. A lord who

---

[17] *Calendar of Patent Rolls, 1330–4*, p. 268. [18] WHR, pp. 268–70.

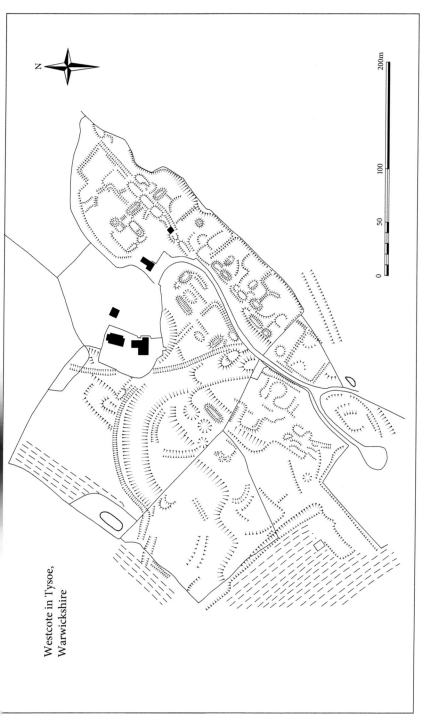

Figure 2.5 Westcote in Tysoe, Warwickshire. The desertion of this village in the fifteenth century means that the plan of the village, unencumbered by modern houses, is visible as earthworks. The curving modern drive to the farmhouse follows approximately the straight line of the original village street, with rows of houses and building plots, at least twelve of them, set on either side of the street. Other houses to the north-west are not so well-ordered (plan by Sarah Wager and the author).

granted a piece of land for assarting, like Thomas Earl of Warwick, may have been regularizing a situation which followed the tenants' initiative: when the lord gave permission for enclosure and cultivation this had already occurred, hence the precision with which the 'new' boundaries could be defined. The lord was ensuring that he received rent and other advantages of lordship from an existing clearing. A lord who appeared before the forest justices accused of assarting, like Richard Siward who was said in the 1240s to hold 58 acres in Feckenham Forest dating back about thirty years, may have directed the clearance of the land by his own employees, or by hiring contractors. Or he may have been facing the court on behalf of his tenants.[19] Similarly a lord who was confronted with protests after common land was enclosed was probably representing tenants who had carried out the enclosure, from which he expected to gain rent. The lord was not controlling the assarting peasants, and was leaving them to shoulder the work and the costs, but they benefited from a partnership in which the lord acted as their defender.

Having presented arguments against regarding lords as the principal instigators of settlement foundation and the extension of cultivation, it should be said that some direct evidence has emerged for a lord enlarging settlements, in the case of Worcester Cathedral Priory on its manors of Crowle, Newnham, and Wolverley in 1336–7. The priory court rolls tell us that the lord (the cellarer, representing the material interest of the monastic community) granted out a total of more than thirty holdings of land to new tenants in three specific locations: on the southern edge of the village of Crowle, and in two woodland hamlets, Bickley in Newnham and Blakeshall in Wolverley.[20] All of these settlements already existed, so that the ventures were enlargements rather than new planned villages and hamlets. The cellarer was seeking to increase the monastery's rent income. The initiatives were probably the result of a new and focused policy of expansion in the period after the great famine of 1315–17 when the priory like all lords faced financial uncertainties. The landscapes created by the Priory fitted into the existing pattern of settlement, adding a concentrated row of houses along a street leading into the nucleated village of Crowle based on strips in the open field, while at Bickley and Blakeshall the woodland hamlets were expanded, and the tenants' land came out of reclaimed waste. The lord provided holdings, but the tenants were expected to build their own houses and barns. The planning of the new house plots involved some consultation with local peasants, as they were expected to help with laying out the new plots.

In general there is little evidence that lords habitually created new settlements for peasant tenants, which contrasts with their ability to remodel landscapes

---

[19] *Rec Feck For*, p. 7.
[20] C. Dyer, 'The Midland Economy and Society, 1314–48: Insights from Changes in the Landscape', *Midland History* 42 (2017), pp. 36–57.

around their residences, in particular laying out gardens, ponds, and spaces for hunting, especially parks. They took their houses and castles out of the villages into a parkland landscape where they could live away from the cares of the everyday world.[21] They sometimes gave their new houses French names which indicated their aim of enjoying their leisure and isolation. Beaudesert in Warwickshire for example, was named in the twelfth century as an imagined wilderness on the edge of the Forest of Arden. A few miles away the Pleasaunce, a moated house with a garden built around 1414–17, served as a retreat accessible by boat across the mere from Kenilworth Castle. The mere itself was a man-made expanse of water a half-mile in length engineered as a defence and to enhance the appearance of the castle in the early twelfth century. In creating new parks the lords were also acting against the interests of peasants, sometimes removing their dwellings and fields to make way for the pastures and woods of the park. If no houses were removed, park pales still extinguished rights of common pasture, or prevented any future encroachments. This type of disruption of peasant lives would have been the result of the emparking of a thousand acres at Northfield (Worcestershire) by the lords of Dudley Castle[22] (Figure 2.6).

Lords sometimes sacrificed their urge to separate themselves by founding new towns at the gates of their castles, manor houses, and monasteries. Berkeley and Tewkesbury in Gloucestershire are examples which appear in embryo in the late eleventh century. By the thirteenth century, the town of Henley-in-Arden had grown beside the castle and park of Beaudesert. Perhaps an orderly planned town in the eyes of the lords gave the castle an appropriate backdrop, and a market made the castle or monastery a hub for the locality. A small town also generated revenues (£10 or £20) from rents, tolls, and court profits. Most new towns, about forty of them in the west midland region, were established by lords in the twelfth or thirteenth centuries not always as adjuncts of their residences but in locations which promised commercial success. Some grew gradually, but in a number of cases lords acted by diverting roads to bring trade to the town, planning the streets, granting privilege, and obtaining market charters.[23] Even in such ambitious schemes peasants had a role, because sites were chosen where unofficial trading activities had arisen from local enterprise, for example when parishioners met on Sundays to trade at the door of an important church. The town's population in its early years was made up of recruits from the country, and later continued to attract peasant migrants from rural backgrounds. Peasants living within about 7 miles of each town provided much of the business flowing through its market. As it prospered, a town could stimulate small settlements to grow nearby,

---

[21] O.H. Creighton, *Designs Upon the Land. Elite Landscapes of the Middle Ages* (Woodbridge, 2009).
[22] S. Mileson, *Parks in Medieval England* (Oxford, 2009); C. Dyer, 'Lords in a Landscape: the Berkeley Family and Northfield (Worcestershire)', *The Fifteenth Century* 14 (2015), pp. 13–37.
[23] M.W. Beresford, *New Towns of the Middle Ages. Town Plantations in England, Wales and Gascony* (London, 1967), pp. 439–41, 498–501.

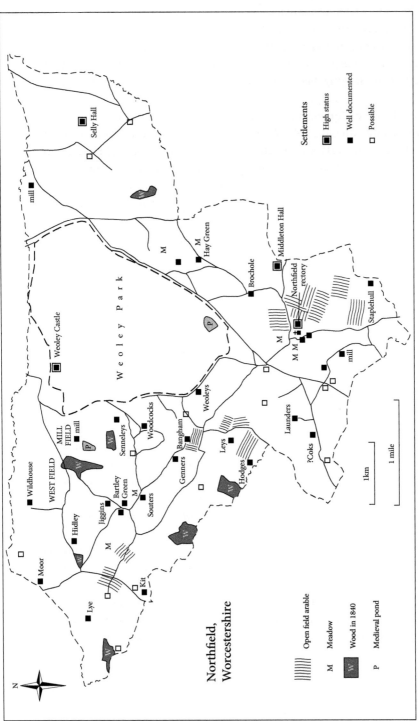

Figure 2.6 Northfield, Worcestershire. This woodland parish was dominated by the lord's park, which contained a castle. Apart from the lord's demesne, occupying fields and meadows to the west of the castle, the rest of the parish was occupied by scattered peasant farms, some clustered around greens, reached by lanes, and associated with patches of arable land, small woods, meadows, and pastures. The settlements date between the pre-Conquest and the thirteenth century; the park was probably created in the thirteenth century (source: note 22).

like Bridgetown in the parish of Alveston which developed across the River Avon from Stratford-upon-Avon (Warwickshire) and caught some passing trade from those crossing the bridge.[24] Down the hierarchy of trading places below the towns were villages with markets, some of them founded by lords who acquired a market charter, perhaps hoping for the growth of a commercial settlement. Some places developed as market centres apparently on the initiative of the villagers themselves, without official encouragement or permission. At Bibury (Gloucestershire), King's Norton (Worcestershire), and Tanworth-in-Arden (Warwickshire) the main evidence is the market place embedded in the plan of the village, and traders and craftsmen who lived around it (see 'Origins of towns' in Chapter 8).

To sum up: the authority of lords in the period 1200–1540 is visible in many parts of the landscape, from parks to new towns. They contributed to colonizing woods and wastes, and forming villages and fields. As their role is examined more closely, their social inferiors can be revealed as active participants in the processes.

Peasants and the making of the landscape

Boundaries were often the result of communities defining a territory so as to combine complementary resources, for example by defining a strip of land which ran from a hillside with pasture and wood, through a section of lowland well suited to arable, and down to river valley meadows with mowable grassland, and ending at the river itself. Such a model allocation of land is found between the Malvern Hills and the River Severn at Hanley Castle, and is likely to have had early origins (see Figure 2.7). Manors would base their boundaries on these pre-existing land units, and these might be written down by lords' officials, but they made no secret of their need to consult local informants about the precise line that they were following. When the monks of Coventry Priory around 1411 gathered information about the small manor of Packwood in the Warwickshire Arden, for a description of the boundary they were clearly relying on the testimony of a local jury of tenants, because at one point the 'metes, divides and bounds' went 'above Bentley Heath on which they have common'.[25] Other landmarks most likely to be known by residents, included two ponds and a small piece of wetland or meadow called 'Tascham sych'. Knowledge of the boundary was not just a matter of describing the limits of their territory when a higher authority enquired. Communities processed round their parish boundary every year on Rogation days (see 'Peasants and religion' in Chapter 10), to make sure that it was known and remembered by everyone, and policed by villagers watching for encroachments.

---

[24] *Reg Wig*, p. 83a. This shows that the hamlet had grown within 44 years of the town's foundation.
[25] *Cov Reg*, p. 55.

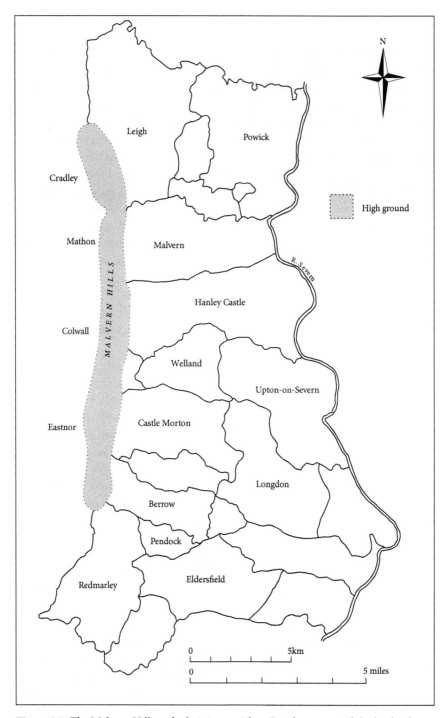

Figure 2.7 The Malvern Hills and adjoining parishes. Parishes occupied the lowlands between the River Severn and the crest of the hills. Arable and meadow were concentrated near the river, and a number of villages shared the pasture on the hills in intercommoning arrangements (see Figures 2.3 and 9.4 for individual parishes in the area). The boundaries come from modern maps, but some were of pre-Conquest origin.

New boundaries were sometimes following an older line. The houses of the villages of Roel and Hawling (Gloucestershire) were located within regular rows of rectilinear house plots. Such planned villages, typical of the Cotswolds are conventionally dated to the eleventh or twelfth centuries, but the banks, stone walls and ditches forming the framework within which the houses were sited are likely to have originated as a Romano-British field system.[26] Local people who were laying out the plots would be sensitive to pre-existing landscape features.

All of this is to say that medieval people lived in a countryside carved into well-defined units of landholding and agricultural management, but some resources were shared. Groups of settlements around a large area of grazing might 'intercommon' the hill, heath, or moor, and manage the pasture collectively. Boundaries would be unenforceable as the sheep and cattle would move across the landscape in search of the best grass. So seven parishes had access to Dunsmore Heath in north-east Warwickshire, and the inhabitants of fifteen parishes pastured their animals on the high ground to the east of the upper Windrush valley in the north Cotswolds, between Broadway in the north and the Guitings in the south.[27] Because these arrangements were of long standing, and worked tolerably well through informal management, they often escaped official record. No single lord or institution was in charge of the intercommoned pastures, so they maintained discipline through persuasion.

The Malvern Hills, a range of extinct volcanoes, were subject to intercommoning (Figure 2.7). They marked a boundary for thousands of years, as a ditch originally dug in the Bronze Age runs along their crest, two hillforts were provided in the Iron Age, and in the Middle Ages the hills marked the western extent of four territories: the kingdom of the Hwicce, the diocese of Worcester, the county of Worcester, and Malvern Chase.[28] The place-name Malvern refers to the bareness of the hills, so over a long period they have been grazed so intensively that the growth of trees was prevented. Some of the animals wandering the hills were deer, as the eastern slopes formed part of the hunting reserves of the king and later the earls of Gloucester: Malvern Forest and later Malvern Chase. To the west the hunting belonged to the bishops of Hereford. The prehistoric ditch was renewed in agreements made in 1287 and 1291 to define the limits of the earl of Gloucester's hunting rights, and it has been known as the 'red earl's ditch', and later the 'shire ditch'. However, cattle and sheep were the predominant livestock on the hills, and they came from a ring of settlements, such as Hanley Castle, Upton-on-Severn, and Castle Morton on the Worcestershire side, and Colwall and Mathon to the west. Early maps (of 1628 and 1744) show access points on to the hill

---

[26] J. Bond and C. Lewis, 'The Earthworks of Hawling', *TBGAS*, 109 (1991), pp. 150–1, 165–70.
[27] C. Dyer, 'Seasonal Settlement in Medieval Gloucestershire: Sheepcotes', in *Seasonal Settlement*, edited by H.S.A. Fox (Leicester, Vaughan Papers 39, 1994), pp. 26–7.
[28] B. Smith, *A History of Malvern* (Leicester, 1964), pp. 25–40, 84–7; M. Bowden, *The Malvern Hills: A Sacred Landscape* (Swindon, 2005).

pasture from the lowland villages. Finds of small quantities of late medieval pottery and two iron knife blades near the south gate of the Iron Age hillfort on Midsummer Hill suggest a temporary settlement for herdsmen staying overnight, perhaps in the summer when cows and ewes were milked at the pasture.[29] Colwall and Mathon paid 8 quarters of oats and some hens and eggs to the lord of Malvern Chase to gain access to the grazing on the eastern slopes. In 1540 people from these two villages were forbidden from 'staff driving' their stock across the shire ditch, that is, deliberately taking a large share of the pasture where Hanley's animals grazed. The scale of the pasture can be judged from the sixteenth-century custom on the Worcestershire side that a villager was restricted to keeping thirty sheep on the village's own pastures, but there was no limit to the numbers that could be kept on the hills.[30]

Pasture on the Malvern Hills is a warning that many features of the peasants' relationships with the landscape were so deeply embedded in their customs and practices that they are not fully documented. Lords' records show more clearly that connections between distant lands or assets could correct imbalances in resources. In the champion and wold country timber, fuel, and hay could be in short supply, and in Warwickshire and Worcestershire Avon valley manors which specialized in grain production were linked to woodlands in Arden, Feckenham, and Malvern, while high Cotswold manors shared in the abundant meadows in the river valleys of the Thames and Severn, or could make hay in the smaller local meadows watered by the Evenlode or Windrush.[31] The extent to which the peasants benefited from these attachments cannot be known for certain, though the occasional grants of timber from remote woods to repair peasant buildings in the fifteenth century (such as trees from Malvern Wood for buildings at Wick Episcopi in the Severn valley) suggest that peasants did not have access by right to quantities of timber. However, peasants from the champion village of Wellesbourne had common rights in the remote Kingswood in the parish of Lapworth.[32]

There is no reason to doubt the role that peasants could play in planning settlements and fields. A group of peasant tenants, who were used to working together, were capable of complex tasks in regulating agriculture in the common fields, and in managing such administrative tasks as tax assessment. Peasants took on a challenging responsibility when the community became farmers of their manor. Farming, that is holding the manor on lease and paying the lord a fixed annual sum, was much used by estates in the eleventh and twelfth centuries, but around

---

[29] Society of Antiquaries, Prattinton V15 68.2; WA, ref. s705:974, BA 9063; S.C. Stanford, *Midsummer Hill. An Iron Age Hillfort on the Malverns* (Hereford, 1981), p. 149.

[30] J.M. Toomey, 'A Medieval Woodland Manor: Hanley Castle, Worcestershire' (PhD dissertation, University of Birmingham, 1997), p. 51; J. Bowen and A. Craven, *Colwall* (London, Victoria County History, 2020), p. 51, Smith, *Malvern*, p. 40.

[31] *RBW*, pp. 103–5, 139–40 shows links between Bredon and Welland and Fladbury and Bradley; *VE*, vol.3 p. 252 shows meadow at Bourton-on-the-Water and Broadwell connected to Eyford.

[32] WA, ref. 009:1, BA 2636, 175/92476; 92482; 92491; *WHR*, pp. 166–8.

1200 a growing number of lords took over direct management by installing officials. Worcester Cathedral Priory persisted in putting manors out to farm, and between 1206 and 1233 six manors were leased to the 'men of the vill'. The villagers, most of them unfree, ran the lord's demesne and collected tenants' rents and dues. They seem to have done this successfully; for example, in 1207 Harvington, which had previously been leased for 12 marks (£8) was put into the hands of the villagers for a rent of 24 marks (£16) and 12 quarters of oats. The estate's confidence in the villagers' abilities was justified, because after a twelve-year lease, they were granted another term of ten years.[33]

The Worcester Priory hamlets of Bickley and Crowle in 1336–7 were to be 'measured by the lord and the vill', or 'measured by the lord and neighbours' suggesting that villagers were equipped with measuring rods which they normally used in allocating land in the fields and meadows. The planning of Westcote village (Figure 2.5) would have required an initial decision by a village meeting, no doubt with consultation with one or more of the lords, but thereafter in a linear village space could be found for new plots and houses by infilling, subdivision of larger plots, and expansion along the main street. In the case of Ufton, based on the map of 1672, the nineteen tenants of 1086 were presumably mainly yardlanders who acquired quite large plots along the two rows on either side of the street. As the numbers of tenants in the next two centuries increased to forty-three the original plots were subdivided and some extra plots added, and the village became a community of half yardlanders by 1279. In the fourteenth and fifteenth centuries as the population declined plots were left unoccupied, and some remained empty in 1672[34] (Figure 2.8). Analysis of Warwickshire village plans shows that most nucleated settlements belonged not to the street or row type (like Ufton) but fall into the 'cluster' or 'agglomerated' category which seem to have developed in an informal and piecemeal fashion.[35]

Orderly rows were scarce in the hamlets and smaller dispersed settlements of the woodlands, where houses might be found in clusters. They were planned in the sense that the boundaries of the plots were agreed, but additions to the settlement could be made on an individual's initiative. Lords or rather their local officials would wish to control the growth of a settlement, as they would keep a record of tenancy and impose rents and services on newcomers, but the neighbours would have a strong interest in managing the encroachments on to public spaces,

---

[33] H. Luard, ed., *Annales Monastici*, vol 4, *Annales Prioratus de Wigornia* (London: Rolls Series, 1869), pp. 391–425 ; Hilton, *Medieval Society*, p. 153.

[34] Balliol College, Estates Map 1, survey E.11.7. It is discussed in N.W. Alcock and D. Miles, 'An Early Fifteenth-Century Warwickshire Cruck House Using Joggled Halvings', *Vernacular Architecture* 43 (2012), pp. 19–27; general arguments for villagers planning their own settlements are made in Williamson and others, *Champion*, pp. 81–100; S. Mileson, 'People and Houses in South Oxfordshire, 1300–1650', *Vernacular Architecture* 46 (2015), pp. 8–25.

[35] B.K. Roberts, 'Village Forms in Warwickshire: a Preliminary Discussion', in *Field and Forest*, edited by Slater and Jarvis, pp. 125–46.

Figure 2.8 Ufton, Warwickshire. A map of 1672 shows the village ranged along one street in a planned layout, with a cluster of houses around the church. The original plots were subdivided between 1086 and 1279, but the subsequent decline in population led to mergers of plots and the abandonment of the southern end of the village (source: Balliol College, Oxford, Estate Map 1, reproduced by kind permission of the Master and Fellows of Balliol College).

and ensuring the good character of newcomers. A hint of the process comes from Hinton-on-the-Green in Gloucestershire in 1266–7, when at the end of a detailed survey of tenants the jury, or perhaps the lord's officials, or both, stated that there were new *bordelli* ('small cottages') 'built without licence', on which rents had been imposed. They recommended that these should be included in the survey, that is given full official recognition.[36]

The role of peasants in small-scale settlement development can be seen in the addition of cottages to existing building plots, sometimes for subtenants, but often to accommodate family members. At Halesowen in Worcestershire the lord occasionally agreed to modifications to the space occupied by tenants, responding to the wishes of the tenants—in 1295 for example Henry Othehul added land adjacent to his messuage, and William le Leche's holding is revealed to have been divided into two (see 'Holding land before 1349' in Chapter 3).[37]

---

[36] *Hist Glouc*, vol 3, p. 61.
[37] J. Amphlett, ed., *Court Rolls of the Manor of Hales, 1272–1307* (WHS, 1910), pp. 320–1, 335.

In woodland landscapes, apparent peasant settlement initiatives took the form of individual farms, each surrounded with small irregular crofts, between which lay patches of pasture and meadow, or small open fields that would be shared by a number of peasants. At Northfield to the east of Halesowen, the western and southern section of the parish was covered with farms, some bearing pre-Conquest names, others apparently having origins in the twelfth and thirteenth centuries, leaving a large area to the north and east where the lord was in exclusive command of his castle, demesne, and park (Figure 2.6).[38]

Throughout this consideration of settlement formation, applied to both nucleated villages and more scattered settlements, lies an assumption that people moved to a new preferred location. One of the explanations for the growth of large compact villages is that peasants left more isolated farms in order to join a larger settlement, and there is some archaeological and place-name evidence for such moves from the early Middle Ages. An oral tradition of a relocation is documented for Stoneleigh (Warwickshire) when estate officials explained the origins of a half-yardland holding at Cryfield. It was held in the 1380s by Richard Thornhale, but his grandfather, William de Thornhale at some time before 1331 had lived at Thornhale in Canley, a neighbouring hamlet. It was said that William was often robbed because 'he lived a long way from the habitation of neighbours', so he arranged an exchange of land in order to to settle in Cryfield which had nine tenants in the late fourteenth century, but may have been bigger at the time of the move.[39] The story could derive from an inaccurate folk memory, but reveals peasant perceptions of their possible role in the nucleation of settlement.

The open fields on which crops were rotated each year according to well-established customs seem to have emerged before the Norman Conquest, but in later centuries they were being adjusted by agreements among the tenants. An area of open field might be enlarged by the addition of areas of newly cleared land, for example at Bishop's Cleeve (Gloucestershire) where assarts on the slopes of the Cotswold edge were added to the common fields by c. 1170.[40] Parts of the field were subject to enclosures, initially a temporary measure to allow crops to be planted in the fallow field, but also more permanent fencing of groups of strips for grazing. A close study of ridge and furrow, the surviving physical remains of the medieval arable, reveals variations and modifications which appear in no written record. Sometimes new building plots on the edge of a village took over the ends of selions, or if the settlement was shrinking in size the ploughing ran over the former house sites (as at Stretton Baskerville in Warwickshire). Cultivators could make the understandable but risky decision to expand the land

---

[38] Dyer, 'Lords in a Landscape', pp. 29–35.
[39] R.H. Hilton, ed., *The Stoneleigh Leger Book* (Dugdale Society, 24, 1960), p. 221.
[40] *RBW*, p. 351.

under corn by extending the strips towards a stream, therefore reducing the amount of meadow, but the ridge and furrow revealing these moves can be notably faint, as if the experiment only lasted some years. Ridges in the woodlands of Warwickshire and Worcestershire could be narrow, with a width as little as 5m compared with 7–8m in the champion. Does this relate to a later date of their formation? In south Gloucestershire on the south bank of the Severn Estuary, in a sample of land between Berkeley and Aust, ridges thought to belong to an early phase of cultivation amount to an area of 5,700 acres, while apparently later ploughing, with a more geometric layout and narrow ridges, totalled 1,100 acres. The later cultivation lay in patches on the edge of presumed pastures, perhaps because they had once been part of the grazing land.[41]

Landscape formation is more easily observed outside the champion districts because the process was still continuing in the documented twelfth and thirteenth centuries. The question, 'who made the landscape?' can be to some extent be answered in the case of the extension of settlements and cultivated land in the woodlands, from deeds and manorial surveys, but also from the forest records. The 1280 eyre (royal court) for Feckenham Forest dealt with offences against forest law in north-east Worcestershire and adjoining parts of Warwickshire.[42] The main offences involved clearing land and enclosing it, that is assarts and purprestures. Of 198 cases, a quarter involved lords of various kinds, from great magnate landholders like the abbot of Evesham to a number of small religious institutions, like the Hospital of St Wulfstan of Worcester and Dodford Priory, and in secular society knights and gentry. These elite holders of land in the Forest accounted for more cleared and enclosed land than the other offenders, because they were said to have cleared large areas. In south-west Warwickshire for example 17 acres were assarted in one village, 23 acres in another, and 43 acres in a third. Some of the areas cleared by lords were so small, such as an acre and a half at Sheriff's Lench and the same at Abbot's Morton, that the inference must be that a lord was paying the penalties, but the work was being done by a tenant increasing the size of a holding. The lord would have benefited from the rents received in the long term.

The great majority of those removing vegetation and enclosing wastes in the Forest came from below the ranks of the gentry. The forest court records give no hint of the status of the offenders, except that it was assumed that they could pay sums of money at a rate of 3s to 4s 6d per acre. The names of fifty-nine offenders or their relatives can be found in the tax lists, notably that of 1275, mostly paying between 1s and 5s, and therefore in the middle ground of rural society, and one in

---

[41] The dimensions of ridges in woodlands derive from observations by D. Pannett and the author; for Gloucs, J.R.L. Allen, 'A Reconnaissance Map of Medieval Alluvial Ploughlands in the Vale of Berkeley, Gloucestershire and Avon', *TBGAS*, 110 (1992), pp. 87–97.

[42] *Rec Feck For*, pp. 119–46.

five paid more than 5s.[43] Twelve of those clearing assarts can be found in manorial surveys near in date to the eyre, and eight of them held less than 15 acres, with the other four below 30 acres, so of middle size. Evidently those converting a parcel of wood or waste into arable land included peasants already in possession of a holding. Those planning the operation needed to have some influence with the manorial officials and the community to obtain their consent. The assarter required time to remove vegetation, followed by hedging and ditching, and the heavy task of the first ploughing. Expenses included the fine to be paid to the forest authorities, and perhaps the employment of labour. Making an assart could well have been supported by a loan of money, so it would have helped if the assarter was credit worthy.

The smallholders could also have had a role in clearance of new land. Of the named offenders in 1280, seventy-nine do not figure in the tax records. Some could have been migrants, or had changed their names, but a proportion were probably exempted from tax because their goods were of low value and fell beneath the taxpaying threshold. A few smallholding offenders can be found in surveys, like Anabel Ervi of Alvechurch who held a messuage and two assarts and no other land, and at Blickley in Hanbury members of the de Blickley family held only assart land. Some of these pioneers may have worked as artisans, like Robert the Roper of Ipsley (who probably made ropes from tree bark or bast) or William le Cupere of Blickley (a maker of barrels).[44]

The main conclusion that emerges from the 1280 proceedings is that peasants of all kinds carried out assarting, including a large number of middling peasants and smallholders. They cleared land often on a small scale, with many holding a half-acre or one acre of newly cultivated or enclosed land. Cumulatively they contributed a great deal to the area of land under cultivation.

Throughout the woodlands of the region older maps can show small and irregular enclosures characteristic of the assarting process, and careful analysis of the landscape can reveal traces of small fields in the form of ditches, banks, and patches of ridge and furrow. The assarters' house sites often survive on roadsides which were once the edge of commons or woods, or the houses that were late abandoned are visible as earthworks or have left surface scatters of pottery. Figure 2.9 shows an assarted landscape at Blakeshall in Wolverley (Worcestershire) as represented on eighteenth and early nineteenth century maps. Some of the assarts carry the name rudding or ridding, referring to the removal of trees and bushes, and one is called Newland. Some preserve the names of former tenants, such as Cole, showing that the plots were in the separate possession of individuals. They were surrounded by hedges and ditches, so the name 'close' is used, with

---

[43] J. Willis Bund and J. Amphlett, eds., *Lay Subsidy Roll for the County of Worcester circa 1280* (WHS, 1893).
[44] *RBW*, 180–1, 221; *Rec Feck For*, pp. 49, 78.

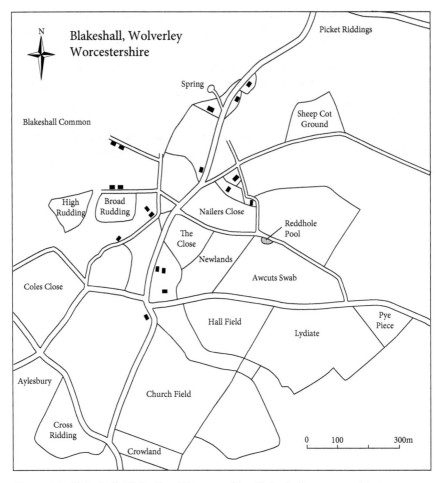

Figure 2.9 Blakeshall, Wolverley, Worcestershire Blakeshall, one township among ten in Wolverley, in 1778 retained much evidence of its development and landscape in the Middle Ages, with scattered houses, small irregular enclosed fields, some bearing assart names like Rudding and Newland, on the edge of a large common (source: WA, ref 970.5, BA 1289).

a common alternative of 'croft'. The irregular shape of the enclosures reflects the process of piecemeal clearance, and lanes and paths were needed to gain access to these small fields. Some of the plots were occupied with houses or cottages, some of which have been abandoned, but others are still occupied by houses that had medieval predecessors.[45] Blakeshall occupied a site on the edge of a large common which still exists, the edges of which had been nibbled away by assarts.

[45] WA, ref. 970.5:197, BA1289.

PEASANTS AND LANDSCAPES 37

At the beginning of the thirteenth century, the Forest of Dean contained large areas of dense woods (Figure 2.10). It would only be in a thinly populated country that wild boar would flourish in such numbers that a hundred of them could be killed in Dean for consumption in the royal household in 1254. Wolves had largely been eliminated in lowland England, but in the 1280s they could still be found in Dean.[46] The area went through a sustained period of development in the twelfth and thirteenth centuries, and the number of households can conservatively be estimated to have increased from 324 in 1086 to more than a thousand by the

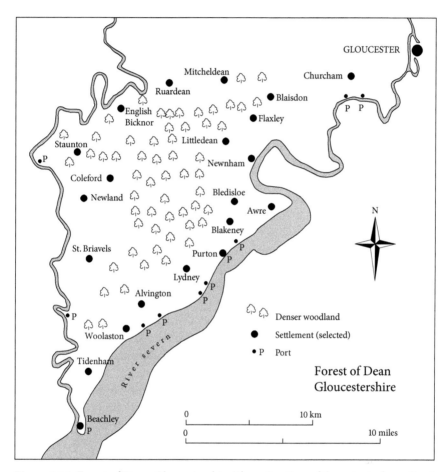

Figure 2.10 Forest of Dean, Gloucestershire The estimation of the extent of woodland depends on sixteenth-century sources. The inhabitants lived in both villages and dispersed settlements (not shown). The river ports gave access to Bristol and other towns (source: *VCH Glouc*, vol. 5, p. 296).

---

[46] *VCH Glouc* vol 5, pp. 285–94, 354–62 (wildlife on p. 290); C.E. Hart, *Royal Forest* (Oxford, 1966), p. 41.

early fourteenth century. Much of that increase was achieved by clearing new land.[47] The forest regard of 1282 records that 94 per cent of the 273 assarts contained 7 acres or less, and two-thirds consisted of an acre or fraction of an acre, suggesting small-scale peasant clearance.[48] Assarts, for which aristocrats were responsible, were being cultivated by peasants: a knight, Henry of Dene of Little Dean, paid for assarting 20 acres and enclosing another 15, but half an acre from this land was sublet to Henry Witelond to build four houses, and he in turn sublet one of them as a cottage to Alexander Hoc for 6*d* per annum. Groups of between three and six individuals cleared a single piece of land, suggesting partnerships to provide labour or raise money. The uncertainties of these ventures are implied by the occasional assart that had not produced a crop. On the other hand, some tenants made efforts to improve their land by marling it, for which purpose pits were dug that were reported to the Forest authorities.

Buildings were added to the assarts and purprestures, mentioned occasionally in Dean, but frequently in enquiries in Feckenham in the 1240s, when dozens of new buildings (sixteen in the small village of Cooksey alone) were said to have been erected mostly by peasants. Some were accommodating animals that grazed in the forest. The assarted land was occasionally held in association with servile holdings. Two tenants at Churcham on the edge of the Forest of Dean, Wymund de Stutebrugge and William Cissmore, held half-yardlands in villeinage and other lands. They were able to add free land to their holdings by acquiring an extra half-acre or acre and a half of assarts.[49] Tenants were attracted to occupy free land in forests and woodlands because their main obligation was a cash rent, and they felt secure under the protection of the common law. Lords offered these advantageous terms in order to gain more tenants and income, and to develop underexploited parts of their estates.

Living in a royal forest was in many ways a disadvantage. In Dean the poor quality of much of the soil and the hilly character of the country did not encourage extensive cultivation of grain, and many peasants had only smallholdings of arable, often a cottage with an acre or two, and rarely more than 15 acres. Individuals worked hard and paid a great deal to acquire new land—4*s* 6*d* per acre was charged by the forest administration in Dean as in Feckenham, and in addition lords took rents and dues from their tenants. Added to those burdens were the constant well-documented complaints that forest officials took extra payments for their own profit. There was much agitation in the thirteenth century against the royal forests, and in an act of conciliation to his subjects at the end of the

---

[47] From figures in A. Farley ed., *Domesday Book* (London, 1783) and P. Franklin, ed., *The Taxpayers of Medieval Gloucestershire* (Stroud, 1993).
[48] C.E. Hart, 'Dean Forest Eyre of 1282' (MA dissertation, University of Bristol, 1955).
[49] *Hist Glouc*, vol 3, pp. 135, 137–8.

century, Edward I redrew the boundaries and greatly reduced the areas under forest law.

For all of the difficulties, the forest offered many benefits. The demands of the crown were not intended to punish enterprising assarters, or to discourage or prevent them. The king needed money, and the sums levied were intended to be affordable: the initial payments were a burden, but they did not continue. Peasants attempted to avoid the penalties of forest law, and they were helped by the inefficiency of the administration. They had their own customs and valued and defended them. In a famous quarrel of the early fourteenth century over the intercommoned pasture on the borders of Alvington and Woolaston, the men of Woolaston drove a hundred sheep off the pasture, which precipitated an agreement between the two monastic lords in 1319 confirming, among other things, the grazing rights of the tenants on both sides.[50]

The common pasture in the Forest of Dean was available without limits, in contrast with the stints imposed in almost all conventional villages. Forest dwellers were able to gather fuel and various types of wood and vegetation, to use for hedging, fodder, litter, and charcoal. Dean was also the source of materials such as iron ore, mineral coal, and various types of stone. Ropes (from lime bark), barrels, and tanned leather could be made from felled trees. It must be rated as one of the most intensively industrialized districts in England (see 'Industry within peasant society' in Chapter 9). Established peasant families can be found among those operating forges in 1282, such as the Jans of Staunton and the Fouls of Ruardean. Peasants who were not drawn into industrial employment could still benefit from supplying the demand from miners, artisans, and labourers for food and drink, or provide transport services for the industries. The forest community benefited from the infrastructure of four boroughs, at least three unofficial market towns (Blakeney, Mitcheldean, and Newland), with roads linking different parts of the forest and taking goods out of the forest, for example to Gloucester, and to small river ports and landing places along the Severn estuary such as Purton. Boats connected the Forest to places up and down the river. Dean had a flexible economy with varied agricultural and industrial resources, and connections with a wide range of customers.

A distinct Dean landscape combined nucleated clusters, even a regular row settlement at English Bicknor, with small hamlets and dispersed farms and cottages, as in other woodlands. Forest settlements and their fields and closes were connected by a network of lanes and roads. In the spaces between settlements were large heaths and commons, to which the word 'meend' ('land held in common') was sometimes applied. At least part of the still visible carpet of cinders from iron forges, and some of the traces of diggings for coal, iron ore, and stone

---

[50] *VCH Glouc*, vol 5, pp. 5, 9.

date back to the Middle Ages. The broad outline of Dean's topography, with its extensive woods protected from destruction, owes much to royal policy, but its intricate detail represents a landscape made by peasants.

The enclosures and the plentiful industrial employment might have encouraged individualism among Forest people, but there was also a need for collective solidarities, such as the common purpose shown by the miners in defending their privileges. The parish had an importance for peasants who otherwise lacked a unifying focus. No less than eight of the Forest villages are known to have had church houses, which were valued assembly points for parish conviviality and fundraising.

Manors in the Forest tended to be small. Their lords did not exercise strong lordship, and tenants owed light rents and services. Parishes could be large and complicated. The modern parish of Newland contains almost 8,800 acres in twenty-two detached parts. Some parcels of land still lack any parochial connections. If the vills chosen for tax assessment in 1327 and 1334 are compared with those named for the taxes of the 1520s an administrative transformation had taken place, reflecting the shifting population. Coleford, a small hamlet in 1349, had become a tax vill with many contributors of its own in 1525, but was linked to Newland in 1522. The lack of administrative continuity makes comparison difficult, but some places seem to have grown in population between the 1320s and the 1520s, in reversal of the normal tendency. This could suggest that the forest dwellers enjoyed opportunities, and were able to benefit from the Forest environment, even when other districts were experiencing hard times.

The distinctive character of the Forest of Dean was expressed in Forest people's sense of identity: they regarded themselves as special and privileged, and very different from the neighbours across the Wye and in the Vale. An incident in 1430, when they rioted and seized grain being carried downriver in boats from Tewkesbury, provoked royal officials to call them 'the whole community of the Forest' (together with the inhabitants of two hundreds between the Forest and the estuary).[51] Belief in the Forest's autonomy, and awareness of the differences between Forest dwellers and their neighbours have persisted into modern times. Did other parts of the region identify themselves as set apart? There are hints of special customs in the Arden, including the use of a 'great acre', and Arden was used in personal names and place names (William de Arden; Hampton-in-Arden) suggesting that people living outside that district thought of it as a coherent territory. Movements of country people (see 'Migration' in Chapter 4) within the boundaries of the Feldon or the wolds resulted from their attachment to familiar landscapes and ways of life.

---

[51] T. Johnson, *Law in Common. Legal Cultures in Late-Medieval England* (Oxford, 2020), p. 126.

Peasants, lords, and the changing landscape after 1350

In examining the making of the west midland landscape in a period of growth, up to the middle of the fourteenth century, peasants had a role alongside kings, lords, and townspeople, but surely in the next phase the lords became much more decisive? As the population thinned in the fourteenth century, especially after the plague of 1349, lords are said in many villages to have expropriated peasants, enclosed the common fields, and converted the arable into grazing for herds and flocks.[52] More careful consideration of the processes shows that just as a range of people and circumstances contributed to the making of villages, so varied social and environmental factors led to their unmaking. To begin with the settlements of the woodlands, both the landscape and the documents record the abandonment of houses in considerable numbers. At Hanbury in Worcestershire a combination of field observation, maps, and documents demonstrates that at least forty houses were left unoccupied, mainly in the later Middle Ages, from a total of more than a hundred inhabited buildings in *c.* 1300. Areas of ridge and furrow now preserved in pasture suggest the retreat of cultivation, but this is not closely dateable. At Pendock, in the same county, about twenty from a total of sixty houses were left uninhabited by the sixteenth century (Figure 2.3).[53] From the tithe records of six parishes in north and west Worcestershire, output of grain and legumes fell by 27 per cent during the first half of the fifteenth century.[54] This was mainly the result of a reduction in the acreage under crops, which was already in process in 1349–1400. One factor leading to a fall in production was the total abandonment of holdings, or the decision by the tenants to favour grazing (see 'Arable and pasture: Managing change' in Chapter 6). The thinning out of the settlements in the woodlands rarely resulted in a complete depopulation of an area of countryside, and similarly, in an agrarian landscape which had always combined pasture and arable, a tipping of the balance in favour of pasture was rarely transformative. The fabric of the historic landscape, with its dispersed settlements, winding roads, enclosed crofts, and areas of common grazing persisted. In the assarted landscape at Wolverley (illustrated in Figure 2.9) some of the closes had contained dwellings before 1350, but after the loss of population remained empty for centuries. The

---

[52] M.W. Beresford, *The Lost Villages of England*, revised ed. (Stroud, 1998); H. Thorpe, 'The Lord and the Landscape', *TBAS* 80 (1965), pp. 38–77.

[53] C. Dyer, *Hanbury: Settlement and Society in a Woodland Landscape* (University of Leicester Department of English Local History Occasional Papers, 4th series, 4, 1991); C. Dyer, 'Dispersed Settlements in Medieval England. A Case Study of Pendock, Worcestershire', *Med Arch* 24 (1990), pp. 97–121.

[54] C. Dyer, 'Peasant Farming in Late Medieval England: Evidence from the Tithe Estimations by Worcester Cathedral Priory', in *Peasants and Lords in the Medieval English Economy. Essays in Honour of Bruce M.S. Campbell*, edited by M. Kowaleski, J. Langdon, and P.R. Schofield (Turnhout, 2015), p. 91.

general impression is that the varied and flexible use of land in the woodlands allowed the inhabitants to absorb the shocks of the later Middle Ages.

In the champion and to a lesser extent in the wolds villages could be reduced drastically in size, and were sometimes totally deserted. Settlements were not abandoned as a direct result of an epidemic, even that of 1349. Rather the widespread tendency for people to migrate was the main cause of empty and decayed houses. Migration was a universal tendency, and can be observed in both woodlands and champion, as serfs were reported to have left the manor without permission, tenants' names disappear, and tenants were reported to be neglecting buildings and allowing them to fall into ruin. Holdings were described as tofts rather than messuages, meaning that the buildings had gone, and land was reported to be lying 'in the lord's hands' or to have been taken on by a tenant as in a process of engrossment. A very rapid turnover of tenants suggests that a village was in terminal decline, like Kingston in central Warwickshire where between 1386 and 1430 few families lasted for more than one generation.[55]

In the nucleated villages of the champion and wolds the abandonment of holdings has left its mark on surviving villages, like Prior's Hardwick in Warwickshire. Modern fields to the east of the modern settlement contain the earthwork remains of tofts (closes in which houses had once stood), house sites, and holloways reflecting the complexity of the settlement's past, with both regular and irregular plot boundaries. Much of the shrinkage must have happened before 1411, when a survey reveals that only seventeen tenants remained of the original thirteenth-century total of forty-four.[56] The centre of the Gloucestershire village of Hazleton was much depleted when its original thirty households halved in number, leaving the earthwork outlines of abandoned houses, and six empty plots where houses once stood.[57] Engrossment is sometimes visible on deserted village sites when a large holding seems to have absorbed its neighbours, only for it in turn to be left to decay.

Peasants decided to leave their houses for a variety of reasons. Occasionally they may have been impoverished, as was clearly the case at Coton in Warwickshire, where the tenants abandoned by c.1300 small houses built of timbers set in the earth. Their possessions were few and of low-quality judging from the small finds and pottery from the excavation.[58] However, some of those leaving villages later in the period were abandoning yardland holdings of 30 acres which should have been capable of supporting a family in some comfort. Excavated houses at Upton in Gloucestershire and Goldicote in Warwickshire where habitation ceased in the late fourteenth century were well built. They do not appear to have been afflicted

---

[55] British Library, Egerton Rolls 2106, 2108; SCLA, DR 98/438, 463a.
[56] Warwickshire County Museum Aerial photograph WAN 6854/32; *WHR*, pp. 203–6; *Cov Reg*, pp. 541–4.
[57] C. Dyer and D. Aldred, 'Changing Landscape and Society in a Cotswold Village: Hazleton, Gloucestershire, to c. 1600', *TBGAS*, 127 (2009), pp. 235–70.
[58] A. Maull and others, 'Excavations of the Deserted Medieval Village of Coton in Coton Park, Rugby' (unpublished report by Northamptonshire Archaeology, Northampton County Council, 2001).

by decay, and were associated with an impressive range of material goods.[59] The migrating inhabitants apparently believed that they could lead a better life in another village, and we can imagine that they left their homes with confidence, not in despair. Not all departures can be described with such optimism. Villages that lost a high proportion of their inhabitants tended to be small and remote, without a parish church, and lacked facilities and much sense of community. In some villages in advanced decline, the manor court had to deal with cases of anti-social behaviour which may reflect some degree of demoralization.[60] One factor affecting the tenants who were engrossing their neighbours' holdings was the lack of workers who could be employed on the large quantities of land that were being accumulated.

Lords often sought to prevent an outward flow of migrants and to encourage newcomers to replace them. They campaigned against the decay of buildings, ordered serfs who had left to return, and allied with the majority of the village community to maintain the rules of husbandry.

A minority of lords adopted a very different policy of removing tenants, but often after a long period of decline. The way was prepared by the engrossing tenants, who prevented newcomers from acquiring land. Some villages were embarking on long term and piecemeal enclosure, which is apparent in the modern hedge lines which follow the curved lines of the ploughed strips in the open fields. Custom prevented lords from evicting the remaining tenants in a decaying village, but they could make life difficult for the inhabitants by enclosing the common pastures or even part of the common arable. The lord's ally in making such changes would have been the leasehold tenant of the demesne (often recruited from the top ranks of the peasantry), who would stand to profit from a rationalization of the manor and the amalgamation of demesne and tenant land. As life became harder tenants moved to occupy vacant holdings which were available in nearby villages, and potential heirs went to take up employment elsewhere.

In the champion major changes in land use are also made apparent in the documents with as much as a third of the land being recorded as pasture in the late fifteenth century (see section on 'Arable and pasture: Managing change' in Chapter 6). Before 1400 most of the pasture lay in shared commons which could not be calculated as a specific acreage. This tendency to expand pasture was obviously being driven to extremes in the case of the deserted villages. Kingston in Warwickshire, which in 1430 had eleven tenants, by 1496 consisted of two closes, East Field and West Field (the former open fields) held by farmers. Five large

---

[59] R.H. Hilton and P.A. Rahtz, 'Upton, Gloucestershire, 1959–1964', *TBGAS* 85(1966), pp. 70–146; P.A Rahtz, 'Upton, Gloucestershire, 1959–1968. Second Report', *TBGAS* 88 (1969), pp. 74–126; P. Thompson and S.C. Palmer, 'Iron Age, Romano-British and Medieval Settlements Excavated on the Transco Newbold Pacey to Honeybourne Gas Pipeline in 2000', *TBWAS* 116 (2012), pp. 1–139.
[60] C. Dyer, 'Villages in Crisis: Social Dislocation, 1370–1520', in *Deserted Villages Revisited*, edited by C. Dyer and R. Jones (Hatfield, 2010), pp. 28–45.

fields were depicted on an estate map of 1697, one of which was called 'Grazing Towne'.[61] The lords' motive for the changes is apparent from the high valuations given to the enclosed pastures that succeeded a village and its fields, which often exceeded £20 and could rise to £40 or £60, far in excess of the rents paid by a decaying village with a handful of tenants with run-down holdings. The process by which a village and its corn fields was transformed into an enclosed pasture is visible in the field as well as in the documents in the case of Weston-juxta-Cherrington in Long Compton parish in Warwickshire. Now sixteen house sites can be identified on both sides of a village street, with the remains of the manor house at the end of the street. At least two other houses stood to the east, and probably another group to the west. There had been twenty-four households in 1279, which had fallen to fourteen in 1353. Then another six were lost, so that when Henry Keble (a London merchant who had become lord of the manor) decided to act in 1509 there were seven houses and a cottage to be 'devastated and destroyed' and allowed to fall into ruin, according to the enquiry into depopulation in 1517. This left thirty-eight people 'without their work, dwelling and occupation'. In 1527 the farmer of Weston left in his will 1,640 sheep and 130 cattle, so the conversion to pasture seems to have been complete.[62] The story of the village's decline is not untypical in the succession of tenants leaving their holdings over many years, followed by the lord closing down the village in a final denouement.

A rather similar sequence of events overtook the village of Westcote (Figure 2.5), which has left the very clear outline of the foundations of the abandoned houses still visible in the landscape. The language used by the reports of the enquiries of 1517 (quoting Warwickshire examples) reflect the different pathways to depopulation, with some forceful statements about lords removing villagers, such as 'the whole hamlet of Barcheston was desolated and annihilated' and people were 'expelled from their houses', but often the actions seem more indirect, such as the lord of Weston Mauduit 'converted' the arable so that people 'departed', or at Shuttington the lord 'allowed the land to fall into decay', and converted it to pasture, so that six ploughs were 'displaced' and people 'withdrew'. The same phrases about 'allowing decay', and people withdrawing were used at Dorsington.[63] The stiff legal language seems to have been describing a variety of processes by which peasants left of their own accord, or departed under pressure, or were directly expelled.

---

[61] *Calendar of IPM*, 2nd ser, Henry VII, vol 1, p. 1052; M.W. Beresford and J.G. Hurst, *Deserted Medieval Villages* (London, 1971), pp. 41–2.

[62] *WHR*, pp. 241–3; SCLA, DR 98/865–6; I.S. Leadam, ed., *The Domesday of Inclosures* (Royal Historical Society, 1897), vol 2, pp. 415–16; E. Rainsberry, *Through the Lych Gate* (Kineton, 1969), pp. 46–7.

[63] Leadam, *Domesday*, vol 2, pp. 395–6, 416–17. I am grateful for the chance to see Spencer Dimmock's translation of documents of the Commissions, including Weston Mauduit and Dorsington.

Most champion and wold villages survived with reduced numbers but with intact open fields. The leading peasants who managed the fields expanded their pastoral resources by converting part of the open field to semi-permanent grazing by turning arable strips into fenced leys. Other enclosures might take the form of small crofts, often on the edge of the open fields. They were able to allow cultivated land to be converted to grazing by intensifying cultivation of a smaller area of arable. Woodland settlements were thinned by piecemeal abandonment of houses, cottages, and areas of cultivation, but a little noticed trend in the century before 1540 was a small-scale resumption of assarting and the building of new houses and cottages, some by lease-holding farmers who were re-organizing their land and moving their farmhouses in consequence, but also cottages were being established on the edge of commons, like Heathhouses in Kingsbury and Rotton Row End in Middleton (both in the Warwickshire Arden).[64]

Conclusion

The proposal that societies were moulded by the variety of land that they occupied has some merits. People also created landscapes, sometimes consciously and deliberately, sometimes by taking actions with unforeseen outcomes. The landscape of the west midland region was the work of many hands stretching back before the Middle Ages: roads and boundaries were a legacy of the prehistoric or Roman periods, while some land is likely to have been under continuous cultivation between the second century and the fourteenth. Roman field boundaries could provide a framework in which medieval fields and settlements developed.

Kings, aristocrats, and the higher clergy all had a direct interest in their own surroundings, and devoted much attention and resources to the gardens and parks around their residences. They protected some landscape features, such as woods, and promoted agricultural expansion, sometimes clearing and cultivating themselves, more often encouraging and sanctioning the work of others. They had a role in settlement planning and the layout of fields, but were selective in their concern: a town for example was a special and valuable asset, and they were likely to be involved in planning its streets and manipulating its communication network. Lay lords often had a transient interest in particular places, making occasional visits to a residence, and, unlike estates held by undying institutions, their tenure tended not to continue over centuries.

---

[64] C. Dyer, 'Peasants and Farmers: Rural Settlements and Landscapes in an Age of Transition', in *The Age of Transition. The Archaeology of English Culture 1400–1600*, edited by D. Gaimster and P. Stamper (Society for Medieval Archaeology Monograph 15, 1997), pp. 61–76, especially pp. 70–1; A. Watkins, ed., *The Early Records of Coleshill c.1120–1549* (DS, 51, 2018), p. 22.

Peasants had a very direct concern with the landscape in which they lived, and every detail had a bearing on their well-being and sense of identity. Boundaries mattered a great deal, and were embedded and renewed in the collective memory. Villagers managed common assets, and maintained their share in intercommoned pastures. They had a role in planning and modifying settlements and fields, and cleared new land. They were responding to encouragement, but also taking the initiative. They infringed the rules by cultivating wastes without authorization, but on occasion they resisted clearance, again in defiance of authority if necessary. Peasants responded to the need to make changes in the landscape when demand for land and food were expanding in the thirteenth century. They scaled down their farming in the fourteenth and fifteenth centuries, leading to inevitable if unplanned reductions in the size and number of settlements. Peasants had a vital role in making the landscape.

3
Peasant society
Landholding and status

Were the social conditions of west midland peasants imposed on them, or could they act to improve or change their circumstances? This chapter will be focussed on themes of inequalities in landholding and legal status, tracing developments throughout the period.

Lords often counted their tenants, or made lists of them, which gives us a picture of a society stratified by the amount of land held and by legally defined tenures and personal status. After a few listings from before 1066, and the comprehensive but brief description of landholding in Domesday Book, more detailed surveys were made by large church estates of their own manors in the twelfth and thirteenth centuries. The state surveyed lands of the laity in the Hundred Rolls of 1279 and the Inquisitions Post Mortem, most informatively between 1250 and 1340. For the rest of the period tenants were listed in rentals, which lacked details.

The surveys show the peasants as subordinates, but modern observers should not accept these partisan documents as an objective depiction of the structure of society. The lords believed that their predecessors had granted land to peasants, and that they continued to be entitled to exercise authority over peasants and to gain a flow of income from them.

An extent (survey) was made in 1299 after the death of John Giffard for his manor of Brimpsfield, in the Gloucestershire Cotswolds.[1] The lord was said to have under his direct control a demesne of 580 acres of arable, with 8 acres of meadow and pasture worth 25*s* (more than a hundred acres). He would also have had access to common pastures. He was obviously able to produce food for his large household, and generate cash from selling surplus grain, wool, and livestock. He enjoyed the status of being the lord of a large manor, reinforced by its castle and associated deer park. Most of the survey was taken up with details of the fifty-nine tenants, giving their names, landholdings, and obligations to the lord. First came the twenty-eight free tenants, most of whom held quarter-yardlands (about 10 acres each) or half-yardlands (20 acres). Yardlands or virgates were the standard unit of landholding, and normally contained about 30 acres of arable land, but

---

[1] S. Madge, ed., *Abstracts of IPMs for Gloucestershire*, part 4, 1236–1300 (British Record Society, 30, 1903), pp. 201–5.

yardlands of at least 40 acres were often found in Gloucestershire.[2] Then the fourteen tenants in villeinage were listed (mostly with half-yardlands); the seventeen smallholders were mostly cottagers or held about 3 acres each. The villein tenants held land by the custom of the manor, and their equivalents in other surveys of this period were called customary tenants or serfs (*servi*). They could be known as *neifs* or *nativi* (born serfs) or bondmen. All of these terms described people who were unfree. The lord benefitted from the tenants' rents, £5 in all from the freeholders, and £2 from the villeins, and from the latter he could call on their labour to do 39 days of ploughing and a thousand days of other work, including cutting and carrying corn in the harvest. Tenants of half-yardlands were very useful to the lord as they each were able to own a plough, harrow, and cart and the draught animals to pull them, so they could contribute to the cultivation of the demesne. Much of the agricultural work that was not being done by the tenants in villeinage was carried out by hired labour, and it was convenient for the lord that there were so many smallholders who needed paid work to supplement their income from the land. In practice, the lord is likely to have chosen to take cash rents rather than labour from the customary tenants, and therefore to employ the smallholders as specialists such as shepherds, and as labourers.[3]

The information about Brimpsfield came originally from manorial officials, who would have consulted local juries of tenants. The voice of the tenants can sometimes be detected when they specified details favourable to themselves. At Brimpsfield the description of the labour services stated that work would not be done for the lord on saints' feast days, and that on Saturdays, work should cease at noon. A jury assisting in a survey of another Cotswold manor at Blockley (also in 1299), reported that a tenant of a yardland, John son of William, was supposed to pay a toll when he sold an ox or horse, but he was able to persuade the jury that this applied only to an ox: 'And he does not owe toll for his horse, as they say'[4] (Figure 3.1).

The details of tenants' obligations were evidently subject to negotiation and compromise, revealing that tenants took a stance and had some influence at least in small matters.[5] On the larger issue of the ordering of society for the benefit of lords, the peasants surely had an alternative model. Judging from the decisions that they were able to make in the manor court about the inheritance of land, they treated their holdings as if they were their property. Their everyday relations with their neighbours, as part of a village community and as parishioners, must have been more important to them than being appendages of a manor serving a lord.

---

[2] For example, on the Gloucester Abbey manors in 1266–7 the median figure was 48 acres: *Hist Glouc*, vol 3, pp. 44–213.
[3] B. Harvey, *Westminster Abbey and its Estates in the Middle Ages* (Oxford, 1977), pp. 225–31.
[4] *RBW*, p. 298.
[5] J.R. Birrell, 'Manorial Custumals Reconsidered', *P&P*, 224 (2014), pp. 3–37.

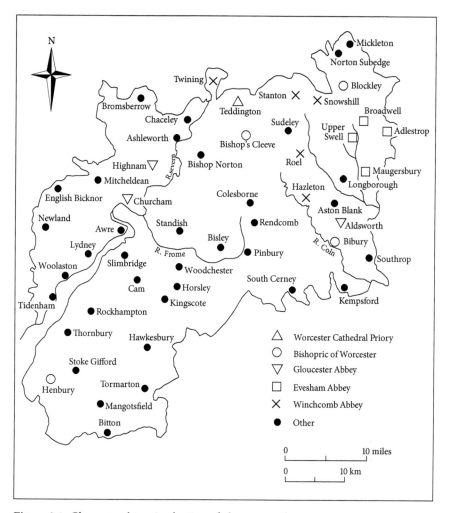

Figure 3.1 Gloucestershire. A selection of places named.

Holding land before 1349

The amount of land held by each tenant was regarded as an important element in defining social rank. In the period 1200–1348 in those districts where landholding was measured in yardlands or virgates, a small minority held more than a yardland (30–40 acres). In most villages, yardlanders occupied the highest rung of the social hierarchy, but as we have seen at Brimpsfield, the half-yardland tenants could form the top layer. Yardlanders were most numerous in the south and east of the region, especially on the Cotswolds and in part of the Vale, and also in the Avon valley and in a scatter of manors in the Feldon of Warwickshire. Half and quarter yardlands are often found in the Worcestershire woodlands and the Arden but in these areas holdings tended not to be measured in yardlands but in acres, or a holding was said to consist of 'a messuage and an assart', or 'a messuage and three crofts'. Smallholdings (mostly between 1 acre and 5 acres) were quite scarce in the Cotswolds, but numerous in woodlands, reaching 62 per cent of the holdings in Warwickshire recorded in 1279 in a cluster of villages in the Arden. Some of these, such as Coundon, were close to Coventry, and proximity to other large towns such as Gloucester and Worcester encouraged the proliferation of smallholdings[6] (Figure 3.2).

A good case can be made for regarding yardlands and their subdivisions, together with smaller holdings called Mondaylands and *averclands* as designed by lords for their own benefit. According to a pre-Conquest document depicting peasant obligations, *The Rules of all Kinds of People*, lords endowed tenants with yardlands, and provided them with livestock and equipment, which enabled them to pay rents and do substantial labour services. The cottars or smallholders would do general labouring tasks.[7]

Lords in the later Middle Ages maintained a policy of preserving the integrity of the standard holdings. This was partly for clarity in levying rents and services on a well-defined unit of tenure, as records of landholding enabled the lord to keep track of the lands and tenants. It was also in the lord's interest that holdings should not be excessively fragmented. The half-yardlanders of Brimpsfield would have four oxen (a number which suggests an unusually large half-yardland), which could be yoked together with the oxen of a neighbour to form the ideal eight-ox plough team for tilling the demesne (see 'Cattle' in Chapter 7). The yardlanders' and half-yardlanders' ability to cultivate their own holdings was also to the lord's advantage as their produce fed the peasants' families, but part would be sold, enabling rents in cash to be paid.

The lord's interests were also served by having a number of smallholdings from which labour could be recruited. At Brimpsfield John Gilebert held a Mondayland, a holding of about 3 acres, for which he was obliged to work on Mondays. The lord would find that day's work useful, but on the other days John would be available to take paid work. There were six other Mondaymen at Brimpsfield, and ten cottagers, so the lord had a plentiful supply of labour for weeding, harvesting, threshing, and mending the fence round the park.

---

[6] *RBW; Reg Wig*; Madge, ed., *IPMs Gloucestershire*; E.A Fry, ed., *Abstracts of IPMs for Gloucestershire*, pt 5, 1302–58 (British Record Society, 40, 1910); *WHR*; *Hist Glouc*; J.Willis Bund, ed., *IPMs for the County of Worcester*, pt. 1, 1242–1299 (WHS, 1894); J. Willis Bund, ed., *IPMs for the County of Worcester*, pt. 2, 1300–1326 (WHS, 1909); HTC; B.A. Lees, ed., *Records of the Templars in England in the Twelfth Century: The Inquest of 1185* (British Academy Records of Social and Economic History, 9, 1935); R.H. Hilton, *Social Structure of Rural Warwickshire in the Middle Ages* (DS Occasional Paper, 9, 1950).

[7] D.C. Douglas, ed., *English Historical Documents*, vol 2, 1042–1189 (London, 1953), pp. 813–16; P.D.A. Harvey, 'Rectitudines Singularum Personarum and Gerefa', *EHR* 108 (1993), pp. 1–22. (yardlands are not named as such in this document, but their existence can be deduced).

PEASANT SOCIETY 51

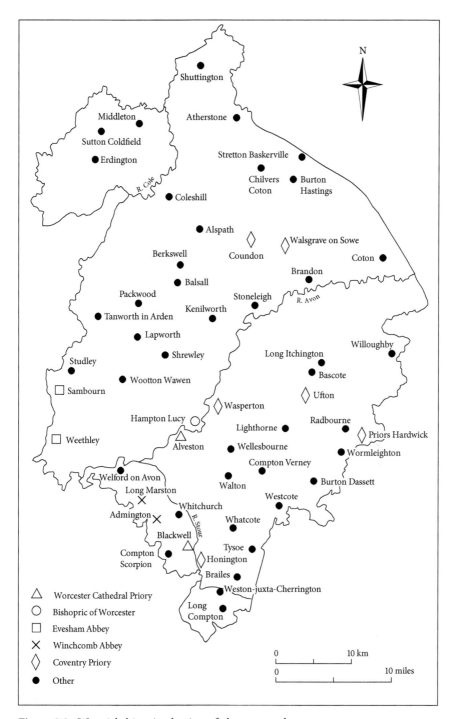

Figure 3.2 Warwickshire. A selection of places named.

The lords kept the standard holdings intact by prohibiting, or only allowing under licence, the splitting of the inheritance between heirs, or the subletting of parcels of land; or the sale by the tenant of part of the holding. In view of the rules that the lords imposed, could peasants have much influence over the possession and transfer of land? In the twelfth and thirteenth centuries everyone involved in decisions about land was under some pressure arising from the growth in population, and the commercial expansion, which together created a greater demand for land and its produce.[8] These underlying tendencies were expressed at local level by the concern of families to provide for younger sons and daughters who were excluded from the main inheritance. They provided the energy behind the movement to create new holdings, either from the demesne, or from clearing land from woods and pastures, or by division of tenures.

Tenants could achieve some of their ambitions for non-inheriting relatives. On some manors, yardlands appear to have been plentiful in the eleventh and twelfth centuries and were subsequently divided. The process can be observed on the Worcestershire manor of Ripple, where in about 1170 there were fourteen full yardlands, but by 1299 only one survived, alongside sixty-two half-yardlands. Twenty-four yardland holdings had already been divided by 1170, and the origin of the other half-yardlands can be detected in a number of statements that two tenants held a yardland together[9] (Figure 3.3). Partible inheritance between brothers or other close relatives can be suggested by identifications of joint tenants as in 1279 at Wasperton (Warwickshire) where Laurence Norman and Robert Norman were named as tenants of a yardland. In three other cases the second tenant lacks a surname, for example, 'William le Bachiler and Sarra', which may well be indicating two members of the same family. The process is recorded at Cleeve Prior at the rather late date of 1351, when Thomas de Yardley, who was 'poor and disabled', surrendered his rights to a yardland to his brother and sister, each of them to hold a half.[10] Lords would also have hoped to increase rents by multiplying tenants, so the interests of both peasants and lords seem to have been converging.

The subdivisions stopped at a point when both lords and peasants probably realized the dangers of taking the process too far. At Ripple in 1299 three half-yardlands were held jointly by two tenants, and therefore heading towards division.[11] However, though the process had begun in that village, it did not continue. Perhaps the lord doubted if tenants of quarter-yardlands would easily pay rents and do services, and peasants understood that such a holding on its own could

---

[8] R.H. Britnell, *Britain and Ireland 1050–1530* (Oxford, 2004), pp. 185–204; J. Langdon and J. Masschaele, 'Commercial Activity and Population Growth in Medieval England', *P&P* 190 (2006), pp. 35–81.
[9] *RBW*, pp. 152–64, 167–71.   [10] *WHR*, pp. 178–9; WCL, E4.   [11] *RBW*, pp. 160, 161.

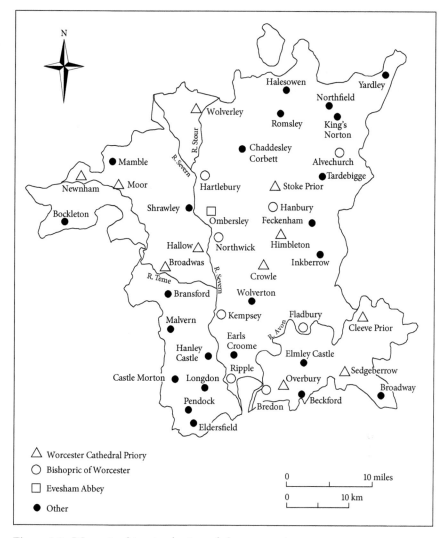

Figure 3.3 Worcestershire. A selection of places named.

not sustain a family. In Warwickshire in 1357, it was assumed that tenants of quarter-yardlands would normally work for wages.[12]

There were many other ways that the apparently rigid structure of standard landholdings could be adapted to the requirements of peasant life cycles. A temporary subdivision could be part of a retirement agreement. The retired couple, or widow or widower, were usually assigned a space in which to live and a promise of food. They were sometimes allowed a part of the land, such as a house

---

[12] B.H. Putnam, *The Enforcement of the Statutes of Labourers* (New York, 1908), Appendix, p. 224.

and one acre for William Walter of Pensax (Worcestershire) in 1315, who was said to be 'destitute and decayed'. A widow of Tibberton in the same county in 1316 drove a hard bargain and was assigned a small house, 4 acres of land, and an acre of meadow from a half-yardland, so about a quarter of the holding.[13] The arrangement did not threaten the main holding in the long term because the land would revert when the old person died.

A special feature of the landholding customs on the Halesowen estate, which might have been a quirk of record-keeping rather than a radical departure from normal practice, was the granting of a parcel of land to relatives such as non-inheriting children. For example, in 1302 a tenant of Romsley gave his brother John son of Mall and Margery his wife a butt of land on which to build, to hold for life for 1 ½*d* per annum.[14] Such a grant enabled the building of a cottage so that those without an inheritance could set up an independent household. The lord licensed these arrangements, but the initiatives came from the peasants.

The short-term division of holdings was also a feature of customary inheritance in relation to widows and their rights of dower. This was a commonplace among free tenants, which is often not fully recorded, but in the Worcestershire manor of Wolverley widows of customary holdings were entitled to dower. Normally widows were allowed free bench of her husband's customary holding, that is to keep the land for life providing that she did not remarry and was not 'corrupted' by extra-marital sexual relations. At Wolverley a widow retained half of the holding in her lifetime. The way this worked is demonstrated by a dispute in 1346 over holdings which had belonged to Roger de Blakesole. The two holdings, a messuage and a half-yardland and a messuage and a quarter-yardland, were claimed by Robert Hobekins. His claim was upheld, but half of the land was being retained as dower by Roger's widow, Matilda. She could not manage the cultivation herself, so she obtained a licence from the lord to lease the land to Richard Hereward. She received in return an annual allowance of grain and so was protected from penury. The danger for the lord was that the half shares might be transferred to new tenants, delaying or preventing the ultimate reuniting of the holding. In this case, in the next year Robert Hobekins surrendered the land to his daughter, also called Matilda, and she married Hereward the subtenant which enabled him to take over all of the land.[15] This custom of dower is unlikely to have been proposed by the lord: he was bending to a well-established tradition among the tenants.

Turning to the numerous holdings in free tenure, these are not fully recorded in manorial courts because lords had limited authority over them. However free

---

[13] WCL, E7; Hereford Cathedral Library, R1162.
[14] *CR Romsley*, p. 48, Z. Razi, 'The Myth of the Immutable English Family', *P&P*, 140 (1993), pp. 3–44, especially pp. 7–9.
[15] WCL, E15.

Table 3.1 Transfers of free land in deeds

Place	Date	Complete holdings	Parcels and plots	Rents	Total
Hanley Castle	1200–1349	14 (30%)	32 (68%)	1 (2%)	47 (100%)
Coleshill	1200–1319	8 (11%)	62 (86%)	2 (3%)	72 (100%)

Sources: *Rec Hanley*; A Watkins, ed., *The Early Records of Coleshill c.1120–1549* (DS, 51, 2018).

land was liable to payment of heriot at the end of a tenancy. New tenants were expected to pay a relief (fixed at one year's rent rather than a variable entry fine), and to do fealty. These obligations were overseen by the manorial court, so that transfers of freeholdings were recorded on the court roll. An alternative guide to the land dealings of free tenants comes from deeds, which throw light on the fragmentation of holdings. Two collections of deeds, from Hanley Castle in Worcestershire and Coleshill in Warwickshire, are analysed in Table 3.1.

Tenants presumably reduced the size of their holdings because they had to sell land to pay debts or because of the stage that they had reached in the life cycle. Land was acquired at the beginning of a landholding career, or to expand the productive capacity of a holding, or to provide for offspring who could not inherit the main holding. Grants by and to lords have been excluded from the sample, to enable a focus on transfers among peasants. The majority of transfers were apparently between unrelated people, that is, 83 per cent at Hanley and 69 per cent at Coleshill. The very large numbers of transfers of parcels—mostly selions or odd acres in the open fields, or crofts which were numerous in these woodland manors—might suggest that the standard holdings were breaking down into fragments under the pressure of inheritance and the land market, but many tenements survived. Free tenants (and their customary neighbours who also acquired free land) took advantage of the flexibility of gaining and disposing of parcels of land and crofts as they were needed, but they valued their yardlands and half-yardlands, either to be inherited, or to be sold at a good price.[16]

A more comprehensive picture of sub-division by free tenants comes from the Hundred Rolls of 1279 which record tenures for 122 villages in east Warwickshire. The surveys are ideal for investigating free peasants' dealings in land, as lords were not directing the activities of these relatively independent landholders. Land was clearly sublet on a large scale. On the woodland estate of Stoneleigh of 1,650 acres held by tenants, 471 acres or 28.5 per cent were recorded as being in the hands of subtenants. In the champion village of Priors Hardwick, from at least 700 acres of tenanted land, 122 ½ acres, or 17.5 per cent, were sublet.[17]

---

[16] The social processes behind the land market are discussed in P.D.A Harvey, ed., *The Peasant Land Market in Medieval England* (Oxford, 1984); R. M. Smith, ed., *Land, Kinship and Life-Cycle* (Cambridge, 1984).

[17] *WHR*, pp. 58–76, 203–6.

Subletting is important for this study because it shows how tenants could add to, or subtract from, or in some other way manipulate the holdings which appear in the official record.[18] The subtenants may have been the people who were involved in agricultural production, including people who were apparently landless, while those said to be tenants were just drawing a rent. At Stoneleigh thirty-five of the fifty subtenants were not also named as tenants, so potentially they gained access to land held officially by others. However some of them were tenants in nearby villages, and one of them served as a juror for compiling the Hundred Rolls and must have been propertied. Six of the subtenants were also letting out land. We find people renting land both from the lord of the manor, and fellow tenants, and then choosing part of their accumulation of land to sublet to others. The whole complex web of tenancy and subtenancy does not present us with a clear alternative pattern of landholding. Among Stoneleigh tenants (excluding subtenants) 60 per cent held 4 acres or less; if tenants and subtenants are added together the percentage of smallholders remains the same.

Was subletting a means by which a tenant could gain a good income from the rents paid by the subtenants? Only occasionally does the rent seem really profitable, like the 10s and 4 horse shoes paid for a half-yardland at Milverton, so in excess of 8d per acre.[19] Subletting could have yielded labour rather than money, for example two tenants of free yardlands at Bishops Tachbrook had cottars as subtenants, who could have been expected to work, not for the lord of the manor, but for a tenant.[20] A non-economic motive would be to help relatives gain a toehold on a holding, like the cottages already noted as being squeezed onto a messuage for a younger son or daughter who was not able to inherit. So Cristiana de Merehule of Lighthorne rented a cottage from a relative, perhaps her father, for 14d.[21]

The subtenants could transform their lives by acquiring access to land, like Reginald de Wolvey of Sowe (now called Walsgrave) who rented a messuage from one tenant and 1½ acres from another. He had the basis for forming his own household, and in feeding his family he was not entirely dependent on wages. There were also opportunities for those at the upper end of the peasantry, like Richard le Bedel of Priors Marston, who managed to accumulate 70 acres by

---

[18] Some of the issues raised by subtenancy are discussed in R.H. Hilton, ed., *The Stoneleigh Leger Book* (DS, 24, 1960), pp. xxxviii–xliv; M.K. McIntosh, *Autonomy and Community. The Royal Manor of Havering, 1200–1500* (Cambridge, 1986), pp. 103–16; M. Tompkins, 'Counting Houses: Using the Housing Structure of a Late Medieval Manor to Illuminate Population, Landholding and Occupational Structure', in *Life in Medieval Landscapes. People and Places in the Middle Ages*, edited by S. Turner and R. Silvester (Oxford, 2012), pp. 225–38.

[19] *WHR*, p. 95.

[20] *WHR*, pp. 188–9; R.M. Smith, 'Kin and Neighbours in a Thirteenth Century Suffolk Community', *Journal of Family History* 4 (1979), pp. 219–56.

[21] *WHR*, p. 199.

combining tenanted and subtenanted holdings.[22] Of course, sublet land was not held by secure tenure, so it was not an unqualified advantage.

As subletting potentially undermined a lord's control of customary land it was not allowed without a licence. Because permission was not always sought, we cannot make an accurate assessment of the quantity of land involved, though the steady stream of reports of illicit subletting raises our suspicion that much went undiscovered and unreported. A note added to the 1299 survey of Bishop's Cleeve (Gloucestershire) reveals a type of subtenant: 'there are many male cottars who owe the lord a one day *bedrip* (reaping service), and their wives do nothing', meaning that the wives had no obligation to the lord.[23] These smallholders presumably owed rent to the tenants from whom they held their cottages, perhaps in the form of work. A list at Eldersfield (Worcestershire) in 1317 contains thirty-five names of people (twelve of them women) who did three *bedrips* for the lord, a common service required of the landless.[24] A number of them seem to have the same name as tenants, so they were presumably related, and others were said to have been earning wages, but their obligation to work suggests that they were not living in the parental household, and some of them are likely to have been subletting cottages.

The cottars and 'little cottars' (*cotterelli*) on some Worcester Cathedral Priory manors were not listed by name but their numbers were given. Two or three appear on some manors in 1314–18, attracting attention at a time of bad harvests, but in 1336–7 a campaign was mounted by the Priory administration to uncover the hidden cottars. Ten tenants each from the manors of Cleeve Prior, Crowle, and Sedgeberrow were all presented for having cottars 'under them', with one, two, or three cottars each, making a total at Crowle of sixteen *coterelli*.[25] The Priory was troubled by subletting without permission, and also because subtenants were believed to be unruly. In 1316 two Cleeve Prior cottars were accused of harbouring malefactors, and a Cropthorne cottar was said in 1318 to have carried off sheaves from the harvest field.[26] However cottars had considerable value to the better-off villagers as a source of labour, and sublets to cottars must have been the secret practice in many villages. Renting out a small parcel for a cottage to be built was not regarded as a heinous crime, judging from the amercements of only 2*d* levied on offenders. Lords were being tolerant of peasants who for a combination of motives, including accommodating family members as well as increasing the pool of labour, were altering the formal structure of landholding. Of course, these cottages were much in demand from the considerable number of those lacking a secure income, and unable to acquire conventional holdings.

The subletting of land for cultivation rather than as building plots was probably on a much larger scale than the proliferation of unofficial cottage holdings. When

---

[22] *WHR*, pp. 140, 142, 210–12.   [23] *RBW*, p. 347.   [24] WA, ref. 705:134, BA1531/69.
[25] WCL, E12, E13.   [26] Hereford Cathedral Library, R1162; WCL, E8.

Table 3.2 Subletting arrangements on Worcester Priory manors before 1349

Quantity of land sublet (in acres)											
Below 1 acre	1	2	3	4	5	6	10	15	22	30 acres	Total
6	3	4	1	1	1	2	2	6	1	4	31
Length of subletting contract (in years)											
1 year	2	3	4	5	6	7	8	9	12	13	20 years	life	Total
0	4	2	7	1	6	1	1	2	1	1	1	2	29

Source: WCL, E series (manorial court rolls).

the authorities investigated subletting, as happened on the Worcester Priory manors of Himbleton (Worcestershire) and Blackwell (Warwickshire) in 1315–16, enough cases were revealed to suggest that many hundreds of acres were being sublet at any time on the whole estate.[27] Most presentments of offenders gave few details, but enough did mention the acreage of the land granted, the rent paid, and the length of the subletting contract. Table 3.2 is based on the subletting arrangements known from the Worcester Priory estate.

The generalization that a high proportion of sublets resulted in a few acres of land being held for a short time, four years or less, is reinforced by the suspicion that lettings of very small parcels for a year were disregarded and escaped notice. Nonetheless, some holdings were half-yardlands or above that size, and could be sublet for more than ten years or even for life. On the Halesowen estate in the early fourteenth century, land was being let for even longer terms of twelve to sixteen years, suggesting that some tenancies of sublet lands were lasting as long as those of conventional holdings.[28]

Customary land could be the subject of complex arrangements, for example when three tiers of tenants were involved. At Alveston (Warwickshire) in 1326 Thomas de Clyve's half-yardland had come into the hands of Adam de Styvyngton, who in turn let it to Thomas Lewelyn for sixteen years.[29] To satisfy the lord's qualms, when a sublet was registered in the manor court the tenant and subtenant could agree about their obligations to the lord. Often the lessor was responsible for rents, but in the second quarter of the fourteenth century the subtenant occasionally took on more responsibilities, even to maintain the buildings. The lessors apparently gained a considerable benefit from a sublet, because they were willing

---

[27] WCL, E7; Hereford Cathedral Library, R1162. On the general importance of subletting, R.H. Hilton, *The English Peasantry in the Later Middle Ages* (Oxford, 1975), p. 131.
[28] R.K. Field, 'The Worcestershire Peasantry in the Later Middle Ages' (MA dissertation, University of Birmingham, 1962), pp. 128, 131, 300.
[29] WCL, E10.

to pay sizeable sums to the lord for a licence, in the range of 2s, 3s 4d, and even 6s 8d. The rent the subtenant paid is rarely recorded, except that in many cases a champart contract was arranged, by which the lessor took a third (or rarely a half) of the crops.

Subletting was not just a matter of transferring control of land and its profits from lord to tenant, and therefore modifying the formal structure of standard tenements, but was a convenient way of managing the various social needs in the peasant community. Land could be sublet to a person holding custody of a child, on condition that the land would revert to the heir when he came of age. Subletting could also offer at least a temporary solution of the problem of non-inheriting children, as when at Newnham (Worcestershire) in 1325 the heir to a yardland sublet half of the holding to his brother. Subletting also came to the aid of tenants who for various reasons could not manage the land themselves. In 1346 John Rolf of Himbleton sublet his land for twelve years because he was disabled, and the new subtenant, William Trigg, paid John's entry fine of 40s (for a quarter-yardland) and agreed to maintain the buildings and land.[30] In the same year Peter de Hardenhull at Hallow in 1346 was reported to be in debt, and sublet his land for seven years, presumably to enable his creditor to recover the money owed. Such a case opens the possibility that undocumented credit negotiations lay behind sublets. Widows also found subletting a convenient way of gaining an income from the land that they held in free bench, so Edward le Newe at Boraston in Newnham (Worcestershire) in 1315 was given a licence to cultivate the land of Edith, widow of Adam Blowe, for 3½ years.[31] Women could also be lessees, as when a holding at Lindridge (Worcestershire) was taken for six years by Cristina atte Nassch and Cristina Haukenes. This was in 1315, a year when a bad harvest made land and grain especially desirable. The lessor was to receive half of the grain, and he would pay the lord's (cash) rent and contributed to the 5s fee for the licence to sublet.[32]

The opportunity that subletting provided the smallholders and other less privileged members of peasant society should not be exaggerated, and those receiving holdings could be from the wealthier end of village society. So we find at Romsley (Worcestershire) that members of three leading families, Henry de Fulfen, William de Yildentre, and Thomas Squier acquired land by licensed subletting in the period 1280–1322.[33]

Our conclusion must be that subletting, both of free and customary land, reveals the ingenuity that peasants applied to mould the apparently rigid landholding structures to meet their needs. There were risks for the tenants as well as the lord in the informality of the arrangements, as experienced by a widow of Overbury in 1315 who wished to recover 6 ½ acres of land sublet by her former husband without licence.[34]

[30] WCL, E10, E15.   [31] WCL, E15, E7.   [32] WCL, E6.
[33] CR Romsley, pp. 36, 41–2, 56, 69.   [34] WCL, E10.

Changing circumstances: Entry fines

A dramatic fall in population changed the circumstances and dynamics of peasant life in the fourteenth century. The underlying influences on the new pattern of landholding, working, and social interaction have been often told and do not need elaborate documentation here. There were problems of high mortality which brought population growth to an end in the first half of the fourteenth century. The Great Famine of 1315–17 was linked with increased death rates, cattle disease, and lasting agrarian problems throughout the region.[35] These problems were invoked by those collecting the new tax of a ninth in 1341, who reported that in some Gloucestershire villages families were abandoning the land and leaving many acres untilled. A few Cotswold settlements were left virtually uninhabited at this time, such as Little Aston in Aston Blank; and nearby Eyford had only one taxpaying household in 1327.[36] The plague epidemic that reached the region at the end of 1348 and spread in 1349 is calculated to have killed about 43 per cent of the male population of the manor of Halesowen. A guide to mortality among tenants of the estates of the bishopric of Worcester comes from the 44 per cent holdings left vacant after the event, and institutions of new clergy in the diocese of Worcester to replace those who had died amounted to 44.5 per cent.[37] All of these figures are based on imperfect data, and it may well be that mortality in the region, taking into account the bias of our sample towards relatively healthy adult males, exceeded 50 per cent. Succeeding epidemics of plague in 1361 and 1369, and of plague and other diseases in the fifteenth century, together with changes in marriage and fertility for which there is little direct documentation, kept the numbers of peasants at a low level until well after 1500. This demographic episode is important background, but as we shall see, peasants were not the prisoners of their circumstances, and they were subject to a wide range of influences including the pursuit of their own aspirations.

An overview of trends in peasant landholding in the long term can be gained from the payment of entry fines. These charges on a tenant taking on a new holding could be profitable for lords, and for tenants represented a major investment. The sums that they were prepared to pay guide us in judging the availability of land, the profits it might give, the strength of peasant ambition, and the fierceness of competition between would-be landholders. The intending tenant would

---

[35] Z. Razi, *Life, Marriage and Death in a Medieval Parish: Economy, Society and Demography in Halesowen 1270–1400* (Cambridge, 1980), pp. 38–43; P. Slavin, *Experiencing Famine in Fourteenth-Century Britain* (Turnhout, 2019), pp. 60–1, 66, 123 finds reduced hay crops and availability of grazing as well as higher grain prices.

[36] *Nonarum Inquisitiones in Curia Scaccarii* (London, Record Commission, 1807), pp. 407–15; C. Dyer, 'The Rise and Fall of a Medieval Village: Little Aston (in Aston Blank), Gloucestershire', *TBGAS* 105 (1987), pp. 165–81.

[37] Razi, *Life, Marriage and Death*, pp. 101–7.

sometimes be paying a price to the seller, but this transaction is hardly ever recorded, so the entry fine is the best guide we have to land values. In deciding the purchase price and the amount of the entry fine such factors as commodity prices, wage costs, and the availability of credit would enter into the calculation. There were also non-economic considerations, such as attachment to family land, and concern for the welfare of relatives. In our own times the future enters into our calculations, and to some extent this was also the case in the Middle Ages, but their future was even more unpredictable than ours. The policy of the lords had an influence, for example when they balanced annual rents against fines, and required a modest fine for a holding of which the rent reflected its 'true value'.

The fines provide an indirect guide to the varied demand for land, which in its broad outlines follows a predictable path. Fines were high in the period 1270–1349, fell to a varied extent in the late fourteenth century, reached a low level in the fifteenth century, and in some places picked up around 1500. Fines can be measured in terms of the amount of money per yardland or per acre, so that a standard high fine before 1349 was 10 marks per yardland, which could be expressed as £6 13s 4d, but people tended to think in marks. Ten marks would have been the benchmark around which the tenant and the estate officials would have negotiated, especially on some manors south of the Avon, such as Sedgeberrow (Worcestershire) and Blackwell (Warwickshire). The rate of fine for individual holdings rose well above the 10 mark level, up to £8, £10, £12, and £14 per yardland. In fact, the highest recorded rate of fine, £4 16s 8d for a quarter-yardland, equivalent to £19 6s 8d per yardland, was paid in 1314 for a holding at Shoulton in Hallow to the north of Worcester.[38] The high price presumably reflected the proximity of the city. On the estate of Winchcomb Abbey, for example at Long Marston (Warwickshire) in the lowland champion country south of the Avon, not far from Blackwell and Sedgeberrow, a fine of 10 marks per yardland (in fact 20 marks for two yardlands) can be found in the 1340s. The equivalent of 12 marks per yardland (6 marks for a half-yardland) was charged on the Cotswold edge at Stanton (Gloucestershire). A yardland at Kempsford (a Cotswold manor on a lay estate) cost £6 13s 4d for a yardland in 1310, and a tenant of the lay lord of Badminton on the south-eastern fringes of the Gloucestershire Cotswolds was prepared to pay £4 6s 8d for a half-yardland, that is at a rate of 13 marks per yardland.[39] On manors with few or no yardlands, the fine has to be calculated per acre. At Eldersfield in the woodlands west of the Severn the fines commonly amounted to 12d per acre before 1349, equivalent to 30s per yardland, and from 1360–99 wavered between 4d and 8d, comparable with a fine

---

[38] WCL, E6.
[39] GA, D678/1/M1/1/1, 2; East Raynham Library, Norfolk, box 25; GA, Badminton Muniments D2700/MAI/1.

Table 3.3 Entry fines on two Worcester Priory manors, 1310–1520 (median rates of fine, per yardland)

	Blackwell/Shipston*	Cleeve Prior
1310–19	£6 13s 4d	£3 15s 0d
1320–9	£3	£5 3s 4d
1330–9	–	£4 2s 0d
1340–9	£9 10s 0d	£6 13s 4d
1350–9	13s 4d	0
1360–9	£1 6s 8d	12 capons
1370–9	3s 4d	6 capons
1380–9	7s 8d	6 capons
1390–9	10s	4 capons
1400–9	£1 6s 8d	6s 8d
1410–19	3s 4d	0
1420–9	13s 4d	3 capons
1430–9	0	6s 9d
1440–9	3 capons	3s 4d
1450–9	13s 4d	3s 4d
1460–9	£1 0s 0d	16 capons
1470–9	11s 5d	–
1480–9	16s 0d	3s 4d
1490–9	5s 0d	15s 8d
1500–9	13s 4d	6s 0d
1510–19	13s 4d	–

*The rural holdings only, excluding fines paid for holdings in the borough of Shipston.
Source: WCL, E1–E95

of 10s–20s per yardland.[40] Perhaps the tenants did not rate the quality of the land very highly, but after the plague they were prepared to pay more than their contemporaries did on the Worcester Priory manors.

No consistent picture emerges of the period immediately before 1349, with a concentration of hard luck stories in the high Cotswolds, with some low entry fines, vacant holdings, and neglected buildings.[41] On some parts of the wolds, and in the lowlands more widely, tenants in the ten years before 1349 seem to have been approaching their acquisition of land with confidence and optimism.

After 1349 our sample manors (Table 3.3) differ considerably with Cleeve Prior fines between 1350 and 1400 being reduced to a token payment of poultry, which had a cash value of 12d at most. After 1400 those acquiring land recovered sufficient confidence to pay at least a few shillings as fines, and a revival in demand is apparent in the 1490s. The peasants of Blackwell and Shipston, perhaps feeling the

---

[40] WA, ref. 705:134, BA1531/69, 69B.
[41] C. Dyer, 'A Medieval Village in a Cotswold Landscape: Pinbury in Duntisbourne Rous', *TBGAS*, 137 (2019), pp. 191–213, especially 209–11.

beneficial influence of their small town, in the fifteenth century tended to offer a single mark, 13s 4d per yardland, apart from reductions in the 1430s and 1440s.

On the Winchcomb Abbey estate, the median fine fell from £2 per yardland in the 1340s to 10s in the 1360s, but then it declined continuously from 2s or 3s around 1400 until between 1440 and 1469 token payments of poultry predominated. Over the whole region tenants were in general paying no more than 13s 4d., and often much smaller sums at the end of the fourteenth century and well into the fifteenth, reflecting the modest rewards of cultivation.

We cannot be sure that lords were always effective negotiators, and this could be reflected in reduced fines when some assertive tenants may have faced down the lord's officials. Lords also exercised patronage and allowed favoured tenants to gain land cheaply. At Ombersley in north Worcestershire, an outlier of the Evesham Abbey estate, fines reached low levels after 1380, and there was no marked revival even after 1500.[42] In the 1470s and 1480s the tenants were systematically depriving the lord of heriot payments, which the abbey's officials seemed to accept, so perhaps they did not drive a hard bargain either on entry fines. The demand for land at Ombersley was probably quite high, suggested by much subletting, and absentee tenants apparently regarded Ombersley holdings as good investments. The soil was high in quality, and there were easy connections to urban markets.

Perhaps low entry fines, if they resulted from institutional weakness, give us an exaggerated impression of the poor returns from cultivation. However, fifteenth-century fines could reflect the market, as in some parts of the region rising rates of fine suggest increased agrarian profits. The people who lived in villages around Bristol were clearly responding to the commercial stimulus. At Stoke Gifford the median fines in the 1420s and 1450s, £2 and £1 6s 8d were considerably higher than any of the places reviewed so far, and they rose decisively to £4 8s 0d and then £7 between 1488 and 1510. Nearby on the Severn estuary, peasants at Rockhampton were paying £4–5 for a yardland for most of the fifteenth century, rising to £8 in 1506–9.[43] A figure of £8 was reached at Henbury-in-the-Salt-Marsh by the 1530s, after a rising trend since the 1460s. Near to the city of Worcester, which was growing in size towards the end of the Middle Ages, tenants were also paying higher fines after 1470 and especially after 1500, up to £4–5.[44] Rural industry may have helped to lift the level of fine that new tenants were prepared to pay, with more than £1 per yardland in and near the clothing district of Bisley during the fifteenth century. At Horsley in the 1470s the rate of fine reached £2–4 per

---

[42] WA, ref 705:56, BA3910/22, 24, 27, 33, 39, 40. For local variations in fines in southern England, including some increases in the late fourteenth century, J. Mullan and R. Britnell, *Land and Family. Trends and Local Variations in the Peasant Land Market* (Hatfield, 2010), pp. 71–83.
[43] GA, Badminton muniments, D2700, MJ11/1/2-5; MJ9/1-3.
[44] C. Dyer, *Lords and Peasants in a Changing Society: The Estates of the Bishopric of Worcester 680–1540* (Cambridge, 1980), pp. 287–91.

yardland, and fines as high as £2 were needed to obtain cottages, presumably because they attracted textile workers.[45]

To sum up, entry fines were an imposition on the peasantry and lords could gain considerable profit from them. If peasants wanted land, they had to pay fines, just as they had to find a purchase price for the sitting tenant. The high fines before 1349 must have saddled buyers and their families with large debts, but a significant number were able to pay the sum required. Land was much more easily obtained after 1349, and especially after 1400, reflecting the reduced income from farming. There were exceptions to the overall story of declining land values, notably the suspicion that some tenants were being given an easy time by slack officials, but also that in some places and at some times, notably around 1500 in south Gloucestershire and near Worcester, land was giving better returns, and tenants could pay higher fines and also gain a good living.

Landholding 1349–1540

After 1349, just as in the pre-plague era, peasant could make choices and influence the acquisition and inheritance of land. No law of nature determined that if there were fewer people and the same amount of land, that holdings should increase in size. Tenants had to make a decision to acquire land, and they made their choices in complex situations. Vacant holdings 'lay in the lord's hands' and the lord's officials judged the capacity of would-be tenants. The tenants themselves had to consider whether they had the necessary equipment and livestock, or enough money to pay for these and also building repairs. They might expect support from their families, and from the wider community, some of whom would act as pledges (guaranteeing rents and building repairs). Much depended on judgements about local conditions, which varied with landscapes, soils, and markets.

The long-term consequences of the decisions made by dozens of individuals resulted in new distributions of land, which are reflected in surveys compiled before and after 1349. Without systematic evidence for subletting arrangements, we rely on the official records of tenancy. No two places experienced the same changes, but broad patterns can be noted. In some cases a drastic fall in numbers was associated with the growth of very large holdings. Priors Hardwick (Warwickshire) in 1279 had forty-two tenants, almost half with half-yardlands. By 1411 the tenants were reduced to sixteen, including four with two yardlands or above. A similarly impressive amalgamation of holdings is found at Wasperton (Warwickshire), where in 1279 twenty-eight of the thirty-four tenants held half-yardlands, but in 1411 of the twenty-one tenants, twelve held more than a yardland,

---

[45] TNA, SC2/175/67.

and seven of them each had three yardlands.[46] The size of the median holding had risen from 15 acres to 60 acres. Similar concentrations of land in the hands of tenants, with two or three yardland holdings appearing in growing numbers, were a feature of the champion villages of all three counties, and the same trend is apparent in the Cotswolds.

Tenants took on large holdings already in existence, or built up accumulations of land by a series of separate transactions because they had the resources to acquire and manage such a holding. However, when a peasant whose grandfather cultivated a half-yardland took on three yardlands, he was not six times more wealthy than his predecessor. A 90-acre holding cultivated on a two-course rotation would require 270 days of ploughing (at a half-acre in a day), and therefore the employment of extra labour. Harvesting and other seasonal tasks would add to the wages bill. After 1375 a smaller area would be ploughed as grain prices fell, and more animals, especially sheep, would be kept on those parts of the field system where grass grew. As sheep numbers were fixed by a stint for each yardland, a three-yardland tenant would be able to keep a flock of at least ninety and possibly 180, depending on the rules in each village.

Priors Hardwick and Wasperton had few smallholders in the late thirteenth century, and the numbers remained low. In many champion villages, while more large holdings were formed, smallholdings shrank drastically in number. Evidently the sons and daughters of cottagers were losing interest in living on a few acres combined with earnings from wages or the profits of a craft. At Priors Marston, the adjoining village to Hardwick, sixty-eight tenants in 1279, more than half of the total, held below a half-yardland, while in 1411 there were five in that category.[47] At Cleeve Prior, a champion village in Worcestershire, there had been eighteen smallholders from fifty-four tenants in 1310, but only one in 1502, among a grand total of seventeen tenants, most of them holding more than a yardland.[48]

The rise of large holdings and the decline in cottagers have been depicted, but sometimes smallholdings survived, and the tenants of middling holdings diminished in number. At the champion village of Ufton (Warwickshire) in the thirteenth century, the twenty-six half-yardlands accounted for a majority among forty-three tenants. By 1411 the half-yardlands had ceased to exist; the number of those with 10 acres or less had fallen to six, and there were nineteen with a yardland or larger holding (see Figure 2.8). The Honington smallholders declined from sixteen to seven in 1279–1411, and only three half-yardlands (compared with eighteen in the thirteenth century) separated the smallholders from the twenty-eight yardlands and double yardlands of 1411.[49] In general the half-yardlander, a very commonly encountered tenant in the thirteenth and early

---

[46] WHR, pp. 178–9, 203–6; *Cov Reg*, pp. 541–4, 549–53.
[47] WHR, pp. 206–12; *Cov Reg*, pp. 530–6.   [48] WCL, C847, C562.
[49] WHR, pp. 155–8, 286–9; *Cov Reg*, pp. 523–6.

fourteenth centuries, had become a scarce species by the fifteenth century. Potential tenants found half-yardlands unattractive because on their own they provided an adequate subsistence but at best a modest surplus. Tenants increasingly used half-yardlands as building blocks in constructing larger accumulations.

In the woodlands smallholdings had been very prominent before 1349, and afterwards they persisted. On the huge Stoneleigh manor in the Arden smallholders were reduced, but in 1392 tenants with 7 acres or less still accounted for 46 per cent of the total.[50] Walsgrave on Sowe (Warwickshire) in a woodland landscape but also on the edge of Coventry, declined in size while its urban neighbour expanded, but holdings below 5 acres still made up a good proportion of the total (28 per cent—it had once been 53 per cent). There was no great increase in large holdings. Counting all of the holdings on Coventry Priory's suburban manors shows tenants with 7 acres and below fell from 48 per cent to 38 per cent.[51] Presumably smallholdings remained attractive in the new post-1349 world for the same reasons that they were a viable basis for a family's survival in the thirteenth century. The tenant's living was built on a combination of an acre or two, access to large commons and woods, the availability of employment in both farming and industry, and the opportunities of work either in or near to the town.

Lords could contribute to the amount of land available to peasants by grants of waste (mostly in the thirteenth century) or parcels of demesne in all periods but in large quantities after about 1380. The lords' main role was to supervise through the manor court the transfer of customary land, ensuring that it descended after death or surrender by inheritance according to custom. This included arranging for widows to take their husband's land as their free bench. Land for which there was no heir came into 'the lord's hands', and he would then expect to grant it to a suitable tenant. A tenant could surrender land into the lord's hands, but would declare that it was for the use of another party (the key phrase was that a grant was being made *ad opus*). This would normally mean the surrendering tenant had sold the land and the lord would grant it to the buyer, keeping a record of the new tenant, and receiving an entry fine.

Peasants had considerable influence over the descent of land, and the lord had limited opportunities to choose his own tenants. He could sometimes discriminate in favour of tenants he preferred when a vacant holding was being granted. He could also evict tenants, or rather using the formal phraseology, tenants could forfeit the holding by failing to pay their rent, or observe rules about cultivation, building repair, and good behaviour. Forfeiture was threatened more often than it was practised. Lords dealing with unsatisfactory tenants, whose offence was most often (especially after 1349) a failure to repair buildings, threatened them

---

[50] Hilton, ed., *Stoneleigh*, p. xli.
[51] D. Greenblatt, 'The Suburban Manors of Coventry, 1279–1411' (PhD dissertation, Cornell University, 1967), pp. 29–31.

first with financial penalties, and with forfeiture as a last resort. Holdings were sometimes forfeit only after the tenant had left the land, like Richard Tederyngton of Stoke in Hawkesbury (Gloucestershire), who in 1435 withdrew from his cottage and cotland 'with all of his goods and chattels in the night, of which nothing came to the lord as heriot'. He had owned a cow worth 5s which should have been the heriot, but he must have driven it before him as he made his escape down dark Cotswold lanes.[52]

Tenants could manipulate the transfer of land, and the motives behind their actions can sometimes be gleaned from the court records. John Clerk was one of the most substantial tenants in Cleeve Prior in 1386. He arrived in the village in 1351, taking over a substantial holding of land left vacant by the epidemic, and serving (at an early age) as one of the harvest reeves. By 1386 when he died, he had accumulated two yardlands and a half-yardland. A court held in October 1386 heard that one yardland had yielded the lord's heriot, an ox worth 14s. The court seems to have expected that his widow, Agnes, would claim the yardland as her free bench, but 'she refused all her right entirely'. It was revealed that 'in her own right' from before her marriage she had inherited from her father a yardland and a half, which shows that John Clerk had expanded his holding by marrying an heiress. Agnes retained her rights to the land and claimed therefore that no heriot was due. Scrutiny of the rolls by court officials found a reference to her land 'six or seven years after the pestilence', so in about 1356. A few months after her husband's death the widow reappeared in court to resolve the heriot problem, under the name Agnes Wille, so she had evidently remarried, perhaps to John Wille, a yardlander since 1380. The subsequent stages of the story are not known, but land once held by the Clerks subsequently came into the hands of William atte Grene and William Carles, who were not identified as relatives. John Wille retired in 1406 and was succeeded by his son, also John Wille.[53]

This history of a married couple and their lands reveal some typical features of the post-plague era, with the rise of a large holding, and its dissolution. Agnes departed from convention by rejecting her free bench, but she had no need of that restricted benefit because she had her own inheritance. She then followed the traditional path for a widow, by remarrying without delay. The Wille holding was inherited, but other lands seem to have been transferred between non-relatives. In this whole fifty-year saga of a family's land changing hands, there were four transfers which apparently did not involve inheritance, and only two cases of inheritance.

The conventional means of acquiring land was by inheritance after the death of both parents, or when both parents or a survivor surrendered the land to the heir, often in order to retire. A widow's free bench gave her the tenure of the holding

---

[52] TNA, SC2 175/52.   [53] WCL, E4, E32, E33, E45.

for life, providing that she did not enter into sexual relations, or remarry. After her death or withdrawal, the land would descend by hereditary succession, normally to the eldest son, or in the absence of sons or daughters to another relative. Hereditary succession was taken very seriously; for example, at Thornbury each vacant holding was publicly proclaimed three times in successive courts, to ensure that heirs could make a claim. In all manors, in the event that rival claimants came forward, the jury in the manor court judged who had the right to take the land, though the lord might influence the decision.

The changing importance of inheritance can be assessed by analysing the transfers of land recorded in the manor court rolls. Many transactions involved land going into, or coming from, the hands of the lord. If we set these aside we can concentrate on land passing between one tenant and another, and these are indicated for a sample of records from the Worcester Priory estate in Table 3.4, which includes inheritance after death and surrenders by tenants in favour or others, distinguishing (as much as is possible) between tenants related to one another and those belonging to different families.

Before 1349 almost two-thirds of the inter-tenant transfers involved identifiable family members. The family's role in the transmission of land diminished after the epidemics, and remained at below a half of the total until the late fifteenth century when there are signs of a recovery in inheritance. If we divide the manors in the champion country from those located in the woodlands of north and west Worcestershire, except in the half-century after the Black Death transfers between family members were more frequent in the woodland manors. Land in the woodlands was not more valuable in financial terms, but perhaps heirs appreciated the flexibility of managing land, and the availability of by-employment. Small differences are apparent between individual manors. At Cleeve Prior, a champion manor where low entry fines after the plague show that demand for land had

Table 3.4 Transfers of land between tenants on the Worcester Cathedral Priory estate, 1300–1500, comparing those within families and between families

	Unrelated parties	Related parties	Total
1300–25	19	33	52
%	37	63	100
1326–50	34	64	98
%	35	65	100
1351–1400	40	37	77
%	52	48	100
1401–1450	29	22	51
%	57	43	100
1451–1500	28	37	65
%	43	57	100

fallen, a very high proportion of transfers between family members before 1350 (76 per cent) fell to 35 per cent in 1351–1400, and continued at that level for the whole of the fifteenth century, without sign of recovery at the end. Blackwell, a manor which included in its boundaries the small town of Shipston, provides a comparison. Excluding the transfers of urban property, the town's influence on its immediate rural surroundings apparently led to a relatively low figure of 59 per cent of holding passing within the family before 1350, and between 48 and 54 per cent for the later periods, including 1501–20. This manor's higher level of entry fine confirms that demand for land was relatively high, which made family holdings more attractive for heirs.

These figures are of course based on inadequate evidence, as the main indication of one tenant being related to another is their shared surname, and the words 'son', 'daughter', or 'brother' only appear occasionally. The number of transactions within families must be regarded as minima, as sons-in-law, who indicate inheritance by daughters, cannot be recognized by their names alone, nor can the names of married daughters, of cousins, and other relatives.[54] A Sedgeberrow dispute draws attention to inheritance problems arising when remarried women had children by different husbands. In 1347 Edith Roggers, a widow, died, leaving a messuage and a yardland and two cottages. Two claimants, Margery le Blake and Sarra le Blake came forward and offered 2s to the court to decide the case. Their names show that they were the children of an earlier marriage, but the court preferred John Roggers, a chaplain and Edith's son by her most recent husband, whose claim might have been helped by his willingness to pay an entry fine of £8.[55]

Other well-documented estates record very similar trends in the proportions of apparently related and unrelated parties in land transfers. On the mainly Cotswold manors of the Winchcomb Abbey estate 61 per cent of transfers were made apparently within the family in the early fourteenth century, falling to 56 per cent in 1357–67, and 23–24 per cent in the period 1367–1466. In the fourteenth-century records of Eldersfield (Worcestershire) free tenants are prominent. Before 1349, transfers between family members accounted for 71 per cent of the total, and in two late fourteenth-century samples the figure slipped to 17 per cent and 14 per cent. The revival in land changing hands within the family after 1500 was especially marked on Worcestershire manors of the bishopric of Worcester, such as Hanbury, Kempsey, and Whitstones.[56]

Young people wishing to acquire land had to accept the disadvantages that accompanied the benefits of inheritance. When their parents were in charge they would be expected to remain on or near to the household, and work on the

---

[54] Z. Razi, 'The Erosion of the Family-Land Bond in the Late Fourteenth and Fifteenth Centuries: A Methodological Note', in *Land, Kinship and Life-Cycle*, edited by R.M. Smith (Cambridge, 1984), pp. 295–304.
[55] WCL, E15.
[56] Dyer, *Lords and Peasants*, pp. 302–5.

holding. The land that they acquired might be burdened with a commitment to maintain their parents, which for Richard Stappe senior of Blackwell included an annual 4 quarters 3 bushels of grain (half of it wheat) and cloth, hose, and shoes.[57]

After 1349 inheritance continued, but on a smaller scale, partly because families were reduced in size, leading to a shortfall of potential heirs. The manorial authorities were constantly complaining of the neglect of buildings and the run-down state of the land. Sons knew about the management of the family land, and if that had been deficient they were reluctant to take on the hard work of bringing weed-infested land and dilapidated buildings back into full production. Filial duty seems to have persisted and some sons and daughters were willing to take on a holding, while parents attempted to strengthen their commitment by the device of joint tenancy. In 1380 at Eldersfield, John Donne, Joan his wife, and John their son were granted a messuage and piece of land, which was of middling size judging from the annual rent that it owed of 4s 6d. In the next year half of a much larger holding with a rent of 30s was acquired by William Russell and William his son.[58] These methods of persuasion could not offset the reduced scale of inheritance, but it continued and revived around 1500.

Throughout the later Middle Ages, but especially after 1349, heirs could acquire land and did not need to wait for the parental holding to become available. That was the only option for most children without any right to the inheritance, though a few might receive land acquired by the father, or be accommodated in a cottage carved out of the messuage.

One route to landholding for single men was to marry a widow and take over the tenancy of her land. Widows were under some pressure to marry, as the villagers would be wary of the moral danger posed by an independent unmarried woman, and they had doubts about a widow's ability to contribute fully to such joint operations as ploughing. Lords feared that a widow's new partner would acquire land without taking on the formal obligations of a tenant. They preferred male tenants who would pay rent and do services, and they readily gave permission for a widow's marriage. Marriages to widows were more frequent in the period before 1349. On the sample of records from the Worcester Priory estate nineteen cases were recorded in that period, and ten after 1349. The practice almost ceased after 1450. A similar pattern of decline after the Black Death prevailed on the manors of Winchcomb Abbey. At Halesowen between 1270 and 1349, 63 per cent of widows married soon after their husband's death, but this decreased to 26 per cent in 1349–1400.[59] Widows presumably preferred not to be pressured into marriage, and neighbours' opinions in favour of their marriage became less urgent. A growing number of widows remarried outside the manor,

---

[57] WCL, E3.   [58] WA, ref. 705: 134, BA 1531/69B.
[59] Razi, *Life, Marriage and Death*, p. 138.

and forfeited their land, as their new husbands probably already had a holding. Men in search of a holding could still benefit from the need of widows to reduce their commitments by taking the land in return for a promise of maintenance, or by taking her land as a subtenant. Christina Batyn of Stoke Gifford (Gloucestershire) was able to maintain her tenancy by obtaining a licence from the lord in 1425 to let 5 acres of her half-yardland to four subtenants, including one who was apparently a relative. One of her neighbours, Juliana Rogers, in 1424 provided herself with a more manageable holding by giving up her half-yardland and took a messuage with a curtilage and 2 acres.[60] One reason for the decline in records of widows attracting marriage partners was the growing trend for husbands and wives to hold land jointly, so that widows took over the holding as a full tenant, avoiding the custom of free bench, and not requiring permission to remarry. At all times of course a single man could acquire a holding by marriage when a daughter held land, because widows were not the only women with property.

An example will show how marriage to a widow might work in practice, and it will be seen how acquiring a widow as a wife connected with other processes in the acquisition and loss of land. Isabella Admont of Cleeve Prior is the central figure. Her husband, Thomas Admont or Admond, was tenant of a full yardland, and a leading figure in Cleeve, who died in 1377, after which Isabella gained the land as her free bench. Her active role in cultivating and managing the holding is suggested by litigation in which neighbours sought to recover debts and detained chattels from her. She owned an ox and was in possession of a plough coulter. She sublet a small part of the land to Thomas Hychen, who seems to have been a business partner, continuing an arrangement of her husband's.

She formed another type of partnership in 1378 (the year after her husband's death) when she was accused of fornication, and her land was declared forfeit. She was able to recover the holding by paying a fine of 2s. The man involved, Richard Wodelond, married her and acquired her land. Richard (like others in the same position) adopted the name of Admont. When Isabella died in 1380 he left the lordship and his chattels were to be seized to pay 8s for Isabella's heriot. Walter Page, Thomas Admont's brother (presumably a stepbrother) went to the court to claim hereditary right to the land, but for the sake of money, not the acres, as he surrendered the land to John Wille, and sold his rights. Wille was evidently upgrading his landholding, as he surrendered a half-yardland that he held as soon as he acquired the Admont yardland. Wille's former holding was called Wille, so he was evidently abandoning a piece of family property. He may have married Agnes, John Clerk's widow with a yardland and a half at her disposal. These people were not seeking stability and took a materialistic view of marriage. Hereditary

---

[60] GA, Badminton muniments, D2700 MJ11/1/2.

Table 3.5 Transfers of land by surrender and grant between unrelated parties on a sample from the records of Worcester Cathedral Priory

Date	1300–1350	1351–1400	1401–1450	1451–1500
No. of transfers between living parties	30	29	19	15
Total transfers in sample	142	157	99	89
%	21	18	19	17

succession was a source of a quick profit rather than a commitment to a particular holding. Richard Admont (previously Wodelond) gained a yardland and then dodged his responsibilities.[61]

Most of those seeking land acquired it from the lord, by the processes of surrender and grant, which show the land market in operation. According to Table 3.5 about a fifth of land transfers on the Worcester Priory estate throughout the period 1300–1500 belonged to this type, focussing on transactions between living and apparently unrelated parties, so as to identify the means by which individuals could acquire land outside the inheritance system. On the manors of the Winchcomb Abbey estate sales of land were on a modest scale in the early fourteenth century, they account for 20 per cent of transfers in 1367–1405, and rose to 40 per cent in 1414–66.

The reversionary agreement provided a method of securing a succession to land for the younger generation. A would-be tenant, often male, would come to an understanding with a sitting tenant, sometimes a relative, but often not, and would pay a fine to the lord, resulting in a record on the court roll for future reference. By the terms of the agreement when the tenant and his wife had died or withdrawn from the tenancy the land would revert to the new tenant. On the Winchcomb Abbey estate, the system was well established by the 1340s (though the term reversion was not always used), but on the Blackwell/Shipston manor it increased after 1376. On the Worcester Priory lands, as a whole it became more frequent towards the end of the fifteenth century. This method of securing a future succession suggests a demand for land, even in times when tenants abandoned holdings and others were reluctant to take them. It could also serve as a device for families to pursue an inheritance strategy, in that sons or daughters without hereditary rights to land could be granted a reversion. It was an alternative to the arrangement of joint tenancy already mentioned.

To sum up the inheritance and transfer of land, peasants were subject to many pressures and stimuli, from lords, custom, population, and the market, but in all circumstances peasants used skills to secure outcomes favourable to themselves.

[61] WCL, E28, E 29, E30.

Serfdom, 1200–1540

The differences between free and unfree peasants were devised by lords and lawyers at the highest levels of society and government. Serfdom was a discriminatory device imposed for purposes of social control, but peasants were not simply victims. They could exercise some influence on the way serfdom worked, and in the long run they opposed and undermined it. The peculiar institution of English serfdom and villeinage needs to be examined, before seeing how peasants coped with it.

The clearly unfree section of the population in Domesday Book (in 1086) were the *servi* and *ancillae* (slaves and bondwomen) who worked on the lord's demesne, often as ploughmen and dairy maids. They were freed in the late eleventh and early twelfth century, granted landholdings, and the males were sometimes called oxmen (*bovarii*); their successors in these smallholdings continued into the later Middle Ages.[62] Already in the early twelfth century the term *nativus* (feminine *nativa*), meaning born into servility, was being used. By 1170 the people previously called villeins were known on both the estate of the nuns of Caen in Gloucestershire, and on the manors of the bishopric of Worcester, as *operarii* (workers), suggesting that their defining characteristic was their obligation to do heavy labour service. Many of them held yardlands or fractions of these, giving them the capacity to work on the demesne with their own implements and draught animals. In Domesday and persisting into the twelfth century the term *villanus* can be translated as villager, and referred to the size of the holding rather than legal status. Villeinage later came to be equated with servility.[63] By the late thirteenth century the unfree status of a substantial proportion of tenants had been firmly established, though they were identified by many terms: *servi* (serfs, a word favoured by the compilers of the 1279 Warwickshire Hundred Rolls), *custumarii* or *consuetudinarii* (customary tenants), *rustici* (rustics), *bondi* (bondsmen), and *nativi* (born serfs). These words seem to have been interchangeable. The people at the time used the English word 'bond', leading to names such as Alice le Bonde.

In the period 1200–1349 bondmen account for about a half of the rural population. The Warwickshire Hundred Rolls of 1279 named 4,437 people, of whom 2,318 (52 per cent) were servile. In the woodlands of the Arden included in that survey 73 per cent were free, and a majority of free tenants are recorded in other sources in the woodlands of west and north Worcestershire. On the other hand, Gloucestershire was predominantly servile, so in the region as a whole, free and unfree were probably evenly balanced. The unfree would have counted for less

---

[62] M.M. Postan, *The Famulus* (EcHR supplement, 2, 1959).
[63] R.H. Hilton, 'Freedom and Villeinage in England', *P&P* 31 (1965), pp. 3–19.

than a half of the population of England, which makes the west midlands a region with a relatively high level of servility.[64]

The unfree section of the population was living under constraints and disadvantages. Only a minority were liable to do heavy weekly labour services, working on the lord's demesne for up to five days per week. In south-east Warwickshire, the burden was much lighter, and a growing proportion of each tenant's obligations throughout the region consisted of cash rents. Labour services were not only performed by the unfree, but as they were major contributors in the following discussion reference will be made to labour services and failure to perform them. The lawyers applied tests for unfreedom, notably liability to tallage, a cash payment often levied collectively, such as £3 from all the serfs in a manor, fines for permission to marry or to leave the manor, or tolls on the sale of beasts. Anyone holding the office of reeve would be identified as a serf, and as serfdom was hereditary, a claim to be free would fail if a father or grandfather could be shown to have acted as a reeve.[65]

Serfs had in theory no access to the king's courts. No higher authority could intervene between the serfs and the lord's justice which was wielded in the manor court according to local customs. Lords claimed to own serfs, and occasionally we find them being conveyed as part of a land transfer. In 1314 Gilbert de Clare earl of Gloucester granted Robert of the Grove of Hanley Castle (Worcestershire) to Sir Roger Tyrel, 'with his whole family (*sequela*) and all their land and chattels'.[66] Lords were anxious to exercise powers as they chose, as when the lord of Kempsford (Gloucestershire), Patrick de Chaworth, in 1258 was said to be able to levy tallage every year in an arbitrary fashion, 'they owe for aid at Michaelmas £5, sometimes more and sometimes less, according to their capabilities and the will of the lord'.[67] The jurors providing information for some villages in the Warwickshire Hundred Rolls did not assign a value in money for aid or tallage as it was levied 'at the lord's will'. In 1299 the customary tenants of Stratford manor (Warwickshire) owed aid at Michaelmas, called *stodynge*, 'which can increase or lessen at the will of the lord, and can each year be great or small'.[68] The tendency in practice for these dues to be fixed at a regular annual sum did not remove the threat to make changes at a whim. Those liable to pay were bound to feel unease at this lack of certainty. Recognition, a collective payment resembling tallage, was imposed on servile tenants at the accession of a new lord, which was an unpredictable event, and the size of the payment was not always clearly fixed. An aim of the unfree peasants throughout medieval Europe, was to achieve some certainty in their obligations and the lords' boasts of arbitrary powers were generally resented.

[64] This is based on the estate surveys cited in note 6 above.
[65] Hilton, 'Freedom and Villeinage', p. 9; M. Bailey, 'Tallage-at-Will in Late Medieval England', *EHR* 134 (2019), pp. 25–58.
[66] *Rec Hanley*, p. 13.   [67] Madge, ed., *IPMs for Gloucestershire*, p. 22.
[68] *WHR*, pp. 265, 269, 270; *RBW*, p. 255.

A claim by lords which was especially prominent in the west midlands was their supervision of the tenants' principal goods or *principalia*, such as their ploughs, carts, brass pots, furnishings, implements, and utensils. Lords claimed that they had once provided their tenants with these items and they could not be sold or transferred. A tenant at Thornbury (Gloucestershire) fell foul of the manor court in 1338 when he took his goods and chattels to nearby Littleton-on-Severn, where he had acquired land 'to the destruction of his native (servile) holding'.[69] Another dimension of the lords' belief that they ultimately owned their serfs' goods was their punishment of unfree tenants who had appeared before courts other than their lords', such as the hundred court or more often the church courts, and incurred penalties. The money that they paid belonged to their lord, or so he claimed, so Robert Jackehonen of Admington (Warwickshire) in 1341 lost 'the lord's chattels' when accused in the church court of sexual misconduct with Alice, his maidservant. Robert found himself, because of his servile status, being punished twice for the same offence, once in the church court and again in his lord's, and having his sins paraded in front of his neighbours on both occasions. Incidentally his neighbours said in the lord's court that he had not committed the offence.[70]

Sexual relations outside marriage were also a matter for the lords' courts when servile women who had strayed were liable to pay *leirwite*. These payments may be linked with the much more frequently levied fine for licence to marry, *merchet*. The marriage fine was mostly paid by the women intending to marry, and it gave them permission to marry wherever and/or whoever they pleased. The cost was not very high, usually 2s, but even such a sum was not easily afforded by a young woman working for 1d per day with many other expenses linked to marriage. Marriage fines involved much more than an inconvenient tax, as phrases could be used in court about the woman gaining some degree of freedom. In 1320 Beatrice daughter of Reynald at Hallow (Worcestershire) was granted her licence as if a general principle was involved: she was 'to be free and quit of all burdens of servitude forever', phrases appropriate to a manumission.[71]

Payments were expected from servile men for permission to leave the manor. Young men often left to seek employment or land without permission or payment. At Thornbury (Gloucestershire) in 1337 the lord complained at the absence of reports on departed *garciones nativorum*, meaning the young sons from servile families, and at Kempsford in the same county in 1309 the homage was given the task of naming the same group.[72] Parents might encourage boys to seek education at schools, which could lead to a career in the church, but they risked financial penalties levied in the manor court, or had to pay for permission, first for school attendance, and again if the son was tonsured. Other restrictions included a

---

[69] SRO, D641/1/4C/1.   [70] GA, D678/1/M1/1/1.
[71] WCL, E9.   [72] SRO, D641/1/4C/1; East Raynham Library, box 25.

prohibition on serfs acquiring free land, unless with the lord's permission, which required a payment. Some paid to escape being compelled to take on the office of reeve of their manor.

This apparently mixed bag of penalties attached to serfdom had a coherent body of policy behind it, which was to supplement the lord's revenues from large payments such as tallage, and by harvesting tolls, licence fees, and amercements if the rules were broken. The lords regarded their serfs as human capital, who should be controlled in such matters as marriage, inheritance, reproduction, and migration, making them available to provide the lord with money and labour. A good example of the use of servile regulation to protect the lords' interests was the toll levied on the sale of oxen and horses, for which a licence was sometimes required. The lord did not wish to find that labour services could not be done because a serf had sold his draught animals. Also, if a substantial sum of money was involved (an ox would often be sold for 10*s*), the lord saw an opportunity to claim a small share. In our minds, and perhaps in the thoughts of the serfs, there must be a suspicion that the whole complex edifice of serfdom was not erected for merely practical and financial reasons, but that the subjection of serfs was integral to the idea of lordship. This might explain the perpetuation of the institution into a period of obsolescence after 1500.

The impositions were experienced by many thousands of peasant families in the west midlands, In theory they were enforced by the lords' courts, and on occasion the steward who presided over the court as the lord's representative insisted on heavy penalties for disobedience, like the £5 amercement demanded in 1337 from the tenants of Overbury (shortly afterwards reduced), and the £20 from the jurors of the Thornbury court in 1339 because they made allegations against the lord's bailiff.[73] These high-handed actions were really a sign of weakness, and illustrate the frustrations felt by the lords in relation to the manor courts, the effectiveness of which depended on the participation of tenants. They were supposed to report all of the infringement of the rules relating to serfs: marriage, *principalia*, tolls, and the others. These would have been regular occurrences in real life, but they appear in the court only occasionally. Exceptionally manorial courts would deal with a full range of cases, notably at Kempsford where tolls on animal sales, departing serfs, and young serfs being ordained as clergy were all reported in the court.[74]

The neglect of regular enforcement of servile dues must have been the result of a deliberate policy of the jurors and others in the court. In the case of a village with dozens of young women marriage fines would have been a regular occurrence, and their absence would have been obvious. Lords were aware of the offence of

---

[73] WCL. E13; P. Franklin, 'Politics in Manorial Court Rolls: The Tactics, Social Composition and Aims of a pre-1381 Peasant Movement', in *Medieval Society and the Manor Court*, edited by Z. Razi and R.M. Smith (Oxford, 1996), pp 162–98, especially p. 185.

[74] East Raynham Library, box 25.

concealment, and some blatant cases were sometimes uncovered, like the departure of Simon Makegive from Broadwas (Worcestershire), which was reported in 1315 after 'the whole vill' had concealed his absence for twenty years.[75] A confrontation at Stoke Prior (Worcestershire) arose in 1297 when the lord of the manor gave a general order that 'all goods and chattels of serfs wherever they are found outside the manor' should be forfeit to the lord. This would have been difficult to enforce, but the jury in the Stoke court claimed (implausibly) that there were no goods held by Stoke serfs outside the manor.[76]

Avoiding the payments and restrictions of serfdom provided no long-term solution to the oppressions inherent in the relationship between lords and serfs. One route to reducing antagonisms involved negotiation arising from tenants' petitions. At the end of the 1299 survey of Bibury (Gloucestershire) the customers 'sought' that those mowing the hay in the lord's meadow should be given 4 bushels of wheat, a wether (mature sheep) worth 18*d*, and a share of the hay. When tenants performed the *bedrip*, or harvest reaping service, they asked for a reward of a sheaf.[77] This was a reasonable request as on other manors it was standard practice to give the hay makers a sheep to eat, and mowers and harvesters commonly received a bundle of hay or a sheaf. We are tempted to link this petition with a separate dispute over the Bibury lord's exclusion of peasants from grazing on the demesne, which may have soured relationships.

Sometimes differences were resolved, as at Romsley (Worcestershire) where labour services had been contentious. In 1327 the customary tenants negotiated with the canons of Halesowen, their lords, to pay cash rather than doing such works as ploughing, mowing, harvesting, and collecting nuts. They paid a fee of 23*s* for this concession.[78]

Collective withdrawal of rents and services was one method of exerting pressure on a lord, best demonstrated at Thornbury (Gloucestershire) where in 1331–5 more than 424 cases were reported of non-performance of labour services, or the work being done badly. Another wave of absenteeism broke out in 1347–8. The protests could be connected with an apparent increase in labour services in 1331, and resentment at a bailiff's behaviour. Perhaps the precise obligations were in doubt, as officials complained that workers had attended but left early. Also in the 1330s the tenants of Teddington and Alstone (Gloucestershire) were amerced more than £4 because they had failed to do labour services over a span of years.[79] This seems to have been a collective withdrawal of labour, not a combination of individuals as at Thornbury.

These relatively small-scale and low-key protests by serfs seem small beer in comparison with the major confrontation between unfree tenants and their monastic lord at Halesowen between 1278 and 1283. The trouble began with the

[75] WCL, E7. [76] WCL, E193. [77] *RBW*, p. 374. [78] *CR Romsley*, p. 82.
[79] Franklin, 'Politics in Manorial Court Rolls'; WCL, E13.

type of piecemeal frictions we have seen elsewhere—the lord demanded high amercements and penalties, such as a 10s marriage fine, and a collective amercement of £10 in 1276 for failing to elect a reeve. Tenants neglected labour services, or avoided marriage fines, and prevented livestock being taken as heriots. They sublet land without permission, and failed to take their corn to be ground at the abbey mill. The tenants showed boldness and confidence in taking their case to the royal courts, hiring lawyers to represent them, making the legal argument that the manor had once belonged to the king, and its ancient demesne status enabled the royal courts to protect the tenants from increases in rents and services.[80] This may have been based on a belief that in the remote past all peasants enjoyed freedom under the king, a radical alternative to the assumption that long ago lords granted land and brought a dependent peasantry into existence. Violent confrontations followed in 1278 and 1282 and the leader of the rebellion, Roger Ketel, died after being ill-treated by the lord's servants. The peasants lost their case in law, but as often resulted from such agitations, the lord thereafter trod more lightly.

The Halesowen agitation resembled dozens of other ancient demesne claims in other parts of England, but it was unusual in the west midlands. The dispute lasted a long time, with a probable beginning in 1252 and a final court case forty years later. It was a significant episode because it reached the courts in Westminster and led to serious violence. The disputes at Halesowen connect with the routines of serfdom, such as the levying of marriage fines and tallage, which occurred on most manors in the region. The main conclusion that we can draw is that just as the official structure of landholding was manipulated and adapted by the tenants, so the restrictions and costs of serfdom were modified, subverted, and questioned by the resistance of the serfs themselves. Mainly through concealment and lack of co-operation, the serfs avoided some of the disadvantages of their unfree condition.

Having considered the unfree before 1349, how did servile peasants cope afterwards? It has been said that there was a 'headlong retreat' from enforcing serfdom from the 1350s as lords realized that the institution was unsupportable in the new circumstances of scarce tenants. It has also been said that lords avoided strong actions in defence of their powers, and decided in the long run mainly on economic grounds that serfdom was not worth defending.[81]

In the west midlands both church and lay lords clung to an institution which reflected their political power. Accordingly, the terms *nativus* or *nativa* (male serf or female serf), often elaborated in the phrase *nativus de sanguine* (serf by blood)

---

[80] Z. Razi, 'The Struggles Between the Abbots of Halesowen and their Tenants in the Thirteenth and Fourteenth Centuries', in *Social Relations and Ideas*, edited by T.H. Aston, P. Coss, C.C. Dyer, and J. Thirsk (Cambridge, 1983), pp. 151–67.
[81] M. Bailey, *The Decline of Serfdom in Late Medieval England* (Woodbridge, 2014). This is based on a sample of south midland manors.

to emphasize the heritability of serfdom, were used more often by clerks writing manorial documents after 1349. Land was sporadically called *native* rather than 'customary'. Peasants may not have been able to read the documents, but the words would have been spoken in the court. The *neifs* of Mathon (Worcestershire) would have been fully aware of the discrimination declared in a custom in 1399 that when a tenancy ended because of death or surrender a free tenant was liable to a heriot of one beast, but a serf owed two.[82] An attempt to claim freedom was launched by Adam le Bedel of Elmley Castle in 1356. He had left the manor but returned to fight his case. The whole homage, that is the jury in the manor court, asserted that he was free born, but the lord would not accept this. He claimed that a large jury of twenty-eight had earlier found in favour of his servile status, and so Bedel remained a *neif*, and the homage was threatened with an amercement of £20 'for various false presentments'.[83] The lord of Elmley was obviously determined that the old world would persist even after the epidemic. Lords could react strongly to insubordination. In 1362 at Eldersfield, when John de Haleford, a serf, left without permission, he was captured and taken into custody. However, as was often the case, coercion was tempered with inefficiency, and he eventually escaped and fled again.[84] Tallage or aid, supposedly agreed as a regular annual rent around 1300, was said in the surveys of the Coventry Cathedral Priory in 1411 to be 'more or less, at the will of the lord', so the lord was clinging to the old formula.[85]

All of these examples tell us that lords persisted in their assertion of powers over servile peasants, not just in the uncertain decades immediately after the Black Death, but in the longer term. Their intransigence was exposed by Adam le Bedel and John de Haleford, who refused to play the role of passive victims. The conflicts continued after the 1360s and throughout the fifteenth century, when lords perpetuated records of servile status, though numbers were diminishing. They met with resistance from the serfs themselves who took no comfort from the reduction in numbers: their neighbours might have been freed, while their own inferiority and subjection continued.

The falling numbers of servile families can sometimes be traced from the individuals who paid servile dues, or who were routinely said to be *nativi*. At Chaddesley Corbett (Worcestershire) members of ten servile families were named in 1375, and by the years around 1440 they had been reduced to four.[86] But serfdom did not go away: censuses of serfs were compiled: at Rockhampton (Gloucestershire), Earl's Croome (Worcestershire), and manors of the bishopric of Worcester, and of Worcester Priory between 1474 and 1519 which recorded more than sixty servile families containing at least 200 named individuals. On the bishopric estate names were still being collected in the 1530s (see 'The size of the household' in Chapter 5).

---

[82] WAM, 21387.   [83] *CR Elmley*, p. 13.   [84] WA, ref. 705:134, BA 1531/69.
[85] *Cov Reg*, pp. 526, 529, 544.   [86] SCLA, DR5/2737-2799.

Many of the adult male serfs would have attended the courts when the censuses were being compiled, and they must have feared adverse consequences. At Teddington, where the names of serfs were gathered in October 1508, Juliana daughter of Robert Heynes paid a 5s fine to be able to 'marry wherever she pleases'. Marriage fines had almost ceased to be collected at that late date.[87] A sense of menace was kept active when periodically a manor court would be told that 'All naifs' goods and chattels are seized in the lord's hands' and lands might be included in the order. These blanket threats were made before 1349 and continued until 1494. Although they were not followed by specific demands for money or confiscation of goods, they reminded everyone of the lords' belief that all of the serfs' possessions ultimately belonged to them. In particular, those chattels identified as principal goods became much more prominent after 1349, and inventories were made in considerable numbers in 1354–1434, in pursuit of the idea that furniture and agricultural implements belonged to the lord and could not be removed from a holding.[88] Serfs must have felt threatened, as not all dues were unchangeable: marriage fines, which were more or less fixed at 2s, were occasionally increased to 5s, 6s 8d, 10s, or 13s 4d., reaching a height of £4 at Honeybourne (Gloucestershire) in 1405.[89] At Halesowen, and specifically at the village of Romsley on the Halesowen estate, the levying of marriage fines, and the rate of such fines, together with a generally high level of financial demands through the court, could have been a factor in provoking a rebellion in 1386 in which the tenants refused to do services and rejected their servile status. The three leaders (including Agnes Sadler) were punished, but afterwards some of the lord's demands were moderated. The Halesowen peasants retained their capacity to rebel, and the abbot needed to summon the aid of a royal commission.[90]

Serfs continued to protest against their burdens by hindering the enforcement of rules and refusing to pay selected unpopular dues. For example, on the bishop of Worcester's estates common fines and recognition fines were withheld in a co-ordinated campaign in 1433–5, and a number of these were eventually removed. At Dumbleton in Gloucestershire a tallage in excess of £4 per annum, called the 'winter gift', a euphemism for a collective tax that was taken rather than given, was not paid after 1425 presumably in a co-ordinated action, and by 1460 the lord accepted the tenants' resistance and pardoned the accumulated debt.[91]

Serfs could escape from their status, or reduce their disadvantages, in various ways. They could purchase manumission, which was not always ruinously expensive. Marriage fines could be grants of freedom as well as licences to marry. General

---

[87] WCL, E92.
[88] R.K. Field, 'Worcestershire Peasant Buildings, Household Goods and Farming Equipment in the Later Middle Ages', *Med Arch* 9 (1965), pp. 137–45.
[89] GA, D678/61.   [90] Razi, 'Abbots of Halesowen', pp. 164–6.
[91] R.E.G. Kirk, ed., *Accounts of the Obedientars of Abingdon Abbey* (Camden Society, new series, 51, 1892), pp. 155, 160.

manumission for a family, not just an individual, could cost as little as 26s 8d (at Eldersfield in 1362) or 53s 4d in 1424 at Hallow. On the other hand the charge could be as high as £8, paid by Richard Bele to Worcester Priory in 1511.[92] Serfs must have asked 'why should a free man pay money to obtain liberty that was unjustly denied?'

Walter Addecokke of Sheperdine in the manor of Rockhampton contested his servile status in 1472. This was a serious matter for the lord of the manor, William Berkeley, who attended the manor court in person, alleging that Addecokke was a villein and serf by blood. Walter came to court with his lawyer. The jury, undaunted by the presence of their lord, found that Walter was free, and his liberty should last for ever, together with that of his four children, and this was confirmed in a document sealed by the lord. Addecokke was determined to prove his case, and he spent money on a lawyer's advice in order to establish a principle.[93] Evidently the issue still mattered to both lord and serf even in the twilight years of serfdom.

The number of serfs diminished primarily by a combination of migration and official inertia. Serfs had left their manors before 1349, but records of departures without licence increased from the 1350s. A total of 346 are known to have left the manors of Worcester Cathedral Priory between 1349 and 1389, increasing in pace to a peak in the 1380s. In 1412 fifty-four were listed, and absentees continued to be noted for the rest of the fifteenth century.[94] On the manors of Evesham Abbey the serfs were still leaving in the later part of the century, with forty-six reported in one court session at Ombersley in 1462, and nineteen at Sambourn (Warwickshire) in 1472.[95] Repeated orders to return, putting pressure on the families of the absentees, were ignored. Migration was a widespread movement throughout society both before and after 1349, and although a serf who had cut contacts with his lord and manor gained his freedom, this was not the only reason for moving.

In the long run, a general relaxation of administrative controls worked in the serfs' favour, as they were mentioned less frequently in the courts and gradually disappeared from view. Before 1349 the various obligations of serfs were enforced patchily because jurors and court officials failed to report breaches of the rules applied to marriage, migrations, and all of the other restrictions. In the fifteenth century this amnesia became habitual, and servile dues ceased to be mentioned. The peasants who managed court business, most of whom were not themselves serfs, kept quiet and helped their neighbours by allowing the irksome and humiliating status of the *nativi* to fade away.

---

[92] WA, ref. 705: 134, BA 1531/69; Hereford Cathedral Library, R1163; WCL, E93.
[93] GA, Badminton muniments MJ9/1–2.
[94] P. Hargreaves, 'Seigniorial Reaction and Peasant Responses: Worcester Priory and its Peasants after the Black Death', *Midland History* 24 (1999), pp. 53–78.
[95] WA, ref. 705:56, BA3910/27; SCLA, DR5/2357.

Sometimes doubt is expressed about the degree to which serfdom stirred resentment in its declining years, but strong antagonism was expressed unequivocally at Elmley Castle by Henry Gybbe, who in 1477 discouraged tenants and serfs from buying firewood in the lord's park. It was explained to the court that he did this because he was a *neif* of the lord's, and that he acted 'out of malice' 'to the lord's disadvantage'. In other words, he expressed his exasperation with his servile condition by seeking to reduce the lord's profits from sales of wood.[96] Plenty of examples already given suggest a general and enduring sense of grievance against unfree status.

Conclusion

The holding defined the character and way of life of the peasantry, and to some extent the amount of land available to them was beyond their control. The proportions of complete yardlands, or half-yardlands, or smallholdings depended on the tenures established in each manor generations before 1200, the level of population, the market for land, and demand for agricultural produce and labour. Constrained by these impersonal forces, individual peasants and communities were limited in the choices that they could make, but the tenants could exert influence over division of holdings, subletting of land, manipulation of the transfer of holdings through inheritance, marriage, and the buying and selling of land. They operated in different economic circumstances, with rises and falls of population and prices, for which the entry fines provide an imperfect index of land values. The rise and slow death of serfdom seems more straightforward, as it is essentially a story of peasants pressing for freedom. In the period of decline lords adopted different positions: some were diehards and others more flexible, and also peasant attitudes ranged from acceptance to vigorous opposition, with a majority eroding servility by non-co-operation.

The connections between serfdom and landholding can be observed at the moment when new tenants took up holdings. The clerks who entered the conveyances on to the court roll chose their words carefully. The phrases used on different landed estates all differed but had generic similarity: 'to him and his according to the custom of the manor'; 'to him and his blood by custom of the manor'; 'to her and her issue according to the custom of the manor'; 'in bondage according to the custom of the manor'; 'to him and his brood (*sequela*) in bondage by the custom of the manor'; 'to him and his heirs and assigns according to the custom of the manor'. An essential feature was the primacy of custom, which meant that any disputes or problems would be decided in the lord's manorial

---

[96] *CR Elmley*, p.181.

court, in which custom would be interpreted by a jury of tenants supervised by the lord's steward. The wording did not always remind the tenants of the servile status of the tenure, but 'villeinage', 'bondage', and 'neifty' were scattered through the records.

The removal of the servile vocabulary is the first change that can be observed in these tenancy records, often in the 1380s. The terms could come back, so at Cleeve Prior after 'in bondage' ceased around 1386, *native* appeared between 1406 and 1428. Peasant preferences must have played a part in the eventual removal of the offending words, as objections may have been voiced in the court, and some of those in authority may have listened.

Peasant opinion must also have influenced the growing practice of making copies of the court record of land transfers available to tenants. These copies rarely survive as documents, though there were once thousands of them kept in small peasant archives. Their existence is recorded if a doubtful matter, such as liability to heriot, could be resolved by producing a copy in court. The first mention of a copy being consulted in the region comes from 1338 at Thornbury, but there are hints of 'writings' earlier.[97] They had become commonplace by 1400. Peasants would have appreciated the utility of written evidence in protecting their interests, as shown when they paid a fee for the court roll to be scrutinized to justify some legal claim. However, they would have much preferred to prove their title with deeds, by which freehold land was conveyed, rather than a copy that emphasized their dependence on the lord's court.

The phrases mentioned earlier which featured in the court records, and of course the copy, come from manors where customary tenure was hereditary in the long term, or 'for ever' as was sometimes said. Tenure for lives was widely practised in various parts of the region, meaning that the lord granted a new tenant, his wife, and their son or daughter with land for their lives. This version of customary tenure was especially prevalent in Gloucestershire, in no apparent geographical pattern: it is found in the Vale, on the high Cotswolds, in the vicinity of Bristol; monastic manors, and those held by lay lords were collecting rents from lands held by tenure for lives. It occurs in contrasting landscapes and social environments in the two northern counties, especially in western Worcestershire. The division between 'copyhold by inheritance' and 'copyhold for lives' can be observed across England in the early modern period.[98] Tenure for lives developed gradually on some manors where inheritance had prevailed. It occasionally appears in the fourteenth century, and more often in the fifteenth and early sixteenth. In Worcestershire, a dozen examples (from 120 conveyances) are found at Kempsey between 1476 and 1512. Three examples are found at Cleeve Prior around 1500,

---

[97] SRO, D641/1/4C/2.
[98] M. Bailey, 'The Transformation of Customary Tenure in Southern England, c.1350–c.1500', *AgHR* 62 (2014), pp. 210–30.

and the same number at Romsley in the 1520s. Life tenure was more frequent at Elmley Castle in the early sixteenth century, with a cluster in the 1530s. Tenure for lives seems to have been preferred by some tenants, who would surrender a holding held for 'to him and his', and then pay a fine to receive the land back for three named lives: 'Richard Buk, Margaret Buk and William Buk their son'. A wife would succeed on her husband's death without the conditions attached to 'free bench' and the son (or daughter if she was named) would follow without danger of inheritance disputes. The chosen heir might not have been the eldest son, as specified by the prevailing customs. This peasant preference cannot be applied to the long-term establishment of tenure for lives as the dominant custom on manors where it could stretch back to the early fourteenth century. The origins of the divergence of customs are not known.

Demand from peasants does partly explain the advance of leasehold tenures. In the thirteenth and early fourteenth centuries, individual customary tenants negotiated with their lords, offering to pay a fine for a new grant of their holding for cash rent, without labour services. These changes must have been to the tenants' advantage because lords sometimes rewarded valued servants with a grant of a leasehold. Dozens of examples are known: they were not very numerous. Leasehold was also used on a larger scale by the radical and profit-seeking lord of the Berkeley estate in c.1295–1312 when the tenants had resisted changes in labour services. Throughout the region after 1349, following a flurry of new leasehold tenures on some manors, there was only a sporadic appearance of 'farms for the term of years' (for between seven and sixty years), in the fifteenth century. Demesne assets like land, meadows, mills, and fisheries were almost all held on lease, but only a few tenant holdings. Customary tenants appreciated the simple cash rent and lack of a long-term commitment that came with leasehold, but while it was adopted wholesale in eastern England, it was relatively scarce in the west midlands.[99]

Lords were not in complete control of tenures and tenant holdings: peasants had some influence.

---

[99] Hilton, *English Peasantry*, pp. 147–60; B. Wells-Furby, *The Berkeley Estate 1281–1417* (BGAS, 2012), pp. 95–118; M. Bailey, *After the Black Death. Economy, Society and the Law in Fourteenth-Century England* (Oxford, 2021), pp. 92–102, 301–7.

4
Peasants changing society

Peasants had some influence over the size and transfer of their holdings, although lords gave the impression that they were in control. Even serfdom could be ameliorated and eroded by peasants. This chapter addresses questions about peasant activities outside the framework of lordship. What use did peasants make of their life chances? How did they deal with their families, neighbours, and wider society? The selected themes highlight different dimensions of peasant lives: migration, social mobility, poverty, and the village community.

Migration

Many pressures combined to discourage medieval peasants from leaving their place of birth and upbringing. Lords would only release serfs from the manor with licence; families expected their offspring to work on the land and in the house; the expectations of inheritance gave sons an incentive to remain; village communities regarded incoming strangers (*extranei*) as a threat, and sought to retain workers in the harvest season. The state after 1349 ordered workers to accept contracts when offered, and forbade them to wander in search of higher paid employment. This array of social and institutional restraints on migration failed, and peasants in considerable numbers ignored the pressures and laws, moved away from their villages, and were replaced by incomers. The scale and pattern of movement can be appreciated in the turnover of names in the records. These show a frequent movement of people both before and after 1349. At Romsley (Worcestershire) with continuous manorial court rolls from 1280 to 1520, half of the surnames changed every twenty years between 1280 and 1340 (see Figure 4.1). The rate of recruitment of newcomers tended to diminish in the late fourteenth century, and after 1420 returned to the same level of mobility as before the plague. Only one name is found at the beginning and end of the series of records. Many similar calculations have been made over shorter periods, which reveal varying degrees of mobility, but never a majority of people remaining over many generations. Hartlebury (Worcestershire) retained some long-staying families (known elsewhere in a later period as 'ancient inhabitants'), but they were a minority, as nine of them persisted through the fifteenth century, and five family names (7 per cent) from 1299 were still traceable among the village's total of sixty-seven in *c.*1490. Henbury-in-the-Salt-Marsh on the Severn estuary had a

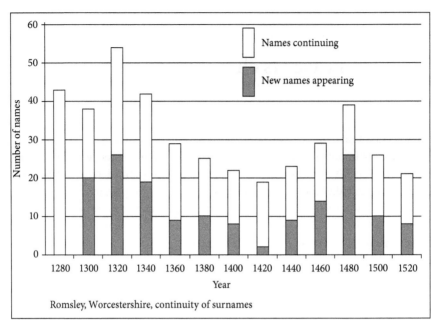

Figure 4.1 Continuity of surnames at Romsley, Worcestershire. Showing the numbers of names persisting, and those of newcomers, over twenty-year periods (source: *CR Romsley*).

similarly stable minority, with a third of the names in 1419 belonging to families holding land in 1299, and a fifth of the ninety-three names of 1432–41 still present around 1500. In most villages, less than 10 per cent of names survived over the whole fifteenth century, and sometimes not a single name from the thirteenth century can be found in the sixteenth. The Severn valley had a more stable population than villages in the Avon valley or on the Cotswolds.[1]

Surnames are an imprecise source of evidence, and generalizations based on them need some caution. Firstly, although surnames were becoming more stable in the late thirteenth century and subsequently, we still find people with aliases and there were occasional changes of name. Secondly, counting surnames in court rolls includes visitors and workers staying for a particular job who would not be expected to be stable residents. If tenants are studied, a greater degree of continuity is found, especially if note is taken of hereditary succession to land through the female line which led to changes of surname.[2] The statistics may therefore exaggerate discontinuity, but nonetheless movement of people was a frequent

---

[1] *RBW*, pp. 191–202, 380–400; WA, ref. 009:1 BA2636/37 (iii), fos. 78–83;/185 92574b;/165/92226 4/4; C. Dyer, 'Were Late Medieval Villages "Self-Contained"?, in *The Self-Contained Village? The Social History of Rural Communities, 1250-1900* (Hatfield, 2007), pp. 6–27.

[2] Z. Razi, 'Family, Land and the Village Community in Later Medieval England', *P&P* 93 (1981), pp. 3–36.

occurrence, as is demonstrated by the newcomers acquiring holdings through the land market, or by marrying widows.

Migrants in the thirteenth century, when many surnames were formed, could be identified by the name of their place of origin. After a move to Wolverton (Worcestershire) from Bransford in the same county, a distance of 7 ½ miles, Walter de Braunsford (or his father) acquired the name which is recorded in the tax list of 1275.[3] There was an element of chance in this, as the choice of name lay with neighbours who might use some other distinguishing feature, such as occupation. The record of names is confined to the villagers with sufficient goods to be liable to tax. After 1350, when surnames formed from place names provide less direct evidence for migration, the manorial authorities recorded the movements of serfs, another imperfect sample.

Even if they were only partially representative of the whole population, both the 'locative' surnames and the lists of serfs can give us insights into the ambitions, circumstances, and motives of some migrants: Where did they go? How far did they travel? Why did they move? What success did they have in their new destination?[4]

From the names in the tax records for Warwickshire and Gloucestershire distances covered by rural migrants can be analysed (see Table 4.1). The people

Table 4.1 Distances between taxpayers' locations, and the places from which their surnames derive, in Gloucestershire and Warwickshire, as recorded in the lay subsidies

Distances	Gloucestershire, 1327	Warwickshire, 1327 and 1332[a]
0–5 km (0–3 miles)	63 (16%)	102 (17%)
5.5–10 km (3.5–6.5m)	99 (26%)	152 (25%)
10.5–15 km (7–9.5m)	39 (10%)	86 (14%)
15.5–20 km (10–12.5m)	25 (7%)	71 (12%)
20.5–30 km (13–19m)	50 (13%)	76 (12%)
30.5–40 km (20–25m)	33 (9%)	46 (7%)
40.5–80 km (26–50m)	52 (14%)	58 (9%)
More than 80 km (50m)	20 (5%)	23 (4%)
Total	381 (100%)	614 (100%)

(a) As two tax lists are available very near to one another in date, their data have been combined. Most names appear in both, but the sample includes the names which appear in only one.

Sources: P. Franklin, ed., *The Taxpayers of Medieval Gloucestershire: An Analysis of the 1327 Lay Subsidy Roll with a New Edition of its Text* (Stroud, 1993); W.F. Carter, ed., 'Subsidy Roll of Warwickshire for 1327', *Transactions of the Midland Record Society* 6 (1902); W.F. Carter, ed., *The Subsidy Roll for Warwickshire of 6 Edward III (1332)* (DS, 6, 1926).

[3] J. Willis Bund and J. Amphlett, eds., *Lay Subsidy Roll for the County of Worcester, circa 1280* (WHS, 1893), p. 25.

[4] Headings for enquiry into migration were originally devised by Ravenstein. They are applied to the west midland evidence in C. Dyer, 'Migration in Rural England in the Later Middle Ages', in *Migrants in Medieval England, c.500–c.1500*, edited by W.M. Ormrod, J. Story, and E. Tyler (Oxford, British Academy, 2020), pp. 238–64.

Table 4.2 Distances from home manor to destinations of *nativi* reported as absent, in Gloucestershire, Warwickshire, and Worcestershire, 1400–99

Distances	
0–5 km (0–3 miles)	79 (21%)
5.5–10 km (3.5–6.5 miles)	71 (19%)
10.5–15 km (7–9.5 miles)	32 (9%)
15.5–20 km (10–12.5 miles)	32 (8%)
20.5–30 km (13–19 miles)	53 (14%)
30.5–40 km (19–25 miles)	33 (9%)
40.5–80 km (26–50 miles)	48 (13%)
More than 80 km (50 miles)	28 (7%)
Total	376 (100%)

Sources: Manorial court rolls of 46 manors.

who moved exercised considerable caution if we focus on the 42 per cent who travelled at most 6 ½ miles to their new destination. On the other hand, an impressive 19 per cent (from Gloucestershire) and 13 per cent (Warwickshire) moved 25 miles or more from their homes. The serfs in the fifteenth century (Table 4.2) confirm the earlier evidence, because 40 per cent of them moved within 6 ½ miles, but they were a little more adventurous, because 20 per cent settled at a distance in excess of 25 miles.

The predominance of short movements is to be expected, and resembles the patterns in later centuries, but there is a surprising absence of evidence for a flow of migrants from the well-populated champion areas into the woodland landscapes that were the scene of assarting and expanding settlements in the twelfth and thirteenth century. In the Worcestershire tax list of 1275, compiled around the height of the colonization movement, a total of 237 surnames derive from place-names (excluding gentry names), and only seventeen names from the woodlands suggest that a taxpayer had originated in a champion settlement in the south-east of the county. Indeed, movement from the woodland to the champion was not uncommon, like the Bransford name at Wolverton mentioned earlier. Names from a sample of Warwickshire villages recorded between 1279 and 1332 (Figure 4.2) reflect a great variety of movements, with relatively few of them having made the journey across the great divide between Arden and Feldon. In the Forest of Dean, which was showing signs of dynamic growth both before and after 1300, few names suggest that settlers came from the obvious recruiting area in the Vale or wolds. After 1349 the pace of assarting and development was slowed or even halted in the woodlands. Industrial activity and pastoral farming might have attracted settlers from the shrinking villages of the champion, but this is not indicated by the movement of serfs.

PEASANTS CHANGING SOCIETY 89

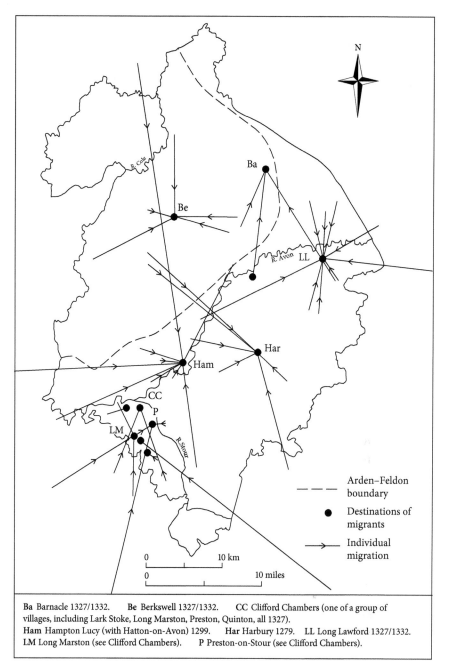

Ba Barnacle 1327/1332.   Be Berkswell 1327/1332.   CC Clifford Chambers (one of a group of villages, including Lark Stoke, Long Marston, Preston, Quinton, all 1327).
Ham Hampton Lucy (with Hatton-on-Avon) 1299.   Har Harbury 1279.   LL Long Lawford 1327/1332.
LM Long Marston (see Clifford Chambers).   P Preston-on-Stour (see Clifford Chambers).

Figure 4.2 Migration patterns in Warwickshire, 1279–1332. Sample villages with surname evidence for inward migration, selected to show a variety of settlements and movements (source: *WHR; RBW;* pp. 264–73; Carter, ed., 'Subsidy Roll 1327'; Carter, ed., *Subsidy Roll 1332*).

Migration was evidently not a reckless pioneering leap into unfamiliar territory, but a move to take up opportunities in landscapes and agrarian economies with which the migrant was familiar. The people who made these cautious moves into places resembling their home village were not hungry paupers hoping for jobs as farmworkers or in woodland crafts, but members of landed families, perhaps looking for a holding.

Migrations were calculated and planned. Peasants might move between villages on the same landed estate, like the tenant named Geoffrey de Offchurch who was living at Wasperton in 1279.[5] Both places, 7 miles apart, belonged to the Warwickshire estate of Coventry Cathedral Priory. Perhaps those who managed the estate encouraged or compelled a move from one manor to another. However, the tenants may have taken the initiative on hearing news of a vacant holding or a marriageable widow that could be carried across the estate by officials or carters. Villages were evidently in contact with one another because they were sited on main roads, or because they visited the same market. The Severn estuary was a corridor along which contacts were made, hence the presence in 1266 of William de Fromptone, most likely from Frampton-on-Severn, at Maisemore to the north of Gloucester, a move of over 10 miles.[6] Long distances could be faced with more confidence if a bold villager made the initial move, and then encouraged others, often relatives, to join him. In 1413 two serfs from Cleeve Prior (Worcestershire), William Holder and Richard Symondes had moved to the distant but high-profile settlement of Wigmore in Herefordshire—had one made an adventurous journey and encouraged the other to follow?[7] The women who formed a sizeable minority of migrating serfs often worked initially as servants, and again presumably had contacts with towns or other villages to inform them of opportunities. Many of the men and women settling in smaller towns came from the hinterland within 7 miles and would have therefore been familiar with the place from journeys to the market (see 'Peasant migration into towns' in Chapter 8).

If people took the risks of migration to better themselves, were they successful? The clearest indications come from those young people who left to acquire education and training, like the sons of serfs attending school who were supposed to obtain permission from the lord. Peasants are known to have featured among the hundreds of clergy ordained by bishops of Worcester in the early fourteenth century, because their names can be traced back to the villages where their families lived.[8] Many other young serfs who left the manor became servants or apprentices, working for a variety of artisans, such as bakers, brewers, carpenters, shoemakers, and weavers. We find those who became servants, many of them young

---

[5] *WHR*, p. 178.   [6] *Hist Glouc*, 3, p. 166.   [7] WCL, E46.
[8] D. Robinson, 'Priesthood and Community: The Social and Economic Background of the Parochial Clergy in the Diocese of Worcester to 1348', *Midland History* 42 (2017), pp. 18–35.

women, living in the households of clergy, gentry, and a Worcester merchant. Employment as a servant could have been a dead end, but with good fortune it would lead to marriage and relative prosperity. Margery Roberd of Harvington (Worcestershire) was reported in 1458 to have moved to Chipping Campden (Gloucestershire) and married a butcher. She is likely to have begun her time in the market town 8 miles from her home village as a servant, and encountered her future husband.[9]

Those who moved to gain land can be found as established members of their adopted community, farming, selling ale, and holding office in the manorial administration. John Reve, a serf of Netherton (Worcestershire), who had acquired land at neighbouring Elmley Castle by 1432, kept at least one pig, and some sheep. He owned a cart. He brewed ale, or at least paid the amercements when his wife Agnes brewed and sold ale. He served intermittently until 1470 on the jury of the manor court. From the late 1460s he was repeatedly reported for neglecting repairs of his buildings, and in the 1470s in his old age faded out of the records.[10] George Underhill, a serf of Hampton Lovett, gained 12 acres at Hartlebury and in the 1480s and 1490s became a leading figure in his village, with a variety of trades as a brewer, baker, and butcher over a twenty-year period. He served on the manorial jury, and as a churchwarden. He infringed the rules by enclosing a croft, neglecting building repairs, and keeping a woman of doubtful morality in his house, but these were characteristic transgressions among villagers, not just immigrants.[11]

Migration was a normal feature of peasant life. People wished to move, and the inhabitants of the villages in which they settled were willing to receive and accept them. Especially in the fifteenth century tenants and labour were in short supply, and a newcomer like Underhill could bring a talent for retail trade that provided a useful service. Knowledge of farming methods or new styles of building, both in domestic houses and churches, could have spread through migration. Beyond the village, when we can identify the town tradesmen and high-status households in which young peasants found a niche, we gain the impression that peasants were kept informed through networks, and some could benefit from patronage. The ambitions of peasant migrants and their attempts to better themselves throws light on their mentality. We can gather stories of success, but some migrants did not find gainful employment, well-off husbands, land, or a place among the village elite.

---

[9] WCL, E64; for servants in towns, P.J.P. Goldberg, *Women, Work and Lifecycle in a Medieval Economy: Women in York and Yorkshire, c. 1300–1520* (Oxford, 1992), pp. 280–304.
[10] *CR Elmley*, pp. 93–179.
[11] R.K. Field, 'Migration in the Later Middle Ages: The Case of the Hampton Lovett Villeins', *Midland History* 8 (1983), pp. 29–48.

Social mobility

Whether peasants relocated themselves, or stayed in their native village, could they achieve social mobility? Disapproval of those who attempted to advance themselves was expressed in legislation against the wearing of expensive clothing by the lower orders. The aristocracy would emphasize the importance of birth and inheritance, which excluded upwardly mobile individuals. However, as well as moving from one rank to another, there could be some internal mobility within social groups, including the peasantry.[12]

Thousands of lives were changed by the acquisition of smallholdings in the twelfth and thirteenth centuries. Domesday recorded many slaves, especially in Gloucestershire where there were 2,140 in 1086, but in subsequent decades they disappeared, to be replaced by smallholders. The slaves had become tenants. At Pinbury in Gloucestershire, for example, nine slaves in 1086 were succeeded by six *bovarii*, four cottars, and three maid servants by *c*.1110.[13] They were burdened with a heavy work commitment, and no doubt their status was still very low, but the few acres held by the ox-men (*bovarii*) and cottars gave them a toe hold in landed society. The holdings granted to former slaves passed through the generations, and can still be traced in later centuries. On the manors of the bishopric of Worcester in 1299 the holdings were called *enchelondi*, with distinctively heavy obligations such as manning the lord's ploughs.

New smallholdings also resulted from the movement to clear land on heaths, moors, and woodland. The assarting movement had only just begun on the manor of Alvechurch in north Worcestershire in *c*.1170, when seven assarts were recorded, but by 1299 twelve tenants held assarts, twenty had 'plots', and another eight had provided themselves with both plots and assarts, or with 'new lands'. Some had occupational names, such as Richard le Coupere or Thomas le Webbe, which suggests that artisans were seeking the security of smallholdings, and others may have been wage workers, either developing land for themselves or buying newly cleared parcels.[14] By gaining land and cottages, whether on their own initiative or by grants, they had added to their security and standing in society as property holders, if only on a small scale. There were many other routes to smallholding, including receiving a parcel for building a cottage on the edge of a messuage (with or without the lord's permission), as a sublet parcel, or from pieces of a freeholding when it was subdivided among daughters, or when fragments were sold (see 'Holding land before 1349' in Chapter 3).

The proliferation of smallholdings in the thirteenth century is often represented as a development that threatened peasant welfare, by encouraging the new tenants to embrace a false promise of security. A marriage might be contracted

---

[12] S. Carocci, 'Social Mobility and the Middle Ages', *Continuity and Change* 26 (2011), pp. 367–404.
[13] *HTC*, pp. 34–5.   [14] *RBW*, pp. 211–26.

and a new household formed on the basis of a small parcel of land which could provide little security in the event of unemployment or a bad harvest. A strong demand for smallholdings suggests that many people thought the risk was worth taking. New smallholdings continued to be acquired by the landless after 1349, such as the servant at Moor (Worcestershire) who was granted a cottage and an acre in 1379; and the three selions let on a short term to Richard, servant of William Offenham at Cleeve Prior in 1395. In 1497 John Reve, a servant of Alveston (Warwickshire), obtained the reversion of a cottage.[15] After 1349 wage earners could afford the rent and could aspire to establish themselves as tenants, though few did so compared with the thousands of new cottagers and smallholders in the period 1200–1320.

Did the tenants of larger holdings experience social mobility? Many tenants owing labour services on their yardlands lost status and incurred financial penalties when their servile status was defined around 1200, but although they were dragged into an inferior legal category, they kept their holdings and remained in the top layer of wealth and responsibility in village society. For example, at Atherstone (Warwickshire) in the early thirteenth century the lord expected customary (servile) tenants with yardlands to fill a supervisory role in the harvest field, attending 'in his own person' for the whole day with all the members of his household (except his wife) 'with an iron fork, and to see that the work is done well'.[16]

In the thirteenth and early fourteenth centuries, the more substantial tenants had the opportunity to acquire extra land, helped by an expanding market for agricultural produce. Deeds sometimes reveal increases in property among free tenants, such as six transactions at Hanley Castle in Worcestershire by Richard Magote in the later years of the thirteenth century and up to 1319, sometimes in association with Richard Ody, once with Richard Apsolon, and sometimes jointly with Agnes, his wife. The amount of land and meadow is not stated, except 'nine selions and their headlands' were conveyed on one occasion. These were clearly sales, as 'a certain sum of silver' was mentioned in three of the transactions, and in 1304 12s was paid for a lease of a parcel of meadow.[17] Producers could accumulate 'sums of silver' in good times, but also were aided in acquiring land by bad harvests which induced those in financial difficulties to put their holdings on the market. At the time of the Great Famine in 1316–17 at Tardebigge (Worcestershire), eight deaths of tenants are recorded in an incomplete series of records, and twenty-three parcels of lands were surrendered and taken by new tenants,

---

[15] WCL, E30, E38, E84.
[16] M. Chibnall, ed., *Select Documents of the English Lands of the Abbey of Bec* (Camden Society, 3rd series, 73, 1951), p. 103.
[17] *Rec Hanley*, pp. 6–7, 10–11, 15.

reflecting a tendency for the better-off to take advantage of neighbours' hardship.[18] These composite holdings according to long term land market studies tended not to last very long, as they were divided by inheritance and sales.

Social mobility was not a matter of the rise and fall of wages which are well documented. In the thirteenth and early fourteenth centuries labourers received a low rate of pay with its purchasing power limited by the high cost of basic food-stuffs. After about 1340 the daily wage in cash rose, and food, especially after 1375, became relatively cheap, but there are doubts about the annual earnings of day labourers. It has been proposed that household incomes were quite high in the fifteenth century because of the combined earnings of the adult male wage earner, wife, and children.[19] Those with land were able to increase the size of their holdings, but they needed skilful management to make profits from their acres at a time of low cereal prices. Individuals could raise their standard of living, but the hierarchy was not transformed. Those cottagers who increased their income still occupied the lower end of village society, and the yardlanders who gained another yardland were still peasants. The relative positions of the top and bottom of village society may have changed, but the gap was still there, as also was the much larger gulf that separated the peasant elite and the lower ranks of the gentry.

Ambitious peasants were provided with new opportunities from the end of the fourteenth century when a growing number of lords, with both large and small estates, gave up direct management and preferred a regular income in the form of the farm (fixed annual rent) paid by a leaseholder. They were encouraged to make this move by the demand among the aspiring farmers, many of whom were peasants, who seem not to have been daunted by the prospect, having previously lived on 30 or 60 acres of land, of taking on the management of a much larger area. John Mannyng and his mother, whose family holding consisted of two yardlands, in 1475–6 leased the 400-acre demesne of Horsley (Gloucestershire) for a rent of £6.[20] Around 1400 lords and farmers typically committed themselves cautiously to quite short terms, for seven to ten years. During the fifteenth and sixteenth centuries the terms lengthened to 60 years or even more, and the rent tended to be reduced. The rents were not high, so that for the large demesne of 400 acres at Horsley the farmer was paying about 3*d*–4*d* per acre. Such rents made it possible for the farmer to make a profit, and peasants found themselves in competition with gentry, clergy, and merchants for the tenancies. Even after 1500 the majority of farmers were of peasant origin, especially in the case of manors (about a tenth

---

[18] WA, ref. b705:128, BA 1188/12. Land transfers were also stimulated among free tenants in Gloucestershire: M. Davies and J. Kissock, 'The Feet of Fines, the Land Market and the English Agricultural Crisis of 1315 to 1322', *Journal of Historical Geography* 30 (2004), pp. 215–30. On the phenomenon in general, P. Schofield, 'Dearth, Debt and the Local Land Market in a Late Thirteenth-Century Village Community', *AgHR* 45 (1997), pp. 1–17.

[19] S. Horrell, J. Humphries, and J. Weisdorf, 'Family Standards of Living Over the Long Run, England 1280–1850', *P&P* 250 (2021), pp. 87–134.

[20] TNA, SC6/855/6;/856/4; SC2/175/67.

of the total) where the demesne was split up into smaller parcels which were attractive to peasant lessees. Even when the formal indentures recorded grants to a gentleman or clerical farmer, other sources suggest that the land was being sublet to local peasants, though of course subtenants would be less likely to make large profits.[21]

The new farmers pursued land management in different ways. To take two Warwickshire examples, one was Roger Heritage of Burton Dassett in 1495 who ran a mixed farm with a strong pastoral dimension, as he cultivated at least a hundred acres of corn, but kept 12 horses, 40 cattle, and 860 sheep, with a rabbit warren in addition. The other was an entirely livestock enterprise managed by Richard Buller in 1527 at Weston-juxta-Cherrington, with 130 cattle and 1,640 sheep. Both demesnes had been mainly arable before 1400[22] (for Weston, see 'Peasants, lords, and the changing landscape after 1350' in Chapter 2).

The wealth of farmers is reflected in their contributions to state taxes. In the poll tax of 1379 the authorities laid down that farmers (among other categories such as franklins) should pay more than the standard tax of 4*d*. In Warwickshire a handful were identified, most paying 12*d*, but a few contributed 3*s* 4*d* and 6*s* 8*d*. From the taxes of 1524 and 1525 (and the assessments included in the military survey of 1522) we gain a more precise valuation of farmers' possessions. They appear at the top of the village hierarchy, paying on goods valued at between £13 and £100 when most taxpayers were rated at £1 to £12. Richard Colchester of Lark Stoke (Warwickshire), for example, had goods valued at £100 in 1522, and £24 in 1525 (the decline probably reflected his skill in negotiating with the tax assessors). Like many farmers he was recruited from outside the village where he held his lease, and by the 1520s was probably specializing in sheep.[23]

The farmers were the richest people in the village, often being ranked as yeomen when the other villagers were rated no higher than husbandmen and labourers. They kept their distance from their neighbours, and did not participate easily in village life. The demesne farm in one Warwickshire village was said in 1480 to be occupied as if it belonged to one manor and the village to another.[24] Taking on a lease was a path to a higher income and limited social advancement, but farmers did not easily progress into the gentry. A few peasant families were able to climb over the fences that protected the exclusive club of the gentry from upstarts. John

---

[21] A useful study with examples from the region is B.F. Harvey, 'The Leasing of the Abbot of Westminster's Demesnes in the Later Middle Ages', *EcHR*, 2nd series, 22 (1969), pp. 17–27.

[22] C. Dyer, 'Were There Any Capitalists in Fifteenth-Century England?', in *Enterprise and Individuals in Fifteenth-Century England*, edited by J. Kermode (Stroud, 1991), pp. 1–24; C. Dyer, *A Country Merchant, 1495–1520: Trading and Farming at the End of the Middle Ages* (Oxford, 2012), p. 149.

[23] *PT*, part 2, pp. 647, 648, 649, 650, 651 etc.; R. Hoyle, ed., *The Military Survey of Gloucestershire, 1522* (GRS, 6, 1993), p. 221; M. Faraday, ed., *The Bristol and Gloucestershire Lay Subsidy of 1523-7* (GRS, 23, 2009), p. 414.

[24] Magdalen College, Oxford, Quinton 56.

Dey from about 1440 acquired parcels of land, some of it freehold, in nine Arden villages, and became lessee of the demesne of the manor of Drakenage. He grew corn, managed a fishpond, and held a mill on lease, but his core activity was grazing cattle at a time of high demand for beef. He was able to style himself as a gentleman in 1471, perhaps helped by the freeholds, and his son Thomas who died in 1489 was also known as a gentleman.[25]

Successive generations of the Andrewes family made money in Warwickshire from grazing livestock, but in the north-east Feldon. Between 1391 and 1444 they acquired land in six villages, but their main residence was a free yardland tenement at the hamlet of Sawbridge. When Thomas Andrewes died in 1496 he held a long lease on Charwelton just across the boundary in Northamptonshire, which he developed as a large sheep pasture. The status of the Andrewes seems to have wavered, as although the two brothers John and Thomas were called gentlemen in 1465, Thomas was being described as a grazier twenty years later, and was even called a husbandman. No doubt conscious of standing at an insecure social boundary, they asserted themselves by outward displays, originally by building a pretentious house at Sawbridge in 1449. Thomas and his wife were commemorated in Charwelton church by a large and high-quality memorial brass around 1496. The family resorted to concocting a fake pedigree and false seal in order to claim a distinguished ancestry, but Thomas Andrewes the second secured an incontrovertible claim to gentry status when he became lord of the manor of Harlestone in Northamptonshire in 1500.[26]

A more frequently travelled path to social advancement took boys to schools, which could have been initiated and were certainly managed by the villagers themselves. Five Worcestershire villages (Hanley Castle, Hartlebury, King's Norton, Rock, and Yardley) are known to have had schools, usually with a chantry priest who acted as schoolmaster, and either the school or the chantry was endowed with land by the early sixteenth century. The endowments consisted of small parcels and rents granted by parishioners, and they were administered by feoffees who collected the rents and paid the schoolmaster. The donors and the feoffees can usually be identified as better-off peasants.[27] More informal arrangements are found at earlier dates, such as the education available at Elmley Castle revealed in 1385 when Robert Pygun was said not to have paid the school fees he owed

---

[25] A. Watkins, 'Cattle Grazing in the Forest of Arden in the Later Middle Ages', *AgHR* 37(1989), pp. 12–25, especially 18–19; C. Carpenter, *Locality and Polity: A Study of Warwickshire Landed Society, 1401–1499* (Cambridge, 1992), pp. 646, 653.

[26] N.W. Alcock and P. Woodfield, 'Social Pretension in Architecture and Ancestry: Hall House, Sawbridge, Warwickshire, and the Andrewes Family', *Antiquaries Journal* 76 (1996), pp. 51–72; Carpenter, *Locality and Polity*, p. 136.

[27] *Rec Hanley*, pp. xv, xvii, xxvii, 69; D. Robertson, ed., *The Old Order Book of Hartlebury Grammar School* (WHS,1904), pp. 209, 218–19; G. Demidowicz and S. Price, *King's Norton: A History* (Chichester, 2009), pp. 43–4; *VCH Worcs*, 4, pp. 327–8; V. Skipp, *Medieval Yardley* (Chichester, 1970), pp. 116–17.

to Richard the chaplain.[28] Young men who had acquired some learning were tonsured and hoped to gain employment as clergy or even to hold benefices, if they could call on the aid of a patron. Some remained in the secular world, and found advantages in engaging in commercial activities if they could read and write, if only in English.

Peasants could seek to improve themselves by moving into towns. Some may have taken to the town knowledge of a craft that they practised in the country, but others moved to become servants and labourers, and acquired skills and experience in the long term. Some achieved wealth and prominence: in Shipston Thomas de Maddeleye, who had probably come from Staffordshire, became lessee of the Shipston mills in 1315 within fifty years of the town's foundation, and became a leading figure.[29] In Coventry, the largest town in the region apart from Bristol, property owners *c.*1300 had names derived from their rural background, such as Geoffrey de Donechirche (Dunchurch) who came from a village a few miles to the east of the city.[30] A few of these migrants can be shown to have reached a high level in the trading hierarchy. William de Wikwan and Anketell de Wykwane are recorded in the 1230s; their unusual name shows that they came from Wickhamford or Childswickham on Worcestershire's border with Gloucestershire.[31] They were merchants with some ambition, as they were selling wine, a consumer luxury, and William was also trading in London. People like the Wikwanes no doubt brought to their new role some commercial acumen, but they also needed resources of cash or credit which may have come initially from their rural background.

Social mobility is usually judged by changes in landholding, income, occupation, and status, but we also ought to take into account such matters as esteem, leadership, and suitability to hold office. Perhaps peasants were trusted to take on administrative tasks by those in authority, and sometimes were selected by their peers, using judgements of their qualities of character and competence rather than just their wealth (see the section on the village community in this chapter).

Poverty

Turning from people who moved up the social hierarchy, to those who lost land and livelihood, the scale of poverty needs to be assessed, and also its causes and possible remedies.

---

[28] *CR Elmley*, p. 46.   [29] WCL, E7.
[30] P.R. Coss, ed., *The Early Records of Medieval Coventry* (British Academy Records of Social and Economic History, new series, 11, 1986), pp. 97, 99, 10, 101.
[31] R. Goddard, *Lordship and Medieval Urbanisation. Coventry, 1043–1355* (Woodbridge, 2004), p. 152.

The poor often appear in documents as an anonymous crowd, like those who received food from monastic almonries. The larger monasteries all had programmes of distributing alms, on a scale which confirms that many paupers were available to receive them, but they and the smaller almshouses and hospitals, like St Mark's at Bristol, were located in towns and aimed to relieve urban poverty. A poor peasant might move to a town to gain access to charity, like John Roose of Kempsey (Worcestershire) who in 1445 gave up his land and went to live on alms in nearby Worcester.[32] In 1535 rural monasteries like the priory at Great Malvern, or the Cistercian houses of Combe and Stoneleigh (both in north Warwickshire), gave out large allowances of cash and food.[33] As monasteries as wealthy as these were scarce in the countryside, and unevenly distributed, the quantity of alms did not match the numbers likely to be in need.

Individuals experiencing poverty can be investigated because the manorial authorities would release named individuals from fines, heriots, and especially amercements, 'because he (or she) is poor'. They would have arrived at this conclusion with advice from the peasant officials in the court, in particular the affeerers who helped to fix financial penalties, using their local knowledge. From the manorial court records of the west midlands, we can extract the names of eighty-eight people who were regarded as too poor to pay sums of money, or who through poverty had to surrender land, or were unable to take on a holding. There were more men than women, sixty-one males compared with twenty-seven females, which reflects the courts' prejudice rather than social reality. In fact, the numbers were probably near to equality because many of the men were married, and their wives shared in their condition. Cases of poverty were scattered quite evenly over the region, but unequally in time, with almost half recorded before 1350, and relatively few in the fifteenth century.

The majority of named paupers, seventy-four in all, are known to have held lands, both before and after they were identified as poor. Their holdings are analysed in Table 4.3. These people had not been entirely dependent on agriculture, and a handful of them were linked to a craft, two as bakers, one a cloth maker, and

Table 4.3 Holdings of land linked with those identified as paupers in manorial records, 1200–1540

Size	Cottage	1–4 ac	5–14 ac	15 ac	16–29 ac	30 ac	30+ ac	Total
unknown 18	16	8	4	14	2	9	3	74
24%	22%	11%	5%	19%	3%	12%	4%	100%

Sources: Manorial court rolls from all documented manors.

[32] WA, ref. 705:4 BA54.   [33] *VE*, vol. 3, pp. 54, 55, 241.

two quarried stone. In their participation in crafts, as well as the distribution of land among them, the sample represents a cross-section of rural society, and is not notably tilted towards smallholders. The human factor was more likely to lead people into poverty than structural imbalances in landholding, climate change, or epidemic disease. They encountered problems at various stages of their life cycle. A youth, John Templer of Middleton (Warwickshire) in 1303 was not admitted to his tithing (which normally happened at the age of 12, when boys became legally responsible), because of his poverty.[34] Young men were sometimes unable to inherit land because they could not afford the entry fine. A greater number could not keep their holdings because they were too poor in their old age. Richard Pytwey of Romsley, said to be poor in 1438, had appeared in the court records for the previous 45 years, so he was probably aged at least 65.[35] Six of the sample were surrendering their land in exchange for a promise of maintenance, either in the form of grain, or a small portion of the holding. Widows figure among these apparently elderly tenants arranging their retirement. Some of those advancing in age were suffering from 'nuclear poverty', because their children did not help them in their declining years, so at Grimley (Worcestershire) in 1326 two tenants, Agnes de Ruggeweye and Adam Atehelme, gave up their holdings in a state of poverty, but no relative came forward to succeed them.[36]

Peasants could encounter difficulties in their middle years, when their children needed to be fed, but were not yet old enough to work. Richard Pleydemore of Northfield (Worcestershire) began an active life in 1424, but met with ill-fortune in 1443 when he surrendered the holding because he was 'impotent' (disabled).[37] As the term life cycle implies, poverty might be temporary, and Agnes Bovetoun of Oversley was judged in 1322 to be too poor to pay an amercement for failing to grind her corn in the lord's mill, but by 1327 she was able to pay 12*d* for the king's taxes.[38]

Poverty could result from inadequacies, which were not specific to any age group. Thomas Robertes of Admington (Warwickshire) seems to have managed his farming badly, so although he held 40 acres of good land (a yardland) the lord found in 1452 that his buildings were in a ruinous state, and he was unable 'to support the burden of the holding'. He was pushed into surrendering the land and moving to another manor on his lord's estate at Sherborne (Gloucestershire).[39] John Muryell of Chaddesley Corbett (Worcestershire) also began his landholding career with a yardland, but surrendered it and moved into a more manageable half-yardland. He did not make a success of that holding either and in 1405 when his widow gave up her tenancy two years after his death the buildings were badly

---

[34] UNMSC, MiM 131/2.   [35] *CR Romsley*, p. 189.
[36] WCL, E10.   [37] BAH, 518086.
[38] SCLA, DR5/2274; Carter, ed., *Subsidy Roll*, p. 29.   [39] GA, D678/62.

decayed.[40] Ruinous buildings were a not infrequent prologue to a tenant giving up land and being identified as poor.

The homeless, wandering paupers make little impact in our records as named individuals, though Simon Lacy of Snowshill (Gloucestershire) in 1342 was said to be wandering about after abandoning his smallholding. Some remained in their community, like Margaret Sterveyn of Elmley Castle, described as a beggar, who in 1385 broke the by-laws by gleaning in the corn field.[41] Others identified as poor were also offending against social norms, by, for example incurring the penalty of *leirwite* for sexual misconduct, and then pleading an inability to pay because of poverty. Contemporary moralists and legislators had much to say about vagabonds and beggars, who were seen to be numerous and to have volunteered to be poor through their idleness. The leading figures in the villages shared some of these negative attitudes toward the wandering poor, who were seen as part of the problem of scarce labour, leading the jurors of Ombersley (Worcestershire) to order the constable in 1496 to supervise vagabonds (see 'Peasants and the state' in Chapter 10).

The great majority of the known poor were not social outcasts or an anonymous underclass, but were members of society who had encountered some misfortune, or through age, infirmity, or widowhood could no longer manage their daily lives. Their payments of amercements and other dues were condoned, perhaps through compassion, but also based on realism. Many people went through the same life cycle and experienced problems similar to those appearing as *pauper* in the official records, but were able to avoid destitution. The maintenance contract by which an old or inadequate person could surrender their land for a promise of food and accommodation was an effective method of securing a steady income. However, this form of social security was only available to those with a landholding. Debt could be a cause of poverty, or a means of gaining temporary relief from it, which may have been the case for Cecilia Rogers of Cleeve Prior in 1320 who owed a relative 27s 6d. Subtenancy could be a means of obtaining an income from land that was difficult for the poor tenant to cultivate, and we find Agnes Bovetoun of Oversley subletting her land when she was experiencing difficulties.[42] Some people afflicted by poverty could themselves become subtenants.

Various practices and measures helped to alleviate poverty. Rectories had an obligation to donate alms to the parochial poor. At Bledington (Gloucestershire) in 1403, after the monastery at Winchcomb acquired the revenues of the rectory, the bishop stipulated that in Lent each year the poor of the parish should be given 8 bushels of wheat and 8 bushels of barley. The bishop felt the need to put the commitment in writing, perhaps because the practice was under threat when a remote religious house took over a parish. The local alms distribution in this case

---

[40] SCLA, DR5/2737,/2750,/2753,/2755.   [41] GA, D678/1/M1/1/2; *CR Elmley*, p. 47.
[42] WCL, E9; SCLA, DR5/2274.

offered no more than a temporary alleviation of hunger—too little was given, and it was a token gesture rather than a targeted response. The date of distribution was based on liturgical priorities, not the time of likely hardship.[43]

The lay congregation rather than the clergy may well have contributed more effectively to poor relief: holy loaves were made available after church services throughout the year, and the poor benefited from handouts of money or food at funerals and weddings. The laity of the parish could maintain a 'common box' to keep funds for charitable purposes, as recommended by Bishop Carpenter of Worcester in 1451, such as the church box at Hagley (Worcestershire) valued at £4 10s 0d in 1522.[44] Those making wills could take some specific and practical steps to help the poor, like William Churchyard of Claines (Worcestershire) who in 1513 bequeathed enough money to provide the poor in winter with fifty pairs of shoes. John Edmunds of Westbury-on-Trym in 1538 wanted poor householders (so not vagrants) to benefit from money to fund the marriages of poor young men and maidens.[45] A community aim to relieve poverty can be found in the by-laws which allowed the poor to glean in the harvest field, and to pick green peas and beans growing in the common fields. Safeguards were attempted to ensure that only those in genuine need should benefit. At Welford-on-Avon (Warwickshire) in 1414 the law reiterated the old principle that 'no-one may collect *pescoddes* in the corn field' if they could work for a day for 1*d* and food. A more elaborate version of these rules at Weston Subedge in 1398 defined those qualifying as 'indigent paupers', forbade collecting peas and beans at night, or selling them at the nearby town of Chipping Campden, or using them to feed pigs.[46]

The survival of the poor may have been helped by the rather patchy provision of parish, village, and individual charity, but much depended on their own efforts, which as well as gleaning involved the practice of a 'cottage economy', as it was described in the nineteenth century, in which many small sources of income were brought together to sustain a family: commons could be scoured for useful and saleable produce such as fuel, fruits and nuts, small birds, rushes, and bracken; modest earnings could be gained from tasks such as spinning in which the elderly and the very young could participate; seasonal work for the short term was available, not just in the harvest but in tasks such as drawing straw, clod breaking, and bird scaring. This can be seen in operation in the early fourteenth century at Bitton in Gloucestershire where the court was concerned that the rushes and gorse on the

---

[43] W. Smith, ed., *Register of Richard Clifford, Bishop of Worcester, 1401–1407* (Toronto, 1976), pp. 136–7.
[44] R.M. Haines, 'Bishop Carpenter's Injunctions to the Diocese of Worcester in 1451', *Bulletin of the Institute of Historical Research* 40 (1967), pp. 203–7; M. Faraday, ed., *Worcestershire Taxes in the 1520s* (WHS, new series, 19, 2003), p. 19.
[45] WA, ref. 008:7, BA 3590/I, vol. 2, fo. 51; ref. 008:7, BA 3585, 1538/46.
[46] King's College, Cambridge, WOA/9; Dorset History Centre, D10/M229/1–5.

common were being over exploited; the gathering of rushes for sale was seen as a particular problem.[47]

Village community

Historians who are impressed by the capacity of peasants to organize themselves, regard villages communities as a practical means of advancing the common good.[48] The origins of local government, popular politics, and even democracy have been seen in the creative self-coordination of the medieval and early modern 'community of the vill'.[49] An alternative view might be to see village administration as an imposition by those in authority. Lords pushed peasants into taking over the farm of the manor (see 'Peasants and the making of the landscape' in Chapter 2) and used them to collect dues such as tallage among themselves. The state made the vill responsible for the assessment and collection of the main direct tax, the lay subsidy, from 1334, and from an early date gave the villagers a range of duties in enforcing law and order, and in military recruitment. The church also gave the parish responsibilities in managing local churches (see 'Peasants and the state' and 'Peasants and religion' in Chapter 10). In fact, the two views are not incompatible; if the villagers managed common assets effectively, above all the fields, outsiders noticed, and took advantage of these administrative capabilities. The peasants co-operated partly because they were compelled, but they also saw advantages in being able to bargain on behalf of the village, and as individuals they hoped to gain in status and sometimes wealth from collaboration.

The village community at work can be seen through the prism of the lord's courts, taking those held by Winchcomb Abbey for 1341–2 (a mainly Gloucestershire estate) as the example, and we can appreciate how the villagers and the lord sometimes pursued similar objectives, but also diverged.[50] The lord expected the villagers of Honeybourne to help in dealing with Roger Herman who had trespassed, probably with livestock in the lord's crops. Herman was required to pay an unusually high amercement of 6s 8d, and 'the whole homage' of Honeybourne were appointed as pledges. The homage (meaning the twelve jurors, or perhaps everyone in court) were being threatened with money penalties to make their neighbour pay, and behave better. Herman was confined in the stocks on the

---

[47] P. Thane, 'Old People and their Families in the English Past', in *Charity, Self-Interest and Welfare in the English Past*, edited by M. Daunton (London, 1996), pp. 113–38; Berkeley Castle Muniments, E1/2/7–E1/2/24; GCR, 137–156.

[48] M. Bourin and R. Durand, *Vivre au Village au Moyen Age. Les Solidarités Paysannes du XIe au XIIIe siècle* (Rennes, 2000).

[49] W.O. Ault, *Open-Field Farming in Medieval England* (London, 1972), pp. 64–78.

[50] GA, D678/M1/1/1–2.

orders of a much-annoyed lord. The homage was in charge of this form of imprisonment, and appear to have taken pity on him, and 'freed him from the shackles', provoking the lord to amerce them the outrageous sum of 13s 4d. The incident demonstrates the community's ability to make collective decisions, and to stand up to pressure from above. The lord knew that they could raise money, and expected them to maintain order among themselves, but underestimated their capacity to oppose him.

In the Winchcomb records of 1341–2, a routine example of enforced cooperation between community and the lord arose in the village of Yanworth where 'all of the customers' (a very high proportion of the whole population) were required to stand surety for the repair of buildings which had come into the hands of a widow after the death of her husband. In theory they would have to pay for the repairs if the widow failed. In the third case at Admington (Warwickshire) a problem of non-payment of taxes revealed a three-cornered relationship between lord, the state, and the village. The 'community of the vill' acting as a collective body brought a plea of debt against Gilbert Ricardes for him to pay 3 ½d as his contribution to the lay subsidy (direct tax). The vill was responsible to the local officials of the royal government for both the assessment and collection of this tax, and the lord of the manor was allowing his court to be the means of disciplining a reluctant payer. A fourth decision of the court shows how the community could be involved in managing a land transfer. Winchcomb Abbey, like many lords in the 1340s, was reducing the size of its demesne by renting out parcels to tenants. At Stanton a total of 41 acres was to be granted collectively to all yardlanders and half-yardlanders (the majority of the tenants), not to be held as a single unit under collective management (as is sometimes recorded), but divided among them 'in proportion to the land and tenements that they hold'. Finally, the Winchcomb courts of 1341–2 recorded collective amercement. It was sometimes a straightforward punishment, as at Roel where 12d had to be paid by all of the customary tenants together for 'contempt'. At Stanton a round sum of 3s 4d could be demanded from 'all customers', and at Sherborne 4s from 'all tenants' because of trespasses committed by their animals, which were normally charged on individuals, but in these cases they were given the collective chore of gathering the money. The Sherborne payment was to apply to both the West End and East End, showing in the case of this divided nucleated village, as for the scattered farms and hamlets in areas of dispersed settlement, that inhabitants had responsibilities to the whole vill. For individual villagers the community was requiring them to pay for collective obligations, but this probably did not seem as oppressive as direct demands from some lord's official, and the community protected them to some extent by bargaining over the payments.

The courts provided an important service for individual villagers because they could bring litigation and thereby settle disputes. In the same series of Winchcomb

Abbey courts, there were dozens of pleadings relating to debts, trespasses, unjust detention, and broken contracts. John de Clyve of Admington could recover 3*s* that he was owed by Robert Prestes for a mare he bought; Robert Colin of Twyning had agreed to provide Henry le Taillour's bullock with winter pasture but failed to do so. In the same village John Huwet obtained a licence to agree with Agnes le Newemon over a debt of 12*d*. These pleas were a contribution to harmony in the community, as they allowed disputes to be aired and resolved, and they often ended in a 'licence to agree' when the parties could attend a love day and settle their differences. The lord gained some profit from small payments made by the litigants, but the whole community could avoid prolonged quarrels among neighbours.

A primary function of the village community was the management of resources, to ensure that the farming system was balanced and disciplined. Much of the regulation must have been the result of following routines well-established before the appearance of the first detailed records in the late thirteenth century. The important decision to begin planting in the open fields, which in return required securing the fences and hedges round the fields, was presumably made in some village meeting hidden from our view. Through the year similar oral deliberations, perhaps conducted very informally, dealt with such matters as the timing of hay making and the beginning of the harvest (see 'Fields and their regulation' in Chapter 6).

The framework of regulation in which the peasants conducted their farming was based on customs transmitted from villager to villager by word of mouth. The rules were sometimes revealed when they were broken, as happened in 1336 at Teddington (Gloucestershire) when Thomas Alvert and John le Reve were said to hold twelve sheep 'beyond the common limit', which shows that the pasture was stinted, and a maximum number of animals permitted. The stint for Teddington is not known at this time, but typically thirty or forty sheep and a dozen larger animals would be allowed for a yardland holding.[51]

Sometimes unwritten customs were reiterated, strengthened, supplemented, or altered by formal ordinances or by-laws agreed in the manor court. Some apparently new harvest regulations were announced in the courts of ten manors on the Worcester Priory estate in July 1337, in anticipation of the coming harvest.[52] The appearance of these by-laws in almost identical form in a succession of manors shows that they were being proposed by the estate officials, though they protected the crops and the welfare of tenants as well as the lord, so peasants may have had a say in their framing. The by-laws were neither new, nor peculiar to the estate or the region, as very similar provisions were made in courts in other parts of the country as early as the 1270s.[53]

---

[51] WCL, E13.   [52] WCL, E13.   [53] Ault, *Open-Field Farming*, pp. 81–6.

One objective of the package of harvest laws was to control gleaning. The practice of allowing the village poor to collect ears of corn left by the harvesters was well-established, though as a concession to help those genuinely in need, not a right. The villagers sought to prevent strangers coming to collect grain. The poor should do their own gleaning, and not employ others. 'Bad gleaning' was prohibited, perhaps referring to gleaners taking ears from the harvested sheaves. Able-bodied potential workers should not glean but accept employment for a penny per day. These were employers' measures, to maximize the size of the labour force, and to reduce harvesters' wages. The producers feared that a proportion of the crop was being stolen. It was accordingly forbidden to pay workers with sheaves, as thieves might claim to be harvesters. These measures were not just directed against the poor and wage earners, as tenants were suspected of dishonesty, hence the law preventing the carting of corn from the fields at night, or on feast days, when honest people would not be working. Villagers were forbidden to have gates, styles, and paths leading into the field from the rear of their closes, lest they use them to steal corn.

The support that this legislation received from the community is shown by the actions of tenants serving as court officials who were responsible for a flurry of presentments after July 1337 for bad gleaning and other harvest offences. These harvest by-laws demonstrate the underlying ambiguities of the village community, which can be identified in all villages over centuries. On the one hand, the laws were represented in the official record as the unanimous will of the people: at Middleton (Warwickshire) in 1312 an order for the repair of the churchyard wall was issued 'by common assent of all of the vill'.[54] On the other hand the laws exposed divisions among the peasants. The leading villagers were ready to join with the lord in making laws that protected their interests, and played a part in enforcement. They were very ready to correct the behaviour of the poor, strangers, and wage earners, but they were reluctant to enforce any curbs on the behaviour of the better-off. Thomas Alvert (or Alvard) of Teddington exceeded the stint of the village's pastures in 1336. In 1327 he was the second highest ranking taxpayer in his village, no doubt already owning a large number of livestock.[55] Such a prominent villager would surely not have been eager to observe the rules and reduce his sheep flock.

Did villages function on the basis of a complementary and harmonious relationship between peasants with holdings of varied size, or were they divided by frictions between the smallholders and their more substantial neighbours? We can analyse the interdependence between those employing labour, and those expecting to be employed. The problem is a complex one because each family went through a cycle of lacking labour in its early stages and becoming

---

[54] UNMSC, MiM 131/7.
[55] WCL, E13; F.J. Eld, ed., *Lay Subsidy Roll for the County of Worcester, 1 Edward I* (WHS, 1895), p. 7.

well-provided as children became old enough to work. Mortality could disrupt this cycle, as is visible in the village of Compton Verney (Warwickshire) in 1279, when eighteen of the forty-five tenants were women, most of them widows. An epidemic must explain so many deaths, which led to a great demand for the labour of the six male cottagers.[56]

Setting aside such special problems, a speculative calculation can be made of a specimen settlement, Honington in Warwickshire, for the year 1279. This was a large village with twenty-five tenants of larger holdings, one or two yardlands each of 32 acres, with nineteen half yardlands, and sixteen smallholders. The number of working days needed for the larger holdings can be calculated on the basis that an acre required fifteen days of work each year, and adding some labour services on the lord's demesne.[57] The annual total of between 9,000 and 12,000 person-days would have been required for the yardlands and double yardlands, of which about 6,000 could have been contributed by the tenants themselves. The smallholders could provide, perhaps 4,000 days, with some from the spare time of the half-yardlanders. The lord was cultivating a demesne of 200 acres each year, and the combination of labour services and the lord's *famuli* (farm servants) would not have covered all of the tasks, creating yet more demand for wage workers. There would not have been a deficit, because household members, wives, children, and living-in servants between them would contribute thousands of person-days to the labour pool of the village.

Among other Warwickshire villages surveyed in 1279, the importance of the family and servant workforce is implied by the villages with many yardlanders and no cottagers at all, for example, at Gaydon and Ascott near Whichford. Priors Hardwick was clearly unbalanced, as it contained only five smallholders, with eight larger holdings and a large demesne and glebe generating a formidable demand for labour. To fill the gap, workers would have come from villages with many cottagers, an obvious candidate being nearby Priors Marston.[58] At the other end of the range of unbalanced societies, were the woodland villages like Stareton with fourteen cottagers, and the ring of villages around Coventry with numerous smallholders. One of those, Binley, might have benefited from its large urban neighbour, but also from its extensive woods with their employment opportunities.[59] The smallholding settlements underline the importance of non-agriculture work, and the necessity of those seeking wages to travel, if only within walking distance.

---

[56] WHR, pp. 248–50.
[57] WHR, pp. 286–90. The numbers of days of work per acre come from C. Thornton, 'The Determinants of Land Productivity on the Bishop of Winchester's Demesne of Rimpton, 1208 to 1403,' in *Land, Labour and Livestock: Historical Studies in European Agricultural Productivity*, edited by B.M.S. Campbell and M. Overton (Manchester, 1991), pp. 183–210; H.S.A. Fox, 'Exploitation of the Landless by Lords and Tenants in Early Medieval England', in *Medieval Society and the Manor Court*, edited by Z. Razi and R.M. Smith (Oxford, 1996), pp. 518–68, especially 544–9.
[58] WHR, pp. 185–6, 203–12, 295–7.   [59] WHR, pp. 73–5, 126–30.

To sum up, the village community before 1349 served the administrative needs of the lords and the state, but also acted collectively in the interests of peasants, moderating the demands of superior authorities, and sometimes able to offer resistance. For the peasants, the prime function of the village was to manage common fields and co-ordinate farming. The different ranks within the village could have been interdependent, with smallholders working for the better-off, though the potential employers and employees were not always evenly balanced.

After 1349 the community was in danger of weakening. The field system was no longer under such pressure as farming was rebalanced, and harvesting became less contentious. There were signs of a loss of functions and authority, for example in the fifteenth century, the manor court ceased to hear so much litigation between tenants, and therefore was not playing such an important part in settling disputes. But in some respects, such as the increase in legislation, the village was becoming more active. Was a factor in the changes in the institution a sharper divide between the better-off tenants and the smallholders and landless? An elite with larger holdings may have been tempted to dominate village affairs.

In some respects, the court became more effective and developed new responsibilities. The fourteenth-century court rolls demonstrate the federal structure of the larger manors. Particularly in the western and southern parts of the region hamlets and small villages reported separately to the manor court, serving as tithings, that is groups with the responsibility of reporting on wrong-doing. At Hawkesbury, for example, Badminton, Kilcott, Stoke, Upton, and Woodcroft all had such a role. There were a dozen subdivisions in Chaddesley Corbett, seventeen at Ombersley, and Hartlebury's business was divided between eight hamlets. Some by-laws applied to the whole territory, but on occasion a law or an 'ordinance' would be announced that applied only to one hamlet. The implication of this is that the inhabitants of each hamlet or tithing held separate meetings before they attended the court. Nucleated villages could be divided into ends, again with some measure of separate government. Broadway in Worcestershire and Sherborne (Gloucestershire) both had two ends. The tenants of Welsh End at Honeybourne (Gloucestershire) were charged with cleaning a pond 'to water their beasts well and competently'.[60] The leading villagers could exercise their influence both in the preliminary small meetings, and again when matters came to the main court.

As the number of by-laws increased, they seemed to become more inclusive, no longer confining themselves to the duties of tenants or the 'homage', but addressing themselves to everyone in the village: 'inhabitants', 'householders', 'residents'. The 'whole vill' or the 'whole community' were expected to amend their behaviour, and 'no-one' was to pasture their sheep on the stubble at the wrong time, and 'no-one' should break hedges. The wide scope of the prohibition of hedge breaking

[60] GA, D678/61.

(to obtain firewood) was necessary as this was an offence often committed by women, children, and servants.

As more people were required to obey the legislation, the scope of the community's responsibilities expanded. Mending roads had always been a duty of the vill, mainly for the benefit of the inhabitants, but also for outsiders crossing the vill's territory. The villagers were told to mend roads with increasing frequency after 1400. The instructions could be specific about the number of cartloads of stone to be carried by those who owned vehicles. At Teddington (Gloucestershire) in 1420, the roads were to be repaired with stone from Bredon Hill, 2 ½ miles away, with each tenant responsible for two cartloads.[61] Water courses attracted much attention, not just the frequent recurrence of orders to scour ditches and prevent roads being flooded, but also measures were taken to prevent the pollution of streams which provided a village's drinking water. The washing of laundry, the disposal of sewage, the cleaning of sheep skins, the retting of flax and hemp, and allowing ducks to swim in the water were all forbidden. 'Wardens of the stream' were appointed in one village to enforce the rules, but repetition of the rules suggest that the laws were not observed. In particular, the ducks swam on. Serious problems of flood control on the shores of the Severn estuary; high tides, storm surges, and the effects of heavy rainfall posed a constant threat, which villages such as Rockhampton counteracted by insisting that gouts (channels with doors to prevent incursions by the sea) and other water control structures were maintained. Catastrophe could not be avoided in an extreme weather event, and in 1483 the peasants of Henbury-in-the-Saltmarsh (along with other villages undocumented) faced severe difficulties from the damage to their buildings, land, and livestock. However, they were able to recover within a few years, demonstrating the strength of the individuals and their collective spirit.[62]

The most striking and enduring achievement of village communities was to raise money to build and maintain parish churches. This responsibility had developed in the thirteenth century, but reached its height in the fifteenth and early sixteenth century with the ambitious perpendicular churches, often with a tall tower, aisles, clerestories, and porches, decorated with wall paintings and stained glass, and furnished with screens and roods. Modern observers are very ready to credit wool merchants and gentry with these buildings, and this was sometimes the case, but very often the peasants contributing collectively were an important source of cash. This expense was sustainable through skilful fundraising which harnessed community contributions by holding events such as church ales and

---

[61] WCL, E48.
[62] C. Dyer, 'Recovering from Catastrophe: How Medieval Society Coped with Disasters', in *Waiting for the End of the World? New Perspectives on Natural Disasters in Medieval Europe*, edited by C. Gerrard, P. Forlin, and P. Brown (Society for Medieval Archaeology Monograph, 43, 2021), pp. 218–38, especially 222–7; GA, Badminton muniments D2700/MJ9/1–2.

dramatic entertainments in purpose-built church houses, which we see springing up at the end of our period (see 'Peasants and religion' in Chapter 10).

As the villages developed their scope, to address their legislation to more people, and to concern themselves with a wider range of public issues, they can also seem to be more divisive, with a particular problem being posed by the shortage of labour. Wage earners had aroused suspicions before 1349, when they were criticized for leaving the village in the harvest for better pay. Those concerns were renewed after 1349, when the harvest by-laws were re-issued, and the manor courts briefly enforced the state legislation on wages and employment (see 'Peasants and the state' in Chapter 10). Servants were singled out for their behaviour, with accusations of breaking hedges at Middleton (Warwickshire), and cutting branches from trees at Ombersley. At Broadway in 1512 servants were said to be playing board games in the afternoon. Wage earners, many of them young, were liable to gamble in the alehouses, or waste their time and energy on games of football and handball. They were seen to be 'badly governed', and to 'live suspiciously'.[63]

The castigations of feckless marginals probably expressed widely held opinions in the village, and do not justify a belief that villages were riven by sharp class divisions. A common judgement is that a wealthy elite were dominating the village institutions and especially the manor court, and pursuing a selfish agenda. Some by-laws discriminated against the smallholders, such as the limit at Ombersley on cottagers keeping more than four pigs 'going at large', and the restriction at Bredon and Hampton Lucy on cottagers on the common keeping more than one animal (usually a cow), or one large animal and a pig.[64]

One remedy for those seeking to employ labour, as the numbers of smallholders shrank was to provide potential workers with accommodation. Before 1349 cottars were encouraged to settle in villages and thus increase the pool of cheap labour. After 1349 as the cottages were surrendered by tenants acquiring land or employment elsewhere, tenants of large holdings added them to their portfolio of land. In 1496 John Felippes of Cleeve Prior (Worcestershire) surrendered his composite holding to Giles Felippes. He was passing on an accumulation which at first looks incongruous, consisting of a total of eight previously separate assets, which totalled three-quarters of a yardland, about 14 acres of land in the fields, described as acres, selions and butts, a croft, and three cottages. He could have been cultivating about 40 acres, but what use could he make of the cottages? He would surely have sublet them, and expect the tenants to pay rent, or

---

[63] UNMSC, MiM131/32; WA, ref 705:56, BA 3910/22; TNA, SC2/210/33. On this type of case, M. K. McIntosh, *Controlling Misbehavior in England, 1370–1600* (Cambridge, 1998).
[64] WA, ref. 705:56, BA 3910/22; C. Dyer, *Lords and Peasants in a Changing Society: The Estates of the Bishopric of Worcester, 680–1540* (Cambridge, 1980), p. 325.

make themselves available to work for him. In modern terminology, they were tied cottages.[65]

The influence of the large landholders should not be exaggerated. Office holding had to be spread widely because there were so many administrative tasks. Those who served in the manorial administration included not just the jurors, tithing men, affeerers, ale tasters, and others in the manor court, and the reeve, beadle, hayward, and woodward running the daily affairs of the manor, but also the harvest wardens, wardens of the stream, co-ordinators of highway maintenance, and those managing the religious institutions, notably the church wardens and the feoffees of the chantries. In addition to the sessions of the court, meetings were held in the hamlets or tithings. Dozens of men (and they were males almost without exception) spent many hours discussing the business of the village, manor, and parish.

At Hartlebury in each year between 1473 and 1485 there were thirty-two offices to fill. About a third of the adult males in the village were occupying these positions each year, and some served only for a year, so in time a considerable proportion experienced office holding. Government was oligarchic in the sense that individuals filled more than one office. Of the thirty-two who served as jurors in the manor court, twenty-two had been 'parishioners' in the church court. They also tended to be better-off, judged in terms of their land holding, as 79 per cent of the jurors held a yardland or two yardlands. However, the yardland at Hartlebury was an unusually small holding of 24 acres at most, and often below 20 acres, and 76 per cent of all tenants held a yardland or two. In any case a few smallholders held office, such as John Gadbury, tenant of a quarter-yardland who was churchwarden in 1472 and manor court juror in 1473. Some individuals from some prominent and well-heeled families as the Ballardes, Bests, and Walls did not hold office, perhaps because they chose not to burden themselves, or were thought unsuitable. The office holders of Hartlebury were not particularly rich, and represent a cross-section of the population, though tilted towards the better-off.[66]

Wealthier tenants tended to be involved in regulating agrarian matters, such as the harvest wardens or harvest reeves who were selected to report not just harvest offences, but agrarian by-laws in general. At Cleeve Prior between three and six of these wardens were elected at regular intervals, making twenty-seven individuals in all between 1375 and 1396. Most of them served for one year, but four appear four or more times. Richard Fisher was selected six times and Nicholas atte Yate five times. Sixteen of them (63 per cent) held 30 acres or more. Richard Fisher

---

[65] WCL, E83. H.S.A. Fox, 'Servants, Cottagers and Tied Cottages During the Later Middle Ages: Towards a Regional Dimension', *Rural History* 6 (1995), pp. 125–54.

[66] R.N. Swanson and D. Guyatt, eds., *The Visitation and Court Book of Hartlebury, 1401–1598* (WHS, new series, 24, 2013); WA, ref. 009:1, BA 2636/169, 192, 37(iii) 98, 306, fos 78–83; S. Dickson, 'Land and Change 1550–1750: The Case of Hartlebury, Worcestershire' (PhD dissertation, University of Birmingham,1999), pp. 93–100.

held only 15 acres, though Nicholas atte Yate was one of the largest landholders with 44 acres. Among the tenants of Cleeve Prior as a whole, 52 per cent held 30 acres or more, so in this influential group quite a high proportion had larger holdings.

These officials had an inconsistent record in their choice of offenders to be presented. Often they did not spare their peers, as in 1389 all of the six who had allowed their horses to stray were current or future harvest wardens, and in 1380 and 1392 harvest wardens (or soon to be harvest wardens) were prominent among those said to have allowed their geese to damage the tenants' growing corn. The wardens could be criticized for neglecting their work in some years, as an absence of reported offences would be more likely to reflect the tolerant (or indolent) attitude of the officials. After a few years without much activity in the first years of the fifteenth century, in October 1405 the Cleeve Prior harvest wardens made a strenuous attempt to enforce the rules, naming nine offenders with pigs in the corn, seventeen who allowed their geese to trespass in the crops, and three whose beasts consumed the lord's barley, amounting to 6 bushels. Another tethered his horse in the lord's corn. Those who broke the rules included many leading villagers, though only one of the harvest wardens was named as an offender. The public exposures of the offences and the payments of amercements that resulted were evidently not trivial matters, as one of the accused, John Holder, who offended three times, responded with evident anger, 'He condemned and contradicted the reeves of the harvest'. He was neither one of the elite nor a smallholder, as he held three-quarters of a yardland, but he had served as harvest warden in 1398 and 1399. The court supported the wardens who had named him in court by amercing him for his outburst the large sum of 3s 4d, but the quarrel did not last long, as a year later Holder was appointed as one of the harvest wardens.[67]

Such investigations of the role of the village in making laws and then attempting to enforce them reveal no systematic conspiracy among the wealthy landholders to manipulate the system to their own advantage.[68] In a complex situation people no doubt believed in the ideals of community discipline and harmony, but in their everyday lives found it difficult to avoid infringing the rules.

Conclusion

The themes of this chapter all show peasants making decisions and changing their lives for themselves. They did not achieve general improvement, as migration did not always lead to the intended 'betterment', opportunities for social mobility

---

[67] WCL, E26–E38; C558.
[68] I. Forrest, *Trustworthy Men. How Inequality and Faith Made the Medieval Church* (Princeton, 2018), pp. 129–213.

were limited, failure of management could leave even a yardlander in poverty, and the village community could not always serve the interests of the 'common good'. However, important changes followed from peasant choices, such as the flow of migrants into towns and the renewal of the population of villages as marriage partners and new tenants came in from outside. The movement of people may have been a channel for spreading ideas, in the realm of farming, house design, the style of parish churches and other innovations. The aim of social mobility was fulfilled for thousands of landless who gained at least a smallholding, hundreds of peasants' sons who joined the ranks of the clergy. A handful of enterprising and ambitious peasants were able to make the transition to become merchants, and, crossing a more challenging frontier, to be accounted members of the gentry. Within peasant society, the demesne farmers and other large-scale accumulators of land lifted themselves out of routine village society. Those who fell into poverty might find the means to gain a living through a maintenance agreement, a loan, subletting land, or self-help, such as managing a 'cottage eonomy'. Individuals and communities adopted measures for easing the lot of the poor. Village communities seem to have been beset by internal problems of the feckless marginal and selfish pursuers of profit, but at the end of the period most of them seem to have overcome their tribulations, and their fields and commons still functioned, the varied population tolerated one another, and they were capable of collective achievements such as renewed parish churches and new church houses.

5
Family and household

Peasants, in the Middle Ages and in other periods, are often thought to have been rooted in their families, but they were much involved in their village and were conscious of the wider horizons of their region and country. Nonetheless, they were brought up in a household and felt a sense of attachment to their parents, siblings, and wider kin. The household worked together: the quality of the holding's management and husbandry depended on the commitment of its members. The form that the peasant family took was partly its own creation, with some manipulation in such matters as marriage from the church and the aristocracy. This chapter examines the size and composition of peasant families and households in the west midlands; then it investigates the space that they occupied, including the size, layout, and quality of the house and its contents; finally it assesses the character and cohesion of families and households.

The size and composition of the household

There are no medieval censuses, but people were counted and listed on various occasions. In 1517–18 when commissions enquired into enclosures, conversion of arable to pasture, and depopulation they reported how many people had been displaced when a house was removed or a plough put out of action. The mean number of people living in an abandoned house in Gloucestershire was 4.9 (from ten villages), and in Warwickshire from sixty-six cases, the mean was 5.66.[1] The figure was likely to include servants as well as tenants, wives, offspring, and relatives. Families can be examined in more detail from lists of serfs compiled by lords, again towards the end of the period. Lords felt the need to keep under observation those who were categorized as personal serfs (*neifs* by blood) and occasionally made records of the male serfs and their children. From five lists dated between 1474 and 1539, 126 families can be analysed, and they contained 299 children.[2] Male offspring outnumbered females, and if this imbalance resulted

---

[1] Based on a translation by Spencer Dimmock, using new MS sources, and also I.S. Leadam, ed., *The Domesday of Inclosures 1517-18* (Royal Historical Society, 1897); I.S. Leadam, ed., 'The Inquisition of 1517: Inclosures and Evictions, part 3', *Transactions of the Royal Historical Society,* new series, 8 (1894), pp. 251–331, especially pp. 280–97.

[2] C. Dyer, *Lords and Peasants in a Changing Society. The Estates of the Bishopric of Worcester 680-1540* (Cambridge, 1980), pp. 230–2; WCL, E 92 (Worcester Priory manors, 1508-9): GA, Badminton muniments, D2700/MJ9/1-2 (Rockhampton, 1474).

from a bias in recording among the male juries and clerks, the numbers can be adjusted, assuming equal numbers of females, to rise to 354. The lists give the fathers' names but omit the mothers, so a figure for them has to be added. On the basis of the children named in the lists, including the omitted wives, the mean family size was 4.37, and if the revision allowing for missing daughters is made, the figure is 4.81. These figures, unlike a census which records people living in the same house, are really genealogies of those who inherited servile status. But like a census they include families at different stages of their life cycle. Children who had left home would still be included, though at some stage (when the children were young) the whole family would have been living together. Wills provide rather similar information, because when the father made his bequests to his children, he would often mention those who were living away. The figures are not dissimilar, deriving from two samples, one of fifty-one and other of thirty-eight, suggesting uncorrected family sizes of 4.66 and 5.20, which could be corrected to 4.89 and 5.40 with an estimate of the missing daughters.[3] The wills are rather later in date than the serf lists, and tend to relate to wealthier people.

The figures in a good number of cases show the number of children after reproduction had been completed. Peasants could not choose the number of children, as those who survived depended on unpredictable mortality. A couple with two children may well have experienced six or seven pregnancies, and then suffered losses from miscarriage and infant and child mortality. A chequered history of the death of partners and remarriage disrupted the reproductive life of many couples, but resulted in the complication that the children in the household had different parents. Margery Gardiner of Claines (Worcestershire) in 1540 made bequests to her two daughters and son, but also mentioned her daughter Eleanor Broke, and asked her son to look after 'my poor daughter Alice'. She had evidently had two or three husbands.[4] Within each marriage the period of fertility and the number of births would be influenced by the age at first marriage, which around 1300 at Halesowen has been calculated as between 18 and 22. The comparable figure for women in Worcestershire villages in the late sixteenth century lay between 22 and 26.[5] We do not know how or when this apparent shift in age occurred, but a rising age at first marriage may have been a factor in delaying recovery from the effects of successive epidemic diseases. Mothers could increase the intervals between births by prolonging breast feeding. Two women were accused before the

---

[3] Dyer, *Lords and Peasants*, p. 394; C. Dyer, *A Country Merchant 1495–1520: Trading and Farming at the End of the Middle Ages* (Oxford, 2012), p. 44. The imbalance between sons and daughters may be explained by factors other than the simple omission of females: M. Kowaleski, 'Medieval People in Town and Country: New Perspectives from Demography and Bioarchaeology', *Speculum* 89 (2014), pp. 573–600.

[4] WA, ref. 008:7, BA3540 1540/25.

[5] Z. Razi, *Life, Marriage and Death in a Medieval Parish: Economy, Society and Demography in Halesowen 1270–1400* (Cambridge, 1980), pp. 58–64; A.D. Dyer, *The City of Worcester in the Sixteenth Century* (Leicester, 1973), pp. 36–7.

Hartlebury church court in the fifteenth century of procuring or attempting abortions, but such practices may not have been widely prevalent.[6]

A minority of households included relatives beyond the standard nuclear family of parents and children. Parents and parents-in-law would be most likely to be accommodated after surrendering their holding to a new tenant. The grain sometimes allowed for maintenance implies that the retired people usually had their own household, and the chamber or building they were allocated suggests that they lived separately (see 'Individuals and communities' in Chapter 10). This does not rule out the occasional integration of the older generation in the same household and at the same meal table, as is implied by a few maintenance contracts, wills, and entries in the poll tax.

Brothers or sisters sometimes shared the tenancy of a holding, and if a sibling was thought incapable of managing a holding (*impotens* was the word used) he or she might be awarded a promise of maintenance. There is no way to judge whether these arrangements resulted in brothers and sisters forming joint households or joining a tenant's household. The will of John Harryes from Charingworth (Gloucestershire) of 1535 required three sons to live in a shared household ('keep household together') until they married, but we do not know if this unusual arrangement was put into effect.[7]

The poll tax of 1381 for parts of Gloucestershire contains a large sample of households and refers to three-generational households, single person households, and other departures from the predominant conventional structure of parents and children.[8] The 1381 tax required that everyone should pay 1s, including parents, children over 15, and servants. The tax was met with hostility and obstruction, with a great deal of concealment, especially of the young, servants, and labourers. The authorities knew about the deception and corruption and ordered a reassessment, which found 478 people in forty-one villages who had been omitted. The two north Gloucestershire hundreds of Salmonsbury and Holford & Greston contained fifty-two villages and the towns of Stow-on-the-Wold and Winchcomb. The towns will be set aside to concentrate on the rural evidence. The tax was paid in the two hundreds by 2,662 people, of whom about a half were described as married couples, without mention of children, servants, or relatives. Many of these households could have included children or servants under 15 years, or the taxpayers hid the young people, or lied about their age. Dishonest under-recording is implied by the inclusion of 116 sons but only eighty-three daughters. A total of 254 households were assessed for tax with more than two members, or with two members, one of which was a relative or servant, not a spouse. Among these the predominant

---

[6] R.N. Swanson and D. Guyatt, eds., *The Visitation and Court Book of Hartlebury, 1401–1598* (WHS, new series, 24, 2013), pp. 165, 244.
[7] TNA, PROB 11/25, fo.311r.   [8] *PT*, part 1, pp. 260–314.

household type, of which there were 111, contained parents and children, mostly a single son or daughter.

A householder's sister, brother, or mother was only occasionally present—four households contained a sister, and four a brother, and in six cases a mother was living with a married couple. Another three mothers each shared a household with a male who lacked a wife: perhaps a widower. Siblings and parents would not have been easily concealed, so there were probably not as many omissions as among the young sons, daughters, servants, and labourers. We can conclude that at least a minority of peasant households contained siblings or mothers, which might accord with the calculation from the detailed reconstitution of families at Halesowen that 16 per cent included such relatives.[9]

Finally, the poll taxes record unusual households which contained two married couples. Four couples were apparently living with a son and his wife, and three households were employing a male servant who was married, so that his wife formed part of the household for tax purposes, and presumably in residential arrangements also. One large household consisted of a married couple, a mother, and two servants, one male and one female, and in a three-generational household at Toddington a single female head, Alice Lyngue, lived with her son John and Joan his wife (who had been married for at least fifteen years), and Cristina their daughter.[10]

Servants often lived in their employers' houses and were committed to work for a period of time, perhaps a year. When surveys were made of landed estates in the twelfth and thirteenth centuries, peasants' servants were already well established and of interest to the lords as a source of labour. Labour services on the lords' demesnes were defined mainly as obligations of individual tenants, and on occasion lords specified that the work should be performed by the tenant himself, *in propria persona*. However on each day when the service was due a proportion of tenants would have been elderly, disabled, or ill. In addition most widows of tenants, though responsible for the rents and service, would have been unused to such heavy work as ploughing. In these circumstances, the tenant would send an able-bodied son or servant to do the work.

On the manors of Alvechurch, Hartlebury, and Hampton Lucy, tenants with full yardlands were expected to attend the *bedrip* with the whole household (*tota familia*).[11] That phrase would include male and female servants as well as sons and daughters, but the tenant's wife and the shepherd were exempt, as neither the house nor sheep could be left unsupervised. The work of the whole household would be the equivalent of that of two or three men, as is clearly stated in the

---

[9] Z. Razi, 'The Myth of the Immutable English Family', *P&P* 140 (1993), pp. 3–44, especially p. 6.
[10] *PT*, pt 1, p. 271.   [11] *RBW*, pp. 206, 233, 277.

customs of Atherstone (Warwickshire) in the early thirteenth century.[12] The *bedrip* was an exceptional labour service owed on a few days of the year, but it gives us an insight into the normal labour needs of the holding. On the day after the household had attended the lord's *bedrip* presumably the same group of workers assembled again to tackle the harvest on the yardland holding. Perhaps a peasant was fortunate enough to have two strong sons, but when the children were very young, or after the teenagers had left home, a servant or two would have been needed to fill the gap.

An occasion similar to the *bedrip* arose when a peasant contributed labour to the village community. John Huys of Claines (Worcestershire) in his will of 1536 wished to contribute to mending the roads in his parish by requiring his *meyny* to spend two days on the task.[13] *Meyny* meant a group, following, or household which would have included family members and servants.

The peasant households were expected to attend the lord's *fustale*. This drinking session may have begun as a paternalistic celebration, binding together the lord and his subordinates, but by 1170 and later it had become a formal obligation, recorded as a manorial custom. Compulsory attendance was accompanied by a contribution to the cost of the drink. It continued sometimes for three days. On the bishop of Worcester's manors wives accompanied their husbands, and at Kempsey in 1170 the *famuli rusticorum* (the servants of the peasants) were expected to attend and pay ½ d each. The Hartlebury *fustale*, also described in 1170, included adult sons and daughters (presumably if they were still living at home) and all male and female servants, though one would remain behind, to keep the house safe.[14] The customs of *bedrip* and *fustale* indicate that each household could commonly contain two or three working males, or their equivalents among females and the young, and it was presumed that peasants with larger holdings would be employing servants, including a specialist shepherd.

In the incomplete Gloucestershire poll tax lists for 1381 there is enough data from seventy-two villages to count 352 servants from a total of 2,982 taxpayers, or 12 per cent of the total. If taken at face value only a small minority of households employed servants and most employers confined themselves to a single servant. This must be an absolute minimum, omitting all servants under 15 years of age as the tax regulation allowed, and concealing illegally a proportion of older servants. Almost a century and a half later, in 1525, tax gatherers in Gloucestershire were again expected to identify servants. The law said that servants should be assessed at 4*d* each, on the understanding that their annual wage amounted to 20*s*. The 4*d* tax would be collected from the employers. This law was applied inconsistently,

---

[12] M. Chibnall, ed., *Select Documents of the English Lands of the Abbey of Bec* (Camden Society, 3rd series, 73, 1951), p. 103.
[13] WA, ref. 008:7, BA 3585, 1536/211.   [14] *RBW*, pp. 85, 206–7.

Table 5.1 Servants taxed in 1525 in four Gloucestershire hundreds (rural population only)

Hundred	Total taxed	Total servants	Percentage
Henbury	320	54	16.9
Kiftsgate	640	145	22.7
Thornbury	153	32	20.9
Westminster	72	20	27.8
All	1185	251	21.2

Source: M. Faraday, ed., *The Bristol and Gloucestershire Lay Subsidy of 1523–1527* (GRS, 23, 2009), pp. 294–309, 408–33.

and servants can only be identified with any confidence in four hundreds (Table 5.1).

Servants made up between 17 per cent and 28 per cent of the taxpaying population in different hundreds in 1525. The taxpaying population who were not servants were mainly heads of households, so if an estimate is made for wives and children the servants amount to about 5 per cent of the whole population. This underestimates the total as servants who received less than 20s in wages (the younger ones for example) were exempt, and no women appear among the servants. The lists rarely link the servants with their employers, so after leaving aside the thirty or so who worked for a monastery and for gentry households, we are left with perhaps 200 servants spread rather thinly over the 400 wealthier peasant households in the sample. Allowing for the omissions, servants could well have accounted for 10 per cent of the population, and could have been employed in a third of all households.

The 1381 lists allow connections to be made between households and their servants. In 254 households which contained children and/or servants from the two sample hundreds in north Gloucestershire, 83 were said to contain servants, mostly only one. These figures are misleadingly small, but they give some useful information. A considerable number of households with servants, fifty-one, consisted of married couples with no recorded children. They may have been childless through infertility or the death of their children, but some may have had young children at the time of the tax, and needed the supplementary labour of a servant or two. Older peasants' children might have left home, again leaving a vacancy that could be filled by a servant. Another twenty-three households with a single head (most likely a widow or widower) also lacked children but needed agricultural or domestic assistance. Not all servants were substitutes for working children, and some ambitious households may have recruited servants as part of a labour force necessary for a large scale of production. Henry Chandeler of Roel, known from other sources as an engrosser of land and owner of a very large flock of sheep, appears in the 1381 poll tax with his wife Alice, two sons called John and

Richard, and John, a servant. The Malverne family of Naunton was also well supplied with labour, with a married couple, a son and his wife, a brother, and a female servant.[15]

The inequalities of village society were probably enhanced by the tendency for the sons and daughters of smaller holdings to seek employment with the wealthier tenants. However, employment as a servant was not confined to the poor, and nor were employers of servants always to be found among the village elite. A period in service was commonplace in the lives of young peasants, and in the absence of apprenticeships in agriculture or housewifery, work in a household would be an opportunity for young men to acquire experience of husbandry, and for young women to learn skills in dairying, brewing, marketing, and household management.[16]

Finally, peasant households might contain people who were neither relatives nor primarily contributors to the work of the holding. Occasionally the outsider was given formal legal recognition, as in the case of Robert Treweman of Hazleton (Gloucestershire) who in 1341 arranged for himself, his daughter Matilda, together with Richard Pecker to hold jointly (*conjunctim*) Robert's yardland holding. Pecker was presumably about to become Matilda's husband, and move into the house, but the agreement did not cover that prospect, nor make reference to residential arrangements.[17] More explicit was an agreement made at Stanton (Gloucestershire) in 1391, that Henry Broun would live with John and Joan Hewes. He had given the lord a fine to become the tenant of the half-yardland holding, which was a common procedure to secure the reversion of land. An unusual feature of the agreement was that Broun and the Hewes would form a single household, sharing the messuage 'with goods and chattels not divided or separated'. If any of the three died, the goods would be shared equally by the survivors. If John Hewes died, Joan would occupy a 'little house called *bourhende* and a small building near the gate with a curtilage', so the joint household would come to an end and Broun would become the sole occupier of the messuage, perhaps with a wife, though his marriage was not mentioned.[18]

Villagers were repeatedly alleged in manor courts to have taken into their houses strangers and malefactors, or to have been harbouring illegal gleaners. The Hartlebury church court was concerned by the keeping of concubines, and an 'alien woman'. The parishioners were told to expel vagabonds from their houses in 1498.[19] The number of unwelcome residents is not given, but no doubt the fear of the unknown led to moralists exaggerating the scale of the problem. A likely explanation for a householder taking a stranger into the house was to gain a small

---

[15] *PT*, part 1, pp. 263, 269; C. Dyer, *An Age of Transition? Economy and Society in England in the Later Middle Ages* (Oxford, 2005), pp. 76–7.
[16] On servants in general, J. Whittle, ed., *Servants in Rural Europe 1400–1900* (Woodbridge, 2017), pp. 1–15.
[17] GA, D678/M1/1/1.   [18] GA, D678/98C.
[19] Swanson and Guyatt, eds., *Court Book of Hartlebury*, p. 251.

income from a lodger, and this 'suspicious' person may well have been an artisan or labourer staying for a short time. Residents who were neither relatives nor servants added to the size of households in a small way.

Historians are tempted to see households in conventional stereotypes, and the model of a married couple, two or three children, and a servant or two can often be observed. However, apparently conventional households could be the result of the merger of two families after remarriage, leading to dilemmas for those deciding on hereditary succession. A woman often became the head of a household, usually as a widow, and such was the rate of mortality and resistance to remarriage, women accounted for 14 per cent of the tenants recorded in the Warwickshire Hundred Rolls of 1279, and 14 per cent also among Thornbury tenants in 1349, rising to 17 per cent of the tenants of the bishop of Worcester in 1299. Rentals compiled in the region after 1349 might record lower figures, below 10 per cent, but 14 per cent of Ombersley tenants in 1419 were female. Among those holding free land in Gloucestershire women appear as parties (often with their husbands) when land was transferred in the royal courts. In 1199–1250 23 per cent were single women or widows, and in the 1251–99 13 per cent, but this figure fell below 10 per cent subsequently.[20] Many female landholders were widows, but not all women in charge of a holding had acquired it after the death of a husband. Felice Jones of Romsley, who first appears as a breaker of hedges in 1313, acquired a holding in 1321, and lost it in about 1333, but a husband is not mentioned.[21] The number of single-person households must have been significant, including those of people who never married, or young people who had left their parental home but had not married, and retired tenants who lived in cottages separate from their original holding. The two sample Gloucestershire hundreds in the 1381 poll tax listed 555 single people, about a fifth of the total, some of them detached from a household by unclear recording, and some who were young and poor and lacking their own dwelling.

This has focussed on the family and household as a 'co-resident domestic group', that is the people who shared a house, ate together, and contributed to the work of the holding and the house. Beyond that important group were a wide range of relatives. We know most about the sons and daughters who were working as servants in other houses, had been settled in nearby cottages, or had acquired land in the same village and had established their own households. They are not very fully documented, but even more difficult to discover are the more distant relatives, the cousins, aunts and uncles, nieces and nephews, and in-laws. The

---

[20] P. Franklin, 'Peasant Widows' "Liberation" and Remarriage before the Black Death', *EcHR*, 2nd series, 39 (1986), pp. 186–204, especially p. 188; *WHR*; *RBW*; R.H. Hilton, *The English Peasantry in the Later Middle Ages* (Oxford, 1975), p. 99; C. Elrington, 'Women Landowners in Medieval Gloucestershire as Seen in Feet of Fines', in *Archives and Local History in Gloucestershire*, edited by J. Bettey, BGAS (2007), pp. 7–16.

[21] *CR Romsley*, pp. 55, 67, 99.

records need to be very full and complete, and the researcher has to be able to devote time and energy to connecting people, often from single oblique references. The work has been done meticulously in records for Halesowen, and it reveals that a high density of kin were living in the settlements of that large manor, but also that kin who moved elsewhere maintained contact with relatives in their original home village. The people in touch with a kin network were provided with useful support in pledging (acquiring guarantors) in court, and in dealing with problems such as indebtedness. For historians the existence of kin networks means that land transfers and maintenance agreements between people with different names and therefore apparently involving different families were really happening between relatives. If other villages followed the Halesowen model the kin networks were largest and most active for the middling and better-off tenants. They survived after the Black Death, but diminished in importance in the fifteenth century.[22]

Space for households

Were peasants' houses effective functional spaces for working, eating, and sleeping, and did they also contribute to the quality of domestic life? Peasant households, whether they lived in villages, hamlets, or isolated settlements, occupied well-defined spaces called curtilages, tofts, or closes, but here the term plots will be used. Commonly they were roughly rectangular in shape, and were surrounded by hedges and ditches, fences, mudwalls, or stone walls. They sometimes originated as the ends of two or three selions or strips in the open fields, which were enclosed in the process of making a row of plots along a street. Less regular shapes with curved boundaries can be encountered more often in woodland settlements where the plot may have originated as an assart or an enclosure out of the waste. A conveyance of land will occasionally give dimensions, such as a grant to a tenant's son at Willoughby (Warwickshire) in c.1250, of land for a new message which was 8 perches by 12 perches (40m by 60m). A plot at Longborough (Gloucestershire) in 1287 was long and narrow, resembling a burgage plot in a town, measuring 94m by 10m.[23] They can also be measured on the ground in deserted settlements, for example, those in the Cotswolds where the boundaries are clearly marked by the earthworks left by collapsed wall foundations. They can be seen on modern maps where the original boundaries seem to have survived. The area calculated from fourteen settlements using landscape evidence varies

---

[22] Z. Razi, 'Family, Land and the Village Community in Later Medieval England', *P&P* 93 (1981), pp. 3–36; Razi, 'Immutable Family'.
[23] Magdalen College, Oxford, Willoughby 61; C.R. Elrington, ed., *Abstracts of Feet of Fines Relating to Gloucestershire, 1199–1299* (GRS, 16, 2003), p. 179. The same source on p. 182 refers to a plot 200 by 100 feet, so c.60m by 30m.

between 900 and 4,500 sq m, with smaller plots measuring 60m by 15m, and larger ones 50m by 90m. The plots were likely to have been decided with some input from both lord and tenant (see 'Lords and landscapes' in Chapter 2). They were ideally large enough to contain at least a yard, a garden or orchard, and space for livestock as well as a dwelling house and barn, and sometimes other buildings (Figure 5.1).

The buildings were the responsibility of the peasant, as is clear from the growing problem arising from the neglect of maintenance after 1349 when the lords put pressure on the tenants to repair and rebuild their houses. Lords sometimes helped, and the details of their work provide information about materials and construction. As early as 1286-7 the lord of Bourton-on-the-Hill in Gloucestershire paid for stone walls (probably foundations) and timber for walls of the house of a former reeve.[24] In the fifteenth century, despairing at the persistence of tenants' neglect, lords throughout the region offered help and inducements in the form of release from rents, cancellation of arrears, and offers of materials, especially the larger timbers from the lords' woods. As a last resort they took on the work themselves, and at Whatcote (Warwickshire) in 1443-5, the duke of Buckingham paid

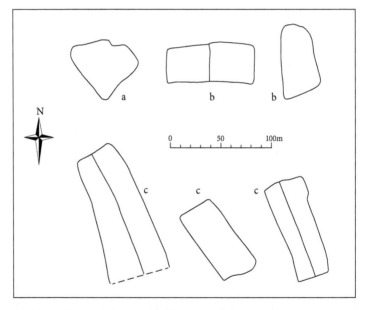

Figure 5.1 Plans of house plots, selected to show shapes and sizes. a) earthworks of boundaries around a house at Hanbury, Worcs. (woodland); b) early map, Welford-on-Avon; Warw. (champion); c) earthworks of walls surrounding houses at Roel/Hawling, Glouc. (wold). The evidence is from the twentieth century; the boundaries are likely to be thirteenth century or earlier.

[24] WAM, 8238.

almost £10 for building work on tenants' houses and barns.[25] These were buildings in peasant style, with no spending on the lime mortar or tiled roofs which would have been normal for the lord's own buildings. A carpenter, mason, and other craftsmen were paid for constructing stone walls, timber roofs, and straw thatch roofs. Timber came from the lord's wood at Great Wolford, and the local centre of the trade at Stratford-upon-Avon, involving cart journeys of 8 and 10 miles.

The peasants normally organized and paid for their own buildings, observing the technical traditions of their region. The conversation between the peasant and the carpenter about a new house would have centred on the design that could be delivered which would have been a timber frame, usually based on crucks, pairs of large curved principal timbers, either standing on or set into a stone wall. In special circumstances a box-frame could have been provided. The roof would have normally been thatched. A major consideration would have been the length, defined by the number of bays.

When manor courts required tenants to rebuild their dwelling houses the size was often specified in bays, varying in number between one and five.[26] As a bay measured approximately 5m by 5m (15 feet by 15 feet using the unit of measurement of the time), this meant that the intention was to build houses between 5m and 25m in length, and about 5m. wide. The great majority were specified as two- or three-bay structures, so 10m to 15m long. An alternative way of defining size was to specify so many couples or forks, meaning pairs of crucks, so that a three-bay house was said to consist of four couples. These standard sizes were translated into real structures on site by builders who had to take account of such practical matters as the lie of the ground surface (some houses had to be terraced into a hillside) or the length of the available timbers. The excavated houses of the thirteenth, fourteenth, and fifteenth centuries accord approximately with the dimensions of the bays, with external length measurements of 11m and 13m at Pinbury, and 11m to 12m at Upton (Figure 5.2).

A house at Bascote was recorded as 8m long, and the smallest house at Burton Dassett Southend reached only 7m, but most of the houses of that settlement varied between 10m and 14m (so 2 or 3 bays), and successive houses built between 1300 and 1450 on three of the excavated plots could have been constructed in four bays as they reached lengths of between 17m and 19m.[27] Widths again agreed

---

[25] SRO, D641/1/2/270, 271, 272.
[26] R.K. Field, 'Worcestershire Peasant Buildings, Household Goods and Farming Equipment in the Later Middle Ages', *Med Arch* 9 (1965), pp. 105–45, especially pp. 112–17; C. Dyer, 'English Peasant Buildings in the Later Middle Ages', *Med Arch* 30 (1986), pp. 19–45, especially pp. 23–4.
[27] S. Litherland, E. Ramsay, and P. Ellis, 'The Archaeology of the Severn Trent Southern Area Rationalisation Scheme, Warwickshire', *TBWAS* 112 (2008), pp. 73–124 (Bascote); N. Palmer and J. Parkhouse, *Burton Dassett Southend, Warwickshire: A Medieval Market Village* (Society for Medieval Archaeology Monograph, 44, 2022), pp. 56–71, 73–138; K3 is on pp. 73, 171–6; J. Hart, A. Mudd, E.R. McSloy, and M. Brett, *Living Near the Edge: Archaeological Investigations in the Western Cotswolds* (Cotswold Archaeology Monograph, 9, 2016), pp 158–93, 208–12 (Pinbury); R.H. Hilton and P.A. Rahtz, 'Upton, Gloucestershire, 1959–1964', *TBGAS* 85 (1966), pp. 70–146; P.A. Rahtz, 'Upton, Gloucestershire, 1964–1968. Second Report', *TBGAS* 88 (1969), pp. 74–126.

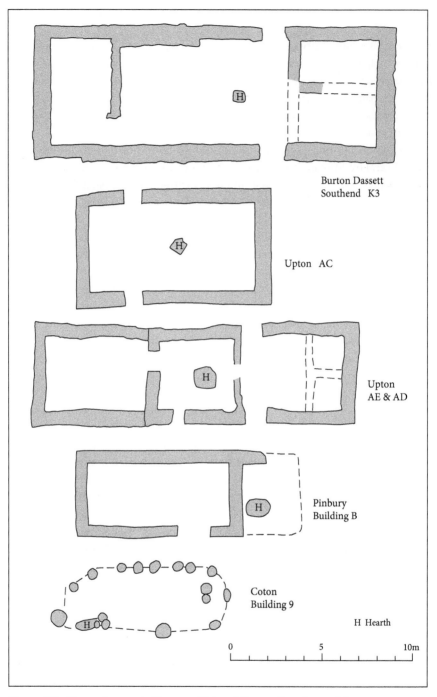

Figure 5.2 Plans of excavated houses. Upton AC was of two bays without apparent space divisions; at Pinbury three bays and two rooms; the Upton house (AE with AD as an addition) totalled three or four bays with a hall and chamber, and a room apparently used for an industrial process; K3 at Burton Dassett Southend was built in four bays with a hall, chamber, and service rooms. All have stone foundations except at Coton, which was based on vertical timber posts). The Upton houses belong to the thirteenth and fourteenth centuries; Pinbury thirteenth century; K3 early fourteenth century; Coton before c.1300 (sources: notes 27, 33).

approximately with the standard bay, varying between 4m and 6m. The largest house excavated at Burton Dassett Southend, K3, which was built in the early fourteenth century, was almost 20m long and 7m. wide. A sample of twenty-four standing peasant buildings, dated between the early fourteenth and late fifteenth centuries, included eleven of three bays, with three of two bays and six of four bays.[28] Later alterations made it difficult to be certain of the original size in some cases. As with the excavated houses, the outcome of the building operation did not produce a house precisely in line with the standard dimensions. Of the surviving houses those of two bays varied in length from 7m to 11m, three-bay buildings could be as small as 10m and as long as 16m, and four-bay structures ranged from 15m to 20m.

The size of the house would have depended on the resources and income of the tenants, and their ability to borrow money (as the cost would usually exceed any cash savings). Timber might be contributed by lords, or purchased, or reused from earlier buildings.

Houses were normally of one storey, but many had at least one upper room, such as four of the still standing houses at Stoneleigh (Warwickshire) and one at Ashow. At Hill Wootton in the same county, a house of the 1470s had a solar built above an end bay: both the ground floor room and the room above are thought to have been used as chambers.[29] A number of standing houses had a cross-wing, that is, a two-storey structure arranged at right angles to the axis of the main house, usually containing two chambers. Cross-wings tended to be late additions, but one of the wings attached to a house at Southam (Warwickshire) seems to have been built at the same time as the main house, in 1418–19, and the same is found at Hanley Castle (Worcestershire) in 1457–8[30] (Figure 5.3). Two of the excavated houses at Burton Dassett Southend had been provided with stairs at one end, to gain access to an upper room. Documents mention first-floor rooms, using the phrase 'lower and upper chamber' at Shirehampton (Gloucestershire), and nearby Henbury in the fifteenth century.[31] In Worcestershire an upper chamber is implied at Crowle in 1406, when reference was made to a lower chamber. The documents also usefully indicate upper storeys rather earlier than is found in the surviving houses and excavated structures: a solar is mentioned at Stoke Prior in 1351, and at Halesowen in 1381.[32] The peasants who commissioned cross-wings, solars, or upper chambers, when most houses consisted of only two or

---

[28] F.W.B. Charles, *Medieval Cruck Building and its Derivatives* (Society for Medieval Archaeology Monograph Series, 2, 1967), pp. 26–32; N.W. Alcock and D. Miles, *The Medieval Peasant House in Midland England* (Oxford, 2013); N.W. Alcock and D. Miles, 'An Early Fifteenth-Century Warwickshire Cruck House using Joggled Halvings', *Vernacular Architecture* 43 (2012), pp. 19–27.

[29] Alcock and Miles, *Peasant House*, HIW-A; ASH-A; STO-C;STO-D; STO-F, STO-G (the codes refer to the CD Rom attached to the book).

[30] Alcock and Miles, *Peasant House*, SOU-A; Hanley Castle house: *Vernacular Architecture* 51 (2020), p. 143; Charles Archive in the Archaeology Data Service, York.

[31] WA, ref. 009:1, BA 2636/165/92225 4/8.   [32] WCL, E45; E 214; BAH, 3279/346369A.

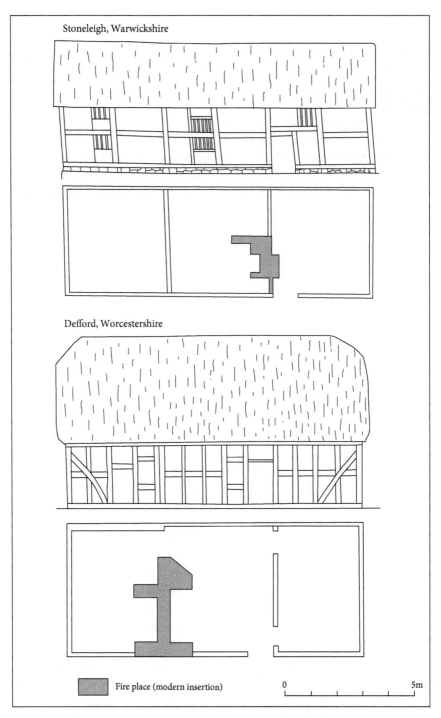

Figure 5.3 Standing buildings. The plans and elevations are partly representing the buildings now visible, but include some element of reconstruction of their appearance when built (Stoneleigh is dated to 1480-2 and Defford is likely to be similar). In both cases, the fireplaces and chimneys were inserted in the early modern period. Both houses are of three bays and consist of three rooms (source: note 28).

three rooms on the ground floor, were choosing to make a considerable addition to the household's accommodation.

Building materials and techniques would give the inhabitants a sense of security and well-being, as well as contributing to their comfort. In the late twelfth and thirteenth centuries the inhabitants of Coton (Warwickshire) lived in quite small buildings (9m by 4m in one case) constructed by setting vertical timbers into the ground (earthfast).[33] This type of timber building was widespread in the twelfth century, and examples have been excavated at Pinbury and Upton, but the inhabitants of those settlements adopted stone foundations with timber walls and roofs after 1200. The timber building tradition continued at Coton through the thirteenth century until the abandonment of the settlement by about 1300. The inhabitants of Coton had a generally low level of material culture, judging from their possessions as well as their houses. The place name, dating back before the twelfth century, refers to a settlement of cottages that seems to have persisted in relative poverty.

The builders of peasant houses in the west midlands (and in many other parts of England) increased the use of stone for walls in the thirteenth century. In the majority the walls were quite low (no more than five courses, up to a height of 30 cm) and narrow; their purpose was to provide a firm foundation for timber-framed walls infilled with wattle and daub panels. At Goldicote a house of the thirteenth and fourteenth centuries was built with notably thick stone walls (90–100cm), suggesting that they were intended to be high enough to support the roof. This is confirmed by pieces of stone window mullion and a door jamb which would have been fitted into a high stone wall. At Burton Dassett Southend a number of houses with wall thicknesses in excess of 55cm could have been built with stone up to the eaves and finds such as a stone door jamb suggest structures mainly of stone.[34] These walls would have been constructed with earth mortar, not lime mortar, which would provide robustness at low cost, as long as the roof prevented rainwater from entering the wall.[35] Among the late medieval peasant buildings still standing, one had high stone walls, at Oxhill (Warwickshire).[36] Most surviving houses had low stone foundations, some supporting a sill beam on which the timber frame was built, but in some cases the base of the crucks rested on padstones. The financial accounts for the construction of tenant building at Whatcote in the 1440s also seem to suggest high stone walls, as both a

---

[33] A. Maull and others, 'Excavations of the Deserted Village of Coton at Coton Park, Rugby' (unpublished report by Northamptonshire Archaeology, 1998).
[34] P. Thompson and S. Palmer, 'Iron Age, Romano-British and Medieval Settlements Excavated on the Transco Newbold Pacey to Honeybourne Gas Pipeline in 2000', *TBWAS* 116 (2012), pp. 72–139; Palmer and Parkhouse, *Burton Dassett Southend*, pp. 160–5.
[35] S. Markley, 'The "Unseen Seen"—Earth Mortared Stone Construction, a Reilluminated Historic Construction Technique in Britain', *Construction History* 33 (2018), pp. 23–43.
[36] Alcock and Miles, *Peasant House*, OXH-A.

carpenter and a mason were employed, and only roof timbers were used, rafters and laths, with no timbers for the walls.

To underline the quality of the Burton Dassett Southend houses, a minority had roofs of slate and ceramic tiles, in a region where thatch predominated. A ceramic tile roof occasionally features in the documents, for example in 1481 at Willoughby (Warwickshire).[37] Peasant houses are often said to have been built from local materials, but the Burton Dassett slates had been carted for more than 20 miles.

What was the peasant household's experience of living in their houses? To modern eyes they seem cramped and uncomfortable, with the small and unglazed windows leaving the inhabitants to suffer from cold and draughts, excessive smoke, a lack of light. However, windows and doors were regarded as important features. At Himbleton (Worcestershire) in 1420, a complaint was made to the manor court that doors and windows had been taken from a house, which shows that they were removable, portable, and of some value.[38] Light-fingered neighbours or tenants terminating their connection with the holding were attracted by the iron fittings, and by the useful boards of which the doors and shutters were made. The ironwork is found when houses are excavated, including iron hinges, studs, and straps for doors, with smaller catches, hasps, hooks, and locks. Stone mullions, jambs, sills, and lintels were very unusual, so door and window openings were wooden. Over the centuries standing and still inhabited medieval houses have been modernized by their successive owners, resulting in the removal of their original fenestration. An important survival is the hall window of a house at Walcot in Haselor (Warwickshire) which measures 1.2m by 1.5m.[39] This was not large by the standard of aristocratic houses, but it brought some light and air into the principal room of the house. Window glass was being introduced into peasant houses at the end of our period, with rare glass fragments at Burton Dassett Southend and a groove to receive glass on a mullion from Goldicote.

The living spaces of the aristocracy provide a model for interiors of medieval houses in general. People assembled for meals and social interaction in the hall, with its essential hearth; the more private chamber was reserved for the head of the household and the inner circle, mainly for sleeping. The service rooms at the 'low' end of the hall provided bread and drink for those eating in the hall. The kitchen might be at this end of the hall, or in a separate building nearby.[40] Peasant houses are often said to have followed this arrangement, with some archaeological

---

[37] Magdalen College, Oxford, Willoughby 45/11. [38] WCL, E48.
[39] Alcock and Miles, *Peasant House*, WAL-A.
[40] M. Gardiner, 'Vernacular Buildings and the Development of the Later Medieval Domestic Plan in England', *Med Arch* 44 (2000), pp. 159–79; M. Gardiner, 'An Archaeological Approach to the Development of the Late Medieval Peasant House', *Vernacular Architecture* 45 (2014), pp. 16–28; C. Dyer, 'Living in Peasant Houses in Late Medieval England', *Vernacular Architecture* 44 (2013), pp. 19–27.

examples such as K3 at Burton Dassett Southend of the early fourteenth century, which was divided into three rooms. At Upton in the thirteenth century, a chamber reached by a ladder (the house AE was built on a slope) provided a clearly separate sleeping space at the high end. Most excavated houses have no obvious divisions at all, or they consisted of two rooms. Standing buildings have been commonly interpreted to have been divided into three, though the use of the service end is not always clear. In excavated peasant houses the 'low' end could have a specialized purpose: in an Upton house it was equipped with stone-built troughs. A similar arrangement was a feature of a Burton Dassett Southend house, suggesting the practice of a craft, perhaps processing sheepskins. A few buildings are found in documents to have had a byre at one end, following the 'longhouse' tradition most commonly encountered in the uplands of the south-west or north. In the west midlands the clearest examples came from the north Worcestershire woodlands, at Northfield and Wolverley, and probably also at Kempsey in the Severn valley.[41]

The documents use the Latin word *domus*, which can be translated as either building or house, though the Middle English word 'house' could be applied to any building, as in carthouse or sheephouse. Dwelling houses were called 'chief house' or 'insethouse'. 'Hall' is sometimes applied to the whole building, but the separate space occupied by the hall is suggested by orders to repair a 'hall and chamber'. Commonly halls and chambers were identified as separate elements within the house in need of repair. Halls were of one or two bays; a chamber commonly consisted of a single bay, except that at Southrop (Gloucestershire) in 1425 a chamber had two bays.[42] A 'hall and kitchen' was specified at Castle Morton (Worcestershire) in 1470.[43] A tripartite division could be implied by the three 'rooms' in a Wolverley house, unless rooms meant bays.[44] Kitchens were rarely mentioned, but bakehouses appear forty-eight times in a sample of the structures mentioned in repair orders, compared with fifty-nine halls and twenty-two chambers. 'Bakehouse' seems to have come to mean 'a building for the processing of food and drink' and the terms kitchen and bakehouse could be interchangeable. In many houses cooking took place in the hall; if two hearths were used in the hall, they might require two roof openings for the smoke, as at Bishops Tachbrook in a house built in 1413/14.[45] At Burton Dassett Southend small post holes and stake holes around a hearth in a hall suggest a structure for supporting cooking equipment.[46]

Hearths were found in excavations as a patch of burnt earth, but often as a more substantial structure of reddened stones. When located near the middle of a

---

[41] Field, 'Worcestershire Peasant Buildings', pp. 115, 134; Dyer, 'English Peasant Buildings', p. 25.
[42] GA, D11718/61/B1.   [43] WAM, 21165.
[44] Field, 'Worcestershire Peasant Buildings', p. 132.
[45] Alcock and Miles, *Peasant House*, BIT-A.
[46] Palmer and Parkhouse, *Burton Dassett Southend*, p. 171.

room, they help to identify a hall. In some standing buildings, traces of a louvre can be found in the roof, designed to aid the escape of smoke from a central hearth. At Burton Dassett Southend, hearths tended in the fifteenth century to be set against a wall, suggesting the presence of a smoke hood, a canopy of wattle and daub contrived to take the smoke out of the room. A standing building at Sutton Coldfield (Warwickshire) was provided with a smoke bay, another device for removing smoke from the hall.[47] These measures would culminate eventually in fireplaces, chimneys, ceilings, and two-storey houses, but not in the west midland peasant houses in the period before 1540. The hall's single open hearth was the only source of heat in the house, as is shown by the roof timbers blackened by soot from the hearth in surviving houses; the beams and rafters in the chamber remained relatively clean. The chamber was mainly used, as inventories reveal, for sleeping and storage.

The possessions, goods, and artefacts recorded from west midland peasant houses are guides to life within the buildings. They are found in such written sources as lists of principal goods, wills, and the hundreds of references in manor court records to objects lost, borrowed, stolen, pledged, seized, taken as heriots (death duties), and used as weapons. Finds from excavations are particularly useful because they include items which were of such low value that they are omitted from documents.[48] These material traces of the peasant past throw light on the extent to which such terms as domesticity and comfort can be applied to households.[49]

For the inhabitants, one of the most important uses of houses was as the location for the preparation and consumption of food and drink. Food was promised to retired tenants, usually in the form of grain and legumes, but also occasionally preserved meat, and garden fruit. Grain as it was threshed was transferred from the barn to wooden chests in the house. The most valuable items of cooking equipment, prominent in the written sources, were copper alloy pots and pans; at least one was owned by almost every household. Vessels for brewing included a lead for heating water, and wooden vats, tubs, and barrels. Many households owned a handmill or quern, of which fragments occur quite frequently in excavations, and are occasionally mentioned in documents. They may have been intended to evade mill tolls at the lord's mechanical mill, but could have had supplementary roles, for milling malt or replacing the lord's mill if it broke down.[50] Wooden kneading troughs for making bread figure in the written sources. Ovens

---

[47] Alcock and Miles, *Peasant House*, SUT-A.

[48] B. Jervis, C. Briggs, and M. Tompkins, 'Exploring Text and Objects: Escheators' Inventories and Material Culture in Medieval English Rural Households', *Med Arch* 59 (2015), pp. 168–92.

[49] For an urban dimension, F. Riddy, '"Burgeis" Domesticity in Late Medieval England', in *Medieval Domesticity: Home, Housing and Household in Medieval England*, edited by M. Kowaleski and P.J.P Goldberg (Cambridge, 2008), pp. 14–36.

[50] S.V. Smith, 'Towards a Social Archaeology of the Medieval Peasantry: Power and Resistance at Wharram Percy', *Journal of Social Archaeology* 9 (2009), pp. 391–416.

are scarce in the archaeological evidence, with a small indoor example at Upton, and one built outside the house at Pinbury, but their absence elsewhere suggests the use of the common oven. This was a seigneurial monopoly, which might be evaded by tenants, or removed by negotiation. In some villages tenants built individual bakehouses, and the common oven was not enforced (see 'Peasants and lords' in Chapter 10, for a dispute over a seigneurial oven).

Excavations have produced numerous finds of knives, which had many purposes, included some used in the kitchen. More specialist items include a metal skimmer from Burton Dassett Southend, and the documents refer (rarely) to spits, mortars, and a frying pan. Mortars occur also as archaeological finds, and they reveal a more sophisticated dimension of peasant cookery, as ingredients for sauces were pounded and ground. Food could be served using pewter dishes, platters, saucers, and salt cellars. The documents show that they belonged to the wealthier village families, who could also own a few silver spoons. Pewter spoons have been found at Burton Dassett Southend. The main types of table ware were of wood (treen) and every household would serve meals on treen plates, dishes, and trenchers, with drinks in wooden cups and bowls.

The abundant ceramics from excavations (pottery is almost unnoticed in documents) provide a wealth of insights into culinary and domestic life. Among the mundane and practical pots and jars which account for the bulk of the pottery some probably were used for storage, but their role as cooking vessels carried indelible traces in the form of sooting from the fire and food residues on the inside of the pot. Shallow bowls probably had a role in dairying. More specialist kitchen wares included scarce dripping pans, used in roasting meat, and pipkins for preparing sauces. In the fifteenth century ceramic cups supplemented the traditional turned wooden drinking bowls; their frequency at Burton Dassett Southend perhaps reflects its semi-urban dimension. Pitchers and jug were in universal use, but in varying quantities. At relatively sophisticated Burton Dassett Southend they accounted for 20.9 per cent of the rim sherds. They were plentiful at Upton, representing a quite affluent house, but they were limited in number at Bascote. At the poorest site, Coton, where occupation ceased by c.1300, only 4 per cent of sherds came from these drink containers. Pitchers and jugs were designed to hold ale, and some had coloured glazes, especially those made at Brill and Boarstall on the western border of Buckinghamshire. West-midland peasants appreciated the splash of colour that they brought to the table.[51]

Were members of the household bound together mainly by sharing food and drink? Was the household providing an environment that could be described as welcoming and offering any domestic comfort? The material arrangements of the house had an emphasis on security, with locked chests for storing clothing, kept in

---

[51] M. Mellor, 'A Synthesis of Middle and Late Saxon, Medieval and Early Post-Medieval Pottery in the Oxford Region', *Oxoniensia* 59 (1994), pp. 111–40.

the most private of rooms, the chamber. The locks and keys from excavations, and the ditches, hedges, or walls around the house plot recall the precaution in the custumals that a household called to attend the lord should leave one of their number to protect the empty house. The chamber's soft bedding and colourful coverlet contrasted with the rather bare hall, with its functional table on trestles that could be dismantled and moved, and its austere and portable benches and forms. Inventories do not include fixed furnishings, and halls could have had benches built against the walls (signs of these were noted at Burton Dassett Southend). At Halesowen in 1381 furnishings built into the structure of a solar were 'pinned fast' and 'nailed fast'.[52] Rooms, and especially halls, may have had more space for relaxation than is conveyed by inventories. At Claines (Worcestershire) a 'painted cloth' was mentioned in 1538 and many halls must have been brightened by such decorative textiles.[53]

We receive inconsistent messages about the social tone of the hall. On the one hand it was a functional space where meals were eaten. A spinning wheel in a hall shows that it could serve as a workplace. On the other hand, lists of possessions in some houses include tablecloths, towels, and a basin and ewer, suggesting some modest ceremonial with a sense of dignity.[54] The inequality within the household would mean that the head of the household or an inner circle would have washed their hands at the meal table, and the head would have had a prominent position at table sitting in a chair, not on a bench.

The excavated artefacts, such as those from Burton Dassett Southend, reveal relaxation, games, and entertainment among those gathered around the hearth after the meal, such as a dice, pegs from a musical instrument, and a design for a nine-mens'-morris board. The hall was also the scene of conversation, storytelling, and reminiscence. Some lively and informative conversation must have rewarded the curiosity of the villagers found listening under the eaves of neighbours' houses, which was an offence occasionally reported in manor courts. Social life could have continued after dark, because peasants owned iron candleholders, and village traders sold tallow candles (sometimes at more than the regulated price).[55]

There were obvious echoes of life in a gentry or urban household in the peasant hall. The hall and chamber arrangement, hand-washing, and social hierarchy all suggest that peasants followed the aristocratic example.[56] Perhaps we are observing different ranks of society, sharing in a common culture? However, many aspects of the peasant hall and house are located within a peasant way of life—cooking at the hall hearth, working in the hall, eating basic foods such as pottage

---

[52] BAH, 3279/346369A. [53] WA, ref. 008:7, BA3585,1538/370.
[54] Field, 'Worcestershire Peasant Buildings', pp. 142–3.
[55] Candle selling was regularly reported at Kempsey in 1475–82, WA, ref. 705:4, BA 54.
[56] Emulation is a theme discussed by M. Johnson, *English Houses, 1300–1800: Vernacular Architecture, Social Life* (Harlow, 2010), pp. 1–17.

and maslin bread—placing the peasant household at some distance from their social superiors.

The spaciousness of a peasant house can be measured scientifically by calculating floor areas. The two-, three-, and four-bay houses recorded in the documents, assuming a bay of roughly 5 m by 15 m would range between 42 and 85 square metres. Standing buildings varied between 37 and 135 square metres but most attained about 90. The excavated buildings at Burton Dassett Southend enable changes in average size to be traced through time: 41 square metres in the thirteenth century, 59 in the fourteenth, and 76 in the fifteenth. This would give space for individuals varying between 8 and 18 square metres if the household contained five people, but if there were seven, allowing for servants and others outside the nuclear family a two-bay house would provide 6 square metres per person. These figures are not dissimilar from those for Indian rural housing in the twentieth century, or for the late medieval south of France.[57] The calculation presumes that people were spread evenly over the house, but we have already seen that the chamber, the sleeping room, was often in the region of 5m by 5m. Perhaps the whole household slept in an overcrowded chamber, or alternatively servants and children might have been sent at night to temporary spaces around the house—in the hall for example, or in an outbuilding. In urban, aristocratic, and monastic housing, and in hospitals and almshouses, in this period private accommodation was increasingly being provided, with individuals being assigned lodgings or small chambers. This tendency in peasant houses led to the addition of upper chambers or solars, or crosswings, though this was much further advanced in south-east England.

The character of family life

The wills that survive from the end of our period expressed eloquently some strong opinions about the duties of family members. They saw the family as a hierarchy, in which children should be brought up in discipline and obedience. John Edmunds of Westbury-on-Trym (Gloucestershire) imagined his family after his own death, urging his wife to provide 'diligent and godly overseeing' of the children, and to bring them up in 'knowledge of God's laws' and in 'honest behaviour and conversation'.[58] He expected that his children would be obedient in the context of the family, but would also behave as good neighbours in the parish and village. A stronger disciplinary tone was struck by Richard Freman of Todenham (Gloucestershire) who in 1535 expected that his daughters when contemplating marriage would be 'ruled, ordered and guided' by their mother and by friends

---

[57] Dyer, 'English Peasant Buildings', p. 42; Palmer and Parkhouse, *Burton Dassett Southend*, p. 171.
[58] WA, ref. 008:7, BA 3585,1538/46.

(which at this period and in this context meant relatives). Roger Heritage of Burton Dassett in 1495 was more harsh in his language, expecting that his daughters would be ruled by his executor in their marriages, and would lose their cash inheritances if they showed an 'evil will or disposition'. His sons would also not receive a cash bequest if they were 'wasters' or 'of evil condition'.[59] The younger generation was clearly expected to be respectful of their elders, and there is evidence of regard for the wisdom of seniors when they were asked to use their memories to resolve disputes and matters of custom. Will makers were not entirely preoccupied with the obedience of children, and their bequests seemed to be motivated by affection and goodwill.

The testators were repeating commonplace and conventional phrases that would be found in contemporary sermons. They were not spontaneously expressing their personal opinions as the words would have come from the clerics who wrote the wills. The wills can still be a guide to the attitudes of the time as the better-off villagers would have accepted phrases that reflected their attitudes. Conventional ideas, merely because they were conventional, could still have real meaning. The emphasis in by-laws on discipline, good order, and sober and responsible behaviour suggest a body of widely held ideas, so evidently the jury of the manor court would have disapproved of 'wasters' just as much as the wealthy farmer Roger Heritage. The values that are found in the wills and the by-laws were judged to be necessary for the co-operative functioning of a family, and an orderly succession between generations.

The church advocated that a valid marriage depended on mutual consent, and the process began with a trothplight agreement made by the couple in which both expressed a commitment to marry. Ideally these exchanges would take place in public, before witnesses, but private expressions of willingness to marry were legally acceptable.[60] In the later Middle Ages solemnization of marriage at the church door became a requirement, but such a religious ceremony was a confirmation of a marriage already agreed and publicly acknowledged. The church's emphasis on consent was designed to establish its authority, as an alternative to the normal practice of negotiating marriages between families. Peasants seem to have accepted the need for the consent of the couple, though they continued to make marriage contracts in which brides were accompanied by dowries of clothing and household goods, and agreements were made about land and inheritance. Families seem to have made oral settlements over marriages which leave little obvious trace in written documents. An exception is an enigmatic legal dispute from Blackwell in 1325 arising from a gift, later withdrawn, of a dress to a bride, Eva de

---

[59] TNA, PROB 11/26, fos 26r-27v; PROB 11/10, fo 231v.
[60] P. Schofield, *Peasant and Community in Medieval England* (Basingstoke, 2003), pp. 90–130.

Hockeley.[61] Wills often mention that the marriage of daughters needed to be funded, with sums such as £5 and £10 being mentioned.

By their licensing of the marriage of female serfs, lords were drawn indirectly into the negotiations. They might attempt to influence the choice of marriage partners by offering a reduced marriage fine if the husband was one of their serfs, and would prefer a husband from the same village. The abbots of Halesowen in the 1370s and 1380s required servile women who married outside Halesowen to lose their claim to inherit land within the manor.[62] Lords also supervised the behaviour of widows, who under the rules of free bench forfeited their former husband's lands if they engaged in sexual relations. Peasants resented marriage fines, but they and lords both favoured rules that established clearly the succession to land. Courts were occasionally asked to resolve the rival inheritance claims of children from successive marriages, and doubts about the validity of marriages would threaten the whole system.

Attitudes towards marriage and family are displayed in the proceedings of church courts, one held by a rural dean for a number of north Worcestershire parishes in 1300; a visitation of parishes for west Gloucestershire, including the Forest of Dean, in 1397; and the series for 1401–1527 from the peculiar court of Hartlebury parish. They heard some matrimonial cases, but most of their business was taken up with accusations of fornication and adultery. Of course these sins were related to the church's teaching on marriage as fornication was defined as sexual relations outside marriage, and adultery was the result of breaking marriage vows. The local laity assisted the church in enforcing the rules by informing the courts of their neighbours' behaviour, just as they did in the manor court. The 'parishioners' acted as a jury of local men, shared some of the values of the canon lawyers and clergy, partly because they were well-versed in Christian morality, and partly because of their interest as possessors of land subject to inheritance, and as responsible heads of households based on the collective commitment of wives, children, and servants. The laity did not habitually flout conventional morality (Table 5.2). The number of offenders were small, seen in the context of the whole population; at Hartlebury there were about two cases reported each year, from 500 parishioners. Of course, not every offence was noticed.

There is no strong impression that marriage was under great threat, and the male parishioners seem to have been willing to defend wives against ill treatment by their husbands. John Michel of Hartlebury was said in 1481 with disapproval to have not allowed his wife to make a will. In west Gloucestershire three husbands were reported to have expelled their wives, and four others were accused of

[61] WCL, E10. [62] Razi, 'Family, Land and the Village Community', p. 25.

Table 5.2 Moral offences reported to west midland church courts, 1300–1527

Court	Fornication	Adultery	Cases involving clergy	Marriage	Incest	Others
North Worcs 1300	47	5	2	1	0	1
West Gloucs 1397	9	12	25	12	4	0
Hartlebury 1401–27	43	35	7	3	2	25

Sources: F.S. Pearson, ed., 'Records of a Ruridecanal Court of 1300', in *Collectanea* edited by S. Hamilton (WHS, 1912), pp. 69–80; A. Bannister, ed., 'Visitation Returns of the Diocese of Hereford in 1397', *EHR* 44 (1929), pp. 444–53; Swanson and Guyatt, eds., *Court Book*.

depriving their wives of food and clothing.[63] Wives were evidently being abused, but voices were raised among the laity to protect them.

Stable marriage was valued in a flexible way, so that when John Waterlade of Hartlebury was accused in 1412 of fornication with Joan Shapster, the couple claimed that they had agreed a trothplight (a secular contract to marry). They were reminded to solemnize the bond in a church ceremony, as if the court was expressing approval of their decision to regularize their relationship.[64] In the manor courts a similar situation arose when a widow was accused of being 'corrupt', but her holding was not forfeit if the man with whom she was accused became her husband, and he paid a fine to take on his new wife's land. A widow often acted as her husband's executor, and also took over the holding which she had already helped to manage. Her subsequent remarriage was regarded in the community as desirable because a productive and well-run holding benefitted from a partnership of husband and wife. The short time, often a matter of months, that separated the husband's death from the widow's remarriage demonstrates practical and realistic attitudes.[65]

The authorities expected the heads of households to pay taxes and rents on behalf of the holding, but also to exercise some supervision over their families and servants. The head had legal responsibility for the mainpast, which meant that he should ensure that his wife, children, and servants kept the peace. A head of a household might be presented to the manor court for offences committed by the mainpast, such as damage caused to hedges in gathering firewood. A married woman's brewing fines would be paid by her husband, without her name being mentioned. Employers were sometimes expected to pay taxes on behalf of servants. The head of household might have been held responsible if his son or

---

[63] Swanson and Guyatt, eds., *Court Book*, p. 227; Bannister, ed., 'Visitation Returns', pp. 448, 451, 452.
[64] Swanson and Guyatt, eds., *Court Book*, pp. 169–70.
[65] Franklin, 'Peasant Widows', pp. 193–4.

servant was not 'sworn in assize', that is, failing to take the oath (to be included in a tithing) to keep the peace on reaching the age of twelve. John Maryote of Willoughby (Warwickshire) in 1504 had to pay 2*d* because his servant Henry had not taken the oath, and another 2*d* for harbouring him against the peace. An extreme example was demonstrated by the killing at Huddington in Worcestershire of Richard Penne by Henry le Palmer, recorded in 1275. Henry was not in a tithing, but was reported to be in the mainpast of Richard le Palmer, his father.[66]

The head of the household took on a leadership role when the lord required a day's harvest services from the whole *familia*. At Atherstone (Warwickshire) in the early thirteenth century the tenant of a large holding attended in the harvest field with an iron fork to symbolize his office, 'to see that the work is done well'. He was rewarded with a meal of bread, ale, and meat or fish. In a similar description of harvest works at Wellesbourne Mountford in 1279 it was said that the tenant acting as a supervisor would eat with the lord, reinforcing the status and authority of the man who was 'above the workers' (*ultra operarios*). The lord aimed to promote hierarchy among his peasants, but the policy may not always have been welcomed by those assigned responsibilities.[67]

Wives lived under their husband's shadow. They had limited legal status; for example, they were not expected to take the oath to keep the peace. They could bring litigation to the manor court, but did so less often than men. On some manors it became more common during the fourteenth century (Eldersfield, Worcestershire, for example) for land to be held jointly by husband and wife, so a widow's rights to hold the land were assured, and she was not restricted by the rules of 'free bench'. When a wife inherited land, her husband gained rights over it, and could sell it. Some apparent safeguards protected the wife's interest, and she was asked in private ('examined sole') to give her consent. This was not primarily to safeguard her rights, but to reassure the purchaser of the land that there would be no subsequent claim.[68]

Women contributed to the production of the holding by working on the garden and looking after poultry, and they could show enterprise in marketing the produce. Agnes Longeman of Cleeve Prior owned seven geese in 1357: these were more than her household would consume and they and their goslings would have been intended for sale.[69] Women's dairying and brewing was partly for household consumption and partly to gain cash. They could profit from the surplus of their

---

[66] Magdalen College, Oxford, EP 67/14; J. Röhrkasten, ed., *The Worcester Eyre of 1275* (WHS, new series, 22, 2008), pp. 366, 447.

[67] Chibnall, ed., *Abbey of Bec*, p. 103; *WHR*, p. 165; J.R. Birrell, 'Peasants' Eating and Drinking', *AgHR* 63 (2015), pp. 1–18.

[68] R.M. Smith, 'Coping with Uncertainty: Women's Tenure of Customary Land in England c. 1370–1430', in *Enterprise and Individuals in Fifteenth-Century England*, edited by J. Kermode (Stroud, 1991), pp. 43–67; J. Whittle, *The Development of Agrarian Capitalism. Land and Labour in Norfolk, 1440–1580* (Oxford, 2000), pp. 131–2.

[69] WCL, E18.

gardens like the beans, peas, and apples sold by women on the streets of Bristol in 1282–4.[70] They also worked in the fields on such tasks as harvesting, weeding, and planting beans, which were traditionally 'women's work'. Once harvested, the corn was threshed by men and winnowed by women. When the Ordinance of Labourers was enforced in 1350 at Blackwell (Warwickshire) husbands and wives were named together and their illegally high joint wage (10*d* per day) showed that each couple worked as a team.[71] Women appeared before the courts for offences committed while milking cows, gathering firewood, and picking peas and beans in the fields. Women can sometimes be found doing 'men's work' such as mowing hay (for which a heavy scythe was normally used): this happened at Madresfield in Worcestershire in 1387.[72]

Joint tenancy between husband and wife could be seen as giving some official recognition of the partnership within a household, and in a rare example of a contemporary assessment of the efficiency of a peasant farm, the tenants at Admington (Warwickshire) in 1341, speaking as a body, praised the 'improvement' achieved in running a holding by Nicholas and Petronilla Shad.[73] Wives' experience of working with their former husbands is suggested by their ability to manage holdings as widows.

Work on the holding by sons and daughters was taken for granted and therefore rarely recorded. They gathered firewood, sometimes damaging their neighbours' hedges as they did so. At Hallow (Worcestershire) a woman was helped by 'boys' in gathering fuel in 1315, and at Southrop (Gloucestershire) in 1381 a son joined his mother in carrying off firewood. In 1395 at Middleton (Warwickshire) the mainpast of each of four tenants, wives, children, and servants, were said to be collecting wood from hedges.[74]

Through the agricultural seasons some jobs were well-suited to young people, such as shepherding, milking, harvesting, and hay making, progressing to the full range of heavy jobs in ploughing, carting, and ditching. At North Cerney (Gloucestershire) in 1381 Richard Reve was described as 'son and servant' of Thomas Reve and his wife Joan, who were judged by the tax assessors as being capable (*potens*) cultivators of land. In the same village a shepherd, John Lomherde, and his wife Beatrice had a son, William, also called a 'son and servant'.[75] Perhaps those compiling the tax list were implying that the young people worked primarily for their parents, though they might also have earned wages from part-time employment with neighbours. The ultimate meaning of the phrase 'son and servant' is

---

[70] M. Sharp, ed., *Accounts of the Constables of Bristol Castle in the Thirteenth and Fourteenth Centuries* (Bristol Record Society, 34, 1982), p. 11.

[71] WCL, E16.

[72] [no editor] *Excerpta e Scrinio Maneriali de Madresfield in Com Wigorn* (1873), 18 (four of the offenders were wives and one a servant).

[73] GA, D678/M1/1/1.

[74] Hereford Cathedral Library, R1162; GA, D11718/61/B1; UNMSC, MiM 131/32.

[75] *PT*, part 1, p. 305.

apparent from an agreement made at Romsley (Worcestershire) in 1398. Thomas Puttewey surrendered his holding to the lord, who granted it back to be held by Thomas, and it would remain to Thomas his son. Thomas junior's elder brother Richard had recently inherited land from his mother, so Thomas junior was being nominated to succeed to his father's holding. This transaction cost Thomas senior 13s 4d for a fine. It was worth the money because Thomas junior would live with his father and 'faithfully serve him' for life. The father would feed and clothe him 'as befits the estate of servant'. Thomas senior had been troubled by the acute labour shortage following the drop in population in the late fourteenth century, and binding his son by contract guaranteed that he would have a worker on call for the rest of his life. The agreement, which was giving formal expression to the normally unwritten understanding between parents and children, shows that 'the cohesive family' could not be taken for granted. Thomas senior must have been uncertain of the loyalty of his son, and was binding him not to leave home to work elsewhere. Such details as the quality of the son's promised food and clothing do not suggest that the son was being treated very generously (though servants' food and clothes were improving at this time). Thomas junior's attitude to all this must be left to conjecture. He apparently inherited the land in 1418 and was still alive in 1444.[76]

Young women recorded as 'daughter and servant' could have done many tasks, but dairying was regarded as a female specialism, though they would also have been useful participants in brewing. In the long run, as arable output fell and peasant holdings developed a pastoral economy, demand may have grown for more female labour, though wives as well as daughters could have done the work.

Parents commonly found ways to provide younger sons and daughters with at least a small amount of land (see 'Holding land before 1349' in Chapter 3), by granting a building plot carved out of the family holding, or by acquiring a parcel by purchase or by assarting, which could be given to a younger son as acquisitions were not included in the main inheritance. A subtenancy would be another way of providing land, though this would not have been a secure holding. Money could be used to fund a good marriage for a daughter, or to purchase land. Fathers would apportion money or goods to demonstrate his intention to treat all children equally: John Edmunds of Westbury (Gloucestershire) in 1538 left £20 each to five children, and William Puffe of nearby Henbury (1540) wished each of his six children to receive £5. The same equality in goods was the ideal of Thomas Dyer of Blockley, who bequeathed to each of his four children a beast and 10 sheep.[77]

Cash bequests of £10 and £20 were not immediately affordable, and the testator was obliging his main heir to find the money out of the land in succeeding years. It might seem unjust treatment of the other children to select one son to inherit

---

[76] CR *Romsley*, pp. 156, 158, 196.   [77] WA, ref. 008:7, BA 3585, 1538/46; 1540/63; 1538/119.

all of the land, but that son might be burdened with his father's debts and bequests. A first-born son, or in some circumstances a younger son selected by the parents to receive the holding on a reversion, was taking on heavy obligations as well as assets. An eldest son might have preferred to buy a holding of his own, and not take on the financial commitments imposed by his father.

To add to the problems of the heir, the transition between the generations was by no means straightforward. A son had to pay attention to the claims of his mother, who could keep the whole holding under the custom of free bench while the son waited. A son who had been living with his parents might continue to share the house with his mother after the father's death. More often the mother occupied the family holding, while the son obtained land or employment elsewhere. In 1536 Richard Freman of Todenham left his son John land at Upper Quinton, 8 miles from Todenham.[78] Fathers might leave livestock and farm implements to a son implying that he had some land, and such bequests are recorded often enough to suggest that it was not unusual for sons to have obtained a holding.

Inheritance involved complex discussions, with much of the negotiation hidden from our view. In theory the courts operated within a framework of customary law, but a full and clear code of rules did not exist. The twelve jurors arrived at conclusions showing some regard for earlier cases, which were recorded in the court rolls, and with a sense that they were applying general principles derived from local customs and the common law. They also had notions of fairness in particular cases, as they knew the people who would be affected by the decision. The judgements were appropriate to particular circumstances, but also had general significance in establishing a new custom.[79]

Families, and particularly the heads of households, made plans and thought ahead, devising 'inheritance strategies', or using 'estate planning' to borrow a modern phrase. Their plans were much influenced by personal preferences rather than general principles. An example will suggest the complexity of the manoeuvres within a family after the death of a tenant. In 1315 at Broadwas (Worcestershire) John Tom's widow, Letice, acquired her husband's holding of two nooks, but surrendered it to the lord. A nook was a quarter-yardland of about 7 acres, so together these were equivalent to a half-yardland, a holding of middling size. Two children, Walter and Lucy, had some claim; Walter surrendered his rights, leaving Lucy as the heir, so male primogeniture, inheritance by the eldest son, had been set aside. Lucy paid a fine so that Letice could keep the land for life, after which Lucy would succeed. Letice had backed out of taking the land immediately after her husband

---

[78] TNA, PROB11/26, fos 26r–26v.
[79] L. Bonfield, 'What Did English Villagers Mean by "Customary Law"?', in *Medieval Society and the Manor Court*, edited by Z. Razi and R.M. Smith (Oxford, 1996), pp. 106–9; J.S. Beckerman, 'Towards a Theory of Medieval Manorial Adjudication: The Nature of Communal Judgements in a System of Customary Law', *Law and History Review* 13 (1995), pp. 1–22; L. Poos and L. Bonfield, eds., *Select Cases in Manorial Courts 1250–1530: Property and Family Law* (Selden Society, 114, 1998), pp. xxvii–xlix.

died, but had she followed the conventional path of free bench, Walter might have succeeded on her death, and Lucy would have been left with nothing. Meanwhile Lucy was arranging to marry William atte Well, so that he would eventually become the tenant of the land. Lucy's prospects of acquiring land made her a very attractive marriage partner. Perhaps this was all a sequence of accidents and impulsive personal decisions, but we suspect that it was planned ahead. Walter Tom could have been persuaded to give up his claim with money, or a promise of maintenance, or perhaps he had acquired land elsewhere. An agreement between John, Walter, Letice, Lucy, and William atte Well could have been made before John died. The lord went along with the project. He received a fine, and had the prospect of a future active male tenant. The community was not directly involved, as the jury was not required to make any difficult judgements. The assembled tenants would have watched and heard the transfers of land and surrender of claims being made in open court, and presumably objections would have been voiced if the transactions were thought irregular.[80]

Servants had in theory a contractual relationship with their employers, unlike the unwritten and unspoken duties and rewards of family members. In practice informal understandings usually required that the servant should be engaged for a fixed period, often a year or a term, which was a half-year either in winter or in summer. Their pay consisted of a combination of cash (rarely more than 10s per annum and often much less), food, clothing, and accommodation. They worked in both agricultural and domestic tasks.[81] They took on responsible jobs requiring some skill, strength, and judgement, like Richard, servant of Henry Sprot of Blackwell who in 1379 drove his employer's cart.[82] A servant did not necessarily work entirely for his or her principal employer, though whether the initiative to take another job came from the servant or his master is not clear. For example, William, servant of William Tony was employed as common herdsman by the vill of Charlton in 1419, to which William Tony gave his consent.[83] Servants took on the role of serving as substitutes for children who were lacking, as was evident from households in the poll tax. This went further than performing tasks that would ordinarily have fallen to children, as when Richard Brocke took on a 2-acre holding at Thornbury (Gloucestershire), which was to be held by himself, his wife, and Alice their servant, showing that in practice she had been adopted as their daughter and heir.[84]

Families and households were supposed to work together and support one another, but frictions and human failings were occasionally exposed. Some households were 'badly governed' and contained prostitutes and suspicious strangers. Court rulings over inheritance might reveal bad feelings and resentments within

---

[80] WCL, E7.   [81] Whittle, ed., *Servants in Rural Europe*.
[82] WCL, E29. The servant was held responsible for the death of a pig with which the cart collided.
[83] WCL, E48.   [84] SRO, D641/1/4C/7.

families. A case at Lindridge (Worcestershire) in 1315 created dissensions in the whole village.[85] A jury decided that John le Bolt son of Margery le Bolt should inherit his mother's cottage, contradicting an earlier decision that the holding should go to Agnes, Margery's niece. John would seem to most observers to have been the obvious heir, but other views prevailed, and local opinion was sharply divided, as seven men were amerced by the court for contempt, objecting to the decision.

A pattern of troubles affected households in the west midlands in the period after 1349, when peasants were facing general disruption. Some problems were the direct effects of high mortality. Fathers died, leaving a small child or no direct heir. Children died leaving parents without assistance and with no immediate successors. Servants and labourers were depleted in numbers, and the survivors expected high pay and better working conditions. An indirect effect of long-term population decline was a higher degree of absenteeism, as vacant land and employment opportunities opened in neighbouring villages. At Southrop (Gloucestershire) in 1381 eleven people gave the lord annually a capon for licence to live outside the tithing (which implied absence from the village). In 1463 at Ombersley twenty-two tenants had sublet their holdings and were living elsewhere, even as far as Bristol. Agnes Meryell claimed in 1477 inheritance of a cottage and croft, although she was living at Lutterworth in Leicestershire.[86] When a tenant of Cleeve Prior, Richard Freman, neglected his yardland holding in 1378, he explained his absence by stating that his wife 'would not live within the lordship'.[87] Young people, among them many serfs, were leaving their manors, including potential workers and potential heirs. The fall in transfers of land between family members reached such an extreme level in the mid to late fifteenth century on some manors that few or no sons chose to take their parents' holding and preferred to live elsewhere. It became difficult to persuade heirs to take an inheritance. At Blackwell in 1397 Constance Jacken inherited a holding when her mother died, but immediately surrendered it to the lord. We will never know why such a decision was made, but it was not uncommon.[88]

In these circumstances relations between the generations might be expected to have deteriorated. As the evidence is anecdotal the proposition could not be proved, and it would be naïve to suppose that family life was harmonious before 1349. The tensions, especially when connected with the problems of inheriting land, the pressure on children to work, and care for the elderly, would always be latent within the peasant family. Maintenance agreements providing for the needs of retired or disabled tenants, both before and after 1349, were registered formally in the court because the parties were distrustful of one another. On occasion, the

---

[85] WCL, E6. [86] GA, D11718/61/B; WA, ref 705:56, BA 3910/27(xi);/27(xvii).
[87] WCL, E28. [88] WCL, E39.

heir or successor had to be reminded by the lord or the community of their obligations. Loyalties within families were not enough to ensure the social security of the parents, showing that the peasant family was not as strong or as caring as is sometimes imagined (see 'Individuals and communities' in Chapter 10). We find after 1349 some surprisingly frank admissions of troubles. In 1352 at Blackwell (Warwickshire) Osbert le Carter decided to accommodate his mother separately after a period when they lived in the same house, but there was so much 'discord and contumely' between them that he feared that his goods might be damaged and his soul would be in danger.[89] Agnes Kyng of Badminton (Gloucestershire) took over her husband's messuage and half-yardland when he died in 1352. After two years she surrendered the land to her son John, but the lord required him not to 'behave badly towards his mother'.[90] This could have been a reference to John's obligation to provide maintenance, but the unusual wording might refer to some past history of friction.

Finally, did households have problems in dealing with the non-relatives under their roofs, the servants? They have some characteristics in common with the children as they were young and might both be involved in those youthful sports and diversions which caused so much disapproval: football, handball, tennis, and dice might all lead to disputes, diverted energy, and lost sleep, all of which attracted the disapproval of employers. They tended to appear in court records accused of illicit fishing or raiding their neighbours' hedges, and in church court records they unsurprisingly encountered disapproval of their sexual behaviour.

The more precise indications of discontent among servants come firstly from the individual complaints that employers did not keep to their side of their contracts by paying them adequately and promptly, and providing clothing and good quality food. For example, John Hyckes of Alveston (Warwickshire), who was employing Alice Swyppe, the daughter of a fellow tenant, was said in 1396 not to have supplied her with linen and woollen cloth for her clothes.[91] Parents took employers to court with complaints on behalf of sons and daughters. Employers resented the tendency for servants to break their contracts and fail to serve for a full year. A typical case was Alice, servant of William Myche of Bilton (Warwickshire), who began her term in Michaelmas 1381 but left before the year was complete.[92] Servants moved from one employment to another, like early modern 'servants in husbandry', to express a sense of independence, but in the case of Henry atte Mule's servant at Horsley (Gloucestershire) in 1354, a rival employer offered inducements to move.[93]

---

[89] WCL, E17.   [90] GA, Badminton Muniments, GA 2700/MAI/1.   [91] WCL, E38.
[92] E. Kimball, ed., *Rolls of the Warwickshire and Coventry Sessions of the Peace 1377–1397* (DS, 16, 1939), p. 125.
[93] TNA, SC2 175/63.

Conclusions

Better-off families in the Middle Ages are understood in general to have lived in households consisting of parents and two or three children with one or two servants. West-midland peasant families accord with that generalization, but qualifications must be made to remember the variants, in particular the many households headed by women, the smaller households of the cottagers, the occasional one-person households, and the complex combinations that included the older generation, siblings, and more than one married couple. This lack of a stereotype does not alter the importance of the household, whatever its composition, as a basic unit of production and consumption.

The space occupied by the household underlines its productive role, because the plots were large enough to accommodate a variety of useful activities such as gardening, with yards and buildings for animals, and the house sufficient to contain between five and seven people. The developing quality and size of houses show peasants investing in a space for working (including crafts), and for accommodating workers. The house was a centre of consumption in that food and drink were prepared and served there, but again the rising quality of the building, and some of its contents, resulted from a greater emphasis on domestic comfort.

A cosy domesticity does not describe adequately the relationships within the household. The prevailing aim was to maintain order and discipline, with a wife as a manager and partner, and children as a workforce. There was limited sentiment, but members had a sense of obligation to one another. The tension between the welfare of others and self-interest could lead to conflict and difficulties in maintaining adequate amounts of labour and securing an orderly hereditary succession. It was on the basis of a rather stern sense of collective welfare that the household conducted the farming, industry, and exchange that will be the subject of the following chapters.

6
Peasants and their crops

This chapter deals mainly with cultivation, and the next with livestock, though separating the two is difficult because they were so closely connected. To make judgements about the effectiveness of the agriculture practised by peasants we must consider the management of fields, methods of husbandry, farming techniques, and the changing balance between arable and pasture.

Fields and their regulation

In the champion districts of the west midland region compact nucleated villages usually divided their land between two fields, occasionally three (see 'The west midland region' in Chapter 2). Crops were grown on one field while the other (in the predominant two-field arrangement) was left fallow, to be reversed in the next year. Each field was subdivided into dozens of furlongs each containing groups of selions, also called ridges or lands. A village's fields contained at least 2,000 of these strips; they were long and narrow, so that the plough turned around as infrequently as possible. A very high proportion of the land lay in arable fields, often in excess of four-fifths, and some villages lacked extensive meadow, pasture, and wood (Figure 6.1 shows a champion village with an almost complete field system, remains of which survived as ridge and furrow until the 1940s). The animals obtained much of their grazing from the vegetation on the fallow field. The typical peasant holding in such villages *c.*1300 was distributed in many strips, evenly divided between the fields. The ploughed land and the common rights were subject to regulation by the community, though the management of the holding was ultimately the responsibility of the individual household. Cotswold fields were organized in a similar way, but often had access to hill pasture. In the woodlands of the north and west, the open fields bore some resemblance to those of the champion, but they occupied a smaller proportion of the village territory; each was relatively small in size, and they numbered at least five. Peasants lived in hamlets or individual farms, each holding strips of land usually distributed unevenly over the open fields, and also a number of crofts, closes, and hedged parcels used for arable or grazing. The closes were thrown open at defined times

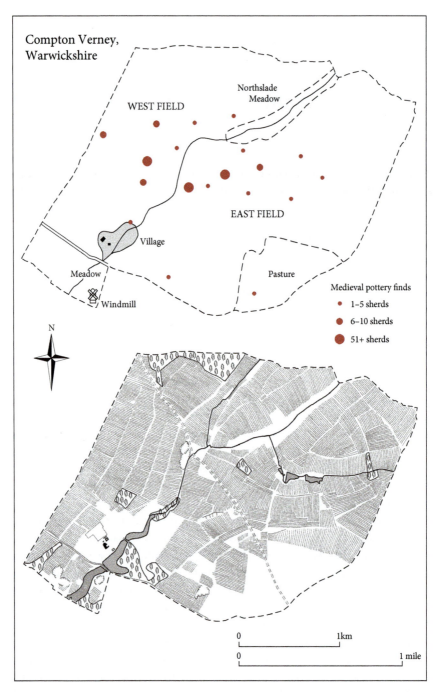

Figure 6.1 Compton Verney, Warwickshire. This two-field Feldon village is shown in the upper map in outline *c.*1300. The modern landscape in the lower map is based on aerial photographs of the 1940s and some field observation. Ridge and furrow represent the survival of strips, headlands, and furlongs on which cultivation ceased *c.*1460. The upper map shows the distribution of pottery from field walking in 1998–9 (see 'Farming methods and techniques' in this chapter) (source: note 75).

for common grazing, along with the open pasture, heath, moor, and meadow, which could be extensive.[1]

What part did peasants play in devising these divergent ways of organizing the countryside? The environment had an underlying influence on types of fields, and it has been argued that the heavy clays of the champion made it essential to have efficient ways of assembling plough teams, for which nucleated villages were well suited. However many open-field villages were cultivating the light gravelly soils of the river valleys, or the stony calcareous earth of the wolds, which did not challenge the ploughman as much as the sticky clay of south-east Warwickshire or Worcestershire. It should be remembered that plough teams had to be brought together by those living in vills formed from groups of hamlets in the woodlands. The environment is not in any case an answer to the question, 'who made the fields?', because the soils, climate, and relief provided a context, not a driving force, and decisions and choices about fields resulted from a range of influences and pressures.[2]

The origins of the fields belong to an early medieval period, when a seventh-century law code refers to peasants regulating shared land, and a general restructuring and intensification of farming has been proposed as occurring in the long eighth century. The earliest evidence for open fields in the west midlands comes from charter boundaries written in the tenth and eleventh centuries.[3] At that date both village communities and estate management by lords could have been involved in setting up fields. The formative factors behind the emergence of the open fields included the definition of specific village territories, later called townships, and sometimes coincident with parishes and manors which typically contained 1,000–3,000 acres. The inhabitants were expanding their ploughed land, in which process arable and pasture needed to be balanced, so that mixed farming could be practised. The best solution was to separate arable from grassland, but to allow livestock onto the corn fields when they were not being cultivated. Rotations and fallowing had to be agreed, co-ordinated, and regulated. In order to secure consent to this coordination of cultivation, the participants were guaranteed equality in the distribution of land, and a fair allocation of good land and less fertile land. Everyone had a stake in the fields, but also in cultivation, because the ploughs, beasts, and labour of cultivation were shared. In order to benefit, everyone also had to accept commitments of work and animals. The fields may originally have been rectangular parcels, but as holdings were divided between heirs,

---

[1] B.K. Roberts, 'Field Systems of the West Midlands', in *Studies in the Field Systems in the British Isles*, edited by A.H.R. Baker and R.A. Butlin (Cambridge, 1973), pp. 188–231; R.H. Hilton, 'Old Enclosure in the West Midlands', *Annales de L'Est* 21(1959), pp. 272–83.

[2] T. Williamson, *Shaping Medieval Landscapes: Settlement, Society, Environment* (Macclesfield, 2003).

[3] M. McKerracher, *Farming Transformed in Anglo-Saxon England: Agriculture in the Long Eighth Century* (Oxford, 2018); D. Hooke, *The Anglo-Saxon Landscape: The Kingdom of the Hwicce* (Manchester, 1985), pp. 154–65, 190–226.

and land held jointly was allocated to individuals, the land was fragmented into smaller subdivisions. The most convenient parcel was a narrow strip, and this was ploughed to form a ridge, for drainage but also to help to define the boundaries between strips, which were not fenced or ditched. The whole arrangement depended on comprehensive multiple contracts between people of similar social rank, and therefore based on the peasant community.[4]

By the time that we can observe in detail the functioning of the fields in the thirteenth and fourteenth centuries both lords and peasants were participating in the routines. Some lords' demesnes consisted of scattered strips intermingled with the holdings of the peasants, meaning that lords rotated their crops and joined in the cycle of common grazing. Lords with 'block' demesnes could not manage the land with complete independence, as common grazing was customary on the demesne when it lay fallow. Lords clearly had an incentive to involve themselves in the management of the field system, because the profit of the demesne was at stake, and the efficiency of peasant farming might have consequences for the lords' rent.[5]

The role of both lords and tenants can be seen in the by-laws announced in the manor court. They sometimes use a conventional formula implying general agreement by the 'whole homage' or 'all tenants'. The role of the lord's representative is given prominence at Southrop (Gloucestershire) in 1409, when the 'steward and the suitors' ordered tenants to arrange for livestock to be supervised (by the common herdsman, we presume). Even when the by-law came from the steward, as at Rockhampton (Gloucestershire) in 1419 it was thought appropriate to add 'by assent of all tenants'.[6]

The by-laws were not focussed on the central disciplines of the arable fields, such as the boundaries between one strip and another, which were potentially controversial. The need to fix stones or posts, and the offence of moving them are mentioned very rarely. Instead, the preoccupations of the law makers and enforcers was to minimize the damage that livestock could cause to crops. The order that pigs should have rings placed in their noses (to discourage them from destructive rooting) was often repeated and clearly not obeyed. When the leading villagers made a serious effort to ensure enforcement of the rules by appointing a panel of harvest reeves or harvest wardens, their principal concern was not the cutting and carrying of the corn. Rather they focussed on preventing animals trespassing in corn fields before the corn had been carried, or on growing crops at other times of the year. This preoccupation with the interface between livestock

---

[4] C. Dyer, E. Thoen, and T. Williamson, eds., *Peasants and Their Fields: The Rationale of Open-Field Agriculture, c.700–1800* (Turnhout, 2018), pp. 1–4, 257–75.
[5] D. Hall, *The Open Fields of England* (Oxford, 2014), pp. 95–105.
[6] GA, D11718/61/B1; Badminton muniments D2700 MJ9/1–2.

and arable lends support to the view that the open-field system originated in the need to co-ordinate cultivation and grazing, and was perpetuated by that priority.

A fundamental question was the membership of the community, and therefore who was entitled to enjoy common rights in the fields and pastures. In 1393 the court at Eldersfield (Worcestershire) identified Thomas Clerk of Stanton (an adjoining village) as keeping seven cattle on a pasture for which he had no entitlement; two years later John Otar was found to be pasturing animals 'but is not a commoner'.[7] More often people were making more general encroachments across boundaries, such as the invasion of Harvington's territory by the men of Sheriff's Lench reported in 1388.[8] These problems often arose from intercommoning arrangements, by which villages shared pastures according to agreed rules, but they did not always work together amicably (see 'Animal welfare' in Chapter 7). Again the livestock's access to the fields, not the arable crops, preoccupied the lawmakers.

In the early fourteenth century opinion in villages and estates was obviously exercised by the problem of the theft of corn in the harvest (see 'Village community' in Chapter 4). Legislators occasionally returned to this problem for the next hundred years. Workers hired from outside the village were regarded as potential thieves. Villagers were told not to pay them with sheaves, as corn given as pay might be confused with stolen crops. Gleaners, usually a small group of elderly and poor women from the village, were regarded with suspicion along with strangers who invaded the harvest fields to glean. Distrust spread to householders and tenants who carted corn at night, and who had entrances into the adjacent fields from the rear of their closes. Perhaps cultivators and estate managers, troubled by disappointing returns, were looking for someone to blame.

The date when the sown field should be closed to livestock, or the beginning and end of hay making, the day when cutting and carrying corn should begin, or the moment when the corn had been removed and the stubble could be thrown open for grazing were crucial events for the cultivators, but they were not decided in by-laws. The time for each event changed from year to year depending on weather patterns. In 1337 at Cropthorne (Worcestershire) a time was given for the beginning of the harvest, but we do not know who authorized this. At Uley (Gloucestershire) in 1479 the completion of the harvest and the opening of the corn field for grazing was decided by the farmer and the bailiff. The day for the end of the harvest at Ham in the Vale of Berkeley (Gloucestershire) was chosen by 'the neighbours' in 1462.[9] These routine but important deliberations were presumably often made by a village meeting, based on local knowledge and wisdom. They probably also prepared matters for the manor court, such as proposals for

---

[7] WA, ref. 705.134, BA 1531/69B.   [8] WCL, E34.
[9] WCL, E13; GA, Badminton muniments D2700 MJ12/1; Berkeley Castle Muniments, A1/1/96 (microfilm).

by-laws. Peasant communities clearly took decisions without the lord's knowledge, and consequently their deliberations were not formally documented.

Changing agriculture: Managing the fields

Peasants had to adjust their farming methods and field organization in the period of growth in the thirteenth century, and they had to adapt in the following centuries to a more thinly settled countryside.

Peasants in the thirteenth century took a leading role in the assarting of land and the extension of the arable area in the woodland landscapes. They have been portrayed in positive terms, as bold initiators of an expanding economy, who worked hard for their own benefit but also for the rest of society. Some scepticism has to be applied to this whole episode, as the growth in population in the woodlands does not seem so great, nor were landscapes everywhere transformed. Occasionally we see the movement of assarts across an area of waste resembling the advance of a frontier, but more often expansion of cultivation took the form of a piecemeal series of small-scale encroachments.[10]

The colonizers faced opposition from powerful interests, including the crown which was enforcing forest law in the thirteenth century, and the great lords who valued their private forests, the chases. They were protecting the habitat of the deer they intended to hunt but the forests could also generate revenue as offenders against the vert (vegetation) could be made to pay substantial penalties. The motives for promoting forest law cannot be easily disentangled.[11] Through the region, individual lords managed woods for their timber, coppice wood, and grazing, and appointed woodwards to make peasants pay if they took trees and underwood without permission. They often surrounded their woods with banks and fences. Parks were created by lords, usually in woodland landscapes, taking in existing woods and wastes, but occasionally former agricultural land. Enclosure with a strong pale kept herds of deer inside, discouraged human intruders, and served as barriers to the further expansion of peasant agriculture. Well over 200 parks are known in the region mainly from the thirteenth and fourteenth centuries, each enclosing as much as 1,000 acres, and commonly between 20 and 400 acres.[12] Lords might also calculate that they could make more profit from

---

[10] T. John, 'Change in Medieval Warwickshire, Domesday Book to the Hundred Rolls of 1279–1280', *Local Population Studies* 59 (1997), pp. 41–53; C. Dyer, *Hanbury. Settlement and Society in a Woodland Landscape* (University of Leicester Centre for English Local History Occasional Paper, 4,1991), p. 28.

[11] R. Jones and M. Page, *Medieval Villages in an English Landscape: Beginnings and Ends* (Macclesfield, 2006), pp. 105–29.

[12] S. Mileson, *Parks in Medieval England* (Oxford, 2009), pp. 45–81. I am grateful to Jane Croom for showing me her list of Warwickshire's medieval parks: she has found ninety.

cultivation, and they themselves cleared their woods and heaths, and allow peasants to colonize in order to gain rents from new tenant holdings.

The attitudes of the peasants were similarly ambiguous. They resented the oppressions of forest law, which cost them money and also made them vulnerable to local forest officials who regularly abused their powers. On the other hand the fines were not so high as to make their assarts unprofitable, and the physical environment of the forest, with its under-utilized land, raw materials, and fuel presented them with opportunities. They also raided lords' woods regularly, and were prepared to pay the fines. Although forest law and lords' preservation of their woods did not prevent the clearance of new land, and was not intended to do so, it does seem to have inhibited peasants and other would-be developers. This discouragement could have been a factor in the survival of considerable areas of wooded land, heaths, and moors at the end of the colonizing movement of the thirteenth century.

Although peasants may have been frustrated by the lords' protection of the natural environment, both lords and peasants showed caution in extending cultivation. They saw the merits of maintaining extensive pastures, and in their own way peasant communities campaigned against the enclosure and cultivation of their common grazing grounds (see 'Peasants and the environment' in Chapter 10). Individual peasants offended by putting hedges or fences around pieces of common land, often on the side of an existing road, and denying neighbours right of entry. They were then free to plough the land and plant crops as they wished. Every new close or croft created in this way deprived those who used the pasture of some grazing land. Each enclosure was small, usually below 2 acres, and made little difference to the capacity of a large common, but a principle was at stake, and cumulatively a succession of encroachments could be damaging to a community. The encloser could obtain permission from the lord, who would (after negotiation) set the terms of tenancy and the annual rent, creating a bond of common purpose between lord and tenant. The community's reaction could take many forms. They could bring a legal action (novel disseisin) alleging that they had been deprived wrongly of pasture rights. When the king's judges held an itinerant court in Warwickshire in 1221 they dealt with seventeen novel disseisin cases.[13] In a typical example three tenants of Ashow in central Warwickshire, on the edge of the Arden, complained that because of Geoffrey de Semilly they had lost common pasture which belonged to their free tenements in the vill. No details are given, but an encroachment on the common was the likely source of the dispute. Geoffrey admitted the disseisin. The parties could come to a settlement. An agreement recorded at Ashleworth in Gloucestershire, around 1240 between the Abbot of St Augustine's at Bristol and Roger de Derneford allowed enclosure in

---

[13] D.M. Stenton, ed., *Rolls of the Justices in Eyre for Gloucestershire, Warwickshire and Staffordshire, 1221, 1222* (Selden Society 59, 1940), p. 233 (Ashow case).

the common of Ashleworth and the wood of Corse. Free tenants objected, but surrendered their rights of common in exchange for payments from the Abbey: William de Morcote received £2 13s 4d, John de Stanton 13s 4d, and so on.[14]

Although the lords arranged the agreements, it was often tenants who made the enclosures, and their neighbours from the same village or nearby villages who raised objections, indicating conflicts of interest among peasants. The disputes could lead to direct action, when groups of objectors removed hedges in the night. They were accused of riotous behaviour, but the groups were mounting a purposeful and disciplined campaign against the offending enclosures, usually without violence.[15] A particularly large scale and persistent episode was provoked by enclosures by people from Alvechurch in north Worcestershire on two commons, West Heath and *Dodenhaleshey*, on which the inhabitants of King's Norton also had rights of grazing.[16] The conflict stretched over the period between 1273 and 1287. Some of the opponents of the enclosures were leading villagers of King's Norton, but these were not just quarrels among the elite of the villages. On the Alvechurch side, a tenant of modest means on the disputed land was Henry de Ickenildestrete (taking his name from a nearby Roman road) who held an acre for an annual rent of 12d at *Dodenhaleshey*, and a plot in the hamlet of Rowney Green.[17]

Small fields with irregular boundaries established in the thirteenth century by peasants such as Henry de Ickenildestrete were visible at West Heath Farm in the late nineteenth century, and also a large area of open heath land survived. Open common pasture can still be seen at Corse, suggesting that opposition to enclosure met with partial success.

Innovations in champion field management also reveal divisions of interest within peasant communities. Demand for cereals and legumes increased in the thirteenth century as the village populations grew. For example, in the group of small villages administered from Tredington (Warwickshire) the forty-eight tenants listed in the late twelfth century had increased to sixty-two by 1299.[18] More grain was needed for bread, ale, and fodder, not just in the producing villages, but also in towns. For example, grain from Tredington, which apparently had a high reputation, was carried as far as Worcester.[19] The cultivated area could not be increased as little waste or wood was left. A possible solution in the champion was to increase the area of arable planted each year by changing from two fields to three, and three

---

[14] D. Walker, ed., *The Cartulary of St Augustine's Bristol* (BRS 10, 1998), pp. 234–8.
[15] C. Dyer, 'Conflict in the Landscape: The Enclosure Movement in England, 1220–1349', *Landscape History* 29 (2007), pp. 21–33.
[16] R.H. Hilton, *A Medieval Society. The West Midlands at the End of the Thirteenth Century* (Cambridge, 1983), p. 152; C. Dyer, *An Age of Transition. Economy and Society in England in the Later Middle Ages* (Oxford, 2005), pp. 58–62.
[17] *RBW*, p. 215.   [18] *RBW*, pp. 280–8, 292–4.
[19] J.M. Wilson and C. Gordon, eds., *Early Compotus Rolls of the Priory of Worcester* (WHS, 1908), pp. 22–3, 31, 40.

fields are known in a handful of villages in central Gloucestershire and in northeast Warwickshire.[20] The great majority of champion villages kept their two fields, not necessarily in a spirit of conservative resistance to change, nor in ignorance of the potential benefits. The practical problems of reordering the whole complex arrangements of furlongs would have been daunting, while the increase in the cultivated area would have reduced the area for grazing, and more frequent cropping might have had negative effects on yields.[21] No doubt the possibilities were debated at village meetings, and usually the opponents of three fields prevailed.

Inhoking provided a more flexible way of increasing the area under cultivation without permanent transformations of the fields. An area of the fallow field would be surrounded by temporary fencing and ploughed and planted, so that part of the field would carry crops in two successive years. This practice became commonplace in villages in south-east Worcestershire and north Gloucestershire by the fourteenth century, for which lords gave permission. The conditions that were sometimes required suggest an awareness of the disadvantages, such as the stipulation by the abbot of Winchcomb that villagers inhoking land at Hailes (Gloucestershire) in 1296 would pay 2d per acre in compensation for the loss of grazing.[22] Conflicting interests emerged from a dispute at Shipston-on-Stour. This agricultural community's economy was stimulated by the adjacent new town, and it had a tradition of antagonism to its lord and quarrelling between neighbours. William Robins, a member of a prominent family, having obtained the agreement of the lord of the manor, fenced off a furlong of the fallow field and in the spring of 1342 planted it with pulse and barley.[23] The Shipston community responded by driving their cattle over the planted area, destroying the crops, and restoring the land to its proper use (in their eyes) as common pasture. Their actions were directed both at the ambitious Robins, and the lord who had supported him. The response to this direct action came from Robins in litigation before the lord's court, in which he claimed compensation for his loss of crops. Smaller scale inhoking continued at Shipston, followed again by litigation similar to that mounted by Robins: in 1378 Henry Mogge's barley was damaged by three tenants, and his pulse was destroyed in a separate incident.[24]

Despite the problems that inhoking caused, the practice persisted. It could be favoured by the community, like the whole homage at Alveston (Warwickshire) which obtained a licence to inhoke two furlongs in 1340. Around Elmley Castle (Worcestershire) the lord gave permission regularly, allowing Little Comberton in

---

[20] Roberts, 'Field Systems', pp. 206–9; Hall, *Open Fields*, p. 262; *VCH Glouc*, 8, pp. 224; 10, pp. 250, 261; 11, p. 194.
[21] H.S.A. Fox, 'The Alleged Transformation from Two-Field to Three-Field Systems in Medieval England', *EcHR*, 2nd series, 39 (1986), pp. 526–48.
[22] D. Royce, ed., *Landboc sive Registrum Monasterii Beatae Mariae Virginis...de Winchelcumba* (Exeter, 1892, vol. 2, pp. 297–8.
[23] WCL, E14.   [24] WCL, E28, E29.

1444 to inhoke a furlong.[25] Elsewhere we find more references to the same practice, called *hechyng*, and to divisions within a field called the *Hiche*. The ultimate development was to call parts of the fields 'every years' land' and to cease to have any fallow, or to intensify cultivation by changing from two fields to four fields. This was more easily achieved than introducing a three-field system, because each of the two fields could be split in two. However in theory it was a very radical modification of the farming system, as instead of a half of the arable fields being cropped each year, three-quarters were planted, and for fallow grazing the animals were confined to the limited space of a quarter of the fields. In practice the imbalance between arable and pasture was avoided by setting aside part of the fields as permanent or at least long-term pasture, often called leys. In addition one of the four courses was devoted entirely to pulse, which was intended as a fodder crop and therefore supported livestock, and in particular sheep. By no coincidence, the first village in the region to be recorded (in 1387) with four fields was Blackwell, next to Shipston[26] (Figure 2.4 shows a village's transition from two to four fields).

The decision to adopt a four-field system was often taken in a shadowy undocumented village meeting, and therefore the first indication comes from a simple statement that a holding was spread over four fields, perhaps many years after the change had been made. An exception was the village of Adlestrop (Gloucestershire) in 1498, where the court of Evesham Abbey approved the inception of the new four-field system, without making clear who was the initiator.[27] The monastery was not involved directly in the agriculture of Adlestrop, as the demesne was being leased by a farmer, though the farmer may have encouraged the lord's interest by recommending a reform of the fields. He had a say in the agreement as he was given an assurance that under the new rules he could drive his sheep through a several field called *le Ferdych*. The tenants had an area 'at the far end of the fields' in *le hechyng*, so they were already cultivating part of the fallow field. However, under the new four-field arrangement they were ordered to plant the *hechyng* according to the old rotation (*ab antiquo*), with fallow years. The new order, made with the assent of all tenants, was to follow the rotation of fallow, barley, pulse, and wheat, 'so that they have four fields' and 'none may sow in a field seed other than that ordered'. The authority of the Abbey added to the strength of the supporters of the change, as we should regard with suspicion the conventional phrase 'with the assent of all tenant'. The balance of farming in favour of pasture was adjusted in parallel with the introduction of the new rotation. No acreages are specified at Adlestrop, but at Welford-on-Avon, a Warwickshire village which had also divided its land into four fields, in the early sixteenth century, 143 acres of the 1,045 acres of potential arable, amounting to

[25] WCL, E1; *CR Elmley*, pp. 112–13.   [26] WCL, E33.   [27] TNA, SC2 175/77.

14 per cent, was described as uncultivated and therefore under grass, much of it 'on the hill', so in a less accessible part of the field system.[28]

The objective of all these changes was to keep as many animals as possible grazing on the fallow field and uncultivated arable, while supplementing their fodder with peas and beans. Arable production could be focussed on a relatively small area on which manure could be concentrated, and where the rotation ensured that wheat (the most valued crop) followed on from the legumes, which would increase the nitrogen available in the soil, and potentially maximize the yield.

Enclosure has been conventionally regarded as an existential threat to traditional field systems, and it has been over dramatized as an imposition by ruthless profiteering lords which in some villages brought the open fields and peasant farming to an end in the fifteenth and sixteenth centuries. Enclosures had a long history, and can be observed in charters and archaeological excavations from before the twelfth century. In the woodlands from c.1150 onwards both old and new closes and crofts could have been seen in their thousands across the region from the Malverns to the Avon, and in the Vale in Gloucestershire.

Enclosed fields were carved out of the woods in the assarting movement of the twelfth and thirteenth centuries, but piecemeal enclosure continued into the fourteenth and fifteenth centuries. Of the nineteen licensed enclosures in the long series of Halesowen records, thirteen belong to the period 1350–1450.[29] A peak in unlicensed enclosures at Ombersley was reached in 1463, when nineteen were the subjects of complaints to the manor court. The statement in the Ombersley court for 1462 that 'John Naissche enclosed a parcel of land in le Brannt' could have two meanings.[30] Firstly enclosure could refer to the erection of a fence, digging a ditch, raising a bank, planting a hedge, or (in the Cotswolds only) building a wall for the first time around a plot of common waste, commonly called an encroachment or purpresture. The same process in an open field could result from an adjacent group of selions or butts on the edge of the field, or near the tenant's house, being brought together by purchase or exchange. Secondly, enclosure could also mean extending a greater degree of control over the separate land by excluding grazing animals in the 'open time', that is, after the harvest or when the close was subject to fallow. The tenant holding the enclosure was expected to leave gates or gaps in the hedge open through which livestock could enter. Again clear divisions of interest set peasants against one another. Those who complained about unauthorized enclosure saw a threat to their ability to feed their animals, and used their influence in the manor court to protect their interests. Those who held the closes

---

[28] GA, P329/1, MI/1.
[29] R.K. Field, 'The Worcestershire Peasantry in the Later Middle Ages' (MA dissertation, University of Birmingham, 1962), pp. 81–4.
[30] WA, ref. 705:56, BA3910/27 (xviii).

wished to reserve any grass that they contained for their own beasts, and valued the option of cultivating their own land in the fallow year. Such tenants could also hope for aid from the lord. A compromise might be found, as at Longdon (Worcestershire) in 1455 after a series of enclosures had been presented as offending against custom. When tenants were making new closes in the waste they were told to observe the custom 'of old' (*ex antiquo*) by allowing access in the open time, but they could choose one close to hold as 'several' for their exclusive use.[31]

The decision to enclose did not always involve confrontation, or at least ways could be found to make the enclosure acceptable to its potential opponents. Tenants went to the lord of Stoke Prior, Worcestershire, in 1351 to seek permission to enclose parcels of meadow. This was a typical project to extend enclosure in an already partly enclosed woodland landscape, adjoining a curtilage and 'a field called Cornecroft', but the neighbours presumably needed to be placated and the applicants secured 'the consent of the whole court'.[32] The community at Bockleton (Worcestershire) treated a potential offender with flexibility. Alice Wyot in 1440 expressed a wish to enclose a field called Denefeld at all times, so preventing any common grazing. She was told that the land should be opened after the harvest each year, and in every third year when it lay fallow. The neighbours however made a concession 'out of love of Alice' that she could keep it completely enclosed in her lifetime, if she gave a half pound of wax to the church.[33] The villagers preferred a community asset to benefit, not the lord.

An apparently paradoxical feature of the regulation of enclosure was that, alongside the reports of unlicensed enclosure which was in particular eroding the amount of available common pasture in the woodlands, another stream of complaints, presentments, and by-laws related to the failure of tenants to maintain their existing hedges. They were required to block gaps and maintain gates. These rules often related to the long and complex hedges that surrounded the cultivated open fields and protected the crops from livestock. The need for precautions continued from the planting of corn in October and November, until the harvest season in the following year when livestock could damage the ripening corn and the cut sheaves. As common fields were cultivated in both champion and woodland landscapes, this fencing and hedging campaign applied everywhere. Individual tenants who suffered from animals straying into the closes around their houses brought pleas of trespass against the owners of the beasts, seeking compensation for grass eaten and gardens trampled. These problems arose from poor maintenance of hedges and fences, the owners of the animals claimed.

The most substantial hedges were formidable topographical features, containing many mature trees, which might be felled, pollarded, and 'shredded' for their

---

[31] WAM, 21161.   [32] WCL, E214.   [33] SRO, D(w)1788/P33/B5.

branches, for which the lord's licence was often required. In about 1500 Thomas Waring, a tenant of John Archer in Tanworth-in-Arden, listed the most valuable trees in woods and hedgerows on the Archer estate.[34] In one hedge he saw twenty-eight great oaks, eleven ashes, and aspens. The hedge also contained coppiced underwood such as hazel. Thick growths of bushes were common elements in hedges throughout the region, which attracted those in pursuit of firewood. Interspersed along the hedge between the trees and bushes, according to illustrations made in the early modern period, were short stretches of fencing, so the hedge might contain 'dead hedge' in addition to the living vegetation. Stone walls surrounded fields in the Cotswolds, at Tormarton in 1495 for example, but even on stone-rich uplands hedges, not walls, predominated. At Kingscote high up above the Stroud valley in 1435 hedges were to be 'pleshed' and at Hawkesbury in the same year also on the hills, and at Stoke Giffard on lower ground, hedges were 'plaited' or 'woven'.[35] The vocabulary is that of living hedges being laid by cutting partly through upright stems of bushes and small trees (pleaching), and bending them to create a dense intertwined barrier, as used to be standard practice in the nineteenth and early twentieth centuries. Such hedges with closely packed and preferably thorny branches would present straying animals with an impenetrable obstacle. Lords' officials sent carts to woods to dig hedging plants, no doubt collecting a number of species, though with a preference for hawthorn and blackthorn. Peasants must have done the same. Hawthorn branches were much in demand for dead hedging, but fencing was regarded (at Hawkesbury in 1468) as inferior to live plants.[36]

So far, the contentious enclosures have been shown to have arisen from closes being hedged or set apart one at a time. 'Enclosure by agreement', by which hundreds of acres of land might be simultaneously divided into a dozen or more closes, required careful negotiation and raised inevitable opposition from those who lost access to the land taken into closes. Ingelstone, a hamlet of Hawkesbury (Gloucestershire) had its fields enclosed in 1467–8.[37] The lord's steward implemented the agreement 'by the assent and consent of all of the tenants'. He delegated to six tenants the task of 'separating and dividing all of the fields between the tenants there' by Michaelmas, the beginning of the agricultural year. It was agreed that the new fences should be made well and competently by Lady Day (25 March), a rather late date. The arrangements for the enclosure, while implying unity among the cultivators, hints at difficulties because first choice of one of the

---

[34] L.D.W. Smith, 'A Survey of Building Timber and other Trees in the Hedgerows of a Warwickshire Estate c.1500', *TBWAS* 90 (1980), pp. 65–73.
[35] Bodleian Library, MS Rawlinson B317; GA, D471/M2; TNA, SC2/175/52; GA, Badminton muniments D2700 MJ11/1/2.
[36] Magdalen College, Oxford, Quinton EP 35/9 (collecting hedging plants in 1430–1); TNA, SC2/175/55.
[37] TNA, SC2/175/55.

new closes was given to Richard Heynes, perhaps to placate a dissenter. The well-documented enclosure of the land of the sixteen 'halfyardland men' at Sambourn (Warwickshire) at some time before 1477 created a new set of fields containing about 240 acres.[38] Again not everyone was on board, as Thomas Beche attempted to pasture his cattle on the enclosed land, presumably thereby claiming his common right. In 1478 the sixteen were ordered that they 'should have all the land within the field called *halfyard grownde* several at all times of year', and they were reminded to repair hedges to keep cattle out. In a separate dispute 'great discord' arose over the allocation of five selions which had been left outside the enclosures when Thomas Roper one of the sixteen claimed two of them. The other fifteen were told to enquire 'to which part they belong'. The course of enclosure was evidently not running smoothly, and we understand the reluctance of villagers to embark on such complex schemes.

The tenants with closes gained the option of cropping in the fallow year and increasing the frequency of crops. Alternatively, the close could be converted to long-term or permanent pasture, which was the case with a Chaddesley Corbett tenant who received approval for building a sheepcote on enclosed land held in severalty called *Scruggesfeldes*.[39] Most of the other changes in land management that we have seen in the period 1350–1540, such as changes in rotation and the introduction of leys, were designed to shift the balance from arable to pasture.

Peasant communities are sometimes idealized, and are portrayed as showing wisdom and cohesion. We have seen that almost all of the adaptations and reforms were accompanied by conflict. These disagreements did not result in much violence, though tempers might have flared when animals found in the wrong place were impounded and then freed by their owner in an act of 'poundbreach'. In other situations, the various mechanism for resolving conflict peaceably seem to have worked.

Modern commentators have identified a drift to an apocalyptic culmination of the endless compromises of peasant farming. One view is that the commons were doomed to a tragic end, as individual ambition was incompatible with the sharing of resources. The land would be ruined by over grazing, and the commons were travelling on a one-way street from community co-operation to individual ownership. This was not the case, and the commons, though mired in controversy, served a vital purpose. They were managed through various agencies, from informal groups of peasants, to village meetings, manor courts, and higher authorities, all of which maintained rules inefficiently but well enough to keep the common

---

[38] SCLA, DR5/2758; C. Dyer, *Warwickshire Farming, 1349-c.1520* (DS Occasional Paper, 27, 1981), p. 26.
[39] SCLA, DR5/2756.

functioning for the benefit of its users.[40] Land was being enclosed gradually from the twelfth century (and before) until *c.*1500 when a fifth of the land in the champion and a third in the woodlands in the west midlands lay in closes. Even by 1640 in England as a whole enclosure had captured less than half (47 per cent), of the land.[41]

Crops and their use

The tithe records of twenty-nine parishes provide a useful guide to peasant crops. Rectors of parish churches were entitled to a tenth of all produce, which included hay, wool, lambs, hens' eggs, and garden produce, but the largest item was the tenth part of the field crops, of grain and legumes. In many cases the tithe was collected, not by a clergyman in charge of the parish, but by a monastery that had appropriated the rectory. Some tithe totals included crops on the lord's demesne, but peasant output made up the majority. In practice the demesne crops were often separated from the main tithe collection, in which case the tithes are a very good guide to the types of grain and legumes grown by peasants.

The sample of documented parishes gives an overview of the region as they represent different landscapes and environments. They stretch in date from the end of the thirteenth century to the late fifteenth, with a bias towards the later part of the period because Worcester Cathedral Priory's records relate to fourteen parishes in the fifteenth century[42] (Figure 6.2).

Peasants in the champion districts of Worcestershire and Warwickshire mainly depended on wheat as their winter corn, with rye and maslin, a mixture of wheat and rye, in some Avon valley parishes. In the spring the champion peasants planted drage (barley and oats mixed) and pulse (peas and beans). In addition to the ten champion parishes to which this generalization applies, in Gloucestershire three Vale of Berkeley parishes could be added, though they grew barley, not drage. Bishop's Cleeve could be included, because although the village itself lay on the edge of the Cotswolds, most of its crops were planted on low lying clay soils. Drage was an especially preferred crop among champion peasants, often

---

[40] M. De Moor, *The Dilemma of the Commoners. Understanding the Use of Common Pool Resources in Long-Term Perspective* (Cambridge, 2015); A.J.L. Winchester, 'Property Rights, "Good Neighbourhood" and Sustainability in the Management of Common Land in England and Wales, 1235–1965', in *Rural Societies and Environments at Risk*, edited by B. Van Bavel and E. Thoen (Turnhout, 2013), pp. 309–29.

[41] J.R. Wordie, 'The Chronology of English Enclosure, 1500–1914', *EcHR*, second series, 36 (1983), pp. 483–505.

[42] WCL, C500–C520, and Hereford Cathedral Library R704 were the *estimationes bladorum* which predicted (without too much inaccuracy) demesne crops and the tithes: C. Dyer, 'Peasant Farming in Late Medieval England: Evidence from the Tithe Estimates of Worcester Cathedral Priory', in *Peasants and Lords in the Medieval English Economy: Essays in Honour of Bruce M.S. Campbell*, edited by M. Kowaleski, J. Langdon, and P.R. Schofield (Turnhout, 2015), pp. 83–109.

accounting for a half of the total. The cultivators of Long Itchington (Warwickshire) another champion parish, grew much drage, but oats were prominent as well as pulse.[43]

Peasant crops were more varied in the woodlands. In western Worcestershire, wheat was preferred, accounting for a third to a half of the total, with varying amounts of barley, drage, oats, and pulse. At Castle Morton a fifth of the output

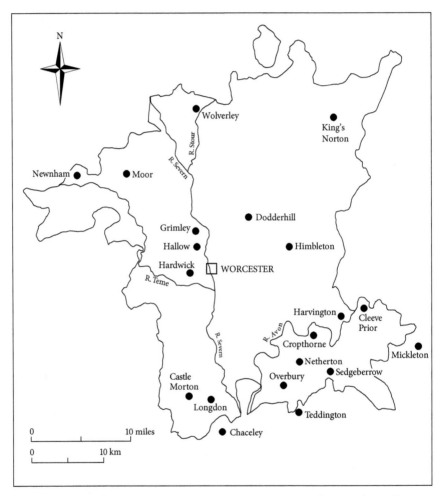

Figure 6.2 Crops from tithe receipts, mainly Worcestershire. The map shows the parishes with evidence; the pie charts the proportions of crops. The Worcester Priory parishes are documented in the fifteenth century, the others in the early fourteenth (sources: notes 42, 44).

---

[43] A. Sabin, ed., *Some Manorial Accounts of St Augustine's Abbey, Bristol* (Bristol Record Society, 22, 1960), pp. 106–8; Corpus Christi College, Oxford, B14/2/3/6; TNA, SC6 1039/14.

PEASANTS AND THEIR CROPS 161

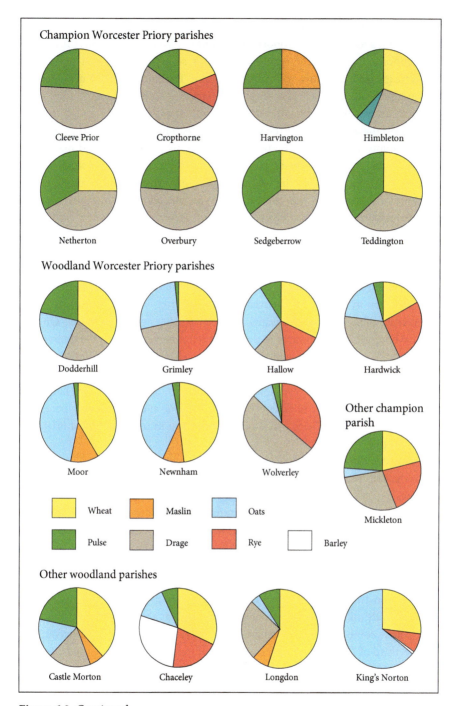

Figure 6.2 Continued

consisted of peas and beans. In the north of the county wheat, rye, or maslin made about a half, a much higher proportion of winter-sown crops than was the case in the champion parishes. The spring sown crops sometimes included drage, but oats were grown in quantity, with very little pulse. The cultivators of King's Norton on the high, cold, and wet plateau of north-east Worcestershire in *c.* 1300 produced an unusually high proportion, 64 per cent, of oats.[44]

What do these tell us about the strategies of peasant production? They made a realistic assessment of the soils and environment, by growing rye and maslin on the sands and gravels of the river valleys, and at Wolverley. Oats were suited to the cold clays of King's Norton. The balance of peasants' crops differed from those of their lords although they were cultivating very similar adjacent land. At Hallow in the fifteenth century the lord favoured rye, and grew very little wheat, while the peasants consistently planted more wheat than rye, perhaps because of their preference for wheat bread. In the spring at Hallow the lord preferred to plant drage and oats, while the peasants grew more pulse. One motive for peasants including much pulse in their rotations could have been to benefit the next grain crop from extra nitrogen in the soil, so the rotation at Adlestrop was specified to have the wheat crop following pulse. Peasants also fed their livestock with pulses. On the seven Worcester Priory manors in the Worcestershire woodlands, the cultivators increased the proportion of winter-sown crops (wheat, rye, and maslin), from 45 per cent at the beginning of the fifteenth century to 54 per cent in 1416–1462. They were supplying their own households with corn for bread, and seeking better returns in the market. At Hallow both the demesne and the peasants increased their pulse planting in 1416, which might have been in response to a short-term rise in the price of pulses.

Before deciding if subsistence or the market had most influence on peasant production, it might help to look at individuals. The grain and legumes collected as tithes represented an aggregate of many individual holdings, all of whom behaved differently, as can be seen by examining the crops harvested after peasants left their holdings, fled after committing a felony, or died, leaving the lord to harvest the crops. Occasionally an individual followed the cropping pattern of his neighbours precisely, such as Walter Longeman of Cleeve Prior in 1374, who planted 2 acres of wheat, 2 acres of drage, and 2 acres of pulse: the tithes of Cleeve typically consisted of one-third of each of those crops.[45] Others had made decisions radically different from their neighbours, such as a tenant of Sedgeberrow in 1417 whose combination of crops included 47 per cent of pulse; pulse accounted for one-third of the tithes of his parish. At Teddington a few years earlier a tenant specialized in drage (46 per cent of the total), compared with 35 per cent of drage in the tithe corn.[46] A clue to interpreting the thinking of individuals can be found in the case of Richard Charlet of Cleeve Prior, who took on lease the parson's

---

[44] WAM, 21034–21037, 21039, 21040, 21043, 21045; WCL, E14.
[45] WCL, E26.   [46] WCL, C510, C505.

glebe, which was not a peasant holding, but at 50 acres (of which 25 acres would have been sown each year) was much the same size as a number of the larger holdings in Cleeve of the mid-fifteenth century. Charlet's choice of crops in 1456 may well have been designed to satisfy the needs of his household, with 46 per cent of the sown area being planted with wheat for making bread, 30 per cent with drage for brewing, 22 per cent with pulse as an ingredient in pottage, but mostly for feeding livestock. The total of grain and legumes that would have been harvested exceeded a normal family's consumption needs, so Charlet would have been able to sell about 7 quarters of wheat and 2 quarters of pulse. Two years later Charlet's priorities had changed totally: 54 per cent of his crops were drage, with 33 per cent of pulse and 13 per cent of wheat. He had evidently decided to grow a large amount of drage with marketing in mind: this relatively rapid change suggests a flexibility in decision-making.[47] Drage was often malted and brewed, and ale consumption was rising.

If Charlet specialized in order to cater for the market, this must explain some of the other unbalanced range of crops grown by individuals, which have already been cited. The woodland parishes expanded their production of winter-sown cereals, including rye, because they could see increased demand from towns along the Severn valley such as Worcester, and from long-distance trade on the river. Rye was eaten in the city of Worcester in the sixteenth century, especially by the less affluent, and in the same period rye figures prominently among the grains kept by householders for family consumption in Coventry.[48] Oats were not much eaten by humans, apart from oatmeal as an ingredient in pottage, but they did have an importance in household consumption as a brewing corn in the absence of barley and drage. Oats were fed both to horses and pigs, and were traded into regions (such as the champion) where they were not much grown. Oats were required in towns for the many horses used for riding and transport.

Archaeological finds of carbonized cereals inform us about their consumption, and confirm the importance of wheat. Grain was charred by accident when it was being dried before being ground for flour, and is sometimes found near the hearth. The grain preserved in this way indicates not just the crops that were grown, but also those that were eaten. On every site, wheat grains were much more plentiful than any other: at Bishop's Cleeve 1,064 wheat grains compare with 135 grains of barley and 106 of oats. A rural site near Moreton-in-Marsh, also in north Gloucestershire, with much wheat (4,293 grains) also had a significant amount of rye (1,330 grains) together with 527 of barley, and 699 of oats, and a few remnants of peas and beans. Quantities of burnt wheat grains are reported

---

[47] WCL, E64; on flexibility of peasant production, B. Dodds, *Peasants and Production in the Medieval North-East: The Evidence from Tithes 1270–1536* (Woodbridge, 2007), pp. 132–61.

[48] A.D. Dyer, *The City of Worcester in the Sixteenth Century* (Leicester, 1973), p. 167; J.M. Wilson, ed., *Accounts of the Priory of Worcester 1521–2* (WHS, 1907), pp. 7–8; M.D. Harris, ed., *The Coventry Leet Book*, part 3 (Early English Text Society, Original Series, 138, 1909), pp. 674–5.

from Burton Dassett, Goldicote, Pinbury, and the other excavated medieval rural sites.[49]

Pulse and oats were fed to animals 'in straw', meaning that the livestock were given peas in their haulm, and sheaves of oats. Straw left after threshing had many functions in the household and on the holding. It provided fodder, litter (for animals), bedding (for people), fuel, and building material. Each type of straw had its own uses: for example, rye straw was valued for thatching, and oat straw was fed to horses and cattle, but it seems unlikely that crops were selected on the basis of these secondary uses.

Medieval peasant households put some effort into their gardens and orchards, and spent time gathering in woods and wastes. The region had a strong reputation for its fruitfulness: in the twelfth century William of Malmesbury, in a passage which belongs to a genre of writing about 'ideal places' extolled the virtues of the Vale of Gloucester, telling his readers that 'even the most bored slacker' would be enthused by the fertility of the crops.[50] He singled out for praise the fruit trees lining the roads. The scale of gardening can be judged by the size of the spaces allotted for it, which could be very small: one at Henbury-in-the-Salt-Marsh in 1376-7 measured 21 feet by 20 feet (7m by 6m), though larger spaces suitable for gardens can be seen behind abandoned houses on village sites, up to 30m by 50m. The excavators of Burton Dassett Southend identified some areas as likely gardens; for example, a space 20m wide and at least 10m long in tenement A. In some places tenants could rent a separate garden which was not part of the house plot, like two parcels of *Plumtrelond* at Bromsberrow (Gloucestershire).[51]

Although the gardens occupied limited space, they were potentially productive through intensive inputs of labour (especially from women), and manure. The total output of apples at Bourton-on-the-Hill (Gloucestershire), a village with about seventy households, in 1295-6 is shown to have attained 255 bushels.[52] The crops have left traces in the botanical evidence from rural excavations, such as apple pips and plum stones. Urban sites are relevant to this enquiry because much of the garden produce is likely to have originated in the countryside and brought into the town for sale. A fifteenth-century latrine at Worcester contained traces of mustard, damson, cherry, pear, apple, gooseberry, fennel, and cabbage.[53] The

---

[49] D. Enright and M. Watts, *A Romano-British and Medieval Settlement Site at Stoke Road, Bishop's Cleeve, Gloucestershire* (BGAS Archaeological Report, 1, 2002), p. 53; M. Watts, ed., *Prehistoric and Medieval Occupation at Moreton-in-Marsh and Bishop's Cleeve, Gloucestershire* (BGAS Archaeological Report, 5, 2007), p.44. For the other sites see notes 27, 33, and 34 in Chapter 5. The report on burnt grain from Burton Dassett Southend can be accessed at https://doi.org/10.5284/1083492.

[50] M. Winterbottom, ed., *William of Malmesbury, Gesta Pontificorum Anglorum* (Oxford, 2007), p. 445.

[51] WA, ref. 009:1, BA 2636/166/92235; Palmer and Parkhouse, *Burton Dassett Southend*, the plant economy report can be accessed at https://doi.org/10.5284/1083492; Gloucester Public Library, R59.2, R59.4, dated 1388-9 and 1487.

[52] WAM, 8247.

[53] J. Greig, 'The Investigation of a Medieval Barrel Latrine from Worcester', *Journal of Archaeological Science* 8 (1981), pp. 265-82.

documents which make most frequent reference to rural gardens are the trespass actions brought to the manor court by tenants whose gardens had been invaded by animals, which might refer to vegetables or herbs being damaged. Cabbages, leeks, and onions were commonly grown, together with such trees as apple, pear, plum, and walnut. Tithe to be collected at Beckford (Worcestershire) in 1487–8 included 'onions and all sorts of herbs', and apples, pears, and crabs, meaning crab apples.[54]

Tenants in retirement were usually promised specific quantities of cereals, but occasionally access to a garden was mentioned, and more specifically fruit from apple and pear trees. An agreement at Elmley Castle in 1470 allowed William Sparke a warden pear tree, and half of the fruit from the pear genet tree that grew in the garden of the house that he was surrendering, showing his regard for these varieties.[55] Peasants grew hemp and flax sometimes in gardens, or in small temporary plots carved out of the common pasture. The fibres could have brought in considerable sums of money, judging from tithe valuation at Monks Kirby in 1411 as high as 13s, indicating that the crop was worth more than £6[56] (see 'Industry within peasant society' in Chapter 9).

Edible plants could be gathered in woods and wastes, and while these sources of free food were especially important for the village poor, they could also add to the diet of the better-off. From rural excavations come evidence for hazelnuts, sloes, blackberries, and elderberries, while urban finds (with likely rural origins) include wild strawberries. The documents focus on the vegetation collected, often because excessive quantities were taken, or some other nuisance caused, including bracken, broom, furze, gorse, and thorns, to be used as litter, fuel, and hedging material, and rushes for strewing. As was the case with the more plentiful and essential field crops of grain and legumes, the purpose of horticulture and gathering was partly, indeed mostly, to satisfy the needs of the household, but some of the produce was sold, hence the archaeological evidence from towns for plants such as bracken, heather and gorse, and complaints in the manor court that rushes, thorns, and furze were being over-exploited for commercial gain (see 'Poverty and industry' in Chapter 9).

Arable husbandry

Peasants expressed views on good and bad husbandry when in the fourteenth century the jurors commented in the manor court on the deficiencies of lords' officials (especially reeves and bailiffs) and specialist employees such as shepherds. The criticisms were encouraged by the estate administrators, following a

---

[54] GA, GDR 40/T2.   [55] CR Elmley, p. 174.
[56] Lincolnshire Record Office, 2 Anc 2/10/1.

well-established medieval technique for checking on the efficiency and honesty of officials. Reeves also had an occasional opportunity to explain their management, for example, in dialogues with auditors. The comments of these ordinary country people who were temporarily occupying office as jurors and reeves bring us near to hearing the voices of peasants, though their views were filtered on being entered into official records.

The criticisms included allegations of corruption, such as a reeve diverting implements and labour from the demesne to work on his own holding.[57] Here the comments will focus on husbandry methods and practices presumed to be based on the peasants' own experiences. They were apparently applying to the demesne the standards of agriculture that they would ideally have practised on their own holdings. An obvious example was the maintenance of fencing to exclude livestock from the sown fields, and reeves sometimes failed to do this.

A repeated complaint concerned the lack of thorough cultivation of the demesne arable. A reeve would cut corners by omitting the headlands, the last part of the field to be ploughed. It was said that the ploughing of the fallow was neglected, and the second ploughing, the *rebinatio*, was not done. This could have reduced yields because repeated ploughing was a means of weed control. The ploughing might be carried out, but not the harrowing that broke up the clods and helped to create a seed bed. Manure might not be spread, or it was 'not spread well'. A reeve justified extra expenditure to the auditors by claiming that he was following good practice by sowing beans by hand, which meant dibbling a hole to receive each seed. A thirteenth-century treatise on estate management from Gloucester Abbey calculated that twelve women could plant 3 acres with a quarter of beans in a day.[58] One reeve hired labour to remove weed seeds from the grain intended for sowing, which was a good practice but led to extra expense.

Criticisms of inadequate demesne cultivation included a lack of weeding, sometimes because it was not done at all, but also because 'it was not well weeded'. Reeves who did carry out weeding would find, perhaps because of earlier neglect, that the land was infested with thistles and removing them needed extra spending. The reeve of Weston-juxta-Cherrington (Warwickshire) complained of the growth of thistles soon after the Black Death, when labour to deal with them was scarce. The managers of the demesnes at Grimley and Wolverley in 1412 blamed a low yield of the rye crop on the growth of tares.[59]

The harvest was always a period of anxiety for cultivators. To save labour, scythes rather than sickles might be used, which reduced the yield because more

---

[57] C. Briggs, 'Monitoring Demesne Managers through the Manor Court Before and After the Black Death', in *Survival and Discord in Medieval Society*, edited by R. Goddard, J. Langdon, and M. Muller (Turnhout, 2010), pp. 179–95.

[58] D. Oschinsky, *Walter of Henley and Other Treatises on Estate Management and Accounting* (Oxford, 1971), p. 473.

[59] SCLA, DR98/865–6; WCL, C506.

grains might be spilled from the ears. Damage would be caused by animals entering the stubble field before all of the sheaves had been carried, and workers had to be closely supervised lest they steal corn. Once brought into the manorial *curia* (farmyard), the stored crops might not be well protected. Juries reported at Netherton (Worcestershire) that in 1389 the barn had defective walls and a poorly maintained roof, and at Blackwell in 1370 a stack of pulse had deteriorated because it was not adequately thatched.[60]

The failings of the reeves and bailiffs provide a useful commentary on husbandry practices, and the same problems were occasionally reported on peasant holdings. From litigation, reports of neglect of ploughing and building repair, and by-laws requiring better cultivation, a picture emerges of fencing in need of maintenance, failure to cultivate, particularly ploughing the fallow, neglect of manuring and non-repair of barns. Many of the criticisms of demesne husbandry were made in the late fourteenth century, when the demesne managers were having to cope with the shortage of labour. The difficulties of recruitment of the full-time demesne servants, such as ploughmen, carters, and shepherds emerged from reports to the courts that the demesne lacked at least one of these important workers for at least part of the year. The gaps must have been filled by hiring workers for short terms.

Peasant holdings cannot be regarded simply as smaller versions of the demesnes, as is apparent from their particular labour problems. They employed servants, but expected them to carry out a variety of tasks. There was not enough ploughing on a 30-acre holding to employ a specialist ploughman, and if a servant did the ploughing, he would be expected to turn his hand in season to ditching, threshing, haymaking, and harvesting. Much of the labour resource of the holding for field work consisted of odd days and weeks of working time gained from family members. The lords' work force consisted mainly of adult males, while the peasants had to make the best use of youths, females of all ages, and the elderly. The lords' workers were contracted to work for a year or half year, but peasant employment was more flexible—a servant might occasionally work for other villagers.

The peasants' shepherd would be a specialist worker, and his duties were regarded as important enough for him to be exempted from the *bedrip*, the harvest service performed by the whole household. These shepherds are rarely mentioned as individuals, but a Shipston court for 1325 dealing with sheep invading the lord's land, criticized 'all of the shepherds of Shipston, except the shepherds of Hugh Baret, Juliana Jenecokes, and Robert Gerveys'.[61] This was at a time when many sheep flocks were no larger than sixty animals, so that employing a shepherd full-time seems a luxury, but the larger flocks of 200 to 300 sheep

---

[60] WCL, E34, E24.   [61] WCL, E10.

which later became more common would keep a worker fully occupied. After the epidemics labour problems might arise from a reduction in the number of children, and the absence of older children who found work or land elsewhere. Family pressure could be exerted on young people to stay at home and work, like those over fifteen years described as 'son and servant' in the 1381 poll tax (see 'Character of family life' in Chapter 5). Labour could be managed effectively in the family context. Weeding, for example, for which demesnes could not recruit and reward sufficient workers, was a relatively light task well-suited to children, women, and the elderly, and could be carried out efficiently by well-motivated workers with manual dexterity, and a willingness to bend down to the task. Cleaning the seed corn by removing weed seeds also benefited from attention to detail and patient endurance of tedium. Family labour would in theory be committed to the work because each worker would benefit, but to that self-interest should be added the moral pressure that could be exerted. A forceful head could remind other members of the household of the benefits of work. The amount of weeding done on a lord's demesne has been calculated at one to two days per acre of crops, some dipping below one per acre. A peasant household with three workers (perhaps including a female and an adolescent) could surely find three working days per acre to deal with 15 sown acres?[62]

In conclusion, the quantity of work applied to peasant holdings and its quality suggests that peasant farming could be well supplied with labour, and did not need to monitor wage costs as did the demesne managers, partly because the holding was organized on different principles. However, the peasants' traditional style of labour-intensive cultivation might have come under strain in the post-plague countryside.

Farming methods and techniques

How effective was peasant agricultural technique, in terms of implements, methods of maintaining or improving fertility, and crop storage? The equipment for farming is well represented in documents and from archaeological excavation and this discussion is based on 383 documentary references to relevant objects, and about 250 finds from excavations. Tools and implements are mentioned in various circumstances, such as lists of the principal goods which tenants were supposed to keep in their houses during a tenancy, or inventories made when a tenant left a holding. But they also feature as heriots, stolen property, loans that had not been returned, and weapons. The heavier pieces of equipment account for a high proportion of the total, around 200 items. These were wains, carts, ploughs, and harrows, together with yokes for oxen, collars for horses, harness, ropes, iron

[62] D. Stone, *Decision-Making in Medieval Agriculture* (Oxford, 2005), pp. 109–13.

chains, and ox goads. The plough, the wooden implement, was valued separately at a few pence, while the iron share and coulter, sizeable pieces of metal, were worth 2s. A fully operational plough with its iron-bound 'foot' (in the west midlands it had no wheels)[63] and all the means of harnessing the oxen would be worth a few shillings, some way behind a wain or cart, which was often valued at 10s. The most expensive vehicles were those with wheels fitted with iron tyres, but of the fifty carts and wains recorded in the west midland documents only fourteen were said to have had wheels of this type. The iron tyres gave the wheels an extended life, and were of particular value for running on hard roads, on journeys to market, for example. Most peasant carts and wains were intended to travel across fields, or on tracks without metalled surfaces, and their loads were sheaves, corn, manure, and wood fuel being transported around the scattered parcels of the holding, or back to the house and buildings.

Ploughs were pulled by oxen, as were wains. After 1340 horse-drawn carts greatly outnumber wains, in the same way that there were more horse harrows than ox harrows. The advance of horse hauling was a comparatively late development. Before 1200 peasants used quite large and heavy ox-drawn vehicles, for which the Latin terms were *plaustrum* and *carrus*, but by the late thirteenth century, even in this conservative region, the technology was changing. At Tredington (Warwickshire) tenants were expected to carry fuel for the lord's hearth in a *plaustrum* in c.1170, but in a cart (*carecta*) by 1299.[64] A horse-drawn vehicle needed a smaller number of animals, and was faster and lighter than a wain, but it carried a smaller load. Horse hauling had increased in the later Middle Ages, and there were more riding horses, but the plough was even in 1500 still pulled by oxen, though there are hints of some mixed teams.

The most frequently mentioned hand tools were forks, either of wood or of iron, with two tines or three, and were mostly intended for moving sheaves or manure. Peasant axes appear often in the records, mainly because on some manors the woodward by custom seized the offenders' axes in response to illicit tree felling or branch lopping. The other tools were used in the successive processes of cultivation: the seedlip from which seed corn was broadcast; hoes and weeding hooks; sickles for cutting corn, wielded by both women and men, forks for pitching sheaves on to carts, and then on to stacks at the barn; ladders and ropes for making and securing stacks, both in the barn and in the yard, flails and winnowing fans, with sieves and riddles used in threshing, and bushel measures and sacks for preparing the grain for sale. A hair cloth would enable grain to be dried over a low fire, or for malting.

For tasks away from the arable fields, scythes cut hay (though sometimes they were used in the grain harvest), and forks had a role in the hay field. An iron rake

---

[63] J. Langdon, *Horses, Oxen and Technological Innovation* (Cambridge, 1986), pp. 127–41.
[64] *RBW*, pp. 281, 293; Langdon, *Horses, Oxen and Technological Innovation*, pp. 246–50.

is mentioned once, suggesting that they were usually made cheaply of wood. Hand tools for digging, mattocks, shovels, and spades, were perhaps most often used in digging ditches along the hedges around the fields, but also for the 'water furrows', for drainage in the fields. Hand digging may have supplemented ploughing in awkward corners or where the oxen trampled the earth when manoeuvring at the end of the strips. Mattocks broke clods which resisted harrowing. Hedges were managed with the aid of axes and billhooks. Sheep shearing was the only task in livestock rearing which required a specific tool, though shears also had domestic uses.

The archaeological finds sometimes coincide with the documentary evidence; for example, sickle and scythe blades are found, though the latter are represented only by fragments. Such large iron tools were too valuable to be discarded, but were recycled by the smith. The trade in scrap and the frequent reworking of worn-out implements explains the absence from archaeological sites of plough shares, coulters, and iron tyres from carts. The smaller fittings from ploughs and carts, often too incomplete and badly corroded to be easily identified, probably feature among the various rings, chain links, staples, and spikes scattered around archaeological sites. Some items are not included in the documents. The number of horseshoes, with seventy-nine from the extensive excavations at Burton Dassett Southend, nine from Upton, nine from Goldicote, three from Pinbury, and as many as thirteen from the poor site at Coton suggests a high level of horse use.[65] Weeding tools are rather sparsely recorded in the documents but blades of hoes, weeding hooks, and spuds, all consisting of sharp iron heads once mounted on long wooden hafts, are routine finds in excavations. They were wielded with precision, with each weed removed individually so as not to disturb the corn, but this method took time.

Numerous finds on settlement sites are hones or whetstones, with eighty-eight from Burton Dassett Southend and seventeen at Upton, of which the documents make no mention. They were needed to sharpen the many blades, including knives, shears, sickles, scythes, and axes. They were employed inside the house, indicated by grooves on them for sharpening needles and pins, but their main use would have been in the fields, and they were kept readily available, with a hole drilled for suspension. They were made of specialist stone, including one type that was imported from Norway. Larger blades, especially those of scythes, could be sharpened (at Upton and Pinbury) with a rotary grindstone.

The archaeological finds reflect social inequalities, which means that metal small finds are much more numerous at sites such as Burton Dassett and Upton, than at the poor hamlet of cottagers at Coton. The documents enable more precise comparisons, and in particular they show that yardlanders and

---

[65] The publication of the excavated sites are to be found in notes 27, 33, and 34 in Chapter 5. The small finds report for Burton Dassett Southend can be accessed at https://doi.org/10.5284/1083492.

half-yardlanders were equipped with ploughs and carts (or wains), and these implements were not included in the inventories of those with smaller holdings. A quarter-yardlander in 1402 at Sedgeberrow (Worcestershire) owned a cart and a harrow, but that stands out as an anomaly.[66] From the small sample of cottagers and smallholders for whom we have lists of possessions it has been suggested that their hand tools may have been used to cultivate their holdings. A striking example was Richard Sclatter of Elmley Castle, an artisan, who owned a spade and a shovel when his goods were recorded in 1457.[67] Perhaps the smallholders dug their land by hand and foot, and it has even been suggested that they produced a more thorough result than that achieved by ploughing. However, spades were not standard possessions among the cottars, but on the contrary were as likely to be owned by the half-yardlanders and yardlanders, and seem to have supplemented the ploughs rather than providing an alternative to them. While a very small holding of an acre or two could have been dug in reasonable time, the tenants who lacked ploughs in the west midlands included quarter-yardlanders with 7 or 8 acres which would have needed many days' work. This was especially arduous work for cultivators with a clumsy wooden spade with a small iron shoe, very different from its efficient modern steel successor.[68] The cultivator's time was limited because, like Richard Sclatter (who roofed buildings with stone slates) they had other paid work to supplement the income from their land.

Smallholders arranged for their land to be ploughed by their better-off neighbours. Those who owned ploughs had spare ploughing capacity. A yardlander in a two-field village would plough 7 or 8 acres in the October to December winter ploughing season, which if he could manage a normal half acre per day would take fifteen or sixteen days. He would be occupied on other days with such tasks as harrowing and sowing, but he would have days when he could transfer his plough and labour on to the land of other tenants. It was a common practice, which is recorded when the arrangement went wrong and a plea of broken contract was pursued through the manor court. Thomas Oweyn of Bockleton (Worcestershire) in 1310 had agreed with Walter de Middelton and John Ragun that they should plough 2 acres, but they did not. At Longdon in the same county in 1378 John Martyn should have ploughed as agreed the land of Alice Notte for two days, and in 1379 William Payn of Alveston (Warwickshire) made a contract for John West to plough 3 acres, but he failed to do so. The Halesowen records between 1270 and 1349 contain fifteen cases in which oxen were hired, thirty-two hirings of ploughs, harrows, and carts, and fifty-seven references to contracts

---

[66] R.K. Field, 'Worcestershire Peasant Buildings, Household Goods and Farming Equipment in the Later Middle Ages', *Med Arch* 9 (1965), p. 138.
[67] *CR Elmley*, p. 148.
[68] J. Myrdal and A. Sapoznik, 'Technology, Labour and Productivity Potential in Peasant Agriculture: England *c.*1000–1348', *AgHR* 65 (2017), pp. 194–212.

to carry out agricultural tasks, including ploughing and harrowing.[69] A will inventory of 1495 includes 21s owed by four people for 'tilling', which refers to a plough owner hiring his implement and labour to neighbours as a source of profit.[70]

The quarter-yardlanders rarely owned a plough, but are found with oxen, revealed when a heriot was taken. If they could contribute an ox or two to the full eight ox team, and presumably their own labour, their land could be worked as a joint operation. Sharing ploughing equipment and pooling beasts to make up a team were widespread practices in medieval England, but are only occasionally documented (see 'Cattle' in Chapter 7). Tenants who did specialist tasks on the demesne, acting as carters or shepherds, who lacked draft animals, were allowed the privilege of the Saturday plough, that is the use of the demesne plough on one day per week.[71]

Ploughing and harrowing created a seed bed and controlled weeds. Documentary sources are not specific about weeds, though thistles and tares were mentioned. Botanical evidence for a wide range of species has come from excavated medieval rural settlements. The presence of weeds in the growing corn is evident from charred seeds which are found mingled with carbonized cereal grains. The species which have left traces at Burton Dassett Southend included corn buttercup, corn cockle, stinking mayweed, and bristly ox tongue, though some of these may have been growing in gardens or on waste ground. The largest plants which would cause problems for the corn crop are the dock, nettle, and plantain found at Coton, and thistle and chickweed at Goldicote. Dock was also present at Bishop's Cleeve, together with knot grass and stinking chamomile.[72]

Manuring the cultivated land was a normal part of the peasant's agricultural routine. Every household kept at least one manure heap, and at Burton Dassett Southend the excavators recognized both concentrated deposits of domestic debris, and dung heaps consisting mainly of organic material.[73] Better-off peasants had dung carts and dung wains for carrying manure, which was collected and spread with dung forks. Manure was a marketable commodity. A legal dispute in 1426 in the borough court of Alcester between two tenants from the nearby village of Sambourn concerned a sum of 7s, which was said to be owed *pro fimo* (for manure).[74] Leasehold requirements that land be manured by the tenant

---

[69] SRO, D(W)1788/P39/B10; WAM, 21123; WCL, E30; Z. Razi, 'Family, Land and the Village Community in Later Medieval England', *P&P* 93(1981), p.10; R.H. Hilton, *The English Peasantry in The Later Middle Ages* (Oxford, 1975), pp. 48–50.

[70] TNA, PROB2/457.

[71] Langdon, *Horses, Oxen*, pp. 235–41; *RBW*, p. 270. This privilege would cover only a fraction of the ploughing needed for a number of holdings, but it shows that lending ploughing capacity was a well-established practice.

[72] See the archaeological reports cited in note 49 of this chapter, and notes 27, 33, and 34 in Chapter 5; the botanical report for Burton Dassett Southend can be accessed at https://doi.org/10.5284/1083492.

[73] Palmer and Parkhouse, *Burton Dassett Southend*, pp. 147–57.   [74] WCRO, CR1886/42.

could result in litigation if the obligation was neglected.[75] Tenants were expected to use manure within the manor or village territory, leading to a by-law at Stoke Gifford in 1423 that no tenant should take manure out of the lordship. The lord presumably did not want a holding to deteriorate in fertility and therefore value, leading to an objection in 1389 when a Teddington (Gloucestershire) tenant took manure to spread on his holding at nearby Beckford.[76]

Manuring practices are reflected in pottery and other artefacts scattered over the surface of modern fields and collected in programmes of archaeological fieldwork. Domestic rubbish, including broken pottery, was spread with manure on the fields, and potsherds were left as an enduring record of the process. A systematic map of the distribution of sherds recovered by field walking allows us to reconstruct the journeys to the medieval fields made by the peasants' dung carts. A complete survey of the ploughed fields of Admington (Warwickshire) shows very marked differences across the township, with notable concentrations of potsherds immediately to the west of the settlement, but also in fields up to half a mile to the north. Similar clusters of sherds have been found to the north of the village of Compton Verney, another nucleated village in the same county[77] (Figures 6.1). By contrast, other fields belonging to these villages have produced very thin distributions of pottery, or none at all. These were certainly cultivated, as they are (or were recently) covered in ridge and furrow, but were either manured 'by the fold' (that is by livestock pastured on the stubble and fallow) rather than 'by the cart', so that manuring left no visible trace, or the land belonged to the lord's demesne, which collected and spread its manure without the addition of domestic rubbish. Furlongs in the open field were probably selected to receive the peasants' carted manure because they had better soils, and would repay the effort, even if this involved a longer cart journey. In other regions, the folding of sheep on the arable was closely regulated in order to maximize deposit of manure on the demesne, but in our region peasants' flocks were not apparently confined at night on the lords' land.

In areas of dispersed settlement, as with nucleated villages, there are similar signs of the selection of particular fields for special treatment. At Pendock (Worcestershire) a great deal of pottery, and therefore manure, was deposited on the largest common field, West Field, but also on land called 'the crofts', where the land was enclosed. Both areas lay near to hamlets (Figure 2.3). The common fields of Hanbury, however, do not seem to have received so much carted manure, and

---

[75] Hilton, *English Peasantry*, p. 50.
[76] GA, Badminton muniments, D2700 MJ11/1/2; WCL, E34.
[77] R.L.C. Jones, 'Signatures in the Soil: The Use of Pottery in Manure Scatters in the Identification of Medieval Arable Farming Regimes', *Archaeological Journal* 161 (2004), pp. 159–88; C. Dyer, 'Medieval Pottery from the Admington Survey', *Medieval Settlement Research Group Annual Report* 13 (1998), pp. 24–5; C. Dyer, 'Compton Verney: Landscape and People in the Middle Ages', in *Compton Verney: A History of the House and its Owners*, edited by R. Bearman (Stratford-upon-Avon, 2000), pp. 66–7.

the densest scatters have been found at Brook End, where much of the land was enclosed, partly as a result of thirteenth-century assarting.[78] One of the advantages of holding land 'in severalty' was the opportunity to spread manure on land controlled completely by the tenant.

The peasant manure heap had its own characteristics. Animal housing, such as a byre, sheepcote, or pigsty, provided a concentrated trampled manure mingled with straw. However peasant animals were often kept in yards or paddocks, and their droppings would have to be collected. The domestic waste, which would have been added may have included human ordure, though latrines and cesspits appear irregularly in documents or excavations. Faeces may have been deposited in wooden vessels and tipped on to the general manure heap. A tantalizing phrase 'domestic manure' described the heap causing a nuisance on the king's highway outside the door of Thomas Clerk of Willoughby (Warwickshire) in 1492.[79]

Peasants were more likely than the managers of the demesne to treat their land with marl. This calcareous subsoil, dug out of deep pits and carted for spreading, improved the texture and chemical properties of the soil in which crops were planted. Demesnes were marled, but not on a sufficient scale to explain the many marlpits in documents. They were regarded as commonplace landmarks when defining boundaries, or they occasionally appear as assets, like the share in a *marlle pytte* in a field called *Swannes pytte* that was leased by John Hoblay of Coleshill in 1414. Very large numbers of water-filled marl pits now dot the countryside. Though undateable, the twelve pits at Compton Verney are likely to belong to the medieval period.[80] Spreading marl was valued so highly that pits were dug to dangerous depths leading to the death of Robert de Upton in a pit at Kempsey (Worcestershire) 'when the earth fell on him', recorded in 1275.[81] Peasants could choose times to extract and spread marl when the round of seasonal agricultural tasks allowed. Lords had to pay workers, or divert labour services to the task, which made them less likely to undertake marling on a large scale.

Once the fields had been prepared by repeated ploughing, harrowing, clod breaking, manuring, and marling, the seed to be sown had to be selected. This often came from the previous year's harvest, but cultivators could change seed by purchase or exchange. Thirteenth-century estate managers believed that sowing seed from another manor could improve yields, but do not mention acquiring different varieties of seed. The written sources scarcely mention types: 'wheat' was a sufficient description, but botanists can identify distinct species and varieties. At

---

[78] These observations are based on the author's field work.
[79] Magdalen College, Oxford, Willoughby EP 68/9.
[80] A. Watkins, ed., *The Early Records of Coleshill* (DS 51, 2018), p. 255; W.D. Shannon, '"An Excellent Improver of the Soil": Marl and the Landscape of Lowland Lancashire', *AgHR* 68(2020), pp. 141–67; Dyer, 'Compton Verney', p. 67.
[81] J. Rohrkasten, ed., *The Worcester Eyre of 1275* (WHS, new series, 22, 2008), pp. 337–8.

Bascote in Warwickshire analysis of surviving chaff suggests a preponderance of free-threshing wheat, with some bread wheat and rivet wheat. At Burton Dassett both rivet wheat and bread wheat had been planted, and they are also found at Moreton-in-Marsh.[82] Each type had advantages and disadvantages, such as rivet wheat's better performance on clay soils, while its spiky ears discouraged birds, and it had some resistance to disease. It needed a long growing season, and it was not always best-suited to bread making. Bread wheat was, as its name implied, good for baking, but did not perform well in poorer soils. Individual peasants could find the best mix of seed for their circumstances by empirical observation, though neighbours could have compared experiences and a collective wisdom would have emerged. Barley came in different varieties, but not on west midland sites. The peasants' corn was apparently not inferior in quality to that grown on the demesne, as occasionally the administrators of the Worcester Cathedral Priory estate sowed their demesne with grain collected as tithe, so deriving their seed from peasant crops.

Seed once planted could be threatened by birds, such as the members of the crow family identified among the bones excavated at Burton Dassett Southend. Hundreds of crows, rooks, and choughs were killed in early sixteenth-century Worcestershire for the Prior of Worcester, and the same methods (with nets) could have been used by peasants, who had strong motives to limit crop damage.[83] As the corn grew it was weeded, and then harvested, a lengthy process that seems to have been hastened by the adoption by the fifteenth century, if not earlier, of the scythe as a supplement to the prevalent sickle. The harvesters would carry the sheaves back to the settlement, which given the field arrangements especially in a champion landscape, might involve a journey of a mile or more. In bad weather some urgency was desirable. Tenants of larger holdings were at an advantage in owning carts, while quarter- yardlanders and smallholders may have borrowed or hired carts, or loaded sheaves onto packhorses.

A major concern, once the sheaves had been carried, was their secure storage until threshing could be completed. Most peasants, even many smallholders, built and maintained a barn. In the documents different Latin words, *grangia* and *horreum*, were applied, but the terms seem to have been synonyms. When orders were made for building repairs from the 1350s a high proportion of the farm buildings mentioned were barns. The size of the building to be repaired or rebuilt was commonly specified as three bays, so about 15m by 5m. They matched dwelling houses in both size and structure, as they were commonly built with stone foundations and timber frames including crucks. At least forty barns built with crucks survive in the west midland. They include buildings that once formed part

---

[82] Archaeological reports cited in note 49 of this chapter, and notes 27, 33, and 34 in Chapter 5; the botanical reports for Burton Dassett Southend can be accessed at https://doi.org/10.5284/1083492; L. Moffett, 'The Archaeology of Medieval Plant Foods', in *Food in Medieval England*, edited by C.M. Woolgar, D. Serjeantson, and T. Waldron (Oxford, 2006), pp. 47–53.

[83] E.S. Fegan, ed., *Journal of Prior William More* (WHS, 1914), pp. 350–2.

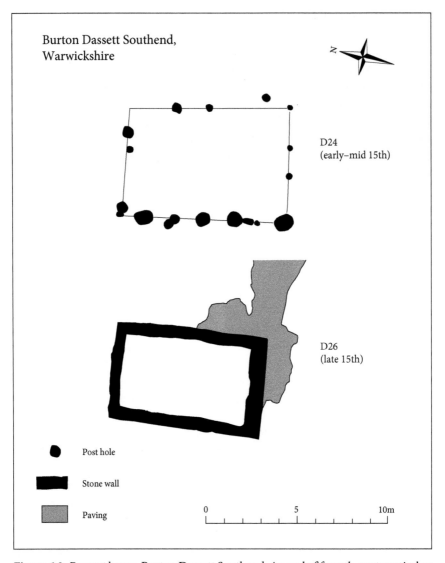

Figure 6.3 Peasant barns, Burton Dassett Southend. An early fifteenth-century timber building was replaced by one with stone foundations in the late fifteenth century. Both were of two bays (source: note 85).

of manorial establishments, monastic granges, or rectory farms, but a number stood next to peasant houses. A four-bay cruck-built barn once attached to a peasant holding at Pendock (Worcestershire) survived in use until the end of the twentieth century.[84] Such survivals tell us something about the durability of the original construction.

---

[84] Field, 'Worcestershire Peasant Buildings', pp. 134–6; N.W. Alcock, ed., *Cruck Construction: An Introduction and Catalogue* (CBA Research Report 42, 1981), pp. 117–19, 121–6, 156–8.

Excavations on village sites include some buildings likely to have been barns. Building A5 at Burton Dassett Southend, dated to the fifteenth century, measured 14.5 m by 4.5 m, and could have been of either three or four bays. It had partially surviving stone foundations and had been timber framed; its wide doors confirm its identification as a barn. Likely barns were found on another five tenements at Burton Dassett Southend[85] (Figure 6.3). A thirteenth-century Gloucester Abbey treatise gives a formula for calculating the volume of stacked sheaves. If this applied to the Burton Dassett Southend barns, they can each be shown to have been capable of storing the crops of a yardland holding.[86] As long as the thatched roofs of barns were maintained (which was not always the case) the heaps of sheaves within them would be kept dry, but rats and mice could not have been excluded by stone foundations, timber-framed walls, and wattle and daub panels. Storage buildings could be constructed on staddle stones, that is, on stone pillars with cover stones resembling large mushrooms. These raised the floor a half metre or so above the ground and would deter the most persistent rat, and also protect the crops from damp. A number of buildings called helms and at least one barn were built on staddle stones on peasant holdings at Bisley (Gloucestershire) in the late fourteenth century, but are not recorded in any other village.[87] Bisley's innovation was not eccentric or a dead end, as it must have contributed to food security, and in modern times buildings on staddle stones became commonplace in the region.

A granary at Burton Dassett Southend protected its contents by means of a storage space above ground level. It was originally constructed in the fourteenth century as a single storey stone-walled building 7m by 5m, but was later enlarged and given an upper storey reached by an external stair. It had a capacity to hold 550 bushels of grain, which suggests that it was built for a cornmonger based in this semi-urban settlement. Peasants, even yardlanders, would sell less than a hundred bushels of grain, and would thresh their crops through the year, consuming and selling as they did so, and they had no need of a substantial granary.[88]

The protection of crops was the main function of peasant barns, but they were multi-functional structures. A 'little hay barn' at Ombersley shows that not just arable crops were stored. Barns housed livestock like the thirty sheep at Shirehampton (Gloucestershire) belonging in 1483 to an elderly couple who had access to part of a barn. They could have sheltered their small flock under cover in winter and in bad weather. Valuable implements such as carts may have been kept in the barn when a tenant had no cart shed. The mixed use of barns might explain

---

[85] Palmer and Parkhouse, *Burton Dassett Southend*, pp. 134, 182–4.
[86] Oschinsky, ed., *Walter of Henley*, p. 475.
[87] C. Dyer, 'Evidence for Helms in Gloucestershire in the Fourteenth Century', *Vernacular Architecture* 15 (1984), pp. 42–5.
[88] Palmer and Parkhouse, *Burton Dassett Southend*, pp. 60, 178–9.

why peasants stacked crops in the yard, like the pulse and hay (in stacks damaged by cattle) at Tibberton (Worcestershire) in 1389.[89]

Conclusion on husbandry and techniques

The changes made by peasants in field organization, their practices in husbandry, and their application of both old and new techniques could have been rewarded by increases in output. We do not have numerous measurements for peasant holdings of the amount of grain produced from an acre, or the ratio between seed sown and grain harvested. Manorial accounts enable us to generalize that on lords' demesnes between 1270 and 1450 harvesters usually gathered in between 8 and 15 bushels per acre, and that grain and legumes yielded between two and five times the seed planted. These figures do not encourage us to have very high expectations for peasant productivity in the west midlands, because the demesnes performed less well than those in other parts of England, especially in the east, and yields were inferior to those found across the North Sea on the near continent.[90]

For comparative figures from peasant holdings, we can only clutch at isolated examples, such as the 7 bushels per acre harvested by the lord of Bourton-on-the-Hill in 1349 from the holdings of tenants who had died in the Black Death. A rather better performance, 9.8 bushels per acre, came from the holding of Walter Shayl of Hatton-on-Avon, whose crops were gathered by his lord after he left the manor. The land of John Kent at Stivichall (Warwickshire) in 1481 produced 11 ½ bushels per acre.[91] All were special cases, as 1349 was an untypical year, Hatton-on-Avon was a village in terminal decline, and the peasants of Stivichall may have been especially stimulated by the influence of nearby Coventry. The peasants' crop yields were not completely different from those of the demesne, but inferior in the case of both Bourton and Hatton where direct comparison can be made.

An indirect indication of the potential performance of peasant arable farming can be made by examining stocking densities. These can be calculated from the arable acreage of a holding and the number of animals, to arrive at an index, suggesting the amount of manure available. The figures have been calculated for demesnes by assigning an index number to various types of livestock, with adult cattle rated at 1.2, horses at 1, and sheep and pigs at 0.1. Demesnes throughout England in 1250–1349 provide average densities of between 41 and 59 per 100 acres (the acreage for grain only, excluding legumes), and between 59 and 92 in

---

[89] WA, ref.705:56, BA 3910/27; ref. 009:1, BA2636/92225 4/8; WCL, E34.
[90] B.M.S. Campbell, *English Seigniorial Agriculture 1250–1450* (Cambridge, 2000), pp. 306–85.
[91] WAM, 8282; Hilton, *English Peasantry*, pp. 201–2.; Dyer, *Warwickshire Farming*, pp. 29–30.

1350–1449, the higher figures reflecting the rising importance of the pastoral dimension in lords' agriculture.[92]

Figures can be calculated for four west midland peasant holdings, dating from 1290 to 1447. The ratios relate to the whole arable acreage of the holdings, including both legumes and grain. The late thirteenth-century example (from Pinbury in Gloucestershire) gives a figure of 68, and three fifteenth-century cases 24, 69, and 193.[93] Such widely scattered results from a tiny sample would not enable the conclusion to be drawn that peasant holdings should have benefited from a relative plenty of manure. The assumption of a direct connection between livestock and cultivation must be doubted, as the peasants' animals deposited much of their manure over the fallow field and common pasture, so peasants gained from it in a general way, but there were limited opportunities for concentrating dung on particular strips and crofts. The stints which limited the numbers of animals that could be kept on the commons by a yardlander and are recorded for a number of villages between 1400 and 1540, can be used to calculate a model stocking density of at least 80, which is higher than that found on most demesnes.[94] The figures leave us without a satisfactory basis for generalization, apart from observing that peasant land was not obviously deprived of manure.

A guide to productivity should come from rent payments, which ought to be related to the output of land. Customary and leasehold rents often varied between 3*d* and 8*d* per acre, and tended not to change, reflecting the arrangements made in some earlier period. Lords felt some restraint from making changes to annual rents, leading to the entry fine rather than the annual rent payment rising and falling with the demand for land. Rents per acre were influenced by the fertility of the soil and profits of cultivation, represented most clearly by the contrast in Gloucestershire between the high rents for customary land of 12*d* in the Severn estuary and the mediocre 4*d*–8*d* often found on the Cotswolds. The most remarkable indication of high yields near the Severn comes from the leasehold rents introduced on the Berkeley estate on such manors as Slimbridge in the late thirteenth and early fourteenth centuries, which reached such astronomic figures as 34*d* per acre.[95] Peasants were prepared to pay such sums, which must mean that they expected to be producing much more than 7 bushels per acre. Relatively high returns must also explain the entry fines of 10 marks (£6 13s 4d) per yardland, around 4*s* 5*d* per acre, found in various parts of the region in the early fourteenth century (see 'Changing circumstances: Entry fines' in Chapter 3).

---

[92] Campbell, *Seigniorial Agriculture*, pp. 172–83.

[93] C. Dyer, 'A Medieval Village in a Cotswold Landscape: Pinbury in Duntisbourne Rouse', *TBGAS* 137 (2019), pp. 208, 209; Hilton, *English Peasantry*, p. 42; SRO, D641/1/4C/7; WA, ref. 705:4, BA 54.

[94] For example, at Oddington (Gloucestershire) a stint of 4 cattle, 3 horses, and 40 sheep on a 30-acre yardland would give a ratio of 79 per 100 acres; GA, D621/M8.

[95] B. Wells-Furby, *The Berkeley Estate 1281–1417. Its Economy and Development* (BGAS, 2012), pp. 89–118.

If the fine was funded by a loan, the repayments over a number of years would have depended on a high and consistent surplus of grain.

An indirect pointer to increasing levels of production comes from the proportion of the region's population living in towns and therefore dependent on rural surpluses for their food. About 12,000 people lived in west midland towns in 1086, double that number in 1200, and around 50,000 in 1300 (see 'Peasant migration into towns' in Chapter 8). There were also workers in rural industries and transport who bought their food, and their horses ate grain and legumes. These rising numbers were being fed from the crops produced beyond the subsistence needs of the rural population.

To step aside from the pursuit of hard data for productivity from uncertain sources, we should trust the people who lived through these times and experienced productivity at first hand. They spent scarce money, time, and effort on technical changes involving clearance of new land, innovations in rotation, enclosures, and techniques such as horse hauling and marling. They did this because they considered that these measures benefited them and the output of their holding. They may not have calculated yield ratios or stocking densities, but they had an empirical understanding of the output of their land. Their judgements were appropriate to their own circumstances. In the period between 1375 and 1520 they sold grain because they needed the money, and if prices were low they produced more to maintain a flow of cash.[96] They lived in those decades when the basic foodstuffs were cheap because they were plentiful, and that made life easier for the poor and the wage earners The producers of grain suffered no great hardship, as their main profits in the market came from livestock, and our attention will now turn to animal husbandry.

Arable and pasture: Managing change

Arable and grassland were not opposites. At regular intervals in the annual cycle of cultivation, livestock were able to find pasturage on the arable. Part of the arable was sometimes called 'frisc', and was uncultivated for a time, but would subsequently be cropped. Faint traces of ridge and furrow suggest that the cultivators temporarily extended the area under the plough, and we know that plots of common pasture might be cultivated with flax crops. The general tendencies are well known: the land under cultivation expanded in the twelfth and thirteenth centuries, and then ceased to grow soon after 1300. The shrinkage in the arable became pronounced from 1350 and it remained in recession around 1500. The

---

[96] D. Farmer, 'Prices and Wages', in *Agricultural History of England and Wales*, volume 3, edited by E. Miller (Cambridge, 1991), pp. 443–55.

underlying causes of these trends are partly related to the rise and fall of the size of the settlements from which the land was cultivated. Many villages doubled in population between 1086 and 1300, and were then halved by the fifteenth century. Demand for grain rose and then fell as the numbers of households diminished, and this was reflected in prices, but the pattern of consumption changed, with an increase in barley and drage as more ale was brewed.

Beginning with the advance of arable before 1300, an impression of the scale of the expansion can be gained from a sample of twenty villages, selected because their landscape history has been the subject of research. An attempt has been made (not without doubts) to estimate the cultivated area in 1086, based on Domesday Book, and again in *c*.1300. For example, at Hanley Castle in the woodlands of Worcestershire, the inhabitants can plausibly be estimated to have been cultivating 1,200 acres in 1086 and 3,000 acres in 1300, representing a growth by 2.5 times. Other woodland villages in the same county grew by almost four times (at Hanbury) and between four and five times at Pendock. Arable in champion and Cotswold villages increased between 1.2 and 1.9 times, with a greater expansion in the case of Burton Dassett. Taken together these villages reflect a countryside experiencing general extension in cultivation, with some significant differences between landscapes.[97] Scientific evidence for changes in vegetation in the Vale of Gloucester come from pollen samples from the fill of a ditch at Haresfield. At the bottom of the ditch deposits of *c*.1200 contain mainly tree pollen, especially from oak and hazel. The upper fill, dating from the mid-thirteenth century, shows a notable reduction in tree pollen and an increase in pollen deriving from cereals, with weeds including those associated with disturbed ground. There was also evidence of grazed grassland.[98]

After 1300 the trends were sometimes contradictory. Some assarting was reported in the Forest of Dean as late as the 1340s. Land was being reclaimed from the marshes of the Severn estuary, but this seems to be an initiative of the Berkeley family rather than the local peasants.[99] However peasants were reported in 1341 leaving their holdings in the Cotswolds, and at the same time land fell out of cultivation.[100] Individual tenants and sometimes groups of them were

---

[97] This is based on a sample of villages on which both detailed documentary and landscape research has been conducted: Glouc: Bibury, Bishop's Cleeve, Hazleton, Hidcote, Pinbury, Roel; Warwicks: Admington, Baddesley Clinton, Compton Scorpion, Burmington, Burton Dassett, Compton Verney, Hampton Lucy, Lark Stoke, Long Compton, Quinton, Welford-on-Avon, Weston-juxta-Cherrington; Worcs: Hanbury, Hanley Castle, Pendock.
[98] M. Brett and J. Hart, 'Land at Quedgley East, Haresfield, Gloucestershire (unpublished report, Cotswold Archaeology, CR0078_1, 2019), pp. 28, 83–6.
[99] E.A. Fry, ed., *Abstracts of the IPMs for Gloucestershire*, part 5, 1302-58 (British Record Society, 40, 1910), p. 315; J.R. Allen, 'A Short History of Salt Marsh Reclamation at Slimbridge Warth and Neighbouring Areas, Gloucestershire', *TBGAS* 104 (1986), pp. 139–55.
[100] *Nonarum Inquisitiones in Curia Scaccarii* (Record Commission, 1807), pp. 407–15; C.R. Elrington, 'Assessments of |Gloucestershire. Fiscal Records in Local History', *TBGAS* 103(1985), pp. 5–16.

Table 6.1 Land use in Gloucestershire from final concords (percentages)

Date	Arable	Meadow	Pasture	Wood	Other	Total
1265–89						
Wold	92	4	2	2	–	100
Vale	94	3	1	2	–	100
1290–1308						
Wold	92	4	2	2	–	100
Vale	94	3	1	2	–	100
1309–30						
Wold	90	5	0	5	–	100
Vale	86	8	3	3	–	100
1331–48						
Wold	84	6	5	5	–	100
Vale	83	8	2	7	–	100
1349–75						
Wold	86	8	0	6	–	100
Vale	85	8	3	4	–	100
1376–94						
Wold	84	6	7	3	–	100
Vale	82	10	4	4	–	100
1395–1416						
Wold	86	7	4	3	–	100
Vale	80	10	7	3	–	100
1418–47						
Wold	70	7	18	5	–	100
Vale	73	10	14	3	–	100
1448–61						
Wold	62	5	29	4	–	100
Vale	65	9	17	9	–	100
1461–81						
Wold	57	12	20	11	–	100
Vale	63	7	25	3	2	100
1484–1509						
Wold	55	8	29	8	–	100
Vale	61	10	24	3	2	100

Source: C.R. Elrington, ed., *Abstracts of Feet of Fines Relating to Gloucestershire 1199–1299* (GRS, 16, 2003); C.R. Elrington, ed., *Abstracts of Feet of Fines Relating to Gloucestershire 1300–1359* (GRS, 20, 2006); C.R. Elrington, ed., *Abstracts of Feet of Fines Relating to Gloucestershire 1360–1508* (GRS, 27, 2013).

abandoning their holdings, such as four of the twenty tenants at Fulbrook (Warwickshire) in 1325.[101] An idea of general developments in the years after 1300 and subsequently can be gained from final concords, that is, records of transfers of land registered in the royal courts, which indicate the use of land mainly on the holdings of free tenants, but also occasionally on demesnes. A typical example will tell us that a conveyance concerned twenty acres of land (meaning arable), an

---

[101] TNA, C134/41/3.

Table 6.2 Reduction in the quantity of crops estimated from thirteen parishes, all on the Worcester Cathedral Priory estate, between 1400–13 and 1416–62

Champion parishes, demesne crops	22%
Champion parishes, tithe corn	13%
Woodland parishes, demesne crops	34%
Woodland parishes, tithe corn	27%

Source: Dyer, 'Tithe Estimates', pp. 90–1.

acre of meadow, and two of pasture. These figures were not based on detailed surveys, but give an impression based on the judgement of contemporary observers. They are imprecise, but inform us of trends over three centuries.[102]

The figures for Gloucestershire in Table 6.1 show clear movements in two regions, the wold and Vale. At the beginning of the series arable was overwhelmingly prominent, partly because the pasture would be associated with a holding, but the quantity could not be given an area—it was a share in a common resource. Similarly it was often taken for granted that each yardland had an acre or two of meadow attached to it. In indicating the size of a piece of land, the amount of arable mattered most, and the rest could be assumed. The dominance of arable in the records can be seen to diminish in the second quarter of the fourteenth century, but decisive movement came in the early years of the fifteenth century, and the rise in pasture seems especially marked after 1448. There are differences in details between the wolds and Vale, but the overall impression is that fifteenth-century Gloucestershire saw a significant move, not just from arable to pasture, but from arable to the types of enclosed or separate pasture that could register with those compiling the final concords. This development was not confined to the wolds where pasture has traditionally been seen as significant, but also in the mixed landscapes of the Vale.

The story is to some extent duplicated in Warwickshire's final concords, but the differences between the landscape divisions is much more pronounced. Both Arden and Feldon are represented by the fines as dominated by arable around 1300, but the first hints of change in the mid-fourteenth century were confined to the Arden, with more land being recorded as wood (13 per cent) and pasture (7 per cent). Significant change according to the final concords for the Arden came in the mid-fifteenth century, when the recorded pasture increased to 45 per cent and remained at that level after 1500. In the Feldon pasture around 1500 stood at 33 per cent, with arable at 57 per cent.[103]

---

[102] M. Davis and J. Kissock, 'The Feet of Fines, the Land Market and the English Agricultural Crisis of 1315–1321', *Journal of Historical Geography* 30 (2004), pp. 215–30.

[103] A. Watkins, 'Cattle Grazing in the Forest of Arden in the Later Middle Ages', *AgHR* 37(1989), p. 21; Dyer, *Warwickshire Farming*, p. 10.

The conclusion that seems to emerge from these impressionistic figures from Gloucestershire and Warwickshire is the importance of the fifteenth century when perceptions of the countryside were revised, and behind that change of mind real developments were presumably taking place. However, perhaps the Warwickshire Feldon, though registering less pasture than in the woodlands, felt the impact of the introduction of grazing land more acutely, as permanent pasture before 1400 had been limited in extent. All of this affected peasants profoundly, and to some extent arose from peasant initiatives.

The extents attached to Inquisitions Post Mortem were focussed on the lords' demesnes, and are therefore not directly comparable with the final concords, but it is useful to see confirmation of the trends, which were clearly shared by lords and peasants in the fifteenth century. Gloucestershire, and especially in the Vale, experienced a surge in pasture and a pronounced drop in arable in the early years of the century, while the same was delayed in Warwickshire until after 1485. As in the final concords, the Arden around 1500 had shed more arable and gained more pasture and wood than the Feldon.[104] From the late fourteenth century onwards demesnes were increasingly coming into the hands of peasant lessees, who could have made decisions to change arable to pasture.

The tithe records from Worcestershire, which reveal so much about the crops grown in different places and times, can also shed light on the volume of arable production at a crucial time in the fifteenth century. Table 6.2 shows that the demesne managers were more ready than the tithe-paying villagers to scale down their arable production, perhaps because they were more sensitive to the decline in market demand. The lords' officials and the peasants resembled one another in that their regional environment influenced their decisions. Lords and peasant alike in the woodlands were more averse to arable cultivation than were their counterparts in the champion. This suggests a serious agricultural recession, but if we had a full series of tithe records, they would show rising output from beef cattle, dairy produce, flitches of bacon, and the other products from animal husbandry. The woodland, already a markedly pastoral countryside, became even more pastoral. This was also the case in the Arden across the county boundary.

The dry statistics of the use of land are valuable in showing unequivocally the consequences of the ups and downs in the numbers of consumers and producers, prices and rents, and all of the other variable factors at work. Change in climate was a factor for which there is little precise information from the region, but which must have been having an influence because it affected the whole of

---

[104] C. Dyer, 'Landscape, Farming and Society in an English Region: Inquisitions Post Mortem for the West Midlands, 1250–1509', in *The Later Medieval Inquisitions Post Mortem: Mapping the Medieval Countryside and Rural Society*, edited by M. Hicks (Woodbridge, 2016), pp. 59–83.

Europe. Relatively warm and stable conditions provided a context for agricultural and urban growth in the thirteenth century; unstable weather was associated with the crises of the fourteenth century; and adverse trends, including falling temperatures, were the backdrop for the recession of the fifteenth century.[105] Climatic adversity, along with the expense of war, civil conflict, shortage of bullion, and successive epidemics all formed the environment in which peasants lived and worked. They did not give up in despair, but adapted to circumstances, and found solutions to many of the problems they encountered.

As well as examining regional and wider statistical trends, we can see how individuals behaved. These people feature in the court proceedings of Cleeve Prior (Worcestershire) and we can trace the reduction in arable farming and understand some of the pressures behind the moves (Figure 6.4). A series of comments begins in 1347 with the statement that 'Robert Droght does not cultivate his land competently', and Henry Long does not cultivate 'as he ought', which might refer to unskilled handling of the plough, or to a departure from the rules of rotation.[106] A more straightforward report came from 1352 when Alice Robynes was said to be allowing her house to decay and leaving her land uncultivated because she was poor and incapable.[107] This appears to have been a social welfare problem with a retreat from arable husbandry as a by-product. A succession of complaints of non-cultivation came mainly from the years between 1374 and 1424, which were followed in 1453–62 by a significant flurry of general orders addressed to 'all tenants'. Specific holdings, from a quarter yardland to whole yardlands were said to be lacking in cultivation, but the neglect did not necessarily mean that there was no ploughing at all. Some tenants did not do their fallow ploughing, or did not double plough the fallow according to the best practice. Some tenants ploughed most of their land but omitted some parcels, like the tenant who ploughed his selions (strips) but not the headlands. Another fault was not to plough at the correct time. A particular problem troubling the people of Cleeve was the consequence of a change in river channels, which left part of the fields on the other side of the river, 'beyond the Avon'. Tenants seem to have co-ordinated their choices by agreeing to leave the inaccessible land lying frisc (uncultivated). They also seem to have collectively chosen land near the village, 'the furlong near the closes of their tenures' to lie uncultivated, according to a report of 1462, finding it convenient to have animals grazing where they could be easily supervised.[108] Most tenants seem to have grown crops on part of their holdings, and left the rest frisc, making the selection on the basis of convenience and fertility. These choices were being made by tenants with large holdings, such as William Carles, who held 64

---

[105] B.M.S. Campbell, *The Great Transition. Climate, Disease and Society in the Late Medieval World* (Cambridge, 2016).
[106] WCL, E15.   [107] WCL, E17.
[108] WCL, E66.

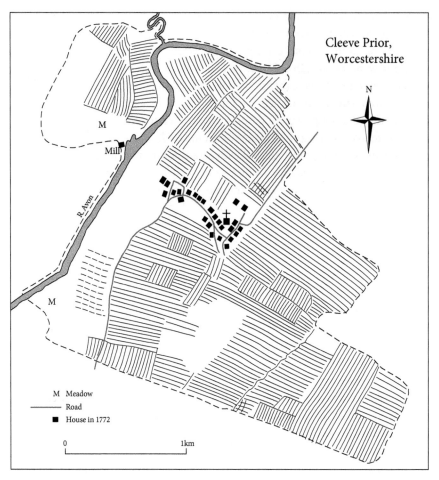

Figure 6.4 Cleeve Prior, Worcestershire. A map of 1772 provides the main evidence for the strips and furlongs of the open fields, supplemented by lidar data and field observation. The nucleated village has a cluster plan; the large arable area is typical of the champion country in the Vale of Evesham. The course of the river changed, hence part of the fields lying on the opposite bank. Village and fields are likely to have been fully formed by thirteenth century (source: WCL, Map 12).

acres in 1420. Faced with the formidable amount of time, effort, and money to plough so many acres, he decided to leave some untilled. In 1447 tenants were grazing horses on the frisc by tethering them, to avoid damaging the crops on adjacent land.[109] A number of tenants at Cleeve Prior used land in the open fields to quarry stone, which prevented cultivation (see 'Industry within peasant society' in Chapter 9). The tithe corn total in Cleeve parish was reduced from 82 quarters

[109] WCL, E61.

around 1402 to 55 quarters near to 1448, meaning a loss to cultivation of at least 200 acres. Behind these totals for the whole village lie many stories of individuals reacting to falling demand.

The reports of non-cultivation at Cleeve Prior serve as a reminder that no development in peasant farming was accomplished without opposition and argument within the community. The reports in the manor court of land lying frisc, being grazed by animals, or being used as quarries came from neighbours reporting the offences against customary land management. Unploughed land could threaten neighbours from the growth of weeds and the straying of animals that escaped their tethers. Uncoordinated conversion to pasture threatened the orderly rotation of crops.

Conclusion

West-midland peasants managed their own fields through largely undocumented village meetings, which communicated with the manor courts. They inherited their fields from earlier periods, but far from being trapped in the legacy of the past made major adaptations. Every move was contentious, but resistance to change was not born from a mindless conservatism, but from rational calculations of disadvantage. Assarting, the enclosure of wastes, changes in rotation, piecemeal enclosure, enclosure by agreement, the protection of existing hedges, the conversion of arable to leys, all met with opposition. Nonetheless changes were made, though those advocating new methods could on occasion be prevented. It cannot be proved that changes led to advances in productivity, but it seems likely that the intelligent, well-informed, and selfish advocates of inhoking, enclosure, adoption of leys, and other measures expected to increase their profits. Reforms to cultivation were likely to have been prevented by those who were liable to lose grazing or crops. The expansion of arable in the thirteenth century, and the rise of pastoralism in the fifteenth, were examples of radical innovations with clear benefits for those pressing them forwards.

In addition to these strategic changes to cultivation, peasants were also making incremental changes to their techniques, in their employment of horses, choice of crops, application of scythes to the grain harvest, provision of secure storage, and modifications in manuring and marling. All of this amounts to an environment of innovation, both large and small, which demonstrates peasant adaptability.

7
Peasant farming
Livestock and pasture

Peasant livestock, taken together, greatly outnumbered those kept by their lords, even in the thirteenth century when demesnes were being managed directly to take advantage of a buoyant market. In the period after *c.*1380 many lords withdrew from managing the land directly, often leasing their demesnes to peasants, so the peasants' share increased to an even higher level. At the same time the income deriving from livestock was increasing as the balance shifted away from arable. A calculation of Gross Domestic Product for England as a whole suggests that the pastoral sector's share rose from about a third of agricultural output around 1300 to almost a half in the 1450s.[1] As peasants were responsible for much of that production, collectively they can be regarded as major contributors to the national economy.

This chapter is concerned with the balance on one hand between the use of animals to feed peasant households and to service holdings with traction and manure, and on the other to maximize earnings from the sale of animals and their produce. Each type of animal, from horses to bees will be considered, assessing their number, age, gender, and management. The central concerns are to assess the importance of the pastoral dimension of peasant farming to the household and as a source of income, and to examine the effectiveness of pastoral activities, including such matters as labour, animal welfare, and the marketing of animals and their products.

Horses

Lists of possessions or inventories show widespread ownership of at least one horse, and a number of individuals owned two or three. A relatively wealthy peasant, Elyas atte Brugge of Abbots Salford (Warwickshire) owned in 1389 a horse, three mares, and two foals. He also had eight cattle.[2] When communities decided to fix stints, which limited the numbers of animals that could be kept on the

---

[1] S. Broadberry, B.M.S. Campbell, A. Klein, M. Overton, and B. van Leeuwen, *British Economic Growth 1270–1870* (Cambridge, 2015), p. 118.
[2] WCL, E34.

common, they often specified two, three, or four horses, much the same as in lists of individuals' livestock. They normally expected that each holding would have more cattle than horses. Horse ownership was rising in the later Middle Ages: when a newcomer to Willoughby (Warwickshire) in 1230 was given livestock at the beginning of his tenancy he received ten cattle and two horses, so a rather lower proportion than prevailed later.[3]

Horses formed a substantial proportion of animals accused of invading sown fields, the lord's demesne, or other prohibited places. At Badminton (Gloucestershire) between 1340 and 1354 thirty-nine horses were listed as causing offence, compared with twenty-five cattle and eighteen pigs. At Kempsford, in the same county, over a longer period in the fourteenth and fifteenth centuries a total of 163 horses were reported in the wrong places compared with 108 cattle. At Eldersfield (Worcestershire) between 1315 and 1336 fifty-nine horses were causing problems, but there were ninety-seven cattle. In 1365–99 in the same village strays were found wandering in the fields and roads without known owners: forty-three sheep, five cattle, and thirty-nine horses. At a much later date, 1466–1518, strays from Brandon (Warwickshire) consisted of thirty-two sheep, eleven cattle, and fourteen horses.[4] Evidently a sizeable horse population was wandering and trespassing around villages throughout the period, and in varied landscapes.

The management of horses led to many complaints, especially when they left their stables or paddocks near the peasant house and were sent to graze on the common pastures. Horses could cause much damage to crops, and one remedy was to tether them, but this was sometimes regarded as ineffective and a complete ban on horses in the common fields was imposed. An alternative control measure was to put the horses into the safekeeping of the common herdsman. At Sedgeberrow in 1336 a keeper of oxen and horses was employed, but Overbury (also in Worcestershire) in 1315 had a 'keeper of the horses'.[5] Younger animals tended to be unruly, and some concern was expressed about the behaviour of geldings.

The varied quality of horses is reflected in the values put on them, from high grade riding horses worth 20s, through middling work horses priced at 6s 8d to 10s down to miserable nags valued at 2s or less. The middle-ranking animals that did useful farm work feature as heriots (death duties), especially when more than one beast was taken, when the horse usually came second to a more highly prized ox. This hierarchy of animals of variable quality resulted from differences in breeding practices. Much unselective breeding resulted from mares and stallions grazing on to the common. The undesirable presence of stallions is acknowledged by the 1533 by-law at Earls Croome (Worcestershire) forbidding 'stoned' horses

---

[3] Magdalen College, Oxford, Willoughby B28.
[4] GA, Badminton muniments D2700 MAI/1; East Raynham library, box 25, 43; WA, ref. 705:134, BA1531/69, 69B; UNMSC, MiM 128/1–128/7.
[5] WCL, E13, E6.

from the commons, but other villages did not attempt to prohibit these animals.[6] More careful small-scale horse breeding was apparently being conducted at Honeybourne and Sherborne (both Gloucestershire) where mares and foals figure among the heriots in 1341–62, with the foals being valued at 10–16s.[7]

Some assessment of the animals can be made from their size. At Bishop's Cleeve (Gloucestershire) two complete horse skeletons have been excavated, from which the height of the living animals at the withers, that is the shoulders, could be estimated at 126cm and 138cm (50–55in), resembling modern Dartmoor and New Forest ponies.[8] Another indication of size comes from surviving horse shoes, which from west midland village sites varied between 9.9cm and 11.9cm in width, whereas the hooves of modern riding horses (not specialized race horses or cart horses) are 12–14cm wide. On the basis of the hoof sizes, the withers height of medieval peasant horses would have been below 156cm.[9] They came in a variety of colours, as they are described as white, grey, black, brown, and red. Their small size must have limited the work that they could undertake, and damage to the bones of the spine of one of the Bishop's Cleeve horses suggests that it struggled to accomplish the tasks required.

Peasant horses had a number of roles. Some were ridden, like a mare from Romsley (Worcestershire) which in 1326 Reginald ate Shawe hired from a substantial tenant, Richard de Honeford, to enable him to go to Alcester, a distance of 16 miles. Reginald overworked his mount, and it died after completing the journey. Honeford valued the animal at 6s 8d, no doubt overstated.[10] Perhaps few horses were intended for riding only, and the unfortunate Romsley mare probably resembled other work animals in being expected to perform a variety of tasks. Specialist riding horses were most likely to be owned by the relatively wealthy, such as the tenant with 3 ½ yardlands at Chaddesley Corbett, who died in 1420 in possession of four horses and a foal, all taken as heriots and valued at 30s, 20s, 16s, and 13s 4d; even the foal was worth 10s.[11] They clearly resembled in price and quality horses that could be found in the stables of the gentry. Horses of middling quality gave their owner not just a serviceable mount but also a marker of status. This is made clear in the case of eight sokemen (free tenants) at Stoneleigh (Warwickshire), mostly with yardland or half-yardland holdings, who were obliged according to the 1279 survey 'to come riding to the great *bedrip*' (harvest service) 'with staves in their hands' to supervise the harvest workers.[12] The tenant associated with the thirteenth-century house excavated at Pinbury (Gloucestershire) may well have been a woodward who needed to ride round nearby Overley Wood: a spur and

---

[6] WA, ref. 705:53, BA111/1 bundle 3.
[7] GA, D678/1 M1/1/1, M1/1/2; D678/65; D678/99.
[8] S. Warman, 'Animal Bone', in *Prehistoric and Medieval Occupation at Moreton-in-Marsh and Bishop's Cleeve, Gloucestershire*, edited by M. Watts (BGAS Archaeological Report, 5, 2007), pp. 86–8.
[9] J. Clark, ed., *The Medieval Horse and its Equipment* (Museum of London, 1995), pp. 29–32, 75–123.
[10] CR Romsley, pp. 80–1.   [11] SCLA, DR5/2774.   [12] WHR, p.69.

harness pendant were found.[13] The ornamental copper alloy harness pendants found on other peasant sites, some of them gilded or enamelled, or even with heraldic decoration, convey the prestige of horse riding, as the attention of onlookers would have been drawn to these trinkets flashing and jingling with the animal's motion.[14]

Most peasants rode horses for mundane tasks around their own villages, to visit fields or to work in them. Rather longer distances would be covered when they called on neighbouring villages or went to towns. Smallholders were included among the horse owners. A cottager at Cleeve Prior in 1416 had an affer (working horse) worth 2s that was taken as a heriot; a black mare valued at 16d was the heriot for the tenant of a cottage and curtilage with 2 acres at Stoke Gifford (Gloucestershire) in 1453.[15] As such tenants with limited landholding also earned wages, a horse would be an asset in finding employment, or carrying tools or materials. Better-off tenants owned horses mainly to haul carts, as the cart was increasingly used by peasants rather than the ox-drawn wain from the thirteenth century onwards.[16] Horses also tended to take over from oxen in pulling harrows. A few horses also powered mills: John Taylour operated a horse mill between 1502 and 1516 at Hanbury (Worcestershire) which lacked a water mill, and where the lord's windmill had long ceased to function.[17] Millers in charge of water and windmills often kept a horse to carry sacks of corn or flour, reminding us of the convenience of packhorses for smaller loads. Packhorses must have been a common sight as so many of the carrying jobs around a peasant holding involved limited quantities of hay, straw, fencing materials, and firewood. Both packhorses and carthorses carrying loads for some distance on roads with hard surfaces needed to be shod, and iron horseshoes are among the most frequently encountered metal finds on excavated village sites. The main use for carts was in the fields and along the lanes and tracks of the village, with a single animal between the shafts, either a gelding (castrated male) or mare. Mares were expected to breed as well as work, and a commonplace scene was a mare pulling a cart while accompanied by a foal, which met with some disapproval because of the potentially skittish behaviour of young horses.[18]

[13] J. Hart and others, *Living on the Edge. Archaeological Investigations of the Western Cotswolds* (Cotswold Archaeology Monograph, 9, 2016), p. 209.

[14] N. Palmer and J. Parkhouse, *Burton Dassett Southend, Warwickshire: A Medieval Market Village* (Society for Medieval Archaeology Monograph, 44, 2022), the report on small finds can be accessed at https://doi.org/10.5284/1083492.

[15] WCL, E47; GA, Badminton muniments D2700, MJ 11/1/2.

[16] J. Langdon, *Horses, Oxen and Technological Innovation. The Use of Draught Animals in English Farming 1066–1500* (Cambridge, 1986), pp. 212–25.

[17] WA, ref. 705:7, BA 7335/64,65. The lord of Quinton (Warwickshire) also tolerated a peasant's horse mill, but the lord of Ombersley (Worcestershire) demanded that one should be removed.

[18] E.g. WCL, E58 'No-one may have any foal over one year following its mother in a cart', at Cleeve Prior in 1443.

Horses were kept on the peasant holding because of their contribution to agricultural tasks and transport, especially for harrowing, carrying, and riding. Peasant horses in southern and eastern England were adopted as plough beasts to the point that they replaced oxen in a significant technological advance during the later Middle Ages. In the west midlands horses made considerable progress in haulage, so that when jurors were reporting on livestock pastured in Feckenham Forest in 1244–6 they found sixty-eight horses compared with 146 of the larger male cattle.[19] By c.1500, using heriots and strays in a sample district on and below the Cotswold edge, horses and oxen were equal in numbers, and many of the horses were high in quality.[20] They may have been beginning to be used in ploughing, perhaps as part of mixed teams, but oxen were still playing a major role in cultivation.

Peasants' horses did not form part of the household's diet, as horse meat was not eaten. A few horse bones found on village sites show signs of butchery, so perhaps the custom changed in famine conditions, or in normal times their flesh was fed to dogs.[21] The only profit from a dead horse normally came from its hide, hence the burial of horse carcasses. Old cattle, sheep, and pigs would not die of old age, but were slaughtered for meat.

Horses made a contribution to the commercial profits of the peasant holding, judging from the number of foals that were reared. Among the animals invading fields at Thornbury (Gloucestershire) between 1328 and 1337 were eighteen mares and sixteen foals. The Eldersfield strays included eleven mares and twenty-five foals. At Longdon (Worcestershire) in the years 1373–83, four mares and twenty foals were counted as strays. These places were all in the Severn valley but a similar picture emerges in the Cotswolds, such as the forty-eight foals among the 163 horses over many years grazing against the rules in fields at Kempsford, and five mares and eleven foals at Hawkesbury.[22] Mares were producing more foals than were needed to replace the village's old stock, so they must have been intended for external sale. Specialist horse breeders can be recognized among the owners of animals found grazing illicitly. For example, at Radbourne in Warwickshire in 1359, two people from the neighbouring villages of Priors Hardwick and Napton-on-the-Hill, allowed in each case five of their foals to cross the boundary. At Middleton (Warwickshire), John atte Hyde had six foals.[23] These animals were being kept in preparation for sale, and evidently the chance of making money, even when the foal was only worth a shilling or two, could not be

---

[19] *Rec Feck For*, pp. 12–14.
[20] C. Dyer, *A Country Merchant 1495–1520. Trading and Farming at the End of the Middle Ages* (Oxford, 2012), pp. 186, 188–90.
[21] J. Hamilton, 'Faunal Remains', in Palmer and Parkhouse, *Burton Dassett Southend*, at https://doi.org/10.5284/1083492.
[22] SRO, D641/1/4C/1; WAM, 21116–21166; East Raynham Library, box 25,43; TNA, SC2 175/41–59.
[23] Cheshire Archives, DCR 35/2; UNMSC, MiM 131/28.

overlooked. Really high returns could be gained by those with high-quality foals to sell, some of which were bought by lords to replenish demesne stock.[24] Older horses could also be sold. The animals were long-lived, up to 12 years according to the bones excavated from west midland village sites, and in that time an animal could have had a number of successive owners.[25]

In addition to selling horses and foals, peasants could earn money from hiring them, either the animal on its own (as in the case of the Romsley mare) or by making a horse and cart available in a haulage contract, which might attract clients within the village, or from nearby towns. At Blackwell, the rural manor containing the small town of New Shipston, horse ownership was generally high, judging from the high proportion of horses taken as heriots, partly because townspeople needed horses for their businesses and would hire them from their rural neighbours.

Cattle

The number of cattle that could be kept by each yardland on the commons was supposedly limited by stints which allowed the tenant between four and nine. The largest number recorded was twelve. A cottager might have been able to keep a cow. Figures for the cattle owned by individuals are based on inventories or lists of possessions of felons or tenants who had gone absent. They show that more substantial tenants owned between four and twelve cattle. Poorer people, even occasionally someone without a tenancy of land, could own a cow. A village's cattle, gathered together to graze in the care of the common herdsman, could reach a formidable total, so that sixty assembled on Lower Swell's fields in 1401. In 1419 two herdsmen were required to supervise the 140 beasts at Charlton (Worcestershire).[26]

Oxen, castrated males that had reached the age of three years, were the essential beasts of burden hauling ploughs, heavy wains, and harrows in the early thirteenth century, but mainly ploughs in subsequent centuries. The oxen were yoked in pairs, and a holding often owned only two or four of them. A remarkably generous stint at Moor (Worcestershire) in 1436 suggests that a yardland holding might have between six and eight oxen (and some 'beasts' as well).[27] Normally a plough needed a six- or eight-ox team, and they would be assembled by bringing together animals from at least two or three holdings. Most yardland and half-yardland holdings owned a plough (the wooden implement with iron fittings) and one, two or three oxen, and smaller holdings might also have one ox. In the late fourteenth-century a tenant with 'a messuage and a croft' and another having 'two

---

[24] J. Claridge, 'The Role of Demesnes in the Trade of Agricultural Horses in Late Medieval England', *AgHR* 65(2017), pp. 1–19, especially p. 19.
[25] Warner, 'Animal Bone'.   [26] TNA, SC2 175/76; WCL, E48.   [27] WCL, E56.

messuages and two crofts' on the Winchcomb Abbey estate, and a quarter-yardlander and a holding with 6 acres at Cleeve Prior, each owned an ox.[28] Such holdings lacked a plough, so the smallholder's ox became part of a composite team made up of animals from other tenants. The contributors would also share the labour, so the smallholder could act on a number of days as one of the two ploughmen. As part of the collective effort, he or she would be entitled to enough days' ploughing to cultivate the few acres of the smallholding, though of course the plough team would spend the most time working on the larger holdings. Such arrangements are implied by the Brimpsfield survey of 1299 with which Chapter 3 began. It assumed (with optimism) that a half-yardland would own four oxen and a quarter-yardland two. It does not state that two, three, or four such tenants should pool their assets to create eight-ox teams, but this would have been the intention. The Brimpsfield document, reflecting the lord's perspective, is only concerned with teams ploughing the lord's demesne, but the same combination of plough beasts could have been applied to the cultivation of the tenants' holdings (see 'Farming and methods and techniques' in Chapter 6).[29]

The values put on peasant oxen suggests their quality. They were regularly said to be worth between 8s to 12s, and in south-west Gloucestershire, presumably under the influence of the Bristol market, they rose to 16s or 20s around 1500, and even to 30s in the 1530s.[30] In the period when lords' demesnes were being managed by the lords' officials, peasant oxen taken as heriots would be added to the demesne livestock, because they were judged not to be inferior to the lords' animals.

Oxen spent many days each year yoked together and pulling either a plough or wain, and as was the case with horses their bones carry signs of the stress related to hard work.[31] When they were not working they grazed with other cattle under the supervision of the herdsman, who was sometimes called 'the keeper of the avers' and there was concern about the damage they could do to the cultivated fields. At night the 'avers' (a generic term for adult male cattle) would be brought to closes and yards adjoining the peasant house where they might receive some supplementary feed (mostly hay and straw). Cattle housing was limited: some holdings had purpose-built byres, and rarely accommodation was provided at one end of the dwelling house (see 'Animal welfare' in this chapter). Otherwise the yard, which was often sunken and fenced, afforded them some shelter.[32] Their manure could add substantially to the peasant's dung hill.

---

[28] GA, D678/65, 99; WCL, E36, E39.

[29] The reality of the eight ox team has been questioned. Perhaps they managed with four.

[30] GA, Badminton muniments MJ11/1/2, 3–5 (Stoke Gifford); MJ 9/1–2, 3 (Rockhampton); WA, ref. 009:1, BA 2636/192 92626 1/12, 168/92339, 165/92225 4/8; 165/92226 1/7.

[31] Hamilton, 'Faunal Remains'; Warman, 'Animal Bone'.

[32] G. Beresford, *The Medieval Clay-land Village. Excavations at Goltho and Barton Blount* (Society for Medieval Archaeology Monograph 6, 1975), pp. 13–18. Sunken yards are clearly visible among the earthworks of west midland village sites, e.g. Norton Subedge (Gloucestershire), Stretton Baskerville, and Wolfhampcote (Warwickshire).

Individual better-off peasant households usually owned two or three cows, and smallholders often had one. Their primary function was to provide the household with dairy produce. A lord's cow yielded between 54lbs and 93lbs of butter and cheese each year on the Berkeley estate in the late thirteenth century.[33] A peasant cow producing 74lbs annually would allow each member of the household an ounce of cheese or butter for each of the days when cheese-eating was permitted. In an agreement of 1483 to maintain Helena Ludlow of Shirehampton (near Bristol) she was promised a cheese, presumably of a standard size, each week.[34] A peasant holding that was keeping two or three cows would be able to provide for the household and have a surplus for sale, bringing in a useful few shillings each year.

Cows were accompanied by their offspring: calves, yearlings, heifers, and bullocks. As they matured the young animals either replaced old oxen or cows, or were sold. Young cattle, especially calves and bullocks, could be sent to market for their meat, and old oxen and cows could end their lives in the same way, sometimes after being prepared by fattening. Old animals (or parts of them), which were less marketable, would be more likely to be consumed in the household.

At Burton Dassett Southend a large sample of bones reveals the importance of cattle as a source of meat, because although sheep outnumbered cattle (based on counting the minimum number of individuals) a cattle carcass weighed ten times more than a sheep carcass, so the villagers ate more beef than mutton. The cattle that were killed and consumed in Burton Dassett Southend were aged between 4 and 9 years, while the younger animals, especially bullocks, are scarce because they were sold in local towns where they fetched a good price. Some Burton Dassett Southend bullocks may have ended their lives in the butchers' shambles of Coventry or even in London (having been sold at Banbury or other local markets). Finds of cattle on west-midland urban sites include animals of all ages, with some younger animals suggesting the preferences of relatively wealthy consumers. Specialist butchers are recorded living and working in some villages, and at Burton and other excavated villages the presence of all parts of the animal, including fragments of skull, suggests that the animals were killed in the village. The urban methods of carcass preparation, for example, by splitting down the spine, were not practised in the country.[35] Bones at Pinbury suggested that after killing the animals in the village, the peasants ate the less desirable parts, such as the head, and the better cuts were taken away for sale.[36]

---

[33] B. Wells-Furby, *The Berkeley Estate 1281–1417. Its Economy and Development* (BGAS, 2012), p. 183.
[34] WA, ref. 009:1, BA 2636/165 92225 4/8.
[35] Hamilton, 'Faunal Remains'; B. Levitan, 'The Animal Bones', in A. Saville, 'Salvage Recording of Romano-British, Saxon, Medieval and Post-Medieval Remains at North Street, Winchcombe, Gloucestershire', *TBGAS* 103 (1985), pp. 130–5; M. Holmes, 'Animal Bones', in L. Whittingham, 'Evidence for Medieval Craft Industry and Occupation...Hales Street, Coventry', *TBWAS*, 122 (2020), pp. 103–7.
[36] M. Holmes, 'Animal Bones', in Hart, *Living Near the Edge*, pp. 186–9.

The quantity of meat that could be obtained from each animal was limited by their relatively small size. An adult bovine at Dassett Southend measured 112–115cm (45–46in) at the shoulder, and similar figures of 108 and 112cm have been calculated for cattle in medieval Droitwich, which are likely to have been brought into the country from peasant holdings. These are significantly smaller than their modern successors which stand at 137–150cm. The edible meat on a medieval cattle carcass is believed to have weighed 240lbs (109kg).[37] The household which slaughtered a beast no doubt ate well for a few days, but much of the animal would have been salted, like that annual quarter of beef allowed to a retired peasant of Blackwell (Warwickshire).[38]

How do we strike the balance between the contribution that cattle made to household subsistence and the profits they yielded in the market? Cattle gave the household haulage, milk, meat, and manure. A modest income would have been generated by dairy produce, and more from the occasional sale of animals, both young and old. By-products of animals slaughtered in the village included hides, and also horns, which at Burton Dassett Southend were removed after slaughter, and probably sold to tanners and horners in towns. As was the case with horses, oxen were profitably hired, and cows could also be rented out for as much as 4*s* to 5*s* per annum.

Most peasants' sales of cattle and dairy produce would have yielded less than 20*s* per annum for even a large holding. Only specialists in the right environment could expect to make large financial gains from keeping cattle. In the Warwickshire Arden the rising demand for beef from the towns from the late fourteenth century stimulated individuals to keep herds as large as sixty animals (at Middleton in 1407).[39] The profitability of the specialism continued and even increased in the fifteenth century when families such as the Deys and the Baillys achieved an impressive rise in their social standing (see 'Social mobility' in Chapter 4). Worcestershire peasants in the thirteenth century can already be seen as cattle herders in Feckenham Forest, and in the fifteenth century in the woodlands in the north of the county there were individuals with as many as the twenty bullocks said to be in the keeping of John Whatecroft at Northfield in 1439.[40] Dairying on a commercial scale was being practised by John Thatcher of Mitton (in Hartlebury parish) in 1476 when he was accused of failing to pay tithes on the output of eleven cows. Thomas Charlecote kept seven cows at Kempsey in 1447. These individuals lived in the Severn Valley and tithe payments suggest

---

[37] Hamilton, 'Faunal Remains'; A. Locker, 'Animal Bone', in *Iron Age and Roman Salt Production and the Medieval Town of Droitwich*, edited by S. Woodiwiss (CBA Research Report 81, 1992), pp. 88, 172–8; B. Harvey, *Living and Dying in England 1100–1540* (Oxford, 1993), p. 228.

[38] WCL, E15.

[39] UNMSC, MiM 131/34; A. Watkins, 'Cattle Grazing in the Forest of Arden in the Later Middle Ages', *AgHR* 37 (1989), pp. 12–25.

[40] *Rec Feck For*, pp. 1214, 21–6; BAH, 518078.

specialized dairying in the river valley villages of Deerhurst and Driffield (Gloucestershire) in the early sixteenth century.[41]

The day-to-day management of cattle was divided along gender lines. Male members of the household looked after the beasts that pulled the plough and wains, while the cows and calves were the responsibility of women. According to a church court, a woman living in the house of Peter Aprice of Hartlebury in 1491 was accustomed to walk from Aprice's house to a pasture called Mytham to milk cows. Such journeys would be followed by the processing of the milk, attested by occasional finds of ceramic bowls used to separate cream.[42]

Peasants must have practised some selective breeding of cattle, judging from the high quality of the oxen that we have noted. West-midland peasant cattle seem often to have been red in colour, and their horns tended to be short, though a medium horned variety is found at Bristol. They rarely owned a bull, and must have relied on the lord's bull when cattle were kept on the demesne. When the demesne was leased out, as at Norton Subedge (Gloucestershire) in 1448, the farmer was expected to provide a common bull, but failed to do so. At Hartlebury the rector usually kept a bull and boar for the benefit of the parishioners, but again was criticized for their absence.[43] When in normal times these animals were being made available to the peasants, the service would presumably have carried a fee, but no trace of these payments has survived.

Sheep

Peasant sheep flocks, added together, exceeded 7,000 at Blockley at the end of the fifteenth century, and 3,000 at Bishop's Cleeve in the late fourteenth.[44] Demesne flocks on a single manor for comparison usually varied between 200 and 600. To us medieval sheep seem small, with a height at the withers (shoulder) for an adult estimated at 55cm (22in) at Burton Dassett, and at Bishop's Cleeve between 49cm (19in) and 56cm (22in). In towns (relevant because of the rural source of their sheep) figures varied between 53 and 61cm, for example with 56 and 57cm on a Bristol site.[45] A comparable measurement for modern animals would be 91cm

---

[41] R.N. Swanson and D. Guyatt, eds., *The Visitation and Court Book of Hartlebury, 1401–1598* (WHS, new series, 24, 2013) p. 216; WA, ref. 705:4, BA54; *VE*, 2, p. 450.

[42] Swanson and Guyatt, eds., *Court Book*, p. 239; R.H. Hilton and P.A. Rahtz, 'Upton, Gloucestershire, 1959–1964', *TBGAS* 85 (1966), pp. 130–1.

[43] L. Higbee, 'Faunal Remains', in R. Jackson, *The Archaeology of the Medieval Suburb of Broadmead, Bristol: Excavations in Union Street, 2000* (Bristol and Region Archaeological Services, 2010), pp. 114–15; Dorset History Centre, D10/M233; Swanson and Guyatt, eds., *Court Book*, p. 239.

[44] Dyer, *Country Merchant*, p. 154; C. Dyer, *Lords and Peasants in a Changing Society, 680–1540* (Cambridge, 1980), p. 329.

[45] Hamilton, 'Faunal Remains'; M. Maltby, 'The Animal Bone', in D. Enright and M. Watts, *A Romano-British and Medieval Settlement Site at Stoke Road, Bishop's Cleeve, Gloucestershire* (BGAS Archaeological Report, 1, 2002), pp. 44–9; Higbee, 'Faunal Remains', p. 110.

(36in). The 'traditional' breed of Cotswold sheep now kept by 'rare breed' specialists are bulky animals, quite unlike their medieval predecessors, and the popular name of 'Cotswold lions' used in the Middle Ages refers to the mane of wool about the sheep's head, not to their physique or temperament.

Wealthy individuals might have sixty-eight sheep, like Elyas atte Brugge of Abbots Salford (Warwickshire) in 1389. Less prosperous tenants making wills around 1500 bequeathed thirty-four sheep in one case, and thirty in another. John Jeffes' inventory, taken at Ailstone (Warwickshire) in 1538, noted thirty sheep.[46] However, a number of lists of possessions and inventories make no mention of sheep, so clearly some individuals chose not to keep them. Stints, of which we have thirty from villages dispersed across the region, allowed a yardland tenant in one village to keep 100 on the common, two set the limit at eighty, and eleven at sixty, and the remainder mainly at thirty or forty.[47] This rationing of grazing might have followed calculations of the pastures' capacity, but one suspects also special pleading by those with large flocks, ever anxious to expand their number.

Those villagers who observed the limits on flocks kept on common pastures had to face up to those grazing very large flocks. This was not just in the Gloucestershire Cotswolds, though two flocks of 300 were reported at Snowshill in 1466, 400 and 200 at Rendcomb in 1435, and perhaps the largest number, in 1442 at Kingscote, when a total of 1,330 tenant sheep included two flocks of 300 and three of 200.[48] Tenants with large numbers occupied the pastures of champion villages, with three having 300 each on the pastures of Long Marston (Warwickshire) in 1453, and at nearby Alveston in 1428 a flock of 200 and three of 100 were reported. Tenants in the woodlands tended to keep smaller numbers, but we still find individuals with 100 at Eldersfield, Longdon, and Stoke Prior.[49]

These figures impress modern historians and at the time must have disturbed the ordinary villagers, but they give a false impression because most tenants kept sheep on a modest scale or did not keep them at all. The villagers of Teddington (Gloucestershire) in 1427 informed the manor court of sheep destroying the lord's meadow (presumably by consuming and trampling the grass intended for hay) which led them to compile a list resembling a census of the village's sheep. This consisted of two tenants with 200 animals, three with eighty, and another five with between eighteen and thirty. The main five offenders were also said to have 'unjustly occupied the common' at another time with between forty and 160 sheep.[50] The large flocks are impressive, but a half of the flocks were of moderate size. Another snapshot of the distribution of sheep can be obtained by analysing the wool purchases of John Heritage, the Moreton-in-Marsh

---

[46] WCL, E34; WA, ref. 008:7, BA3585, 1538/242.
[47] A sample is given in Dyer, *Country Merchant*, p. 186; Dyer, *Lords and Peasants*, p. 325.
[48] GA, D678/95; SRO, D641/1/4M/1; GA, D471/M2.
[49] GA, D678/62; WCL, E53; WA, ref. 705:134, BA 1531/69B; WAM, 21125; WCL, E223.
[50] WCL, E52.

Table 7.1 Estimates of the size of the flocks of those selling wool to John Heritage, 1503

Quantity of wool (in lbs)	Below 28	28–139	140–251	252–363	364–727	728 +
No. of sheep per owner	15 (or less)	16–79	80–143	144–207	208–415	416 +
No. of owners	7	21	14	4	5	1
%	13	40	27	8	10	2

Source: WAM, 12258, fos. 9r–13r.

woolmonger of 1497–1520, whose business catered for both large and small producers. A significant number of his suppliers owned 200–400 animals, and he bought a good proportion of fleeces from those keeping a hundred sheep, but more than a half of those selling him wool were pasturing less than eighty (Table 7.1). Cottagers owned sheep as can be seen from their heriots, for example, at Hawkesbury in the Cotswolds from forty-six payments of heriot between 1394 and 1500, six were cottage holdings where the 'best beast' was a ewe and lamb, or a young sheep, a hoggaster. Another eight cottagers were better off, in that they had a cow to be taken as a heriot, but they may have owned sheep as well.[51]

In the *Valor Ecclesiasticus* of 1535, a comprehensive survey of church property, tithe records often exclude details, but the clerks working on parts of the west midlands did not consistently abbreviate the entries. One group of thirty parishes in eastern Gloucestershire, many in the Cotswolds, were the benefices of rectors (they had not been taken over by monasteries), and the main products, corn, hay, mills, personal tithes, and so on were valued separately. The wool and lamb totals are a guide to the importance of sheep in each parish. They come in round sums such as 30s, 48s, and 60s, which were estimates but not fictions. Wool and lambs together made 48 per cent of the total of tithes for Colesbourne parish, a high point on the western edge of the Cotswolds, and only 3 per cent of the tithes at Corse in the woodlands on the west bank of the Severn. Such a low figure was exceptional, and in 15 of the 30 parishes wool and lambs accounted for 33 per cent of the value of the tithes, or a higher figure, and these sheep products were worth at least 25 per cent in another seven parishes.[52] As a check on the reliability of the tithe assessments in the *Valor*, they can be compared with tithe accounts compiled for rectories operating their own administration. The rectory of Bishop's Cleeve, a village mainly in the lowlands though with some upland pasture, in 1389–90 derived 12 per cent of its tithe income from wool, and 7 per cent from lambs, so at 19 per cent was not too far below Gloucestershire parishes in the *Valor*.[53]

---

[51] TNA, SC2 175/46–56.   [52] VE, 2, pp. 436–51.
[53] Corpus Christi College, Oxford, B/14/2/3/1.

The tithes demonstrate the importance of arable for peasant farming, with 60 per cent or 70 per cent of the tithe values deriving from corn in some parishes, but in eleven parishes the grain tithe fell below 50 per cent of the total, and in thirteen others lay between 51 and 59 per cent. The wool and lamb totals made up a good part of the tithe values, but milk, calves, and piglets helped to push up the proportion of tithes derived from pastoral farming. The tithe record did not accurately reflect the balance between the income from arable and pasture, because although wool and lambs accounted for the main revenues from sheep keeping, 'milk and calves' were not the only outputs from cattle. The main point is that in a significant number of villages pastoral revenues exceeded those from corn-growing, and this re-orientation had come in the late medieval period, and especially after 1400 when the use of land changed (see 'Arable and pasture: managing change' in Chapter 6). Peasant sheep keeping had played a major role in moving the rural economy's centre of gravity.

If the wool and lamb tithes are considered separately, they reveal differences in sheep management across Gloucestershire. At Colesbourne, wool tithes were valued at 48s (implying wool production worth £24) and lamb tithes at 5s. The likely explanation of the relatively low figure for lambs was that the village's extensive hill pasture was occupied by wethers, which were hardy adult animals able to cope with cold winds. Wethers are recorded on uplands elsewhere in the region, such as Hawkesbury.[54] Ewes through the winter and spring were kept in sheltered valleys, and lambs were more plentiful at lowland villages such as Driffield and Hatherop, with lamb tithes valued at 20s and 18s 4d, respectively. These were in south Gloucestershire, but high lamb tithes are also found in the Vale to the north, at Swindon and Badgeworth. Again the pattern found in the tithes is confirmed by other sources, as at Twyning also in the Vale in 1443 where a stint in 1443 limited to forty-five the number of ewes 'and their issue', with no mention of wethers.[55]

The parishes which produced the wool and lambs were not dependent entirely on the resources within their boundaries. A problem for those keeping livestock on the hill pastures was gaining access to hay for winter fodder. Duntisbourne Rouse had plenty of hill pasture, and its wool tithes were worth 60s but its hay was worth only 6s. In the adjoining parish of Daglingworth the manor had a link with Latton in Wiltshire, and other similar connections with the extensive meadows of the Thames valley helped to feed hill sheep in the Cotswolds. But these arrangements benefited the demesne sheep, and peasants may have had to purchase hay, and depended a good deal on peas, oats, and even drage as fodder crops.

The big estates practised transhumance, which meant that large flocks of ewes and lambs, or young sheep, belonging to Westminster Abbey or the bishops of Worcester, would be driven on to summer pasture on the Cotswold hills in

[54] TNA, SC2 175/58.   [55] GA, DA678/94.

May, to return to the valleys in October. Peasant sheep could follow the same pattern, sometimes without leaving their own village territory, at Hanley Castle (Worcestershire) for example, the sheep could be kept in the Severn valley in the winter, and occupy pasture on the Malvern Hills in summer. The same advantage was enjoyed by villages lying in the lowlands around Bredon Hill, such as Kemerton (Worcestershire). Many peasants did not have rights to customary grazing on high ground, but individuals could negotiate access to seasonal pasture. The tithe customs for Beckford (Worcestershire) gave details on how tithe should be levied on those who 'take in sheep for summering', referring to Beckford people selling their common rights on the slopes of Bredon Hill to outsiders from lowland villages.[56] Another device was for a sheep owner in a nearby village to acquire land in a place with hill pasture and gain access to its commons. This may explain why tenants of Teddington held land in neighbouring Beckford.[57] The predominant method for gaining seasonal pasture was to pay cash for 'summering' and 'wintering', which caused much controversy in the villages which received the flocks, leading to accusations that 'he receives the sheep of strangers', or that tenants 'sold agistment', or they granted *haverage* or *harfold* without licence. Those who offended by selling access to common pasture are named, but the strangers remain unidentified, suggesting a network of contacts over some distance. The villagers who caused complaint by selling summer pasture rights in the uplands, might themselves have sought lowland winter pasture for their sheep.

In addition to the thirty Gloucestershire parishes, the *Valor* gives enough details for seventeen parishes scattered over Worcestershire to inform us about sheep and other animals in both champion and woodland landscapes. The information is less detailed, as each item was not listed separately. Instead, corn and hay were valued together, as were wool and lambs. And the other tithes, including piglets, calves, geese, and flax, were combined under the heading 'lesser tithes'.[58] Taken together corn and hay were assessed at 78 per cent of the total, with 16 per cent for wool and lambs, and 6 per cent for 'lesser tithes'. So the peasants of Worcestershire, though deriving a higher proportion of their agricultural output from arable and meadow than their counterparts in Gloucestershire, obtained income from sheep that was far from negligible. The parish with the highest tithe assessment deriving from wool and lambs was Broadway, with 23 per cent. This was a large parish straddling the Cotswold edge and it attracted a large number of flocks belonging to strangers, revealing a persistent minority ready to make a profit from the sale of common rights.[59] The smallest share of tithe revenue deriving from sheep among the Worcestershire parishes was 3 per cent for Mamble in the wooded north of the county, where the peasants gave priority to pigs, as did those at Eastham and Clifton-on-Teme.

---

[56] GA, GDR 40/T2. [57] WCL, E34.
[58] *VE*, 3, pp. 261–79. [59] TNA, SC2 210/33.

The tithe assessments show that sheep were a widespread presence, especially important in the high Cotswolds but also in champion and woodland communities. The value of the corn in the 1535 calculations was based on the price the tithes fetched in the market, but only part of the peasant crop was sold, and the rest was consumed in the household. Wool on the other hand was almost entirely for sale, except some held back for spinning. This was still contributing cash to the household budget, as the yarn would be sold. The wool of thirty adult sheep would be sold for 14s to 24s, and 100 fleeces would be worth between 47s and 83s (depending on the location of the pasture and the fluctuations of price).[60] For many peasants the proceeds from wool paid their rent and taxes, and helped to fund capital investment and consumer spending.

Other sources of income included the sale of old wethers and ewes, animals showing signs of disease, sterile ewes, and sometimes surplus lambs. Sheep skins (woolfells) were sold perhaps to be processed in the village, or more often went to a fellmonger in a town. At times sheeps' cheese was available for sale. It was produced by the lord's officials on the manor of Minchinhampton (Gloucestershire) and is likely also to have been made by peasants.[61] Fees gathered for *haverage* enabled tenants with common rights but no sheep of their own to draw income from other people's animals.

In view of the income that sheep could generate, why did some peasants have only a modest number or did not keep them at all? Perhaps in particular places and times the price of wool was a deterrent: for example, it was lower in Worcestershire than on the Cotswolds, and dipped everywhere in the mid-fifteenth century. Sheep were liable to disease, such as liver fluke, and needed care to prevent and treat scab and foot rot with expensive remedies such as tar. They were also vulnerable to theft, attacks from dogs, and a tendency to wander. Shepherds were employed to look after peasant flocks full-time, and some peasants built expensive sheepcotes. In short, sheep were troublesome and potentially costly.

What did sheep contribute to the peasant household, as distinct from their earnings in the market? They trod their droppings into the surface of the fields when folded, and if they were housed in a sheepcote, or penned in an enclosure, they left useful deposits of dung. We do not know if their milk and cheese contributed regularly to the diet of the household, though peasant sheep might have been milked by smallholders who lacked a cow. Sheep were an important source of meat for household consumption. At Dassett Southend about 40 per cent of the bones recovered, and more than a half of the minimum number of individual animals represented by the bones, came from sheep. The figure was rather higher on Cotswold sites, and much higher (based on the number of bones) at Upton.[62]

---

[60] T.H. Lloyd, *The Movement of Wool Prices in Medieval England* (EcHR supplement, 6, 1973).
[61] TNA, SC6 856/23.
[62] S. Yealland and E.S. Higgs, 'The Economy', in Hilton and Rahtz, 'Upton', pp. 139–43.

However, even in a village with an abundance of sheep, mutton consumption was exceeded by beef. Those who owned sheep valued them primarily as wool producers, and did not kill them until they reached their fourth or fifth year. Most surplus and superannuated animals would have been sold alive, to be killed in towns, so only a minority were consumed in the household. The presence of skull bones suggests that some were slaughtered in the village, and shows that all parts of the animal were consumed. A by-product of processing the carcass was tallow, from which candles were made for lighting the household or for sale.

On balance, dead or alive, sheep were of more value to the peasants as a source of cash than as contributors to household subsistence. Wool, and the other saleable products from sheep, yielded more income than any other source, often including the sale of corn.

Goats

Goats had a negative reputation in the Middle Ages, partly because of their destructive effect on vegetation.[63] Among modern historians they are assumed to have lived on marginal, low quality land, and to have been kept by the poor; they epitomized the self-sufficiency of the disadvantaged. Peasant goats are mentioned in documents because of the damage that they caused. For example, in 1315 a man and woman of Knighton-on-Teme (Worcestershire) in the manor of Newnham, were said to have allowed goats to enter the lord's wood of Cornwood.[64] This report was connecting the goats to an area of assarting on the edge of a very large wood.

In Feckenham Forest in 1242–6 seventeen people were said to own goats in the manor of Feckenham, with between one and fifteen of the animals each. Most flocks were small, with twelve of them containing four animals or a lesser number. In another list compiled in 1244–6 ten people were said to have fifty-three goats. These goat owners were not very poor. They owned other animals, and their names linked them to well-established local families. The goats grazed in a royal forest, but the many oxen and horses listed alongside the goats, and other evidence in the period for fields and pastures, suggests that Feckenham resembled many other productive and well-cultivated woodland landscapes. So the goats did not represent some primitive survival, but belonged to a normal cross-section of peasant society living in a developed though still evolving landscape. Nor did they disappear in the new world that emerged after the Black Death, as in 1362

---

[63] C. Dyer, 'Alternative Agriculture: Goats in Medieval England', in *People, Landscape and Alternative Agriculture*, edited by R. Hoyle (AgHR Supplement, 2004), pp. 20–38.
[64] WCL, E7.

seventeen people owned goats, mostly in small numbers though one had six, and the largest flock contained twelve.[65]

The peasants of Feckenham kept goats primarily as a source of dairy produce for their own households. Most of the animals were females, and their owners were evidently prepared to devote time to milking, or rather were content that their wives and daughters would take on the task. The animals saved their owners' labour by finding their own food in the rough pastures and areas covered in bushes and trees. These were low-cost animals, enhancing the variety of the household's diet, and accorded well with households aiming at self-sufficiency. However, they could also be a source of cash, as those who chose to keep a dozen of the animals must have been aiming at a saleable surplus of cheese. Other sources of commercial profit were the kids much in demand in aristocratic households: for example, three meals with kids were served to the bishop of Hereford when his household stayed at Prestbury (Gloucestershire) in February 1290, no doubt supplied by peasant goat keepers from the Cheltenham area. Another pocket of goat keeping was revealed when the Duke of York's household spent Christmas in Malvern Chase in 1409. Kids were also available to the household in Bristol Castle in 1226, probably being reared in the royal forest of Kingswood.[66] A limited market for the meat of adult goats is suggested by the few goat bones found on urban domestic sites at Droitwich and Warwick.[67] Droitwich was of course located on the edge of Feckenham Forest. Goats, though small in number, illuminate a niche species in a specialist landscape, and show peasants as opportunists seeking supplies of dairy produce for their households and sometimes commercial profit.

Pigs

Pigs are often regarded as peasant animals, but large numbers were kept in towns, and pork was prominent in aristocratic diet.[68] Pigs were quite thinly spread through peasant society, in the sense that many individuals owned one or two adults, from which offspring were bred. Lords levied pannage on pigs at a rate of ½ d or 1d on each animal, depending on age. This payment was for access to the

---

[65] *Rec Feck For*, pp.12–14, 21–6, 168, 170.

[66] J. Webb, ed., *Roll of the Household Expenses of Richard de Swinfield Bishop of Hereford* (Camden Society, 1854–5), pp. 51, 52; J. Toomey, ed., *A Household Account of Edward Duke of York at Hanley Castle, 1409-10* (WHS, new series, 24, 2013), pp. 87, 89, 91–3; C. Woolgar, ed., *Household Accounts of Medieval England*, part 1 (British Academy Records of Social and Economic History, new series, 17, 1992), pp. 147–50.

[67] J.D. Hurst, ed., *A Multi-Period Salt Production Site at Droitwich. Excavations at Upwich* (CBA Research Report, 107, 1997), p. 103.

[68] U. Albarella, 'Pig Husbandry and Pork Consumption in Medieval England', in *Food in Medieval England. Diet and Nutrition*, edited by C.M. Woolgar, D. Serjeantson, and T. Waldron (Oxford, 2006), pp. 72–87.

acorns and beechmast in the lords' woods in October in preparation for slaughter in November. Typically between ten and thirty households in a village paid pannage, and most of them owned between one and four animals each. They were especially numerous at Leigh, at the northern end of the Malvern Hills in north-west Worcestershire, where pannage was paid in 1381 for 236 animals, with individual herds as large as ten, fourteen, and eighteen.[69] The probability of evasion makes us regard these as minimum figures. In inventories and lists of individuals' possessions numbers can be quite large, like the Broadwas tenant in 1388 who owned a sow, six pigs, and eight piglets, and John Jeffe of Ailstone in 1538 had twelve swine (alongside nine cattle and thirty sheep).[70] Pigs were often not included among the livestock subject to stints, though at Ombersley no cottager was to have more than four pigs 'in the fields or at large'. Other places allowed much larger numbers: in the thirteenth century a stint as high as twenty was quoted at Willoughby (Warwickshire).[71]

By-laws show that pigs were spread over every part of the region; in champion villages such as Alveston or Sedgeberrow as well as in the woodlands, those keeping pigs were ordered to keep the animals under control, and to ring them or yoke them to limit the amount of damage they would cause by rooting. Such complaints and large pannage payments allow 'pig villages' to be identified. They are most often encountered in the woodlands and the Vale of Gloucester, though Hawkesbury, a Cotswold village with extensive woodlands is included, and the champion village of Cleeve Prior (Worcestershire). Pig bones recovered in excavations of village sites could amount to 10 per cent of the total, but at Upton and Goldicote fell as low as 4 per cent and 6 per cent.[72] They are under-represented because of the relative fragility of the bones of younger animals.

Unlike cattle and sheep, pigs were not always concentrated in the hands of the wealthy; less affluent pig owners include John Passe of Kempsey (Worcestershire) who held 6 acres, but in 1394–5 paid pannage on thirteen pigs, which made him one of the leading pig-keepers in his village.[73] Pigs were relatively low in cost; they were kept in small and cheaply built sties, and their food came partly from foraging and rooting on waste land. Poorer tenants may have fed a share of their gleanings in the harvest field to a pig.

Pig keeping involved an annual routine of taking the animals to pannage in the lord's wood. For most animals the woods were local and the journey short, but in addition long-distance, large-scale expeditions were mounted to very extensive woods with substantial feeding opportunities. The annual pannage reported to be

---

[69] TNA, SC2 210/53.   [70] WCL, E34; WA, ref. 008:7, BA 3585, 1538/242.
[71] WA, ref. 705:56, BA3910/22(x); Magdalen College, Oxford, Willoughby B28.
[72] Yealland and Higgs, 'The Economy'; S. Hamilton Dyer, 'Animal Bones', in P. Thompson and S. Palmer, 'Iron-Age, Romano-British and Medieval Settlements Excavated on the Transco Newbold Pacey to Honeybourne Gas Pipeline in 2000', *TBWAS* 116 (2012), pp. 120–8.
[73] WA, ref.705:4, BA54.

normally paid to the lord of Malvern Chase in the late fifteenth century, £21 8s 1½d would suggest that hundreds of animals converged on the woods around Welland.[74] In the early thirteenth century, pigs from the demesnes of Cotswold and Severn Valley manors were driven to feast on the acorns of Malvern, and presumably if peasants were willing to pay the fee their pigs could join them.[75] Robert Fippus of Castle Morton (in the Chase) in 1373 was said to be occupying the common with forty pigs belonging to 'strangers'.[76] Similar arrangements were made in the Forest of Dean, where pannage generated an annual income for the crown in the thirteenth century that varied between £20 and £26.[77] The forest administration welcomed the 'pigs of strangers' for the profits they generated for the crown, and the unofficial pickings of forest officials.

After their encounter with the woodland acorns, many pigs were killed, traditionally around 11 November, and certainly towards the end of the year. The animal bones from rural settlements show that their lives ended at around 15 months, when they had reached a good size.[78] The pannage records show that some survived into a second year. The meat and offal that could not be preserved would have been eaten soon after slaughter, by the household and dispersed among neighbours. The main contribution to long-term meat supplies were the two sides of bacon (flitches) obtained from each carcass, which after salting and smoking could be preserved for months. The bacon was displayed in the smokey atmosphere of the roof of the house, available for consumption. At Mathon in 1383 a flitch was too easily accessible, as a neighbour's dog entered the house, seized the bacon, and ate it.[79] Fresh pork in November, preserved bacon and probably sausages (or puddings as they were called) provided the household with a source of meat through much of the year. The fresh meat and salted joints of beef and mutton would have been available more irregularly, and were more likely to feature in the diet of the better-off.

Keeping pigs belonged to a part of the village economy in which money had a limited role. The pigs fended for themselves and their owners did not need to make fields or crofts available to them. The cost of employing the village swineherd was shared among the pig owners. Boars seem to have run about the village, so their owners did not apparently have to be paid for their services. The whole village faced low-level disruption from the misbehaviour of wandering animals, which was perhaps tolerable because most households derived some gain from small-scale pig keeping.

Pigs contributed to the subsistence of peasant households but they also brought in cash. Flitches of bacon were sold, as when Richard Golafre in 1384 bought one

---

[74] *Rec Hanley*, p. 131.   [75] WA, ref. 821, BA 3814, fo. 51 (White Book of Worcester).
[76] WAM 21116.
[77] M.L. Bazeley, 'The Forest of Dean and its Relations with the Crown During the Twelfth and Thirteenth Centuries', *TBGAS*, 33 (1910), pp. 153–286, especially p. 222.
[78] Hamilton, 'Faunal Remains'; Holmes, 'Animal Bones'.   [79] WAM, 213879.

from Richard Bele of Chaceley.[80] Bacon also figured among the peasants' sales to towns, but live animals were sent to market by the large-scale pig owners, like Denise Holdwyn of Longdon whose twenty animals in 1387 were said to have damaged crops worth 10s.[81]

Poultry

Poultry, meaning cocks and hens, pullets, capons, ducks, geese, and doves, were not very profitable, and consequently receive limited attention from contemporary documents and modern historians. Although a hen in the thirteenth century was worth only 1*d* and a goose 2*d*, peasants devoted time and energy to rearing them.

Poultry, especially hens, could be found in every landscape, settlement, and household. The lords of manors assumed that all tenants would have at least one hen or pullet, sometimes more, that could be paid in an annual rent. The payments were partly symbolic and marked the ritual of the calendar, with eggs owed at Easter and hens at Christmas. More valuable birds might be demanded in special payments, such as a capon paid to the lord for permission to live away from the manor.

Rent demands sometimes grew into burdensome obligations, like the expectation (recorded in 1279) that six tenants of Whatcote (Warwickshire) should each bring to a compulsory Christmas meal in the manor house a cock and three hens and a loaf of bread.[82] The lord was supposedly hosting a celebration, but the peasants were emptying their henhouses. The Christmas dinner custom was widespread, though it was normally on a smaller scale than at Whatcote. An expansion of lords' demands for poultry came in the late fourteenth century when tenants were required to pay six capons, rather than cash, on taking on new land.

The numbers of poultry owned by most peasants are consistently recorded as a cock with three, four, or five hens. Pullets, the product of breeding within the small flock are less consistently mentioned; as is also the case with capons, which were larger and fatter birds resulting from the castration of young males. Geese were much more unevenly distributed, and a minority of peasants owned a gander and two or three females. Modest poultry-keeping by individuals amounted to formidable quantities for whole communities. The hens of Bishop's Cleeve in 1390 produced 10,800 eggs, surely an under-assessment by the tithe collectors. The numbers of new geese being reared, 300, should again be regarded as a minimum.[83]

---

[80] WAM, 21124.   [81] WAM, 21125.   [82] *WHR*, pp. 271–2.
[83] Corpus Christi College, Oxford, B/14/2/3/1.

The rents and tithes are a guide to the poultry produced and consumed by peasant households. Enough eggs could have been laid in the spring and summer months to provide each member of the household with an egg on most days. They would also have had occasional opportunities to eat poultry meat judging from the bones recovered from excavations. At Burton Dassett more than 200 chicken bones and a hundred goose bones were found, but this does not reflect accurately the scale of poultry consumption as most bones were too fragile to survive.[84] Most hens after a period of useful egg production, ended their days on a meal table, but as the Whatcote Christmas dinner suggests, poultry were reserved for special occasions.

The cock and hens spent their days in or near to the plot occupied by the peasant house and outbuildings, and obtained part of their diet from plants, invertebrates, and grain scattered from ricks and barns. They could be fed small quantities of 'hen corn', which was inferior grain. The birds could have occupied a purpose-built hen house, like the structure excavated at Bishop's Cleeve based on six vertical posts set in the ground, measuring 1m by 1.5m.[85] Alternatively they may have roosted in the roof of a barn or other building. Poultry were in the care of peasant women, who combined feeding and egg collecting with their many other tasks: when the theft of a hen was reported to the manor court, the owner or the accused, or both, were often women. Hens were easily stolen, or taken by mistake, because they wandered around the village. Geese were not as closely associated with houses and settlements, as they grazed the commons and fields, and tended to go on to land where they were unwelcome. They were associated with both men and women. Ducks were kept in smaller numbers, and gravitated towards ponds and streams, where they attracted complaints by polluting the water.

The homely images of poultry scratching in gardens and yards and ducks swimming in the common stream, with eggs and the occasional festive bird being consumed in the household, suggests a model of self-sufficiency. Poultry keeping also had a significant commercial dimension. An internal village market is implied by the lord's demands for six capons for an entry fine, as few individuals would own so many, and they would need to be purchased. Sales of poultry and eggs beyond the village would explain the twelve hens belonging to John Momeford of Hampton Lucy in 1538; similarly in 1373 John Thoury of Elmley Castle claimed to own a cock and fourteen hens.[86] An incident at Halesowen in 1358 offers a glimpse of the marketing of eggs, when Roger atte Lowe's dog bit Robert atte Brok's pack horse which was carrying a basket of eggs to market. Atte Lowe valued the 300 eggs that were broken at 18*d*.[87] Geese were more often produced on a scale far beyond the consumption of even a prosperous household.

---

[84] Hamilton, 'Faunal Remains'.   [85] Enright and Watt, *Stoke Road, Bishop's Cleeve*, p. 16.
[86] WA, ref. 008:7 1538/241; *CR Elmley*, p. 17.   [87] BAH, 3279/346342.

At Cleeve Prior, ninety-five birds were offending in their grazing in 1357, including flocks belonging to individuals of twelve, sixteen, and forty. A cart load of geese was taken from Cleeve to market in 1390, presumably part of a routine trade, but made visible to us by litigation over the canvas cover.[88] Both geese and hens were in demand for meat in towns, and could be sold directly in the street by huxters (female traders). They were also gathered together on a larger scale by poulterers (see 'Marketing animals' in this chapter).

Peasants may have been stimulated to produce more poultry by rising prices as demand increased after 1350 and especially in the fifteenth century. The market encouraged peasants to own dovecots. Lords had no monopoly on dove keeping, and the monastic lord of the manor of Hawkesbury (Gloucestershire) far from discouraging dovecots, valued the rent that they produced and pressured tenants at Kilcott and Hillesley in 1408 and 1409 to keep them in good repair.[89] A number of peasant dovecots were located near towns, for example, around Worcester, because few doves were consumed by peasants' households, and the birds, regarded as a luxury, were sold in towns. Possession of a dovecot, though not an exclusive privilege of lordship, still brought some prestige as well as economic benefits.[90]

Bees

Bees could be found on lords' demesnes, such as the manor of Oldington near Kidderminster (Worcestershire) in 1281–2 which kept seven beehives, and 5 gallons of honey were sold for 2s 11d (in the subsequent two centuries honey prices rose to 12d per gallon).[91] However these manorial hives were unusual, and peasants were the main keepers of bees in the late medieval west midlands. Halesowen Abbey was entitled to multiple heriots, which meant that on the death of a tenant the Abbey's officials could take a number of animals, sometimes a cart, and occasionally a beehive. In 1393 Henry Wiliames died and his heriot (and an additional payment called 'custom') consisted of an ox, a cow, a heifer, a calf, a horse and a young sheep, worth in total 21s 6d, and in addition a hive (*ymbe*) of bees worth 18d.[92] Other examples scattered over the region indicate the wide dispersal of beekeeping. A debtor in Elmley Castle in 1373 owed honey and wax worth 2s, almost certainly the produce of a single hive. When Richard Sainter of Longdon was drowned in the Severn in 1470 his possessions included six cattle and two

---

[88] WCL, E18, E35.   [89] TNA, SC2 175/48.
[90] C. Dyer, 'Peasants and Poultry in England, 1250–1540', *Quaternary International* 543 (2020), pp. 113–18.
[91] TNA, SC6 1070/5.   [92] BAH, 3279/346372.

pigs, along with a hive of bees.[93] On the Gloucester Abbey estate at Upleadon and Churcham in 1266–7 *honilond* holdings, often between 3 acres and 8 acres, paid a rather high rent in honey (or the money equivalent) of a gallon or two for an acre.[94] The impression we gain from such instances is that the ownership of bees was commonplace among peasants, rich and poor, and that individuals might own four or more hives.

Stray swarms, recorded alongside stray animals, show that beekeeping was spread over the whole region, but was especially common in woodland landscapes. At Ombersley five were reported in one year, 1380, and in the long run of Chaddesley Corbett records between 1375 and 1442 seventeen swarms were reported.[95] Flowers were presumably plentiful in hedges, pastures, and woods, in contrast with the champion's limited lengths of hedgerow and extensive cultivation. The swarms were regarded as significant assets, to be pursued, captured, and put in the care of a reliable and skilled local person. The bees were rarely claimed and their owners, and their temporary keeper would add them to his or her hives. The swarms were valued, and probably undervalued, in the courts at between 4*d* and 2*s*, though most were judged to be worth 12*d* or less. An important variable was the time of year when the swarm appeared. A complete hive with bees, wax, and honey could be said to be worth 3*s* 4*d*, and we have seen already that a hive's wax and honey together were valued at 2*s*. A hive is said to have been capable of yielding at least a pound of wax and a gallon of honey. If a peasant had four hives, their output would have exceeded in cash terms 7*s* per annum, more than the income that came from a cow or 10 sheep. The apparently trivial and small-scale pursuit of beekeeping, which involved little work by the owner, could yield some impressive results.

Beekeeping was sufficiently profitable to attract investment and complexities of management. Fractions of hives were a feature of Halesowen; where a victim of the Black Death in 1349, Richard de Chirlet, had available to be taken for his heriot a horse, three cows, a cart, and a quarter of a hive. When John Hichecoks from the hamlet of Illey died in 1362, holding a half-yardland, the lord's officials took three animals and half of a hive, valued at 12*d*.[96] The fractions show that the hives could be shared assets, in which partners invested and took their portion of the proceeds. This was set out in detail at Alveston (Warwickshire) in 1353 when John Symonds leased to Richard Vicar four beehives worth 8*s*, with lessor and lessee each agreeing to take half of the profits. Three tiers of tenancy were arranged at Hartlebury in the early fifteenth century, involving the churchwardens, the owners of the hives, who

---

[93] *CR Elmley*, p. 17; WAM, 21165.   [94] *Hist Glouc*, 3, pp. 128, 136–7.
[95] WA, ref. 705:56, BA3910/39; SCLA, DR5/2737–2799.
[96] BAH, 3279/346321/346343.

leased them to two brothers, who in turn rented them to others who tended the bees and collected the honey.[97]

Those who kept bees were venturing into the trade in luxuries. Honey and wax could only be afforded by the wealthier consumers. Perhaps the beekeeper's family was allowed a taste of honey, but he or she had to take advantage of the price of 8*d* to 12*d* per gallon (more than Gascon wine) and sell as much as possible. Similarly the wax was much in demand for lighting the houses of the aristocracy, and for the candles essential for church liturgy. Peasants could light their halls, but only with cheap tallow candles. All of the outputs of the peasant beehives were sold in a market with European dimensions, satisfying the sweet tooth of the aristocracy with honey, though Mediterranean sugar was offering growing competition, and the wax from English peasant hives helped to fill the gap left because imports from the Baltic did not satisfy the demand from the English church.[98]

Animal husbandry on the peasant holding

To gain an overview of peasant pastoralism we can attempt to assess the role of livestock in the household and holding, in comparison with the contribution of animals and their products to a saleable surplus. Much of the meat and dairy produce consumed by the household came from the holding's own animals and birds. The livestock of the holding also provided traction for ploughs, means for riding, and transport. Manure made the arable more fertile. The old mares, horses, oxen, cows, ewes, and wethers were often replaced from among the young animals bred on the holding.

A high proportion of the money made by peasants derived from their pastoral activities. The cash from wool sales covered rents and other expenses. A steady income came from the dairy produce of cows but also occasionally from ewes and goats. Hens' eggs gave a small but useful return. The by-products of the death or killing of animals included hides and woolfells, tallow, and horn. Bees' products, wax and honey, were all sold. An irregular source of income came from disposing of animals, either young cattle or horses not needed for replacement purposes, or old stock. Most of the animals being sold for butchery left the village alive, but some meat went to market, especially bacon. In hard times, after a bad harvest or some unexpected expense, an animal could be sold. In good times as well as bad, livestock were hired, not just the larger draught animals or cows, but also poultry and beehives.[99]

---

[97] WCL, E17; Swanson and Guyatt, eds., *Court Book*, pp. 159, 179, 202, 220.

[98] A Sapoznik, 'Bees in the Medieval Economy: Religious Observance and the Production, Trade, and Consumption of Wax in England, c.1300–1555' *EcHR*, 72 (2019), pp. 1152–74.

[99] On the renting of geese, P. Slavin, 'Goose Management and Rearing in Late Medieval Eastern England, c.1250–1400', *AgHR*, 58 (2010), pp. 1–29, especially pp. 26–8.

The distinction between self-sufficiency and exchange depicts peasant life in excessively simple terms. Documents, such as inventories, are concerned with ownership, not agricultural reality. When a well-off peasant, probably a yardlander, Elyas atte Brugge of Abbots Salford, died shortly before 1389, his animals were listed as six horses, eight cattle, and sixty-eight sheep.[100] The numbers of animals resemble the limits on a yardland declared as stints in a number of villages, and we would expect that they would bring prosperity to their owners in straightforward rewards. The complicated management of animals practised by people like atte Brugge can be investigated in litigation around his time. At Harvington (Worcestershire), an Avon valley manor near to Salford, in 1379 John Colyns leased to Richard May twelve ewes to keep for four years. Perhaps he did not have access to enough pasture or hay to keep them through the winter, or his shepherd could not cope with all of them, especially at lambing. After two years the ewes had produced eighteen lambs, beside tithe payments of two lambs, which would be quite near to one lamb each year for each ewe, suggesting that May had looked after them quite well. Colyns at this point took them back, with the lambs, because he said that May was not feeding them properly.[101]

John Stappe, who belonged to a well-established family at Blackwell (Warwickshire), sought grazing because his village had limited amounts of permanent pasture. He planned to fatten two oxen in preparation for selling them on 11 November 1379, when butchers bought cattle for slaughter. Stappe put the animals in the care of Walter Sclatter of Longdon, adjacent to Blackwell, which was not a lease but a grazing contract. Sclatter intended apparently to keep the oxen with his own cattle, partly on the common and partly in his own several (enclosed) land. In practice he fed his own cattle in the several, and sent the oxen on to poor land, so that (according to Stappe) they almost starved. Stappe took the animals back and paid Sclatter no money.[102] There were many other small-scale arrangements, such as the renting out of cows, which manorial lords did in the fourteenth century, but was also common among peasants. John Loyte of Hartlebury was said in 1411 to have leased a cow for 3s. In 1359 Walter le Webbe complained that at Cakemor in Halesowen he had rented two oxen from the 3 May to Robert le Berneward and Agnes his wife, but they failed to return them. A speculation, in view of the date, is that the animals were being used (with others) for the ploughing of fallow land, which would have begun in May.[103]

These examples reveal a world in which grazing was unevenly distributed between villages, and among households. Some peasants were unable to profit from animals because they could not afford to buy them, or they lacked plough beasts. Wealthy peasants had more animals than they could conveniently feed or supervise. Leasing, or forming partnerships, or matching the animals to the

---

[100] WCL, E34.   [101] WCL, E30.   [102] WCL, E30.
[103] Swanson and Guyatt, eds., *Court Book*, p. 169; BAH, 3279/346342.

pasture, all show peasants making the most efficient use of resources, ideally to the mutual advantage of the parties. These complicated arrangements mean that Elyas atte Brugge's well-stocked holding could have included sheep which were rented out, or were 'summering' on a distant hillside. An ox might have been sent for fattening in the next village, and a horse could have been hired by a neighbour. He might also have been receiving other peasants' animals because Salford villagers had access to large meadows. The income from atte Brugge's animals could have been divided between a number of households, thanks to leasing and pasturing arrangements.

The pastoral sector was often drawn into complex financial arrangements which meant that owning a flock of sheep or a few cows did not simply result in a regular flow of cash. Peasants were often in debt, and would make arrangements to sell future production. Wool was commonly sold before the sheep were sheared. Sales in general were based on credit, so after an initial small sum of earnest money, the full payment on an ox or a stone of wool would be delayed for months. No part of the pastoral economy was exempt from these complications, so that even beehives were held in shares.

Intricate financial arrangements are appropriate to production connected to the international trading network. The price that a peasant received for wool depended on the fortunes of the Flemish cloth industry, and the profit of a beehive was linked to imports of Mediterranean sugar and Baltic wax. The marketing of animals and animal products must have impacted on peasant activities, and raised their confidence. From the early thirteenth century when demand increased for pastoral products, they could pay their rents in cash, and adopt new approaches to rotations and land management. It was not an accident that the moves to enclose parcels of land on the commons coincided with growing profits from dairying and wool production, or that inhoks were designed to provide more fodder crops. Pastoral farming was changing in line with wider developments, such as technical innovation leading to the rising use of horses, or the entrepreneurial spirit shown by fifteenth-century cattle farmers who took advantage of the upsurge in beef consumption. Status came from association with some animals, as a well-off peasant knew as he rode into town on a good horse with ornaments hanging from its harness.

Pastoral farming incurred lower commitments of labour than cultivation. Even the intensive demands of milking and sheep shearing could not compare with the routine of ploughing through the year and the surge of work for many hands in the harvest. Labour could be saved by co-operation in the village community to employ a herdsman, sometimes called the 'common servant'. Some peasants employed their own shepherds but they could put their animals into the custody of the common herd, and in some villages specialist herdsmen were responsible separately for horses, cattle, and swine. The surname Gateherd (goatherd) suggests another specialized herding task.

The common herds came to the attention of the authorities when an appointment was disputed, or, much more frequently, problems arose in collecting money to pay their wages. At Harvington in 1420 litigation about a breach of contract showed that the tenants made a collective agreement with a herd, John Robertes, to serve them from Michaelmas to Michaelmas (29 September), the standard employment period for servants.[104] This was not a typical arrangement, however, as Robertes was also appointed to serve as hayward (*messor*), and it was agreed that he could keep his own cattle with those of the village. He was ranked higher in status than most herds, who tended to be young and landless. There are examples of villages employing a tenant's son, or a tenant's servant might be delegated or loaned to the village. The herd's job may not have been a very attractive one, leading the villagers at Broadwell (Gloucestershire) in the early sixteenth century to build collectively a cottage for the herd.[105] At Sutton-under-Brailes (Warwickshire) in 1379–80, the lord of the manor paid the common herd 15*d* to look after ten beasts over the harvest season of two months.[106] If that was the standard rate of pay, and the herd looked after sixty villagers' animals for the whole year, he would have received about £2, which was not a high wage.

Herds were criticized for allowing animals to stray into planted fields or other protected areas, or even to cross the boundary into the next village. As such errors were reported only occasionally, perhaps they did their work effectively? More likely the mistakes were so commonplace that they were not worth mentioning in court, and the herd was too poor to pay financial penalties. At Overbury in 1497 when the tenants of Overbury and adjoining Conderton were told not to pasture sheep on Bredon Hill in the winter at night without a keeper, it suggests a serious dereliction of responsibility. On the other hand, the community reacted with a by-law to restore a better standard of care.[107]

The more intensive labour required in managing animals and their produce tended to be undertaken by women. The tasks were often located near the house, notably the daily routines of feeding pigs and poultry, as well as dairying. Cheese-making, like brewing, involved a practical knowledge of chemistry. Women acquired these skills from training at home followed by accumulated experience, and just as families sought to persuade sons to maintain their interest in the holding, so young women would have been assets to be encouraged. The connection between dairying and a female labour force can be detected in individual villages, such as Weston Mauduit (Warwickshire), a small village in the Avon valley. Its meadows suggest a dairying economy, and in 1381 five of its ten households contained a resident daughter.[108]

Men looked after oxen and horses, as a natural extension of working with the animals in ploughing and carting. Shepherding was mainly done by men, who applied

[104] WCL, E48.   [105] TNA, SC6 Henry VIII/4047.   [106] GA, D1099 M31/46.
[107] WCL, E85.   [108] *PT*, part 1, p. 277.

remedies for disease and supervised lambing, when they were expected to sleep alongside the flock. Women would wash demesne sheep before shearing, so they probably carried out the same task with peasant flocks. If sheep were milked, and goats certainly were, women did the work, and made the butter and cheese afterwards.

Animal welfare

The concept of animal welfare was not one that featured in the range of priorities of medieval peasants who owned and managed livestock. They knew that ill-treatment reduced the value of the animal, so the owner of a dog that attacked a cow, for example, was expected to pay for the financial loss. Perhaps there was a perception that animals had some mental capacity. Clerks writing court rolls referred to a pig running into the road 'voluntarily' and a dog biting a pig 'maliciously'. Dogs were kept in many peasant households, as is shown by the discarded bones of domestic animals which often carry evidence of gnawing. Aggressive attacks on domestic animals were occasionally reported. They had their uses, for guarding houses and domestic animals, and controlling vermin, especially rats, but we do not know the extent to which they were regarded as pets and companions. Fables and folklore often used the device of intelligent animals to transmit moral messages, and they figure symbolically in wood carvings, portraying doctors as monkeys, foxes as priests, and rabbits hunting men. However, these portrayals do not seem to have influenced the daily routine of contacts between people and their livestock.[109]

An important goal was to keep animals adequately fed, though in the constant struggle to separate livestock from arable crops the welfare of the owners of the corn took priority. The pinch point which troubled many villages around early August came when the fallow field had been given its summer ploughing and could not be grazed. The corn field that was being harvested contained sheaves waiting to be carried, and some corn was still uncut, so animals should have been excluded.

Animals faced fodder shortages at other times. In mid-winter the grass had stopped growing, and animals were kept away from rain-soaked grassland that was liable to be damaged by being 'poached' from trampling hooves. Ample quantities of hay provided part of the answer, but peasants rarely had access to enough meadow. A calculation made by a lord's managers, at Stoke Bishop (Gloucestershire) in 1380–1 assigned to the demesne's eight oxen hay from 10 acres of meadow, which was worth 14s if sold. Each ox was receiving hay

---

[109] J. Aberth, *An Environmental History of the Middle Ages. The Crucible of Nature* (Abingdon, 2013), pp. 169–76.

worth 1s 9d.[110] Most peasants did not have the option of feeding on that scale. A yardland rarely had as much as 4 acres of meadow, from which at least eight cattle and horses were fed, and sheep also needed hay. The importance of fodder crops such as peas and beans is apparent.

The by-laws fixing stints were focussed on the problem of sharing grazing fairly. The quotas allowed for each unit of arable, such as forty sheep for each yardland, suggest careful calculation, but other considerations may have been village politics dominated by self-interested better-off villagers. Some villages in the mid-to-late fifteenth century give the impression that they were moving towards realistic restraints on stocking levels. A by-law at Roel (Gloucestershire) in 1452 reiterated the *levant et couchant* principle which should have been etched on the mind of every sheep owner, that no-one should keep over the winter any sheep outside the 'close, fold or house', which refers to the enclosure and building at the rear of the dwelling house.[111] Another way of expressing this was to limit the number of animals that could be pastured in the summer to those kept in the winter. In theory this could be the basis of a precise calculation of the quantity of animals that tenants could keep, but the real world, for example, one which allowed strangers to buy access to the common pasture, made figures very hard to judge accurately. A fresh start seems to have been attempted at Long Marston (Warwickshire) in 1453, when 'it was ordered by common assent that [four named men] should supervise and extend [meaning assess] each yardland', and they should recommend 'how many sheep each tenant ought to hold both in summer and winter so that no-one of them should overburden the common pasture'.[112] This reform, based on evidence, measurement, and fair judgements, seemed to be motivated by an aim to match resources to demand, which in modern language would be called sustainability. A similar idea and even the key word was expressed in an order at Willoughby (Warwickshire) in 1498 that 'tenants should enquire how many more sheep the common can sustain'.[113] These ventures seemed to be moving away from blaming individuals towards allocating pasture on a rational basis. The examples come from villages in wold and champion landscapes which had limited amounts of permanent common pasture.

Villages sometimes had safety valves which allowed access to pastures beyond their boundaries. A number of these were survivals from a remote past, such as the connection between Wellesbourne (Warwickshire) and Kingswood, part of the woodland village of Lapworth at a distance of 12 miles. The peasants of Wellesbourne, according to customs recorded in 1279, could feed their pigs, graze animals, and collect firewood in this area of pasture and trees, very different from their mainly arable Avon valley settlement with a 'grove' of limited extent.[114] Such connections between south-east and north-west Warwickshire had been

---

[110] WA, ref. 009:1, BA2636/171/92416.   [111] GA, D678/62.   [112] GA, D678/62.
[113] Magdalen College, Oxford, Willoughby EP 68/1.   [114] WHR, pp. 165–6.

commonplace in the early middle ages. Later sources also show that in the north and west of the county woods were intercommoned, allowing the livestock of two or more settlements to graze in the same wood, a practice no doubt dating back many centuries. Fifteen examples have been recognized, involving the inhabitants of large settlements in the case of Stoneleigh and Kenilworth. An area of heath pasture to the east of Coventry was grazed by people from Binley, Brandon, and Brinklow, and further south pasture was shared between Salford Priors in Warwickshire and the Worcestershire villages of Atch Lench and Abbots Morton.[115] Much of the land subject to these joint grazing arrangements belonged in the category of wood pasture, referring to grazing under widely spaced trees. Communities in other woodland landscapes also shared common land, such as on the high ground between Alvington and Aylburton on the southern edge of the Forest of Dean. Upland pastures that were available to villages on the slopes of the Malverns and Bredon Hill (see 'Peasants and the making of the landscape' in Chapter 2) to which can be added the heaths of Dunsmore in north Warwickshire, and the heath that was shared by a dozen villages in four shires to the east of Moreton-in-Marsh. It could be argued that these facilities which allowed peasants to graze animals beyond their village boundaries were ancient arrangements dating back from before the Conquest, and not reflecting the resourcefulness of the late medieval peasants. This is not entirely the case, as these intercommoned pastures were liable to dispute, and encroachment, requiring the peasants to be vigilant and ready to defend their rights (Figure 7.1).

Peasants could buy pasture, like John Stappe fattening his oxen, or many others paying for common rights in villages where they did not belong. The most abundant source of pasture could be on the lord's demesne, or a park that was not being reserved solely for deer, and some lords gained a considerable revenue from the sale of agistment.[116]

The controversies around pasture arose from the need to feed animals, yet we have little direct evidence for their nutritional status. A stray sometimes died before it could be claimed by its owner, but strays were likely to have been in poor condition. An occasional accusation was made that an animal or animals that had been impounded had died because they had been deprived of food and water. These were specific circumstances, and if there was a general problem one might expect that animals being valued as heriots would be described as weak or sickly, but this was rare.

Animal bones show signs of stress, such as the indication that horses and oxen had suffered from hauling heavy loads. A depression on a sheep's horn core from

---

[115] S. Wager, *Woods, Wolds and Groves: The Woodland of Medieval Warwickshire* (British Archaeological Reports, British series, 269, 1998), pp. 27–136.

[116] Agistment in Estmedow, the lord's several close, at Quinton, Gloucestershire in 1473 enabled twenty tenants to pasture 32 cows, 7 calves, 6 bullocks, 9 oxen, and 9 'animals' for a total of £3 11s 11d: Magdalen College, Oxford, Quinton EP 35/5.

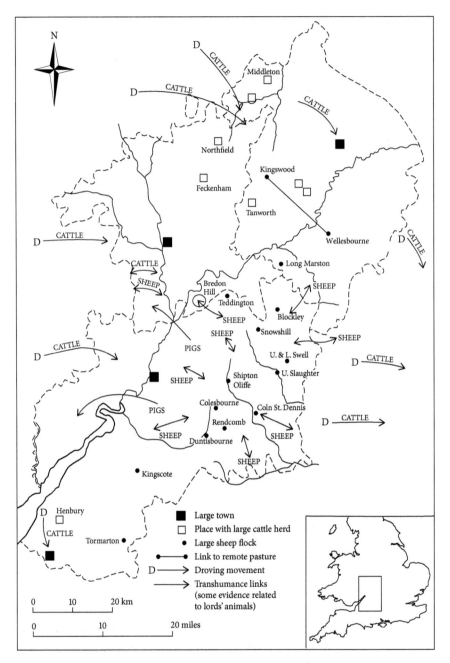

Figure 7.1 Remote pastures, transhumance, and droving. This impressionistic map shows movements of livestock, some seasonal use of high and low ground, some droving to markets, thirteenth to sixteenth century.

Bristol has been suggested, along with examples from other regions, as a possible indicator of poor nutrition, but such evidence is not abundant.[117] Animal size could be seen as a result of poor feeding conditions. The heights of cattle, horses, and sheep of the thirteenth to fifteenth centuries which can be calculated from bones, all point to their small size by modern standards. A reduction in size has been detected in the early middle ages, and has been linked to the introduction of open fields and consequent restrictions on pasture in the tenth and eleventh centuries.[118] Animal bones excavated at Dudley Castle on the Worcestershire/Staffordshire border show an increase in size from the late fourteenth century, and similar changes have been detected in other parts of England, though with variations in dating, so in some cases the change came after 1500. In the case of Dudley improved nutrition could be related to landscape changes in north Worcestershire and south Staffordshire where the animals might have fed.[119] A high proportion of land at Halesowen and Northfield within a few miles of Dudley was being managed by peasant tenants in enclosed pastures, and this was a feature of the whole district. No size increase is apparent at Burton Dassett, in a district where cattle and sheep tended to be grazed on fallows in open fields and on common pastures. However, we cannot leap easily to a causal connection between body size and the management of pastures.

Peasants could have contributed to the welfare of livestock by housing them. It was once thought that peasant houses, especially in the thirteenth century, would have a byre reserved for cattle at one end of the dwelling, but actual cases in the west midlands are scarce. An excavated complex of buildings at Upton (Gloucestershire) included a thirteenth-century house with an end room which had no residential purpose, but its fittings, including a wide trough, suggested an industrial use. Separate from the two dwelling houses at Upton was a building for animals, either cattle or sheep.[120] A peasant house might be described as combining a dwelling and byre but it is rare, with only three clear examples out of hundreds of documentary references to buildings (see 'Living space' in Chapter 5). Among a sample of 375 buildings with identified functions tenants were ordered to repair, mainly after 1350, many were dwellings, and of the remainder 152 were barns, 24 sheepcotes, 11 byres, 7 dovecotes, 6 pig sties, and 5 stables. Although these figures demonstrate a

---

[117] L. Strid, 'Animal Bone Reports on Bristol Finzel's Reach', BRSMG 2007.28 (unpublished report, Oxford Archaeology); U. Albarella, 'Depressions on Sheep Horncores', *Journal of Archaeological Science* 22 (1995), pp. 699–704.

[118] M. Holmes, 'Does Size Matter? Changes in the Size of Animals Throughout the English Saxon Period (AD 450–1066)', *Journal of Archaeological Science* 43 (2014), pp. 77–90.

[119] R. Thomas, *Animals, Economy and Status: Integrating Zooarchaeological and Historical Data in the Study of Dudley Castle, West Midlands (c.1100–1750)* (British Archaeological Reports, British series, 392, 2005), pp. 39, 47; R. Thomas, M. Holmes, and J. Mams, '"So bigge or bigge may be": Tracking Size and Shape Changes in Domestic Livestock in London (AD 1320–1900)', *Journal of Archaeological Science* 40 (2013), pp. 3309–25.

[120] P.A. Rahtz, 'Upton, Gloucestershire, 1964–1968. Second Report', *TBGAS* 88 (1969), pp. 74–126.

variety of specialist buildings, they cannot support the notion that peasant farms were commonly provided with a full range of accommodation for livestock. A wealthy tenant of Sutton-under-Brailes (Warwickshire) in 1507 was said to have a dwelling house, barn, stable, sheepcote, and dovecot, but so much livestock accommodation on a single holding was unusual.[121] Many tenants provided themselves with a house and a barn, and animals would have been sheltered by means of temporary and ad hoc arrangements. Pig sties and hen houses need not have been elaborate structures (see 'Poultry' in this chapter). Buildings could have been sublet from neighbours, and within the holding flexibility in use helped to find room when necessary. A widow at Elmley Castle (Worcestershire) in 1474 was to keep twenty sheep 'in a building of the said cottage', which was clearly not a dedicated sheepcote. At Overbury (Worcestershire) in 1496 tenants were told that calves should not accompany cows into the fields, but rather should be kept in a building.[122] Not every holding would have a byre, so perhaps the unfortunate animals were put in a barn? Barns were for crop storage, but they were only full of corn for a few months, leaving space for other functions. A more formal division is suggested by the 'barn and stable under one roof' at Adlestrop (Gloucestershire) in 1498, and the 'barn with sheepcote' at Wichenford (Worcestershire) in 1473.[123] Livestock that were not allocated space in a barn, or could not be squeezed into temporary accommodation could have been given some protection in yards or huddled in 'shelter sheds' or under other forms of temporary roofing. Peasant animals must be thought of as hardy creatures with shaggy coats. Although contemporary opinion among lords' managers thought it desirable that animals be kept in buildings, peasants could not afford to build and maintain substantial housing for the variety of animals that they kept.[124]

Deaths from disease among demesne animals were recorded from year to year in manorial accounts, and also in reports to the manor courts by the *cadavatores* who gave details of which animals had died, and apportioned blame, if appropriate, among the lord's employees. The two worst episodes of epidemics were the sheep scab outbreaks of the 1270s and 1280s, and the cattle plague (probably rinderpest) after 1318.[125] Peasant animals suffered from endemic diseases and the exceptional epidemics, and this is signalled in a chronicle entry for 1277 recording the deaths of 'almost all of the sheep'.[126]

The lords' shepherds combatted disease by applying tar and grease, and the same treatment was used by some peasants, such as John Persons, a tenant of

---

[121] WAM, 8362.   [122] *CR Elmley*, p. 176; WCL, E82.
[123] TNA, SC2 175/77; R.K. Field, 'Worcestershire Peasant Buildings, Household Goods and Farming Equipment in the Later Middle Ages', *Med. Arch* 9 (1965), p. 136.
[124] C. Dyer, 'The Housing of Peasant Livestock in England, 1200–1520', *AgHR* 67 (2019), pp. 29–50.
[125] P. Slavin, 'Mites and Merchants: The Crisis of English Wool and Textile Trade Revisited, c.1275–1330', *EcHR* 73 (2020), pp. 885–913; P. Slavin, 'The Great Bovine Pestilence and its Economic and Environmental Consequences in England and Wales, 1318–50', *EcHR* 65 (2012), pp. 1239–66.
[126] H.R. Luard, ed., *Annales Monastici*, vol. 4, *Annales Prioratus de Wigornia* (Rolls Series, 1869), p. 473.

Sutton-under-Brailes (Warwickshire), who acquired a barrel of tar worth 6s in 1504.[127] The practice of veterinary medicine is rarely documented. On the Pershore demesne in 1344 an ox was treated with 'mixed blood', and the Worcester Priory sheep reeve in 1445–6 arranged for hoggasters (two-year-old sheep) to be castrated and 'treated' for a payment of 16d.[128] These procedures seem to have been carried out by an outsider, as also at Chilvers Coton (Warwickshire) in 1310–11 when 'bark wos' (medicine from tanning bark) was given with 'other medicines' to an ox 'with the work of the *curator*'.[129] The last word means the person who cures, which presumably refers to a veterinary practitioner. The experts on animal disease who were brought in to deal with specific problems, were not apparently regular employees of the lord, but members of the local community. They could have gained their knowledge from oral tradition transmitted through families and based ultimately on trial and error. Individuals were likely to have acquired a reputation for having special skills and access to remedies. Smiths combined fitting horseshoes with treating equine ailments, again drawing on practice and experience. Such an individual was Richard le Marshal who treated a horse belonging to the abbot of Halesowen in 1366.[130] Demand for veterinary treatment must also have come from peasant owners of animals.

Peasants brought litigation to the manor court when they suffered losses from the ill-treatment of their livestock. Typical circumstances arose when a neighbour's beast found its way into a close and trampled or ate grass or crops. The tenant who suffered damage could react strongly, and violently expel the offending animal with kicks and blows from a stick. Dogs might be encouraged to join the fray. The assaults could have resulted in cuts, loss of a tooth or eye, or lameness; the animal's ability to work could be impaired, or it might even be killed. In addition to these encounters on enclosed land, animals grazing in the wrong place in the open fields or common pasture might be impounded, and left in the small enclosure provided as a pound. Animals were also liable to be maltreated when they were loaned or hired, and in particular horses could be overworked. Animals were injured by carts on the roads, and they sometimes hurt one another, most often when dogs attacked. In 1397 at Chaddesley Corbett (Worcestershire) thirty sheep were said to have been killed by dogs in a single incident, and while this was one of the worst cases, it was one of many.[131] The main consequence of an act of cruelty was the payment of damages by the perpetrator, though owners of dangerous dogs could be amerced and ordered to keep the animal under control.

Modern observers with humane attitudes towards animals are repelled by their treatment in the Middle Ages. We can offer the rational explanation that animals suffered as a by-product of the shortage of pasture and inadequacy of fencing, and

---

[127] WAM, 12258, fo. 17r.   [128] WAM, 22121; WCL, C3.   [129] TNA, SC6 1038/20.
[130] Society of Antiquaries, MS 535.   [131] SCLA, DR5 2742.

we know that the church taught that animals lacked souls. Sadistic practices such as bull-baiting tended to take place in towns, but in the country the Shrovetide custom at Badsey (Worcestershire) (and many other parishes) in the early sixteenth century involved throwing sticks at a tethered cock.[132] To focus on farming practices, despite their limited resources peasants' best interest was served by keeping well-fed, contented, and productive animals, and many of their actions were intended to achieve that goal.

Marketing animals and animal products

Given that the ultimate purpose of much pastoral farming was commercial gain: where and how were animals and their products sold? Lords presumed that peasants would attend local markets; for example according to a survey made in 1299, it was expected that the sale of draught animals by tenants of the Worcestershire manor of Bredon would take place at Evesham and Pershore, nearby market towns.[133] Westminster Abbey's officials at Bourton-on-the-Hill in 1326–7 proclaimed strays at the markets held at Chipping Campden and Stow-on-the-Wold in the belief that crowds of local people might include the owners of the animals.[134] The purchase of cattle in 1378 by William Cocks of Alspath near Coventry shows that peasants had wide horizons, as he ignored the markets near to his home, and bought three cows at Nuneaton (Warwickshire), presumably following the reputation of the market or of the cattle reared in its surroundings.[135]

Peasants with livestock and produce to sell would expect to find buyers in towns, either in the marketplace, or through some other means of meeting, in an inn for example. The sale of dairy products and poultry might have been in breach of the regulations, because the producers would sell outside the market to dealers who would profit from resale. The town authorities were attempting to control prices, but in fining the traders they gained some revenue. The important point for our enquiry into peasant pastoral production is that the number of offenders and frequency of offences, in towns such as Coventry, Droitwich, and Nuneaton shows the substantial flow of cheese, butter, eggs, and poultry coming from the country, and this was a trade that is otherwise rarely recorded. It must have made a significant contribution to the earnings of many peasant households. Sales of livestock in towns resulted in court cases if the animal was not delivered, or was

---

[132] E.A.B. Barnard, *Churchwardens' Accounts of the Parish of Badsey with Aldington* (Hampstead, 1913), pp. 9–22; R. Hutton, *The Rise and Fall of Merry England: The Ritual Year, 1400–1700* (Oxford, 1994), p. 19.
[133] *RBW*, p. 95.   [134] WAM, 8272.
[135] A. Watkins, *Small Towns in the Forest of Arden in the Fifteenth Century* (DS Occasional Paper, 38, 1998), p. 13.

of poor quality, or if the money was not paid. A problem arose when William Brid of Pinvin (Worcestershire) sold a horse to a Worcester man at Pershore in 1334, and was owed 2s 6d of the purchase price. A debt of 6s 8d resulted when John Botull of Studley (Warwickshire) sold an ox to John Harvy of Stratford-upon-Avon in 1500.[136] These were transactions that went wrong, and the majority proceeded successfully and left no evidence.

The peasants travelled to the town on horses or on foot with baskets of produce, but there were occasions when townspeople went to the country to buy, especially when they were intending to obtain high-quality goods in bulk. The Fraternity of the Holy Cross at Stratford-upon-Avon held gatherings with food and drink through the year, but the annual feast was on a lavish scale. The officials of the Fraternity would ride into the countryside before the great event, collecting in 1426–7 some 167 geese and 168 pullets from many suppliers. In 1431–2, the expedition lasted for four days in order to buy geese, pullets, pigs, and sheep.[137] This proactive approach to food purchase was also adopted by large aristocratic households, which were facing the problem of meeting a large scale of demand from many small-scale and scattered producers.

Some trade in livestock did not involve towns at all, but was conducted in village markets, both those established by charter, like that at Monks Kirby (Warwickshire) with its butchers' shambles, or unofficial venues such as Knowle in the same county where again butchers are known to have traded.[138] Often both buyers and sellers lived in the country, sometimes in the same village but also at a distance. Most transactions were conducted by 'private treaty' or 'at the farm gate'. The advantage of the public market was that it brought buyers and sellers together at the same time, whereas the other methods depended on networks, local knowledge, and go-betweens. Beyond the regulation of an official market the manor courts could resolve differences. The buyer might complain that he had been misled, as when William Prescotte of Whitstones assured William Adam in 1392 that an ox was healthy and suited for the plough. The delivery of the animal or the payment might be delayed. A sum of 10s for an ox sold at Moor (Worcestershire) on 2 February 1388 should have been paid by 24 June 1388, but it was still outstanding in the following year. More often the payment was made in instalments and these were not completed, as when a horse was sold at Stoneleigh for 7s 4d but after two years (in 1479) the seller claimed that he was still owed 4s 4d.[139]

Many sales of animals or their products drew the seller into the business dealings of merchants and middlemen. Some of these were fellow villagers who

---

[136] WAM, 21939; SCLA, DR75/4.
[137] [W.J. Hardy] ed., *Stratford-on-Avon Corporation Records: The Guild Accounts* (Stratford-upon-Avon Corporation, 1880), pp. 17, 23.
[138] WCRO, CR 2026/3; C. Dyer, 'The Hidden Trade of the Middle Ages: Evidence from the West Midlands', in C. Dyer, *Everyday Life in Medieval England* (London, 2000), pp. 294–5.
[139] WA, ref. 009:1, BA2636/173 92448; WCL, E34; SCLA, DR18/30/24/15.

operated as entrepreneurs on a small scale. John Deye of Ombersley was a dairyman, perhaps leasing cows. He sold cheese to thirteen villagers for a total of 1s 9 ½d, a fraction of a larger business. His near contemporary in the same village was Henry atte Mere, who traded as a butcher. He bought animals including horses and was grazing sheep and feeding pigs in the village. He was also amerced for selling meat at excessive profit, a standard charge against all butchers, and his meat was said to be diseased.[140] The trade in pigs seems to have attracted specialists, like the 'merchant' of Wickhamford (Worcestershire) who bought twenty-one piglets from Pershore Abbey in 1381–2, probably to sell them for rearing.[141] Dealing in horses led villagers to acquire foals with the intention of selling them, and a more specialized and large-scale approach is suggested by the occupational description of a taxpayer as a *courser*, meaning a horse dealer, at Winchcomb, where the fair had a reputation for its horse trade that stretched as far as Kent.[142] The staple court of Bristol in 1510–13 was mainly concerned with large-scale credit arrangements between urban merchants. However, six husbandmen and yeomen from villages to the west of the town, including Clifton and Henbury, had dealings with Bristol merchants and butchers involving sums that varied between £7 and £35. The likely background was the sale of cattle, up to twenty at a time, which had been acquired by enterprising peasants in their home villages.[143]

Poulterers acted as contacts between the many rural small-scale producers and wealthy households or the consumers in towns. The household of the wealthy Warwickshire knight, William Mountford, obtained poultry from the wife of John Baggeslowe who lived at Blyth, a hamlet south of Coleshill near Mountford's manor house. She sold sixty geese to Mountford in the late summer of 1434 and he acquired forty pullets from another trader, Margery Clerk. Peasant women evidently played a major role in the poultry trade, relying on a network of contacts over neighbouring villages to assemble birds from many suppliers which could be sold on to urban poulterers such as those in fourteenth-century Coventry.[144] Honey and wax attracted the attention of middlemen, reflected in the occupational personal name Honymonger (at Badminton, Gloucestershire) in 1341; Alexander and Juliana Honemon lived at Earls Croome in Worcestershire in 1275.[145]

The most complex and profitable of entrepreneurial ventures was the trade in wool, with its many branches and layers of commercial activity. In the thirteenth century the Italian companies made contracts with major producers, many of

---

[140] WA, ref. 705:56, BA 3910/39.
[141] F.B. Andrews, 'The Compotus Rolls of the Monastery of Pershore', *TBAS* 57 (1933), p. 32.
[142] *PT*, part 1, p. 273; D.L. Farmer, 'Marketing the Produce of the Countryside 1200–1500', in *The Agrarian History of England and Wales*, vol. 3, 1348–1500 (Cambridge, 1991), pp. 381–2.
[143] E.E. Rich, ed., *The Staple Court Book of Bristol* (Bristol Record Soc., 5, 1934), pp. 107, 133, 135, 145, 165–6.
[144] Woolgar, ed., *Household Accounts*, part 2, pp. 440, 442.
[145] GA, Badminton muniments, D2700 MA1/1; J.W. Willis Bund and J. Amphlett, eds., *Lay Subsidy Roll for the County of Worcester ca. 1280* (WHS, 1893), p. 26.

them monasteries, in which they paid for the wool in advance of the shearing of the sheep, sometimes committing the producer for some years ahead. This was relevant to the peasants who kept sheep, because the monasteries would increase the amount of wool that they sold by including the *collecta*, that is, wool bought in their locality, often from peasant producers. A contract by Llanthony Priory (sited in Gloucester) in 1319 envisaged the purchase of wool by the monastery if their own flocks did not produce the amount promised.[146]

Wool was also sold in markets in such places as Northleach (Gloucestershire) and Stratford-upon-Avon (Warwickshire) in the fourteenth century. A high proportion of peasant wool was bought by woolmongers, also known as woolmen and woolbroggers (brokers) who bought directly from the producer. The procedure is well documented from the account book of John Heritage of Moreton-in-Marsh, who was active in the first two decades of the sixteenth century.[147] He made a bargain with the sheep owner early in the year, agreeing a price and quantity, and paid a small sum in earnest money. After the sheep were sheared and wool delivered the woolman paid the money due in instalments that could extend over the whole year. Although not many records of the transactions exist (other than in Heritage's account book) buying wool before shearing was the subject of legislation, so it must have been a general practice. There were many woolmongers, so the peasant producers could change from one to another to obtain the best price or promptest payment. Woolmongers were often based in small towns, of which Northleach was the most celebrated, but they could be found in a rural setting, like John Spencer of Defford (Worcestershire) who bought Pershore Abbey's tithe wool in 1379–80, and presumably also dealt in the fleeces of his peasant neighbours.[148]

Woolmen often handled sheepskins (wool fells), but there were other specialist dealers, the fellmongers, two of whom were trading in Stow-on-the-Wold in 1381.[149] They would buy fells brought in by producers, who had skinned animals that had been butchered but more often were the casualties of disease and old age, and sell them on to the white tawyers who processed the skins, usually in towns.

Lords bought peasant livestock as they often did not breed enough replacements from their own animals. On some Worcester Priory manors in the late fourteenth century, new oxen were regularly obtained, but the source is not identified. On the Warwickshire estate of John Brome of Baddesley Clinton in 1444–5 William Colletts, a carpenter who also held land, sold two oxen to Brome.[150] Peasants also supplied aristocratic households, like that of William Mountford of Coleshill,

---

[146] R.H. Hilton, *A Medieval Society. The West Midlands at the End of the Thirteenth Century* (Cambridge, 1983), p. 180.
[147] Dyer, *Country Merchant*, pp. 100–31.   [148] Andrews, 'Compotus Rolls', p. 22.
[149] *PT*, part 1, p. 264.
[150] SCLA, Ferrers MSS, 800. Throughout the country demesnes bought horses from peasants: Claridge, 'Agricultural Horses', p. 19.

which was sold butter worth 2s 6d by the wife of William Jeke, a tenant of Gilson, a hamlet of Coleshill.[151]

Animals were not always sold or leased, but changed hands through loans, gifts, bequests, and as seigneurial dues. At Cleeve Prior in 1370 Richard Fisher borrowed a mare from John de Alvechurch which died in unknown circumstances.[152] Livestock often figure in peasant wills, because as cash was scarce, children were left cattle or horses, and sheep were used to reward servants, or bequeathed to more remote relatives and godchildren. Wills recorded the last gifts of those who were about to die, but they may have been continuing earlier transfers of animals to sons setting up their own farms. Peasant animals went to the lord when heriots, the best beasts, were taken by manorial officials. They might be sold back to the widow or heir, or added to the demesne stock, saving the lord the expense of buying oxen or horses from peasants. Mortuary payments allowed the rector or vicar to take the second-best animal. In these respects, as in many others when we consider the continuing importance of self-sufficiency, the market was not exercising a complete dominance over peasants' pastoral farming.

Conclusion

West-midland peasants did not practise mixed farming out of habit or tradition, but because arable and pasture were interlocked. Corn-growing needed animal traction and manure. The animals benefited from a share of the produce of the harvest for litter and fodder. Peasants kept animals and poultry as contributors to the household's food consumption as even small-scale allowances of cheese, bacon, and eggs meant that peasant diet was not based exclusively on cereals and vegetables. Combined with the expectation of occasional meat meals (after a pig killing for example), and seasonal feasts like the reap goose in September and chicken at Christmas, the peasants' livestock were adding greatly to the quality of their lives.

Peasants developed complex arrangements for feeding livestock. The main resource, the pasture on fallows, stubbles, and meadows that became available through the cycle of cultivation, harvest, and hay making, was subject to much regulation. Beyond the grazing linked to the open fields were the enclosures, sometimes subject to common grazing, wood pasture, intercommoning, agistment, the trade in hay, and the use of fodder crops. The regulations and controversies give the impression that the pasture supply was always teetering on the edge of failure, but animals seem not normally to have starved.

Pastoral farming responded to market conditions, and decisions about the numbers of cattle, sheep, pigs, and poultry were influenced by demand. Peasants

---

[151] Woolgar, ed., *Household Accounts*, p. 443.   [152] WCL, E24.

were conscious of costs, and were cautious in providing housing for livestock, or increasing expenditure on wages. Animals were an important source of cash for peasants, and this was obtained in many ingenious ways, through hiring as well as sale, and many credit devices, including advances of cash (in the case of wool). Payments for animals were delayed or made in instalments. Sometimes the producer could engage directly with the purchaser, but very often the animals or their produce were bought by a dealer or monger.

Animal husbandry is often regarded as a more individual activity than cultivation, but pastures were managed in common and the interests of those sharing the facilities were supposed to be observed, leading to the stinting of grazing. The pooling of beasts in plough teams and the employment of the common herd were central to the operations of the village community. Occasionally, however, a better-off peasant could display status as an individual by riding a well-equipped horse, or building a dovecot.

8
Peasants and towns

In 1354 at Horsley in a country of steep valleys and wooded slopes in central Gloucestershire Henry atte Mulle complained that Henry Croumere, with whom he was in legal dispute, had taken away his horse.[1] Without this animal he could not travel to town (probably Tetbury or Minchinhampton) to trade (a literal translation would be 'to merchandise') and do business (*negocium*). We must suppose that especially on market day, on Wednesday in the case of Tetbury, people like Henry atte Mulle on horseback, or leading a packhorse loaded with grain, carts full of hay, firewood, or geese, men on foot driving an animal, women bringing baskets of eggs, fruit, and vegetables, all converged on the town. This chapter will examine peasant involvement in towns and assess the consequences of the interaction between town and country. As well as drawing on the evidence from the twenty best researched places, special attention will be given to the well-documented town of Alcester. A town is taken to have been a dense and permanent settlement with inhabitants pursuing a variety of non-agricultural occupations, mostly in manufacturing and trade.

Origins of towns

At the end of the twelfth century the larger towns of the region were well established. Bristol, Gloucester, Warwick, and Worcester had been planned and encouraged by kings, lay magnates, bishops, and monasteries. Tamworth and Winchcomb had strong associations with the region's past rulers. Droitwich was a special case as a centre of salt production of much interest to kings and local magnates.[2]

Before the twelfth century a number of smaller towns were beginning to grow, at Berkeley, Cirencester, Coventry, Evesham, Pershore, Tewkesbury, and Thornbury. They began a trend, which led to the appearance of more than forty towns between

---

[1] TNA, SC2 175/63.
[2] D. Palliser, ed., *Cambridge Urban History of Britain*, vol. 1, 600–1540 (Cambridge, 2000), pp. 609–19 on the origins of these towns, with references. Publications since then include J. Maddicott, 'London and Droitwich, c.650–750: Trade, Industry and the Rise of Mercia', *Anglo-Saxon England* 34 (2003), pp. 7–58; N. Baker and R. Holt, *Urban Growth and the Medieval Church: Gloucester and Worcester* (Aldershot, 2004); S. Bassett, 'The Middle and Late Anglo-Saxon Defences of Western Mercian Towns', *Anglo-Saxon Studies in Archaeology and History* 15 (2008), pp. 180–239; *VCH Staffordshire*, 12, pp. 15–16 (for Tamworth).

the late twelfth and early fourteenth centuries.[3] A half of the prime movers of these towns were major secular lords, barons, and earls. A third were monasteries or bishops, and the remainder lesser lay lords, such as knights. Towns apparently owed their existence to the rich and powerful (Figure 8.1).

The 'new town' model, which emphasizes the role of the lord, can be applied to many of these urban developments. The sequence of events began with a lord, eager to gain profit and status. The lord, or the estate officials, identified a site with a road junction or river crossing (or both), and altered the road layout so as to maximize the flow of traffic along a main street. Plots of land were measured and defined, and tenants encouraged to take them up by grants of liberties and privileges. These benefits often included burgage tenure, so tenants were freeholders, paying a fixed money rent, and able to sell or dispose of their plot as they wished. A market charter would be obtained from the Crown, and the new venture would be advertised as an opportunity for new settlers.[4]

Even if the new town model is thought to have been the normal pattern of urban development, the lords depended on the settlers' decision to move to the town. Lords pushed some subordinates into taking up new plots, but they had limited powers, so the townspeople were mainly volunteers. Oversley (Warwickshire) was laid out as the apparent first stage of a small town at the gate of a twelfth-century castle, but the site proved to be unattractive, people moved away, and the would-be town failed by about 1225.[5] An offer from a lord needed to be matched by a sustained response from people prepared to move and then stay. As Oversley faltered, nearby Alcester on a more advantageous site, was growing.

Lords might attempt to compel tenants to trade in their markets. The abbot and convent of Halesowen made an agreement in 1363 with their tenants that any of them selling grain would firstly take it to the market of Halesowen borough. Similarly, Worcester Priory in 1342 ordered people at Blackwell and Shipston to offer cattle for sale at Shipston market before selling them privately. When in 1423 Thomas Lette of Shipston took four pigs to the market at nearby Brailes, he was charged by the Worcester monks a toll of 1*d*, which would have been paid if the

---

[3] R.H. Hilton, *The English Peasantry in the Later Middle Ages* (Oxford, 1973), pp. 76–94; R.H. Hilton, 'Lords, Burgesses and Huxters', *P&P* 97 (1982), pp. 3–15; R.H. Hilton, 'The Small Town and Urbanisation—Evesham in the Middle Ages', *Midland History* 7(1982), pp. 1–8; R.H. Hilton, 'Small Town Society in England before the Black Death', *P&P* 105 (1984), pp. 53–78; R.H. Hilton, 'Medieval Market Towns and Simple Commodity Production', *P&P* 109 (1985), pp. 1–23; R.H. Hilton, 'Low Level Urbanisation: the Seigneurial Borough of Thornbury in the Middle Ages', in *Medieval Society and the Manor Court*, edited by Z. Razi and R.M. Smith (Oxford, 1996), pp. 482–517; R.H.C. Davis, *The Early History of Coventry* (DS Occasional Paper, 24, 1976).

[4] M.W. Beresford, *New Towns of the Middle Ages. Town Plantations in England, Wales and Gascony*, new edition (Gloucester, 1988).

[5] C. Jones, G. Eyre-Morgan, S. Palmer, and N. Palmer, 'Excavations in the Outer Enclosure of Boteler's Castle, Oversley, Alcester, 1992–93', *TBWAS* 101 (1997), pp. 1–98.

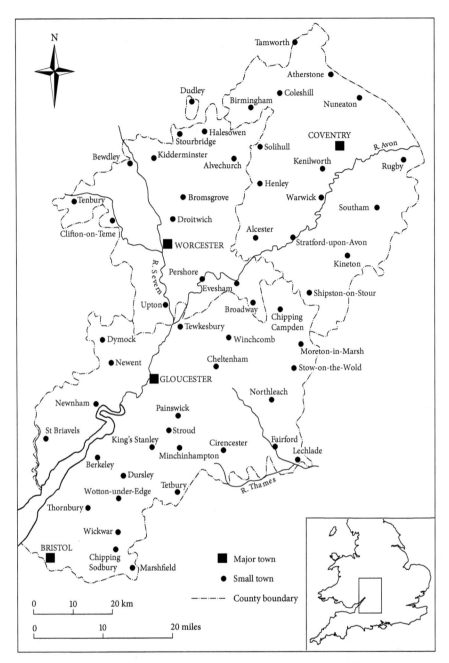

Figure 8.1 Towns in the west midlands. This omits less-certain candidates for urban status, such as Redditch, Knowle, and Mitcheldean. Some towns were sited on landscape frontiers, such as the Cotswold edge. There were notable gaps, such as west Worcestershire and the centre of the Cotswolds. Most of the towns were established by 1300; Stourbridge and Stroud later.

sale had been conducted properly in Shipston marketplace.[6] Normally buyers and sellers were not pressured to use a particular market.

Townspeople did not just respond to initiatives from above. Some sites for new towns were chosen because traders and artisans had already established themselves. Plots and houses at Burton Dassett Southend (Warwickshire) were planned in 1280–1300, following a market charter of 1267, in the hope of founding a new town. For a time, it was known as Chipping Dassett. However significant occupational surnames, with two people called Marchaund, occur among the tenants of 1279, who do not look like recent arrivals, and excavation suggests that an area of plots resembling those found in towns had come into existence before 1250.[7] Bretford (Warwickshire) is another apparent new town established by a lay lord with a market charter, town plan, new bridge, diverted main road, and burgage tenure in the early thirteenth century. However, a town had already begun to develop, as in the year of the charter, 1227, the tenants, some of whom were pursuing trades and crafts, were already living at Bretford and probably operating an informal market.[8] In both cases the lords were catching up with unofficial developments, which they did not discourage, but sought to control.

The formative phase of some towns takes us back to the minster churches of the period 670–850. Markets were held near churches on Sundays, when those gathered for religious services could stay to buy and sell. Coleshill had a prominent minster church, with an adjoining marketplace (Figure 8.2). In the early thirteenth century, the market was held on Sundays, and dated back before 1200. The embryo of a town plan, with houses ranged along a single main street, could have begun to form before 1200, marked by irregular building plots still visible in modern times around the church. A similar development can be observed next to the church at Cheltenham, another early minster.[9]

The town plan can suggest that a town grew without a grand scheme imposed by a lord. Roads could meet in an irregular pattern suggesting an original rural settlement, or that groups of incomers established themselves at road junctions. Thornbury's four main streets now converge on a space called 'The Plain', and there is a similar irregularity in the layout of Tetbury, a town in which a minster had an early influence. Phrases such as 'primary towns' or 'organic towns' have been coined to describe these towns that emerged gradually without a single master plan.[10]

---

[6] Z. Razi, 'Family, Land and the Village Community in Later *Medieval* England', *P&P* 93 (1981), pp. 3–36, especially p. 30; WCL, E2; E51.
[7] N. Palmer and J. Parkhouse, *Burton Dassett Southend, Warwickshire: A Medieval Market Village* (Society for Medieval Archaeology Monograph 44, 2022), pp. 54–70.
[8] C. Dyer, 'New Towns in the Middle Ages: Lessons from Bretford in Warwickshire', *TBWAS* 120 (2018), pp. 75–92.
[9] A. Watkins, ed., *The Early Records of Coleshill c.1120–1549* (DS, 51, 2018), pp. 30–7; A. Craven and B. Hartland, *Cheltenham Before the Spa* (London, 2018), pp. 18–25, 133–4, 138.
[10] R. Leech, *Small Medieval Towns in Avon. Archaeology and Planning* (Bristol, Committee for Rescue Archaeology in Avon, Gloucestershire and Somerset, 1975), pp. 21–5; R. Leech, *Historic Towns in Gloucestershire. Archaeology and Planning* (Bristol, Committee for Rescue Archaeology in Avon, Gloucestershire and Somerset, 1982), pp. 86–9.

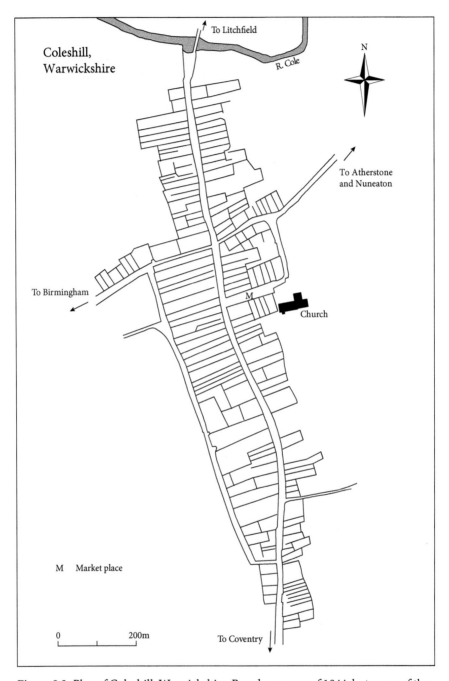

Figure 8.2 Plan of Coleshill, Warwickshire. Based on a map of 1844, but many of the property boundaries date from before 1300. Those on the eastern side of the main street, both to the north and south of the church, belonged to a rural settlement and the initial growth of a trading centre around the church and the marketplace. The regular tenements on the west side, with a back lane, probably belong to a phase of urban planning in the twelfth and thirteenth centuries. The roads leading to other towns suggest Coleshill's role as a trading hub (source: note 9).

Lords varied greatly in their influence over urban growth. Stratford-upon-Avon was founded in a single act of planning in 1196, with a grid of streets, a wide market street, and probably a new bridge. The king issued a market charter, and the privileges of the new burgesses were set out in a document which was not granted to them, but written for the lord's archives. A great lord, a bishop, promoted the ambitious plan as a display of power and lordly magnificence. The lord's officials administered the borough, but with a very light rein, and the townspeople found that their religious fraternities served as a route to practical autonomy.[11] Not much grandeur was on display at Bromsgrove, with its single main street along which in the 1260s and 1270s plots were laid out. Two lords, Worcester Priory and the king (or rather his officials) co-ordinated the early stages, but showed little interest in further co-operation, or in promoting the town. The town was not a borough, so its tenants had no special privileges, but they succeeded in leading an urban way of life and governing the town informally.[12] The lord of the rural estate of Tardebigge (Worcestershire), the Cistercian abbey of Bordesley, indicated no ambition to found a town at all, which did not accord with Cistercian ideals of rural isolation. Nonetheless in the fourteenth and fifteenth centuries a loose collection of innkeepers, artisans, and traders assembled a short distance from the monastery, in the tithing of Redditch which reported business to the manor court.[13] Perhaps it should not be called a town, but it had some urban characteristics. These examples show that lords could be zealous planners of towns, or promoters at a distance, or just interested observers of urban growth.

Alcester was a town with an early history combining various strands of urban development. The town lies at a point where the river Alne joins the river Arrow, flowing out of the woodland landscapes of north and west Warwickshire. The Arrow continues four miles south to join the Avon, which drains the champion country of the south and east of the county. Alcester had been a Roman town, served by two major roads, one running west to east joining Droitwich and Stratford, the other linking the Fosse Way in the Cotswolds to Watling Street to the north of Arden. Three other significant roads complete the picture of Alcester as a well-connected place (Figure 8.3).

Alcester could be called an 'organic town' because its irregular streets and plot boundaries suggest piecemeal growth. Roads join at the town centre, crossing the Arrow by two bridges, with two foci, to the north a triangular marketplace, and to the south a space that may have been a second marketplace. The rows of regular plots along Bleachfield Street give it the character of a planned suburb.

---

[11] R. Bearman, ed., *The History of an English Borough: Stratford-upon-Avon, 1196–1996* (Stroud and Stratford, 1997), pp. 1–79.

[12] C. Dyer, *Bromsgrove: A Small Town in Worcestershire in the Middle Ages* (WHS Occasional Publication, 9, 2000).

[13] C. Dyer, 'The Hidden Trade of the Middle Ages: Evidence from the West Midlands of England', *Journal of Historical Geography* 18 (1992), pp. 141–57.

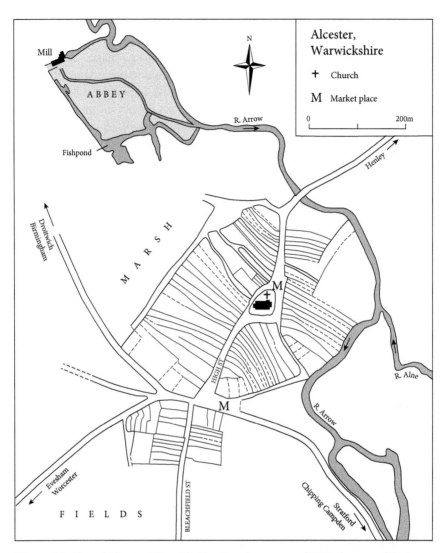

Figure 8.3 Plan of Alcester, Warwickshire. Based on a map of 1754, the core of the town was contained within the walls of its Roman predecessor. The irregular pattern of boundaries suggests a piecemeal growth 1000–1300, in contrast with the planned suburb of Bleachfield Street. The church in the marketplace replaced the early minster church, which was moved to the meadows when it was refounded as an abbey (source: note 14).

The main built-up area north of Bleachfield Street lay within the Roman walls, which defined an oval area, but the Roman town had been largely abandoned in the early Middle Ages, with its defences as a short-lived legacy.[14] A minster

---

[14] P. Booth and J. Evans, *Roman Alcester: Northern Extra-Mural Area* (CBA Research Report 127, 2001); S. Cracknell and M. Jones, 'Medieval Kiln Debris from School Road, Alcester', *TBWAS* 94 (1985–6), pp. 107–22.

church founded within the walled area is the likely source of an elaborately carved and decorated ivory crozier head of the eleventh century. An eleventh-century legend claimed that a royal council had been held at this 'celebrated place' in 709. The story has been discounted but the author may have been encouraged to embroider the past because he was impressed in his own day by Alcester's Roman origins (still visible in its walls), its minster church, and role as the centre of a royal estate.[15]

In about 1138/9 the minster church was refounded as a small Benedictine monastery in the meadows a quarter mile from the original site.[16] It was replaced in the town by a church dedicated to St Nicholas, sited in the main marketplace like other churches with this dedication, which was probably serving an existing town. Indications of the town's early beginnings include pottery of the eleventh century from the southern part of the town. Also the rents that were charged for holdings in the town, recorded in the sixteenth century, consist of small sums of 2 ½d, 3d, 4d, and 6d rather than the standard 12d per plot, resembling rents found in towns before the Norman Conquest. The market needed no charter after 1200 as it had already been established, though it was renewed in c.1274. A further indication of Alcester's early development is the pottery industry, which was established in the twelfth century and continued into the thirteenth. The kilns were sited between the Abbey and the medieval town, and are likely to represent an early but short-lived urban industry.[17] The town seems to have had deep roots, dating back to the twelfth century and probably before 1100. It had grown on royal demesne, but in the twelfth and later centuries came into the hands of lay aristocratic families. Kings tended to be benevolent and distant lords, and their successors, the Botreaux and the Beauchamps, intervened in only limited ways.

All of this is relevant to our theme because the townspeople came together in complex movements over a long time and are likely to have moved from the nearby countryside, which in 1086 was quite densely settled, especially to the south of Alcester. We do not know their origin in the early days of the town, but the surnames of townspeople recorded in c.1300 reflect the movement of villagers mostly from within five miles. The minster and the lords had a role in these processes, but did not plan the town or exercise close control over it.

---

[15] D. Wilson, *Anglo-Saxon Art. From the Seventh Century to the Norman Conquest* (London, 1984), p. 194; M. Lapidge, 'The Medieval Hagiography of St Ecgwine', *Vale of Evesham Historical Society Research Papers* 6 (1977), pp. 77–94; L. Roach, *Kingship and Consent in Anglo-Saxon England* (Cambridge, 2013), p. 86.

[16] *VCH Warwickshire*, 2, pp. 59–61; D Styles, 'The Early History of Alcester Abbey', *TBAS* 64 (1941–2), pp. 20–38.

[17] BAH, 272798 (dated to 1545; WCRO, CR1886/218; S. Letters, *Gazetteer of Markets and Fairs in England and Wales to 1516*, part 2 (List and Index Society, Special Series, 33, 2003), p. 357; Cracknell and Jones, 'Kiln Debris'.

Peasant migration into towns

Peasants moved in large numbers into towns to take up a new way of life. Information about peasant migration comes from town dwellers' family names, which were based on villages of origin. The name of William of Saynebyr, who was a tenant at Chipping Campden in 1273, derived from Saintbury, his (or his father's) home village a mile and a half from the town. The list of tenants of 1273 can be supplemented from other sources of similar date to give a sample of fifty surnames, and 44 per cent of them came from places within 10 miles[18] (Figure 8.4). Northleach seems to have been founded in 1220, and a survey was made in 1266-7. Analysis of this and other early sources shows that 71 per cent of those with names deriving from places came from within 10 miles.[19]

What types of peasant were motivated to move? The social structure of their village of origin provides a clue. For example, Thomas de Upton of Campden and Gilbert de Haselton at Northleach came from villages where most tenants were yardlanders.[20] It seems to follow that the migrants were representative of the better-off villagers, and it is possible that these people gave up their holdings of 30 acres of land, or at least sublet them, and moved into a new town to take up a craft or trade. However, a yardland gave its tenant a good income and security, and the sons of the more substantial tenants, not the tenants themselves, were likely to have migrated, with some financial help from their families.

The migration by members of better-off peasant families may not be the whole story, because peasants with substantial holdings did not predominate in all of the villages from which migrants came. Robert de Brokthrop migrated to Northleach before 1266; as his village of Brookthorpe in Gloucestershire was socially diverse with a proportion of smallholdings, he may not have belonged in the top ranks of landholders.[21] If families held cotlands a relative's entry into town society might have received some support, so the migrant was not fleeing from misery. Our observations are biased in favour of well-documented peasants and the better-off townspeople who held burgages, and there is likely to have been a lower class of penniless migrants who lived as lodgers, servants, or subtenants.

The country dwellers transferring to the town needed skills and experience to make a living in a new urban environment. Some arrivals may have been practising a craft or trade in the countryside so they were bringing their existing skills into a commercial centre with better opportunities. Country craftsmen in the thirteenth century might be identifiable from their names, for example, in Chipping Campden's area of influence the villages of Ilmington and Quinton, from which burgesses were recruited included among their late thirteenth-century tenants

---

[18] S. Madge, *Abstract of the IPMs for Gloucestershire*, part 4, 1236–1300 (British Record Society, 30, 1903), pp. 63–9, 80–3.
[19] *Hist Glouc*, 3, pp. 176–9; *VCH Glouc*, 9, pp. 106–11.
[20] *RBW*, pp. 300–2, 314–16; GA, D678/Safe 3, fos 21 and 22.   [21] *Hist Glouc*, 3, pp. 140–6.

PEASANTS AND TOWNS 237

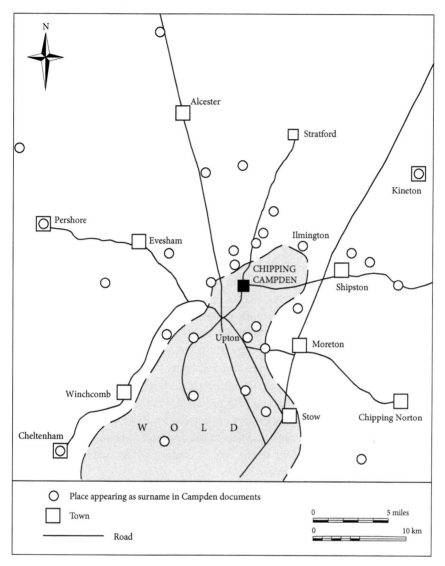

Figure 8.4 Migration into Chipping Campden, Gloucestershire. The origin of the early migrants into the town is recorded in the surnames of the population of 1273. They came from villages which used the town's market, along a dense road network, which connected the town with both the wold to the south and the champion to the north (source: Madge, *IPMs*, pp. 63–9, 80–3).

people called barker (tanner), smith, carpenter, and carter, and in neighbouring villages lived a chapman, cook, smith, and tailor.[22] These people (or their fathers) had transferable skills appropriate to founding a business in a new town. Many

[22] *RBW*, pp. 327–30.

stayed in the country, but some were able to move or they encouraged their sons to do so. Providers of food and drink figure prominently in urban occupations, and this is very apparent at Halesowen in the unique records of its first days from about 1270. An influx of women transferred to the town the activities they had previously practised in the country: brewing ale, baking bread, and selling flour (probably oatmeal). They also prepared flax for spinning and weaving.[23] They would be encouraged by the urban environment to brew more, sell more, and generally quicken the commercial pace.

The villages of origin of the townspeople can hint at the mechanics of migration. One method of recruitment was for news to travel across a landed estate. Gloucester Abbey's borough of Northleach recruited from other Abbey manors, even from Brookthorpe at a distance of 17 miles. Markets must have been great opportunities to spread news of opportunities in towns, and to build confidence if a visitor from the country observed a crowd of buyers and sellers. Many new townspeople came from places within the zone of trading contacts, and the villages of origin of Campden's burgesses were well placed on the road network.

Towns were often sited strategically in relation to the frontiers of landscapes, so that Alcester attracted immigrants from the woodland and champion of Warwickshire, and people from both the wolds and the champion of the Avon valley looked to Campden on the edge of the wolds. Lines of towns were strung out along the divide between Arden and Feldon in Warwickshire, and down the Cotswold edge from Campden to Chipping Sodbury. Across the landscape boundaries complementary products were traded—in the case of Alcester wheat and other grains from the champion were carried to the woodland, and timber, firewood, bacon, cheese, honey, and oats in the opposite direction. The origins of the town dwellers confirm the town's role in connecting landscapes through its people as well as its commodities.[24]

By contrast Birmingham seems to have drawn people from its own specialized woodland landscape. It was granted a market in the mid-twelfth century, and was clearly developing actively in the 1230s. By 1296 and 1344, when two rentals name many tenants, who had moved from the pastoral landscapes to the north-east and north-west, with a number from hamlets in south Staffordshire. One came from a village on the road to Coventry, Alspath.[25] No name suggested that anyone travelled from the champion country to settle in the clearly prosperous and expanding Birmingham.

The great majority of contacts between town and country depended on the road system which was being improved in the period of urban growth between

---

[23] Hilton, 'Small Town Society', pp. 60–6.
[24] For the general point of complementary hinterlands, see H. Carter, *The Study of Urban Geography* (London, 1995), pp. 41–51.
[25] G. Demidowicz, *Medieval Birmingham: the Borough Rentals of 1296 and 1344-5* (DS Occasional Papers 48, 2008).

1180 and 1330 by the building of bridges.[26] Worcester on the west midlands' only navigable river, the Severn, received migrants from riverside villages, such as Apperley (Gloucestershire), recorded in 1275.[27]

To sum up the contribution that peasants made to the expansion of towns until c.1300. The focus is on the smaller towns because they had the closest relationship with the peasants, and they were either founded or were still in an early stage of growth in the thirteenth century. The larger towns had begun much earlier, but were continuously receiving newcomers from the villages. Bristol names from the early fourteenth century, many of them belonging to members of the elite, show that people came from other towns such as Oxford, but some derive from villages within 10 miles. From Gloucestershire came people from Beachley, Bitton, Hawkesbury, and Tockington.[28] Coventry was expanding in the thirteenth century, and displayed its power of attraction by gaining many citizens from other towns at a distance of 20 miles and more. But shorter distance migrations had originated in villages within 10 miles such as Dunchurch, Maxstoke, and Pailton, all within 10 miles, suggesting that local peasants hoped for a good living in a burgeoning commercial centre.[29]

The large towns had been able to increase their inhabitants by c.1300 to about 14,000 in the case of Bristol, with 5,000 at Gloucester, 5,000 at Coventry, and 3,000 for Worcester, accounting for about a tenth of the 260,000 people estimated (and probably underestimated) to have lived in the three west midland counties.[30] The smaller towns, about sixty of them with populations between 300 and 1,500, could together account for 24,000, so the 'urban ratio' lay in the region of 20 per cent. The towns' inhabitants included many former peasants, or people recently descended from peasants.

West-midland peasants continued their connections with towns, so that a third of serfs recorded as leaving their manors in the period 1350–1500 moved into towns (see 'Migration' in Chapter 4). Among the fifteenth-century sample, twenty-one went to towns outside the region, including London, Calais, and Salisbury. Sixty travelled to larger towns in the region such as Bristol and Gloucester, but especially to Coventry and to some extent Worcester, which were increasing their populations in part of the period. The other migrants with known urban

---

[26] D. Harrison, *The Bridges of Medieval England. Transport and Society, 400–800* (Oxford, 2004), pp. 54–9, 138.

[27] J.W. Willis Bund and J. Amphlett, eds., *Lay Subsidy Roll for the County of Worcester circ 1280* (WHS, 1893), p. 4.

[28] S.A.C. Penn, 'The Origins of Bristol Migrants in the Early Fourteenth Century: The Surname Evidence', *TBGAS* 101 (1983), pp. 123–30.

[29] R. Goddard, *Lordship and Medieval Urbanisation. Coventry, 1043–1355* (Woodbridge, 2004), pp. 137–55; P. Coss, ed., *Early Records of Medieval Coventry* (British Academy Records of Social and Economic History, new series, 11, 1986), pp. 81–2, 97–101, 299–300.

[30] B.M.S. Campbell, 'Benchmarking Medieval Economic Development: England, Wales, Scotland, and Ireland, c.1290', *EcHR* 61 (2008), pp. 896–945, for the population of the region; the main source for urban population is Palliser, ed., *Cambridge Urban History*.

destinations were spread over twenty smaller towns, including Chipping Campden, Evesham, Pershore, Tewkesbury, and Winchcomb.

The records of migrations by serfs can tell us what they did in the town in which they settled. A dozen of the serfs who went to towns were reported to be 'with' a named town dweller, so Katherine Alvard of Bevere (Worcestershire) in 1476 was said to be 'with William Josse' of Worcester, and this is likely to mean that she was entering a household as a servant.[31] For a young woman working as a servant was an informal version of apprenticeship, by which experience of household management and such domestic (and money-making) skills as brewing were acquired. Occupations being pursued by departed male serfs often as servants included brewing, baking, shoemaking, and weaving. One was with a carpenter, another with a 'troughman' which must mean a woodworker producing kneading troughs. Mostly these 'placements' were with independent artisans, pursuing their craft in their own houses, like John Yate, a baker of Coventry, whose shop, we are told was near Broadgate in the city. He was reported in 1428 to be employing John Porter from Hartlebury, who was aged 16.[32] Some found work in the brewhouse or bakehouse at Evesham Abbey.[33] Rural immigrants in towns found marriage partners in towns, like Agnes Robyn, a Sambourn serf who had married Thomas Suard of Evesham by 1472, just as in York couples met through the woman's employment.[34] Agnes of the Feld of King's Norton (Worcestershire), presumably from a peasant background, was apprenticed to a Coventry purse maker, Robert Raulot, in 1345.[35] At the end of our period an abundance of records of apprenticeship from Bristol throws light on routines of recruitment which had probably been in existence (though undocumented) for many years. Between 1532 and 1539 the names are known of apprentices, their place of origin and parentage, together with details of the masters and their occupations. Young people were drawn to Bristol from a large area, including south-western counties, but to focus on our region sixty-seven came from towns, including Coventry, Worcester, and Birmingham, but mainly from the urban centres of the Severn valley such as Gloucester, Tewkesbury, and Berkeley (Figure 8.5). Eighty-six with rural origins had parents identified as husbandmen, yeomen, and labourers, many of whom are revealed by their appearance in the tax assessments of the 1520s as belonging to a wide spectrum of peasant society with goods valued in a range from 20*s* to £10. Some parents in the countryside had occupations as artisans. Masters who took on country apprentices were practising thirty-two crafts, the most frequent being hoopers (barrel makers) and whitetawyers (processing sheepskins). The rural

---

[31] WA, ref. 009:1, BA2636/175/92482.   [32] WA, ref. 009:1, BA2636/169/92372.
[33] WA, ref. 705:56, BA3910/27.
[34] SCLA, DR%/2359; P.J.P. Goldberg, *Women, Work and Life Cycle in a Late Medieval Economy: Women in York and Yorkshire c. 1300–1500* (Oxford, 1992), pp. 158–202.
[35] R. Goddard, 'Female Apprenticeship in the West Midlands in the Later Middle Ages', *Midland History* 27 (2002), pp. 165–81.

PEASANTS AND TOWNS 241

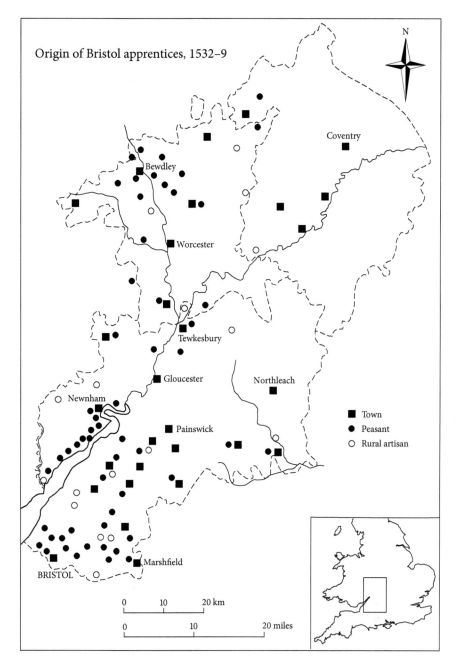

Figure 8.5 Origins of apprentices at Bristol, 1532–9. The map marks the towns and villages from which apprentices originated. Bristol's influence was strongest in south Gloucestershire but extended up the Severn to north Worcestershire (source: Hollis, *Apprentice Book*).

recruits were concentrated in the Severn valley, with a number from such villages as Iron Acton, Pucklechurch, and Westbury-on-Trym. The gaps in the eastern Cotswolds and Warwickshire suggest the rival attraction of apprenticeships in Oxford and Coventry. The places sending recruits included villages in north Worcestershire such as Chaddesley Corbett and Rock, from which boys went to Bristol, not a difficult journey because they lay in the hinterland of Bewdley, a busy river port from which a succession of boats travelled down the river. Not all of the apprentices were male, as they included Selia Tovy from Broadwas (Worcestershire) who went to learn the art of housewifery in the household of a Bristol mercer.[36]

In addition to the stream of young country people gaining a practical education by working as servants or serving as apprentices, many sons of servile families attended schools, for which their fathers were supposed to obtain permission from their lord, or face a fine when their sons' education became public knowledge. Some schools had been endowed in villages (see 'Social mobility' in Chapter 4). Most of the schools in the region were held in towns, twelve of them in Warwickshire alone. Very small towns such as Bromsgrove and Shipston made some provision for education.[37] Most of the available places would have been taken by town boys, but the steady flow of references in the court rolls to the education of serfs' sons must mean that rural pupils attended urban schools.

Serfs left their village to better themselves in the town, but they did not always succeed. There are hints that the first move did not go well, because the absentee was reported in a succession of towns. One who went to Coventry had initially moved to Cirencester. Another apparently found that Worcester suited him better than Droitwich. Many of the migrants were young, and doubtless expected to find rewarding employment, and eventually to practise a craft. This optimism was not shared by those who moved in a state of poverty, like John Taylor of Kempsey who in 1462 withdrew to Worcester, and left his holding of 6 acres in the lord's hands.[38] He was expecting perhaps to live in the city like many others from alms or casual employment.

After they moved, townspeople did not forget their rural origins. In making their wills they made bequests to rural relatives and churches in their native village. John Hands or Hannys of Stratford-upon-Avon, probably the wealthiest person in the town when he died in 1473, had been born in the village of Hidcote Bartrim (Gloucestershire) and left £3 6s 8d to the church there; he also bequeathed property in the village to his son.[39] In the town where Hands made his fortune the archive of the Fraternity of the Holy Cross shows people from town and country

---

[36] D. Hollis, ed., *Calendar of the Bristol Apprentice Book 1532–1565* (Bristol Record Soc.,14, 1949).
[37] I. Green, *Warwickshire Readers, c1520–c1750: Their Schooling and Their Books* (DS Occasional Papers 51, 2015), p. 5.
[38] WA, ref. 705:4, BA54.
[39] S. Appleton and M. Macdonald, eds., *Stratford-upon-Avon Wills* vol. 1 (DS, 52, 2020), pp. 65–6.

transferring urban property. Members of the Kyngton, alias Walker, family had an interest in two adjacent shops in the 'Middlerow', a major retail attraction in Stratford's town centre. Richard Kyngton was a husbandman of Tidmington, Walter Kyngton lived at Charlecote, and was also called a husbandman, and Robert Kyngton belonged to Alveston. William Walker, father of Robert, had been the heir of Isabella Walker of Loxley, daughter of Emota Colyns of Compton Wynyates, and one of these women had probably been married to a townsman. All of the villages lay within 12 miles of the town.[40] Deeds from the rural Compton Verney archive record that the Jones family held a yardland by free tenure at Compton in the late fourteenth century, and a family member was John Jones junior, called a chaplain in 1362. Another John Jones was a tenant in 1406, and the holding had come into the hands of Agnes Jones by 1434. She had been married to Henry Wilkyns of Compton, but when he died she married Thomas Baret of Stratford-upon-Avon, giving him the tenancy of a freehold yardland.[41] These bonds of kinship and marriage between townspeople and country dwellers made movement of people a commonplace event, but also allowed the flow of funds, so that for example rural money could have been invested in urban businesses.

Occupations and commerce: Peasant influence on towns

Towns, and in particular the largest towns, connected with wealthy elites based in the countryside. Lay aristocrats and leading churchmen joined urban fraternities (such as Coventry's Trinity Guild) and drew rents from urban property. Merchants of Bristol and Coventry traded in wine and spices for rich consumers, and top-of-the-range craftsmen made expensive and specialized products for rich clients, such as armour, or church organs. All of this was remote from the everyday world of peasants.

Peasants were not cut off from the larger towns. Gloucester, for example, around the year 1400 licensed annually a hundred or so 'foreign' traders for a shilling or two each. To select a sample year, in 1380 villagers who paid their fees lived within 10 miles and brought bread, ale, grain, malt, and fish into the town.[42] Peasants living near all of the region's larger towns would have taken advantage of such market opportunities.

Most peasants lived in the neighbourhood of small market towns, and the occupations of the townspeople reflect the varied needs of the less affluent, but still numerous, rural population that visited their shops and markets. The number

---

[40] SCLA BRT 1/2/408; M. Macdonald, ed., *The Register of the Guild of the Holy Cross of Stratford-upon-Avon* (DS, 42, 2007), p. 359.
[41] SCLA, DR98/31a, 33, 34, 35, 38, 39, 40, 83, 90, 92, 93, 96.
[42] *VCH Glouc*, 4, pp. 46–50.

Table 8.1 Occupations in Alcester, 1380–1504

Food and drink:	baker, brewer, butcher, fishmonger, miller, spicer
Textiles:	weaver
Clothing:	hosier, tailor
Leather:	corviser (shoemaker), glover, saddler, tanner
Wood:	bowyer, cooper, collier, sawyer, wheeler
Metal:	ironmonger, smith
Building:	carpenter, glazier, mason, thatcher
Services and miscellaneous:	barber, chandler, chaplain, clerk, ostler (innkeeper)

of separate occupations helps us to recognize a town and judge its rank. A large town such as Worcester had more than fifty trades and crafts according to such sources as the 1381 poll tax.[43] Most small towns could muster twenty or thirty, which reflected the needs of those coming to the town as consumers.

Shipston's court rolls of 1310–1520 record nineteen occupations. This modest spread of trades and crafts would be expected in a very small town with only 300 inhabitants. At another small town, Bromsgrove, twenty occupations are recorded, but unlike many small towns there were significant concentrations of crafts, with six weavers in 1393, and five tanners in 1500.[44] Cotswold towns in 1381 provided a living for a rather large number of different trades and crafts such as thirty-five at both Chipping Campden and Winchcomb, and twenty-eight at Stow-on-the-Wold. The Cotswold towns were unusual because their trading population included merchants, that is, large-scale dealers in wool, though in the three mentioned here there were only one or two in each town, so it is misleading to call them 'wool towns'.[45]

Table 8.1 shows the twenty-nine occupations recorded for Alcester, drawing on evidence from court records, especially those of the borough court of the fifteenth century. The variety of occupations at Alcester seems appropriate for a community of about 600 people.

In the case of Alcester, anyone living within a few miles of the town could attend the market and sell their produce, and also buy the goods that were not available on their holding or in their village. The table shows that peasants' purchases could include sea fish, such as dried cod and red herrings, shoes and harness, a barrel or tub, a cartwheel, or horseshoes. A visitor from the country might wish to negotiate with a carpenter about building work. Alcester's list of occupations included two luxury trades: glaziers who worked on high-status buildings, and a spicer, who presumably sold pepper, ginger, sugar, and dried fruits mostly in

---

[43] C. Barron, 'The Fourteenth-Century Poll Tax Returns for Worcester', *Midland History* 14 (1989), pp. 1–29.
[44] C. Dyer, 'Small-Town Conflict in the Later Middle Ages: Events at Shipston-on-Stour', *Urban History* 19 (1992), pp. 183–210, especially p. 189; Dyer, *Bromsgrove*, pp. 29–31.
[45] Hilton, *English Peasantry*, p. 79.

demand by aristocratic and wealthy clerical households. The ostlers of Alcester had as their main clientele travellers on the main roads who could afford the accommodation and meals. Alcester's traders were evidently not exclusively concerned with the less affluent consumers, but the ordinary people of the villages were more numerous, and in combination had more spending power.

Some occupations were probably omitted by chance from Alcester's records. Most towns had at least one cook selling takeaway meals, who sometimes broke regulations by intervening in the market for food and pushing up prices, like the cooks at Halesowen who bought poultry before it could be offered to the general consumer. A draper selling cloth retail was frequently encountered in towns. If a weaver was working at Alcester, a fuller or dyer might also be expected, and indeed at Alcester (although she was not called a dyer or dyster, the female equivalent) Matilda Brown in 1462 was said to have agreed to dye some cloth.[46] These three trades seem to have been present in the town in the thirteenth and early fourteenth century if the personal names of cook, dyer, and linen draper are taken as evidence for occupations.[47] And finally, life in small towns often included some entertainment. A musician is occasionally mentioned, notably in 1462 when a lawsuit was brought by John Pyper of Atherstone (Warwickshire) against John Pyper of Nuneaton. Townspeople and visitors to both towns evidently could expect to hear the sound of the 'baggepype'.[48]

The peasant visitors needed to be confident that when they arrived at the market with a load of corn or an animal that there would be a good prospect of finding a buyer and the price would be fair. They also expected that the goods that they wished to buy would be of high quality and not overpriced. The town's authorities needed to reassure those coming from the country, who were probably suspicious of the cunning ways of townspeople.[49] Confidence would be built if any disputes could be settled, which was possible if outsiders as well as the townspeople had access to the borough court to recover debts, to obtain redress if a trespass had occurred, or to deal with broken contracts, goods retained, or deception. The problems that led to these lawsuits were not everyday occurrences, but the bargains that went wrong give us a sample that began as routine transactions. The ideal record of these cases would name the litigant and the place of residence, the transaction that led to the dispute, and the value of the goods or animals, or the sum of money in the case of a debt. However, the clerk tended to abbreviate the entry, and often all that is given is the names of the parties, the type of action

---

[46] WCRO, CR1886/156.
[47] W.F. Carter, ed., *The Lay Subsidy Roll for Warwickshire of 6 Edward III (1332)* (DS, 6, 1926), p.6; A.J. Gwinnett, *A History of Alcester* (Alcester, 1953), corrected by BAH, MS 3068/7/1.
[48] A. Watkins, *Small Towns in the Forest of Arden in the Fifteenth Century* (DS Occasional Paper, 38, 1998), p. 12.
[49] J. Davies, *Medieval Market Morality. Life, Law and Ethics in the English Marketplace,1200-1500* (Cambridge, 2012), pp. 270-3.

(for debt for example) and little else. In the borough court records for Alcester between 1424 and 1504 much of the litigation was between inhabitants of Alcester, and there were occasional disputes arising from dealings between traders from Alcester and those from seven urban centres within twelve miles. Country people are identified in a minority of cases.

A standard procedure in the Alcester court was to take a distraint of goods, to bring pressure to bear on the litigant to attend court and pay any money owed. Alcester's residents were distrained by taking household utensils, such as a brass pot or a pewter dish, but a visitor from the country might lose a horse or the goods it was carrying. In 1439 John Mase of Great Alne had a horse and 4 bushels of barley taken, together worth 10s, and William Knoll of Kinwarton was distrained by 2 bushels of barley worth 20d.[50] The plea initiated by Richard Haselholt, a leading Alcester townsman, against Nicholas Cockes of Cleeve Prior in 1462 led to distraint by a sack and 4 bushels of barley worth 2s. 6d.[51] Cockes was a prominent villager in Cleeve, and he clearly had a surplus of grain to sell. The grain taken in distraint, is evidence for an important element in the town's trade. Incidentally, the peasants were taking grain to market by packhorse, which seems to have been the main means of transporting goods.

The surviving court records for Alcester contain thirty-five other examples of people from named villages owing money, or being owed money by Alcester residents, giving rise to a plea of debt. This is a minimum number of encounters between town and country as the clerks did not consistently record the place where litigants lived. The legal cases encourage us to think of the town as a source of credit for peasants. Usually credit was given when a sale was agreed, so it was really a delayed payment, but occasionally a cash loan had been arranged. This could lead to a plea in the court with no reference to a sale or other dealing between the parties, such as the claim in 1468 that Henry Bovy of Coughton owed money to two Alcester men.[52] A dozen debt pleas arose from transactions between two parties, neither of whom lived in Alcester, but in different villages, such as Cock Bevington the home of Thomas Laurans in 1486, and Marlcliffe near Bidford, where John Yeven lived.[53] Did these pleas arise from bargains struck in Alcester, perhaps in the marketplace and therefore to be resolved in the Alcester court? Or was it simply that the parties looked to the Alcester borough court as a trusted and effective settler of debts? In either case it strengthens the idea of the market town as a hub for its rural surroundings.

The litigation in the borough court can be mapped (see Figure 8.6) and helps to define Alcester's hinterland or sphere of influence, the cluster of rural settlements belonging to thirty-six villages mostly within 8 miles. Debts and other causes of litigation show villages within a similar radius in a number of west midland towns

[50] WCRO, CR1886/144.   [51] WCRO, CR1886/156.   [52] WCRO, CR1886/167.
[53] WCRO, CR1886/176.

PEASANTS AND TOWNS 247

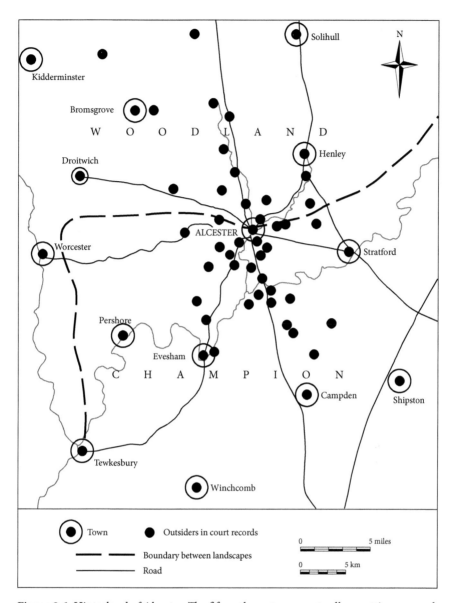

Figure 8.6 Hinterland of Alcester. The fifteenth-century court rolls sometimes record the place of residence of litigants, often those owing money to Alcester traders. This indicates the town's zone of influence, which notably included both the champion country to the south and the woodland to the north.

such as Atherstone and Nuneaton in north Warwickshire, Stratford and Shipston in the south, and at Pershore and Droitwich in Worcestershire.[54] Each town's hinterland contained between 4,000 and 10,000 people, and territories overlapped, so that many country dwellers could choose between two or three towns.

The commodities that appear in the records of Shipston include pulse, hay, malt, and a calf. Thornbury had a more pronounced specialism in textiles, so its traders dealt in grain and malt, but also wool and cloth. Atherstone and Nuneaton were located on the edge of the woodlands, so charcoal figures among the goods subject to dispute, as did cattle and dairy produce.

The market gave opportunities for middlemen and entrepreneurs, who are identified in town courts as forestallers and regraters, who intercepted goods before they reached the market. At Coleshill in 1383 peas and oats were being acquired by a trader (who was a carpenter) from nearby Maxstoke, John Ambresley. He resold them, and was therefore accused of regrating.[55] A rural tenant of Halesowen, Thomas Hulle, was identified as a bagger or badger (cornmonger) in the 1420s and 1430s. He did not always co-operate with the court, but in other ways was a conventional tenant of a middling holding, with a customary half yardland and a toft held as a freehold. During the period of food shortage and high prices in 1438 two men broke into his house, perhaps in pursuit of stored grain.[56] In years of bad harvests food traders took on a high profile: in the famine year 1316 a baker called Rosa le Meleward of Eldersfield (Worcestershire) was accused of selling bread of low weight (against the assize) and retailing oatmeal.[57] Rural entrepreneurs also operated in the meat trade, such as Simon Hayne of Attleborough (Warwickshire) who presumably bought livestock around his rural base, and sold meat in Nuneaton market for twenty years between 1389 and 1409.[58]

Most of the documented middlemen were town-based, like John Harry and John Odeston of Nuneaton who were accused of forestalling eggs, milk, and butter in 1390, and at Droitwich in the early fifteenth century six forestallers, four of them women, were said to be dealing in foodstuffs, and specifically in eggs, doves, and fowl.[59] Perhaps the offences were routine, and the authorities were finding a way of imposing a tax on traders. In Coventry, a large town with a huge demand, in 1380-1 nine women and a man were said to have regrated doves, geese, capons, butter, eggs, cheese, and other 'small victuals' in six separate cases.[60] The products all came from the country, and presumably peasant women were meeting with town traders, many of them women, and welcoming the chance to sell their

---

[54] C. Dyer, 'Market Towns and the Countryside in Late Medieval England', *Canadian Journal of History* 31 (1996), pp. 17–35.; Watkins, *Small Towns*, pp. 24, 25.
[55] Watkins, ed., *Records of Coleshill*, p. 48.
[56] BAH, 3279/346393, 346, 404, 346, 406; *CR Romsley*, pp. 180, 181, 188–9.
[57] WA, ref. 705:134, BA 1531/69.   [58] Watkins, *Small Towns*, p. 17.
[59] Watkins, *Small Towns*, p. 19; BAH, photostatic copy of Droitwich court rolls, vol. 3, no. 296.
[60] E.G. Kimball, ed., *Rolls of the Warwickshire and Coventry Sessions of the Peace, 1377–1397* (DS, 16, 1939), pp. 37, 38, 43, 48, 54.

produce in a single transaction rather than spending hours retailing in the market place, in the street, or door-to-door.

Manufactured goods could also be bought in bulk and distributed, as was the case at Charingworth (Gloucestershire) reported in 1424, when John Vicarye bought a hundred ropes of bast at Shipston-on-Stour.[61] The ropes were made from the bark of lime trees, and were probably sold at Shipston by a dealer from the Arden who bought them from ropers working in the woodland. Vicarye would not have needed so many ropes, and must have acquired them in order to sell them around the villages of north Gloucestershire. Town-based grain merchants plied their trade in the champion villages around the lower Avon valley and the eastern banks of the Severn. In the 1380s, thirteen cornmongers from Tewkesbury and seven from Cheltenham collected formidable quantities of grain, 600 quarters in one case and 540 quarters in another, mainly from peasant producers, presumably for shipment down the river Severn to Bristol.[62] On a much more modest scale urban artisans were selling loaves of bread in the villages, in north Warwickshire for example where bakers from Coleshill (Warwickshire) in the late fifteenth century were taking bread for sale in four nearby villages.[63]

A striking feature of the borough of Alcester was its custom of granting for a fee, usually 12*d*, the 'liberty within the borough to buy and sell freely', or in another version to have the 'liberty and franchise of the vill'. This meant that individuals, eight of them in 1438, fourteen in 1463, eight in three batches in the late 1460s, and another eleven in 1475, were gaining the same privileges as burgesses, and indeed when five townspeople in 1462 'are made new burgesses', they also paid a fee of 12*d*. Some of these purchasers of access to the borough were tenants of properties in the town which were not burgages, and therefore they did not enjoy the privileges of burgesses. At least two lived in Bleachfield Street, which lay outside the borough. Others were active in the urban economy: four sold ale, and another four were involved in pleas of debt or trespass. Some were country dwellers with ambitions to trade, like John Smyth who paid his fee in 1438. He came from Dunnington, 3 miles to the south-west and was renting a shop in Alcester.[64] Birmingham had a similar arrangement by which 'rent payers' (*censarii*) paid 2*d* or 4*d* for access to the town's market. Eighty-five of them were listed in 1296 but some traces of the institution survived into the sixteenth century. About twenty-six of those paying in 1296 seem to have been resident in the town, but names such as John, son of Gregory of Smethwick, suggest that they came from rural settlements within a 10-mile radius. Some may have moved into Birmingham, but a substantial number seem to have been country dwellers who either brought produce into the town, or sought work in the town.

---

[61] WCL, E51.   [62] Hilton, *English Peasantry*, p. 89.   [63] Watkins, *Small Towns*, p. 16.
[64] WCRO, CR1886/143.

As well as their country produce, peasants sold their labour in the towns, and appear in the records as servants, day labourers, and artisans. Urban authorities, such as the Bristol fullers in 1381, were so concerned by competition from rural fullers that they prohibited (no doubt unsuccessfully) receiving cloth for finishing that had been fulled in the country.[65] Coventry citizens were told in the early sixteenth century not to deal with fullers who worked outside the city.[66] These resentments tended to be expressed in hard times, so the rural cloth workers were not always so unwelcome.

Rural workers in the building industry tended to live near towns. The name 'carpenter' seems to cluster around Coventry according to the 1332 tax list, and carpenters were identified in the 1379 poll tax, with three at Stivichall and four at Bulkington and its adjacent hamlet of Ryton, both within 5 miles of Coventry.[67] At Bristol between 1295 and 1322 construction projects on the castle brought into the workforce people living on the castle's rural estate. The villagers of Mangotsfield paid the constable a modest rent for permission to quarry, presumably with a view to selling stone in the town. In 1295 fifteen masons were employed on the castle work, who probably travelled from some distance but thirty labourers seem to have lived on the castle estate, including John de Camey, a customary tenant of Mangotsfield.[68]

The fraternity of the Holy Cross at Stratford in the fifteenth century paid for constructing and maintaining its own guildhall, almshouses, and schoolhouse, and also invested heavily in dozens of rent-paying properties in the town. Stone, timber, and tiles were mostly obtained from the woodland landscapes to the north of the town, and some of the leading carpenters came from the Arden: John Bromefeld lived at Rowington, Thomas Parsons at Tanworth, and Henry Perkyns at Haseley. They supplied timber from sources near to their homes as well as building houses. They were probably landholders, as Thomas Parsons is recorded to have been, though we do not know if he worked the land himself or let it for rent.[69]

Peasant consumption and towns

Townspeople were responding to peasants' consumption demands. The peasant possessions most frequently encountered are indicated in Table 8.2, with the

---

[65] F.B. Bickley, ed., *The Little Red Book of Bristol* (Bristol, 1900), pp. 15–16.
[66] M.D. Harris, ed., *The Coventry Leet Book*, part 3 (Early English Text Society, Original Series 188, 1909), pp. 659, 704–5, 723.
[67] Carter, ed., *Lay Subsidy*, pp. 43, 50, 53, 60; *PT*, part 2, pp. 653, 688–9.
[68] M. Sharp, ed., *Accounts of the Constable of Bristol Castle in the Thirteenth and Early Fourteenth Centuries* (Bristol Record Society, 34, 1982), p. 37; S.A.C. Penn, 'A Hidden Workforce: Building Workers in Fourteenth-Century Bristol', *TBGAS* 109 (1991), pp. 171–8.
[69] T.H. Lloyd, 'The Medieval Gilds of Stratford-upon-Avon and the Timber-Framed Building Industry' (MA dissertation, University of Birmingham, 1961), 154, 169; SCLA, DR37/76. A tiler from Lapworth, Thomas Staffordshire, was another Arden-based worker employed by the guild.

Table 8.2 Peasant possessions, classified by materials

From written documents	
Textiles	tablecloth, towel, cushion, banker, painted cloth, coverlet, sheet, blanket, mattress, carpet, sack, canvas cover
Clothing	chemise, hose, doublet, hood, cap, kerchief, shirt, supertunic, gown, robe, tunic, coat
Leather	shoes, belt, harness, traces, bridle, saddle, sheath, horse collar
Wood*	table, bench, form, stool, chair, cupboard, almery, chest, ark, barrel, tub, trough, bucket, stand, cup, seed-lip, plough, cart, harrow, flail, rake, sieve, riddle, goad, whip, hames, spinning wheel, wych (a bin), bushel measure, bow and arrow
Metal (iron)*	knife, spade, fork, mattock, rake, scythe, sickle, weeding hook, axe, auger, saw, tyres (on wheels), plough share, coulter, clout, tines of harrow, heckle, comb, door furniture (locks and keys, hinges, hasps, studs), frying pan, spit, tripod, trivet, andirons
Metal (non-ferrous)	pots, pans, lead vats, basin, ewer, pewter dishes, pewter spoons, silver spoons
Ceramic	tiles
Stone	quern, mortar
Miscellaneous	rope, hair cloth, sack
From archaeological evidence	
Metal (iron)	knife, shears, scythe, sickle, weeding hook, spud, needle, lock, key, hinge, door stud, hasp, horseshoe, ox shoe, bit, spur, curry comb, chisel, punch, awl, reamer, arrowhead
Metal (non-ferrous)	dress accessories, e.g. buckle, belt end, harness fitting, brooch, mount
Ceramic	pottery, tile, ridge tile
Stone	quern, mortar, whetstone, door pivot, spindle whorl, grindstone
Bone	flute/pipe, dice, comb, toggle
Miscellaneous	glass smoother

* a number of items, e.g. plough, bucket, spade, were made of a combination of wood and iron, and have been rather arbitrarily classified here.

variety of garments, utensils, implements, and furnishings specified in documentary and archaeological evidence. The size of this great collective inventory might give an impression of peasant affluence, but of course these things were spread unevenly over many households, and individuals often lacked some basic furnishings or implements. On the other hand, the list understates peasant consumption, as the documents tended to omit cheap items, such as pottery, and archaeological finds from sites which are not waterlogged exclude objects made of wood and leather. To appreciate the urban role in peasant consumption we need to know where, how, and by whom these objects were made, exchanged, and distributed.

Wooden implements such as flails for threshing corn, or the handles of spades or scythes, could have been made, or at least mended or replaced, in the home.

One type of spindle whorl was cast from lead in urban workshops, but the simple and even clumsy discs of stone or reused ceramics could have been fabricated without specialist skills. Musical pipes made by inserting holes for fingering in a hollow bird bone appear to have been home-made. Repair work on metal implements and utensils may have been attempted by peasants, but the small quantities of slag and metal-working residues found on excavated rural sites were probably left by itinerant tinkers. The great majority of the items listed in Table 8.2 were made by specialists.

The materials used often came from the countryside: wood and timber, the fibres used in cloth (wool and flax), iron, and stone. A good deal of processing and manufacture was country-based, for some cloth and tanned hides, and most potting and tile making. However there were major cloth industries in Bristol and Coventry for at least part of our period, and on a smaller scale in clothing towns in south Gloucestershire and north Worcestershire. Normally every town, like Alcester, had a weaver and dyer. Non-ferrous metal working was in particular an urban industry, and the larger scale bell makers or founders who made the brass pots owned by almost every peasant household were confined to the more important towns such as Worcester.[70] Copper alloy dress accessories would also be made in large towns, and the designs are sometimes so close to finds from London that they are likely to have been made in the capital, though then distributed through provincial traders down to small-town retailers.[71] Ironworking was widely distributed because so many horse owners required a local shoeing service, but country smiths probably made knives and agricultural implements, and sharpened blades. Smiths and ironworkers operated in towns, for example, a specialist maker of arrowheads was working at Solihull in 1475–6, and an arrow maker paid the poll tax at Rugby in 1379.[72] Tailors are found scattered through the villages, but concentrated in some towns. In 1381 three tailors and three shepsters (dressmakers) are recorded in Lechlade, and ten tailors and three shepsters in the much larger centre of Cirencester.[73] Tanners also congregated in towns, for example, at Bromsgrove; shoes were occasionally made in the country, but many country people went to towns for their leather goods. Woodworkers such as coopers and wheelwrights were often town-based, though turners and coopers can be found operating in woodland rural settlements. A wealthy consumer in 1392–3 bought wooden utensils, such as a tub, buckets, and pails, at Chipping

---

[70] H. Dalwood and R. Edwards, *Excavations at Deansway, Worcester, 1988–9: Romano-British Small Town to Late Medieval City* (CBA Research Report 139, 2004), pp. 107–10, 187–90, 378–86, 432–5.

[71] G. Egan, 'Urban and Rural Finds: Material Culture of Country and Town c.1050–1500', in *Town and Country in the Middle Ages*, edited by K. Giles and C. Dyer (Society for Medieval Archaeology Monograph 22, 2005), pp. 199–210.

[72] SCLA, DR37/114; *PT*, part 2, p. 674.   [73] *PT*, part 1, pp. 290, 294–7.

Campden, probably at the fair, and these goods may also have been obtained there by ordinary consumers.[74]

Houses were the most expensive and complex of peasant acquisitions. Some elements of self-help were involved, because the peasant household's own labour could have contributed to such tasks as preparing the site and digging clay for walling. The labour of the mason, carpenter, dauber, and roofer could have been recruited in both country and town. Four carpenters were living in Southam in 1379, who must have found work in the surrounding villages as well as in the small town.[75] Masons and slaters could also be town-based. The building materials were often sourced locally, in particular stone, clay, sand, rods, wattles, and thatching straw, but timber was frequently brought from a distance or purchased. The lord of the manor of Whatcote in the 1440s built peasant houses and barns, using much the same methods as peasants if they had been arranging the work.[76] The larger timbers were purchased at Stratford-upon-Avon, a major distribution centre. While they were in the town the lords' officials also purchased nails and the iron fittings for the doors and shutters.

Even if goods were made in the country, the town was still the place from which they were distributed, as towns served as centres of communication for dealers and middlemen. Wealthy mercers and drapers handled linen and woollen cloth (and other goods). The leading traders were concentrated in large towns such as Coventry, but there was a drapery in a town as small as Rugby where small-scale retailers would offer cloth presumably of a type and quality appropriate for less affluent rural customers.[77] Litigation can record the purchase of cloth by a peasant consumer, such as John Bynethetown of Bricklehampton (Worcestershire), who was said in 1335 to owe John de Pendock of Pershore 16*d* for cloth bought. The small sum suggests that it was only part of the original purchase price. Bynethetown was listed among the taxpayers of his village in 1327, and he paid 7*d*, so was not very wealthy.[78]

An intricate network connected rural consumers, urban traders, and industrial workers in the countryside. Pottery was made from the thirteenth century into modern times at Chilvers Coton (sometimes called Potters Coton) in north Warwickshire. Potters are sometimes supposed to have travelled round villages and towns to sell their wares, but more likely middlemen were involved. George Bayly alias Potter in the early years of the sixteenth century held land and perhaps a kiln in Chilvers Coton, and took a leading role in Nuneaton, where he was rated highly in the town's tax assessment of 1525.[79] He and others from Nuneaton are

---

[74] Corpus Christi College, Oxford, B/14/2/3/4.   [75] *PT*, part 2, p. 669.
[76] SRO, D641/1/2/270, 271.   [77] SRO, D641/1/2/274.
[78] WAM, 21940; F.J. Eld, ed., *Lay Subsidy Roll for the County of Worcester 1 Edward I* (WHS, 1893), p. 50.
[79] E.A. Gooder, 'Clayworking in the Nuneaton Area', in *Pottery Kilns at Chilvers Coton, Nuneaton*, edited by P. Mayes and K. Scott (Society for Medieval Archaeology Monograph 10, 1984), pp. 10–11.

likely to have organized the distribution of pots so that they reached Coventry, towns such as Southam and Warwick, and every rural settlement within a 20-mile radius. The highly competitive pottery trade could present consumers with a choice of wares from a number of centres of manufacture. An example of successful marketing by Bayly's predecessors was the dominance of Chilvers Coton pottery at Burton Dassett Southend, 24 miles from the kilns. From excavations of the settlement occupied between c.1220 and 1500, 14,000 pieces of Chilvers Coton ware were recovered, far exceeding the market share of its two main rivals at Deritend (near Birmingham) and Brill/Boarstall in Buckinghamshire.[80]

Peasants in Alcester's hinterland were not entirely tied into local markets. They also acquired, through a chain of middlemen, overseas imports, notably the chest of *pruis* owned by a Cleeve Prior tenant, which was a piece of furniture imported from the Baltic and named from Prussia, and at Weethley a whetstone imported from Norway was owned and subsequently lost or discarded by a villager. In the hinterlands of other Warwickshire towns pieces of lava quern stones (from hand mills) found at Burton Dassett Southend had originated in the Rhineland, and also from the same part of Germany a tenant of Weston-juxta-Cherrington around 1500 owned a drinking jug of German stoneware, and a similar find comes from Barston in north Warwickshire.[81] These exotic imports would have been bought locally, from a retailer in a market town, or perhaps at a fair. Overseas trade was of course flowing in the other direction, with exports to the continent of Cotswold wool, Gloucestershire cloth, and grain from the Severn valley. The profits from this commerce may have made a small contribution to the level of consumer spending in the region.

Finally, Table 8.2 does not include foodstuffs, yet these must have featured among the purchases by peasants in their local towns. Salt, essential for making cheese and curing bacon came from Droitwich along a well-established network of roads to all parts of the region. Peasants were familiar with sea fish. Herring, served to workers harvesting demesne crops, would have been appreciated in peasant households as nutritious, tasty, and relatively cheap. Herring bones from the excavations at Pinbury (Gloucestershire), were likely to date from the thirteenth century. The demand was met mainly by urban fishmongers, though herring were being sold by a shop in Chaddesley Corbett village in 1441.[82] The town could also offer the better-off peasants food and drink superior to that in their own households or in the village, such as the pies and meals prepared by the cook

---

[80] Palmer and Parkhouse, *Burton Dassett Southend*; the pottery report can be accessed at https://doi.org/10.5284/1083492.
[81] WCL, E51; Palmer and Parkhouse, *Burton Dassett Southend*; small finds report can be accessed at https://doi.org/10.5284/1083492; W. Burnett, 'Barston: An Archaeological Survey of an Arden Parish', *TBWAS* 112 (2008), p. 28; whetstone and stoneware from Weston are finds made by the author.
[82] For harvest workers receiving fish, WCL, C705 (Overbury); WAM 27694 (Knowle); for Pinbury, see J. Hart and others, *Living Near the Edge* (Cotswold Archaeology Monographs 9, 2016), p. 187; Chaddesley shop: SCLA, DR5/2798.

Table 8.3 Households and expenditure in the hinterland of Alcester (Warwickshire) 1327

Status	Number	Percentage	Spending (each)	Spending (total)
Smallholders	600	40	20s	£600
Middle holdings, e.g. ½ yardland	500	33	8s	£200
Larger holdings e.g. 1 yardland	400	27	20s	£400
TOTAL	1,500	100		£1,200

Note: smallholders are estimated to have bought basic foodstuffs, which middling and larger holdings would have produced for themselves.

who traded in most towns, white bread (wastel) made from finely sieved flour, and high-quality ale such as the 'best ale of Bristol town' relished by a widow of Shirehampton according to an agreement of 1483.[83]

The accumulated value of peasant consumption for the town can be estimated, firstly by calculating the size and population of the hinterland. Returning to Alcester, we have already noted that it dominated a rural area formed of thirty-six tax-paying villages. In 1327 they contained 614 taxpayers; estimating the number of households exempt from tax and the size of the household leads to a total of 7,500 people living in 1,500 households. Table 8.3 indicates the stratification among the households, and estimates the amount of money they had to spend each year. The total of £1,200 represents the potential consumer expenditure for Alcester and its surroundings. In practice, village traders or another town could have been favoured for some purchases. Alcester might have had 120 households in 1327, so a notional share of consumer spending of £10 each could have been the basis of the town's economy.

Peasants and changing fortunes of towns

Towns throughout Europe mostly multiplied and expanded in the thirteenth century, and then experienced varying fortunes in the next two centuries. Westmidland towns followed the same trend. Changes in peasant numbers and welfare ought to have connected with the ups and downs experienced by towns, especially smaller towns, which were most closely entwined with the surrounding countryside.

The conventional picture of the rural scene in the late twelfth and thirteenth centuries highlights the expansion over new land, the increase in the rural

---

[83] TNA, SC2 210/71 (Wastel bread at Pershore); WA, ref. 009:1, BA2636/165/92225 4/8.

population, and the production of a surplus for exchange, all of which are found in the west midlands. More than thirty places appear to have been emerging as towns in the thirteenth century, and a dozen had apparent twelfth-century origins. Some were new towns founded in a single act of planning. Towns like Alcester grew over a long period and other places can be shown to have expanded piecemeal from an analysis of their plans. Bewdley and Brinklow both apparently began in the thirteenth century from an initial core along a main street, and added groups of plots (plan units) in stages.[84] Estimating population can be based on surveys of tenants and tax records, but the numbers of people that lived in each burgage cannot be known, nor how many people were exempted from taxation. Evesham had embryonic origins before the Norman Conquest, and by 1200 had gathered almost 1,000 inhabitants. In the next century it could have reached over 1,500 especially if part of the adjacent settlement of Bengeworth was integrated into the town. Chipping Campden from a starting point before 1200, had about 525 people in 1273. Stratford was founded in 1196, had more than a thousand inhabitants by 1252, and could have attained near to 2,000 in the early fourteenth century. Birmingham may have been developing around a market in the mid-twelfth century, and could have had 1,250 inhabitants in 1296. Northleach, a small place getting off to a late start in *c.*1220, is likely to have grown to 430 by 1266.[85]

Urban growth of the thirteenth century amounted to a major social change, with the newly founded or rapidly growing small towns by 1300 together providing a living for thousands of people. The new town dwellers were taking on quite small plots of urban land with insufficient space to live from agriculture: at Chipping Sodbury, for example, a town with at least 800 inhabitants in the thirteenth century, the borough was assigned a territory of 107 acres, filled with streets and burgage plots with no space for large fields.[86] Such towns were dependent on making an income from crafts and commerce, in order to buy foodstuffs from the country.

A productive symbiosis between urban and rural ways of life, did not always work, as not all towns achieved much growth. Moreton-in-Marsh struggled to reach a population of 300, and remained small throughout the Middle Ages, though its people seem to have practised enough non-agricultural activities for it to be regarded as urban. That test has not been passed by Alvechurch, Clifton-on-Teme, Prestbury, and St Briavels, though they were all boroughs.

---

[84] T.R. Slater, 'English Medieval New Towns with Composite Plans: Evidence from the Midlands', in *The Built Form of Western Cities*, edited by T.R. Slater (Leicester, 1990), pp. 60–82; K.D. Lilley, 'A Warwickshire Medieval Borough: Brinklow and the Contribution of Town-Plan Analysis', *TBWAS* 95 (1993–4), pp. 51–60.
[85] Hilton, 'Evesham', pp. 3–4; Madge, ed., *IPMs for Gloucestershire*, 63–4, 80–3; Bearman, ed., *Stratford-upon-Avon*, p. 44; Demidowicz, *Medieval Birmingham*, p. 26; *Hist Glouc*, vol. 3, pp. 176–9.
[86] Beresford, *New Towns*, p. 441.

The proliferation of markets and fairs indicates the surge in the promotion of commercial activity before 1350, which includes more than fifty rural markets in the three shires that made up the region. The lords who founded them by obtaining a royal charter chose sites which would be likely to attract local peasants, but in most cases the market did not flourish.[87] Peasants were not confined within the official market network. For example, Bibury in Gloucestershire was a village which retained some vestiges of its former importance as the site of a minster church and estate centre, and was well-sited in a river valley served by some major long-distance roads. It was divided between two lords, which may have encouraged peasant enterprise. A space in the centre of the village, now known as 'The Square' resembles a marketplace. In 1327 Robert le Chapman (meaning 'trader') paid his tax at Bibury, and later in the century an unusual number of brewers plied their trade there. In 1381 those paying the poll tax included a 'merchant', three carpenters, a butcher, a tailor, a brewer, and a smith. A butcher was recorded in the early fifteenth century.[88] Other villages with unofficial markets are scattered over the region, including Mitcheldean and Newland in the Forest of Dean, and various woodland settlements such as Chaddesley Corbett in Worcestershire and Tanworth-in-Arden in Warwickshire. Lords made no direct profits from these activities, and they seem to be the result of villagers seeking the convenience of a nearby local market, at which no tolls were required.

In the late fourteenth and fifteenth centuries rural society was shrinking, with houses abandoned in almost every settlement, while some villages were in terminal decline. This was echoed in the towns like Warwick and Winchcomb which have been said to have been stagnating. John Leland, observing towns in the 1540s, reported that Thornbury had been a clothmaking centre, 'but now idleness much reynithe there'.[89] Transfers of properties in the courts of Pershore included some tofts, meaning that houses had decayed, and the authorities were making agreements with new tenants to rebuild or repair dilapidated buildings. Upton-on-Severn was well placed as a river port serving a woodland hinterland in south-west Worcestershire, but in 1429–30 'various burgages' were lying in the lord's hands for a lack of tenants, and so complete was their abandonment that the sites of the burgages were not known, and former tenants could not be traced. The tolls of the market and fair, once worth 12s, had ceased to yield any revenue.[90] Lechlade's market and fair generated little income for the lord of the town in the fifteenth century, and at nearby Fairford the rents from the borough were much diminished.[91] Towns that had been successful only in a low key began to lose any

---

[87] Letters, *Gazetteer*, part 1, pp. 139–50; part 2, pp. 357–64, 380–4.
[88] C. Dyer, 'Landscape and Society at Bibury, Gloucestershire, to 1540', in *Archives and Local History in Bristol and Gloucestershire*, edited by J. Bettey (BGAS, 2007), pp. 75–6.
[89] Hilton, 'Evesham', p. 7; L. Toulmin Smith, ed., *Leland's Itinerary in England and Wales* (London, 1909), vol. 5, p. 100.
[90] TNA, SC2/210/72,73, 74; WA, ref.705:139, BA 8397/1.   [91] *VCH Glouc*, 7, pp. 78,115,117.

claim to be urban, for example at Brailes and Bretford. Rural markets were lost from sight. In Warwickshire, for example, more than twenty markets authorized by royal charters had ceased to function by 1600, and most of them had failed many years before that date.[92]

Signs of distress were not universal. Perhaps reports of declining rents and market tolls resulted from slack administration and concealment by officials. In some towns when houses deteriorated they were rebuilt and repaired, by the lord of the town at Rugby in the 1440s, and by a major property owner (the Fraternity) at Stratford-upon-Avon throughout the fifteenth century.[93] The expenditure on buildings was a vote of confidence in the long-term future of the town. The improvement in the urban fabric is reflected in the number of timber-framed houses of the fifteenth and early sixteenth centuries, some dated by dendrochronology, which are still visible (or partly hidden by modern brick or stone facades) along the streets of Alcester, Bewdley, Droitwich, Henley-in-Arden, Pershore, Shipston-on-Stour, Tewkesbury, and Winchcomb. Population figures are as uncertain in this period as before 1349, but recovery from plague mortality is suggested by Chipping Campden's 600 people in 1381, compared with the estimate of 525 in 1273. It remained at about 600 in the early sixteenth century. Northleach's expansion has been attributed to its importance as a base for three major families of woolmongers. In the fifteenth century, burgages had been divided in half to accommodate more tenants, and new building partly filled the marketplace, raising the population in the long term from 430 in 1266 to about 600 in the early sixteenth century.[94] Birmingham had some wool merchants in the early fourteenth century, but its metal industries and tanning sustained its later growth, from 1,250 in 1296 to around 2,000 in the early sixteenth century.

Northleach and Birmingham moved forwards by specializing, but towns which catered for all comers with a wide range of crafts and trades, such as Alcester, Evesham, Nuneaton, and Stratford fared reasonably well, and these are the most relevant to gauging the continued importance of the towns' interactions with peasants.[95] New urban life could be breathed into previously obscure settlements at Stourbridge and Stroud, and centres of trade which did not quite qualify as towns developed and expanded, for example, at Knowle (Warwickshire) and Redditch (Worcestershire).[96] These were all in woodland landscapes, and they benefited from the development of pastoralism and industry. A final reassurance of the health of the urban sector was a town's ability to survive the stress test of disaster. Birmingham had suffered a great fire around 1300, but seems to have recovered, as might be expected of that vigorous centre in a period of opportunity,

[92] W. Barker, 'Warwickshire Markets', *Warwickshire History* 6 (1986), pp. 161–75.
[93] SRO, D641/1/2/269, 272, 274, 275; Bearman, ed., *Stratford*, pp. 50–3.
[94] *VCH Glouc*, 9, pp. 107, 110–11, 128.
[95] Palliser, ed., *Cambridge Urban History*, pp. 636–7.
[96] Dyer, 'Hidden Trade'.

but Shipston-on-Stour in 1478, when it was holding its own at a time of falling population and vacant land in its champion hinterland, had most of its houses destroyed in a fire, but carried on trading and was largely rebuilt within five years.[97]

How could towns manage to avoid decline? Although the number of people in their hinterlands fell often below 5,000, and although the grain trade had diminished in volume and profitability, the towns that had emerged by 1300 continued to occupy niches in the marketing network. They adapted to the shift in farming from arable to pasture by developing their handling of livestock and animal products, raising the profile of butchers, tanners, and fellmongers in the later part of the period. The better-off section of the rural population benefited from larger holdings and changes in farming methods. The remaining smallholders received increased rewards from employment and were able to keep at least a few animals.

However, there is limited direct evidence for the assumption that clothing worn by peasants increased in quality. The agreements for the maintenance, usually of retired tenants sometimes specify the clothing and shoes to be provided annually. They mention lengths of woollen cloth of 2 ¾ yards and 3 ells, or complete garments such as a tunic with hood. The amount of money per person varied between 2s for a boy's clothing to 4s for the cloth allowed to a retired yardlander and the same for a widow giving up a half yardland. Although they range in date between 1318 and 1483, no upward or downward trend can be detected, though they seem to be suggesting that peasants were buying cloth for about 1s per yard. These contracts, in clothing as well as food, seemed to be repeating a customary standard which defined a minimum rather than reflecting actual consumption. National legislation in 1463 and 1483, fixing limits on the quality of cloth that could be worn by labourers, implied that without legal restraint they would wear cloth worth 2s per yard.[98] Many peasants would surely expect to dress at least as well as a labourer, so perhaps, contrary to the evidence of the maintenance contracts, more money was being spent generally on clothing in the late fifteenth century?

A rare opportunity to judge changes in peasant possessions over a long period comes from the pottery. The high point of design came in the thirteenth century, when among the pots available in our region the jugs from the Brill/Boarstall kilns were decorated with colourful glazes and elaborate surface treatment with strips of applied clay and rouletting. The Chilvers Coton potters made some very elaborate jugs, including examples with moulded human faces, clearly intended to serve as a point of attraction and comment at the meal table where they would be

---

[97] Z. Razi, 'The "Big Fire" of the Town of Birmingham', *TBWAS* 88 (1976–7), pp. 135; C. Dyer, 'Recovering from Catastrophe: How Medieval Society in England Coped with Disaster,' in *Waiting for the End of the World? New Perspectives on Natural Disasters in Medieval Europe*, edited by C. Gerrard and others (Society for Medieval Archaeology Monograph 43, 2021), pp. 227–31.

[98] C. Given-Wilson and others, eds., *The Parliament Rolls of Medieval England, 1275–1504* (Woodbridge, 2005), vol. 13 p. 11; vol 14, p. 459.

used to serve ale.[99] However these more elaborate pots seem to have been intended mainly for the urban market. A high proportion of the wares deriving from villages consisted of rather drab and functional cooking pots with little elegance of form and minimal decoration. Towards the end of the Middle Ages, the potters seem to have been responding to more refined consumer preferences, or perhaps the potters were educating the taste of their customers by introducing new techniques and designs. The technical quality changed with the advent of 'midland purple' with harder-fired fabric and a better finish. Towards the end of the fifteenth century so-called Cistercian ware appears, which was well-fired, thin-walled, and glazed inside and out. Drinking cups in this ware offered a very superior alternative to the wooden drinking bowls in everyday use for centuries.[100]

Houses and other buildings also allow us to trace changes in consumption over the centuries. The amount of accommodation seems to have increased in the late fourteenth and fifteenth centuries with the occasional addition of cross-wings to one storey houses, adding an extra chamber on the first floor (see 'Space for households' in Chapter 5). At Burton Dassett Southend the floor area of houses, and therefore the amount of space available for each member of the household, expanded. Roofs of stone tiles were being provided at the same settlement before 1350, but both slates and ceramic tiles, though by no means common, appear more often in the fifteenth century. The hearth in the hall was moved from the centre of the floor to near a wall, which implies that smoke was removed not from a louvre at the apex of the roof, but by means of a smoke hood, an internal chimney suspended over the fire. This increased the potential warmth and comfort of those using the hall. There is some direct evidence from housing therefore that peasants enjoyed better living standards in the later part of our period.

Peasants and money

Money pervaded the west midlands in the late Middle Ages. Lords promoted towns and markets partly to enable tenants to sell produce and pay their rents and dues in cash. Peasants preferred money rents; for example, customary tenants aspired to pay fixed cash rents like free tenants. Money penetrated deeply into everyday social practices and habits of thought, enabling values to be attached, for example, to damage to a garden. Coins were not very plentiful, leading to forms of barter, and payments were often delayed or made in instalments. In the end cash had to be handed over, and individuals accumulated coins for that purpose.

---

[99] M. Mellor, 'Oxfordshire Pottery', *Oxoniensia* 59 (1994), pp. 17–217, especially pp. 111–40; *Chilvers Coton*, edited by Mayes and Scott, pp. 62, 68, 159, 164.

[100] M.R. McCarthy and C.M. Brooks, *Medieval Pottery in Britain AD 900–1600* (Leicester, 1988), pp. 471–6.

The use of coins is indicated most directly by the thousands that survive, often worn by handling and after being rubbed against the inside of a purse. Because small sums were needed for everyday transactions, farthings to buy the smallest standard loaf, for example, and because the official mints did not produce enough halfpence or farthing coins, the penny coin would be cut into halves and quarters, and would circulate in that mutilated but useful form. The coins, both whole and cut into fractions, can be identified, counted, and analysed to provide insights into the flow of commerce in the region. Coins that belonged to peasants, or of which peasants had been the last owners before they were lost, can be found in village excavations. Such finds are few. At Upton, for example, a house occupied for a century and a half by a relatively well-off peasant family, and excavated carefully in the twentieth century, yielded two medieval coins.[101] Hundreds of silver pennies must each year have passed through the hands of the members of the family, but each penny was too valuable to lose. Our sample of coins therefore comes mainly not from houses and villages, but from the fields, where coins might have been mislaid by those working the land, or more often lost in the home, and carted with the domestic refuse into the fields.

All of the known medieval coins from the west midlands, 2,186 in total up to 2013, have been analysed in a study of their date of minting and the places where they were found. The sample included Herefordshire alongside our three counties.[102] Most were found by metal detectorists, and their distribution (mainly in Gloucestershire and Warwickshire), reflects the areas in which these amateurs have chosen to search. Alcester and its vicinity has attracted detectorists because it is known as a major Roman site and therefore rich in finds of that period. As a by-product, 229 medieval coins, an unusually large number for a relatively small area, have been recovered. The quantity does not tell us that medieval Alcester was exceptionally wealthy or commercially active, just that modern detectorists have singled it out for their attention.

In a separate sample, medieval coins recorded from Warwickshire increased in the thirteenth century, peaked around 1300, and fell after 1351 to quite low levels in the next two centuries (Table 8.4). In the region as a whole, the rate of coin loss, and presumably therefore the use of coins, increased dramatically around 1200, and attained a maximum towards the end of the thirteenth century. They reached only low levels in the fifteenth century. The dates refer to the year of minting, not the years of circulation, so although fewer coins were minted after 1351, part of the old stock of coins produced in the thirteenth and early fourteenth centuries continued in use. Also, more gold coins were circulating,

---

[101] C. Dyer, 'Peasants and Coins: The Uses of Money in the Middle Ages', *British Numismatic Journal* 67 (1998), pp. 30–47.

[102] M. Andrews, 'Coin Use and Circulation in the Medieval West Midlands, c.1066–1544AD' (MA dissertation, University College, London, 2013).

Table 8.4 Single coin finds from Warwickshire, 1066–1544

Date	No. of dated coins	%
1180–1247	48	17
1247–1279	50	18
1279–1351	94	34
1351–1412	26	9
1412–1464	32	11
1464–1544	30	11
Total	280	100

Source: Dyer, 'Peasants and Coins', pp. 36–8.

but are not visible among the coin finds because, given that many of them were worth 6s 8d, their owners took even more care than they did with silver to ensure that they were not lost.

Coins in the whole region were found in 295 parishes, though concentrated near urban centres or places where markets were held. Setting aside the extraordinary case of Alcester, whereas the average parish with finds has produced seven coins, fourteen coins or more have been found at small towns: Coleshill, Dymock, Newent, Nuneaton, Pershore, and Stratford. The Alcester series gives us a sense of an especially steep rising curve between 1180 and 1279 (Table 8.5), which should be connected with the expansion of the cultivated area and commodity production in the surrounding countryside. Money circulated in the villages in the payment of wages, the sale of produce, and cash rents and then flowed into the hands of traders and artisans in the market town. The sharp decline in loss of coins minted after 1351 at first seems inconsistent with the apparent lively state of the town as depicted in the fifteenth-century records. While the countryside was experiencing a falling population and a decline in cultivation, the large landholdings and increased pastoralism should have stimulated commercial exchanges. The explanation is partly that old coins and gold were circulating, but also that the reduced population in the country meant that the amount of money per head was not reduced as much as the global figures suggest.[103]

Town and country: Cultural connections

Towns acquired institutions and cultures which set them apart from those of the countryside. We are impressed by the advanced institutions of Bristol, modelled on those of London, and celebrated in the mayor's book compiled by Robert

---

[103] J.L. Bolton, *Money in the Medieval English Economy, 973–1489* (Manchester, 2012), pp. 258–95.

Table 8.5 Single coin finds from Alcester parish, 1100–1544

Date	No. of dated coins	%
1100–1135	5	2
1135–1158	0	0
1158–1180	6	3
1180–1247	41	18
1247–1279	80	35
1279–1351	61	27
1351–1412	21	9
1412–1464	10	4
1465–1544	5	2
Total	229	100

Source: Andrews, 'Coin use'.

Ricart in 1478–9. The book was designed to define the town's liberties and to enable them to be defended by civic officials. It describes the annual cycle of ceremonies and processions, and gives the text of speeches to be delivered.[104] A peasant encountering such an occasion might have felt out of place.

Most towns, especially the smaller ones, were governed by their lords. At Alcester each year, the jury of twelve took an oath at the lord's view of frankpledge (the court leet) and the officers were elected: bailiffs, constables, ale tasters, tasters of meat and fish, and the 'collectors of the common money'. By a local peculiarity, as a legacy of a time when the lordship of the town was divided between two lords, there were two bailiffs and two constables. Alcester seems to have attracted the attention of the local aristocracy to an unusual extent. In 1444 it was united under a single lord from a branch of the Beauchamp family, who were often resident and could intervene in the town's affairs, by announcing a by-law for example. A number of other local lords held property in the town and also exercised some influence: these were the Burdets of Arrow, the Rous family of Ragley, the Throckmortons of Coughton, and perhaps Alcester Abbey, though it kept a low profile. An unusual by-law of 1475, during the Wars of the Roses, forbade tenants and residents from wearing clothing (which refers to livery) or signs (that is, badges) of any lord or gentleman other than Richard Beauchamp, the lord of the town.[105] This suggests that townspeople had been recruited into affinities, seen by Beauchamp as divisive.

A typical compromise allowed the leading townspeople to occupy positions in the lord's administration, and thus to exercise some authority. Administrative responsibility was not narrowly concentrated, as twenty-six men were involved in

---

[104] P. Fleming, ed., *The Maire of Bristowe is Kalender* (Bristol Record Society, 67, 2015).
[105] *VCH Warw*, 3, pp. 12–17; WCRO, CR1886/173D.

the government of the town each year. From its beginning, Northleach was not under the total control of its monastic lord, as in about 1220 a 'composition' between the Abbot of Gloucester and the burgesses gave considerable power to the bailiff appointed by the lord, but also allowed two burgesses to 'see that our officers do not ill treat them'.[106] In a village the lord was in charge, often rather remotely, and offices of bailiff or reeve, beadle, jurors, affeerers, woodward, ale tasters, and others would have been occupied by senior, experienced, and often better-off men. In both town and country lords' authority was mediated through local people, and depended on the co-operation and consent of the community.

An important development in civic life was marked by the emergence of fraternities such as 'the guild of Warwick' and the Holy Cross fraternities in Birmingham and Stratford.[107] These began as religious associations, organizing funerals, and maintaining a chantry priest or priests to pray for the souls of the departed. The strength of the fraternity lay in its promotion of sociability, giving opportunities for townspeople to meet, eat and drink together, and settle disputes. Fraternities developed other functions and by the end of the Middle Ages they were funding civic buildings, bridges, roads, public clocks, almshouses, and schools. They had become 'shadow governments' in the towns, usually without antagonizing the lords. Alcester lacked such a well-organized fraternity, but townspeople were drawn into managing the St Mary's chantry attached to the parish church, which funded a school and maintained the town's two bridges.[108] In the west midland countryside a few fraternities had a rural base, including the village guild at Aston Cantlow, a few miles from Alcester. The closest parallel to an urban fraternity in a village would be the groups of feoffees who were charged with running the landed endowment of a chantry, employing the priest as a schoolteacher. This is documented at Hanley Castle and Hartlebury in Worcestershire around 1500, but probably originated at an earlier date. Villagers who felt the need to belong to a fully developed fraternity could join those based in towns, so the Stratford fraternity welcomed hundreds of country members. The fraternity of Knowle, a Warwickshire place which did not develop fully into a town, provided a focus for peasants, artisans, and gentry from a wide radius.[109]

Mutual support and opportunities to socialize were functions of the rural parish. Groups within villages based on age cohorts held social gatherings and contributed to parish funds. The social (and fundraising) dimension of the parish was given a stronger institutional focus when churchwardens towards the end of the Middle Ages built church houses to accommodate church ales. Finally, there

---

[106] N. Herbert, 'Northleach: New Light on the Making of a Gloucestershire Town', in *Archives and Local History*, ed. Bettey, pp. 17–26.
[107] VCH Warw, 8, pp. 423–4, 479; R.A Holt, *The Early History of the Town of Birmingham 1166–1600* (DS Occasional Paper, 30, 1985), pp. 12–13; Bearman, ed., *Stratford-upon-Avon*, pp. 59–79.
[108] VCH Warw, 3, pp. 9, 19–20.
[109] W.B. Bickley, ed., *Register of the Guild of Knowle* (Walsall, 1894).

are enigmatic references to guildhalls in villages, often no more than a passing reference in a field name, which suggests that in the thirteenth century or earlier guilds had existed. There may be a connection with the occasional reference to 'ales' meaning drinking sessions which survived into the later Middle Ages as the lord's fustale and the parish church ale. So villagers congregated to drink together and raise funds but did not form voluntary associations with many functions on the scale or durability of those in towns.

Coventry's cycle of plays depicting biblical episodes was enacted in the streets, uniting the citizens who through their crafts would organize the performances.[110] Country people would no doubt have come to the city to be impressed by these displays of civic culture. Alcester could obviously not mount such an event, but in 1421–2 Lady Katherine Beauchamp, spending much of the year in her nearby manor house, gave 20*d* 'to the players' for a play (*interludum*) in Alcester'.[111] The term interlude suggests a rather short piece of light entertainment, which was judged to be suitable for an aristocratic lady as well as local people. Villages held their own performances also, and bands of villagers put on plays, dances, and musical events not just for their neighbours but for a more sophisticated audience. Prior More of Worcester between 1518 and 1535 gave rewards to groups of local villagers who visited his household and entertained the assembled clergy, servants, officials, and guests. They included the 'Martley players', 'dancers of Claines', and men and women of Grimley who 'syngeth on May morning'. He made a generous donation to the church ale at Grimley 'and a play' which suggests that drama contributed to parish fund-raising. Some plays were secular in content, such as those with Robin Hood themes[112] (see 'Individuals and communities' in Chapter 10).

Towns developed their own memories of the past so that the inhabitants shared traditions. Coventry's legend of Lady Godiva unified the people of the city, who would have appreciated its message about successful resistance to taxation. A small town such as Alcester could perpetuate a legend relating to the town's past that appeared in different versions. The town, it was said, was visited by the bishop of Worcester and founder of Evesham Abbey, St Ecgwine, or alternatively by St Chad, bishop of Lichfield. So the story is set in the remote past, around either 670 or 700. The bishop attempted to preach a sermon but was frustrated either by the loud hammering of smiths, or because people ignored his words. The good bishop cursed those who refused to listen, and the town was swallowed up into the earth. The lessons that the story conveyed include the obvious morals that preaching deserved a respectful hearing, saintly bishops should be received with honour, and that sinners deserved punishment. The legend resembled an

---

[110] R.W. Ingram, ed., *Coventry* (Toronto, Records of Early English Drama, 1981), pp. xv–xviii.
[111] WA, ref. 705:99, BA5540/2.
[112] E.S. Fegan, ed., *Journal of Prior William More* (WHS, 1914), pp. 88, 91, 308, 309, 327, 405.

origin myth as it explained why Alcester people in the Middle Ages encountered walls and building remains (of Roman date) under their houses and gardens; they quarried the remains to recycle the building stone. Finds of Roman iron slag suggested a link to the noisy smiths. The power of the legend was that it showed local people that Alcester had been important, and encouraged pride in past glories: 'the town hath been a great thing'.[113]

A quite separate legend concerned a small hill a short distance outside the town on the Roman road to Stratford-upon-Avon, called Alcock's Arbour, a name first documented in 1480. It was said to have been the place where a notorious robber, Alcock, buried his treasure. The hill is part of a Roman site, and the discovery of Roman coins is likely to have been the basis of the legend. However, there was evidently some connection with the fifteenth-century town, as John Alcock appears in the borough court rolls, mainly as a brewer and seller of ale in the 1460s and 1470s. The legend explained the strikingly prominent hill, and people were engaged by the idea that a notorious criminal had once lived among them.[114]

These legends with their false memories embedded in the local landscape contributed to Alcester people's sense of belonging and their loyalty to a longstanding community. We know about the stories because they were recorded by the monks of Evesham Abbey, by John Leland, and by William Dugdale. The small group of clergy associated with the parish church and its chantries may have helped to perpetuate the memories, but there was clearly a strong oral tradition among the townspeople.

Memories in the countryside are often perpetuated in minor place names which were once connected to legends now forgotten. Puckeput (Puck's pit) from the thirteenth century is a reference to a supernatural phenomenon, a malicious or mischievous sprite, but we do not know why this word was connected to a pond or depression near Maisemore (Gloucestershire). Clerkenleap in Kempsey (Worcestershire) seems to refer to a real or imagined event, either a suicide or an athletic feat by a clergyman.[115] St Chad, who appears in one version of the Alcester legend, is remembered by a well and chapel for pilgrims at Chadshunt (Warwickshire) and an association is strengthened by the village having been a possession of the bishops of Lichfield. The well predates the saint, however, because the Latin word *funta* (meaning well or spring) forms part of the place-name.[116] Just as the people of Alcester valued the idea that in a remote past their

[113] VCH Warw, 3, p. 12; J. Sayers and L. Watkiss, eds., *Thomas of Marlborough. History of the Abbey of Evesham* (Oxford, 2003), pp. 45–51; Toulmin Smith, *Leland's Itinerary*, 2, p. 51.
[114] VCH Warw, 3, p. 110; WCRO, CR1886/164, 170C, 173d.
[115] A.H. Smith, *The Place-Names of Gloucestershire* (English Place-Name Society, 38-41, 1960–5), part 3, p. 262; A. Mawer and F.M. Stenton, *The Place-Names of Worcestershire* (English Place-Name Society, 4, 1927), p. 145.
[116] VCH Warw., 5, p. 34; M. Gelling, *Signposts to the Past: Place-Names and the History of England* (London, 1978), pp. 83–6.

town had been 'a great thing', country people who lived near Roman villas and other sites used long established place names such as those ending in –cester and –chester (Woodchester, for example) or the field name *chestles* referring to stone buildings. We know that peasants of the thirteenth and fourteenth centuries were aware of the past, because they picked up Roman coins in the fields and kept them. The coins that have been found at Upton and Pinbury (both in Gloucestershire) in peasant houses are likely to have been recognized as belonging to a period before the finders' time.[117]

Although traditions may have encouraged a sense of unity, many commentators have remarked on the amount of interpersonal violence suggestive of underlying tensions in both towns and villages. To indicate the amount of fighting that could occur at Alcester, in 1468 thirteen assaults were reported to the Easter view of frankpledge, and ten in another violent year in 1475.[118] The courts mention the shedding of blood in some of these incidents and refer to weapons such as knives. Assaults were also reported in the views held in villages, but especially acute conflicts were generated by markets and fairs in towns, when country people could have been involved.

Gatherings of large numbers of people carrying goods and money, and consuming much ale, attracted criminals and were occasions for disorder. The anonymity of the marketplace was an opportunity for the sale of stolen property, like the three oxen brought by thieves to Worcester market in 1324. Also those intent on doing harm to an enemy would find him at an event that he was likely to attend: so the notorious gang led by Malcolm Musard beat Thomas of Chetynton at Blockley fair in 1305.[119] However markets had more fundamental reasons for being scenes of contention, as access led to controversy over the payment of toll, and over the tendency of traders to interfere with the flow of goods in search of larger profits. Negotiating a sale was surrounded by controversy over price, payment for the goods, provision of credit, the quality of the goods, and their delivery after purchase.

At Alcester a small example of these problems arose in 1462 in the case of Nicholas Cockes of Cleeve Prior, whose barley was seized in distraint in a dispute with Richard Haselholt of Alcester, an office holder of some substance. Later in the year Haselholt brought a plea of trespass against Cockes, alleging that he had conspired to assault him, valuing the damages at 34s. The sum of money was certainly exaggerated, and the whole affair may have been blown up by Haselholt to make a good case in the court. The incident shows how sales and rather clumsy procedures for the recovery of debts, could lead to threatening behaviour.[120]

---

[117] Smith, *Gloucestershire*, part 3, p. 110; P.A. Rahtz, 'Upton, Gloucestershire, 1964–8', *TBGAS* 88 (1969), p. 110; Hart and other, *Living near the Edge.* p. 178.
[118] WCRO, CR 1886/170C, 173D.   [119] Hilton, *Medieval Society*, pp. 255, 261.
[120] WCRO, CR1886/156.

Collective violence on a larger scale was alleged in about 1400, when people from Alcester and Stratford were carrying corn and other foodstuffs northward to Birmingham, Coleshill, Walsall, and Dudley.[121] This must have been in response to food shortage, as 1400–2 were years of high prices following poor harvests. The south of Warwickshire normally sent wheat and barley to the northern towns, but the inequalities in supply would have made the need for trade and grain more acute in a bad harvest year. Evildoers (in the words of the complaint), covering their faces (which proved their sinister intent), ambushed the packhorses. Women and children riding on the horses fell to the ground, and the sacks were cut and the corn scattered. As usual, the record is concerned to establish that a really serious offence has been committed, rather than offering an explanation. Consumers resentful of the high prices of corn in the market should have welcomed new supplies which would bring prices down. Perhaps the corn was intercepted by farmers and corndealers in the north of Warwickshire who were fearful that competition would reduce their profits? More likely the 'evildoers' came from among consumers in the southern part of the Arden, in the vicinity of Henley-in-Arden and Solihull, who were hoping that the corn could be sold in their area and not carried to the northern towns as intended. If this was the reason for the interception, it would have some similarity to the 'food riots' of modern times when crowds in times of dearth took measures to bring supplies into the market at reduced prices. An incidental detail was that a journey to a distant market could apparently take on the character of a family outing.

A parallel episode in 1428, another poor harvest year, led to the interception of boats carrying wheat and barley from Worcestershire and Gloucestershire down the River Severn towards Bristol. The boats were seized at Minsterworth near Gloucester and the grain taken away.[122] As people from the Forest of Dean had been involved in similar interruptions to the grain trade in 1401 and 1409, it seems that they had been behind the seizure at Minsterworth. This was stated explicitly after an incident in 1433 when boat loads of grain were attacked at a time of high food prices, and Tewkesbury traders denounced the wild people of the Welsh border, and the lawlessness of the community of the Forest of Dean.[123] Again this was not a simple matter of theft, but an attempt to divert supplies to a region without large corn crops.

To return to Alcester, a report of 1408–9 relates to violence in Alcester marketplace when henchmen (yeomen and servants, so members of his household) of Thomas Burdet, lord of the manor of Arrow beat and wounded tenants of the Earl of Warwick from Tanworth-in-Arden.[124] Tanworth belonged to Alcester's

---

[121] *Calendar of Patent Rolls*, Henry IV, vol. 1 1199–1401, pp. 552–3.
[122] B. Sharp, *Famine and Scarcity in Late Medieval and Early Modern England. The Regulation of Grain Marketing, 1256–1631* (Cambridge, 2016), pp. 137–9.
[123] T. Johnson, *Law in Common. Legal Cultures in Late-Medieval England* (Oxford, 2020), p. 126.
[124] British Library, Egerton Roll 8772.

hinterland, and its tenants would be expected to have traded in the market. The quarrel may have arisen over the payment of market toll, as a result of Tanworth people claiming that they were exempt. Or was there a rivalry between markets, as Tanworth had a marketplace, but no market charter? Something similar arose at Shipston-on-Stour which was in competition with the earl of Warwick's borough and market at nearby Brailes. In 1377–80 a Shipston tenant, Margaret atte Broke, was said to have procured men of Brailes to beat the Shipston reeve, and William Smith encouraged the tenants of the earls of Warwick to make a disturbance in Shipston market. Two years later no one in Shipston dared arrest 'disturbers of the peace' who were tenants of the Earl of Warwick, it was alleged.[125] The Burdet family, who caused trouble at Alcester, held manors near to Shipston, and their aggression spread to the town when the young and disorderly Nicholas Burdet launched attacks in April and June 1413. Both raids took place on Fridays, so the day before market day; in the second event, two Shipston tenants were killed.[126] Burdet's gang seem to have been targeting a faction in the town who were allied to Worcester Priory (see 'Peasants and lords' in Chapter 10).

Peasants needed to bring their surplus produce to urban markets, but they were evidently treading into potentially dangerous waters, where arguments were liable to be stirred by issues such as the price of corn in years of scarcity. In addition, access to markets and toll payments were disputed. And a final ingredient was the apparent readiness of gentry like the Burdets to interfere in the political lives of market towns.

Conclusion

An influential view of medieval urbanization portrays the kings, monks, bishops, and secular lords as setting wheels in motion, after which townspeople and country dwellers gave the process momentum. But traders and peasants (often the same people or closely connected) were not just responding to stimuli from above, but gathered at river crossings or near important churches before charters were issued and town plans devised. Towns grew through peasant migration, not just as the pioneering generation, but through a continuing flow of rural recruits. The peasant who remained on the land influenced the development of the towns as producers by keeping the market supplied with surplus crops and livestock, and as consumers by demanding that the townspeople provide a wide range of goods and services. Towns grew as the country expanded, and through reciprocal stimulation, peasants produced and marketed more, and increased their consumption. After 1350 the reduction in the number of

---

[125] WCL, E27, E30.   [126] Dyer, 'Small-town Conflict', pp. 205–7.

those using the towns' services caused some restructuring, but not disaster. Peasants were fewer but not poorer.

Urban civic consciousness cannot be matched in the country, yet we can find self-government and avoidance of lordly dominance in both towns and villages. There are even rural versions of dramatic performances, unifying myths, and a sense of a common past.

9
Peasants and industry

The Middle Ages are sometimes described as belonging to a pre-industrial age, which ignores the large numbers of people who worked at least part-time in industrial or non-agricultural activities. In the west midlands crafts and manufactures could be concentrated in towns, most intensively in Droitwich's salt boiling, but also clothmaking employed many people at times in Coventry and Bristol, and in smaller south Gloucestershire towns such as Stroud and Dursley. Worcester became a cloth centre towards the end of our period. Most towns provided a living for artisans practising a range of skills, and their strength lay in their ability to satisfy the varied needs of their hinterlands (see 'Occupations and commerce' in Chapter 8). Here we are concerned with the thousands of country people engaged in crafts, or in activities ancillary to industry, who probably exceeded in number the town-based manufacturing workers.

Three districts with especially concentrated industrial activity can be identified in the later Middle Ages: the Forest of Dean; the Frome valley including Bisley and Minchinhampton; and the settlements around Birmingham in north-west Warwickshire and north-east Worcestershire. However, crafts were scattered over the countryside, with groups of artisans in pockets such as the potters of Chilvers Coton and Hanley Castle, and individuals and small clusters working as smiths, tailors, and carpenters dispersed in many villages (Figure 9.1). The prevalence of dual occupations, or the phenomenon called by the French 'pluriactivity' makes it difficult for us to pin a label on a person or a household. Juries required to identify people's status and occupations might in the mid-fifteenth century describe William Huntley of Churcham (Gloucestershire) as a yeoman, husbandman, and tailor.[1] The balance between his agricultural and craft work would have varied with the seasons. His household could well have included a daughter who span woollen yarn, and a wife with a brewing and ale-selling sideline. The lack of specialization shows up in the archaeological record: for example, when an iron chisel is found in a peasant house, is this evidence that a peasant might occasionally have built a stone wall, or even worked part-time as a mason, or that the household at some time employed a specialist (but forgetful) artisan?[2]

---

[1] R. Goheen, 'Peasant Politics? Village Community and the Crown in Fifteenth-Century England', *American Historical Review* 96 (1991), p. 48.

[2] R.H. Hilton and P.A. Rahtz, 'Upton, Gloucestershire, 1959–1964', *TBGAS* 85 (1966), pp. 70–146, especially pp. 119–20.

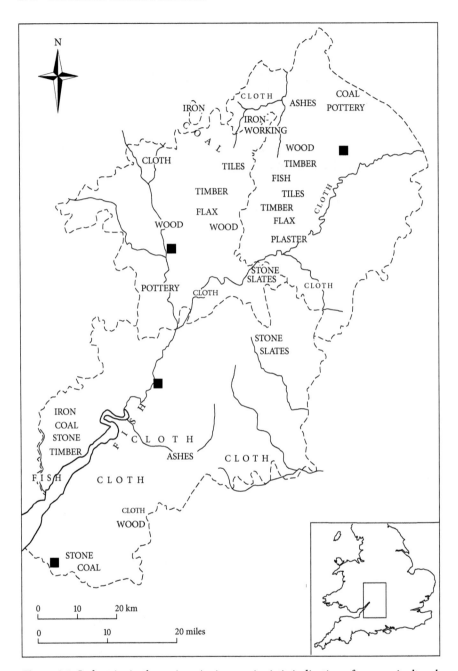

Figure 9.1 Industries in the region. An impressionistic indication of non-agricultural activities and products in the countryside.

To what extent did peasants take on non-agricultural occupations on their own initiative, or did they join in enterprises devised by elites, both aristocratic and urban? Were they driven to participate by poverty, or were they in a position to advance themselves and seek profits? To explore these questions, four themes will be proposed, which could be described as models of industrialization: lords as creators of industry, the urban entrepreneur promoting manufacture, poverty as a spur to industrial employment, and the dual economy, generated within peasant communities.

The role of lords in creating industry

Lords of many kinds founded rural industrial enterprises which could be on a large scale and well-documented. Cistercian monks have a strong reputation for practical profit-seeking both in their organization of farming and in founding industries. Flaxley Abbey in the heart of the Forest of Dean was in a good position to manage ironworking, and its itinerant forge is recorded in 1258.[3] The ironworking establishment about which we have the most detailed knowledge was organized by Bordesley Abbey in north-east Worcestershire. The waterpowered forge developed from the late twelfth century, and flourished with renewals of buildings and machinery until the late fourteenth. Excavation has revealed an elaborate water control system, with a mill powering bellows and hammers, producing a wide variety of metalwork, including weapons, nails, and tenterhooks. These were partly for use on the monastic estates, and partly for sale. The written sources contain no mention of this enterprise.[4] Lay lords as well as monasteries invested in ironworking, and in the Worcestershire industrial zone, near Dudley, Roger de Somery in 1291 was profiting from a coal mine and an iron mine associated with two great forges. A member of the gentry in the Warwickshire woodlands, John Brome in the mid-fifteenth century set up a tile house at Baddesley Clinton to exploit an abundance of fuel and clay in order to supply roof tiles to nearby towns. Brome also developed a stone quarry.[5]

As consumers the aristocracy had a limited part in stimulating local rural industry by their consumption as they tended to obtain their cloth, metalwork, and high-quality leather goods from outside the region. However, their spending on buildings led to purchases of local materials such as stone, timber, and tiles,

---

[3] *VCH Glouc* 5, p. 145.
[4] G.G. Astill, *A Medieval Industrial Complex and its Landscape: The Metalworking Watermills and Workshops of Bordesley Abbey* (CBA Research Report, 92, 1993).
[5] J. Hunt, *Lordship and Landscape. A Documentary and Archaeological Study of the Honor of Dudley c.1066–1322* (British Archaeological Reports British Series, 264, 1997), p. 81; C. Dyer, 'A Small Landowner in the Fifteenth Century', *Midland History* 1 (1972), pp. 8–9.

and they employed local labour. Examples of technical innovation in building were the prestigious brick houses constructed towards the end of our period, of which the first at Fulbrook (Warwickshire) was conceived by the Duke of Bedford in the 1430s. Although the bricks were made locally, on site, the expertise probably came from visiting artisans from the Low Countries.[6]

Both lords and peasants contributed to the emergence of one type of rural artisan, the village smith. In the early Middle Ages kings, aristocrats, and leading churchmen took a strong interest in ironworking for strategic military and economic reasons, and smiths, who could be itinerant, or attached to an estate centre, had a special status.[7] A smith was active at Bidford-on-Avon (Warwickshire), a royal estate centre, judging from a ninth-century deposit of ironworking debris and iron objects in a small hoard that apparently served some commemorative or ritualistic purpose.[8] In the Domesday Book, smiths are mentioned in Worcestershire in eight places, and as they were listed with villeins and bordars they were apparently tenants with land. In the early twelfth-century survey of Pinbury in Gloucestershire the forge is mentioned alongside the mill and the church, and the smith may have been one of the tenants.[9]

In the twelfth and thirteenth centuries, lords of all kinds—bishops, monasteries, and lay lords—are recorded as setting up smiths' holdings on their manors. The tenants were responsible for ironworking for the lord, in parallel with those tenants serving as a shepherd, ploughman, or carter. The amount of land assigned to smiths varied in size from smallholdings to standard yardlands or half-yardlands on customary or servile tenures. The holdings would owe the usual combination of cash and labour, with servile dues such as tallage, toll on the sale of animals, and marriage fines. However, the smith would not be liable to rents and labour services if he served the lord as an ironworker. These specialist duties were vaguely described: at Blackwell (Warwickshire) in 1240 the smith with a cotland was 'to work on the iron of the ploughs',[10] but usually the smith was expected to make or repair the ironwork of each plough (they varied in number between two and six). The largest pieces of iron were the coulter and share, but presumably the smith's duties extended to the smaller fittings such as chains, and the iron on the plough's foot at the front of the plough. Additional tasks would be shoeing horses, either on the front feet of two animals, or all four feet for one animal. On the estates of the nuns of Caen in Gloucestershire (Minchinhampton and its attached manors) an extra task in the late twelfth century was to provide

---

[6] C. Dyer, 'A Landscape for Pleasure: Fulbrook, Warwickshire, and John Duke of Bedford in the Fifteenth Century', *Warwickshire History* 15 (2013–14), pp. 239–50, especially pp. 244–5.

[7] D. Hinton, *A Smith in Lindsey. The Anglo-Saxon Grave at Tattershall Thorpe, Lincolnshire* (Society for Medieval Archaeology Monograph 10, 2000), pp. 111–15.

[8] S. Hirst and T. Dickinson, 'The Archaeology of Bidford-on-Avon: Excavations 1970–94', *TBWAS* 23 (2021), pp. 109–13, 143–50.

[9] *HTC*, pp. 34–5.   [10] *Reg Wig*, pp. 66a–66b.

seven scythes and seven weeding hooks, which was reduced to five of each of these implements by 1306. In the same year a smith with a smallholding had lighter duties, shoeing one horse and sharpening axes and scythes. The smiths on the Caen estate were expected to attend to the iron hinges on the doors of particular manorial buildings. For all of their jobs around the manor they provided their own iron and steel, but were accorded various privileges, such as a crop of wheat from an acre of demesne land, and the right to pasture animals, oxen in one case, ewes in another. Trees could be taken from the demesne wood to make charcoal for the forge.[11]

On other estates the lords would provide the metal, though some came from recycling the parts being replaced. The smith's duties might include the sharpening of the bills that were used to recut the grooves on millstones. At Fladbury, according to the survey of 1299, if he carried out this task the smith could have his own corn ground without paying toll.[12]

An earlier arrangement (in c.1170) on the manor of Northwick (Worcestershire) assigned the smith two acres of rye and two acres of oats on the demesne, but the usual practice was to provide land.[13] On the bishop of Worcester's estate the idea of endowing a smith with land for the service of ironworking had been adopted on five manors by c.1170, and had spread to eleven of the nineteen manors surveyed in 1299.

Problems arose as was common in many feudal relationships based on the exchange of land for services. At Hampton Lucy, after the death of Richard Smith in the early thirteenth century, the smith's holding lay uncultivated and the house stood empty. Potential tenants resented the servile dues, and the lord eventually persuaded a new smith to take on the land by removing the liability to pay toll, pannage, and marriage fines.[14] Enforcing the performance of service became difficult, so that smiths on the Worcester Priory manors of Cleeve Prior and Cropthorne in 1337 'did not do the iron work as agreed'.[15] The days of the smith's tenement were numbered, and lords increasingly engaged smiths to work on ploughs who were free agents, working for an agreed price, or for wages.

The tenant smith's work for the lord, even the many tasks at Minchinhampton, occupied a fraction of his time and he must have lived by working for money for his peasant neighbours. Smiths holding tenements in return for doing the lords' ironwork had previously worked independently, and some smiths continued to hold land through the twelfth and thirteenth centuries without special obligations, like Thomas Faber (Smith), a smallholder of Hanbury in c.1170, or the holder of a quarter-yardland at White Ladies Aston in 1299 called John Faber (both in Worcestershire).[16]

---

[11] *HTC*, pp. 64, 80, 127–8, 129–30. [12] *RBW*, pp.131. [13] *RBW*, p. 37.
[14] *RBW*, pp. 268–9. [15] WCL, E13. [16] *RBW*, pp. 89, 176.

The breakdown of the system of smiths' tenements left a scatter of independent smiths over the countryside, providing a service for both lords' demesnes and peasants. The old arrangements were not forgotten immediately. Coventry Priory noted that Simon Smith of Honington (Warwickshire) in 1411 held a yardland for 12s rent, and recalled that the former tenants of the holding had once performed a smith's duties.[17]

How many smiths were working in the countryside? The collectors of the 1379 poll tax in Warwickshire did not record occupations systematically, but in a total of ninety-one villages they found smiths in thirty-four, suggesting their presence in at least one village in three.[18] If that figure was applied across the three counties of the region, there were 400 rural smiths in the late fourteenth century. Allowance should be made for undercounting in the poll tax, and for clusters in the specialist industrial districts such as the four smiths in 1381 at Little Dean in the Forest of Dean, but Dean was unfortunately not fully documented.[19] There may well have been more than 500 rural smiths working in the region around 1380.

To sum up the development of rural smiths, in the twelfth and thirteenth centuries lords anchored smiths on manors. Some smiths operated independently even in the hey-day of the tenant smiths, and the whole craft slipped out of seigneurial control in the fourteenth century. Lords had helped to spread smiths over the countryside, and they gained a secure place in village society. Some smiths could have been the descendants of the itinerant or estate craftsmen of the early Middle Ages. Others came into the craft as the commercial world expanded in the twelfth and thirteenth centuries. They needed both equipment and training, funded perhaps by their families. The tools were expensive, judging from the value of 16s 8d put on an anvil at Blackwell (Warwickshire) in 1395.[20] In 1391 the lord of Long Marston (Warwickshire) listed the smith's tools as *principalia*, not just the anvil but also a *forehammer* (heavy hammer), a pair of tongs, *hurthestoff* (equipment around the hearth), a *wosshel* (unknown), a grindstone with an iron spindle and bellows.[21] They are not valued, but are likely to have been worth much more than 20s, especially if allowance is made for the lesser tools omitted, such as small hammers, punches, and files. A smithy excavated at Burton Dassett Southend indicates the investment and skill deployed[22] (Figure 9.2). The building (facing on to the main street with easy access) measured 12m by 5m, so it was smaller than some houses, but with solidly constructed stone foundations. It was occupied from the early thirteenth century to the early fifteenth, and may have had some space for a rather cramped domestic life. The single room (with partitions or screens in some phases of occupation) contained a hearth and an anvil.

---

[17] *Cov Reg*, p. 546.   [18] *PT*, part 2, pp. 642–89.   [19] *PT*, part 1, p. 260.
[20] WCL, E38.   [21] GA, D678/98C.
[22] N. Palmer and J. Parkhouse, *Burton Dassett Southend, Warwickshire: A Medieval Market Village* (Society for Medieval Archaeology Monograph, 44, 2022), pp. 60–3, 184–7; a specialist report can be accessed at https://doi.org/10.5284/1083492.

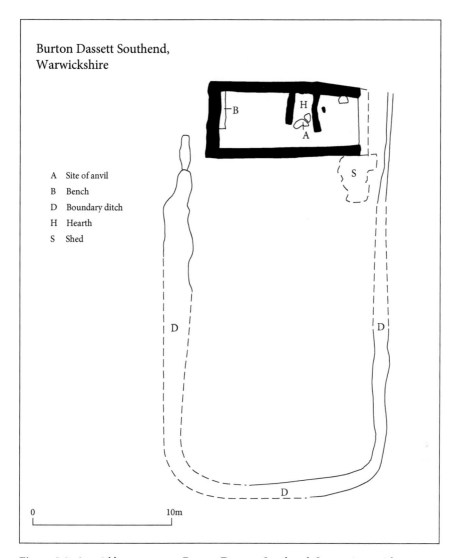

Figure 9.2 A smith's tenement at Burton Dassett, Southend. Successive smiths occupied this building over two centuries. In the early fifteenth-century phase shown here, the layout of the workshop can be identified. The building had stone walls, and the plot was defined by a boundary ditch (and probably a hedge) (source: note 22).

A block of stone and stone troughs were part of the equipment. We can imagine the implements described in the Long Marston list, such as the bellows, deployed around the hearth. Metallurgical experts who have examined the site's debris, mainly slag and hammerscale, have noted evidence for a wide range of processes– hot forging, cold work, and fire welding. For example, the smiths who worked here could make iron tools with steel edges. They concluded that the building was occupied by general smiths (over many generations) 'manufacturing and repairing a range of domestic and agricultural artefacts'. They would have acted as farriers, as horse shoeing was in demand from customers visiting the market as well as residents. However, the quantity of slag suggested that the work had not been continuous. The smith worked part-time or seasonally, so he fitted into the 'dual economy', summed up in the Gloucestershire poll tax of 1381 by a taxpayer described as 'a smith and cultivator'.

The craft had a strong hereditary tradition, so that skills, specialized buildings, and expensive equipment often passed from father to son. The excavation of the Burton Dassett Southend smithy did not produce pottery or finds which suggested that the successive tenants enjoyed great prosperity, and the same conclusion emerges from the tax records or court roll evidence from other villages. Working as a smith was a steady living, but it did not usually lead to wealth.

Urban entrepreneurs and rural industry

Town-based entrepreneurs could play a central role in the origins of rural industry. For a long period between the thirteenth and the nineteenth centuries over much of Europe rural industries were based on artisans with family members working in their own homes often to supply distant markets. The term proto-industrialization was applied rather reluctantly in England, but the organization of production and distribution was essentially the same as on the continent.[23] The entrepreneurs who oversaw manufacturing and marketing might be based in the country, but were often urban merchants who could take advantage of the infrastructure and communication links of the town to buy materials and distribute goods. They had access to credit networks through which the commerce could be funded. The entrepreneur, a clothier in the case of textile manufacture, operated a putting-out system which could erode the independence of the artisan and eventually led to a wage-earning labour force.

In the west midlands in the Stroudwater district cloth making had begun by c.1170–1200, but then greatly expanded in the following two centuries when in the hamlets in the valley of the river Frome between Stroud and Chalford manufacture was concentrated around a growing number of fulling mills (Figure 9.3). The cloths came in various colours and qualities, but the most celebrated were marketed as 'Bristol reds' or 'Stroudwaters', and were sent to London and Bristol to be distributed, and often sold on the continent. The Stroudwater evidence is not abundant, but John Benet of Cirencester who died in 1497 seems to have had the right connections and characteristics to identify him as a town-based entrepreneur

---

[23] S. Ogilvie and M. Cerman, *European Proto Industrialization* (Cambridge, 1996).

PEASANTS AND INDUSTRY 279

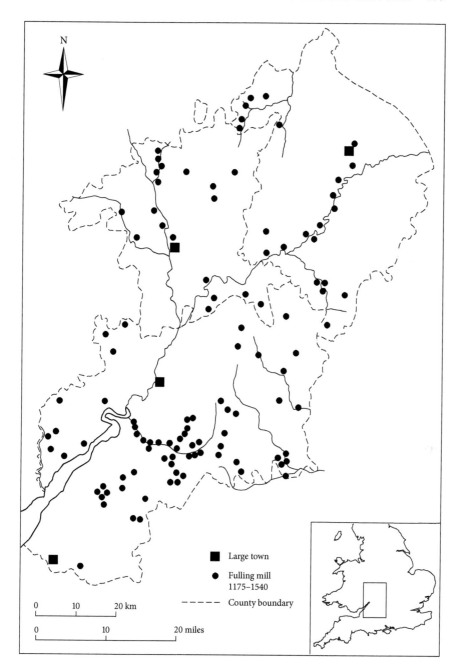

Figure 9.3 Distribution of fulling mills. The mills can be traced in a great variety of documents, dated between 1180 and 1540. Many are only mentioned once, and may not have worked for a long span of time.

with significant links to the rural industry.[24] His will reveals that he had houses in Stroud, Ebley, and the nearby small town of King's Stanley, and sublet a house in Rodborough. Four churches and chapels in Stroudwater received bequests from him. He owned a fulling mill, and also cloth shears (for trimming the knap) which suggested that he employed workers skilled in finishing cloth. Four female servants benefited from his will, as did nine employees.

Robert Rychards was a clothier of Dursley, a small town in the deep valley of the river Ewelme, 5 miles to the south-west of Stroud. His will and inventory of 1492 indicate the scale of his business, as he was in process of selling forty cloths, most of them red, worth £116.[25] He had an apprentice, three servants, and nine other employees. We can follow through the various processes of cloth manufacture from his possessions and bequests, beginning with raw wool worth £5 10s. 0d, and proceeding to the large quantity of yarn worth £48, which must have been the result of employing dozens of spinners in Dursley itself and the surrounding countryside. He left money to the parish churches of Cam and Slimbridge, so perhaps some of his spinners lived there. Three broad looms appear in the inventory, but although weavers may have worked in his house, he was probably also putting out yarn to weavers living and working in their own houses. The cloth would have been fulled in one of the local mills, and the fullers would have been responsible for the tentering and shearing. Dyeing was done on Rychards's own premises, where he had a dyehouse equipped with a 'great furnace' and two 'great vats'. He had a store of madder (a red dye) and alum (the chemical mordant needed for the dyeing process). He bought the imported dyestuffs and alum from Bristol, and sold the finished cloths in London, where at the time of his death he had three packs containing eighteen cloths. The ultimate purchasers were continental merchants with German names like Gerard von Wesel, Herman Kyng, and Herman Bytterweke. Rychard's business, like all clothiers and other medieval traders, depended on credit. The purchasers of his cloth owed him more than £200, but the executors of his will regarded these as 'good debts' (meaning that payment was expected). Rychards no doubt owed money to his suppliers of wool, and his spinners, weavers, and fullers, but like his customers, would pay eventually. Merchants such as Benet and Rychards had the wide contacts and experience to enable them to obtain imported dyestuffs, oil, alum, and soap that were needed for cloth manufacture, to sell cloth overseas, to organize finance, and manage the various stages of production and marketing.

The Stroudwater cloth industry seems to have developed in accord with the earlier characterization of proto-industries, because the independent weavers,

---

[24] TNA, PROB11/11, fo. 90r; E. Carus-Wilson, 'Evidences of Industrial Growth on Some Fifteenth-Century Manors', *EcHR*, 2nd series, 12 (1959), pp. 190–205; R. Perry, 'The Gloucestershire Woollen Industry, 1100–1690', *TBGAS*, 66 (1945), pp. 49–137.

[25] TNA, PROB11/9 fo 142v; PROB2/57.

fullers, dyers, and shearmen of the early stages became a work force of wage earners, judging from the 1525 tax for four of the main clothmaking villages in Bisley hundred, where of 209 taxpayers, 106 were paying tax on wages of 20s, and another sixty-six were assessed on goods of 40s, among whom were likely to have been some receiving wages.[26]

Other clothmaking centres in the west midlands were in no way as concentrated as in south Gloucestershire, but there are signs of the influence of urban entrepreneurs among those who took on the leases of fulling mills. They were outsiders and sometimes connected to a town, like the lessee at Sherborne in the eastern Cotswolds in 1342 who came from Winchcomb, or in 1465 William Yronmonger of Chipping Campden took on the Tredington (Warwickshire) mill. The tenant of the new Wolverley mill in 1482 in north Worcestershire came not from a town but from an industrial district at Tettenhall in Staffordshire, and other fulling mills in other villages tended to be held by men called Touker or Walker (both meaning 'fuller') as if they came, with some experience and expertise, from other clothmaking places.[27] It was not unusual for them to be given the responsibility of repairing or maintaining the mill, or even building or rebuilding it, suggesting that they were bringing capital to the project as well as experience.

Entrepreneurs both urban and rural had a part in the co-ordination of the Stroudwater industry. Fourteen clothiers from Dursley are recorded in the Common Pleas records for the period 1480–1500, and thirteen clothiers or clothmen from Stroudwater who seem to have been homegrown, and countrybased. Their origin might be traced back to c.1170–1200, when already 'fuller' appears as a not uncommon surname at Avening and Minchinhampton.[28] A family called 'de Rodborough' moved the short distance from Rodborough to Minchinhampton enabling Richard de Rodborough in 1241 to acquire a free yardland, and Thomas de Rodborough, perhaps his son, was well enough established by 1250–70 to witness a deed. The name Thomas reappears in 1306, perhaps belonging to another generation, holding a yardland and a half (for riding services) and two half yardlands, so with a total of 75 acres. Such a substantial land holder would be called franklin in the thirteenth century, and in the fifteenth a yeoman. He rented a fulling mill at Brimscombe in the Frome valley, a mile from the main settlement of Minchinhampton, and also paid an annual rent for water rights attached to a mill in Bisley on the north bank of the Frome.[29] Perhaps his interest in fulling was as an investor drawing rent from mills, or perhaps he was

---

[26] M. Faraday, ed., *The Bristol and Gloucestershire Lay Subsidy of 1523–1527* (GRS, 23, 2009), pp. 398–403.
[27] GA, D678/1/M1/1/2; WCL, E70, E75, E80.
[28] J.S. Lee, *The Medieval Clothier* (Woodbridge, 2018), pp. 121–2, 124–5; *HTC*, pp. 57, 61, 64, 66, 69, 70, 71, 81, 85.
[29] C. Elrington, ed., *Abstract of Feet of Fines Relating to Gloucestershire 1199–1299* (GRS, 16 2003), p. 74; *HTC*, pp. 26, 115, 118.

playing a more active role in the industry, but the family's history suggests the mechanisms by which a well-off land holder might be drawn into clothmaking in that district. A later clothier from Rodborough, Edward Haliday, who died in 1519 holding a fulling mill and a dyehouse, was the son of a fuller.[30] Rural clothiers in Suffolk, Kent, and Yorkshire have been traced back to families of artisans, especially fullers and dyers, and from better-off peasants. The clothiers who emerged out of a landed background tended not to cut themselves off from their origins but pursued dual occupations in which they combined some farming with clothmaking. A Bisley clothier owned 200 sheep, and a Chalford fulling mill was held with a half yardland and a close.[31]

The north Warwickshire iron industry could have been co-ordinated by ironmongers based in Birmingham. The first reference to such a specialist was in 1448.[32] Traders in iron wares, especially weapons emerged more prominently in the early sixteenth century. John Coke, William Smythe, John Browne, and Richard Russell were selling the heads of bills (infantry weapons) to the king in 1511–13, and also bridle bits.[33] Their activities were on such a scale that they must have received orders from royal officials and then commissioned the blade smiths to produce the goods. In normal times their role, judging from the activities of their successors, was to supply bar iron to the blade smiths and other specialists in and around Birmingham, and to find markets for the finished products.[34] Some metalworking artisans judging from their wills still retained some independence, and were in contact with their own customers. Gloucester entrepreneurs might have been active in the Forest of Dean iron industry, but although many artisans in the city worked with iron brought from Dean, such as smiths, cutlers, and wiredrawers, there were very few traders described as a 'hardwareman' or ironmonger who were likely to have been distributing iron wares.[35]

In smaller industries connections can be found between urban traders and rural workers. Gypsum was quarried near Stratford-upon-Avon in the fifteenth century, and was burnt to make plaster. The presence in the town of a 'plastermonger' in 1445–6 suggests that a townsman was arranging the sale of the product.[36] In other places lime was produced in a similar way, and marketed over considerable distances, but if there were dealers in lime they must have been based in the country

---

[30] Lee, *Medieval Clothier*, p.125.
[31] Lee, *Medieval Clothier*, pp. 272–81; N. Amor, *From Wool to Cloth. The Triumph of the Suffolk Clothier* (Bungay, 2016), pp. 190–6; Perry, 'Woollen Industry', p. 112'; *VCH Glouc*, vol. 11, pp. 20–30.
[32] R.A. Holt, *The Early History of the Town of Birmingham 1166–1600* (DS Occasional Paper, 30, 1985), p. 20.
[33] *Letters and Papers of Henry VIII*, vol. 1, part 1, p. 501; vol. 1 part 2, p. 1512.
[34] W.H.B. Court, *The Rise of Midland Industries, 1600–1838* (Oxford, 1938), pp. 36–42.
[35] J. Rhodes, ed., *Terrier of Llanthony Priory's Houses and Lands in Gloucester, 1443* (GRS, 30, 2016), pp. 203, 218, 253.
[36] *Reg Guild*, p. 196.

near the lime pits and lime kilns, probably at producing villages such as Wootton Wawen (Warwickshire).[37]

Poverty and industry

A long-running debate about the modern industrial revolution concerned the effect it had on lowering or improving the living standards of industrial workers, and it has also been proposed that prevalent high wages in the eighteenth century stimulated the adoption of labour-saving machinery.[38] In the thirteenth century the labour force was increasing in size, and employment in agriculture was insufficient to support a large population of cottagers and smallholders, so they turned to industrial employment. Those who were developing industries were encouraged to do so by the plentiful supply of cheap labour. The labour force was expanded not just by the growing numbers of men, but also by the females and children who were considered to be well-suited to some types of industrial work.

The workforce was often to be found in woodland districts, with their abundant raw materials and fuel. Smallholders proliferated in woodland landscapes because freeholdings tended to be divided by inheritance and the land market, and new cottages could be built on the edge of commons. Commercialization gave smallholders chances of gaining income from retail trade or casual employment, which tempted people to marry and begin a new household. Timber and wood generated employment opportunities, both for skilled specialist wood workers such as turners and cartwrights, but also the less skilled workers who felled trees, lopped branches, or cut coppice wood. A specific and long-standing activity was the harvesting of wood fuel for the Droitwich salt works, which extended 12 miles and more from the town. In 1294 at Romsley (10 miles distant) a cartload of the lord's underwood was cut illicitly for carriage to the salt town.[39] Woods within easy reach of the Severn, at places such as Ribbesford and Shrawley, periodically had their underwood felled and carted to the river for transport by boat for major consumers such as Tewkesbury Abbey and Worcester Priory.[40] Many artisans, or makers of iron in bloomeries relied on wood fuel and charcoal, and the potash used in cloth making was produced by ashburners clearing vegetation and burning it in woods in north Warwickshire (to supply Coventry) and around

---

[37] T.H. Lloyd, *Some Aspects of the Building Industry of Stratford-upon-Avon* (DS Occasional Paper, 14, 1961), p. 20.
[38] R.C. Allen, *The British Industrial Revolution in Global Perspective* (Cambridge, 2009).
[39] *CR Romsley*, p. 41.
[40] T. Wakeman, 'On the Kitchener's Roll of Tewkesbury Abbey', *Journal of the British Archaeological Association*, 15 (1859), pp. 318–32; J.M. Wilson and C. Gordon, eds., *Early Compotus Rolls of the Priory of Worcester* (WHS, 1908), p.19.

Stroud in Gloucestershire. Consequently a living could be made by wielding axes and billhooks.

Two examples, Tidenham and Hanley Castle, can be used to demonstrate how non-agricultural employment developed in woodland landscapes, in which the many smallholders needed a source of income. Tidenham was a large estate to the south-west of the Forest of Dean occupying a peninsula between the rivers Wye and Severn. It combined arable land with abundant woods and areas of open pasture with dispersed settlements. In 1306 a survey listed 144 tenants, and of these 110 held 11 acres or less and twenty-eight of them also held a fishery. Fish traps in the tidal waters of the two rivers survived in use until modern times, and very similar medieval predecessors have been excavated. They consisted of fences based on wooden stakes driven into the riverbed, closely woven with rods, which guided the fish into funnel-shaped basket-work 'putts'. Judging from their rents, between 2*d* and 6*s* 8*d*, the fisheries varied greatly in the size of their catch. Most paid the lord less than 2*s*, and presumably the fish that were caught were worth more. Another eighteen fisheries were held by people without recorded landholding. Perhaps these were landless, or they held land as subtenants or from another lord. Including these in the calculation, and adding them to the tenants of 11 acres or less, 16 per cent of the tenants of Tidenham were using the fishery either as a major means of support or as a significant supplement to a relatively small holding. Some of the Tidenham fisheries were operated by tenants with large and middling holdings, so fishing was not practised entirely by the less well off.[41] Constructing the fish traps, cutting the timber posts, rods, and withies kept many workers busy, and labour was also required to process the fish, such as salting the salmon. This productive activity did not spring into existence with the thirteenth-century growth in population and commerce, as fish traps at Tidenham are fully recorded before the Conquest.

At Hanley Castle in Malvern Chase, pottery making was clearly linked to those lacking much land. Arable land and meadow lay near the River Severn on the eastern side of the parish, but with plenty of wood and pasture to the west. Settlements called ends were strung along the roads that ran to the west from the river (Figure 9.4; see also Figure 2.7). Hanley manor had at least a hundred holdings, most of them not large, with thirty-two of them in 1296 each consisting of 6 acres. The manorial surveys note the potters separately, thirteen of them in 1296, ten in 1315. There is no evidence that they held land, but each paid the lord a standard rent of 6*d* per annum for clay and wood fuel. Evidently the potters were either subtenants, or tenants of the small manor of Hanley Hall, or were landless. They dug numerous clay pits, some of them on common land on roadsides, and

---

[41] E.A. Fry, ed., *Abstracts of IPMs for Gloucestershire* part 3, 1302–58 (British Record Society, 40, 1910), pp. 63–72; S. Godbold and R.C. Turner, 'Medieval Fishtraps in the Severn Estuary', *Med Arch* 38 (1994), pp. 19–54.

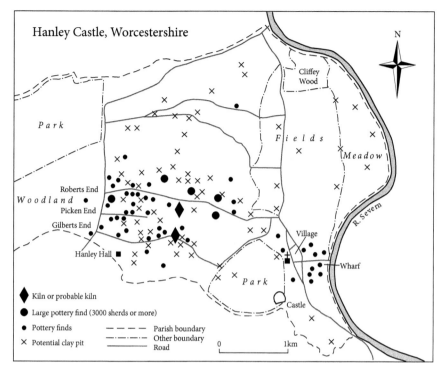

Figure 9.4 Hanley Castle. Potters in a landscape. One kiln has been excavated, and the existence of another has been detected, but hundreds would have been active over the three centuries of the medieval industry. The intensity of manufacture is suggested by numerous clay pits and scatters of potsherds, some very large, focused on the various 'ends' (hamlets), and the roads leading to them. The woods to the west of the ends provided fuel. The finds in the east of the parish, near the wharf, probably relate to settlement and agriculture, not manufacture (source: note 42 and Worcestershire Historic Environment Record).

probably kept livestock on the extensive pastures which lay next to the western 'ends'. A survey of 1349 said that all of the potters were dead.[42] A factor in this may have been that in addition to deaths among those making pots, the epidemic left jobs and land vacant elsewhere, and some potters moved away from their arduous and not very well rewarded occupation. However, a new generation took up the craft, and the industry flourished into the seventeenth century, at times on a larger scale than before 1350. Pottery making at Hanley can be located from a single excavated kiln and one probable kiln site, but mainly from scatters of pottery and roofing tiles which occur throughout the western end of the parish, including

---

[42] *Rec Hanley*, pp. 130, 143, 146, 147, 149, 154; D. Hurst, 'A Medieval Production Site and other Medieval Sites in the Parish of Hanley Castle: Results of Fieldwork in 1987–1992', *Transactions of the Worcestershire Archaeological Society*, 3rd ser., 14 (1994), pp. 115–28.

some very dense concentrations containing thousands of pottery fragments. In the same industrial zone, dozens of clay pits are still visible as ponds. Finds in the river by the quay show that pottery and tiles were distributed by boat.

Suburbs provided other contexts for smallholders using industrial employment to make ends meet. The urban fringes gave access to the town to migrants who often held cottages or only a few acres of land. Coventry Cathedral Priory held a ring of property around the edge of its city, at such places as Walsgrave on Sowe and Coundon, where the proportion of smallholdings in 1279 was high, at 48 per cent with 7 acres or below, compared with only 10 per cent of such tenants on its more rural manors. The numbers of suburban smallholdings on the Priory estate declined subsequently, but still amounted to 38 per cent of the total in 1411.[43] The names of the tenants in 1279 give a few indications of connections between them and the adjoining Coventry. Among Walsgrave tenants, Henry Taylor, may be the same Henry Taylor who held property in the city. William le Cooper and Ralph le Feur (Smith) of the same village are not listed as urban tenants, but may have supplied city customers with barrels and ironwork.[44] In the suburb of Gloucester on the eastern side of the city that belonged to Gloucester Abbey in 1266-7 the names of two weavers, a parchment maker, baker, dyer, wheelwright, skinner, and fuller suggest an interaction between the smallholders and cottages of Barton Street, Brook Street, and Newland and those living within the walls. Likewise, the smallholders in the northern suburb of Worcester in 1299 belonging to the manor of Northwick included a baker, collier, tiler, smith, hooper, and plumber. A century earlier, when occupational surnames were scarce, we still find a parchment maker, smith, and potter.[45] The relatively low pressure on space in Worcester's northern suburbs attracted the potters and tile makers who could dig for clay. In all of the examples we have examined there was scope for small-scale agriculture and horticulture, with opportunities to graze animals on extramural pastures, so the dwellers of the suburbs retained connections with the peasant way of life. The inhabitants on the urban fringe no doubt gained less than those within the walls, but they need not have feared poverty, as some were pursuing some well-rewarded crafts.

Gathering and scavenging on commons and in woods cannot be regarded as industrial, but they should be mentioned in a survey of non-agricultural activities, especially if they contributed to the supply of fuel and raw materials for artisans. The resources of the commons were especially important for the cottagers who often lived on the edge of woods and wastes. The courts sought to licence and control gathering activity, for example for thorns and furze, which were cut

---

[43] D. Greenblatt, 'The Suburban Manors of Coventry 1279-1411' (PhD dissertation, Cornell University, 1967), pp. 29-31.

[44] *WHR*, pp. 140-1; P.R. Coss, ed., *The Early Records of Medieval Coventry* (British Academy Records of Social and Economic History, new series, 11, 1986), p. 381.

[45] *Hist Glouc*, vol.3, pp. 73, 149-64; *RBW*, pp. 7-10, 11, 13, 57-9.

and carried for hedging materials and fuel. They were concerned that overuse would endanger supplies for the community. Outsiders who had no right on the common were taking vegetation for sale, leading at Stoke Prior (Worcestershire) in 1400 to an order to find out who was cutting furze and gorse in the heath.[46] Rushes, gathered for strewing in the household were being taken for sale. In 1435 at Upton Warren (Worcestershire) Cristina, wife of John Walker, and the wife of Nicholas Sharp, were carrying rushes out of the parish and selling them in Worcester, it was said for 4s 0d. One of the women was the wife of a smallholder.[47] Brief reference should also be made to peasants as hunters. Pursuit of deer and other beasts of the chase were prohibited under forest law in royal forests and many lords had rights of free warren which protected smaller game. Peasants were occasionally accused under forest law of setting out with bows and dogs to kill deer but more often they are seen to be opportunists, taking advantage of finds of dead or wounded deer, which they took back to their homes. They sold the carcasses, contributing to the illicit trade in venison. Peasants probably aspired to be hunters, and equipped themselves with arrows with heads suitable for shooting game (which are found in excavations), and accompanied by their dogs sometimes infringed the lords' privilege of warren by taking rabbits and game birds. This was on a very small scale, as they consumed negligible quantities of meat from wild animals and birds, judging from the scarcity of game among bones recovered from peasant sites.[48]

Spinning and brewing could also supplement the incomes of country people with limited resources. Clothmaking was ever-present as a rural craft which expanded in episodes between 1350 and the early sixteenth century with growth both in exports and home demand. Around 1540 approximately 142,000 spinners would be employed in England, or 16 per cent of the female population over the age of 12.[49] If 5 per cent of English cloth was produced in the west midlands, 7,000 workers, mainly women, would have been engaged in spinning, but as most of them worked part-time, the total making some contribution would have exceeded 10,000. The numbers would be smaller in 1400 or 1300 as rather less cloth was produced in the countryside, but still thousands of peasant households would have been gaining income from this source. These calculations are all based on woollen cloth, but linen manufacture provided employment for many spinners as thousands of yards of linen were made every year. Spinning was so commonplace, so firmly bound into the routine of households, that it receives little notice in documents. Daily life depicted in misericords often included a

---

[46] WCL, E223   [47] WA, ref. 705:100, BA 1120/12.
[48] J.R. Birrell, 'Peasant Deer Poachers in the Medieval Forest', in *Progress and Problems in Medieval England*, edited by R. Britnell and J. Hatcher (Cambridge, 1996), pp. 68–88.
[49] C. Muldrew, '"The Ancient Distaff" and "Whirling Spindle". Measuring the Contribution of Spinning to Household Earnings and the National Economy in England, 1530–1770', *EcHR* 65 (2012), pp. 498–526.

woman with a distaff, such as one from Ripple (Worcestershire) showing a couple sitting at their fireside, with the woman spinning in her 'leisure' time. Spindle whorls, discs of lead, stone or bone that weighted the end of the spindle, are found in excavations of west-midland peasant settlements, with four at Pinbury, nine at Upton, eight at Dassett Southend and three at Coton (a community of poor cottars).[50] Lead whorls are also found in fields, in one case from the Forest of Dean.[51] Spinning wheels were included in the inventories of cottage tenants, like Richard Sclatter of Elmley Castle in 1457. Wealthier tenants also owned them, perhaps to add another strand to their many sources of income, but the money generated by spinning made a real difference to the income of cottagers.[52] If the spinners or rather spinsters kept their earnings, the craft gave women the potential for some small measure of financial independence.

The brewing and selling of ale was quite commonly pursued by relatively wealthy households as a means of making profitable use of their surplus of grain. Brewing gave the wives of well-off tenants the opportunity to develop a business of their own. Smallholders and other poorer producers, such as widows, operated under the disadvantage of having to buy their malting grains. However, if they could not afford expensive brewing equipment, it could be hired, like the brewing lead at Overbury in the 1420s made available for 2 ½d.[53] Those too poor to brew could still participate in the trade by acting as tranters, retailing the ale brewed by others.

There is clearly a connection between poverty (or at least the prospect of poverty) and non-agricultural work. Potting and fishing could attract the landless, and cottagers and smallholders can be identified spinning, brewing, and gathering thorns and rushes. The tenants of smallholdings also included many skilled workers, notably in the suburban settlements outside large towns. The woods offered chances for unskilled workers preparing fuel for industries and households. However, the people who used the fuel were often workers with skills, equipment, and buildings who expected more from manufacturing than merely to achieve self-sufficiency.

---

[50] J. Hart, A. Mudd, E.R. McSloy, and M. Brett, *Living Near the Edge: Archaeological Investigations in the Western Cotswolds* (Cotswold Archaeology Monograph, 9, 2016), pp. 182–3; Hilton and Rahtz, 'Upton', pp. 113–16; P. Rahtz, 'Upton Gloucestershire 1964–1968', *TBGAS* 88 (1969), pp. 105, 107; Palmer and Parkhouse, *Burton Dassett Southend*, pp. 206, 209; A. Maull and others, 'Excavations of the Deserted Medieval Village of Coton at Coton Park, Rugby' (unpublished report by Northamptonshire Archaeology, 1998).

[51] Portable Antiquities Scheme, accessible at https://finds.org.uk/database, GLO 65E15; E.R. Standley, 'Spinning Yarns: The Archaeological Evidence for Hand Spinning and its Social Implications', *Med Arch* 60 (2016), pp. 266–99.

[52] *CR Elmley*, p. 148; R.K. Field, 'Worcestershire Peasant Buildings, Household Goods and Farming Equipment in the Later Middle Ages', *Med Arch* 9 (1965), pp. 138, 142.

[53] J.M. Bennett, *Ale, Beer, and Brewsters in England* (New York, 1996), pp. 39–48, 51–6; WCL, C721.

Industry within peasant society

In exploring peasant industries that were not promoted by lords, managed by urban entrepreneurs, or practised by smallholders and the landless, a starting point is provided by royal forests and woodland landscapes in general.

The Forest of Dean covered thirty-three parishes in the far west of Gloucestershire, and supported the largest concentration of industry in the west midlands (Figure 2.10). Its natural resources combined thousands of acres of woods with geological deposits rich in minerals. Industries in Dean had deep historical roots, and expanded in the thirteenth century. In 1282 the lease of iron-ore mines brought £46 to the crown. The medieval mines of Dean were not just the simple bell pits found elsewhere, but deep trenches and tunnels which needed to be propped with timber. They were worked by privileged free miners who had rights of access and were able to take trees, according to customs defined in the later Middle Ages, but which went back to the thirteenth century. The ore was roasted and crushed (by 'stamping') before being smelted in forges, of which forty-three were reported in 1270 and sixty in 1282, falling to forty-nine in 1317 and thirty-three in the 1430s. In addition, cinders left from earlier workings were smelted. The fuel for smelting, wood charcoal, was prepared in pits of which 2,685 were recorded in the royal demesne woods in 1282. Not all of the iron ore was processed in the forest, and thousands of loads were carried to the banks of the Wye and Severn to be carried by boat to be smelted elsewhere. Coal was also mined for export from the Forest.[54]

All of these activities required a prodigious amount of timber and wood, so that the royal enquiry of 1282 found thousands of stumps of oak and beech trees which had been felled for charcoal burning and other purposes. There was much complaint at the damage to the woods, especially by felling that had not received permission from the forest authorities; however, some woods survived. Timber was worked into building timber, barrels, cartwheels, and boats, and the bark sold for tanning. Lime bark (bast) was made into rope. The underwood was cut for fuel and fencing. Both timber and wood were taken out of the Forest by the roads leading eastwards to Gloucester, and by boat from river ports, of which twelve were recorded on the Severn and Wye in 1282.[55] They connected Dean both upriver to Gloucester and Worcester, and downstream to Bristol. As well as wood products and the output of the mines, the boats carried illicit venison for the wealthy households of Bristol. The numerous coal mines produced the fuel for the manufacture of ironwares. Large quantities of crossbow bolts, horseshoes,

---

[54] *VCH Glouc.* vol. 5, pp. 326–7, 339, 346, 347.
[55] C.E. Hart, *The Regard of the Forest of Dean in 1282* (Forest of Dean Local History Society, 1987), pp. 23–43; C.E. Hart, 'The Dean Forest Eyre of 1282' (MA dissertation, University of Bristol, 1955); *VCH Glouc*, vol. 5, pp. 326–46; C.E. Hart, *Royal Forest* (Oxford, 1966), p. 28.

and agricultural implements came from the ironworks of Dean for widespread distribution. Dean iron was manufactured into wire, knives, and implements of all kinds in Gloucester. Quarries in the Forest were a source of sandstone for building, limestone for burning into lime (using local coal), specialized stones for millstones and grindstones, and oxide and ochre to make red and yellow paint.[56] Not all industries were related to the specialized resources of the Forest, as at least six fulling mills served the clothmakers in or near to the forest.[57]

Some of the many tasks itemized here were carried out by specialist workers, such as the free miners, and there would have been much wage work associated with the forges, the mines, and charcoal burning. In 1282 when the crown needed experienced tree fellers to open up routes for new roads for the campaigns in north Wales, they found a hundred recruits in Dean, presumably men who normally worked for wages.[58]

Peasant artisans offended against the vert in the Forest by taking trees, building houses, digging marl pits, and making enclosures. Those named were usually landholders, who were breaking forest law in pursuit of both their agricultural and industrial work. In Dean in 1282 the offenders included a carpenter, a cooper, two charcoal burners, three smiths, and a roper, judging from their occupational surnames. There were also textile workers, two weavers, a shearman, and a tailor. Those involved in the food trades as butcher, baker, and cook may have been trading with the forest workers, as charcoal burners, miners, and quarrymen needed to be fed.[59] Peasants were equipped for hauling with carts, and some owned ox-drawn wains suited for carrying heavy timber. In the specialized and concentrated industrial scene of Dean, there was plenty of scope for the peasant to become involved in manufacture, or to provide services.

The Forest of Feckenham in north Worcestershire and west Warwickshire lacked Dean's tracts of land covered with large trees, and the underlying geology was not rich in minerals apart from the salt deposits at Droitwich. However there was still an impressive range of occupations in the records of the 1270s and 1280s. Setting aside the artisans from the town of Alcester (two smiths, a carpenter and a wheelwright) in order to focus on rural crafts, fifteen occupations can be identified from the surnames, with six charcoal burners, six smiths, an arrow smith, a lorimer (making iron horse bits), together with woodworkers: a carpenter, cooper, hooper, and sawyer. Clothmakers included three weavers, and a shearman, and there was also a potter and roper. Food traders, a baker, and four cooks, also offended against forest law.[60] The offences committed by all of these people with occupational surnames arose from their holding of land, so if they were still pursuing the occupations from which they took their names, they belonged to the dual economy. From woodlands outside royal forests specialist woodworkers produced

---

[56] *VCH Glouc.* vol. 5, p. 337.
[57] *VCH Glouc.* vol. 5, p. 345.
[58] Hart, *Royal Forest*, pp. 50–1.
[59] Hart, 'Dean Forest Eyre'.
[60] *Rec Feck For.*

items for particular niches in the market. Ladders were being made at Romsley (Worcestershire) in 1485, and yokes in 1382 at Bisley (Gloucestershire). Hurdle making was a feature of the woodlands of Hawkesbury (Gloucestershire).[61]

Industrial activity spread over quite a large area of north-west Warwickshire, north-east Worcestershire, extending into south Staffordshire. This territory was adjacent to royal forests, but can be characterized as a woodland landscape with a combination of rather poor quality arable (oats were much grown), pasture, heath, and some wood. Land was often held in small hedged crofts. At the centre lay the town of Birmingham and its suburb of Deritend, with a population in 1300 of 1,250, and probably near to 2,000 in the early sixteenth century (see 'Peasants and changing fortunes of towns' in Chapter 8). The area was connected by road to the coal mines of Pensnett, Dudley, and Halesowen to the west. Drove roads from the west brought cattle from north Wales and then on to London, and wool came from Shropshire. Eastwards roads went to Coventry, the regional capital, but also to the east coast ports. Grain came from the south, from the Avon Valley, and roads to the south-west connected it to the Severn and ultimately Bristol by boat. The area was most famous for its smiths and other ironworkers, and it produced many blades, notably for scythes, knives, and weapon bills, but tanners and clothmakers were important. The application of water power for sharpening blades is found at neighbouring Halesowen as early as 1346, when Hugh le Cotiler was using a water mill to sharpen knives and axes.[62] Mills are recorded in the early sixteenth century on the small River Rea and lesser streams near to Birmingham including two fulling mills and a number of blade mills. Artisans, often just individuals, and industrial mills worked in the villages around Birmingham, at Aston, Bordesley, Edgbaston, Erdington, Handsworth, Harborne, Northfield, and Yardley.[63] When the central government needed iron wares and especially bills for infantry soldiers in 1511–13 they negotiated with men based in Birmingham, but also with William Smyth of Bickenhill to the east, and Richard Parkys of Sedgley to the west. The wooden poles on which the bill heads were fitted were supplied by William Bradford of Hanbury in Feckenham Forest.[64]

A varied and adaptable society seems to have developed at King's Norton, 5 miles south-west of Birmingham under the remote lordship of the crown, which meant that the inhabitants enjoyed relative freedom, and held land under the customs of ancient demesne. Various lesser lords and church institutions held sub-manors which wielded limited power over tenants. King's Norton people demonstrated their independent spirit by defending common rights if outsiders

---

[61] *CR Romsley*, p. 259; TNA, SC2/175/8, SC2/175/58.   [62] BAH, 3279/346313.
[63] Holt, *Town of Birmingham*, p. 18; *VCH Warw*, vol. 7, pp. 253–69; A. Beardwood, ed., *The Statute Merchant Roll of Coventry, 1392–1416* (DS, 17, 1939), p. 61.
[64] *Letters and Papers of Henry VIII*, vol. 1, part 2, pp. 1512, 1515.

encroached.[65] Their settlements were dispersed, and their lands included some open field but much enclosure, as well as the common pastures and heaths. King's Norton lay in the parish of Bromsgrove, but its religious life was centred on a chapel which grew in size to accommodate the population of a thousand, and became larger than most parish churches. Next to the chapel was an open space, the Green, surrounded by houses and probably the venue for an unchartered market. Leland, visiting in the early sixteenth century mentioned wool staplers living near the church. Clergy attached to the chapel taught in a school.[66] In the late thirteenth century, surnames indicate nine non-agricultural occupations, and more reliable descriptions of trades and crafts around 1500 record a total of fourteen. Mercers, drapers, and food traders were included, but also artisans: textile workers, makers of clothing, a shoemaker, a tanner, a carpenter, a wheelwright, and smith. Ceramic tiles were made and traded as far as Stratford-upon-Avon. Pastoral farming had apparently developed a commercial speciality, as the prior of Worcester in 1535 was buying King's Norton cheese.[67]

A great quantity of imported Spanish iron came to King's Norton from Bristol, by boat (trow) up the Severn, and by cart overland, probably from the river port of Bewdley. These cargoes are recorded in 1539 and 1540, but the trade was well established by then. Richard Chamber, yeoman, received 11 tons, and William Reynolds 3 tons, the two men paying almost £60 in total for the iron over two years.[68] Chamber and Reynolds were presumably middlemen who sold smaller parcels of the metal to working artisans. Their customers could well have been smiths and cutlers in Birmingham and the nearby villages. The Spanish iron was of a high quality, and was used for specialized products, perhaps in combination with cheaper metal from the west midlands. Even artisans on the fringes of Dean with abundant nearby sources of iron had uses for Spanish iron.[69]

Turning from concentrations of industrial activity, the scatter of peasant craftsmen over the countryside were well placed to respond to the needs of their neighbours for building workers, those making textiles and clothing, and suppliers of food and drink.

Building workers are traditionally headed by the masons. They were quite thinly and unevenly spread. For example, there were twenty people with the Mason or Machom surname in Gloucestershire paying tax in 1327 compared

---

[65] A.F.C. Baber, ed., *The Court Rolls of the Manor of Bromsgrove and King's Norton* (WHS, 1963), pp. 4–10; C. Dyer, *An Age of Transition?* (Oxford, 2005), pp. 60–1.

[66] A. Baker, 'A Study of North-Eastern King's Norton: Ancient Settlement in a Woodland Manor', *TBWAS* 107 (2003), pp. 131–49; G. Demidowicz and S. Price, *King's Norton. A History* (Chichester, 2009), pp. 13–40, 50.

[67] E.S. Fegan, *Journal of Prior William More* (WHS, 1914), p. 403.

[68] J. Angus and J. Vanes, eds., *The Ledger of John Smythe 1538-1550* (Bristol Record Society, 28, 1974), pp. 41–3.

[69] Smythe supplied smiths at Westbury-on-Severn and Woolaston: Angus and Vamnes, eds., *John Smythe*, pp. 32, 40.

with thirty-two carpenters. In the sixty-seven villages covered by the poll tax records in 1381 only five masons were identified.[70] A growing number of peasant houses from the thirteenth century onwards were built on stone foundations, and a minority had stone walls up the eaves, but the mainly low walls of rubble without lime mortar would not have taken much of the mason's time. Their main sources of work were high status ecclesiastical, aristocratic, and urban buildings. A mason with a long-term engagement with an aristocratic employer was John Monfort, who worked on the earl of Warwick's castle at Elmley (Worcestershire) and in 1382 acquired a cottage, a croft, and three selions. Such masons with smallholdings form another category of peasant artisans. Some masons supplied stone as well as working and laying it, and at Elmley they obtained licences to open a quarry. The quarries were small in size, for example, one on Bredon Hill measured 40 feet by 40 feet.[71] Rural carpenters were often employed on high-status and urban buildings, but a high proportion of their work was done for peasants. This helps to explain their numbers, and their tendency to be based in the country. Combining two documents, an eyre roll and a lay subsidy, both compiled in 1275, twenty-nine carpenters are listed for Worcestershire, only three of whom lived in a town (for comparison, only nine Mason or Macun names, three of them urban, appear in the same sources) (Figure 9.5). Similarly, fifteen of the twenty carpenters named as taxpayers in Warwickshire in 1332 were rural.[72]

They tended to be based in woodland landscapes, though in the poll tax of 1381 thirteen taxpayers described as carpenters appeared in Cotswold villages. A notable feature of the poll taxes was the clustering of carpenters, with groups near Coventry at Bulkington and Stivichall (see 'Occupations and commerce' in Chapter 8). Three of them can also be found at some distance from a town, for example at Bibury (Gloucestershire).[73] Perhaps the consumers benefited from a group of carpenters operating in one place, and likely to compete over price and quality of service. There might have been advantages for the carpenters in being able occasionally to work together. They often did minor jobs which took only a few days, but the carpenter who was paid 6s 8d for extensive repairs to a peasant house and barn at Whatcote in 1443–4 probably worked for sixteen days (at 5d per day).[74] Most carpenters worked as individuals, were widely spaced across the country, and consequently travelled quite long distances to work.

Carpenters demonstrated their technical skills and their accomplishments in design in work that still survives in the form of standing buildings. The twelfth and thirteenth centuries saw the adoption of a number of innovations that seem

---

[70] P. Franklin, ed., *Taxpayers in Medieval Gloucestershire* (Stroud, 1993); *PT*, part 1, pp. 260–308.
[71] *CR Elmley*, pp. 27, 128, 161.
[72] J. Röhrkarsten, ed., *The Worcester Eyre of 1275* (WHS, new series, 22, 2008); J. Willis Bund and J. Amphlett, eds., *Lay Subsidy Roll for the County of Worcester, circa 1280* (WHS, 1893); W.F. Carter, *The Lay Subsidy Roll for Warwickshire of 6 Edward III (1332)* (DS, 6, 1926).
[73] *PT*, part 1, p. 294.   [74] SRO, D641/1/2/270.

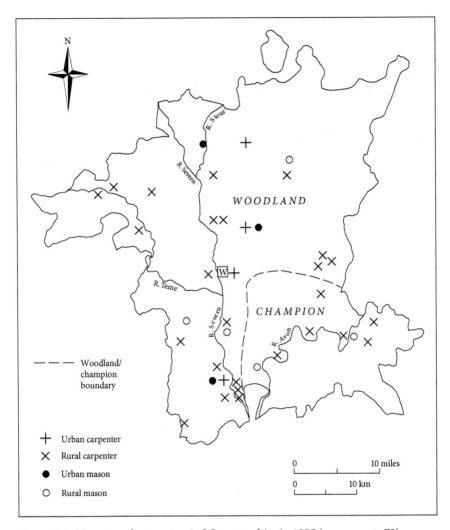

Figure 9.5 Masons and carpenters in Worcestershire in 1275 (source: note 72)

to be interconnected. Stone foundations were widely adopted, and in some circumstances stone walls to full height were being constructed. Timbers were neatly cut from the tree in a systematic conversion into a squared form which could then be assembled with mortice and tenon joints into a timber frame. In the west midlands crucks provided the basis of the frame, and they were fixed in a horizontal sill beam, or stood on padstones, or were embedded in a stone wall. Once the cruck-based timber frame and stone walls had been adopted, carpenters worked within that method of construction, which may have limited their scope for individual choice in layout and technique. However no two buildings were identical and each craftsman solved constructional problems in slightly different ways. For example, a variety of methods were used to join pairs of cruck blades together at the apex of the roof. Some carpenters employed unusual joints requiring considerable skill, such as the 'joggled halvings' in one Warwickshire house.[75] The arrangement of timbers could vary, with the use of curved braces in addition to the geometric squares of conventional framing, and the occasional extravagant use of timber in close studding. In deciding on the design of a house the carpenter was consulting with the client who was commissioning the work.

Although they displayed much skill, carpenters did not enjoy a high status in the hierarchy of crafts. They appear in court stealing trees, and had a reputation for unreliability, by failing to do agreed work. William atte Toun of Mathon in the 1380s and 1390s did not just let a client down, but also seems to have threatened a neighbour.[76] Some may have depended entirely on the earnings of their craft, but they could hold quite large amounts of land. Some were smallholders, like the carpenter with a cottage and 4 acres at Elmley Castle, but William atte Toun, a serf, seems to have been tenant of a yardland. In 1384 a carpenter of Madresfield (Worcestershire) was granted freehold lands in Madresfield and Baldenhale (part of Malvern) consisting of many pieces of land including a close, 17 selions, 5 dayworks, and 5 butts. Three years later he was told to pay in the manor court an unusually punitive amercement of 10s for felling and carrying off timber from land he held from the lord of Madresfield in order to build a house on a piece of land that he had purchased. He may have offended his lord, but he was also making full use of his lands.[77]

New rural buildings were mostly thatched, and roofs needed frequent repair and maintenance. The thatchers' craft was not as specialized as others in the building trade, and it was not a frequent occupational description. Slaters and tilers, who covered the roofs of high status or urban buildings with stone slates and ceramic tiles had a higher profile, and they appear in the poll tax and holding land in the villages. Only a small proportion of peasant houses were provided with these expensive roofs, though sometimes the louvre or smoke vent on a thatched roof was surrounded by a patch of slates or tiles to prevent fire.

Roofing slates had to be quarried in places with suitable stone, and the products of Cotswold villages such as Guiting and Snowshill were sent over a wide area. At Cleeve Prior (Worcestershire) the local limestone, lias, was probably being exploited before 1350, but it first attracted official attention in 1357 when tenants

---

[75] J.T. Smith, 'The Problems of Cruck Construction and the Evidence of Distribution Maps', in *Cruck Construction: An Introduction and Catalogue*, edited by N.W. Alcock (CBA Research Report, 42, 1981), pp. 5–24; N.W. Alcock and D. Miles, *The Medieval Peasant House in Midland England* (Oxford, 2013); N.W. Alcock, P. Barnwell and M. Cherry eds., *Cruck Buildings: a Survey* (Donington, 2019); N.W. Alcock and D. Miles, 'An Early Fifteenth-Century Warwickshire Cruck House...Joggled Halvings', *Vernacular Architecture* 43 (2012), pp. 19–27.

[76] WAM, 21,377, 21,383, 21,387.

[77] CR Elmley, p.122; WA, ref. 970.5:99, BA892/1, no. 177; Anon, *Excerpta e Scrinio Maneriali de Madresfield in Com Wigorn* (1873), pp. 20–1.

were ordered not to sell stone slates without the lord's licence. In 1365 the requirement for a licence was extended to include the extraction of the stone as well as the sale of the slates.[78] The lord was not opposing the industry, but expected to make money from it. From 1386 until 1421 individuals were amerced for digging slates. Of the seven offenders reported in 1387 three held yardlands, and another three half-yardlands with additional acres, so quarrying had become a sideline for relatively well-off tenants.[79] Presumably employees were doing the actual quarrying and slate making. It later became clear that the source of the stone was not a distant hillside, but strips of arable land in the open fields, where the stone lay near the surface. Eventually, in the 1390s, the offending tenants agreed to seek the lord's licence. In 1392 one of the four tenants digging stone paid 2s 4d to make and sell 1,000 slates and in the next year another tenant was told to pay 6d for the sale of three cartloads of slates. The lord's licence fee in 1406 cost seven tenants, some of whom were selling building stone rather than slates, a total of 9s 10d.[80] The lord's intervention shows us the scale of the industry, which was clearly able to send many thousands of slates onto the market. Perhaps the licence fees were set at a level which allowed the lord a share of the revenues without discouraging the industry. The tenants seem to have decided that they were paying too much, withdrew their cooperation, and paid no fees, which led the lord in 1406 to ask for an enquiry as to who was digging stone. The lord meanwhile shifted his grounds for intervening which must initially have been based on asserting his mineral rights, but in 1421 the quarries were said to be on servile land, which the lord claimed to control. A new objection to quarrying in 1420–1 was concern about damage to the fields, and tenants were told to restore the land so that it could be cultivated again.[81]

To sum up, a considerable proportion of Cleeve Prior tenants, nine in one year (1421) extracted stone for roofing slates from quarries on strips in the open fields. The profits were not very large, as a thousand slates would have sold for about 5s, but it was evidently worthwhile, especially if the lord's licence fees could be avoided. Cereals were becoming less profitable, and the cultivators of Cleeve were leaving parts of the arable unplanted (see 'Arable to pasture' in Chapter 6) The episode illustrates peasant adaptability, as an accident of geology gave them the opportunity, and they acquired new skills, or recruited skilled workers, and perhaps developed distribution and marketing networks. The production of slates was an example of peasants responding to consumer demand, as townspeople and a few peasants turned from thatch to expensive but durable and fire-proof roofing materials. Ceramic roofing tiles were made in woodland production centres, including Baddesley Clinton, Hanley Castle, and King's Norton, all of which supplied

[78] WCL, E18, E21.   [79] WCL, E33.   [80] WCL, E36, E45.   [81] WCL, E45; E49.

towns. Coventry was served by a large-scale production site on its outskirts at Stoke.[82]

The building industry in general remained active because demand moved from one social group to another. Elite buildings needed a large labour force before about 1280, but after that castles and monasteries gradually reduced their programmes of construction. Peasant buildings enjoyed a boom in the period 1380–1500, nor were timber buildings in some towns being neglected in the period 1430–90, so this could have been a good time to be a carpenter. The workers were often based in the country and followed dual occupations, combining their craft with a peasant holding.

A trade in cloth aimed at local consumers is implied by the drapers and draperies (groups of stalls) in market towns. A few drapers lived in the country, according to the 1379 poll tax at the small and otherwise primarily agricultural Warwickshire village of Radbourne and also at Birdingbury not far away. Richard Calwe of Northfield (Worcestershire), a rural draper was reported to be the victim of robbery in 1445, in which he claimed to have lost cash totalling £6 and possessions including 2 yards of blanket, a relatively cheap woollen. The stolen items included a gown of *must devylers*, which was an imported cloth from Montivilliers in Normandy, and probably the draper's own rather superior clothing.[83] Less affluent consumers might have bought Welsh cloth or the cheap woollens from Kendal in the north-west. The favoured colours were blue and russet (grey).

Rural clothmaking is made visible by references to fulling mills, some of which paid rents to manorial lords. Fullers could be pursuing their trade while cultivating land, like the fuller at Eastington (Gloucestershire) in 1439 who held 14 acres.[84] The significance of mills should not be exaggerated. Lords did not initiate an industry by building a mill, but rather the lord's officials noticed weavers at work, and seized the opportunity to gain revenue. Mills might also be built by local people who paid rent for use of the water.[85] Once established, the mill could encourage further advances in cloth making. The intense development of the Stroud district, with at least thirty mills, could not be matched in any other part of the region, but at various times a total of 112 mills are known to have existed, and that is a minimum (see Figure 9.3). Loose groupings can be seen in the western part of the Forest of Dean, in the valley of the Coln in south Gloucestershire, along the rivers Stour and Avon in Warwickshire, and the Stour and Severn in Worcestershire, and in villages around Birmingham. Mills were not just serving

---

[82] *VCH Warw.* Vol. 8, p. 101.   [83] *PT*, part 2, pp. 669, 672; BAH, 518089.
[84] *VCH Glouc*, vol.10, p. 132.
[85] R. Holt, *The Mills of Medieval England* (Oxford, 1988), pp. 152–8; Carus Wilson, 'Industrial Growth'.

their immediate vicinity, and a weaver is known to have travelled 17 miles to have his cloth fulled.

Tailors and shepsters (female dressmakers) made contact with their rural clients by establishing themselves in market towns, but also in the country. The surname 'tailor' is found in nineteen rural locations in Worcestershire in 1275, and many others would have been too poor to contribute to the tax.[86] Later records reveal tailors and shepsters in nineteen villages among the sixty-seven in the surviving Gloucestershire 1381 poll tax records, including two tailors at Chedworth, a tailor and two shepsters at Up Ampney, and three tailors at Dowdeswell.[87] In the Warwickshire poll tax of 1379 of ninety-one villages documented, fifteen contained tailors, with two each in three places, but in this list most crafts were undercounted. To explain these numbers, which are comparable with smiths and carpenters, many peasants evidently expected their clothes to be made by specialists. The dialogue between customer and craftsperson might have led to shifts in fashion in rural clothing. Unlike some peasant societies, English countrymen kept up with the new styles, as we find men's garments described mainly as tunics until the late fourteenth century, and after that they were wearing gowns, doublets, and coats. This meant that they moved from loose clothes to the tight-fitting styles which had been adopted originally at the royal court.[88] The tailors were adept at keeping one foot in the world of fashion, and another in the soil, as they are found holding land, and not just smallholdings. A fifteenth-century Churcham (Gloucestershire) tailor was also described as a husbandman and a yeoman.[89]

Woollen cloth seizes our attention because it has such a high profile in the life of the region and the nation. Yet linen undergarments were much worn, and no bed was complete without linen sheets, made from spun flax fibres, or *hurden* sheets woven from hemp. Flax and hemp were widely grown in small quantities, which means that they feature as a minor item in valuations of tithes. They were prominent in woodland landscapes, leading to the sale of the flax and hemp tithe at Wootton Wawen (Warwickshire) in 1453 for 22s 1d; this implies that the whole crop was valued at £11, which might mean at least 30 acres devoted to these crops.[90] At Hanbury in Worcestershire and other woodland villages, parcels of common pasture were planted with flax, and more widely flax and hemp were grown in gardens or enclosed crofts.[91] The widespread cultivation of the two crops is evident from the complaints of the pollution caused by retting the plants in streams and ponds, to separate the fibres. Equipment for preparing yarn from the fibres, heckles (combs with metal teeth), and spinning wheels, appear in inventories, but linen weaving is sparsely recorded. A rare example was Thomas

---

[86] Willis Bund and Amphlett, *Lay Subsidy circa 1280*.   [87] *PT*, part 1, pp. 288, 299, 305.
[88] F. Piponnier and P. Mane, *Dress in the Middle Ages* (New Haven, 1997), pp. 63–8, pp. 86–9.
[89] Goheen, 'Peasant Politics', p. 48.   [90] Kings College, Cambridge, WoW 223.
[91] C. Dyer, *Lords and Peasants in a Changing Society: The Estates of the Bishopric of Worcester, 680–1540* (Cambridge, 1980), p. 321.

le Webbe of Cleeve Prior, who was the subject of a complaint in 1357 that he had detained 3 ells of linen cloth promised to John Bell of Bidford-on-Avon (Warwickshire).[92] Linen weaving leaves no material traces, apart from a glass smoother for finishing linen found in the excavations of a rural settlement at Goldicote (Warwickshire).[93] The production of linen might have had a low profile because it was a commonplace small-scale part-time activity in many villages, in which, as in the Thomas le Webbe case, the weaver sold cloth direct to customers. If women played a large part in linen weaving as well as spinning, this would have been a factor in the craft's invisibility. Although not much co-ordination by entrepreneurs is apparent, the occasional rural mercer (who traditionally dealt in non-woollen textiles) is mentioned, and the surname Linendraper appears at Alcester in the thirteenth century, so perhaps there was some marketing of the cloth by middlemen (see 'Occupations and commerce' in Chapter 8).

In considering the long-term changes in demand for cloth in the region, although between the 1340s and the 1520s the numbers of those buying and wearing cloth declined, people may have bought more per head and demanded higher quality textiles. Support for this suggestion comes from the sumptuary laws of 1363–1533 alleging that the lower ranks of society were wearing clothes previously associated with their social superiors, but does this prejudiced source mean that clothing standards were generally rising? The west-midland maintenance agreements for retired tenants occasionally promised new garments annually, and tell us something about the clothes and their value, but they do not indicate an increase in expenditure on textiles or garments. This may be a problem of this source, which was concerned with defining minimum provisions (see 'Peasants and changing urban fortunes' in Chapter 8). Perhaps the best indication of rising demand for cloth comes from the new fulling mills built in the fifteenth century, which were part of a national trend for more industrial mills. In England as a whole, the percentage of mills used in industry grew from 6 per cent of the total around 1300 to 23 per cent in the 1530s. In the west midlands the increase was more modest, in the same span of time from 3.5 per cent to 11 per cent.[94] The regional difference can be explained in the modest size of the west-midland cloth industry compared with the intensity of clothmaking found in Berkshire, Kent, and Wiltshire, where many fulling mills came into operation in response to rising cloth exports. Nonetheless the healthy state of mechanical fulling in the west midlands would be compatible with an appetite among consumers in the region for more and better clothing.

---

[92] WCL, E18.
[93] P. Thompson and S. Palmer, 'Iron Age, Romano-British and Medieval Settlements Excavated on the Transco Newbold Pacey to Honeybourne Gas Pipeline in 2000', *TBWAS* 116 (2012), p. 115.
[94] J. Langdon, *Mills in the Medieval Economy. England 1300–1540* (Oxford, 2004), pp. 40–7.

Only three shoemakers appear in the villages covered by the poll tax, and a few more feature in manorial court records. Clothing could be mended, altered, even made at home, as is shown by finds in excavations of scissors, shears, needles, and thimbles. Making shoes would have been a greater challenge and most shoes would have been bought in market towns. Leather workers in general were scarce in the west midland countryside, with a single glover recorded at Shustoke in Warwickshire, and only a few instances of skinners sometimes revealing their unwelcome presence by cleaning sheepskins and fouling the water in a stream.[95]

Consumption of freshwater fish expanded in the later Middle Ages, in parallel with the demand for meat. Throughout the period the rents paid for pond and river fisheries reflect the profits that could be made from selling the catch. Two lessees were willing in 1329 to pay £13 6s 8d per annum for a large pond at Lapworth (Warwickshire), which would enable them to take pike, bream, tench, perch, roach, and eels.[96] A very high rent, £20 in 1506, was paid for Framilode weir on the Severn, with a potential for large catches of salmon and lampreys. Most river fisheries carried a lesser rent, but the sums were equivalent to a middling holding of land. For example, 13s 4d was paid for two lengthy stretches of the river Avon at Welford-on-Avon (Warwickshire), by two prominent local tenants in 1450. Similar rents for fisheries on the same river further downstream at Cleeve Prior, again attracting peasant lessees, remained at much the same level through the depression of the mid-fifteenth century, suggesting a sustained demand for fish.[97] Tenants were attracted to acquire fishing rights in minor streams, like the Bow Brook at Walcot in Allesborough (Worcestershire) for 20d rent.[98] A steady flow of complaints about illicit fishing shows that poachers realized that they could make quick profits from catching and selling fish, from rivers and ponds which could not be closely policed.

Among the fishing techniques practised, the most drastic employed at Adlestrop in 1402 (and elsewhere) was to build a temporary dam across a stream, and take the fish that were penned in behind it, though the lessees of the fishery had to be reminded to remove the dam afterwards to prevent floods.[99] On larger rivers, as at Tidenham, weirs or fences were designed to direct the fish into basket-work traps, and the weirs attached to mills traditionally were used to catch eels. The use of 'machines' and 'engines' (presumably traps or just nets) was regulated by manor courts. It was probably the fear that efficient devices might endanger stocks, that led the authorities at Brandon (Warwickshire) in 1475 to order that no tenant should fish in the lord's 'several waters' except with 'an angle rod'.[100]

---

[95] *PT*, part 2 p. 658; WCL, E51 (by-law at Teddington on pollution).
[96] *Calendar of Ancient Deeds*, vol. 5, p. 173, A11597.
[97] Gloucester Cathedral Library, Register C, pp. 130–2; Kings College, Cambridge, WOA 5; WCL, E30, E32, E52, E54, E61; Hereford Cathedral Library, R1163.
[98] TNA, SC2 210/9.   [99] TNA, SC2 175/76.   [100] UNMSC, MiM 128/4.

As well as leasing fisheries from lords, peasants in some circumstances could create their own fishponds. The large parish of Tanworth-in-Arden (Warwickshire) is known to have contained twenty fishponds, some of which seem to have been made by peasants, notably John Smith who in 1332 acquired an open ditch which he converted into a pond by damming a water course. It was later called Smythespool.[101]

All of those with access to fisheries aimed at supplying the market rather than obtaining fish for domestic consumption. Peasants probably ate eels and small fish, but their main ambition was to catch the larger species which would be consumed by aristocratic, monastic, and wealthy urban households. Salmon and pike had a high status but other species fetched good prices. The Trinity Guild at Coventry gave a lavish breakfast in March 1458 (in Lent) and served bream which cost 18*d* each, and they paid 5*d*, 8*d*, and 10*d* each for tench.[102]

The rural food and drink trades enabled peasants to enhance the profits from agricultural produce, aiming at peasant consumers. In the court records bakers appear sporadically and in small numbers, paying amercements for selling loaves of low weight. Butchers are rather more commonly encountered, normally appearing before the court for selling meat at excessive profit (see 'Marketing animals' in Chapter 7). Some villagers probably bought both meat and bread in towns, though urban bakers would visit villages (see 'Occupations and commerce' in Chapter 8). Most peasant households did not need to buy loaves because they baked their own bread, either in ovens in their house or bakehouse, or in the common oven. Bakers and butchers presented to the manor courts were often landholders, and can therefore be regarded as part of the dual economy. Cooks were mainly town-based, but in Eldersfield in 1390 Edward and Roger Viteler (a significant name) were making and selling pies.[103]

Large numbers participated in brewing ale, many of them women. They were regulated in price, the use of measures, and quality. The authorities wished to make sales accessible, by insisting that a stake was placed outside the alehouse when ale was available, and sometimes they attempted to establish a rota of brewers. It seems that every seller of ale, both the brewers and the tranters who bought ale from the brewers and sold it, was liable to pay a small sum (often 2*d*–4*d*) supposedly for breaking the rules, but really as a tax on trading. In an increasingly common practice, a frequent brewer paid an annual sum (perhaps 12*d*) for exemption from a succession of small fines.

---

[101] M. Aston and C.J. Bond, 'Warwickshire Fishponds', in *Medieval Fish, Fisheries and Fishponds in England*, edited by M. Aston (British Archaeological Reports, British Series, 182, 188) part 2, pp. 417–34, especially p. 431.

[102] G. Templeman, ed., *The Records of the Guild of the Holy Trinity, St Mary, St John the Baptist and St Katherine of Coventry* (DS, 19, 1944), pp. 180–1.

[103] WA, ref. 705:134, Box 69B.

Numbers of brewers varied greatly between places, and from year to year. The court of a large manor in its peak years, like Hawkesbury (Gloucestershire) in the 1390s, would deal with thirty-five brewers in a year.[104] Elsewhere there might be only four. Men were named as brewers, but were usually being made responsible for their wives' breaches of the rules, and the women were named in the court when they were widows or single women. Numbers of brewers tended to fall in the fifteenth century, suggesting not a decline in ale production or drinking but a concentration of the trade in fewer hands, with more specialization and a more pronounced commercialism. Brewers included all ranks of village society, from better-off tenants to landless. At Cleeve Prior in 1405–6 two women, one a widow, and six men were named. Three of the brewers were yardlanders, one was a smallholder, and probably two others held some land. One seems to have been a tenant's son who at one time worked as the lord's swineherd.[105]

The larger scale brewers were supplementing their incomes by selling part of their grain surplus. Two tenants with large holdings at Hampton Lucy (Warwickshire) in 1516–17 each brewed 12 quarters of malt in a year, enough to make 720 gallons, so if the ale was sold at 1*d* per gallon their turnover would have been £3 in a year.[106] They was probably really selling more gallons than they admitted at more than 1*d*. At the other end of the social spectrum brewing and ale-selling could bring a modest income to a poor household ('Poverty and industry' in this chapter).

The alehouses were dwelling houses in which drink was sold. At Burton Dassett Southend such an establishment of the fifteenth century has been excavated and identified by the number of cups found in or near to the house, made of Cistercian ware, the new glazed pottery of the late fifteenth century. The design of the house was unusual with an upper storey reached by an external staircase, and a one-bay hall with a hearth in the corner where the ale may have been served.[107] The alehouses attracted customers by providing space where dice, cards, and other games could be played, though in the view of respectable villagers the establishments encouraged gambling, idleness, and worse when suspicious women were present.

Ale varied in strength, quality, and flavour. Traditionally it was brewed from drage in the champion, barley on the wolds and in the lower Severn valley, and oats in the north of the region. Towards the end of our period, in 1491–2, in the vicinity of Bristol at Almondsbury, the lord of the manor gave the haymakers bread, cheese, butter, and beef, accompanied by *cervisia bera*, meaning beer, a hopped drink originally from the Low Countries and probably spreading from the cosmopolitan port of Bristol.[108] The drink was presumably bought from a

---

[104] TNA, SC2 175/46. [105] WCL, E45a.
[106] WA, ref. 009:1, BA 2636/165/92221.
[107] Palmer and Parkhouse, *Burton Dasett Southend*, pp. 131–4.
[108] A. Sabin, ed., *Some Manorial Accounts of St Augustine's Abbey, Bristol* (Bristol Record Society, 22, 1960), p. 91.

brewer in the village, showing that it was spreading through the countryside. Beer, already popular in eastern England, had arrived and was now about to conquer the west, turning the craft into an industry.[109]

Conclusion

Peasants participated in non-agricultural activities, loosely called industries, and even played an initiating role. Their contribution can be described, but cannot easily be quantified. The 1381 poll tax for Gloucestershire, the record nearest to an occupational census, suggests that 26 per cent of the male population were engaged in some form of industry. This includes both town and country. If the urban element is set aside, the percentage falls to 14 per cent. This is a misleading understatement. The tax records fifty rural brewers, which is a clearly low count for sixty-seven villages. At Kempsford the poll tax identifies three brewers, but the court rolls of 1376–7 name fourteen of them. The comparable figures from Bibury were one brewer in the poll tax and nine in the court records.[110] The tax assessors must have noted the most persistent or the most prominent brewers only, or those exhibiting their ale stake on the day of the assessment. The rest would be entered in the tax list as *cultores* (cultivators), thus hiding from view at least three hundred households with significant involvement in the craft.

The size of the industrial sector would be much expanded if the women identified as wives without reference to an occupation could be included. Wives were active in tasks alongside their husbands, as weaving for example needed two pairs of hands, or they could have practised some completely different skill. The tax collectors cannot be expected to reflect part-time work such as spinning or wood cutting in their one-word occupational descriptions.

Lords made a contribution to industrial development, by building fulling mills, by opening up quarries, developing iron forges, and contributing to the infrastructure of roads, bridges, and ports. Urban entrepreneurs and middlemen marketed the products of pottery kilns and ironworks, and above all co-ordinated the various processes that went into the large scale cloth production in the Stroudwater and Dursley districts. The numerous small-scale industries were not refuges from desperate poverty, but were created by independent producers who developed pottery manufacture, or were able to cultivate flax and hemp and weave linen without being dominated by town-based middlemen. They combined skilled craftsmanship with trade in commodities, so the carpenters from the woodlands provided timber for their buildings. They began a new industry in the

---

[109] Bennett, *Ale, Beer, and Brewsters*, pp. 43–59, 77–97.
[110] *PT*, part 1, pp. 291–2, 294; East Raynham Library, box 43; GA, Badminton muniments, D4431/1/M1/2/1; D678/63.

Cleeve Prior slate quarries, made their own fish ponds, and took up the new craft of beer brewing. The enterprise shown by an isolated craftsman in an unexpected place deserves to be noticed. The lord of Tysoe (Warwickshire) in 1465–6 was rebuilding his windmill, and needed a brass bearing. He would surely have had to commission a specialist founder or bellyeter in a big town? The skills that he needed could be found in the village of Alderminster, where John Tyngker earned his living normally as a tinker, repairing pots and pans in nearby villages.[111]

The best way to assess the importance of industry in peasant society would not be to count the specialist artisans like John Tyngker and calculate them as a percentage of the population, but to estimate the amount of time spent throughout the population on agricultural and non-agricultural tasks. Tyngker might have devoted half of his hours on metalworking, but a weaver spent more time at the loom, while an occasional brewster might produce ale on average a few hours per week. Children, always part of the workforce, helped to make pots. Any figure from these speculations would be impressionistic, but it would be surprising if less than a third of peasants' working time was engaged in non-agricultural tasks. The proportion of rural incomes gained from non-agricultural sources in 1500 has been estimated at 20 per cent.[112]

The other significance of peasant industry was that it put down markers for future development. The theme of this chapter has been innovation: large scale rural clothmaking; the package of techniques used in cruck building; expanding use of stone as a building material; the diffusion of smiths and villages; and the changes in design and quality in rural pottery making, all involved peasant artisans and entrepreneurs of peasant origin. In industry, as in farming, peasants could be initiators.

---

[111] SRO, D641/1/2/275.
[112] J. Oldland, 'The Clothiers' Century, 1450–1550', *Rural History* 29 (2018), pp. 1–22.

10

Peasant outlook, values, perceptions, and attitudes

Discovering the thought processes, mentality, and values of people who did not write is a great challenge for historians. An attempt will be made here to examine the west midland peasants' outlook by dividing up their world into relationships with the state, their lords, and religion, and then enquiring into their perception of the environment, and sense of the individual's role in the family and the community.

Piers Plowman

The poem that scholars have agreed to call *Piers Plowman*, the author of which may have been William Langland, is firmly rooted in the west midlands.[1] The language is the dialect of the west midlands, and the work belongs to a group of alliterative poems characteristic of the region—a typical example of alliteration is the description at the beginning of the poem of the rural scene as a *fair feld full of folk*. A number of the manuscripts of the latest version of the poem, judging from a detailed study of their dialect, seem to have been written in south-west Worcestershire or nearby, around the southern end of the Malvern Hills (see Figure 2.7).[2] A woodland landscape reminiscent of that part of Worcestershire is recalled by references in the poem to a croft, hedges, tree stumps (stocks), a moated house, and a hill called a *berw* (C text) or *bergh* (B text).[3] The author was probably born and brought up in the west-midland region, spent some time in London, and may have returned to his country of origin at least briefly. *Piers Plowman* went through successive revisions, now known as an A text of the 1360s, a B text written in the 1370s, and C text of the 1380s. It may have had local origins, but it was known and read in all parts of England. Piers, a peasant, is a central figure to whom the author attributes a range of attitudes and opinions. An honest and virtuous peasant speaks to us, but Piers's views cannot be treated

---

[1] J.A. Alford, ed., *A Companion to Piers Plowman* (Berkeley, CA, 1988); A. Cole and A. Galloway, eds., *The Cambridge Companion to Piers Plowman* (Cambridge, 2014).
[2] M.L. Samuels, 'Dialect and Grammar', in *Companion*, ed., Alford, pp. 201–21.
[3] R.W.V. Elliott, 'The Langland Country', in *Piers Plowman: Critical Approaches*, edited by S.S. Hussey (London, 1969), pp. 226–44.

uncritically as the voice of the common man. However, the author is unusual in his interest in ordinary people, his idealization of some of them, and his apparent understanding of their lives.[4] Very few peasants could have read the poem, but they had heard about it, and were aware of its contents, judging from letters written at the time of the 1381 revolt.[5]

The poem begins on the Malvern Hills with an imaginary person who falls asleep and has a vision of society. It refers elaborately to the very old idea of three orders.[6] Firstly the hard-working and productive peasants are contrasted with wasters, minstrels, and beggars. They are followed by the clergy, among them friars, priests, and bishops, who are portrayed in unflattering terms. Finally the king appears with his knights, nobles, and councillors, who are said to be potentially beneficial for the rest of society. John Gower, a contemporary of the Piers Plowman poet, made much of the three orders of workers (peasants), those who pray (the clergy), and warriors (secular aristocrats) who were committed to serve each other and receive benefits in return. However, Gower was highly critical of the failure of all three orders to play their part.[7] The *Piers Plowman* poet says that the peasants should work 'for profit of all the people'. In particular, ploughmen were expected 'to till and travail (work)'. This is a static and conservative model, but the poet is very aware of change, so that in his view the mutual obligations are in need of reform; for example, social ills are blamed on the corrupting power of money. In the later version of the poem, the C text, the poet, concerned by any possible association with the revolt of 1381, distances himself from radicalism. He expresses hostility to social mobility, and laments that the offspring of bondmen (serfs) can become bishops.[8]

The peasant Piers Plowman appears towards the end of the fifth section of the poem (in the B text) as the loyal servant of Truth. Piers is presented initially as a ploughman in the sense of a servant or *famulus* whose job was to cultivate a lord's demesne. Unlike some real ploughmen of the 1370s, Piers has stayed with the same employer for many years, and is a contented and motivated worker. A group of virtuous pilgrims ask him to guide them in a search for Truth, but first he must cultivate a half-acre. Some of the pilgrims offer to help in the work, and Piers asks women to sew sacks. Piers rejects the offer of help with ploughing from the

---

[4] Among a number of literary scholars who discuss this theme, M. Stokes, *Justice and Mercy in Piers Plowman: A Reading of the B Text Vision* (London, 1984); R. Lister, 'The Peasants of Piers Plowman and Its Audience', in *Peasants and Countrymen in Literature*, edited by K. Parkinson and M. Priestman (Roehampton, 1982), pp. 71–90.

[5] R.F. Green, 'John Ball's Letters. Literary History and Historical Literature', in *Chaucer's England: Literature in Historical Context* (Minneapolis, 1992), pp. 176–200.

[6] The brief summary that follows is based on the B text: G. Kane and E. Talbot, eds., *Piers Plowman: The B Version* (London, 1975).

[7] D. Green, 'Nobility and Chivalry'; D. Lepine, 'The Papacy, Secular Clergy and Lollardy', in *Historians on John Gower*, edited by S. Rigby and S. Echard (John Gower Society, 12, 2019), pp. 141–65, 243–69.

[8] D. Pearsall, ed., *Piers Plowman: An Edition of the C Text* (London, 1979), pp. 100–1.

knight, on the grounds that an aristocrat protects society and should not do manual work. He renews the three orders contract between peasants and aristocrats by making the knight agree to deal with the idle wasters, to hunt harmful wildlife, and not oppress his tenants, nor ill-treat his bondmen. Later Piers makes a will which takes the form of a contract between him and the church, recalling his prompt payment of tithe, and expects that the parish priest will pray for his soul. Piers speaks with authority in dealing with the knight and priest.

In the ploughing of the half-acre, Piers is represented as a self-sufficient tenant, and no longer as an employee. He owns a plough, a team of oxen, a cart, and a cow and calf, and refers to 'my croft', and 'my hedges'. The half-acre is clearly only a small part of the holding that Piers works. Normally the owner of a plough and cart would have at least a half-yardland (see 'Arable husbandry' in Chapter 6). Piers sets some of the pilgrims to weed and dig, but the wasters refuse to work. Piers shows sympathy for the poor who deserve help, but denounces the workshy, expressing attitudes similar to those found in fourteenth-century legislation at both manorial and national level. Hunger appears as a remedy for those who are idle, and in general food provides insights into social relations. Piers describes his own frugal diet of bread made from beans and bran, oat cakes, dairy produce, and vegetables. He complains that the wasters deserve nothing better than peas and beans. Beggars and labourers express aspiration for a better life by demanding high-quality foods such as white bread and well-cooked meat and fish.

A climax in the poem takes us to the spiritual goal pursued by Piers, an assurance of salvation of his soul. He is promised a pardon, but when he sees the document, he rejects it as inadequate and tears it in half. At this point the person whose dream has provided the substance of the poem wakes, still on the Malvern Hills.

In this complex work of religious literature, the peasant Piers was chosen as a virtuous advocate of a social order based on obligations and reciprocal benefits, untainted by the sins that abounded around him. He stood up for hard work, honesty, independence, and a zealous search for salvation, in contrast with Hawkyn, who unscrupulously sought profit in many spheres, including ignoring boundaries between open-field strips to steal a neighbour's corn. This well-informed contemporary's depiction of peasant ideas is the best contemporary source available to us, though we can supplement and sometimes modify the poet's perspective from other often indirect evidence.

Peasants and the state

Piers Plowman shows respect for the king, and shares with the reformers who were most vocal in the Good Parliament of 1376 a belief that the king could be a force for good if only he was not badly or corruptly advised. A similar analysis was voiced by the rebels of 1381 who sought to remove 'traitors' and forge an alliance between ruler and people.

West-midland peasants were aware of the 1381 revolt, but did not participate fully.[9] Throughout the period under scrutiny they were drawn into the administration of the law at village level in the view of frankpledge held by the lord of the manor at which males at the age of 12 swore 'to bear faith to the lord king of England' to become part of a tithing which was obliged to keep the peace and report wrong-doing. The view was the main point of contact for most peasants with royal justice, but they were also liable to serve on the juries of the royal courts. Jurors who took part in the Worcestershire eyre of 1275 appear in the lay subsidy paying in tax between 8*d* and 10*s*, and mostly between 1*s* 6*d* and 6*s* 0*d*, so they were recruited from both middling and better-off peasants.[10] The rural jurors who took part in the proceedings before the Justices of the Peace in Warwickshire in 1381 were drawn from the upper end of peasant society, with a franklin from Tanworth-in-Arden, a free yardlander from Compton Verney, and the tenant of two free yardlands at Wasperton. Another juror, John Harryes, can be found at Wormleighton owning twenty pigs and twenty other animals.[11] A similar conclusion has been drawn for the peasant jurors in the Gloucestershire quarter sessions in the fifteenth century; one of them was known as a yeoman, husbandman, and tailor, and was said to have overstocked the common at Minsterworth.[12] The jury at the view of frankpledge followed routines of electing a constable (an officer under the king), dealing with small crimes such as minor assaults and thefts, and supervising the self-help police measure of the hue and cry. Occasionally they participated in the enforcement of specific royal statutes, presumably when encouraged to do so by the lord's steward who presided over them. At Blackwell in September 1350, the year after the Ordinance of Labourers had sought to control post-plague wages, sixteen workers, half of them women, were amerced for taking as much as 5*d* per day, and 10*d* per day for a pair of harvesters. In Warwickshire, in cases brought under the Statute of Labourers of 1351 in the Justice of the Peace sessions in the 1350s and 1380s jurors provided information about workers and made judgements on them, although the offenders

---

[9] R.H. Hilton, *Bondmen Made Free: Medieval Peasant Movements and the English Rising of 1381* (London, 1973), p. 165; Z. Razi, 'The Struggles between the Abbots of Halesowen and Their Tenants in The Thirteenth and Fourteenth Centuries', in *Social Relations and Ideas: Essays in Honour of R.H. Hilton*, edited by T.H. Aston and others (Cambridge, 1983), pp. 151–67, especially pp. 165–6.

[10] J. Röhrkarsten, ed., *The Worcester Eyre of 1275* (WHS, new series, 22, 2008); J. Willis Bund and J. Amphlett, eds., *Lay Subsidy Roll for the County of Worcester, circa 1280* (WHS, 1893).

[11] E.G. Kimball, ed., *Rolls of the Warwickshire and Coventry Sessions of the Peace 1377–1397* (DS, 16, 1939), p. 101; for Harryes, Northamptonshire Record Office, Spencer roll 216. On the general finding, J. Masschaele, *Jury, State and Society in Medieval England* (Basingstoke, 2008).

[12] R. Goheen, 'Peasant Politics? Village Community and the Crown in Fifteenth-Century England', *American Historical Review* 96 (1991), p. 48.

were sometimes their neighbours.[13] The peasants on the juries were acting under pressure, but among them would have been those who as employers regarded the labour laws as protecting their interests.[14] Parliamentary legislation took on the problems of vagrancy in the fifteenth century, and again a body of peasant opinion supported measures against idleness, echoing Piers Plowman's criticism of wasters. A year after the statute of 1495 'against vagabonds and beggars' the twelve jurors of Ombersley (Worcestershire) ordered the constable to identify vagabonds, beggars, and strangers, and not to permit them 'to live here against the statute'. They were also in favour of enforcing the statute's provisions on servants' wages.[15] In dealing with the law of tenancy in the manor court, peasants encountered common law practices, and seemed aware indirectly of the results of Edward I's legislation.[16]

Military service carried burdens which were unlikely to have been welcomed, though they did not necessarily arouse organized opposition. Armies of foot soldiers could be raised by commissions of array, which gave a shire a quota of troops. In 1345 Edward III needed archers for his French campaigns, and fifty were to be supplied by Gloucestershire, forty by Warwickshire, and twenty from Worcestershire, reflecting the unequal populations of those counties The quotas were subdivided among the villages, so in response to a 1295 requirement by Edward I's government for a Welsh campaign four soldiers were to be recruited in Halesowen, but the four were defrauded by a villager who offered to go in their place for a fee, and then disappeared.[17] In preparation for military service peasants were expected to possess arms, and to acquire skills with the bow at the village butts. They seemed to accept this expense and trouble, but in varying degrees of enthusiasm, depending on their perception of possible threats. The military survey in 1522 in a sample of twenty villages mainly in the north and west of Worcestershire assessed the taxable wealth of 665 people. Almost a half, 304, owned arms of some kind; forty-two, mostly gentry, had armour. The peasants (157 of them) were mainly armed with bills (long poles with a blade attached), and 105 were described as archers.[18] In Gloucestershire little commitment to military preparedness was apparent in twenty villages in the safety of the eastern Cotswolds, with twenty armed men from 305 householders, but in the west in villages such as

---

[13] WCL, E16; Kimball, ed., *Sessions of the Peace*, pp. 95, 159, 163, 166.; B.H. Putnam, ed., *The Enforcement of the Statutes of Labourers during the First Decade after the Black Death* (New York, 1908), Appendix, pp. 223–7.

[14] L.R. Poos, 'The Social Context of the Statute of Labourers Enforcement', *Law and History Review* 1 (1983), pp. 27–52.

[15] WA, ref. 705:56, BA 3910/22(x).

[16] R. Smith, 'The English Peasantry, 1250–1650', in *The Peasantries of Europe*, edited by T. Scott (Harlow, 1998), pp. 33–71, especially pp. 353–4.

[17] H.J. Hewitt, *The Organization of War under Edward III, 1338–62* (Manchester, 1966), pp. 36–47; G.C. Homans, *English Villagers of the Thirteenth Century* (Harvard, 1941), p. 330.

[18] M.A. Faraday, ed., *Worcestershire Taxes in the 1520s* (WHS, new series, 19, 2003), pp. 1–21.

Blaisdon and Churcham almost everyone owned weapons, presumably reflecting the nearness of the Welsh border.[19] War was usually distant, but impinged on the countryside when grain for feeding soldiers was taken compulsorily, in return for promises of compensation which was often delayed and then inadequate. A peasant became a victim of purveyance when a quarter of wheat was taken from John Jones of Compton Verney in 1347 by the sheriff of Warwickshire.[20] The lords of manors fended off demands for much larger amounts with bribes to the purveyors, which peasants could not easily afford.

Peasants assisted the state, under some compulsion, in assessing and collecting direct taxes. In the lay subsidies up to 1332 local assessors had a role, and subtaxers were named in the 1327 lists. The value of movable goods was calculated for each householder, and a fraction of the value was due in tax, a twentieth in 1327, and a fifteenth in 1332. The poorer villagers were exempt. A new approach taken in 1334 persisted for the whole medieval period, with a quota of taxation assigned to each vill, often within the range of £1 10s 0d to £6. The vill was told to make its own assessments of individuals, and although the tax was called 'the fifteenth', vills calculated individual obligations in any way they chose. The villagers would rather not have paid the taxes, which came at irregular intervals, and sometimes in a cluster, but they seem to have accepted their duty, and perhaps were convinced that the community of the realm had given its consent in parliament on each occasion.[21] They did not find this extension of self-government difficult, as they were used to apportioning lump sums in their payments to the lord such as tallage, and they delivered the money on time. In contrast the poll taxes in 1379 and 1381 were widely evaded, because the tax seemed unjust, assessments were not sufficiently graduated with very few exemptions, and the local community had little part in the administration. The lay subsidy continued at the same level of assessment for decades, and vills petitioned for abatements, leading to the reduction of the burden for the whole country in 1433 and 1446, with some allowance for the changed circumstances of individual communities.[22]

Did the taxpayers in each vill believe that the lay subsidy was fair and acceptable? This was a matter for the internal government of the village, not the lord of the manor. A dispute at Quinton (Warwickshire) in 1430 reveals the lord complaining to the vill that he was expected to contribute too large a share. The disagreement revealed that the tax was based on each taxpayer contributing 4d for each large animal (cattle and horses). This would mean that a wealthy tenant with eight

---

[19] R. Hoyle, ed., *The Military Survey of Gloucestershire, 1522* (GRS, 6, 1993), pp. 72–85, 87–93, 195–207.
[20] J.R. Maddicott, *The English Peasantry and the Demands of the Crown* (Past and Present Supplement, no. 1, 1975), pp. 15–34; TNA, E213/382.
[21] W.M. Ormrod, 'England in the Middle Ages', in *The Rise of the Fiscal State in Europe c.1200–1815*, edited by R. Bonney (Oxford, 1991), pp. 19–52.
[22] M. Forrest, 'Patterns of Economic Change in the South-West during the Fifteenth Century', *EcHR* 70 (2017), pp. 423–51.

cattle and four horses would pay 4s, and a cottager with a cow, 4d, which seems transparent and reflected unequal wealth.[23]

Some villages lacked clarity in their assessment and seemed to favour the better-off. A rare list of taxpayers has survived for Brandon (Warwickshire) in 1497.[24] It is headed 'The sessement of the xv peny', still preserving the memory of the 'fifteenth'. The total was for £2 13s 3d, and it covered the two vills of Brandon and Bretford. In 1334 Brandon had paid £3 10s 0d and Bretford £2 1s 6d, making £5 11s 6d.[25] The drastic reduction must mean that the authorities had been persuaded that Bretford, once a small functioning market town, had lost most of its population and taxable value. In the fourteenth century seventeen people were taxed at Bretford, but in 1497 only two Bretford taxpayers were included.

The village community of Brandon, represented no doubt by its leading figures such as Richard Collett and Thomas Bossy, decided how much their neighbours should contribute. There were thirty-five assessments, mostly named individuals, but 'two widows' were not named, and three pieces of land were assessed without a tenant or owner. There was no appraisal of goods, or counting of animals, but instead payments seem to have been based on impressionistic valuations of land in round shillings. The six top payers were rated at between 3s and 9s, then seventeen at 1s, 2s, or 2s 6d, and another twelve paid between 2d and 6d (Table 10.1). These included the widows, together with labourers and cottagers.

Table 10.1 Tax assessment at Brandon (Warwickshire) 1332 and 1497

1332									
Tax paid	2d	3d	4d	6d	10d	1s–1s 11d	2s–2s 11d	3s–12s	total
No. of payers									
Brandon	-	-	-	-	-	11	2	8	21
Bretford	-	-	-	-	1	8	3	5	17
1497									
Tax paid	2d	3d	4d	6d	10d	1s	2s–2s 11d	3s–9s	total
No. of payers									
Brandon and Bretford	3	2	6	1	-	12	5	6	35

Sources: Carter, ed., Lay Subsidy (1332), pp. 42–3; UNMSC, MiM 128/6.

Contemporaries said that the leading villagers did not pay their fair share, and it seems unlikely that a substantial leaseholder like Richard Collett was only four times wealthier than the average villager. The people at the bottom might appear to have been making a token payment, but 4d was a day's wages, and before 1334 the least well-off were completely exempt (see Table 10.1). The leading villagers

---

[23] Magdalen College, Oxford, Quinton EP 35/9.   [24] UNMSC, MiM 128/6.
[25] R.E. Glasscock, ed., *The Lay Subsidy of 1334* (British Academy Records of Social and Economic History, new series, 11, 1975), p. 323.

made a bargain with the state in which they were given the authority to govern their community, and efficiently delivered the agreed amount of taxes. At places like Brandon, the well-to-do paid less than was just, and the poor had to accept regressive taxation.

From around 1200 peasants were gradually being included in the political life of the kingdom. Magna Carta made concessions to 'free men', a category mainly confined to the aristocracy; however, all those holding land freely, including many peasants, were being brought within the jurisdiction of the royal courts. Peasants were expected to pay direct taxes in 1207, 1225, and 1232. King John in an extraordinary episode in 1209 during his conflict with the Pope insisted that all free men should swear an oath of allegiance to him.[26] Peasants' interests were affected by the agitations over Forest Law after 1217, and in the west midlands the forests of Horwell and Ombersley in Worcestershire were disafforested (after a large payment) in 1218.[27] The king's influence was felt in particular over the royal demesne manors such as Bromsgrove and King's Norton in Worcestershire, Feckenham in the same county, and in Gloucestershire King's Barton and the forest of Kingswood attached to Bristol Castle. Tenants on such demesne manors were not subject to the disadvantages of serfdom, and peasants on former royal demesnes (ancient demesne) valued the protection from lords' arbitrary demands that the king might provide. Changes in the law, such as the rules relating to enclosure of common land (in 1236), royal enquiries into the judicial power of lords (from 1278) and the growing number of direct tax demands all pushed peasants into contact with politics at the highest level.

Did peasants take sides in aristocratic disputes, both in opposition to the crown, and between factions? Lists of rebels made after the collapse of the baronial reform movement of 1265 consisted mainly of knights and gentry who had fought for Simon de Montfort, but 'the men of Bromsgrove and [King's] Norton' were included.[28] The people of this royal manor were taking a bold position as Henry III in 1263 had granted the manor to Roger Mortimer, a royal supporter. Perhaps, as was said by the villagers of Peatling Magna (Leicestershire) also in 1265, the people of Bromsgrove believed that the barons were acting for 'the welfare of the community of the realm'.[29] Regard for Simon de Montfort was widely shared, as individuals from the region experienced miracles performed at the tomb of the baronial leader when he became a posthumous popular saint. Roger Horsman of Buckland in Gloucestershire and a woman from Dunchurch in Warwickshire

---

[26] M. Jurkowski, C.L. Smith, and D. Crook, *Lay Taxes in England and Wales, 1188-1688* (Kew, 1998), pp. 7-8, 12-15; J.R. Maddicott, 'The Oath of Marlborough, 1209: Fear, Government and Popular Allegiance in the Reign of King John', *EHR* 126 (2011), pp. 281-318.

[27] R.R. Darlington, ed., *The Cartulary of Worcester Cathedral Priory (Register 1)* (Pipe Roll Society, 76, 1962-3), p. 173.

[28] J. Hunt, 'Families at War: Royalists and Montfortians in the West Midlands', *Midland History* 22 (1997), pp. 1-34, especially p. 4.

[29] D.A. Carpenter, 'English Peasants in Politics, 1258-1267', *P&P* 136 (1992), pp. 3-42.

were cured of paralysis after they visited the earl's tomb.[30] They and their neighbours appealed for the 'saint's' help because they were convinced of his virtue.

In the early years of Edward II's reign the earl of Warwick, Guy de Beauchamp, formed part of the magnate faction opposed to the king's misrule under the influence of Piers Gaveston. Gaveston was seized by the barons in Oxfordshire in 1312, and taken by way of Elmley Castle (Beauchamp's Worcestershire stronghold) to Warwick where he was executed. Adam Lese of Charlton in Cropthorne (near Elmley) appeared before the manorial court in October 1315 accused of 'trespasses that he did in slandering and other iniquities towards the earl of Warwick and other magnates promulgated by him for the whole time past'. Lese was ordered to pay £4, a huge sum, due in three instalments over a year. He would have had problems in paying as he was assessed for the subsidy a few years later at 14d, but he was eventually pardoned by his lord, Worcester Cathedral Priory, and let off the amercement. The dispute over Gaveston's influence divided local opinion as the then bishop of Worcester was a staunch royalist, but the Priory seems to have taken a different view judging from its treatment of Lese. A few years later some Worcestershire peasants supported Thomas of Lancaster in his rebellion against Edward II in 1321–2.[31]

Thomas Beauchamp, earl of Warwick between 1369 and 1401, an opponent of Richard II, may have stirred popular interest in politics in the region, and certainly his tenants and supporters, and those of his rivals, were active in local disputes.[32] More is known about the fifteenth-century peasants who became part of the affinities recruited by aristocrats (see 'Peasants and lords' in this chapter), but a rising in Gloucestershire in 1463–4 supported by peasants, artisans, and merchants seems to have been a popular movement, though with unknown motives. There are more indications of political activity at the end of the Wars of the Roses. In February 1485, when Richard III was establishing his rule after usurping the throne in 1483, John Lyndrych of Alcester complained that by order of Robert Charlette, a leading Cleeve Prior villager, he had ridden round Worcestershire ' labouring (we might say lobbying or persuading) various gentlemen and officers of the lord king'. He did this on behalf of a relation of Robert's who had committed 'various trespasses' against the king. John claimed expenses of 2s 8d and 6s 8d 'for his labour'.[33] Evidently villagers might be drawn into the suspicion and distrust surrounding the king's rule at local level. A year later, when Humphrey Stafford launched a rebellion against Henry VII his followers, presumably previously

---

[30] J.O. Halliwell, ed., *The Chronicle of William de Rishanger... The Miracles of Simon de Montfort* (Camden Society, 1840), pp. 70, 100–1.
[31] Hereford Cathedral Library, R1162; C. Valente, *The Theory and Practice of Revolt in Medieval England* (Aldershot, 2003), pp. 141–6.
[32] A.K. Grundy, *Richard II and the Rebel Earl* (Cambridge, 2013), pp. 128, 169–70; Valente, *Practice of Revolt*, pp. 189–91.
[33] R.H. Hilton, *The English Peasantry in the Later Middle Ages* (Oxford, 1975), pp. 71–3; WCRO, CR1886/175.

recruited into his affinity, included a number of Worcestershire peasants (see 'Peasants and lords' in this chapter).

Peasants had an important role in working for the state as jurors, soldiers, taxpayers, and tax gatherers. They were not blindly following instructions, but could take sides in the various political contests. They probably saw themselves as part of the 'community of the realm' to use contemporary language, and as participants in 'political society' in current historical terms.[34]

Peasants and lords

The social cohesion idealized in *Piers Plowman* in the late fourteenth century worked imperfectly. Lords were conscious of their deficiencies, like Bishop Wakefield of Worcester, making his will in 1395, who left £100 to be distributed among 'my poor tenants, and especially those who were injured by me'.[35] What level of consciousness did peasants have of their ill-treatment by lords: Were they simply discontented, or did they make serious criticisms of the social hierarchy?

Lords could behave in a paternalistic way, as if they were conscious of the need to win over tenants and prevent resentment or unrest. There were (rare) moments of compassion when individual poor tenants were given grain.[36] Tenants performing their labour services of mowing hay were treated to a meal, as at Idlicote (Warwickshire) in 1279 when they received a wether (adult sheep), a cheese and eight white loaves, and afterwards they could take a bundle of grass for their own use. These rewards which are recorded on many manors with variations in details, could resemble a competitive sporting event as each mower lifted as much grass as possible on his scythe.[37] The manorial administrators sometimes used language to soften the harshness of demands, calling the much disliked tallage 'aid' or a 'gift'.

A 'good lord' showed flexibility in conducting manorial business. Decisions about hereditary succession to customary holdings were left to the jury in the manor court. Lords facilitated succession planning by allowing the reversion of holdings after the death or withdrawal of a sitting tenant. A widow who was found to be 'corrupt' by engaging in sexual relations lost her holding, but could recover the land with a fine. Subletting, though forbidden, was tolerated in practice. Lords resisted fragmentation of holdings which threatened the integrity of tenures, but when demand for land fell after 1350 a lord would offer tenants a few acres to add to their existing holdings, allowing a vacant holding to be split.

---

[34] T. Johnson, *Law in Common: Legal Cultures in Late-Medieval England* (Oxford, 2020), pp. 269–75.
[35] W.P. Marett, ed., *A Calendar of the Register of Henry Wakefield Bishop of Worcester 1375–95* (WHS, new series, 7, 1972), pp. xliv–xlvi.
[36] B. Wells-Furby, *The Berkeley Estate 1281–1417: Its Economy and Development* (BGAS, 2012), p. 130.
[37] *WHR*, pp. 194, 231, 248, 275, 286, 294, 310.

A lord by these measures served the estate's own interests in maintaining an income stream from rents, but the tenants also gained.

On their side, tenants seem to have accepted lords' decisions which were potentially offensive to them. Evictions were quite unusual, and usually followed flagrant breaches of the customary rules. The neighbours may have approved as they could be adversely affected by an absent or neglectful tenant. Tenants collaborated with a lord, usually accepting the duty of holding office in the lord's administration, as reeve of the manor or a juror in the court, partly because they benefited in terms of status and material gain.

Tenants could show respect for their lord with acts of deference such as new year gifts, received by William More, Prior of Worcester Cathedral Priory. The donors in 1524 and 1525 included well-heeled people such as officials of the Priory, or wealthy tenants of the bishopric estate for which More acted as surveyor. Ordinary peasant tenants of the Priory's manors of Crowle and Grimley gave More a capon or two, and a pig was provided by Thomas Turnar of Grimley, perhaps in the hope of a favour in return.[38]

Manorial courts accepted in a matter-of-fact way that a tenant was receiving support from some local member of the gentry. At Sambourn (Warwickshire), where Evesham Abbey was the lord, in 1473 Joan Mulleward, widow of John Mulleward, was given licence to live off the manor and sublet her cottage 'at the instance of Humphrey Stafford' (lord of Grafton near Bromsgrove and steward of a number of estates). At Long Marston in 1391 John Smyth was accused of causing 'waste and destruction' on his yardland holding, and William Grevel, the Campden wool merchant who founded a line of landed gentry, intervened to arrange for Smyth to make a financial settlement with his lord, Winchcomb Abbey.[39] Evidently peasants found it useful in dealing with their lords to cultivate influential allies.

The military survey of 1522 for Worcestershire took an interest in those who were attached to local gentry because in the event of an emergency, men with military capabilities would serve in the retinues of such important local figures as Humphrey Stafford, Gilbert Talbot, and William Compton, all knights. The largest group of retainers belonged to the affinity of Thomas Grey, marquis of Dorset, some in the town of Droitwich, but also in neighbouring villages, with eight in Hanbury, seven in Feckenham, and four in Bentley Pauncefoot.[40] Grey's large affinity gave him a reputation for promoting disorder, but mainly around his base in Leicestershire. Clearly peasants of all kinds were prepared to attach themselves to these leading figures, providing them with support when serving on juries, or turning out with weapons. They divided their loyalties because they had

---

[38] E.S. Fegan, ed., *Journal of Prior William More* (WHS, 1914), p. 203.
[39] SCLA, DR5/2537; GA, D678/98C.
[40] Faraday, ed., *Worcestershire Taxes*, pp. 8–9, 35–6, 40–2, 60–2.

also sworn to be the faithful men of the lord of their manor. An extreme example of the problems arising were the bands, better described as gangs, assembled by Nicholas Burdet to launch two raids on Shipston-on-Stour in 1413, in which two Shipston tenants were killed. Burdet's followers included William Juggement and John Bromley of Cleeve Prior. Bromley appears in the Cleeve records as John Muleward, who held the manorial mill on lease. Juggement was a smallholder. They went hunting together, breaking their lord's privilege of free warren.[41] Their lord was of course Worcester Cathedral Priory, and the victims of the raids at Shipston belonged to a faction among the Priory tenants which supported their lord against a group of rebels. The men who in 1486 turned out in aid of Humphrey Stafford in his rebellion against Henry VII were respectable tenants of Bromsgrove and Hanley Castle, who included a juror, a bailiff, and a forester.[42]

Strong loyalty to a lord by peasants was reported in the petition of widows of Painswick (Gloucestershire) in 1442, after sixteen men went to war in France with their lord, John Talbot, and eleven of them did not return. The widows asked for, and received, special consideration because of their loss, including exemption from heriot and the custom that they would lose their free bench if they remarried.[43] Peasants were prepared to follow their lord into danger, and to develop relationships of service with lords who could offer patronage. These relationships could have been based on calculations of self-interest, but they could also become involved in ill-judged ventures.

Peasants seem to have adopted elements of aristocratic language so that a word such as 'honourably' was introduced into the court records as if it was used by jurors or other suitors. Peasants may have had regard for aristocratic symbolism, like the heraldic shield which featured on a copper alloy harness mount from Dassett Southend.[44] A seal used by Tanworth-in-Arden peasants in 1335 and 1346 included a hunting motif, a hawk seizing a duck, recalling an aristocratic sport. Others incorporated into their design a shield.[45] Peasant houses were divided into halls and chambers, just like the residences of the aristocracy, though only one of the many houses excavated at Burton Dassett Southend followed the full aristocratic model of a three-fold plan with hall, chamber, and rooms at the

---

[41] TNA, KB9/202/42, 43, 44; *Calendar of Patent Rolls, 1413–16*, p. 111; *1416–22*, p. 147; WCL E45, E46, E49, E51, E52. Their animals damaged crops when they grazed on the land of both lord and tenants, but that was not unusual.

[42] C. Dyer, 'The Political Life of the Fifteenth-Century English Village', *The Fifteenth Century* 4 (2004), pp. 135–57, especially p. 149.

[43] W. St Clair Baddeley, *A Cotteswold Manor: Being the History of Painswick* (London, 1929), pp. 105–6.

[44] Palmer and Parker, *Burton Dassett Southend*, small finds report can be accessed at https://doi.org/10.5284/1083492.

[45] A. Sutherland, 'Non-Armorial Personal Seals and the Expression of Identity in Rural English Communities, c.1175–1349' (PhD Dissertation, University of Leicester, 2020), Appendix, pp. 137–55.

end for services[46] (Figure 5.1). Perhaps aristocratic culture was pervasive and unavoidable, and a few peasants, with difficulty, promoted themselves into the gentry.

Peasants had good reason to distrust and resent their lords. They knew that in speech and writing they were described with words that disparaged them: villein, serf, neif, rustic, and churl were all insults. Lords seemed to relish assertions of their authority over customary tenants, like the announcements made in manorial courts at intervals that the neifs, their goods and chattels and holdings, had been seized into the lord's hands. A rare direct encounter between lord and peasant has been recorded by an abbot of Westminster, William de Curtlington, who met Henry Melksop of Todenham (Gloucestershire) in 1321. The abbot told him of a generous (in the abbot's view) offer to cancel a debt of accumulated payments from the customary tenants who had refused selectively to do some labour services they regarded as unjust. Melksop 'did not deign to open his mouth to thank us'. Melksop presumably thought that the tenants had been wronged by the original demand for services, and therefore no payment was justified, and no thanks were required. The angry abbot withdrew the offer to cancel the debt. It would be hard to imagine a wider social gap than that separating a customary peasant with a holding of 27 acres and the great lord of a huge estate.[47]

In addition to claims to legal control, assertions that the property of the unfree belonged to the lord, and expectations of tenants' gratitude, lords could seize opportunities to make impositions. Officials of Worcester Cathedral Priory in 1314 decided at Alveston (Warwickshire) that seven yardlands that had paid 6s 8d per annum should have their rents raised to 10s, and at Harvington rents of six half-yardlands once set at 10s were increased to 12s to reach their 'true value'. At Cleeve Prior in 1378 the succession to a half-yardland was disputed. A tenant was ejected and the rightful heir installed, only to be charged a fine of 20s at a time when a fine was usually six capons.[48] A lord could arbitrarily increase dues like Winchcomb Abbey's officials moving from manor to manor on the estate in 1405, charging a leirwite of 20s (normally 2s), marriage fines of 20s and £4, and unusually high entry fines. These charges are just examples from many similar episodes after 1349. Although competition to acquire land had fallen, lords were still making high demands, using their social power to counteract the economic pressure to reduce rents.[49]

The tenants' response to such assertiveness was to attempt to bargain, and to react to unrealistic demands by quietly refusing to comply. This was easier to carry out after 1349 when tenants became scarce. A tenant would agree to take a holding provided there were no labour services attached, and no payment of tallage (this was in 1362, immediately after the second outbreak of plague), or if a

---

[46] Palmer and Parker, *Burton Dassett Southend*, p. 73.
[47] B. F. Harvey, *Westminster Abbey and its Estates in the Middle Ages* (Oxford, 1977), p. 231.
[48] WCL, E7, E28.   [49] GA, D678/61.

lord decided to increase the rent on a vacant holding, no tenant stepped forward.[50] Lords threatened the relatives of serfs who had left the manor with financial penalties unless they secured their return, but no serfs returned and no penalties were levied.

The campaign against the common oven at Cleeve Prior shows how tenants could quietly secure a concession, but also demonstrates the tenacity of a determined lord. The common oven was like the lord's mill, a seigneurial monopoly. The lord rented out a smallholding on which an oven was built, and its tenant undertook to bake the tenants' loaves, knowing that the lord would enforce the 'suit of oven', that is to compel villagers to use the common oven. Tenants were not allowed to have ovens in their homes. The rent for the oven at Cleeve was 6s 8d in the early fourteenth century, falling later to 5s reflecting the decline in the number of households. The tenant of the oven did not need to bake well, and in 1384 the whole community brought a plea of trespass against the baker for the poor quality of the bread.

The tenants resisted by not sending their loaves, thereby reducing the oven's income so that its tenant could not afford repairs. As the building and the service it provided deteriorated, the tenants were even more justified in baking at home. This cycle was evident in 1340–1 when the tenant failed to repair the bakehouse, and 'served his neighbours badly', so the villagers 'withdrew their suit'. This recurred in the 1350s, and again after the oven was repaired in 1398, when tenants were reminded to bring their bread to be baked. In 1403, with the common oven in disrepair, Nicholas Tailor was amerced for building an oven on his holding 'against the custom of the manor'. The problem was settled by compromise in 1412. The lord gave a licence to twenty-one tenants to build bakehouses on their holdings, and they paid sums of 2d, 3d, and 4d for the concession. This charge became an annual additional rent and was still being paid ninety years later.[51] The lord lost his monopoly, but not his revenue, as the accumulated licence fees brought in as much money as the common oven had done. The tenants gained the principle of baking their bread as they wished, and removing a humiliating restriction. They had achieved this goal by the tactic of co-ordinated non-co-operation.

The monopoly of the oven was only one example of the many impositions and restrictions to which peasants objected, and which they resisted by breaking rules, taking their corn to mills other than their lord's, selling animals without paying tolls, felling trees on customary land without permission, and many other small-scale actions or inactions. These were not just avoiding payment, but often arose from a point of principle. If we take all aspects of the lord–tenant relationship, and identify the points of friction that were most often singled out for protest or at least non-compliance, it is possible to suggest their alternative view of

---

[50] WCL, E20; E28.
[51] The whole series of Cleeve court records from E1 to E46; C559; C563.

lordship. They did not express the radical rejection of lordship like rebels in south-eastern England in 1381. They could however envisage a world in which lords received cash rents from their tenants, without all the extra dues associated with servility. Free tenants paid a rent and a relief (a year's rent) on taking on a holding, and all tenants aspired to that simple and honourable position. The customary tenants' hostility towards particular obligations can be identified from thirteenth-century agreements made by individuals to buy exemption from labour services, and after 1350 the dues that they chose not to pay if they were negotiating to take a holding, or the payments that were refused collectively, or those that were concealed. These included recognitions (paid collectively to a new lord), tallage, marriage fines, tolls on the sale of animals, labour services, chevage (head money for being absent from the manor), suit of mill, woodpenny, and others. They could still campaign for the reduction in the cash 'rent of assize', leading to such sharp confrontations as the bargaining at Lighthorne (Warwickshire) in which the tenants threatened in 1437 to leave the village, compelling the lord to reduce the rent of each yardland from 15s 6d per annum to 10s 6d. Tenants at Cheltenham refused to pay some rents and it needed an arbitration between 1445 and 1452 to bring the rent total down from just over £10 to £6 13s 4d.[52]

Entry fines could be high, over £10 per yardland before 1350, but fines do not seem to have been refused by tenants, nor were demands made for their removal. The market forces that usually decided the level of fines was apparently accepted as a fact of life. Heriots were more controversial, although they were supposed to be paid by free tenants and therefore not usually regarded as a mark of servile status. They represented a considerable burden, as tenants with multiple holdings would owe a 'best beast' for each holding resulting in two or three oxen or other valuable animals worth as much as 30s being taken by the lord. Tenants would arrange with the lord to pay a fixed sum in cash instead of an animal, and another route to avoid the full impact was for an incoming tenant to pay an entry fine which supposedly included a sum for the heriot. Families at Ombersley resorted to subterfuge, as after 1464 a growing number of tenants were claimed to have nothing more valuable than a sheep as their 'best beast'. The deception was exposed in 1478 by Thomas Jones, who had been an unsuccessful claimant for a half-yardland holding, and offered to pay the lord 5s to compensate him for the inadequate pair of sheep worth 20d paid by the family of his predecessor, Richard Jones.[53] The lord, Evesham Abbey, responded weakly to this revelation of fraudulent practices, and continued to accept sheep from holdings likely to have possessed oxen and valuable horses.

---

[52] R.H. Hilton, 'Gloucester Abbey Leases of the Late Thirteenth Century', in *English Peasantry*, pp. 139–60 (individual agreements); Hilton, *English Peasantry*, pp. 67–9 (collective negotiations).
[53] WA, ref. 705:56, BA 3910/27 (xvii).

Some places developed a tradition of resistance and rebellion, notably Halesowen and Thornbury (see 'Serfdom, 1200–1540' in Chapter 3). The tenants of the manor of Blackwell, which included two villages, Blackwell and Old Shipston, and the small town of New Shipston, resisted and protested repeatedly. The chapel at Shipston served as a symbol of self-government and independence before 1300. Campaigns of non-co-operation on such matters as marriage fines and suit of mill were active from the early fourteenth century onwards. The antagonisms were notable for acts and threats of violence against manorial officials. Strong language was used, with expressions of contempt for the lord in 1342, and in 1378 a demand that they should explain to the lord in person their refusal to do weeding services was described by a tenant as 'foolishness'. The townspeople's discontent encouraged their rural neighbours. The townsmen claimed that Shipston had been a royal estate, and this mistaken belief, with its implications of 'ancient demesne' privileges may have raised the peasants' hopes.[54] These prominent examples of conflict were not exceptional aberrations, as dozens of villages won small victories in their tussles with their lords.

Blackwell and Shipston were not threatened by enclosure around 1500, as was the case in dozens of champion villages, but while some seem to have been undermined and overwhelmed by pressure from their lords, organized resistance was attempted at Shuckburgh (Warwickshire) and with success at Longborough (Gloucestershire).[55] Truculent refusals to pay modest rents or perform a few labour services were much more common than strong opposition to enclosure and usurpation of common pasture which threatened the very existence of the village.

To conclude, deferential peasants and paternalistic lords formed part of the story of west-midland rural society in our period. However, if they were to maintain their flow of income lords had to maintain pressure on their tenants. Peasants established limits to co-operation, and pursued selective campaigns against impositions such as suit of oven. Their goal was that free and customary tenants alike would owe an annual cash rent (preferably a low one) with perhaps a payment at the beginning of a tenancy; in short, peasants looked forward to the day when all tenants would be freeholders.

Peasants and religion

The church in the early Middle Ages was hierarchical, ruled from the top, promoted by kings, and developed a rural network of churches under aristocratic

---

[54] WCL, E14, E28; C. Dyer, 'Small-Town Conflict in the Later Middle Ages: Events at Shipston-on-Stour', *Urban History* 9 (1992), pp. 183–210; Hilton, *English Peasantry*, p. 61.

[55] C. Dyer, *An Age of Transition?* (Oxford, 2005), pp. 67–70; C. Dyer, *A Country Merchant* (Oxford, 2012), pp. 171–2.

patronage. In the later Middle Ages, parish churches were propertied institutions with rights to collect tithe, and had often begun as profitable assets of landed estates. Peasants were expected to learn from the church's teaching, observe its moral codes, attend its services, and fund its clergy through tithes and rent. Given these entrenched institutions and their powerful grip on society, how could peasants have any influence on religious life?

In the twelfth and thirteenth centuries, parishioners, who originally had a very limited role, were increasingly active in the management of religious life. They could take initiatives, for example, founding chapels to fill gaps when small villages and hamlets lacked their own places of worship. In eastern England, chapels were sometimes endowed with collective grants of land by peasant communities. The same may have happened in our region at Oldbury, on the Halesowen estate, where the chapel was built on customary land which was presumably once part of a peasant holding.[56] Most of the dozens of chapels in our region are very poorly documented, or are known only from archaeological evidence, which suggests that they were founded informally, without written grants of land. The chapel of Shipston-on-Stour in the parish of Tredington, was apparently in existence by the twelfth century, serving the village before the foundation of the town. The rector of Tredington resented the loss as part of his parish slipped out of his control, and the lord of the manor feared that the chapel enabled his tenants to assert some independence, especially as the chaplain was appointed and paid by the community.[57] A common ambition among those attending chapels was to gain rights of burial, but the rectors opposed the idea as mortuary payments accompanied each funeral. The burials that are sometimes found in excavations at chapels show that congregations might flout the rules.[58]

In the later Middle Ages the church expected that the lay parishioners would be responsible for the upkeep of the church building and its goods (furnishings, ornaments, and vestments), and for the churchyard. The chancel would be built and maintained by the rector, leaving the rest of the building, that is nave, aisles, porch, tower, and steeple to the laity. Churchwardens were responsible for gathering funds and spending them on the parish's needs, for which they would be answerable to the parishioners, sometimes preparing written financial accounts.[59] Lay parishioners also participated in church courts, where they provided information about the sins of their neighbours, and commented on the state of the church building and the conduct of the clergy (see 'Character of family life' in Chapter 5).

The clergy could represent the aristocratic domination of the church because the sons of landed gentry were sometimes presented to a benefice on their family's

---

[56] *VCH Worcs*, vol. 3, p. 150.   [57] Dyer, 'Small-Town Conflict', pp. 196–7.
[58] Such discoveries have been made at Lark Stoke (Warwickshire).
[59] C. Burgess, 'Pre-Reformation Churchwardens' Accounts and Parish Government: Lessons from London and Bristol', *EHR* 117 (2002), pp. 306–32.

estate. A rural rectory could resemble a secular manor, with a glebe that functioned as a demesne, and peasant tenants who owed rents and services. The rectory could be built in the style of a manor house, and the household staffed with servants like that of a manorial lord.

However, the social distance between peasants and clergy was not always so great. Many glebes were no larger than a peasant holding, and the parish clergy followed the same farming routines as their peasant neighbours. Often rich rectors were absentees, and the clergyman who served the parish was a stipendiary priest of modest status. A growing number of rich rectories were taken over by monasteries, who appointed vicars inferior to rectors in status and income. In larger parishes a team of clergy were carrying out a variety of duties, including priests serving chantries for annual stipends not much larger than the wages of a skilled artisan. By the fourteenth century a growing number of the ordained clergy were of peasant origin, even the sons of serfs, who had attended local schools (see 'Social mobility' in Chapter 4). The combination of these low-born clergy and the management of parish life by the community leads to the conclusion that local churches were no longer under complete aristocratic domination.

The region's most informative churchwardens' accounts come from Halesowen, beginning in 1487.[60] Halesowen's large and impressive church building stood near the centre of an extensive parish with a population in the region of 1,500 (Figure 10.1). The small borough occupied streets around the church, but most of the parishioners lived in a dozen hamlets and villages. The widely spread settlements developed their own sense of belonging, and three of them, Frankley, Oldbury, and Romsley, had their own chapels. Frankley's chapel even had its own churchwardens. The outlying chapels acknowledged their connection to Halesowen by paying for lights in the parish church. The Halesowen churchwardens, who each served for a year or two, represented a cross-section of rural society, including the richest villager John Mucklowe, who paid 7s to the lay subsidy of 1524 (his goods had been valued at £14), but the majority of wardens were of more modest means and contributed between 1s and 3s 6d. Henry Melley, who paid 1s tax on his lands, had inherited two half-yardlands held in villeinage in 1520, and a free holding of unknown size, so he was well-provided. One churchwarden was assessed in the lay subsidy on wages and paid 4d.[61] For comparison a half of the twenty-one churchwardens who appear in the fifteenth-century Hartlebury church court records held two yardlands or above (not a very large holding in this village, but still quite substantial), so there was a bias towards the better-off, but five had half-yardlands or cottages.[62]

---

[60] F. Somers, ed., *Halesowen Churchwardens' Accounts (1487–1582)* (WHS, 1952, 1953).

[61] M.A. Faraday, ed., *The Lay Subsidy for Shropshire 1524-7* (Shropshire Record Series, 3, 1999), pp. 32–3; *CR Romsley*, p. 276.

[62] R.N. Swanson and D. Guyatt, eds., *The Visitation and Court Book of Hartlebury, 1401–1598* (WHS, new series, 24, 2013); WA, ref. 009:1, BA 2636//37(iii), fos.78–83.

PEASANT OUTLOOK, VALUES, PERCEPTIONS, AND ATTITUDES   323

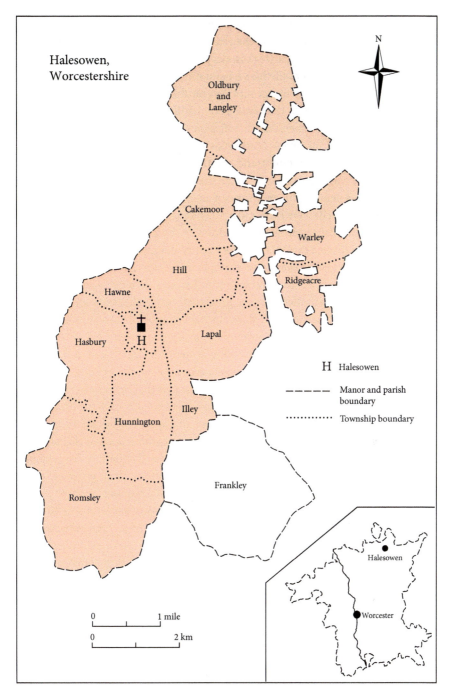

Figure 10.1. Halesowen parish. The parish coincided with the manor, but Frankley, a chapelry, had a different lord. The church was sited in the borough at a little distance from the Abbey. The boundaries were formed by 1300; defining them simply posed difficulties in the north (source: Z Razi, Life, *Marriage and Death in a Medieval Parish: Economy, Society and Demography in Halesowen 1270–1400* (Cambridge, 1980), p. xiv).

The agricultural and the liturgical year followed different but overlapping calendars. The universal church began the year on 25 March, known as Lady Day in England, but villagers and the lords of manors preferred 29 September (Michaelmas) because it marked the end of the harvest and the beginning of winter ploughing. The Halesowen churchwardens' accounting year followed agricultural practice by choosing 29 September after 1507, and also in 1487–8. In the intervening years, the churchwardens began their term of office on either 11 November (Martinmas) or 25 November (St Catherine). Martinmas had agricultural significance as the end of the pastoral farming year, and the traditional date for killing animals. St Catherine's day was a special event in Halesowen: a chapel in the north aisle of the parish church was dedicated to her, with an altar on which a light was kept burning, and on her day bells were rung and a priest sang mass. For the rest of the year, both parish and village celebrated the usual feasts of Christmas, Easter, and Whitsun, and these were the occasions for church ales in the years that they were held. Special days at Halesowen were St Stephen's day (26 December) and Relics' Sunday in early July. The churchwardens kept banners in good repair for use on processions, among them the collective progress through the fields and along the parish boundary on the Rogation days (in the week before Ascension Day, so usually in May) which were important events in an agricultural community because in practical terms they renewed memories of boundaries, and they were also the occasion for the ritual of blessing the crops. At Hanbury (Worcestershire) in c.1530 the rogation procession helped a witness in a church court to remember tithe obligations, and at Shuckburgh (Warwickshire) around 1500 the procession was prevented from gaining access to common land by an enclosing lord.[63]

In most parishes about forty feast days would be commemorated through the year, and these days set aside for religious devotion created dilemmas for peasants who were expected to desist from work. The Hartlebury church court heard of individuals who had worked on seven named saints' days, four of them in the harvest season, and clearly a peasant would be tempted to work on a holiday to bring in crops. The Halesowen churchwardens' sources of income reflected the agrarian way of life, as they hired out cows, let parcels of land that they had been given for rent, and charged for grazing road-side pasture. Their counterparts at Hartlebury rented out beehives. At Halesowen the regular annual revenues, together with bequests, and fees for burial inside the church, provided enough income (£2 or £3 per annum) to cover the routine expenses of wax, oil, and minor repairs. If the churchwardens embarked on larger building projects, such as a rood loft or extensive roof repairs they held a church ale, which would yield between £2 and £4. Ales were rooted in village tradition and could be held for a number of purposes, including fundraising for charity. At Halesowen's event food

---

[63] TNA, E328/25/1, 2, 3, 6, 7; Dyer, *Age of Transition*, p. 69.

was provided as well as drink, and the wardens were spared paying for a church house and its upkeep as the ales seem to have been held in the houses of the wealthier wardens such as John Mucklowe. The ales celebrated the unity of the community in both religious and secular matters.[64]

Each parish raised funds in different ways. At Badsey (Worcestershire) ales were held but they were not very profitable, yielding 1s 11d in one year and 2s 3d in another.[65] Instead, the wardens were funded by groups resembling informal fraternities, who must have held celebrations, in which ale no doubt featured, and collected money. The young men formed one group, the young women (maids) another, and the 'little maids' a third. 'Cock money' was raised at an event on Shrove Tuesday when sticks were thrown at a tethered cock. Hartlebury funded parish expenditure in a more sober and systematic fashion, by collecting money through an assessment of wealth, so that a tenant with a yardland was expected to contribute 3s 4d to a new bell tower.[66] In the long run such methods of collecting funds developed in most parishes into a rating system, but in the early sixteenth century church ales were still important events in many parishes, and to hold them church houses were being built throughout the region.[67]

The churchwardens gathered money to provide the material basis for a satisfying liturgical and spiritual experience. The laity assembled in the nave of the church witnessed on the other side of the screen the clergy performing elaborate rituals using the books, vestments, vessels, incense, and other items provided by the wardens. The congregation would be impressed visually by the colours and designs of textiles, glass, wall paintings, glazed floor tiles, and statues, and also by the sounds of the bells, organ, and singing. The smell of incense completed the impact of the service on the senses. The parishioners in the Hartlebury court thought it important that images and rituals should be visible, and they asked that the parish clerk at Easter should at the appropriate time draw back the cloth hanging in the church at Easter so that the congregation could see the altar.[68]

The parishioners, as represented by the churchwardens expected impressive displays which needed regular renewals in structures and furnishings. At Halesowen, for example, every few years some improvement was made, like the new rood loft that was installed in 1530–2 at great expense. Church buildings themselves reflect this desire for additions which often had a liturgical purpose, so aisles accommodated extra altars and side chapels for chantries, porches provided spaces for weddings, and towers with bells contributed to funeral rituals. No doubt these

---

[64] K. French, *The People of the Parish: Community Life in a Late Medieval Diocese* (Philadelphia, 2001).
[65] E.A.B. Barnard, ed., *Churchwardens' Accounts of the Parish of Badsey with Aldington from 1521 to 1571* (Hampstead, 1913), pp. 9–22.
[66] Swanson and Guyatt, eds., *Hartlebury*, p. 185.
[67] For example, there were eight in Forest of Dean parishes, *VCH Glouc*, vol. 5.
[68] Swanson and Guyatt, eds., *Hartlebury*, p. 258.

matters were discussed by the laity and the clergy, but the wardens held the purse strings and must have made the final decisions. In some parishes the local aristocrats were major players, and throughout the region churches survive such as Sudeley (Gloucestershire) and Weston-on-Avon (Warwickshire) where wealthy patrons funded much of rebuilding (the lord bequeathed £50 in 1480 in the case of Weston) and dictated the architecture, insisting that the tombs of the family would be prominent features.[69] In many cases, although local gentry might have made a large contribution to building work, the funding was a collective effort and the wardens had some say in the cost, scale, and style of the building. Some parish churches were rebuilt without any visible input from lords, and it is known that in addition to the community's fund raising, local peasant families paid for particular features, such as windows.[70] Judging from the quantity of rebuilding, especially in the century before the Reformation, and the quality of the buildings, the parishioners were strongly motivated. They were enthusiasts for providing appropriate spaces for the celebration of the mass and other ceremonies, but they were also expressing their pride in their communities and seeking to impress parishioners, travellers, and visitors.

The work on the fabric had a significance for our understanding of the religion of the peasant parishioners. The churchwardens at Halesowen chose in 1512–13 to employ a painter (from Birmingham) to depict a Doom. This has been covered or removed subsequently, but such paintings in other churches occupy the space above the chancel arch, visible to everyone in the nave. At the top of the painting, Christ presided over the last judgement, with the souls of the righteous on his right hand enjoying the splendours of the celestial city, and the sinners to the left suffering the torments of hell.[71] This was reinforcing the message of sermons and was designed to persuade sinners to reform, threatening punishment but also giving hope of salvation. A social message was being conveyed that moral distinctions were more important than social rank on the day of judgement, as the wealthy and powerful (bishops for example) were depicted among the damned. Sermons of the late fourteenth century gave egalitarian ideas a sharp edge by assuring the poor that they would sit beside God and join in the judging of the rich.[72] Church courts, with strong lay participation, dealt more immediately with those accused of sins and sought to correct their behaviour. Although the courts

---

[69] N. Saul, *Lordship and Faith: The English Gentry and the Parish Church in the Middle Ages* (Oxford, 2017); C. Pickford and N. Pevsner, *Warwickshire* (The Buildings of England, New Haven and London, 2016), p. 702.

[70] G. Dark, *Church Building and Society in the Later Middle Ages* (Cambridge, 2017); Dyer, 'Political Life', p. 156 for the case of Bledington's windows, funded by peasants.

[71] Although the Doom has not survived, there were paintings of the life of St Nicholas: M. Gill, 'The Lost Wall Paintings of Halesowen Church', *Transactions of the Worcestershire Archaeological Society*, 3rd series, 16 (1998), pp. 133–42.

[72] J.A. Ford, *John Mirk's Festial. Orthodoxy, Lollardy and the Common People in Fourteenth-Century England* (Woodbridge, 2006), pp. 76–9.

were mainly concerned with points of law, it could still be said in 1496 at Hartlebury that church attendance was 'for the salvation of souls'. The court took seriously the notion that parents should educate their children in religious matters, hearing that Thomas Holmer of Hartlebury was accused of preventing his sons from attending church, and that he failed to instruct them in the catholic faith. None of our sources had occasion to mention the laity's participation in the mass, perhaps because it was so widely accepted as a central moment in which the congregation came together. They were supposed to share in a sense of connection with the whole community of the faithful, and with the divine order.[73] The written sources say little about individual acts of piety, though there were occasional references to pilgrimage, like the Hartlebury parishioner who went to Rome. Visits to shrines explain the metal badges and *ampullae* used to contain holy water from places of pilgrimage which are found in fields where they were lost, or more likely mislaid in the home and incorporated in the household refuse.[74] Badges from the Marian cult centre at Walsingham in Norfolk have been found at Highnam, Maiseyhampton, and Westbury-on-Severn in Gloucestershire, so the faithful were prepared to travel considerable distances.[75] 'Beads', presumably rosary beads, are sometimes mentioned in court records as goods lost or stolen, and individual beads are found on excavated rural settlements.

The sources are also deficient in recording indifference, scepticism, and dissent. Thomas Holmer of Hartlebury evidently lacked enthusiasm for the church's religious teaching and contemporaries clearly suspected that a failure to observe Sundays and saints' days might point to unbelief. Much of the heresy in the region was based in towns, though the occasional offender was identified in the country, like John Walcote, who was discovered at Hazleton in Gloucestershire in 1425, but when put on trial in Worcester agreed to abandon his heretical beliefs and performed an elaborate public penance. His was apparently an isolated case, though other named individuals were reported in the region at about the same time, and we might wonder how and where they came into contact with heresy.[76]

Peasants experienced a religion that was full of colourful ceremony, which gave them an alternative to the ordinariness of their daily routines. Their willingness to participate in parish life with its raising of substantial funds and ambitious projects suggests not just an acceptance of conventional worship, but also that they subscribed to the teaching of the church on morality and salvation that underpinned the whole edifice of organized religion. The universal preoccupation of

---

[73] Swanson and Guyatt, eds., *Hartlebury*, pp. 186, 248; W.H. Campbell, *The Landscape of Pastoral Care in Thirteenth-Century England* (Cambridge, 2018), pp. 122–35.

[74] Portable Antiquities Scheme, accessible at https://finds.org.uk/database, ampulla from Hartlebury, WAW 2ADFFD; another from Blaisdon (Gloucestershire) has a T which apparently shows that it came from the shrine of Thomas Beckett at Canterbury: GLO 89CA21.

[75] Portable Antiquities Scheme, accessible at https://finds.org.uk/database, GLO BD3800; GLO A14B8D; GLO SE9448.

[76] I. Forrest, *The Detection of Heresy in Late Medieval England* (Oxford, 2005), pp. 102, 136, 180.

the age, shared by peasants and reflected in *Piers Plowman*, was the question 'How can I save my soul?' Clergy composing sermons, such as John Mirk, based at Lilleshall in Shropshire, 20 miles from Halesowen, could defend the validity of popular religious devotion. He demonstrated this with a story of a husbandman teaching monks about the intensity of his spiritual experience gained from a vision of the punishment of sinners in hell.[77]

Peasants and the environment

Country people showed their awareness of landscape by their incorporation of terms such as 'filden' or 'feldon', 'Arden', and 'wold' into minor place names and personal names.[78] Patterns of short distance migration (see 'Migration' in Chapter 4) indicate a preference to stay within familiar landscapes, suggesting a sense of identity.

While people might have been attached to local landscapes, did they also have an understanding of the problems posed by the imbalances of the environment and the harm that might arise from excessive exploitation of resources? Was their main aim the short-term pursuit of a living, or did they farm the land with the intention of conserving fertility and preventing degradation?[79] Open-field farmers in particular have been criticised for their conservatism, but perhaps they persisted in their two-course rotations and stinted pastures because they correctly feared that innovation would have adverse consequences.

Peasants are said to have ignored provident restraints as they gave priority to the welfare of themselves and their households. A criticism of medieval agriculture in general was the tendency in the thirteenth century to extend cultivation over infertile land or to plough beyond the realistic limits. They asserted the sandy soils of Wolverley (Worcestershire) for example, or founded new settlements on land now rated as unsuitable for arable farming. Landscape indications of this extension of ploughing (though not always securely dated) include the cultivation terraces on steep hillsides (strip lynchets), such as those near Wotton-under-Edge, or in the lowlands the ridge and furrow encroaching on meadows which were liable to flooding. Having sensibly adopted a two-course rotation, probably in the pre-Conquest period, they risked a loss of fertility by planting on the fallow and reducing the amount of pasture. Over the period between 1350 and 1520 they converted some arable to grazing, but a threat came from overburdening common pastures with ever-larger flocks and herds, leading to the gloomy

---

[77] Ford, *Mirk's Festial*, pp. 99–100, 147.
[78] S. Wager, *Woods, Wolds and Groves: The Woodland of Medieval Warwickshire* (British Archaeological Reports, British Series, 269, 1998), pp. 167–8; on the general background, S. Kilby, *Peasant Perspectives on the Medieval Landscape* (Hatfield, 2020).
[79] P. Warde, *The Invention of Sustainability. Nature and Destiny, c.1500–1870* (Cambridge, 2019).

prediction of 'a tragedy of the commons' (see 'Changing agriculture: managing the fields' in Chapter 6). The management of woods will help to clarify the dilemmas that they faced, and their behaviour in the face of ecological threats.

Peasants could be regarded as the enemies of woods and their tendency to remove trees and vegetation was an obstacle to sustainability. Lords protected manorial woodland from encroachment and over-exploitation. Royal forests practised conservation on a large scale, as courts dealt with long lists of those who felled trees and assarted woodland in the period of expansion in the thirteenth century. The king expected to profit both from timber, wood, and industrial activities, and to generate revenue from enforcing Forest Law. Parks were designed both to protect deer, and to maintain useful woods. Both inside and outside parks lord managed wood pastures to grow larger trees and graze animals, and by fencing coppices to promote the growth of underwood (often hazel and thorns). Underwood and larger trees could be combined if the woods were managed as 'coppice with standards'. Underwood was cut on cycles of five to eight years, and larger trees were felled occasionally. The larger trees were kept as a store of wealth to be realized when cash was short. Trees could be cropped, having their branches lopped or pollarded for use without felling, and bark from these operations sold to tanners. Applying forestry management to the woods enabled them to be maintained and renewed. Commercial exploitation of woods, for example for industry, was allowed under licence, and supposedly supervised by the lords' officials.[80]

Peasants appear in the lords' records as disrupting the orderly management of woods. They had access to woods, having the right to pasture animals among the trees, and under the customary rules of *housbote*, *heybote*, and *firebote* they could take a limited number of trees or a quantity of underwood for building, fencing, and fuel. They were supposed to exercise these rights under supervision, but instead entered the woods as they wished and helped themselves to more than they were entitled. Exasperated woodwards, as well as recommending financial penalties, confiscated axes that were being used illegally. Peasants also grazed animals to excess, and introduced the most destructive livestock, pigs and goats. Owners of pigs took more than their share by collecting fallen acorns and carrying them away. The underwood was endangered by breaking the fences and allowing livestock to browse the growing shoots. Coppice growth was cut illicitly to supply charcoal burning, ashburning, and hurdle making.[81] Many of these offences reduced the value of woods without destroying them. Unauthorized assarting however devastated areas of woodland by permanent removal of vegetation.

---

[80] A. Watkins, 'The Woodland Economy of the Forest of Arden in the Later Middle Ages', *Midland History* 18 (1993), pp. 19–36, especially pp. 22–4.
[81] Watkins, 'Woodland Economy', pp. 25–8.

Woods were not the only sources of trees and useful vegetation. Hedges could be sources of fuel, especially in the woodland districts with their numerous crofts and closes. Even in champion country the parish boundary could be marked by a stout hedge, and the common fields were surrounded by discontinuous hedges supplemented by fences. The village itself had many hedges enclosing house plots, and additional crofts. Especially attractive for those gathering firewood were the dense growths of bushes and trees which were landmarks in the local landscape, like the 'Hedge' at Sambourn (Warwickshire) which became a minor place-name.[82] Periodically trees in hedges were felled without licence, and the timber sold. On open land, especially on the common pasture, thickets of bushes grew, typically hawthorns, blackthorns, gorse, and broom, and they were in demand for fuel and fencing. The lord's court, concerned by the over-exploitation of this resource, attempted to limit the cutting of the thorns to those with common rights, and forbade their collection for sale. A similar problem was posed by the cutting of shoots of willow trees which again were taken by outsiders in excess.

The picture that comes from a simple reading of the court records of lords defending woods from misuse by peasants is of course a misleading oversimplification. The protection of woods, trees, and bushes by the authorities did not aim to prevent the taking of timber and underwood, but rather to collect revenue. The financial penalties could be seen as licence fees, showing that lords (and the officials in charge of the royal forests) accepted the loss of some of the assets as long as money was paid. They were also themselves capable of removing woods to make way for profitable agriculture, to 'approve' it in their language (meaning improve). Peasants tended to enclose and cultivate an acre or two at a time, whereas lords were capable of clearance on a much larger scale, such as the 200 acres in Dean by the Abbot of Tintern in 1282, or the 23 acres which William de Botreaux, lord of Alcester assarted at King's Coughton (Warwickshire) before 1280.[83]

Peasants appreciated the long-term utility of woods. Like everyone they relied on timber for building material and underwood for fuel and fencing. They were especially dependent on the implements and utensils made in or near woods using the available raw materials, and many of the craftsmen were peasants pursuing dual occupations as ploughwrights, cartwrights, turners, and coopers. The majority of the animals grazing in wood pastures, and most of the pigs being fattened on acorns belonged to peasants. They had a strong vested interest in the survival of woods.

Manorial woods, which were defended by the lord's officials, especially the woodwards, figure prominently in the documents. The most comprehensive

---

[82] SCLA, DR5/2357.
[83] C.E. Hart, 'The Dean Forest Eyre of 1282' (MA dissertation, University of Bristol, 1953), p. 160; *Rec Feck For,* p. 133.

record, in Domesday Book, omitted woods that brought no revenue to lords. This continued, so that thirteenth-century surveys and extents only include demesne woods, and sometimes give the impression that a manor was provided with either a few acres of wood or no wood at all. Champion and wold landscapes which have sometimes been described as 'treeless' were dotted with 'groves' usually with one for each township. An example is Aston Blank (Gloucestershire) (see Figure 2.4) which had a single grove of 30 acres in the middle of its field system in 1752. Most groves contained enough wood for the village's fuel and fencing, though timber would have to be brought in from large remote woods. Common woods, managed by the villagers, could be large and can be discovered by careful historical detective work. Some notable examples have been identified in the large Arden townships of north Warwickshire, at Temple Balsall (where Balsall Wood contained 350 acres in 1538), Lapworth (with Kingswood, where people from Wellesbourne had common rights), Knowle Wood (called Chessett Wood in the Middle Ages), Solihull Wood (containing 400 acres) and Yardley Wood just over the boundary in Worcestershire. In Meriden parish were two large common woods, one called Meriden Shelfs and a wood in Alspath township. Berkswell's common wood, Beechwood, was not so extensive (Figure 10.2). These woods often no longer exist, having been removed in modern times, like Balsall Wood which became Balsall Common, and is now covered with the houses of an outer suburb of Coventry. The loss of common woods was not the inevitable consequence of peasant mismanagement, as many of them, like Balsall Wood, survived into the sixteenth century.[84] The smaller groves of the champion and wolds were similarly kept unscathed and often still exist, as in the case of Aston Blank.

Peasants defended woods in which they had common rights from appropriation and encroachment by direct action and legal process. In the Forest of Dean the abbot of Flaxley complained that Richard of Blaisdon, who was not acting alone, destroyed the bank around the wood at Timbridge in 1231.[85] The obstacle had been raised by the abbot to exclude local people, and he apparently succeeded. In Arden Geoffrey de Langley faced 'a serious contention' involving two free tenants, Richard and William de Pinley in the 1230s. Langley planned to 'improve' the wood and other land at Pinley; his opponents took legal action that forced a negotiation and settlement in which the de Pinleys were bought off with a grant of land (a half-acre each) and other concessions.[86]

Collective action was taken by Warwickshire tenants who complained that by enclosing or assarting woods lords were depriving them of right of pasture and

---

[84] This paragraph depends on Wager, *Woods, Wolds and Groves*, especially pp. 79–94.
[85] *Curia Regis Rolls*, 13, p. 359; 14, pp. 10, 82–3, 315–16; C. Elrington, ed., *Abstracts of Feet of Fines Relating to Gloucestershire 1199–1299* (GRS 16, 2003), p. 46.
[86] P.R. Coss, *Lordship, Knighthood and Locality. A Study of English Society c.1180–c.1280* (Cambridge, 1991), pp. 103–6.

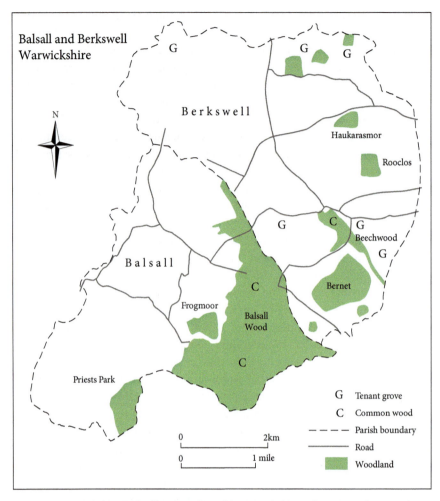

Figure 10.2 Woods in Balsall and Berkswell, Warwickshire. The two Arden parishes had plentiful woodlands, including common woods, and a number of groves (source: Wager, *Woods, Wolds and Groves*, pp. 86–9).

customary access to woods for house repairs and fencing. The men of Stoneleigh in 1290 petitioned the king because Stoneleigh Abbey by assarting was threatening their right of estovers (*housbote*, *heybote*, and *firebote*) in the lord's woods, together with their customary pasture for livestock and pigs in particular, and the gathering of nuts. They claimed that their rights were vital to them, and that they would be impoverished by their loss. A similar dispute at Middleton in 1269 led to the lord Philip Marmion taking to court fifty-one people who entered his wood and cut and carried off trees. These apparent acts of theft were really cases of exercising disputed common rights. We do not know the perspective of the offenders because they did not attend the court, perhaps after being discouraged from doing so.[87]

As well as large woods that served whole communities, small groves were held by peasants as part of their portfolios of landholdings, again using Warwickshire examples. Richard Colyns of Tanworth-in-Arden in 1351 was holding three fields (*campos*), a meadow, and two groves for 21*d*. The phrase 'plots of wood' was sometimes used at Tanworth. Groves appear elsewhere in the Arden, with twenty-nine in 1553 at Berkswell, and in 1327–8 eight tenants held groves at Wroxall[88] (Figure 10.2). Sambourn tenants around 1500 held 'coppices' rather than groves. As with other parts of their holdings, they were supervised, and were presented in the court for felling trees without licence or failing to keep fences in repair. At this village these small private woods survived and appear on a map of 1746.[89] The hedges which were subject to attack by those gathering firewood often belonged to peasants, and they joined in the efforts to defend them. Similarly the protests against large-scale removal of thorns, furze, and broom on commons came from the village community represented by the manor court.

To sum up, lords and peasants over-exploited woods and removed great quantities of natural vegetation by clearing land for agriculture. Peasants also can be found protesting against enclosure and clearance when it threatened their interests. Many woods survived the threats of the Middle Ages, only to be felled and converted into agricultural land in the disafforestations of the seventeenth century, notably in Feckenham Forest. The destruction of woodland continued in subsequent centuries.

The conclusion must be that although peasants abused their customary rights and damaged woods on occasion, a strong body of opinion within the village favoured preserving woods and making use of their resources on a scale that prevented their destruction. When manor courts heard of attacks on woods, hedges, and thorn thickets beyond the customary limits the jurors and other court officials named the offenders in the court, and joined in deciding their amercements.

In the case of woodland management, as in more general issues of maintaining equilibrium between cultivation and pasture, or between individual profit and the common good, much depended on checks and balances within village society. For every move to exploit resources irresponsibly and selfishly, there were counteracting tendencies among those favouring restraint and neighbourly co-operation. Wise policies on calculating stints like those advocated at Long Marston in 1453 (see 'Animal welfare' in Chapter 7), were presumably widely shared, if not often expressed so explicitly. Peasants may not have advocated sustainability in the

---

[87] J.R. Birrell, 'Common Rights in the Medieval Forest: Disputes and Conflicts in the Thirteenth Century', *P&P* 117 (1987), pp. 22–49, especially pp. 46, 48–9.
[88] Bodleian Library, MS Top. Warwick C1; Wager, *Woods, Wolds and Groves*, pp. 88–9, 90, 96.
[89] SCLA, DR5/2360; Wager, *Woods, Wolds and Groves*, p. 112.

modern sense, but the village community promoted compromise between different interest groups which helped to prevent the disastrous degradation of the environment.

Individuals and communities

The poem *Piers Plowman* deals rather obliquely with issues of community and family. A discordant band who might be seen as representing the lower end of village society began to help Piers in his work but failed. Piers has a family but is presented as a self-reliant individual who advocates social collaboration without much prospect of achieving it. As an alternative to Piers's upright morality, Hawkyn the 'active man' appears initially as a dishonest trader, but also boasts of the typically peasant offence, in an open-field setting, of ploughing over the boundary of his strip of ploughland, encroaching on his neighbour, and in the harvest reaching over with his sickle to cut corn from the crops growing on the next strip.

To what extent did peasants consider the welfare of others in their decision making? This section is focussed on the culture of community, the treatment of the older generation within families, and the morality of trade.

The collective life of the village is seen in a fresh perspective from the financial accounts of John Wickwane, abbot of Evesham, and William More, prior of Worcester, compiled in 1456-7 and 1518-36.[90] These wealthy ecclesiastics lived in an aristocratic style, in large houses full of servants, administrators, and guests, eating and drinking well and welcoming a varied range of professional entertainers, including minstrels, jugglers, and musicians. The abbot and prior and their companions found time for villagers to present dramatic performances. Towns such as Evesham and Pershore were represented by their players, but our focus is on the villagers. Some were connected to church events, like the church ale at Grimley, 'and a play', for which Prior More gave a reward of 7s 6d. He was both rewarding the players, and supporting church funds. Across the country, we know of churchwardens enhancing the experience of the church ale with drama. Grimley belonged to the Priory estate, but villages without that connection were welcomed at the Prior's residence, such as the Martley players as part of the celebration of the feast of the Nativity of the Blessed Virgin Mary on 8 September 1519.[91] The abbot of Evesham gave 3s 4d to the tenants of Broadwell for playing before their lord, and the same sum for a group from Upper Swell at Christmas. Both were on the Evesham estate, but Northfield was not, and its players received only 12d.

---

[90] WA, ref. 705:56, BA3910/33(iv); Fegan, ed., *More*.
[91] Fegan, ed., *More*, pp. 90–1, 308.

The content of the plays is not usually recorded. Those that were held on church festivals elsewhere had a religious content, like the 'Christmas game' at Ashburton in Devon which featured God, Christ, Herod, and devils. A very elaborate play at Bassingbourn (Cambridgeshire) told the life of St George, complete with a dragon.[92] Others were entirely secular: among plays performed before Prior More were 'Robin Hood, Maid Marion and others' performed by tenants of Cleeve Prior in July 1531 (for 6s 8d), 'Robin Hood and Little John' by an Ombersley group in May 1535, and 'Robin Hood and his men' was put on for an event connected with Tewkesbury Bridge, though no village was mentioned. The prior gave 12d to the Robin Hood box at Claines in 1530. In addition to plays More saw performances by 'dancers of Claines' at Midsummer, and he heard 'men and women singing on May morning' at Grimley, for which he gave 3s.[93]

These performances could be dismissed as clumsy rustic affairs, which would be received with disdain by the elite audience, or at best were attended as a duty with paternalistic tolerance. The obvious parallel is the rude mechanicals' play in a *Midsummer Night's Dream*, written only sixty years after Prior More's last years. Perhaps we should have higher expectations. Grimley's repertoire suggests a village with a tradition of music and drama, and the more distant places like Martley and Northfield had apparently acquired reputations that travelled far. If the audience had found the plays tedious, they would surely have discouraged the performers, but instead they received them and gave them substantial rewards.

Mounting a play suitable for presentation outside the village shows leadership and organization, and a commitment of time. A high level of participation is suggested by Cleeve Prior's play which required a sizeable cast if Robin Hood was accompanied by an appropriate band of outlaws: at this time Cleeve had about twenty households. At Coventry the obligation to perform in the city's drama cycle caused much debate among the participating fraternities, with understandable reluctance to commit to the task, but also some pride in the achievement. Perhaps the Worcestershire villagers experienced a similar combination of problems and rewards. Another implication is that literacy had become sufficiently widespread for the players to acquire a script, and that at least some of them had the ability to read it. A play book was used for the St George play at Bassingbourn, and the text of a Robin Hood play survives.[94] The brief references to the plays are enough to suggest that village communities could achieve a level of complexity, sophistication, and organization.

Villagers were also challenged by the difficult cultural decisions that they had to take in modifying and building parish churches. Much church architecture of

---

[92] A. Hanham, ed., *Churchwardens' Accounts of Ashburton, 1479–1580* (Devon and Cornwall Record Society, new series, 15, 1970), p. xi; D. Dymond, ed., *The Churchwardens' Book at Bassingbourn, Cambridgeshire 1496–c.1540* (Cambridge Record Society, 17, 2004), pp. lx–lxviii.
[93] Fegan, *More*, pp. 87, 309, 327, 332, 388, 405.
[94] R.B. Dobson and J. Taylor, *Rymes of Robin Hood* (London, 1976), pp. 203–7.

the fourteenth and fifteenth centuries was commissioned by churchwardens and the parishioners they served. Peasants found themselves negotiating with masons, carpenters, glaziers, painters, and carvers about the form of the whole building, or an aisle or tower, or about details of tracery, size of windows, images, the scenes and figures to be included in glass windows and wall paintings, and the design and decoration of screens and rood lofts. If aristocratic patrons and rich donors contributed funds, their preferences would have carried great weight. The views of the clergy would have to be taken into account; the advice of the craftsmen must have been crucial, and note would be made of the work that had been done on neighbouring churches; but the final decision lay with the leading parishioners and particularly the churchwardens. We are presented with evidence for the end product and must presume the long processes of thought and debate that lay behind the eventual result.

Concern for the welfare of the older generation is a useful test of the extent to which society was dominated by self-interested individualism or a willingness to make sacrifices for others. This was a dilemma for family members faced with elderly relatives unable to support themselves, and for the wider community.

Maintenance agreements recorded the surrender of a holding by a tenant wishing to retire from fully active farming, in exchange for a promise of food and other benefits from the successor.[95] Of sixty-five examples where names are given, thirty-two of those taking on the holding were clearly relatives, and the remainder have surnames that differed from that of the departing tenant. A few of these at least were related in some way, for example as sons-in-law. One of the interpretations of these transactions is that they were in essence commercial contracts, in which the retiring tenant was selling the holding in return for an annuity. The old people were calculating the demand for land and could drive a hard bargain, while the new tenants were taking a risk that the old person would encumber the holding for a long time. However, this view of the agreement as a product of the market does not accord with the hint in some agreements that a son or daughter or some other relative was motivated by family loyalty, or at least by a sense of duty. There was also a broader social perception that the elderly should not sink into poverty. On the Worcester Priory estate in the 1340s, the custom was stated that 'if an heir entered by licence of the lord into land, the widow should receive (annually) from the heir 3 cronnocks of rye, a cronnock of barley and a quarter of oats' (a cronnock was 4 bushels). This clearly stated a principle supported by the lord of the manor, and set a standard that would avoid disputes. At Ombersley in 1416, it was said that the allowance of grain (a very basic 4 bushels of rye and

[95] R.M. Smith, 'The Manorial Court and the Elderly Tenant in Late Medieval England', in *Life, Death and the Elderly*, edited by M. Pelling and R.M. Smith (London, 1991), pp. 39–61; M. Page, 'Manor Courts and the Retirement of Customary Tenants on the Bishop of Winchester's Estates before the Black Death', *Southern History* 35 (2013), pp. 23–43.

4 bushels of barley or drage) was 'according to custom', which again meant that the community and the lord were involved in the agreement.[96]

The notion that the maintenance of the elderly was required by custom might be contradicted or modified. In 1314 at Hallow (Worcestershire), on the Worcester Priory estate, the holding of a poor couple, Simon and Matilda le Tornour, was granted to an unrelated tenant, and the lord 'out of charity' ordered the new tenant to provide them with an annual allowance of wheat, rye, peas, and oats.[97] Perhaps charity rather than custom was invoked because the new tenant was not an heir? At Ombersley in 1464 William Bishop's son-in-law took over the holding, granting the standard customary quantity of rye and barley, but in addition twenty-two selions of land, probably amounting to 5 acres, the right to lop trees, grazing, and other benefits, 'as a grant of alms', because of William's poverty, and by licence of the lord.[98] Again the idea of charity was being introduced, so these agreements were neither commercial, nor enforced by custom. Perhaps the generous extra allowance of land was the charitable element? A more straightforward case involved Roger Bele of Sedgeberrow in 1315, who surrendered his holding to his son John. 'The whole court' found that Roger should be granted a house and an acre of land for life, and the lord consented to this.[99] Here it seems that the son was under no precise obligation to provide for his father, and the community acting through the court pressured John to do the decent thing, with support from the lord.

Reluctance by successors, including relatives, to provide for the older generation must have led Worcester Priory officials to record their statement of custom in the 1340s. Individual agreements were being made throughout the region because of distrust, as old people valued a record in the court roll so that new tenants could be held to their commitments. One of the earliest agreements, made in 1281 for a Halesowen widow, Agnes Brid, gave an unusual amount of detail to protect her from non-compliance by the new tenant. The contract specified the dimensions of the house to be built for her, and the number of doors and windows. In addition to grain, she was to receive coal and firewood, and arrangements for their delivery were agreed; penalty payments were due if this did not happen.[100] Other agreements contain similar hints of distrust, and two cases arose from a failure by the new tenant to keep to promises made. The retired people could also be at fault, and an agreement for a Teddington widow in 1326 raised the possibility that she might be 'contentious'. A son from Blackwell who was supporting his mother had to move her into separate accommodation because, he alleged, she was unbearably quarrelsome.[101] Both sides were protected by the written word.

---

[96] *Reg Wig*, p. 7; WA, ref. 705:56, BA 3910/24.
[97] WCL, E7.   [98] WA, ref. 705:56, BA3910/27 (ix).   [99] WCL, E7.
[100] J. Amphlett, *Court Rolls of the Manor of Hales, 1272–1307* (WHS, 1910), pp. 166–8.
[101] WCL, E10; E17.

The accommodation arrangements specified in thirty-five maintenance agreements are a guide to the daily experience of contact between the generations. The retired person or couple would live in their successors' household in three cases. In sixteen examples they were to live in the same house, but occupy a specified chamber. At Burton Dassett Southend, an excavated house had been provided with a first-floor chamber reached by a stair built on the end of the building. Cross-wings and upper storeys gave the inhabitants of houses more privacy, and allowed the elderly to be separated. The remainder of the retired peasants would be assigned their own building, like the new house built for Agnes Brid. On the sites of abandoned villages the foundations of a small buildings are sometimes visible at the back of a close, which may have been to accommodate a widow or elderly couple. An existing building such as a bakehouse, cart-house, barn, or sheepcote could be converted to a dwelling. If the retired people were to receive land, or keep livestock, they could be assigned part of a barn or other outbuilding. The conclusion must be that the generations wherever possible lived apart. The younger generation who were willing to support old people did not wish to share their lives with them in the same household.

To sum up, family loyalties should not be exaggerated. The limited attachment of young people to their households and villages is evident from land transfers and migration (see 'Landholding after 1349' in Chapter 3, and 'Migration' in Chapter 4). The new tenants who took on an elderly peasant's holding were not compelled by an enforceable custom to guarantee food, clothing, and accommodation for life, but they were under pressure from the community and the lord. Such agreements were probably more prevalent than we are aware, because they were often based on informal verbal understandings. Those taking on land were guided by their consciences, and they must have had in mind that they would one day be old themselves, a point made forcefully in a fourteenth-century moralistic poem, in which a young son chides his father for ill-treating his grandfather.[102] They were also aware of the harm that neglecting the elderly would cause to their reputation. In spite of all of these tendencies that favoured making agreements and keeping them, some old people apparently had to give up their holdings without written assurance of subsequent support.

The maintenance agreement might also throw light on the dilemmas facing medieval peasants (and those attempting to interpret them) because they tell us about levels of consumption. Piers Plowman is portrayed as living very frugally, with an emphasis on a diet of oats and beans, and the poet evidently approved because he criticised the selfish greed of the labourers and beggars who demanded better food: white bread, and plenty of meat and fish. The food allowances for old people justify the view that peasants lived austerely, consuming cheaper cereals,

---

[102] Homans, *English Villagers*, pp. 154–6.

and with only occasional hints of meat and dairy products. The explanation must be that the purpose of the agreements was to define a minimum, on the assumption that the retired people would have other sources of food or money. When the diets of wage-earners were specified, such as the food allowances for harvest workers at Wibtoft (Warwickshire) in 1402–3, they were given ample quantities of meat. They would not eat so well outside the harvest season, but they would not be reverting to oats and beans. A retired peasant who had held a yardland would surely not have been expected to live less well than a landless farm servant or labourer.[103] The same applies to the cheap clothing promised to retired peasants, which did not change through the late fourteenth and fifteenth centuries, whereas contemporaries complained of the high quality of labourers' clothing (see 'Peasant consumption' in Chapter 8). There may have been notions in communities that it was virtuous to live modestly, but in general individual peasants were raising the standard of their consumption through the period, and the generations living around 1500 were better fed, better clothed, and more comfortably housed than their predecessors before 1350.

Finally, difficult decisions had to be made about exchange and commerce in the village. Did peasants, like Hawkyn in *Piers Plowman*, pursue profit to their own advantage, or were they restrained in their dealings, mindful of the common good, and aware of the advantages of reciprocal honesty? Peasants were familiar with the profits of farming. A holding could be said to have been improved in value (annual return) by 20s, meaning its surplus income from year to year had increased by that amount. Peasants in general could pursue many strategies to raise profit, for example, by changing the crops that they grew even from one year to another to take advantage of movements in price.[104] Those with larger holdings could store crops in a barn over the winter in order to thresh and sell them in the spring and early summer as prices rose. The 'hungry time' in May and June was the profitable time for those with crops to sell. Lords' officials spoke of land being rented at its 'true value', or when demand for land slackened after the Black Death they let a holding at a low rent but hoped that someone would come to offer more. Such language and the concept of obtaining the best price would be familiar to peasants. A peasant from Henbury (Gloucestershire) told his executors to arrange a transfer of land 'the beste chepe they can'.[105] The competition between market towns was based on calculations that sellers could be attracted to the markets where they would get good prices and plenty of buyers. We know how fickle peasants could be from the account book of John Heritage of Moreton in Marsh. He

---

[103] British Library Add Roll 49,762. Harvesters' food cost 44s 4d: bread (23 per cent); ale (32 per cent); meat (41 per cent); fish (2 per cent) and dairy produce (3 per cent).
[104] B. Dodds, *Peasants and Production in the Medieval North-East. The Evidence from Tithes, 1270–1536* (Woodbridge, 2007), pp. 134–44.
[105] WA, ref. 008:7, BA3510, 1538/46.

had a few regular clients who sold their wool to him every year but many after one or two sales moved on to others. They were searching for the best deal.[106]

However the question we are addressing is not whether peasants wished to buy cheap and sell dear, but if they did so selfishly and by flouting morality. Litigation alleged bad practices, such as selling oxen incapable of work while claiming that they were strong and healthy.

The retail sale of foodstuffs was regulated by the various assizes enforced in the view of frankpledge. Here we see the 'just price' transposed into practical law enforcement, as the weight of loaves and cost of ale varied with grain prices, and butchers were not expected to make excessive profits. Villagers participated as ale tasters, jurors, and affeerers advising on amercements, so they all knew about the morality of price fixing. Lending money raised more serious problems as charging excessive interest led to the serious charge of usury, which the church regarded as a grievous moral offence.[107] Lenders were entitled to receive damages, because they suffered from losses caused by the absence of the money loaned. In the manor court the original claim for damages was often reduced by the court, so at Cleeve Prior in 1389 Geoffrey Blacberd, who was owed 2s, claimed 6d in damages but was awarded 4d, which was still a rather high rate of 17 per cent.[108]

Peasant credit is often represented as exploitation, with those with cash to spare (beneficed clergy, widows, tenants with very large holdings, traders) being identified as 'money lenders' who habitually advanced cash in order to make a profit. An alternative expectation would be that better-off tenants lent money to their poorer neighbours, creating dependency and perpetuating social inequality. To test these negative interpretations of the operation of credit in a peasant society seventy-two pleas of debt or related litigation recorded for Cleeve Prior between 1314 and 1377 have been analysed. Most were probably not attempts to recover cash loans, but resulted from delays in payments for goods or wages. Of the 112 individuals appearing as owing or being owed money, only eight were outsiders, so the credit relationships were being formed among Cleeve villagers. Few of those lending or being owed money appear more than once, so specialist 'money lenders' were not identifiable. Instead of the rich exploiting the poor the 'lenders' and the 'borrowers' had a very similar profile of landholding, they held a half-yardland, a yardland or a mill. The debts had arisen from the normal interactions of peasant society, as people bought and sold, paid for work done, or advanced cash in small quantities (less than 5s) for short terms.[109] Loans to cottagers and smallholders would not be the subject of litigation as there was no point in

---

[106] Dyer, *Country Merchant*, pp. 106–7.
[107] J. Le Goff, *Your Money or Your Life. Economy and Religion in the Middle Ages* (New York, 1990).
[108] WCL, E34.
[109] C. Briggs, *Credit and Village Society in Fourteenth Century England* (Oxford, 2009), pp. 149–75.

attempting to recover loans from those without large resources. We might speculate that poorer people were involved in an informal credit network in which small loans were made for short terms without records.

Conclusion

The poem *Piers Plowman* presented its readers with an idealistic vision of a harmonious world in which everyone did their duty, but this was difficult to achieve and contrasted with the reality of a sinful society corrupted by money and self-interest. The peasant Piers stood for honest peasant values of simplicity, hard work, morality, and frugality, who was opposed by lazy wasters, greedy labourers, and the scheming deceiver, Hawkyn.

West-midland peasants supported the state by participating in law enforcement and co-operating in tax collection. These commitments to public life also show some self-interest because they gained from practising self-government sanctioned by higher authority. Like the rest of the 'political society' to which they aspired to belong, they took sides in political disputes at the highest level. They were not openly or comprehensively opposed to their lords, and were complicit in manorial government. They were even drawn into affinities of aristocrats who were not their lords, and became involved in dangerous adventures. In dealing with their lords they fought their own corner, and resisted impositions and restrictions which they saw as unjust. In pursuing a goal of freedom, they undermined repressive institutions. Peasants belonged to church congregations, and attempted to be good Christians, believing in the salvation that Piers Plowman made his explicit goal. As active managers and members of their parish, they moulded religious practices that accorded with their way of life. In dealing with the natural world they had no conception of conservation, but their exploitation of natural resources was subject to internal checks and balances within peasant society combined with some pressures from outside. In consequence, profit-seeking by individuals was restrained and patterns of land use benefited the whole community. The same complex of motives can be seen in the interactions between individuals, their families, and the village. The older generation was not automatically supported by the family and community but was saved from destitution by a complex mixture of filial duty, community pressure, charitable impulses, intervention by the lord, and pangs of conscience. People were caught up in community efforts which had a meaning for the participants beyond individual self-interest. They participated in dramatic and musical performances, which could be connected with parish fund-raising and collective endeavours. Their plays are lost, but tangible outcomes were the church buildings, which survive in their hundreds.

Conclusion

A regional study has the advantage of being specific and concrete, but local examples enable us to understand more about general approaches to the past, so reference has been made to sustainability, social mobility, sense of identity, proto-industrialization, and popular culture. Firm generalizations are made difficult by the paradoxes of peasant history. Peasants can be presented as egalitarian, recorded as holding similar amounts of land as many as their neighbours, sharing the legal and social status of other villagers, and by the rules of the common fields having equal access to resources. However, some peasants were finding ways of gaining in wealth, by developing new land and by buying or leasing land. They could raise their status by taking on offices, by building a house with a cross wing, or by riding a better horse with a decorated harness. Many broke the rules of the common fields, by keeping too many animals on the pastures and not preventing them from trampling their neighbours' crops, while participating in the village community, acting together to manage common assets for the good of all. The definition of peasants included their closely knit families, working together and living under the patriarchal authority of the head of the household. Families had to cope with tensions developing into disputes, and younger members left home for other households and villages, even abandoning their inheritance and leaving their ageing parents to negotiate support with an unrelated successor. Peasants combined subsistence farming, in which the crops were consumed by the household, with production for the market. They admired ideals of frugality and sparse living, while consuming foodstuffs and manufactures which they purchased. They even acquired luxury goods, such as Prussian chests and stoneware drinking vessels. They were primarily agricultural producers, but were drawn into manufacture, not just by taking on trades and crafts as an individual, such as working as a carpenter, but also becoming involved, as entrepreneurs as well as workers, in large-scale industries aimed at distant markets. Villages could not be self-sustaining communities satisfying their needs among themselves. They sold produce in the towns, and bought goods not easily obtained in the country. They hired lawyers occasionally, and employed building workers habitually.

General conclusions about the results of peasant initiatives and activities are best reached by looking at the end of the period and surveying the countryside after more than three centuries of change. The brave new world of the sixteenth century may seem far removed from everyday life of west-midland peasant communities. The Tudor monarchy, new forms of government, Protestant reform, audacious voyages to new worlds, a renaissance culture, and the beginnings of the scientific revolution, all suggest a clear break with the past. However, the advances made by peasants helped to make these novelties possible.

In the period up to 1540 the collective needs of the whole of society, but especially decisions made by peasants, tilted the balance of farming in the west midlands. A peasant-led movement had brought more acres under the plough in the thirteenth century. Subsequently the region became more pastoral. The numerous livestock on pastures of all kinds by 1500 were not just promoting the profits of their owners, but also stimulating commerce in the market towns and satisfying consumer demand for a diet with plenty of meat. The size of peasant holdings were crucial to their well-being and position in the social hierarchy. Holdings were assigned to them, but they could also adjust their size by such means as negotiated subdivisions at inheritance, and by subletting. The fragmentation of landholding stimulated by population growth and commercialization in the thirteenth century did not overwhelm the landholding structure. Larger holdings survived and pressures from lords and communities prevented, for example, the wholesale colonization of wastes by smallholdings. At important stages of the subdivision of standard holdings, the process was halted so that yardlands were not all divided into halves and quarters. Those decisions were made by lords and the peasant tenants themselves. After 1349, with demographic pressure relaxed, more land became available for tenants, both in composite holdings of previously separate units, and in demesne land held on lease. In the west-midland region generally tenants of larger holdings, such as yardlands, formed an important section of society, and some very large holdings exceeding 60 acres emerged. These units of land holding were accumulated and kept in existence by the choice of their tenants.

The holdings that survived and emerged at the end of our period were farmed in new ways. Peasants are often thought to have been conservative and resistant to change, but the three centuries of this enquiry were marked by a series of innovations. In the thirteenth century, land was being converted to arable, and cultivation became more intensive as parts of the open field lying fallow were fenced off and planted with spring sown crops, some intended for fodder. In the fourteenth century, and not just after 1349, arable was turned into grass leys, and open fields were subdivided so that four fields were being worked, enabling three-quarters of the land to be cropped each year. At the same time the enclosure movement that was already active in the thirteenth century in the woodlands spread to the open fields, some of which were enclosed by agreement. These changes all needed approval by lords and they sometimes encouraged them. There were damaging enclosures by lords of champion villages in the fifteenth and early sixteenth centuries, but many other changes came from peasant initiatives.

Through all these complex changes in the holding, management, and use of land, peasants were gaining more control of their lives and their holdings.

Serfdom was a restriction on personal freedom, but was intimately linked to tenancy. In practice it can be said with some justification that serfdom fell short of controlling peasants' landholding, but financial penalties were attached to the lack of freedom. The powers over serfs claimed by lords were a constant threat looming over the lives of the peasantry. The peasants undermined servile institutions by non-cooperation, and eroded the authority of lords consistently from the early days of imposition around 1200 through to its dying days around 1500. Customary and servile tenants aimed to gain the same control over land as their free neighbours, and by 1500 they were paying cash rents, owing no labour services, were no longer subject to tallage or marriage fines, and could practice the same type of succession planning as free tenants in arranging for the transmission of land to the next generation. Copyhold for lives and reversion agreements provided means for selecting heirs.

Peasants acquired artisan skills and developed rural industries which overshadowed the industrial initiatives of lords. The countryside was peppered with individual enterprises, with weavers, tailors, building workers, turners, coopers, and many others, reaching a higher density in woodlands and concentrations in Forest of Dean. The emergence of a major clothmaking district in south Gloucestershire owed much to urban entrepreneurs, but the peasants held fulling mills and rural clothiers emerged from an artisan and peasant background. The industry was based on peasant weavers and spinners drawn into activities initially to supplement their agricultural work. Peasants played active roles in the growth of an urban network throughout the region. Of course lords promoted towns and to some extent chose sites at the beginning of urban growth, but peasants made the towns by settling in them in their thousands, and by replenishing the numbers of townspeople over the centuries. Towns were numerous and populous because of their close relationship with the rural population.

Peasants possessed individual freedoms in the period, not just because they shook off serfdom, but they also escaped from the close control of families, hence their ability to migrate. The relationship was not antagonistic because families helped their young by finding them positions as servants in suitable households, supporting them if they were not well treated, and helping to set them up in new lives with grants and bequests of livestock, implements, or cash. Women showed an independent spirit in managing holdings when necessary, finding opportunities in commerce and crafts both in country and in town, and as widows sometimes resisting pressure to remarry.

And although it could suit those in authority that peasants formed strong communities, the main impetus to work together and observe the rules of open-field farming came from those most directly involved. The strength of communities grew in the thirteenth and fourteenth centuries as they took over new functions such as tax collection, developed their legal skills in the manor courts, and took over responsibility for the management of the parish church. Far from declining after 1349 or 1400, they became more active in church fund raising, dramatic performances, road building, and framing the rules of social control. They believed themselves to be part of political society, so when the state moved against vagabonds they joined in the campaign, but they collected money in the 'common box' to relieve their own poor. As poor laws were introduced from 1536, the parish became the unit of local government capable of managing the welfare system.

The end of the peasantry has often been regarded as an essential part of the modernization of society, and the years around 1500 are claimed as part of the dying process, but the west midlands does not fit this pattern. A different type of peasant emerged after three centuries of change, but they are recognizable still as peasants. In some respects they participated in modernization. In a region that was not in the forefront of industrial growth, the suggestion can be made that a third of working time was devoted to non-agricultural tasks. Historians analysing occupational specialization in the early modern period believe that the growing industrial sector in the sixteenth century marked a stage in the trend to an upward spiral of production and consumption in later centuries. The prehistory of that trend towards 'the first industrial country' began before 1500. Wider cultural and political developments point to the same element of continuity over the period between 1200 and 1800, such as the literacy of the fifteenth century, or the 'shared understanding of governance'.[1] Peasants had created the conditions for these important changes, and their contributions deserve wider recognition.[2]

---

[1] L. van Zanden, *The Long Road to the Industrial Revolution: the European Economy in a Global Perspective, 1000–1800* (Leiden, 2009).
[2] T. Johnson, *Law in Common. Legal Cultures in Late-Medieval England* (Oxford, 2020), p. 269.

Glossary

acre area of land equivalent to 0.40 hectare. A modern association football pitch is 1¾ acres

agistment grazing rented to others; sometimes the rent paid for pasture

amercement a penalty in money levied in a manorial court, typically between 1*d* and 4*d*

assart cleared land, converting wooded or wasteland for agricultural production

aver adult cattle, but sometimes any large animal

bailiff official employed by a lord to manage one or more manors

bay unit of building, usually applied to timber buildings, about 15 feet by 15 feet, or 5m by 5m

bedrip, benrip reaping service owed to the lord of the manor. See *boon*

blade mill water mill equipped with a grindstone for sharpening blades, e.g of knives, scythes, or weapons

bloomery a forge producing blooms, that is lumps of iron, by smelting iron ore with intense heat from charcoal

bondman unfree tenant, also neif, villein, serf

boon collective labour service, owed to the lord of the manor by all tenants on a limited number of days, often in the harvest season. See *bedrip*

bushel unit of volume, for measuring grain, equivalent to 36 litres; one bushel of wheat would feed an individual for a month

butt a small parcel of land, usually a selion of short length

byre building to accommodate cattle

capon castrated male fowl

chamber room in a house often used for sleeping and storage

champart method of renting land, usually between peasants, by which the tenant owes a fraction of the crop, often a half or a third ('the third sheaf')

champion a type of landscape with extensive open fields (from the French word *champ*, meaning field). Champion settlements tend to be nucleated villages

chase a forest held by a lord other than the king; a private hunting reserve

chattels movable goods such as house furnishings or farm equipment

chevage (Latin *capitagium*) *either* a collective payment, often called a common fine, owed to a lord, *or* a payment by an individual serf for permission to live away from the manor

church house building near a church containing a large room for gatherings, often for holding church ales, built and managed by churchwardens

close See *croft*

common law the legal system practised by the royal courts

court roll document recording the business of a manorial court

croft (or close) a piece of enclosed agricultural land, often small, and often held by a single tenant

cruck a vertical timber forming a pair, usually curving, on which the timber structure of a building was based. Also called a fork (*furca*)

curtilage a small enclosed piece of land, containing a house or near to a house or cottage

customary law, custom the rules and legal system used by manorial courts, which varied locally

daywork small measure of land, usually a fraction of an acre

deed document recording a transfer of free land or rent

demesne land reserved for the use of a lord, either cultivated directly, but commonly leased to a tenant, often between a fifth and a third of the area of a manor

dower share of a holding retained by a widow, usually a feature of freeholdings

drage a spring-sown grain crop consisting of a mixture of barley and oats

engrosser an individual tenant who accumulated land by taking over previously separate holdings

entry fine payment to the lord by a tenant taking a customary holding which varied with the size of the holding and such factors as the demand for land. See *relief*

extent survey of a manor including both demesne and tenant land, valuing the assets

eyre court session held by itinerant royal justices

fallow cultivated land allowed to rest without a planted crop, usually for a year

farmer tenant holding an asset, often land, on lease ('at farm'). From *c.*1380 many farmers were lessees of demesne land, often in excess of 100 acres each

Feldon the champion district of south and east Warwickshire, with open fields

feoffees trustees with legal responsibility for holding property

forge see *bloomery*

free bench the custom that a widow should hold her husband's land after his death in her lifetime

frisc uncultivated land, previously arable

fulling mill water mill equipped with wooden hammers powered by a water wheel for treating woollen cloth to give it a close woven (felted) texture

furlong a subdivision of a field, consisting of at least ten strips or selions

fustale a drinking session organized by the lord, compulsory for tenants

gentleman lowest aristocratic rank, intermediate between yeomen and esquires

gentry the lesser aristocracy, including knights, esquires, and gentlemen

gleaning collecting ears of corn left after corn has been cut

glebe land and other assets held by a parish clergyman as part of a benefice

gout a tidal door, to enable water to flow into the sea, and to prevent seawater reaching the land; also applied to the channel leading to the door

hamlet a small rural settlement, often consisting of less than ten households

haulm stems and stalks left after threshing peas and beans, like the straw from grain crops

haverage the practice of granting access to outsiders' animals on a common pasture

heckle a tool with iron teeth used in preparing flax and hemp fibres for spinning

heriot due on death or surrender by a tenant, usually the best beast or chattel, but sometimes more; later a cash payment

homage formal recognition of the superiority of a feudal lord, by extension a group owing allegiance to a lord, often a jury but also those attending a manorial court

hue and cry popular policing, by which a victim of crime 'raises the hue' by calling out their neighbours to pursue the offender

hurden cloth woven from hemp (so inferior to linen) used to make bed sheets

husbandman a category of peasants defined in terms of size of holding (6–50 acres) and other indicators of status, intermediate between labourer and yeoman

inhok (also hich) a part of a field, usually one designated as fallow, cultivated often in the short term, though sometimes every year

intercommoning an understanding between neighbouring settlements to share a common

inventory list of possessions, usually giving values

Justices of the Peace prominent local people, gentry and above, commissioned by the Crown to hold courts and enforce the law

lay subsidy royal tax based on the valuation of the goods of the laity

leirwite payment to a lord levied on servile women accused of incontinence

mainpast a household for whom a head had legal responsibility

350 GLOSSARY

manor organization to enable a lord to gain revenue from the land and tenants

manumission formal procedure for granting freedom to a serf

marl pit a pit dug to extract subsoil to be spread on arable land

marriage fine see *merchet*

maslin winter-sown grain crop, consisting of a mixture of rye and wheat

merchet a fine for a lord's permission for the marriage of a female serf

messuage a house and associated buildings on a small plot of land, often with a yard, garden, etc.

mile unit of length, equivalent to 1.61km

mondayland tenant holding owing labour service on Mondays, usually a smallholding

neif (also *nativus/nativa*) bondman, serf, villein, so unfree individual

nucleated village a compact settlement, usually with ten or more households, common in champion and wold landscapes

open field an area under cultivation subdivided among tenants, without fences or hedges except on its perimeter, subject to agreed routines of cropping and fallowing

padstone single stone acting as foundation for a timber, for example, a cruck

pannage the practice of feeding pigs in the autumn in woods on acorns and beechmast, but also the payment for feeding pigs in this way

park a fenced area of grassland and woodland in the exclusive control of a lord, often to keep deer

partible inheritance inheritance custom by which a holding was divided among heirs

pill a creek or inlet in the Severn estuary, often modified for drainage purposes

pound a small enclosure in which animals straying or trespassing were confined

primogeniture inheritance custom by which the holding descended complete to the eldest son

***principalia* (or principal goods)** chattels (agricultural and domestic) belonging to a customary holding, deemed to be the property of the lord

purpresture an enclosure of land, often waste, usually for agricultural use or for a building

putt wickerwork container attached to a fish trap, in which the fish were confined

quarter unit of volume for measuring grain, containing 8 bushels, equivalent to 290 litres

recognition a collective payment, similar to tallage, owed by customary tenants on the accession of a new lord

rector clergyman holding a parish as his benefice

reeve a lord's official, himself a customary tenant, managing a manor, that is the cultivation of the demesne, and sometimes collecting tenants' rents

relief payment to the lord by a new tenant of a free holding, the sum limited to one year's rent. See *entry fine*

reversion by a process in a manorial court a would-be tenant could acquire a right to the holding in the future, after the tenant(s) had died or withdrawn

retting a process to place flax or hemp plants in water until the softer parts had rotted, allowing the fibres to be separated for spinning and weaving

rhine (or reen) a water course, often taking water from an area of wetland, and draining into an estuary or the sea

ridge and furrow the still visible earthworks of cultivation, reflecting the pattern of subdivision of the field into furlongs and strips and selions

royal forest area of land placed under forest law, administered by special officials and courts. Forests included woodland and waste sheltering deer for hunting, and also settlements and fields

selion a long narrow strip of land in an arable field with boundaries defined by wooden or stone markers at the end

serf also neif, bondman, villein, an unfree person, often a tenant

sheepcote (also sheep house) building for sheltering sheep, especially in winter

sill beam horizontal beam on which a timber frame for a building could be constructed

solar upper room in a dwelling

stint limit on the number of animals that could be grazed on common land

stocks timber device for detaining wrongdoers; a stock was a tree stump

surrender the legal procedure by which a tenant gave up a holding, initially to the lord, but usually a new tenant took the land

tallage collective payment to a lord by customary tenants, also called aid, larder silver, etc. It was used as a legal test of unfree status

timber and wood timber refers to substantial material used for building, implements, etc. wood from younger trees was used as fuel, fencing, wattling, etc.

tithe levy of one-tenth of all produce owed to the parish clergy

tithing a group of males aged 12 and over sworn to keep the peace and to report wrongdoing to the view of frankpledge

toft plot of land once for a building, but on which no building was standing

toll a fee paid on a sale in a market; payment owed to the lord when a customary tenant sold a horse or ox

tonsure distinctive hairstyle which identified ordained clergy

transhumance practice of driving animals from one pasture to another

trothplight a marriage contracted between the parties by mutual consent and exchange of promises

vert the vegetation in a royal forest protected under forest law

vicar clergyman holding a benefice that had been appropriated by a religious house, inferior in status and wealth to a rector

view of frankpledge (often just view) a court, often held by a lord annually, to hear presentments by tithings of petty crimes and public nuisances

village (also vill) a settlement often with between 10 and 50 households; also a unit of government and taxation (see *hamlet* and *nucleated village*)

wain heavy two-wheeled vehicle drawn by oxen; carts were horse-drawn

waste land not subject to cultivation, and not in separate ownership, often used as common pasture

wether adult castrated male sheep

wold originally, woodland, but in 1200–1540 a landscape on high ground, with much arable and often access to pasture

wintering providing pasture in winter for livestock (as distinct from summering)

woodward manorial official supervising and protecting woods

yardland (often called a virgate) a standard holding of land, often in the region of 30 acres of arable, though varying from place to place between 12 acres and 64 acres, with meadow and access to pasture and wood

yeoman from *c.*1400 the highest rank of peasant, superior to a husbandman, holding usually between 50 and 150 acres

Bibliography

Primary printed sources

J. Amphlett, ed., *Court Rolls of the Manor of Hales, 1272–1307* (WHS, 1910).
F.B. Andrews, 'The Compotus Rolls of the Monastery of Pershore', *TBAS* 57 (1933).
J. Angus and J. Vanes, eds., *The Ledger of John Smythe 1538–1550* (Bristol Record Society, 28, 1974).
S. Appleton and M. Macdonald, eds., *Stratford-upon-Avon Wills*, vol. 1 (DS, 52, 2020).
A.F.C. Baber, ed., *The Court Rolls of the Manor of Bromsgrove and King's Norton* (WHS, 1963).
A. Bannister, ed., 'Visitation Returns of the Diocese of Hereford in 1397', *EHR* 44 (1929), pp. 444–53.
E.A.B. Barnard, *Churchwardens' Accounts of the Parish of Badsey with Aldington* (Hampstead, 1913).
F.B. Bickley, ed., *The Little Red Book of Bristol* (Bristol, 1900).
J.R. Birrell, ed., *Records of Feckenham Forest, Worcestershire, c.1236–1377* (WHS, new series, 21, 2006).
J. Caley and J. Hunter, eds., *Valor Ecclesiasticus temp Henry VIII* (Record Commission, 6 vols. 1810–34), 6 vols.
W.F. Carter, ed., 'Subsidy Roll of Warwickshire for 1327', *Transactions of the Midland Record Society* 6 (1902).
W.F. Carter, ed., *The Subsidy Roll for Warwickshire of 6 Edward III (1332)* (DS, 6, 1926).
M. Chibnall, ed., *Select Documents of the English Lands of the Abbey of Bec* (Camden Society, 3rd series, 73, 1951).
M. Chibnall, ed., *Charters and Custumals of the Abbey of Holy Trinity Caen* (British Academy Records of Social and Economic History, new series, 5, 1982).
P.R. Coss, ed., *The Early Records of Medieval Coventry* (British Academy Records of Social and Economic History, new series, 11, 1986).
P. Coss and J.C. Lancaster Lewis, eds., *Coventry Priory Register* (DS, 46, 2013).
D. Crouch, ed., *The Newburgh Earldom of Warwick and its Charters 1088–1253* (DS, 48, 2015).
R.R. Darlington, ed., *The Cartulary of Worcester Cathedral Priory (Register 1)* (Pipe Roll Society, 76, 1962–3).
G. Demidowicz, *Medieval Birmingham: The Borough Rentals of 1296 and 1344–5* (DS Occasional Paper 48, 2008).
F.J. Eld, ed., *Lay Subsidy Roll for the County of Worcester, 1 Edward I* (WHS, 1895).
C.R. Elrington, ed., *Abstracts of Feet of Fines Relating to Gloucestershire, 1199–1299* (GRS, 16, 2003).
C.R. Elrington, ed., *Abstracts of Feet of Fines Relating to Gloucestershire 1300–1359* (GRS, 20, 2006).
C.R. Elrington, ed., *Abstracts of Feet of Fines Relating to Gloucestershire 1360–1508* (GRS, 27, 2013).
M. Faraday, ed., *Worcestershire Taxes in the 1520s* (WHS, new series, 19, 2003).

M. Faraday, ed., *The Bristol and Gloucestershire Lay Subsidy of 1523-7* (GRS, 23, 2009).
A. Farley ed., *Domesday Book* (London, 1783).
E.S. Fegan, ed., *Journal of Prior More* (WHS, 1914).
C. Fenwick, ed., *The Poll Taxes of 1377, 1379 and 1381*, 3 parts (British Academy Records of Social and Economic History, new series, 27, 29, 37, 1998, 2001, 2005).
R.K. Field, ed., *Court Rolls of Elmley Castle, Worcestershire 1347-1564* (WHS, new series, 2004).
P. Franklin, ed., *The Taxpayers of Medieval Gloucestershire* (Stroud, 1993).
E.A. Fry, ed., *Abstracts of IPMs for Gloucestershire*, pt. 5, 1302-58 (British Record Society, 40, 1910).
R.E. Glasscock, ed., *The Lay Subsidy of 1334* (British Academy Records of Social and Economic History, new series, 11, 1975).
W. Hale, ed., *Registrum Prioratus Beatae Mariae Wigorniensis* (Camden Society, 1865).
J.O. Halliwell, ed., *The Chronicle of William de Rishanger... The Miracles of Simon de Montfort* (Camden Society, 1840).
[W.J. Hardy] ed., *Stratford-on-Avon Corporation Records: The Guild Accounts* (Stratford-upon-Avon Corporation, 1880).
M.D. Harris, ed., *The Coventry Leet Book*, 4 parts (Early English Text Society, Original Series, 134, 135, 138, 146, 1907-13).
W. Hart, ed., *Historia et Cartularium Monasterii Sancti Petri Gloucestriae*, 3 vols (London, Rolls Series, 1867).
R. Hewlett, ed., *The Gloucestershire Court of Sewers 1583-1642* (GRS, 35, 2020).
R.H. Hilton, ed., *The Stoneleigh Leger Book* (DS, 24, 1960).
M. Hollings, ed., *Red Book of Worcester* (WHS, 1934-50).
D. Hollis, ed., *Calendar of the Bristol Apprentice Book 1532-1565* (Bristol Record Soc., 14, 1949).
R. Hoyle, ed., *The Military Survey of Gloucestershire, 1522* (GRS, 6, 1993).
T. John, ed., *The Warwickshire Hundred Rolls of 1279-80* (Records of Social and Economic History, new series, 19, 1992).
G. Kane and E. Talbot, eds., *Piers Plowman: The B Version* (London, 1975).
E. Kimball ed., *Rolls of the Warwickshire and Coventry Sessions of the Peace 1377-1397* (DS, 16, 1939).
R.E.G. Kirk, ed., *Accounts of the Obedientars of Abingdon Abbey* (Camden Society, new series, 51, 1892).
I.S. Leadam, ed., *The Domesday of Inclosures* (Royal Historical Society, 1897) 2 vols.
B.A. Lees, ed., *Records of the Templars in England in the Twelfth Century: The Inquest of 1185* (British Academy Records of Social and Economic History, 9, 1935).
H. Luard, ed., *Annales Monastici*, vol. 4, *Annales Prioratus de Wigornia* (London: Rolls Series, 1869).
M. Macdonald, ed., *The Register of the Guild of the Holy Cross, Stratford-upon-Avon* (DS, 42, 2007).
S. Madge, ed., *Abstracts of IPMs for Gloucestershire, part 4, 1236-1300* (British Record Society, 30, 1903).
Nonarum Inquisitiones in Curia Scaccarii (London, Record Commission, 1807).
D. Oschinsky, *Walter of Henley and Other Treatises on Estate Management and Accounting* (Oxford, 1971).
D. Pearsall, ed., *Piers Plowman: An Edition of the C Text* (London, 1979).
F.S. Pearson, ed., 'Records of a Ruridecanal Court of 1300', in *Collectanea* edited by S. Hamilton (WHS, 1912), pp. 69-80.

L. R. Poos and L. Bonfield, eds., *Select Cases in Manorial Courts* (Selden Society, 114, 1998).
B.H. Putnam, *The Enforcement of the Statutes of Labourers* (New York, 1908).
E.E. Rich, ed., *The Staple Court Books of Bristol* (Bristol Record Soc., 5, 1934).
J. Rhodes, ed., *Terrier of Llanthony Priory's Houses and Lands in Gloucester, 1443* (GRS, 30, 2016).
J. Röhrkasten, ed., *The Worcester Eyre of 1275* (WHS, new series, 22, 2008), pp. 337–8.
D. Royce, ed., *Landboc sive Registrum Monasterii Beatae Mariae Virginis...de Winchelcumba* (Exeter, 1892), 2 vols.
A. Sabin, ed., *Some Manorial Accounts of St Augustine's Abbey, Bristol* (Bristol Record Society, 22, 1960).
M. Sharp, ed., *Accounts of the Constables of Bristol Castle in the Thirteenth and Fourteenth Centuries* (Bristol Record Society, 34, 1982).
L.D.W. Smith, 'A Survey of Building Timber and other Trees in the Hedgerows of a Warwickshire Estate c.1500', *TBWAS* 90 (1980), pp. 65–73.
F. Somers, ed., *Halesowen Churchwardens' Accounts (1487–1582)* (WHS, 1952, 1953).
D.M. Stenton, ed., *Rolls of the Justices in Eyre for Gloucestershire, Warwickshire and Staffordshire, 1221, 1222* (Selden Society 59, 1940).
R.N. Swanson and D. Guyatt, eds., *The Visitation and Court Book of Hartlebury, 1401–1598* (WHS, new series, 24, 2013).
G. Templeman, ed., *The Records of the Guild of the Holy Trinity, St Mary, St John the Baptist and St Katherine of Coventry* (DS, 19, 1944).
M. Tompkins, ed., *Court Rolls of Romsley 1279–1643* (WHS, new series, 27, 2017).
J. Toomey, ed., *Records of Hanley Castle, Worcestershire, c.1147–1547* (WHS, new series, 18, 2001).
J. Toomey, ed., *A Household Account of Edward Duke of York at Hanley Castle, 1409–10* (WHS, new series, 24, 2013).
L. Toulmin Smith, ed., *Leland's Itinerary in England and Wales* (London, 1909), 6 vols.
D. Walker, ed., *The Cartulary of St Augustine's Bristol* (BRS, 10, 1998).
A Watkins, ed., *The Early Records of Coleshill c.1120–1549* (DS, 51, 2018).
J. Webb, ed., *Roll of the Household Expenses of Richard de Swinfield Bishop of Hereford* (Camden Society, 1854–5), 2 vols.
J. Willis Bund, ed., *IPMs for the County of Worcester*, pt. 1, 1242–1299 (WHS, 1894).
J. Willis Bund, ed., *IPMs for the County of Worcester*, pt. 2, 1300–1326 (WHS, 1909).
J. Willis Bund and J. Amphlett, eds., *Lay Subsidy Roll for the County of Worcester circa 1280* (WHS, 1893).
J.M. Wilson, ed., *Accounts of the Priory of Worcester 1521–2* (WHS, 1907).
J.M. Wilson and C. Gordon, eds., *Early Compotus Rolls of the Priory of Worcester* (WHS, 1908).
C. Woolgar, ed., *Household Accounts of Medieval England*, 2 parts (British Academy Records of Social and Economic History, new series, 17, 1992; 18, 1993).

Secondary sources

J. Aberth, *An Environmental History of the Middle Ages: The Crucible of Nature* (Abingdon, 2013).
N.W. Alcock, ed., *Cruck Construction: An Introduction and Catalogue* (CBA Research Report 42, 1981).
N.W. Alcock, P. Barnwell, and M. Cherry, eds.,*Cruck Building: A Survey* (Donington, 2019).

N.W. Alcock and D. Miles, 'An Early Fifteenth-Century Warwickshire Cruck House Using Joggled Halvings', *Vernacular Architecture* 43 (2012), pp. 19-27.

N.W. Alcock and D. Miles, *The Medieval Peasant House in Midland England* (Oxford, 2013).

N.W. Alcock and P. Woodfield, 'Social Pretension in Architecture and Ancestry: Hall House, Sawbridge, Warwickshire, and the Andrewes Family', *Antiquaries Journal* 76 (1996), p. 51-72.

J.R.L. Allen, 'A Short History of Salt-Marsh Reclamation at Slimbridge Warth and Neighbouring Areas, Gloucestershire', *TBGAS* 104 (1986), pp. 139-55.

J.R.L. Allen, 'A Reconnaissance Map of Medieval Alluvial Ploughlands in the Vale of Berkeley, Gloucestershire and Avon', *TBGAS*, 110 (1992), pp. 87-97.

R.C. Allen, *The British Industrial Revolution in Global Perspective* (Cambridge, 2009).

N. Amor, *From Wool to Cloth: The Triumph of the Suffolk Clothier* (Bungay, 2016).

G.G. Astill, *A Medieval Industrial Complex and its Landscape: The Metalworking Watermills and Workshops of Bordesley Abbey* (CBA Research Report, 92, 1993).

M. Aston and C.J. Bond, 'Warwickshire Fishponds', in *Medieval Fish, Fisheries and Fishponds in England*, edited by M. Aston (British Archaeological Reports, British Series, 182, 1988) part 2, pp. 417-34.

W.O. Ault, *Open-Field Farming in Medieval England* (London, 1972).

M. Bailey, 'The Transformation of Customary Tenure in Southern England, c.1350-c.1500', *AgHR* 62 (2014), pp. 210-30.

M. Bailey, 'Tallage-at-Will in Late Medieval England', *EHR* 134 (2019), pp. 25-58.

N. Baker and R. Holt, *Urban Growth and the Medieval Church: Gloucester and Worcester* (Aldershot, 2004).

M.L. Bazeley, 'The Forest of Dean and its Relations with the Crown During the Twelfth and Thirteenth Centuries', *TBGAS* 33 (1910), pp. 153-286.

R. Bearman, ed., *The History of an English Borough: Stratford-upon-Avon, 1196-1996* (Stroud and Stratford, 1997), pp. 1-79.

J.S. Beckerman, 'Procedural Innovation and Institutional Change in Medieval English Manorial Courts', *Law and History Review* 10 (1992), pp. 197-252.

J.S. Beckerman, 'Towards a Theory of Medieval Manorial Adjudication: The Nature of Communal Judgements in a System of Customary Law', *Law and History Review* 13 (1995), pp. 1-22.

J.M. Bennett, *Women in the Medieval English Countryside: Gender and Household in Brigstock before the Plague* (Oxford, 1987).

J.M. Bennett, *Ale, Beer and Brewsters in England* (Oxford, 1996).

M.W. Beresford, *The Lost Villages of England* (London, 1954, revised edition, Stroud, 1998).

M.W. Beresford, *New Towns of the Middle Ages: Town Plantations in England, Wales and Gascony* (London, 1967; new edition, Gloucester, 1988).

M.W. Beresford and J.G. Hurst, *Deserted Medieval Villages* (London, 1971).

J.R. Birrell, 'Common Rights in the Medieval Forest: Disputes and Conflicts in the Thirteenth Century', *P&P* 117 (1987), pp. 22-49.

J.R. Birrell, 'Peasant Deer Poachers in the Medieval Forest', in *Progress and Problems in Medieval England*, edited by R. Britnell and J. Hatcher (Cambridge, 1996), pp. 68-88.

J.R. Birrell, 'Manorial Custumals Reconsidered', *P&P* 224 (2014), pp. 3-37.

J.R. Birrell, 'Peasants' Eating and Drinking', *AgHR* 63 (2015), pp. 1-18.

J.L. Bolton, *Money in the Medieval English Economy, 973-1489* (Manchester, 2012).

L. Bonfield, 'What Did English Villagers Mean by "Customary Law"', in *Medieval Society and the Manor Court*, edited by Z. Razi and R.M. Smith (Oxford, 1996), pp. 103-16.

C. Briggs, *Credit and Village Society in Fourteenth-Century England* (Oxford, 2009).
C. Briggs, 'Monitoring Demesne Managers through the Manor Court Before and After the Black Death', in *Survival and Discord in Medieval Society* edited by R. Goddard, J. Langdon, and M. Muller (Turnhout, 2010), pp. 179-95.
R.H. Britnell, *Britain and Ireland, 1050-1530* (Oxford, 2004).
E. Britton, *The Community of the Vill* (Toronto, 1977).
S. Broadberry, B.M.S. Campbell, A. Klein, M. Overton, and B. van Leeuwen, *British Economic Growth 1270-1870* (Cambridge, 2015).
A.D. Brown, *Popular Piety in Late Medieval England: The Diocese of Salisbury, 1200-1550* (Oxford, 1995).
B.M.S. Campbell, *English Seigniorial Agriculture 1250-1450* (Cambridge, 2000).
B.M.S. Campbell, 'The Agrarian Problem in the Early Fourteenth Century', *P&P* 188 (2005), pp. 3-70.
B.M.S. Campbell, 'Benchmarking Medieval Economic Development: England, Wales, Scotland, and Ireland, c.1290', *EcHR* 61 (2008), pp. 896-945.
B.M.S. Campbell and K. Bartley, *England on the Eve of the Black Death: An Atlas of Lay Lordship, Land and Wealth, 1300-49* (Manchester, 2006).
S. Carocci, 'Social Mobility and the Middle Ages', *Continuity and Change* 26 (2011), pp. 367-404.
C. Carpenter, *Locality and Polity: A Study of Warwickshire Landed Society, 1401-1499* (Cambridge, 1992).
D.A. Carpenter, 'English Peasants in Politics, 1258-1267', *P&P* 136 (1992), pp. 3-42.
E. Carus-Wilson, 'Evidences of Industrial Growth on Some Fifteenth-Century Manors', *EcHR*, 2nd series, 12 (1959), pp. 190-205.
F.W.B. Charles, *Medieval Cruck Building and its Derivatives* (Society for Medieval Archaeology Monograph Series, 2, 1967).
N. Christie and P. Stamper, eds., *Medieval Rural Settlement: Britain and Ireland, AD 800-1600* (Oxford, 2012).
J. Claridge, 'The Role of Demesnes in the Trade of Agricultural Horses in Late Medieval England', *AgHR* 65 (2017), pp. 1-19.
J. Clark, ed., *The Medieval Horse and its Equipment* (Museum of London, 1995)
P.R. Coss, *Lordship, Knighthood and Locality. A Study of English Society c.1180-c.1280* (Cambridge, 1991).
W.H.B. Court, *The Rise of Midland Industries, 1600-1838* (Oxford, 1938).
A. Craven and B. Hartland, *Cheltenham Before the Spa* (London, 2018).
O.H. Creighton, *Designs Upon the Land. Elite Landscapes of the Middle Ages* (Woodbridge, 2009).
H.C. Darby and I B. Terrett, *The Domesday Geography of Midland England* (Cambridge, 1954).
J. Davies, *Medieval Market Morality. Life, Law and Ethics in the English Marketplace, 1200-1500* (Cambridge, 2012).
M. Davies and J. Kissock, 'The Feet of Fines, the Land Market and the English Agricultural Crisis of 1315 to 1322', *Journal of Historical Geography* 30 (2004), pp. 215-30.
G. Demidowicz and S. Price, *King's Norton: A History* (Chichester, 2009).
T. de Moor and J. L van Zanden, 'Girl Power: The European Marriage Pattern and Labour Market in the North Sea Region in the Late Medieval and Early Modern Period', *EcHR* 63 (2010), pp. 1-33.
M. de Moor, *The Dilemma of the Commoners: Understanding the Use of Common Pool Resources in Long-Term Perspective* (Cambridge, 2015).

B. Dodds, *Peasants and Production in the Medieval North-East. The Evidence of Tithes, 1270-1536* (Woodbridge, 2007).

A.D. Dyer, *The City of Worcester in the Sixteenth Century* (Leicester, 1973).

C. Dyer, *Lords and Peasants in a Changing Society: The Estates of the Bishopric of Worcester 680-1540* (Cambridge, 1980).

C. Dyer, *Warwickshire Farming, 1349-c.1520* (DS Occasional Paper, 27, 1981).

C. Dyer, 'English Peasant Buildings in the Later Middle Ages', *Med Arch* 30 (1986), pp. 19-45.

C. Dyer, 'The Rise and Fall of a Medieval Village: Little Aston (in Aston Blank), Gloucestershire', *TBGAS* 105 (1987), pp. 165-81.

C. Dyer, 'Dispersed Settlements in Medieval England: A Case Study of Pendock, Worcestershire', *Med Arch* 24 (1990), pp. 97-121.

C. Dyer, 'Were There Any Capitalists in Fifteenth-Century England?' in *Enterprise and Individuals in Fifteenth-Century England*, edited by J. Kermode (Stroud, 1991), pp. 1-24.

C. Dyer, *Hanbury: Settlement and Society in a Woodland Landscape* (University of Leicester Department of English Local History Occasional Papers, 4th series, 4, 1991).

C. Dyer, 'The Hidden Trade of the Middle Ages: Evidence from the West Midlands of England', *Journal of Historical Geography* 18 (1992), pp. 141-57.

C. Dyer, 'Small-Town Conflict in the Later Middle Ages: Events at Shipston-on-Stour', *Urban History* 19 (1992), pp. 183-210.

C. Dyer, 'Market Towns and the Countryside in Late Medieval England', *Canadian Journal of History* 31 (1996), pp. 17-35.

C. Dyer, 'Rural Settlement in Medieval Warwickshire', *TBWAS* 100 (1996), pp. 117-32.

C. Dyer, 'Peasants and Farmers: Rural Settlements and Landscapes in an Age of Transition', in *The Age of Transition: The Archaeology of English Culture 1400-1600*, edited by D. Gaimster and P. Stamper (Society for Medieval Archaeology Monograph 15, 1997), pp. 61-76.

C. Dyer, 'Peasants and Coins: The Uses of Money in the Middle Ages', *British Numismatic Journal* 67 (1998), pp. 30-47.

C. Dyer, 'Compton Verney: Landscape and People in the Middle Ages', in *Compton Verney: A History of the House and its Owners*, edited by R. Bearman (Stratford-upon-Avon, 2000).

C. Dyer, *Bromsgrove: A Small Town in Worcestershire in the Middle Ages* (WHS Occasional Publication, 9, 2000).

C. Dyer, 'Villages and Non-Villages in the Medieval Cotswolds', *TBGAS* 120 (2002), pp. 11-35.

C. Dyer, 'Alternative Agriculture: Goats in Medieval England', in *People, Landscape and Alternative Agriculture*, edited by R. Hoyle (AgHR Supplement, 2004).

C. Dyer, 'The Political Life of the Fifteenth-Century English Village', *The Fifteenth Century* 4 (2004), pp. 135-57.

C. Dyer, *An Age of Transition? Economy and Society in England in the Later Middle Ages* (Oxford, 2005).

C. Dyer, 'Were Late Medieval Villages "Self-Contained"?' in *The Self-Contained Village? The Social History of Rural Communities, 1250-1900* (Hatfield, 2007), pp. 6-27.

C. Dyer, 'Conflict in the Landscape: The Enclosure Movement in England, 1220-1349', *Landscape History* 29 (2007), pp. 21-33.

C. Dyer, 'Landscape and Society at Bibury, Gloucestershire, to 1540', in *Archives and Local History in Bristol and Gloucestershire*, edited by J. Bettey (BGAS, 2007), pp. 62-77.

C. Dyer, 'Villages in Crisis: Social Dislocation, 1370-1520', in *Deserted Villages Revisited* edited by C. Dyer and R. Jones (Hatfield, 2010), pp. 28-45.

C. Dyer, *A Country Merchant, 1495-1520: Trading and Farming at the End of the Middle Ages* (Oxford, 2012).

C. Dyer, 'Living in Peasant Houses in Late Medieval England', *Vernacular Architecture* 44 (2013), pp. 19-27.

C. Dyer, 'Peasant Farming in Late Medieval England: Evidence from the Tithe Estimations by Worcester Cathedral Priory', in *Peasants and Lords in the Medieval English Economy: Essays in Honour of Bruce M.S. Campbell*, edited by M. Kowaleski, J. Langdon, and P.R. Schofield (Turnhout, 2015), pp. 83-109.

C. Dyer, 'Lords in a Landscape: The Berkeley Family and Northfield (Worcestershire)', *The Fifteenth Century* 14 (2015), pp. 13-37.

C. Dyer, 'Landscape, Farming and Society in an English Region: Inquisitions Post Mortem for the West Midlands, 1250-1509', in *The Later Medieval Inquisitions Post Mortem. Mapping the Medieval Countryside and Rural Society*, edited by M. Hicks (Woodbridge, 2016), pp. 59-83.

C. Dyer, 'The Midland Economy and Society, 1314-48: Insights from Changes in the Landscape', *Midland History* 42 (2017), pp. 36-57.

C. Dyer, 'New Towns in the Middle Ages: Lessons from Bretford in Warwickshire', *TBWAS* 120 (2018), pp. 75-92.

C. Dyer, 'The Housing of Peasant Livestock in England, 1200-1520', *AgHR*, 67 (2019), pp. 29-50.

C. Dyer, 'A Medieval Village in a Cotswold Landscape: Pinbury in Duntisbourne Rous', *TBGAS*, 137 (2019), pp. 191-213.

C. Dyer, 'Migration in Rural England in the Later Middle Ages', in *Migrants in Medieval England, c.500-c.1500*, edited by W.M. Ormrod, J. Story and E. Tyler (Oxford, British Academy, 2020), pp. 238-64.

C. Dyer, 'Peasants and Poultry in England, 1250-1540', *Quaternary International* 543 (2020), pp. 113-18.

C. Dyer, 'Recovering from Catastrophe: How Medieval Society in England Coped with Disaster', in *Waiting for the End of the World? New Perspectives on Natural Disasters in Medieval Europe*, edited by C. Gerrard and others (Society for Medieval Archaeology Monograph 43, 2021), pp. 218-38.

C. Dyer and D. Aldred, 'Changing Landscape and Society in a Cotswold Village: Hazleton, Gloucestershire, to c. 1600', *TBGAS*, 127 (2009), pp. 235-70.

C. Dyer, E. Thoen, and T. Williamson, eds., *Peasants and Their Fields: The Rationale of Open-Field Agriculture, c.700-1800* (Turnhout, 2018).

G. Egan, 'Urban and Rural Finds: Material Culture of Country and Town c.1050-1500', in *Town and Country in the Middle Ages*, edited by K. Giles and C. Dyer (Society for Medieval Archaeology Monograph 22, 2005).

F. Ellis, *Peasant Economics* (Cambridge, 1993).

D. Enright and M. Watts, *A Romano-British and Medieval Settlement Site at Stoke Road, Bishop's Cleeve, Gloucestershire* (BGAS Archaeological Report, 1, 2002).

R.K. Field, 'Worcestershire Peasant Buildings, Household Goods and Farming Equipment in the Later Middle Ages', *Med Arch* 9 (1965), pp. 105-45.

R.K. Field, 'Migration in the Later Middle Ages: The Case of the Hampton Lovett Villeins', *Midland History* 8 (1983), pp. 29-48.

H.P.R. Finberg, *Gloucestershire: An Illustrated Essay on the History of the Landscape* (London, 1955).

J.A. Ford, *John Mirk's Festial: Orthodoxy, Lollardy and the Common People in Fourteenth-Century England* (Woodbridge, 2006).

H.S.A. Fox, 'The Alleged Transformation from Two-Field to Three-Field Systems in Medieval England', *EcHR*, 2nd series, 39 (1986), pp. 526–48.

H.S.A. Fox, 'Exploitation of the Landless by Lords and Tenants in Early Medieval England', in *Medieval Society and the Manor Court*, edited by Z. Razi and R.M. Smith (Oxford, 1996), pp. 518–68.

P. Franklin, 'Malaria in Medieval Gloucestershire: An Essay in Epidemiology', *TBGAS*, 101 (1983), pp. 111–22.

P. Franklin, 'Peasant Widows' "Liberation" and Remarriage before the Black Death', *EcHR*, 2nd series, 39 (1986), pp. 186–204.

P. Franklin, 'Politics in Manorial Court Rolls: The Tactics, Social Composition and Aims of a pre-1381 Peasant Movement', in *Medieval Society and the Manor Court*, edited by Z. Razi and R.M. Smith (Oxford, 1996), pp. 162–98.

P. Freedman, *Images of the Medieval Peasant* (Stanford, CA, 1999).

K.L. French, *The People of the Parish: Community Life in a Late Medieval Diocese* (Philadelphia, 2001).

M. Gardiner, 'Vernacular Buildings and the Development of the Later Medieval Domestic Plan in England', *Med Arch* 44 (2000), pp. 159–79.

M. Gardiner, 'An Archaeological Approach to the Development of the Late Medieval Peasant House', *Vernacular Architecture* 45 (2014), pp. 16–28.

M. Gardiner and S. Rippon, eds., *Medieval Landscapes* (Macclesfield, 2007).

M. Gelling, *Signposts to the Past: Place-Names and the History of England* (London, 1978).

C. Gerrard, *Medieval Archaeology: Understanding Traditions and Contemporary Approaches* (London, 2003).

M. Gill, 'The Lost Wall Paintings of Halesowen Church', *Transactions of the Worcestershire Archaeological Society*, 3rd series, 16 (1998), pp. 133–42.

S. Godbold and R.C. Turner, 'Medieval Fishtraps in the Severn Estuary', *Med Arch* 38 (1994), pp. 19–54.

R. Goddard, 'Female Apprenticeship in the West Midlands in the Later Middle Ages', *Midland History* 27 (2002), pp. 165–81.

R. Goddard, *Lordship and Medieval Urbanisation: Coventry, 1043–1355* (Woodbridge, 2004).

R. Goheen, 'Peasant Politics? Village Community and the Crown in Fifteenth-Century England', *American Historical Review* 96 (1991), pp. 42–62.

P J.P. Goldberg, *Women, Work, and Life Cycle in a Medieval Economy: Women in York and Yorkshire c.1300–1520* (Oxford, 1992).

J. Greig, 'The Investigation of a Medieval Barrel Latrine from Worcester', *Journal of Archaeological Science* 8 (1981), pp. 265–82.

R.M. Haines, 'Bishop Carpenter's Injunctions to the Diocese of Worcester in 1451', *Bulletin of the Institute of Historical Research* 40 (1967), pp. 203–7.

D. Hall, *The Open Fields of England* (Oxford, 2014).

H.E. Hallam, ed., *Agrarian History of England and Wales*, 2, 1042–1350 (Cambridge, 1988).

B.A. Hanawalt, *The Ties that Bound. Peasant Families in Medieval England* (Oxford, 1986).

P. Hargreaves, 'Seigniorial Reaction and Peasant Responses: Worcester Priory and its Peasants after the Black Death', *Midland History*, 24 (1999), pp. 53–78.

D. Harrison, *The Bridges of Medieval England. Transport and Society, 400–1800* (Oxford, 2004).

C.E. Hart, *Royal Forest* (Oxford, 1966).
J. Hart, A. Mudd, E.R. McSloy, and M. Brett, *Living Near the Edge: Archaeological Investigations in the Western Cotswolds* (Cotswold Archaeology Monograph, 9, 2016).
B.F. Harvey, 'The Leasing of the Abbot of Westminster's Demesnes in the Later Middle Ages', *EcHR*, 2nd series, 22 (1969), pp. 17–27.
B. F. Harvey, *Westminster Abbey and its Estates in the Middle Ages* (Oxford, 1977).
B. Harvey, *Living and Dying in England 1100–1540* (Oxford, 1993).
P.D.A. Harvey, ed., *The Peasant Land Market in Medieval England* (Oxford, 1984).
P.D.A. Harvey, 'Rectitudines Singularum Personarum and Gerefa', *EHR*, 108 (1993), pp. 1–22.
J. Hatcher, *Plague, Population and the English Economy 1348–1530* (London, 1977).
R.H. Helmholz, *Marriage Litigation in Medieval England* (Cambridge, 1974).
N. Herbert, 'Northleach; New Light on the Making of a Gloucestershire Town', in *Archives and Local History in Bristol and Gloucestershire*, edited by J. Bettey (BGAS, 2007), pp. 17–26.
H.J. Hewitt, *The Organization of War under Edward III, 1338–62* (Manchester, 1966).
M. Hicks, ed., *English Inland Trade 1430–1540: Southampton and its Region* (Oxford, 2015).
R.H. Hilton, *Social Structure of Rural Warwickshire in the Middle Ages* (DS Occasional Paper, 9, 1950).
R.H. Hilton, 'Old Enclosure in the West Midlands', *Annales de L'Est* 21 (1959), pp. 272–83.
R.H. Hilton, 'Freedom and Villeinage in England', *P&P* 31 (1965), pp. 3–19.
R.H. Hilton, *A Medieval Society: The West Midlands at the End of the Thirteenth Century* (London, 1966).
R.H. Hilton, *Bond Men Made Free: Medieval Peasant Movements and the English Rising of 1381* (London, 1973).
R.H. Hilton, *The English Peasantry in the Later Middle Ages* (Oxford, 1975).
R.H. Hilton, 'Lords, Burgesses and Huxters', *P&P* 97 (1982), pp. 3–15.
R.H. Hilton, 'The Small Town and Urbanisation—Evesham in the Middle Ages', *Midland History* 7 (1982), pp. 1–8.
R.H. Hilton, 'Small Town Society in England before the Black Death', *P&P* 105 (1984), pp. 53–78.
R.H. Hilton, 'Medieval Market Towns and Simple Commodity Production', *P&P* 109 (1985), pp. 1–23.
R.H. Hilton, 'Low Level Urbanisation: The Seigneurial Borough of Thornbury in the Middle Ages', in *Medieval Society and the Manor Court*, edited by Z. Razi and R.M. Smith (Oxford, 1996), pp. 482–517.
R.H. Hilton and P.A. Rahtz, 'Upton, Gloucestershire, 1959–1964', *TBGAS* 85 (1966), pp. 70–146.
B.P. Hindle, *Medieval Roads* (Princes Risborough, 1982).
S. Hirst and T. Dickinson, 'The Archaeology of Bidford-on-Avon: Excavations 1970–94', *TBWAS* 23 (2021).
R.A. Holt, *The Early History of the Town of Birmingham 1166–1600* (DS Occasional Paper, 30, 1985).
R. Holt, 'Whose were the Profits of Corn Milling? The Abbots of Glastonbury and their Tenants, 1086–1350', *P&P* 116 (1987), pp. 3–23.
G.C. Homans, *English Villagers of the Thirteenth Century* (Cambridge, MA, 1941).
D. Hooke, *The Anglo-Saxon Landscape: The Kingdom of the Hwicce* (Manchester, 1985).
S. Horrell, J. Humphries, and J. Weisdorf, 'Family Standards of Living Over the Long Run, England 1280–1850', *P&P* 250 (2021), pp. 87–114.

J. Hunt, *Lordship and Landscape. A Documentary and Archaeological Study of the Honor of Dudley c.1066–1322* (British Archaeological Reports British Series, 264, 1997).

D. Hurst, 'A Medieval Production Site and other Medieval Sites in the Parish of Hanley Castle: Results of Fieldwork in 1987–1992', *Transactions of the Worcestershire Archaeological Society*, 3rd ser., 14 (1994), pp. 115–28.

R. Hutton, *The Rise and Fall of Merry England. The Ritual Year, 1400–1700* (Oxford, 1994).

T. John, 'Change in Medieval Warwickshire, Domesday Book to the Hundred Rolls of 1279–1280', *Local Population Studies* 59 (1997), pp. 41–53.

M. Johnson, *English Houses, 1300–1800. Vernacular Architecture, Social Life* (Harlow, 2010).

T. Johnson, *Law in Common. Legal Cultures in Late-Medieval England* (Oxford, 2020).

R Jones, 'Signatures in the Soil: The Use of Pottery in Manure Scatters in the Identification of Medieval Arable Farming Regimes', *Archaeological Journal* 161 (2004), pp. 159–88.

R. Jones and M. Page, *Medieval Villages in an English Landscape: Beginnings and Ends* (Macclesfield, 2006).

M. Jurkowski, C.L. Smith, and D. Crook, *Lay Taxes in England and Wales, 1188–1688* (Kew, 1998).

S. Kilby, *Peasant Perspectives on the Medieval Landscape* (Hatfield, 2020).

S. Knight, *Robin Hood: A Complete Study of the English Outlaw* (Oxford, 1994).

M. Kowaleski, 'Medieval People in Town and Country: New Perspectives from Demography and Bioarchaeology', *Speculum* 89 (2014), pp. 573–600.

M. Kowaleski, J. Langdon, and P.R. Schofield, eds., *Peasants and Lords in the Medieval English Economy* (Turnhout, 2015).

B. Kumin, *The Shaping of a Community. The Rise and Reformation of the English Parish c.1400–1560* (Aldershot, 1996).

J. Langdon, *Horses, Oxen and Technological Innovation: The Use of Draught Animals in English Farming 1066–1500* (Cambridge, 1986).

J. Langdon, *Mills in the Medieval Economy: England 1300–1540* (Oxford, 2004).

J. Langdon and J. Masschaele, 'Commercial Activity and Population Growth in Medieval England', *P&P* 190 (2006), pp. 35–81.

J.S. Lee, *The Medieval Clothier* (Woodbridge, 2018).

R. Leech, *Small Medieval Towns in Avon: Archaeology and Planning* (Bristol, Committee for Rescue Archaeology in Avon, Gloucestershire and Somerset, 1975).

R. Leech, *Historic Towns in Gloucestershire: Archaeology and Planning* (Bristol, Committee for Rescue Archaeology in Avon, Gloucestershire and Somerset, 1982).

S. Letters, *Gazetteer of Markets and Fairs in England and Wales to 1516*, 2 parts (List and Index Society, Special Series, 32, 33, 2003).

K.D. Lilley, 'A Warwickshire Medieval Borough: Brinklow and the Contribution of Town-Plan Analysis', *TBWAS* 95 (1993–4), pp. 51–60.

S. Litherland, E. Ramsay, and P. Ellis, 'The Archaeology of the Severn Trent Southern Area Rationalisation Scheme, Warwickshire', *TBWAS* 112 (2008), pp. 73–124.

T.H. Lloyd, *Some Aspects of the Building Industry of Stratford-upon-Avon* (DS Occasional Paper, 14, 1961).

T.H. Lloyd, *The Movement of Wool Prices in Medieval England* (EcHR supplement, 6, 1973).

J.R. Maddicott, *The English Peasantry and the Demands of the Crown* (Past and Present Supplement, no. 1, 1975).

S. Markley, 'The "Unseen Seen" –Earth Mortared Stone Construction, a Reilluminated Historic Construction Technique in Britain', *Construction History* 33 (2018), pp. 23–43.

J. Masschaele, *Jury, State and Society in Medieval England* (Basingstoke, 2008).

M.E. Mate, *Daughters, Wives and Widows after the Black Death. Women in Sussex, 1350–1535* (Woodbridge, 1998).

A. Mawer and F.M. Stenton, *The Place-Names of Worcestershire* (English Place-Name Society, 4, 1927).

P. Mayes and K. Scott, *Pottery Kilns at Chilvers Coton, Nuneaton* (Society for Medieval Archaeology Monograph 10, 1984).

M.R. McCarthy and C.M. Brooks, *Medieval Pottery in Britain AD 900–1600* (Leicester, 1988).

M.K. McIntosh, *Autonomy and Community: The Royal Manor of Havering, 1200–1500* (Cambridge, 1986).

M.K. McIntosh, *Controlling Misbehavior in England, 1370–1600* (Cambridge, 1998).

M. Mellor, 'A Synthesis of Middle and Late Saxon, Medieval and Early Post-Medieval Pottery in the Oxford Region', *Oxoniensia* 59 (1994).

S. Mileson, *Parks in Medieval England* (Oxford, 2009).

S. Mileson, 'People and Houses in South Oxfordshire, 1300–1650', *Vernacular Architecture* 46 (2015), pp. 8–25.

S. Mileson, 'Openness and Closure in Later Medieval Villages', *P&P* 234 (2017), pp. 3–37.

E. Miller, ed., *Agrarian History of England and Wales*, 3, 1350–1500 (Cambridge, 1991).

C. Muldrew, '"The Ancient Distaff" and "Whirling Spindle": Measuring the Contribution of Spinning to Household Earnings and the National Economy in England, 1530–1770', *EcHR* 65 (2012), pp. 498–526.

J. Myrdal and A. Sapoznik, 'Technology, Labour and Productivity Potential in Peasant Agriculture: England c.1000–1348', *AgHR* 65 (2017), pp. 194–212.

S. Ogilvie and M. Cerman, *European Proto Industrialization* (Cambridge, 1996).

J. Oldland, 'The Clothiers' Century, 1450–1550', *Rural History* 29 (2018), pp. 1–22.

W.M. Ormrod, 'England in the Middle Ages', in *The Rise of the Fiscal State in Europe c.1200–1815*, edited by R. Bonney (Oxford, 1991), pp. 19–52.

M. Page, 'Manor Courts and the Retirement of Customary Tenants on the Bishop of Winchester's Estates before the Black Death', *Southern History* 35 (2013), pp. 23–43.

D. Palliser, ed., *Cambridge Urban History of Britain*, vol. 1, 600–1540 (Cambridge, 2000).

N. Palmer and J. Parkhouse, *Burton Dassett Southend, Warwickshire: A Medieval Market Village* (Society for Medieval Archaeology Monograph, 44, 2022).

S.A.C. Penn, 'The Origins of Bristol Migrants in the Early Fourteenth Century: The Surname Evidence', *TBGAS* 101 (1983), pp. 123–30.

S.A.C. Penn. 'A Hidden Workforce: Building Workers in Fourteenth-Century Bristol', *TBGAS* 109 (1991), pp. 171–8.

R. Perry, 'The Gloucestershire Woollen Industry, 1100–1690', *TBGAS*, 66 (1945), pp. 49–137.

L.R. Poos, 'The Social Context of the Statute of Labourers Enforcement', *Law and History Review* 1 (1983), pp. 27–52.

L.R. Poos, *A Rural Society after the Black Death: Essex 1350–1525* (Cambridge, 1991).

M.M. Postan, *The Famulus* (EcHR supplement, 2, 1959).

M.M. Postan, ed., *The Agrarian Life of the Middle Ages* (Cambridge Economic History of Europe, vol. 1, 2nd edn, 1966).

O. Rackham, *The History of the Countryside* (London, 1986).

J.A. Raftis, *Tenure and Mobility. Studies in the Social History of the Medieval English Village* (Toronto, 1964).

P.A. Rahtz, 'Upton, Gloucestershire, 1959–1968. Second Report', *TBGAS* 88 (1969), pp. 74–126.

Z. Razi, *Life, Marriage and Death in a Medieval Parish. Economy, Society and Demography in Halesowen 1270–1400* (Cambridge, 1980).

Z. Razi, 'Family, Land and the Village Community in Later Medieval England', *P&P* 93 (1981), pp. 3–36.

Z. Razi, 'The Struggles Between the Abbots of Halesowen and their Tenants in the Thirteenth and Fourteenth Centuries', in *Social Relations and Ideas*, edited by T.H. Aston, P. Coss, C.C. Dyer, and J. Thirsk (Cambridge, 1983), pp. 151–67.

Z. Razi, 'The Myth of the Immutable English Family', *P&P* 140 (1993), pp. 3–44.

Z. Razi and R.M. Smith, eds., *Medieval Society and the Manor Court* (Oxford, 1996).

S.H. Rigby, ed., *A Companion to Britain in the Later Middle Ages* (Oxford, 2003).

S. Rippon, *The Severn Estuary. Landscape Evolution and Wetland Reclamation* (Leicester, 1997).

B.K. Roberts, 'A Study of Medieval Colonization in the Forest of Arden, Warwickshire', *AgHR* 16 (1968), pp. 101–13.

B.K. Roberts, 'Field Systems of the West Midlands', in *Studies in the Field Systems in the British Isles*, edited by A.H.R. Baker and R.A. Butlin (Cambridge, 1973), pp. 188–231.

B.K. Roberts, 'Village Forms in Warwickshire: A Preliminary Discussion', in *Field and Forest: An Historical Geography of Warwickshire and Worcestershire* (Norwich, 1982); edited by T.R. Slater and P.J. Jarvis, pp. 125–46.

B.K. Roberts and S. Wrathmell, *Region and Place: A Study of English Rural Settlement* (London, 2002).

D. Robinson, 'Priesthood and Community: The Social and Economic Background of the Parochial Clergy in the Diocese of Worcester to 1348', *Midland History* 42 (2017), pp. 18–35.

W. Rösener, *Peasants in the Middle Ages* (Cambridge, 1985).

A. Sapoznik, 'Bees in the Medieval Economy: Religious Observance and the Production, Trade, and Consumption of Wax in England, c.1300–1555', *EcHR* 72 (2019), pp. 1152–74.

P. Schofield, 'Dearth, Debt and the Local Land Market in a Late Thirteenth-Century Village Community', *AgHR* 45 (1997), pp. 1–17.

P.R. Schofield, *Peasant and Community in Medieval England, 1200–1500* (Basingstoke, 2003).

P.R. Schofield, *Peasants and Historians: Debating the Medieval English Peasantry* (Manchester, 2016).

T. Scott, ed., *The Peasantries of Europe* (Harlow, 1998).

T. Shanin, ed., *Peasants and Peasant Societies* (Harmondsworth, 1971).

B. Sharp, *Famine and Scarcity in Late Medieval and Early Modern England: The Regulation of Grain Marketing, 1256–1631* (Cambridge, 2016).

V. Skipp, *Medieval Yardley* (Chichester, 1970).

T.R. Slater, 'English Medieval New Towns with Composite Plans: Evidence from the Midlands', in *The Built Form of Western Cities*, edited by T.R. Slater (Leicester, 1990), pp. 60–82.

T.R. Slater, *Edgbaston: A History* (Chichester, 2002).

T.R. Slater and P.J. Jarvis, eds., *Field and Forest: An Historical Geography of Warwickshire and Worcestershire* (Norwich, 1982).

P. Slavin, 'The Great Bovine Pestilence and its Economic and Environmental Consequences in England and Wales, 1318–50', *EcHR*, 65 (2012), pp. 1239–66.

P. Slavin, 'Peasant Livestock Husbandry in Late Thirteenth-Century Suffolk: Economy, Environment and Society', in *Peasants and Lords in the Medieval English Economy*, edited by M. Kowaleski, J. Langdon, and P.R. Schofield (Turnhout, 2015), pp. 3–26.

P. Slavin, *Experiencing Famine in Fourteenth-Century Britain* (Turnhout, 2019).

P. Slavin, 'Mites and Merchants: The Crisis of English Wool and Textile Trade Revisited, c.1275–1330', *EcHR* 73 (2020), pp. 885–913.

A.H. Smith, *The Place-Names of Gloucestershire* (English Place-Name Society, 38–41, 1960–5), 4 parts.

B. Smith, *A History of Malvern* (Leicester, 1964).

R.M. Smith, 'Kin and Neighbours in a Thirteenth Century Suffolk Community', *Journal of Family History* 4 (1979), pp. 219–56.

R.M. Smith, ed., *Land, Kinship and Life-Cycle* (Cambridge, 1984).

R.M. Smith, 'Coping with Uncertainty: Women's Tenure of Customary Land in England c.1370–1430', in *Enterprise and Individuals in Fifteenth-Century England*, edited by J. Kermode (Stroud, 1991), pp. 43–67.

R.M. Smith, 'The Manorial Court and the Elderly Tenant in Late Medieval England', in *Life, Death and the Elderly*, edited by M. Pelling and R.M. Smith (London, 1991), pp. 39–61.

R.M. Smith, 'The English Peasantry, 1250–1650', in *The Peasantries of Europe*, edited by T. Scott (Harlow, 1998).

W. St Clair Baddeley, *A Cotteswold Manor: Being the History of Painswick* (London, 1929).

E.R. Standley, 'Spinning Yarns: The Archaeological Evidence for Hand Spinning and its Social Implications', *Med Arch* 60 (2016), pp. 266–99.

S.C. Stanford, *Midsummer Hill: An Iron Age Hillfort on the Malverns* (Hereford, 1981).

D. Stone, *Decision-Making in Medieval Agriculture* (Oxford, 2005).

J. Thirsk, ed., *Rural England: An Illustrated History of the Landscape* (Oxford, 2000).

R. Thomas, *Animals, Economy and Status: Integrating Zooarchaeological and Historical Data in the Study of Dudley Castle, West Midlands (c.1100–1750)* (British Archaeological Reports, British series, 392, 2005).

R. Thomas, M. Holmes, and J. Mams, '"So bigge or bigge may be": Tracking Size and Shape Changes in Domestic Livestock in London (AD 1320–1900)', *Journal of Archaeological Science* 40 (2013), pp. 3309–25.

P. Thompson and S.C. Palmer, 'Iron Age, Romano-British and Medieval Settlements Excavated on the Transco Newbold Pacey to Honeybourne Gas Pipeline in 2000', *TBWAS* 116 (2012), pp. 1–139.

H. Thorpe, 'The Lord and the Landscape', *TBAS* 80 (1965), pp. 38–77.

M. Tompkins, 'Counting Houses: Using the Housing Structure of a Late Medieval Manor to Illuminate Population, Landholding and Occupational Structure', in *Life in Medieval Landscapes: People and Places in the Middle Ages*, edited by S. Turner and R. Silvester (Oxford, 2012), pp. 225–38.

C. Valente, *The Theory and Practice of Revolt in Medieval England* (Aldershot, 2003).

E. Vanhaute, *Peasants in World History* (London, 2021).

S. Wager, *Woods, Wolds and Groves: The Woodland of Medieval Warwickshire* (British Archaeological Reports, British series, 269, 1998).

P. Warde, *The Invention of Sustainability: Nature and Destiny, c.1500–1870* (Cambridge, 2019).

A. Watkins, 'Cattle Grazing in the Forest of Arden in the Later Middle Ages', *AgHR* 37 (1989), pp. 12–25.

A. Watkins, 'The Woodland Economy of the Forest of Arden in the Later Middle Ages', *Midland History* 18 (1993), pp. 19–36.

A. Watkins, *Small Towns in the Forest of Arden in the Fifteenth Century* (Dugdale Society Occasional Paper, 38, 1998).

M. Watts, ed., *Prehistoric and Medieval Occupation at Moreton-in-Marsh and Bishop's Cleeve, Gloucestershire* (BGAS Archaeological Report, 5, 2007).

B. Wells-Furby, *The Berkeley Estate 1281-1417: Its Economy and Development* (BGAS, 2012).

J. Whittle, *The Development of Agrarian Capitalism: Land and Labour in Norfolk, 1440-1580* (Oxford, 2000).

J. Whittle, ed., *Servants in Rural Europe 1400-1900* (Woodbridge, 2017).

C.J. Wickham, 'How Did the Feudal Economy Work? The Economic Logic of Medieval Societies', *P&P* 251 (2021), pp. 3-40.

T. Williamson, *Shaping Medieval Landscapes: Settlement, Society, Environment* (Macclesfield, 2003).

T. Williamson, R. Liddiard, and T. Partida, *Champion: The Making and Unmaking of the English Midland Landscape* (Liverpool, 2013).

A. J. L. Winchester, 'Property Rights, "Good Neighbourhood" and Sustainability in the Management of Common Land in England and Wales, 1235-1965', in *Rural Societies and Environments at Risk*, edited by B. Van Bavel and E. Thoen (Turnhout, 2013), pp. 309-29.

C.M. Woolgar, D. Sergeantson, and T. Waldron, eds., *Food in Medieval England* (Oxford, 2006).

C.R. Young, *The Royal Forests of Medieval England* (Leicester, 1979).

Index

Note: Tables and figures are indicated by an italic '*t*' and '*f*', respectively, following the page number.

For the benefit of digital users, indexed terms that span two pages (e.g., 52–53) may, on occasion, appear on only one of those pages.

Abbots Morton (Worc) 34, 216–17
Abbots Salford (Warw) 188–9, 198, 212–13
Adam, William, of Claines 223
Addecokke, Walter, of Rockhampton 81
Adlestrop (Glouc) 154–5, 162, 219–20, 300–1
Admington (Warw) 18, 75, 99–100, 103–4, 138, 173
Admond (Admont), Isabella 71–2; Richard (formerly Wodelond) 71–2; Thomas 71, all of Cleeve Prior
Ailstone (Warw) 198, 204–5
Alcester (Warw) 172–3, 190–1, 229, 233–5, 234*f*, 238, 244*t*, 244–9, 247*f*, 252–6, 255*t*, 258–9, 263*t*, 261–9, 290–1, 298–9, 330
Alcester Abbey 263
Alcock, John, of Alcester 266
Alderminster (Warw) 303–4
ale 4, 91, 117, 131, 136–7, 162–3, 181, 249, 288, 301–3, 324–5
Allesborough, *see* Pershore
Almondsbury (Glouc) 302–3
Alne, river 233
Alspath, *see* Meriden
Alstone (Glouc) 77
Alvard (Alvert) Katherine, of Claines 240–2; Thomas, of Teddington 104–5
Alvechurch (Worc) 35, 92, 116–17, 152, 256; Rowney Green in 152
Alveston (Warw) 58–9, 143, 153–4, 171–2, 198, 205, 210–11, 242–3, 317
Alvington (Glouc) 39, 216–17
Ambresley, John, of Maxstoke 248
Andrewes, John; Thomas (first and second), of Sawbridge 96
Apperley (Glouc) 239
apples, *see* horticulture
apprentices, apprenticeship 90–1, 240–2, 241*f*
Aprice, Peter, of Hartlebury 197
Apsolon, Richard, of Hanley Castle 93–4
Archer, John, of Tanworth-in-Arden 156–7
Arden 24–5, 27, 30, 40, 45, 49–50, 66, 73–4, 88, 95–6, 151–2, 183–4, 196–7, 233, 238, 249, 268, 330–1, 333

Arrow, river 10–12, 233
artisans 35, 39, 90–1, 97–9, 236–8, 240–2, 271, 274–8, 280–2, 286, 289–91
Ascott (Warw) 106
Ashburton (Devon) 335
Ashleworth (Glouc) 151–2
Ashow (Warw) 125–7, 151–2
Aston (Warw) 291
Aston Blank (Glouc) 14, 16*f*, 60, 330–1; Little Aston in 60
Aston Cantlow (Warw) 264
Atch Lench (Worc) 216–17
Atehelme, Adam, of Grimley 98–9
Atherstone (Warw) 93, 116–17, 137, 245–8
Attleborough (Warw) 248
Aust (Glouc) 33–4
Avening (Glouc) 281–2
Avon, river; Bristol Avon 18–20; Little Avon 10–12; Warwickshire Avon 10–12, 14–18, 25–7, 30, 61–2, 85–6, 155, 159–60, 233, 238, 249, 291, 297–8, 300
Avonmouth (Glouc) 19–20
Aylburton (Glouc) 216–17

Bachiler, William le; Sarra, of Wasperton 52
Baddesley Clinton (Warw) 273
Badgeworth (Glouc) 200
Badminton (Glouc) 61–2, 107, 189, 224; Little Badminton, *see* Hawkesbury
Badsey (Worc) 221–2, 325
Baggeslowe, John, of Blyth near Coleshill 224
Bailly, family, of Middleton 196–7
Baldenhall, *see* Malvern
Ballarde, family, of Hartlebury 110
Baltic Sea 210–11, 254
Banbury (Oxon) 195
Barcheston (Warw) 43–4
Baret, Hugh, of Shipston 167–8; Thomas, of Stratford 242–3
barley 159–64, 246, 336–7, *see* drage
barns 121–2, 130–1, 175–8, 176*f*, 219–20, 338, 339
Barston (Warw) 254

Bascote, *see* Long Itchington
Bassingbourn (Cambs) 335
Batyn, Christina, of Stoke Gifford 70–1
Bayly, George (alias Potter), of Nuneaton 253–4
Beachley (Glouc) 239
beans 166, 307
Beauchamp family, *see* Warwick, earls of
Beauchamps of Powicke 263; Lady Katherine Beauchamp 265; Richard Beauchamp 263
Beaudesert (Warw) 24–7
Beche, Thomas, of Sambourn 157–8
Beckford (Worc) 164–5, 172–3, 200–1
Bedel, Adam le, of Elmley Castle 78–9; Richard le, of Priors Marston 56–7
Bele, John; Roger, of Sedgeberrow 337; Richard, of Chaceley 80–1
Bell, John, of Bidford-on-Avon 298–9
Benet, John, of Cirencester 278–80
Bengeworth (Worc) 255–6
Bentley Pauncefoot (Worc) 315–16
Berkeley (Glouc) 25–7, 33–4, 84, 149, 179–80, 195, 228–9, 240–2
Berkeley family, lords of Berkeley 181–3; William Berkeley 81
Berkeley, Vale of 17, 149–50, 159–60
Berkswell (Warw) 330–1, 332*f*, 333
Berneward, Robert le; Agnes le, of Halesowen 212
Best, family, of Hartlebury 110
Bevere, *see* Claines
Bewdley (Worc) 240–2, 255–6, 292
Bibury (Glouc) 25–7, 77, 257, 303
Bickenhill (Warw) 291
Bickley, *see* Knighton-on-Teme
Bidford-on-Avon (Warw) 274, 298–9; Marlcliffe in 246
Bilton (Warw) 143
Binley (Warw) 106, 216–17
Birdingbury (Warw) 297
Birmingham (Warw) 10–12, 18–19, 238, 240–2, 249, 253–6, 258–9, 264, 268, 271, 282, 291–2, 297–8; Deritend in 291
Bishop, William, of Ombersley 337
Bishop's Cleeve (Glouc) 33–4, 57, 159–60, 163–4, 172, 190, 197–9, 207–8
Bishops Tachbrook (Warw) 56, 129
Bisley (Glouc) 63–4, 177, 271, 280–2, 290–1
Bitton (Glouc) 101–2, 239
Blacberd, Geoffrey, of Cleeve Prior 340
Black Death 68–71, 79, 120–1, 166, 178, 203–4, 210–11, 339–40
Blackwell (Warw) 57–8, 61–3, 62*t*, 68–70, 72, 134–5, 137–8, 142–3, 153–4, 166–7, 193, 196, 212, 229–31, 274–8, 308–9, 320, 337. *See also* Shipston-on-Stour

Blaisdon (Glouc) 309–10
Blaisdon, Richard of 331
Blake, Margery le; Sarra le, of Sedgeberrow 69
Blakeney (Glouc) 39
Blakeshall, *see* Wolverley
Blakesole, Matilda de; Roger de, both of Wolverley 54
Bledington (Glouc) 100–1
Blickley, family of, of Hanbury 35
Blockley (Glouc) 48, 139, 267; Upton in 42–3, 123, 124*f*, 128–31, 170–1, 202–3, 205, 219–20, 236, 261, 266–7, 287–8
Blythe, river 10–12, 224
Boarstall (Bucks) 131, 253–4, 259–60
Bockleton (Worc) 156, 171–2
Bolt, John le; Margery le, of Lindridge 141–2
bondmen, *see* serfs
Bordesley Abbey (Worc) 233, 273, 291
Bossy, Thomas, of Brandon 311
Botreaux, family, lords of Alcester 235; William de 330
Botull, John, of Studley 222–3
boundaries 27–30, 40, 233, 324
Bourton-on-the-Hill (Glouc) 122–3, 164–5, 178, 222
Bovetoun, Agnes, of Oversley 99–100
Bovy, Henry, of Coughton 246
Bradford, William, of Hanbury 291
Brailes (Warw) 229–31, 268–9
Brandon (Warw) 189, 216–17, 300–1, 311–12, 311*t*
Bransford, Walter de, of Wolverton 87
Bransford (Worc) 87–8
Bredon (Worc) 109, 222
Bredon Hill (Worc) 18, 108, 200–1, 214, 216–17
Bretford (Warw) 231, 257–8, 311
brewing, *see* ale
Bricklehampton (Worc) 253
Brid, Agnes, of Halesowen 337–8
Brid, William, of Pinvin 222–3
Brill (Bucks) 131, 253–4, 259–60
Brimpsfield (Glouc) 48–50, 193–4
Brimscombe (Glouc) 281–2
Brinklow (Warw) 216–17, 255–6
Bristol (Glouc and Somerset) 63–4, 97, 98, 137–8, 142, 151–2, 194, 197, 204, 217–19, 223–4, 228, 239–43, 241*f*, 249–50, 252–5, 262–3, 268, 271, 278–80, 289–92, 302–3, 312; Bristol, St Augustine's Abbey, abbot of 151–2
Broadwas (Worc) 76–7, 140–1, 204–5, 240–2
Broadway (Worc) 29, 107, 109, 201
Broadwell (Glouc) 214, 334

Brocke, Richard, of Thornbury 141
Brok, Robert atte, of Halesowen 208-9
Broke, Eleanor, Claines 114-15; Margaret atte, of Shipston 268-9
Brokthrop, Robert de 236
Brome, John, of Baddesley Clinton 225-6, 273
Bromefeld, John, of Rowington 250
Bromley, alias Muleward, John, of Cleeve Prior 315-16
Bromsberrow (Glouc) 164
Bromsgrove (Worc) 233, 242, 244, 252-3, 291-2, 312-13, 315-16
Brookthorpe (Glouc) 236, 238
Broun, Henry, of Stanton 119
Brown, Matilda, of Alcester 245
Browne, John, of Birmingham 282
Brugge, Elyas atte, of Abbots Salford 188-9, 198, 212-13
Buckingham, duke of 122-3
Buckland (Glouc) 312-13
Buk, Margaret; Richard; William, of Kempsey 83-4
building industry 122-3, 250, 253, 273-4, 292-7, 294f, 325-6, 335-7
Bulkington (Warw) 250, 293; Ryton in 250
Buller, Richard, of Weston-juxta-Cherrington 95
Burdets of Arrow 263; Burdet, Nicholas 268-9, 315-16; Thomas 268-9
Burton Dassett (Warw) 95, 123-34, 124f, 163-4, 170-5, 176f, 177, 181, 195-8, 202-3, 208, 217-19, 231, 253-4, 259-60, 276-8, 277f, 287-8, 302, 316-17, 338
Bynethetown, John, of Bricklehampton 253

cabbages, see horticulture
Caen, nunnery of 73
Calais 239-40
Calwe, Richard, of Northfield 297
Cam (Glouc) 280
Cam river 10-12
Camey, John de, of Mangotsfield 250
Canley, see Stoneleigh
Carles, William, of Cleeve Prior 67, 184-5
Carpenter, John, bishop of Worcester 101
Carter, Osbert le, of Blackwell 142-3
carts 18-19, 148, 168-72, 175, 283-4, 295-6, 307
Castle Morton (Worc) 29-30, 129, 159-60, 205-6
cattle 48, 50, 95-6, 169, 172, 193-7, 212, 214, 223
Chaceley (Glouc) 206-7
Chaddesley Corbett (Worc) 79, 99-100, 107, 125-7, 158, 190-1, 210, 221, 240-2, 254-5, 257

Chadshunt (Warw) 266-7
Chalford (Glouc) 278-82
Chamber, Richard, of King's Norton 292
Chandeler, Alice; Henry; John; Richard, of Roel 118-19
chapels 291-2, 320-2
Chapman, Robert le, of Bibury 257
Charingworth (Glouc) 115, 249
Charlecote (Warw) 242-3
Charlecote, Thomas, of Kempsey 196-7
Charlet, Richard, of Cleeve Prior 162-3
Charlette, Robert, of Cleeve Prior 313-14
Charlton, see Cropthorne
Charwelton (Northants) 96
Chaworth, Patrick de, holder of the probable barony of Kempsford 74
Chedworth (Glouc) 298
Cheltenham (Glouc) 204, 231, 249, 318-19
Chetynton, Thomas of 267
Chilvers Coton (Warw) 220-1, 253-4, 259-60, 271
children 59, 99, 107-8, 113-16, 133-4, 138-40, 167-8, 283, 304
Childswickham (Glouc) 97
Chipping Campden (Glouc) 90-1, 101, 222, 236-40, 237f, 244, 252-3, 255-6, 258, 281, 315
Chipping Sodbury (Glouc) 238, 256
Chirlet, Richard de, of Halesowen 210-11
church, parish 42-3, 100-1, 108-9, 134-5, 159-62, 199, 221-2, 231, 235, 264-6, 278-80, 306-7, 320-8, 335-6
church houses 40, 108-9, 325
Churcham (Glouc) 38, 209-10, 271, 298, 309-10
Churchover (Warw), Coton in 42-3, 124f, 127, 131, 170-2, 287-8
Churchyard, William, of Claines 101
Churn, river 10-12
Cirencester (Glouc) 18-19, 228-9, 242, 252-3
Cissmore, William, of Churcham 38
Claines (Worc) 101, 114-15, 117, 131-2, 265; Bevere in 240-2; Northwick in 275, 286; Whitstones in 69, 223
Clare family, see Gloucester, earls of
Cleeve Prior (Worc) 52, 57, 62-3, 62t, 65, 67-9, 71, 83-4, 90, 92-3, 100, 109-11, 137-8, 142, 162-3, 184-5, 186f, 187, 191, 193-4, 205, 208-9, 226, 246, 254, 267, 275, 295-6, 296-7, 300, 302-4, 313-14, 317-18, 335, 340-1
Clerk, Agnes (later Wille); John, of Cleeve Prior 67; Margery, of Coleshill 224; Thomas, of Willoughby 149, 174
Clifton (Glouc) 223-4, 256
Clifton-on-Teme (Worc) 201

clothmaking, clothing 63–4, 244, 248, 250, 252–3, 257–9, 271, 278–82, 286–8, 290–2, 297–9
clothiers, *see* clothmaking, merchants
Clyve, John de, of Admington 103–4; Thomas de, of Alveston 58–9
Cock Bevington, *see* Salford Priors
Cockes, Nicholas, of Cleeve Prior 246, 267
Cocks, William, of Alspath 222
Coke, John, of Birmingham 282
Colchester, Richard, of Lark Stoke 95
Coleford (Glouc) 40
Colesbourne (Glouc) 199–200
Coleshill (Warw) 54–5, 174, 225–6, 231, 232*f*, 248–9, 262, 268; Gilson in 225–6
Colin, Robert, of Twyning 103–4
collective organizations 19–20, 29–31, 102–11, 147–50, 213–14, 216, 335, 337
Collett, Richard, of Brandon 311–12
Coln, river 10–12, 297–8
Colwall (Herefs) 29–30
Colyns, Emota, of Compton Wynyates 242–3; John, of Harvington 212
Colyns, Richard, of Tanworth-in-Arden 333
Combe Abbey (Warw) 98
common herdsmen (including swineherds) 141, 148, 189, 193–4, 206, 213–14
common rights 29, 39–40, 147–9, 151–2, 155–6, 158–9, 329–33
Compton, William, knight 315–16
Compton Verney (Warw) 105–6, 146*f*, 173–4, 242–3, 308–9
Compton Wynyates (Warw) 242–3
Conderton (Worc) 214
conservation 150–2, 331–4
Cooksey (Worc) 38
Cooper, William le, of Walsgrave 286
copyhold, *see* customary tenure
Corse (Glouc) 151–2, 199
Cotiler, Hugh le, of Halesowen 291
Coton, *see* Churchover
cottages, cottagers, cottars 32, 35–8, 43–5, 47–8, 50, 54, 57, 63–4, 66–7, 92–3, 101–2, 105–6, 109–10, 127, 141–2, 193, 286
Coughton (Warw) 246, 330
Coundon (Warw) 49–50, 286
Coupere, Richard le, of Alvechurch 92
Coventry (Warw) 18–19, 49–50, 66, 97, 106, 163, 178, 195, 216–17, 222–4, 228–9, 238–43, 248–50, 252–3, 265–6, 271, 283–4, 286, 291, 293, 296–7, 301, 330–1, 335
Coventry Priory (Warw) 27, 66, 78–9, 90, 276, 286
credit, *see* debt

Cropthorne (Worc) 18, 57, 149–50, 275, 313; Charlton in 141, 193
Croumere, Henry, of Horsley 228
Crowle (Worc) 24, 31, 57, 315
crucks 123, 127–8, 175–6
Cryfield, *see* Stoneleigh
Cupere, William le, Hanbury 35
Curtlington, William de, abbot of Westminster 317
customary tenure 53–4, 57–9, 82–4, 314–15, 317

Daglingworth (Glouc) 200
Dean, Forest of (Glouc) 10–14, 37–40, 37*f*, 88, 135, 181–3, 205–6, 216–17, 257, 268, 271, 273, 276, 282, 284, 287–92, 297–8, 331
debt 59–61, 71, 100, 103–4, 125, 245–8, 317, 340–1
Deerhurst (Glouc) 196–7
Defford (Worc) 126*f*, 225
Dene, Henry of, of Little Dean, knight 37–8
Dene, river 10–12
Derneford, Roger de, of Corse 151–2
Deritend (Warw), in Aston (adjacent to Birmingham) 253–4
Derneford, Roger de, of Corse 151–2
Dey family, of Drakenage 95–6, 196–7; John; Thomas, son of John 95–6
Deye, John, of Ombersley 223–4
Dodford Priory (Worc) 34
Donechirche, Geoffrey de, of Coventry 97
Donne, Joan; John; and John, of Eldersfield 70
Dorsington (Warw) 43–4
Dowdeswell (Glouc) 298
dower 54
drage 159–63, 336–7, *see* barley
Drakenage (Warw) 95–6
drama 265, 334–5
Driffield (Glouc) 196–7, 200
Droitwich 18–19, 196, 204, 222–3, 228, 233, 242, 246–9, 254–5, 258, 271, 278, 290–1, 315–16
Droght, Robert, of Cleeve Prior 184–5
Dudley (Worc) 24–5, 217–19, 268, 273, 291
Dumbleton (Glouc) 80
Dunchurch (Warw) 239
Dunnington, *see* Salford Priors
Dunsmore (Warw) 29, 216–17
Duntisbourne Rouse (Glouc) 200; Pinbury in 92, 123, 124*f*, 127, 130–1, 163–4, 170, 179, 190–1, 195, 254–5, 266–7, 274, 287–8
Dursley (Glouc) 271, 280–2, 303–4
Dyer, Thomas, of Blockley 139
Dymock (Glouc) 262

Earls Croome (Worc) 79, 189–90, 224
Eastham (Worc) 201

Eastington (Glouc) 297-8
Ebley (Glouc) 278-80
Edgbaston (Warw) 291
Edge Hill (Warw) 10-12
Edmunds, John, of Westbury-on-Trym 101, 133-4, 139
education, *see* apprenticeship, schools
Eldersfield (Worc) 57, 61-2, 69-70, 78-81, 137, 149, 189, 192-3, 198, 248, 301
Elmley Castle (Worc) 18, 20, 78-9, 82, 91, 96-7, 100, 153-5, 165, 170-1, 208-10, 219-20, 287-8, 292-3, 295, 313
employment, *see* wage-earning
enclosures 21, 33-6, 43-5, 150-2, 155-8
English Bicknor (Glouc) 39-40
entry fines 60-4, 62*t*, 99, 179-80, 317, 319
Erdington (Warw) 291
Ervi, Anabel, of Alvechurch 35
Evenlode, river 10-12, 30
Evesham (Worc) 18, 222, 228-9, 239-42, 255-6, 334
Evesham Abbey (Worc) 14, 22, 63, 81, 240-2, 315, 319; abbot of 34, 334
eviction, *see* forfeiture of holding
Ewelme, river 280
Eyford (Glouc) 60

Faber, John, of White Ladies Aston 275
Faber, Thomas, of Hanbury 275
Fairford (Glouc) 257-8
family values 68-9, 72, 86-7, 115, 120-1, 132-4, 136, 142-3
famine (and bad harvests) 60, 93-4, 184-5, 192, 248, 268
farmers 30-1, 43-5, 94-6, 149-50, 154-5, 184
Feckenham (Worc) 203-4, 312, 315-16; Feckenham Forest 12-14, 22-4, 30, 34, 38-9, 192, 196-7, 203-4, 290-1, 312, 333
Feld, Agnes of the, of King's Norton 240-2
Felippes, Giles, of Cleeve Prior; John, of same 109-10
Feur, Ralph le, of Walsgrave 286
fields 14, 18-20, 22, 33-6, 40-5, 104, 145-58, 184-5, 189, 214, 295-6, 328-9
Fippus, Robert, of Castle Morton 205-6
fish, fishing 95-6, 254-5, 284, 300-1
Fisher, Richard, of Cleeve Prior 110-11, 226
Fladbury (Worc) 18, 275
flax 165, 298-9
Flaxley (Glouc); Timbridge in 331
floods 19-20, 108, 300-1
food 129-33, 162, 164-5, 180, 195, 202-3, 206, 208-9, 223, 248-9, 254-5, 268, 301, 307, 338-9

food trades 162-3, 222-3, 236-8, 240-3, 245, 248-9, 254-5, 257-8, 290-1, 301
Forest of Dean, *see* Dean
forfeiture of holding 43, 66-7, 315
forks (for dung, hay, sheaves, straw etc) 93, 137, 169-70
Fosse Way 18-19, 233
Foul family, of Ruardean 39
Frampton-on-Severn (Glouc) 90
Frankley (Worc) 322, 323*f*
fraternities 233, 242-3, 250, 258, 264
free holdings, free tenants 38, 47-8, 54-6, 55*t*, 73-81, 83, 120, 283-4, 318-20, 331
Freman, John; Richard, of Todenham 133-4, 140
Freman, Richard, of Cleeve Prior 142
Frome, river 10-12, 278-82
Fromptone, William de, of Maisemore 90
Fulbrook (Warw) 181-3, 273-4
Fulfen, Henry de, of Romsley 59

Gadbury, John, of Hartlebury 110
games, *see* sports
gardens, *see* horticulture
Gardiner, Margery, of Claines 114-15
gathering (of vegetation) 101-2, 165, 286-7
Gaydon (Warw) 106
gentry 95-6, 263, 268-9, 315-17, 325-6
Germany, trade with 254, 280
Gerveys, Robert, of Shipston 167-8
Giffard, John, lord of Brimpsfield 47-8
Gilebert, John, of Brimpsfield 50
gleaning 101, 105, 149
Gloucester 10-12, 18-19, 164, 181, 228, 239-43, 282, 286, 289-90
Gloucester Abbey 166, 177, 209-10, 238, 286; abbot of 263-4
Gloucester, earls of 12-14, 29-30, 49-50; Gilbert de Clare 74
goats 203-4
Goldicote (Warw) 42-3, 127-8, 163-4, 170, 172, 205, 298-9
Gower, John, poet 306
Grafton, near Bromsgrove 315
grain, *see* barley, drage, maslin, oats, rye, wheat
grain trade 163, 180, 246, 248-9, 268, 339-40
Great Alne (Warw) 246
Great Wolford (Warw) 122-3
Grene, William atte, of Cleeve Prior 67
Grevel, William, of Chipping Campden 315
Grey, Thomas, marquis of Dorset 315-16
Grimley (Worc) 98-9, 166, 265, 315, 334-5
Grove, Robert of the, of Hanley Castle 74

Guitings (Guiting Power and Temple Guiting) 29, 295–6
Gybbe, Henry, of Elmley Castle 82

Hagley (Worc) 101
Hailes (Glouc) 153
Haleford, John de, of Eldersfield 79
Halesowen (Worc) 32–3, 54, 58, 60, 70–1, 77–8, 80, 114–16, 120–1, 125–7, 131–2, 135, 155–6, 171–2, 210–11, 217–21, 229–31, 236–8, 245, 248, 291, 309–10, 321–7, 323*f*; Cakemor in 212; Oldbury in 321–2, *see also* Romsley
Halesowen Abbey (Worc) 209–10; abbots of 135, 229–31
Haliday, Edward, of Rodborough 281–2
Hallow (Worc) 61–2, 75, 138, 162, 337; Shoulton in 61–2
Ham (Glouc) 149–50
hamlets 14, 31–3, 107, 322
Hampton Lovett (Worc) 91
Hampton Lucy (Warw) 109, 116–17, 208–9, 275, 302; Hatton-on-Avon in 178
Hanbury (Worc) 35, 41–2, 69, 122*f*, 173–4, 181, 191, 275, 291, 298–9, 315–16, 324
Handsworth (Staffs) 291
Handys alias Hannys, John, of Stratford-upon-Avon 242–3
Hanley Castle (Worc) 27, 29–30, 54–5, 74, 93–4, 96–7, 125–7, 181, 200–1, 264, 271, 284–6, 285*f*, 296–7, 315–16
Harborne (Staffs) 291
Hardenhull, Peter de, of Hallow 59
Haresfield (Glouc) 181
Harlestone (Northants) 96
Harry, John, of Nuneaton 248–9
Harryes, John, of Charingworth 115
Harryes, John, of Wormleighton 308–9
Hartlebury (Worc) 85–6, 91, 96–7, 107, 110, 114–17, 135–6, 197, 210–12, 240–2, 264, 322, 324–7; Mitton in 196–7
Harvington (Worc) 30–1, 90–1, 149, 212, 214
Harvy, John, of Stratford-upon-Avon 222–3
Haseley (Warw) 250
Haselholt, Richard, of Alcester 246, 267
Haselor (Warw) 128; Walcot in 128
Haselton, Gilbert de, of Northleach 236
Hatherop (Glouc) 200
Hatton-on-Avon, *see* Hampton Lucy
Hawkesbury (Glouc) 66–7, 107, 156–7, 192–3, 198–200, 205, 239, 290–1, 302; Ingelstone in 157–8; Kilcott in 107, 209; Little Badminton in 107; Stoke in 66–7, 107, 209; Upton in 107; Woodcroft in 107
Hawkyn (in *Piers Plowman*) 334, 339–41

Hayne, Simon, of Attleborough 248
Hazleton (Glouc) 42, 119, 327
hearths 128–30, 132, 163, 260
hedges 138, 156–7, 330
hemp 165
Henbury-in-the-Salt-Marsh (Glouc) 63–4, 85–6, 108, 125–7, 164, 223–4, 339–40; Shirehampton in 125–7, 177–8, 195, 254–5
Henley-in-Arden (Warw) 268
Hereford, bishops of 43, 204
heresy 327
Hereward, Richard, of Wolverley 54
heriots 54–5, 66–7, 71–2, 77–8, 172, 189–91, 194, 198–9, 201, 209–10, 217, 226
Heritage, John, of Burton Dassett and Moreton-in-Marsh 198–9, 225, 339–40; Roger, of Burton Dassett 95, 133–4
Herman, Roger, of Honeybourne 102–3
Hewes, John and Joan, of Stanton 119
Heynes, Juliana; Robert, of Teddington 80; Richard, of Ingelstone, in Hawkesbury 157–8
Hichecoks, John, of Halesowen 210–11
Hidcote Bartrim (Glouc) 242–3
Highnam (Glouc) 326–7
Hill Wootton (Warw) 125–7
Himbleton (Worc) 57–9, 128
Hinton-on-the-Green (Glouc) 31–2
Hobekines, Matilda; Robert, of Wolverley 54
Hoblay, John, of Coleshill 174
Hoc, Alexander, of Little Dean 37–8
Hockeley, Eva de, of Blackwell 134–5
Holder, John; William, of Cleeve Prior 90, 111
Holdwyn, Denise, of Longdon 206–7
Holmer, Thomas, of Hartlebury 326–7
Honemon, Alexander; Juliana, of Earls Croome 224
Honeybourne (Glouc) 80, 102–3, 107, 189–90
Honington (Warw) 65–6, 106, 276
Hood, Robin, fictional outlaw 5–6, 265, 335
horses 48, 169, 175, 188–93, 246
Horsley (Glouc) 63–4, 94–5, 143, 228
Horsman, Roger, of Buckland 312–13
horticulture 121–2, 137–8, 164–5
Horwell (Worc), in Severn Stoke and Defford 12–14, 312
hospitals 34 (Worcester); 98 (Bristol)
houses 6, 14, 24, 31–3, 37–8, 41–5, 121–33, 124*f*, 126*f*, 244–5, 250, 253, 257–8, 260, 292–5
Huddington (Worc) 136–7
Hulle, Thomas, of Halesowen 248
hunting 12–14, 24–5, 29–30, 286–7, 315–17
Huntley, William, of Churcham 271
Huwet, John, of Twyning 103–4
Huys, John, of Claines 117

INDEX 373

Hychen, Thomas, of Cleeve Prior 71
Hyckes, John, of Alveston 143

Ickenildestrete, Henry de, of Alvechurch 152
Idlicote (Warw) 314
Ilmington (Warw) 236–8
Ingelstone, see Hawkesbury
inheritance 3–4, 52, 54–5, 59, 67–72, 68t, 83–4, 139–42, 314–15
inhok 153–4, 213
intercommoning 29–30, 39, 149, 216–17
Ipsley (Warw) 35
Iron Acton (Glouc) 240–2

Jackehonen, Robert, of Admington 75
Jans family of Staunton 39
Jeffs, John, of Ailstone 198, 204–5
Jeke, William, of Coleshill 225–6
Jenecokes, Juliana, of Shipston 167–8
John, son of Gregory, of Smethwick 249
Jones, Agnes, of Compton Verney 242–3; Felicity, of Romsley 118–19; John, of Compton Verney 242–3, 309–10; Richard, of Ombersley 319; Thomas, of Ombersley 319
Josse, William, of Worcester 240–2
Juggement, William, of Cleeve Prior 315–16
juries, jurors 48, 76–9, 81, 91, 109–10, 263, 308–9, 315–16

Keble, Henry, of London 43–4
Kemerton (Worc) 200–1
Kempsey (Worc) 69, 83–4, 98, 117, 128–9, 174, 196–7, 205, 242
Kempsford (Glouc) 61–2, 74–6, 188–9, 303
Kendal (Westmorland) 297
Kenilworth (Warw) 24–5, 216–17
Kent, John, of Stivichall 178
Ketel, Roger, of Halesowen 77–8
Kidderminster (Worc) 209–10; Oldington in 209–10
King's Barton (Glouc) 312
Kingscote (Glouc) 156–7, 198
King's Norton (Worc) 18, 21–2, 25–7, 96–7, 152, 160–2, 240–2, 291–2, 296–7, 312–13
King's Stanley (Glouc) 278–80
Kingston (Warw) 42–4
Kingswood (Glouc) 12–14, 30, 216, 312, 330–1
Kinwarton (Warw) 246
kitchens, including bakehouses 129–31, 318
Knighton-on-Teme (Worc) 24; Bickley in 24; Newnham in 59, 203
Knoll, William, of Kinwarton 246
Knowle (Warw) 21–2, 223, 258–9, 264, 330–1
Kyng, Agnes; John, of Badminton 142–3

Kyngton, Richard, of Tidmington 242–3; Robert, of Alveston 242–3; Walter, of Charlecote 242–3

labour services 53–4, 73–4, 77, 106, 116–17, 317–18, 320
Lacy, Simon, of Snowshill 100
Lancaster, earl of 313
land market 3–4, 55t, 66, 68t, 71–2, 72t, 93–4
land use 14–22, 33–9, 41–8, 145–8, 151–2, 180–7, 182t, 200, 216–17
Langley, Geoffrey de, knight 331
language, English 5–8, 12, 305–6
Lapworth (Warw) 30, 216–17, 300, 330–1
Lark Stoke (Warw) 95
Latton (Wilts) 200
Laurans, Thomas, of Cock Bevington 246
law 5–6, 74–5, 77–8, 107–8, 111, 136–7, 140, 245–8, 308–9, 312
Leadon, river 10–12
leasehold tenure 30–1, 43, 84, see farmers
Leche, William le, of Halesowen 32
Lechlade (Glouc) 14–17, 252–3, 257–8
Leigh (Worc) 204–5
legumes, see beans, pulse
Lese, Adam, of Charlton in Cropthorne 313
Lette, Thomas, of Shipston 229–31
Lewelyn, Thomas, of Alveston 58–9
Lichfield (Staffs) 18–19; bishops of 265–7
Lighthorne (Warw) 56, 318–19
Lilleshall (Shropshire) 327–8
Lindridge (Worc) 59; Moor in 92–3, 193, 223
linen 236–8, 287–8, 298–9
literature 5–6, 164, 265–6, 305–8
litigation (in manor courts) 103–4, 107, 153, 164–5, 171–2, 208–9, 212, 221, 223, 245–8, 340–1
Little Aston, see Aston Blank
Little Avon, river 10–12
Little Comberton (Worc) 153–4
Little Dean (Glouc) 37–8, 276
Littleton-on-Severn (Glouc) 75
Llanthony Priory (Glouc) 224–5
local government 10–12, 29, 40, 107–8, 262–4, 308–9
Lomherde, Beatrice; John; William, of North Cerney 138–9
London 18–19, 97, 195, 239–40, 252–3, 262–3, 278–80, 291, 305–6
Long, Henry, of Cleeve Prior 184–5
Longborough (Glouc) 121–2, 320
Long Compton (Warw) 43–4; Weston-juxta-Cherrington in 43–4, 95, 166, 254
Longdon (Worc) 14–17, 155–6, 171–2, 192–3, 198, 209–10, 212

Longeman, Agnes, of Cleeve Prior 137-8; Walter, of same 162-3
Long Itchington (Warw) 159-60; Bascote in 123-5, 131, 174-5
Long Marston (Warw) 61-2, 198, 216, 276-8, 315, 333-4
Lowe, Roger atte, of Halesowen 208-9
Low Countries 19-20, 273-4, 302-3
Lower Swell (Glouc) 193
Loyte, John, of Hartlebury 212
Ludlow, Helena, of Shirehampton 195
Lutterworth (Leics) 142
Lyndrych, John, of Alcester 313-14
Lyngue. Alice; Joan; John, of Toddington 116

Maddeleye, Thomas de, of Shipston 97
Madresfield (Worc) 137-8, 295
Magote, Agnes; Richard, of Hanley Castle 93-4
maintenance agreements 53-4, 98-100, 115, 142-3, 165, 299, 336-9
Maisemore (Glouc) 90, 266-7
Maiseyhampton (Glouc) 326-7
Makegive, Simon, of Broadwas 76-7
Mall, John son of, of Romsley 54
Malmesbury, William of 164
Malvern (Worc), Chase 29-30, 204-6, 284-6; Forest 12-14, 29-30; Hills 10-12, 27, 28f, 29-30, 200-1, 204-5, 216-17, 305-7; Priory 98; Baldenhall in 295
Mangotsfield (Glouc) 250
Mannyng, John, of Horsley 94-5
manure 172-4, 178-9
market forces 63-4, 152-3, 163, 255-6, 258, 261-2, 278-80, 296-7, 300
marl 37-8, 174
Marlcliffe, *see* Bidford
Marmion, Philip, lord of Middleton 331-3
marriage 3-4, 67-72, 92-3, 101, 114-15, 134-6, 140-1, 240-2
marriage fine (merchet) 74-8, 80-1, 274-5, 317-20
Marshal, Richard le 220-1
Martyn, John, of Longdon 171-2
Martley (Worc) 265, 334-5
Maryote, John, of Willoughby 136-7
Mase, John, of Great Alne 246
maslin 159-62
Mathon (Worc and Herefs) 29-30, 78-9, 206, 295
Maxstoke (Warw) 239, 248
May, Richard, of Harvington 212
Meleward, Rosa le, of Eldersfield 248
Melksop, Henry, of Todenham 317
Melley, Henry, of Halesowen 322

merchants (including clothiers) 97, 223-5, 231, 243-4, 253, 278-83
Mere, Henry atte, of Ombersley 223-4
Merehale, Cristiana de, of Lighthorne 56
Meriden (Warw), Alspath in 222, 238, 330-1
Meryell, Agnes, of Lutterworth 142
Michel, John, of Hartlebury 135-6
Middleton (Warw) 98-9, 105, 109, 138, 192-3, 196-7, 331-3
Middleton, Walter de, of Bockleton 171-2
migration 42-4, 66-7, 81, 85-91, 87t, 88t, 89f, 235-43, 237f
mills 4-5, 77-8, 97, 191, 275, 315-16, 318-20; fulling mills 278-82, 279f, 289-91, 297-9; metal-working mills 273, 291
Milverton (Warw) 56
Minchinhampton (Glouc) 202, 228, 271, 274-5, 281-2
mining 39-40, 273, 289-90
Minsterworth (Glouc) 268, 308-9
Mirk, John, writer of religious literature 327-8
Mitcheldean (Glouc) 39, 257
Mogge, Henry, of Shipston 153
Momeford, John, of Hampton Lucy 208-9
monasteries (including minsters) 17, 27, 63, 77-9, 98, 100-1, 159, 228-31, 233-5, 238, 240-2, 273
Monfort, John, of Elmley Castle 292-3
Monks Kirby (Warw) 165, 223; Pailton in 239
Montfort, Simon de, baronial leader 312-13
Montivilliers (Normandy) 297
Moor, *see* Lindridge
More, William, Prior of Worcester 265, 315, 317-18, 334-5
Moreton-in-Marsh (Glouc) 14-17, 163-4, 174-5, 198-9, 216-17, 225, 256, 339-40
Mortimer, Roger, lord of King's Norton 21-2, 312-13
Mountford, William, knight 224
Mucklowe, John, of Halesowen 322, 324-5
Mule or Mulle, Henry atte, of Horsley 143, 228
Mulleward, Joan, of Sambourn 315
Muryell, John, of Chaddesley Corbett 99-100
Myche, William, of Bilton 143

Naissche, John, of Ombersley 155-6
Napton-on-the-Hill (Warw) 192-3
nativi, neifs, *see* serfs
Netherlands, *see* Low Countries
Netherton (Worc) 18, 91, 166-7
Newemon, Agnes le, of Twyning 103-4
Newent (Glouc) 262
Newland (Glouc) 39-40, 257
Newnham, *see* Knighton-on-Teme
Norman, Laurence; Robert, of Wasperton 52

INDEX   375

North Cerney (Glouc) 138–9
Northfield (Worc) 18, 24–5, 26*f*, 33, 99, 128–9, 196–7, 217–19, 291, 334–5
Northleach (Glouc) 225, 236, 238, 255–6, 258–9, 263–4
Northwick, *see* Claines
Norton Subedge (Glouc) 197
Norway 170, 254
Notte, Alice, of Longdon 171–2
Nuneaton (Warw) 222–3, 245–9, 253–4, 258–9, 262

oats 159–64, 302–3, 307, 336–7
Odeston, John, of Nuneaton 248–9
Ody, Richard, of Hanley Castle 93–4
Offchurch, Geoffrey de, of Wasperton 90
Offenham, William, of Cleeve Prior 92–3
Oldbury, *see* Halesowen
Oldington, *see* Kidderminster
office-holding 110–11, 263–4, 308–9, 315
Ombersley (Worc) 12–14, 63, 81, 100, 107, 109, 120, 142, 155–6, 177–8, 204–5, 210, 223–4, 307, 312, 319, 335–7
Otar, John, of Eldersfield 149
Othehul, Henry, of Halesowen 32
ovens 130–1, 318–19, *see also* kitchens and bakehouses
Overbury (Worc) 59, 76, 189, 214, 219–20, 288
Oversley (Warw) 98–9, 231
Oweyn, Thomas, of Bockleton 171–2
Oxford 239–42
Oxhill (Warw) 127–8

Packwood (Warw) 27
Page, Walter, of Cleeve Prior 71–2
Pailton, *see* Monks Kirby
Painswick (Glouc) 14–17, 316
Palmer, Richard le; Henry le, of Grafton Flyford 136–7
parks 21–2, 24–5, 47–8, 50, 82, 150–1, 329
Parkys, Richard, of Sedgley 291
Parsons, Thomas, of Tanworth-in-Arden 250
Passe, John, of Kempsey 205
Payn, William, of Alveston 171–2
Peatling Magna (Leics) 312–13
Pecker, Richard, of Hazleton 119
Pendock (Worc) 14, 15*f*, 41–2, 173–6, 181
Pendock, John de, of Pershore 253
Penne, Richard, probably of Huddington 136–7
Pensax (Worc) 53–4
Pensnett (Staffs) 291
Pershore (Worc) 18, 220–3, 228–9, 239–40, 246–8, 253, 257–8, 262, 334; Allesborough in 300; Walcot in 300
Pershore Abbey 223–5

Persons, John, of Sutton-under-Brailes 220–1
pigs 109, 204–7, 223–4
pilgrimages 326–7
Pinbury, *see* Duntisbourne Rouse
Pinley (Warw) 331
Pinley, Richard de; William de, of Pinley 331
Pinvin (Worc) 222–3
place-names 5–6, 14, 19–20, 24–5, 27, 29–30, 35–6, 39–40, 43–4, 154–5, 266–7, 305–6, 328
Pleydemore, Richard, of Northfield 99
ploughs 168–72, 193–4, 274–5, 307
poll tax, *see* tax
popular culture 132, 143, 264–7, 334–5
Porter, John, of Hartlebury 240–2
pottery 8, 29–30, 34–6, 131, 173–4, 235, 253–4, 259–60, 284–6, 285*f*
poultry 62–3, 111, 137–8, 207–9, 224
poverty 52–3, 92–3, 97–102, 98*t*, 307, 337, 340–1
Prescotte, William, of Whitstones 223
Prestbury (Glouc) 204, 256
Prestes, Robert, of Admington 103–4
Priors Hardwick (Warw) 42, 55, 64–5, 106, 192–3
Priors Marston (Warw) 56–7, 65, 106
productivity 178–80
proto-industrialization 278–83, 291–2
Pucklechurch (Glouc) 240–2
Puffe, William, of Henbury-in-the-Saltmarsh 139
pulse 159–64
Puttewey, Richard; Thomas, of Romsley 98–9, 138–9
Pygun, Robert, of Elmley Castle 96–7
Pyper, John, of Atherstone and Pyper, John, of Nuneaton 245

quarrying 282–3, 289–90, 292–3, 295–7
Quinton (Warw) 140, 236–8, 310–11

Radbourne (Warw) 192–3, 297
Ragun, John, of Bockleton 171–2
Raulot, Robert, of Coventry 240–2
Redditch (Worc) 233, 258–9
reeve 74, 109–10, 165–7, 315
Rendcomb (Glouc) 198
rent 47–8, 56, 60–1, 74, 94–5, 109–10, 136–7, 179–80, 314–15, 317–19
retirement, *see* maintenance agreements
Reve, Agnes; John, of Elmley Castle 91; Joan; Richard; Thomas, of North Cerney 138–9; John, of Alveston 92–3
Reve, John le, of Teddington 104
Reynald, Beatrice daughter of, of Hallow 75
Reynolds, William, of King's Norton 292
Ribbesford (Worc) 283–4

Ricardes, Gilbert, of Admington 103
Ricart, Robert, of Bristol 262–3
Ripple (Worc) 52–3, 287–8
rivers 10–12, 18–19, 39, 90, 238–42, 257–8, 283–4, 289–90, 300–1
roads 18–19, 39, 90, 108, 229, 231, 233, 238–9, 244–5, 289–91
Roberd, Margery, of Harvington 90–1
Robertes, John, of Harvington 214; Thomas, of Admington 99–100
Robins, William, of Shipston 153
Robyn, Agnes, of Sambourn 240–2
Robynes, Alice, of Cleeve Prior 184–5
Rock (Worc) 96–7, 240–2
Rockhampton (Glouc) 79, 81, 108, 148; Sheperdine in 81
Rodborough (Glouc) 278–82
Rodborough, Richard de; Thomas de, of Minchinhampton 281–2
Roel (Glouc) 29, 103, 118–19, 122*f*, 216
Rogers, Cecilia, of Cleeve Prior 100; Juliana, of Stoke Gifford 70–1
Roggers, Edith; John, of Sedgeberrow 69
Rolf, John, of Himbleton 59
Romano-British period 29, 45, 152, 261, 265–7
Romsley (Worc) 54, 59, 77, 80, 83–6, 86*f*, 98–9, 120, 138–9, 190–1, 193, 283–4, 290–1, 322
Roose, John, of Kempsey 98
Roper, Robert the, of Ipsley 35; Thomas, of Sambourn 157–8
Rous family, lords of Ragley 263
Rowington (Warw) 250
Rowney Green, *see* Alvechurch
Rugby (Warw) 252–3, 258
Ruggeweye, Agnes de, of Grimley 98–9
Russell, Richard, of Birmingham 282; William, of Eldersfield 70
Rychards, Robert, of Dursley 280
rye 159–64
Ryton, *see* Bulkington

Sadler, Agnes, of Halesowen 80
St Briavels (Glouc) 256
Saintbury (Glouc) 236
Sainter, Richard, of Longdon 209–10
Salford Priors (Warw) 216–17; Dunnington in 249; Cock Bevington in 246
Salisbury 239–40
salvation 307, 326–8
Sambourn (Warw) 81, 157–8, 172–3, 240–2, 315, 330, 333
Sawbridge, *see* Wolfhampcote
Saynbyr, William of, of Chipping Campden 236
schools 90–1, 96–7, 242, 291–2

Sclatter, Richard, of Elmley Castle 170–1, 287–8; Walter, of Longdon 212
scythes 137–8, 166–7, 169–70, 175, 274–5, 291, 314
Sedgeberrow (Worc) 57, 61–2, 69, 162–3, 170–1, 189, 205, 337
Sedgley (Staffs) 291
Semilly, Geoffrey de, of Ashow 151–2
serfs 47–8, 73–83, 87–8, 90–1, 113–14, 306, 317–18
servants 90–1, 106–9, 115–20, 118*t*, 136–9, 141, 143, 167–8, 213–14, 240–2, 278–80, 306–9
Severn estuary 14–17, 19–20, 33–4, 63–4, 85–6, 90, 108, 179–83
Severn, river 10–12, 11*f*, 14, 18–19, 27, 30, 61–2, 85–6, 128–9, 163, 179–80, 192–3, 196–7, 200–1, 205–6, 209–10, 238–42, 249, 254, 268, 283–6, 289–92, 297–8, 300, 302–3
Shad, Nicholas; Petronilla, of Admington 138
Shapster, Joan, of Hartlebury 136
Sharp, Nicholas, of Upton Warren 286–7
Shawe, Reginald ate, of Romsley 190–1
Shayl, Walter, of Hatton-on-Avon 178
sheep 96, 104–5, 116–17, 177–8, 197–203, 199*t*, 212, 216, 225, 281–2
Sheperdine, *see* Rockhampton
Sherborne (Glouc) 99–100, 103, 107, 189–90, 281
Sheriffs Lench (Worc) 34, 149
Shipston-on-Stour (Warw) 62–3, 68–9, 72, 97, 153–4, 167–8, 229–31, 242, 244, 246–9, 258, 268–9, 315–16, 320–1, *see also* Blackwell
Shirehampton, *see* Henbury
Shoulton, *see* Hallow
Shrawley (Worc) 283–4
Shuckburgh (Warw) 320, 324
Shustoke (Warw) 300
Shuttington (Warw) 43–4
Siward, Richard 22–4
Slimbridge (Glouc) 19–20, 179–80, 280
smiths 220–1, 265–6, 274–8, 277*f*, 282
Smith, John, of Tanworth-in-Arden 300–1; Richard, of Hampton Lucy 275; Simon, of Honington 276; William, of Shipston 268–9
Smyth, John, of Dunnington 249; John, of Long Marston 315
Smyth, William, of Bickenhill 291
Smythe, William, of Birmingham 282
Snowshill (Glouc) 100, 198, 295–6
social hierarchy 49–50, 94–6, 106, 109–11, 119, 137
Solihull (Warw) 252–3, 268, 330–1
Somery, Roger de, lord of Dudley 273
Southam (Warw) 125–7, 253–4

Southampton 18–19
Southrop (Glouc) 129, 138, 142, 148
spades 169–71
Sparke, William, of Elmley Castle 165
Spencer, John, of Defford 225
sports and pastimes 109, 132, 143, 302, 314, 316–17
Sprot, Henry, of Blackwell 141
Squier, Thomas, of Romsley 59
Stafford, Humphrey, of Grafton 313–16
Stanton (Glouc) 61–2, 103, 119, 149
Stappe, John, of Blackwell 212, 217; Richard, of same 69–70
Stareton (Warw) 106
Sterveyn, Margaret, of Elmley Castle 100
stints 104–5, 179, 188–9, 193, 198, 204–5, 209–10, 216, 333–4
Stivichall (Warw) 178, 250, 293
Stoke, *see* Hawkesbury
Stoke Bishop (Glouc) 215–16
Stoke Gifford (Glouc) 63–4, 70–1, 156–7, 172–3, 191
Stoke Prior (Worc) 76–7, 125–7, 156, 198, 286–7
Stoneleigh (Warw) 33, 55, 66, 125–7, 126*f*, 190–1, 216–17, 223, 331–3; Cryfield in 33; Thornhale in 33
Stoneleigh Abbey 98, 331–3
Stour, river 10–12, 297–8
Stourbridge (Worc) 258–9
Stow-on-the-Wold (Glouc) 115–16, 222, 244
Stratford-upon-Avon (Warw) 25–7, 74, 122–3, 222–3, 225, 233, 242–3, 246–8, 250, 253, 255–6, 258–9, 262, 264, 266, 268, 282–3, 291–2
Stretton Baskerville (Warw) 33–4
Stroud (Glouc) 14–17, 258–9, 271, 278–80, 283–4, 297–8
Stroudwater (Glouc) 278–82, 303–4
Studley (Warw) 222–3
Stutebrugge, Wymund de, of Churcham 38
Styvyngton, Adam de, of Alveston 58–9
Suard, Thomas, of Evesham 240–2
subletting of land 55–9, 58*t*, 94–5, 100, 109–10, 139
Sudeley (Glouc) 325–6
Sutton Coldfield (Warw) 21, 129–30
Sutton Chase 12–14
Sutton-under-Brailes (Warw) 214, 219–21
Swindon (Glouc) 200
Swyppe, Alice, of Alveston 143
Symonds, John, of Alveston 210–11
Symondes, Richard, of Wigmore 90

Tailor, Nicholas, of Cleeve Prior 318
Talbot, John, lord of Painswick 316; Gilbert, knight 315–16
tallage 74–6, 78–80, 102, 274–5, 310, 314, 317–19

Tame, river 10–12
Tamworth (Staffs and Warw) 228
Tanworth-in-Arden (Warw) 21, 25–7, 156–7, 250, 257, 268–9, 300–1, 308–9, 316–17, 333
Tardebigge (Worc) 93–4, 233
tax; lay subsidies 87*t*, 87–8, 95, 99, 103, 118, 240–2, 255, 280–1, 293, 298, 310–12, 311*t*; poll tax 95, 115–20, 138–9, 252–3, 276, 293, 297–8, 303
Taylor, Henry, of Walsgrave 286
Taylour, John, of Hanbury 191
technology 153–5, 166, 169, 174–5, 177, 276–8, 291, 297–9
Teddington (Glouc) 77, 80, 104–5, 108, 162–3, 172–3, 198–201, 337
Tederyngton, Richard, of Hawkesbury 66–7
Teme, river 10–12
Temple Balsall (Warw); Balsall Common, Balsall Wood 330–1, 332*f*
Templer, John, of Middleton 98–9
Tetbury (Glouc) 228, 231
Tettenhall (Staffs) 281
Tewkesbury (Glouc) 25–7, 40, 228–9, 239–42, 249, 258, 268
Thames, river 10–12, 30
Thatcher, John, of Hartlebury 196–7
Thornbury (Glouc) 67–8, 75–7, 83, 120, 141, 192–3, 228–9, 231, 248, 257–8, 320
Thornhale, *see* Stoneleigh
Thornhale, Richard; William, of Stoneleigh 33
Thoury, John, of Elmley Castle 208–9
Throckmortons of Coughton 263
Tibberton (Worc) 53–4, 177–8
Tidenham (Glouc) 284, 300–1
tile and slate making 273, 295–7
Timbridge, *see* Flaxley
tithes 4–5, 159–63, 160–1*f*, 184, 199–202, 207, 320–1
Tockington (Glouc) 239
Todenham (Glouc) 133–4, 140, 317
Toddington (Glouc) 116
Tom, John; Letice; Lucy; Walter, of Broadwas 140–1
Tormarton (Glouc) 156–7
Tornour, Simon le; Matilda le, of Hallow 337
Toun, William atte, of Mathon 295
Tovy, Selia, of Broadwas 240–2
transhumance 29–30, 200–1, 205–6, 216–17, 218*f*
Tredington (Warw) 152–3, 169, 281, 321
Trent, river 10–12
Treweman, Matilda; Robert, of Hazleton 119
Trigg, William, of Himbleton 59
Turnar, Thomas, of Grimley 315

Twyning (Glouc) 103–4, 200
Tyngker, John, of Alderminster 303–4
Tysoe (Warw) 303–4; Westcote in 22, 23f, 31, 43–4

Ufton (Warw) 31, 32f, 65–6
Uley (Glouc) 149–50
Underhill, George, of Hartlebury 91
Up Ampney (Glouc) 298
Upleadon (Glouc) 209–10
Upper Swell (Glouc) 334
Upton, *see* Blockley and Hawkesbury
Upton, Robert de, of Kempsey 174; Thomas de, of Chipping Campden 236
Upton-on-Severn (Worc) 29–30, 257–8
Upton Warren (Worc) 286–7
urban influence 49–50, 62–3, 66, 239, 243–4, 247f, 250–1, 255t, 255, 278–83, 293–5, 339–40

vagabonds 100, 119–20, 308–9
Valor Ecclesiasticus 199–202
Vicar, Richard, of Alveston 210–11
Vicarye, John, of Charingworth 249
villages 2, 7–8, 20, 22, 25–7, 29–31, 33, 42–5, 101–11, 121–2, 171–2, 180–1, 193–4, 257, 264–7, 276, 298, 334–5
Viteler, Edward; Roger, of Eldersfield 301

wage-earning 47–8, 50, 52–3, 65–6, 85–6, 92, 94, 105–6, 109–10, 143, 149, 250, 278, 280–1, 308–9
wains 168–71
Walcot, *see* Haselor, and Pershore
Walcote, John, of Hazleton 327
Walker, Cristina; John, of Upton Warren 286–7; Isabella, of Loxley 242–3; William, of Stratford-upon-Avon 242–3
Walsall (Staffs) 268
Walsgrave-on-Sowe (Warw) 56–7, 66, 286
Walsingham (Norf) 326–7
Walter, William, of Pensax 53–4
Waring, Thomas, of Tanworth-in-Arden 156–7
Warwick, earls of 12–14, 18, 21–4, 235, 263, 268–9, 292–3, 313–14
Warwick 228, 253–4, 257–8, 313
Wasperton (Warw) 52, 64–5, 90, 308–9
Waterlade, John, of Hartlebury 136
Watling Street 10–12, 233
weapons 267, 309–10
Webbe, Thomas le, of Cleeve Prior 298–9; Walter le, of Halesowen 212
weeding hooks 169–70, 274–5
weeds, weeding 166–8, 172, 175
Weethley (Warw) 254
Welford-on-Avon (Warw) 101, 122f, 154–5, 300

Welland (Worc) 205–6
Wellesbourne (Warw) 30, 137, 216, 330–1
West, John, of Alveston 171–2
Westbury-on-Severn (Glouc) 326–7
Westbury-on-Trym (Glouc) 101, 139, 240–2
Westcote, *see* Tysoe
Weston-juxta-Cherrington, *see* Long Compton
Weston Mauduit (Warw) 43–4, 214
Weston-on-Avon (Warw) 325–6
Weston Subedge (Glouc) 101
Westminster 78
Whatcote (Warw) 122–3, 127–8, 207, 253, 293
Whatecroft, John, of Northfield 196–7
Whichford (Warw) 106
White Ladies Aston (Worc) 275
Whitstones, *see* Claines
Wibtoft (Warw) 338–9
Wichenford (Worc) 219–20
Wick Episcopi (Worc) 30
Wickhamford (Worc) 97, 223–4
widows 54, 59, 66–72, 98–100, 105–6, 114–15, 120, 135–6, 138, 302, 316, 336–7
Wigmore (Herefs) 90
Wikwan(e), Anketell de; William de, of Coventry 97
Wiliames, Henry, of Halesowen 209–10
Wilkyns, Henry, of Compton Verney 242–3
Wille, Agnes; John, of Cleeve Prior 67, 71–2
William, John son of, of Blockley 48
Willoughby (Warw) 121–2, 128, 136–7, 174, 188–9, 204–5, 216
Winchcomb (Glouc) 102–3, 115–16, 223–4, 228, 239–40, 244, 257–8, 281
Winchcomb Abbey 61–3, 69–72, 100–4, 153, 193–4, 315, 317
Windrush, river 10–12, 29–30
Witelond, Henry, of Little Dean 37–8
wheat 159–64, 174–5
wills 7–8, 113–15, 117, 133–4, 171–2, 242–3, 278–80
Wodecroft, *see* Hawkesbury
Wodelond, Richard, of Cleeve Prior 71–2
Wolfhampcote (Warw), Sawbridge in 96
Wolverley (Worc) 24, 54, 128–9, 162, 166, 328–9; Blakeshall in 24, 35–6, 36f, 41–2, 281–2
Wolverton (Worc) 87–8
wolves 37–8
women 4, 98, 105–8, 120, 135, 137–9, 197, 204, 214, 224, 236–8, 240–2, 271, 278–80, 286–8, 298, 301–3, 308–9, *see also* widows
Woodchester (Glouc) 14–17
woods and forests 12–14, 21–4, 30, 34–40, 37f, 66, 106, 122–3, 150–1, 183, 216–17, 238, 253, 283–6, 289–91, 295, 329–34, 332f
Woolaston (Glouc) 39

Wootton Wawen (Warw) 282–3, 298–9
Worcester 10–12, 18–19, 29–30, 49–50, 60, 63–4, 79, 98, 163–5, 209, 228, 238–44, 252–3, 267, 271, 286, 289–90
Worcester, bishops and bishopric 60, 69, 73, 79–80, 90–2, 101, 120, 200–1, 265–6, 275, 313–14
Worcester Cathedral Priory 22, 24, 30–1, 57–8, 61–2, 68, 70–2, 79–81, 104, 159–62, 160–1*f*, 174–5, 183*t*, 225–6, 229–31, 233, 275, 291–2, 313, 315–17, 336–7
Wormleighton (Warw) 308–9
Wotton-under-Edge (Glouc) 328–9
Wroxall (Warw) 333

Wye, river 40, 284, 289–90
Wyot, Alice, of Bockleton 156

Yanworth (Glouc) 103
Yardley (Worc) 18, 21–2, 96–7, 291, 330–1
Yardley, Thomas de, of Cleeve Prior 52
Yate, John, of Coventry 240–2
Yate, Nicholas atte, of Cleeve Prior 110–11
Yeven, John, of Marlcliffe 246
Yildentre, William de, of Romsley 59
York 240–2
Yronmonger, William, of Chipping Campden 281